Daw 3/18 £9.99 ®

MIDDLESBROUGH COLLEGE
LEARNING RESOURCES CENTRES
CLASS: 342·42 Smi
ACCESSION: 00107690
LOCATION: Loan

CORE STATUTES ON
PUBLIC LAW & CIVIL LIBERTIES 2017–18

Learning Resources Centre
Middlesbrough College
Dock Street
Middlesbrough
TS2 1AD

MIDDLESBROUGH COLLEGE
LEARNING RESOURCES CENTRE
WITHDRAWN

D1323840

The *Palgrave Core Statutes* series

Core EU Legislation	Paul Drury
Core Statutes on Commercial & Consumer Law	Graham Stephenson
Core Statutes on Company Law	Cowan Ervine
Core Statutes on Contract, Tort & Restitution	Graham Stephenson
Core Statutes on Criminal Justice & Sentencing	Martin Wasik
Core Statutes on Criminal Law	Kate Cook, Mark James & Richard Lee
Core Statutes on Employment Law	Dominique Lauterburg
Core Statutes on Evidence	Christina McAlhone, Simon Cooper & Jonathan McGahan
Core Statutes on Family Law	Frances Burton
Core Statutes on Intellectual Property	Margaret Dowie-Whybrow
Core Statutes on Property Law	Peter Luther & Alan Moran
Core Statutes on Public Law & Civil Liberties	Rhona Smith, Eimear Spain & Richard Glancey
Core Documents on International Law	Karen Hulme
Core Documents on European and International Human Rights	Rhona Smith

MIDDLESBROUGH COLLEGE
LEARNING RESOURCES CENTRES
CLASS No. 342 . 42 Smi
ACCESSION 00107690
LOCATION L

CORE STATUTES ON PUBLIC LAW & CIVIL LIBERTIES 2017–18

Rhona Smith, Eimear Spain & Richard Glancey

Learning Resources Centre
Middlesbrough College
Dock Street
Middlesbrough
TS2 1AD

MIDDLESBROUGH COLLEGE
LEARNING RESOURCES CENTRE
WITHDRAWN

 macmillan education   palgrave

This selection © Rhona Smith, Eimear Spain & Richard Glancey 2017

All rights reserved. No reproduction, copy or transmission of this publication may be made without written permission.

Crown Copyright/public sector material is licensed under the Open Government Licence v3.0.

EU material is © European Union, http://eur-lex.europa.eu/, 1998–2017. Under the terms of the permission, it requires to be stated that only European Union documents published in the *Official Journal of the European Union* are deemed authentic.

The extracts from the Convention for the Protection of Human Rights and Fundamental Freedoms, and from the European Court of Human Rights are © Council of Europe.

No portion of this publication may be reproduced, copied or transmitted save with written permission or in accordance with the provisions of the Copyright, Designs and Patents Act 1988, or under the terms of any licence permitting limited copying issued by the Copyright Licensing Agency, Saffron House, 6–10 Kirby Street, London EC1N 8TS.

Any person who does any unauthorized act in relation to this publication may be liable to criminal prosecution and civil claims for damages.

The authors have asserted their rights to be identified as the authors of this work in accordance with the Copyright, Designs and Patents Act 1988.

PREFACE

The enclosed materials represent the core statutes and additional instruments for undergraduate study of Public (Constitutional and Administrative) Law. We have edited the materials to focus on those aspects of the materials most commonly required for private study and examination. Thus some statutes are extracted. For the full text of the instruments, recourse should be had to The National Archives or one of the paper or online consolidated version providers. Where possible, prospective amendments are marked in italics. Otherwise, unless indicated, text is presented as accurate at the dissolution of Parliament on 3 May 2017. Students should consult www.legislation.gov.uk for statutes enacted after that date.

Rhona Smith
Eimear Spain
Richard Glancey

CONTENTS

ALPHABETICAL LIST OF CONTENTS

MAGNA CARTA (1215)

(1)   FIRST, THAT WE HAVE GRANTED TO GOD, and by this present charter have confirmed for us and our heirs in perpetuity, that the English Church shall be free, and shall have its rights undiminished, and its liberties unimpaired. That we wish this so to be observed, appears from the fact that of our own free will, before the outbreak of the present dispute between us and our barons, we granted and confirmed by charter the freedom of the Church's elections – a right reckoned to be of the greatest necessity and importance to it – and caused this to be confirmed by Pope Innocent III. This freedom we shall observe ourselves, and desire to be observed in good faith by our heirs in perpetuity.

    TO ALL FREE MEN OF OUR KINGDOM we have also granted, for us and our heirs for ever, all the liberties written out below, to have and to keep for them and their heirs,

(9)   The city of London shall enjoy all its ancient liberties and free customs, both by land and by water. We also will and grant that all other cities, boroughs, towns, and ports shall enjoy all their liberties and free customs.

(29)   No free man shall be seized or imprisoned, or stripped of his rights or possessions, or outlawed or exiled, or deprived of his standing in any other way, nor will we proceed with force against him, or send others to do so, except by the lawful judgement of his equals or by the law of the land. To no one will we sell, to no one deny or delay right or justice.

British Library Board. All Rights Reserved (MS Cotton Augustus II 106)

THE BILL OF RIGHTS (1688)
(1 Will. & Mar. sess 2, c. 2)

An Act declaring the Rights and Liberties of the Subject and Setleing the Succession of the Crowne

Whereas the lords spirituall and temporall and comons assembled at Westminster lawfully fully and freely representing all estates of the people of this realme did upon the thirteenth day of February in the yeare of our Lord one thousand six hundred eighty eight present unto their Majesties then called and known by the names and stile of William and Mary Prince and Princesse of Orange being present in their proper persons a certaine declaration in writeing made by the said lords and comons in the words following viz

Whereas the late King James the Second by the assistance of diverse evill councillors judges and ministers imployed by him did endeavour to subvert and extirpate the Protestant religion and the lawes and liberties of this kingdome

By assumeing and exerciseing a power of dispensing with and suspending of lawes and the execution of lawes without consent of Parlyament.

By committing and prosecuting diverse worthy prelates for humbly petitioning to be excused from concurring to the said assumed power.

By issueing and causeing to be executed a commission under the great seale for erecting a court called the court of commissioners for ecclesiasticall causes.

By levying money for and to the use of the Crowne by pretence of prerogative for other time and in other manner then the same was granted by Parlyament.

By raising and keeping a standing army within this kingdome in time of peace without consent of Parlyament and quartering soldiers contrary to law.

By causing severall good subjects being protestants to be disarmed at the same time when papists were both armed and imployed contrary to law.

By violating the freedome of election of members to serve in Parlyament.

By prosecutions in the Court of King's Bench for matters and causes cognizable onely in Parlyament and by diverse other arbitrary and illegall courses.

And whereas of late yeares partiall corrupt and unqualifyed persons have beene returned and served on juryes in tryalls and particularly diverse jurors in tryalls for high treason which were not freeholders.

And excessive baile hath beene required of persons committed in criminall cases to elude the benefitt of the lawes made for the liberty of the subjects.

And excessive fines have beene imposed.

And illegall and cruell punishments inflicted.

And severall grants and promises made of fines and forfeitures before any conviction or judgement against the persons upon whome the same were to be levyed.

All which are uterly and directly contrary to the knowne lawes and statutes and freedome of the realme.

And whereas the said late King James the Second haveing abdicated the government and the throne being thereby vacant his Highnesse the Prince of Orange (whome it hath pleased Almighty God to make the glorious instrument of delivering this kingdome from popery and arbitrary power) did (by the advice of the lords spirituall and temporall and diverse principall persons of the commons) cause letters to be written to the lords spirituall and temporall being protestants and other letters to the severall countyes cityes universities boroughss and cinque ports for the choosing of such persons to represent them as were of right to be sent to Parlyament to meete and sitt at Westminster upon the two and twentyeth day of January in this yeare one thousand six hundred eighty and eight in order to such an establishment as that their religion lawes and liberties might not againe be in danger of being subverted, upon which letters elections haveing beene accordingly made.

And thereupon the said lords spirituall and temporall and commons pursuant to their respective letters and elections being now assembled in a full and free representative of this nation taking into their most serious consideration the best meanes for attaining the ends aforesaid doe in the first place (as their auncestors in like case have usually done) for the vindicating and asserting their auntient rights and liberties, declare

1   That the pretended power of suspending of laws or the execution of laws by regall authority without consent of Parlyament is illegall

That the pretended power of dispensing with laws or the execution of laws by regall authoritie as it hath beene assumed and exercised of late is illegall.

That the commission for erecting the late court of commissioners for ecclesiasticall causes and all other commissions and courts of like nature are illegal and pernicious.

That levying money for or to the use of the Crowne by pretence of prerogative without grant of Parlyament for longer time or in other manner than the same is or shall be granted is illegal.

That it is the right of the subjects to petition the King and all commitments and prosecutions for such petitioning are illegal.

That the raising or keeping a standing army within the kingdome in time of peace unlesse it be with consent of Parlyament is against law.

That the subjects which are protestants may have arms for their defence suitable to their conditions and as allowed by law.

That election of members of Parlyament ought to be free.

That the freedome of speech and debates or proceedings in Parlyament ought not to be impeached or questioned in any court or place out of Parlyament.

That excessive baile ought not to be required nor excessive fines imposed nor cruell and unusuall punishments inflicted.

That jurors ought to be duly impannelled and returned.

That all grants and promises of fines and forfeitures of particular persons before conviction are illegal and void.

And that for redresse of all grievances and for the amending strengthening and preserving of the lawes Parlyaments ought to be held frequently.

And they doe claime demand and insist upon all and singular the premises as their undoubted rights and liberties and that noe declarations judgements doeings or proceedings to the prejudice of the people in any of the said premises ought in any wise to be drawne hereafter into consequence or example. To which demand of their rights they are particularly encouraged by the declaration of his Highnesse the Prince of Orange as being the only meanes for obtaining a full redresse and remedy therein. Haveing therefore an intire confidence that his said Highnesse the Prince of Orange will perfect the deliverance soe farr advanced by him and will still preserve them from the violation of their rights which they have here asserted and from all other attempts upon their religion rights and liberties.

The said lords spirituall and temporall and commons assembled at Westminster doe resolve that William and Mary Prince and Princesse of Orange be and be declared King and

Queene of England France and Ireland and the dominions thereunto belonging to hold the crowne and royall dignity of the said kingdomes and dominions to them the said prince and princesse dureing their lives and the life of the survivour of them. And that the sole and full exercise of the regall power be onely in and executed by the said Prince of Orange in the names of the said prince and princesse dureing their joynt lives and after their deceases the said crowne and royall dignitie of the said kingdoms and dominions to be to the heires of the body of the said princesse and for default of such issue to the Princesse Anne of Denmarke and the heires of her body and for default of such issue to the heires of the body of the said Prince of Orange.

And the lords spirituall and temporall and commons doe pray the said prince and princesse to accept the same accordingly. And that the oathes hereafter mentioned be taken by all persons of whome the oathes of allegiance and supremacy might be required by law instead of them and that the said oathes of allegiance and supremacy be abrogated.

I A B doe sincerely promise and sweare that I will be faithfull and beare true allegiance to their Majestyes King William and Queen Mary

Soe helpe me God

I A B doe sweare that I doe from my heart abhorr, detest and abjure as impious and hereticall this damnable doctrine and position that princes excommunicated or deprived by the Pope or any authority of the see of Rome may be deposed or murdered by their subjects or any other whatsoever. And I doe declare that noe forreigne prince person prelate, state or potentate hath or ought to have any jurisdiction power superiority preeminence or authoritie ecclesiasticall or spirituall within this realme.

Soe help me God

Upon which their said Majestyes did accept the crowne and royall dignitie of the kingdoms of England France and Ireland and the dominions thereunto belonging according to the resolution and desire of the said lords and commons contained in the said declaration. And thereupon their Majestyes were pleased that the said lords spirituall and temporall and commons being the two Houses of Parlyament should continue to sitt and with their Majesties royall concurrence make effectuall provision for the settlement of the religion lawes and liberties of this kingdome soe that the same for the future might not be in danger againe of being subverted, to which the said lords spirituall and temporall and commons did agree and proceede to act accordingly.

Now in pursuance of the premises the said lords spirituall and temporall and commons in Parlyament assembled for the ratifying confirming and establishing the said declaration and the articles clauses matters and things therein contained by the force of a law made in due forme by authority of Parlyament doe pray that it may be declared and enacted that all and singular the rights and liberties asserted and claimed in the said declaration are the true auntient and indubitable rights and liberties of the people of this kingdome and soe shall be esteemed allowed adjudged deemed and taken to be and that all and every the paritculars aforesaid shall be firmly and strictly holden and observed as they are expressed in the said declaration. And all officers and ministers whatsoever shall serve their Majestyes and their successors according to the same in all times to come. And the said lords spirituall and temporall and commons seriously considering how it hath pleased Almighty God in his marvellous providence and mercifull goodness to this nation to provide and preserve their said Majestyes royall persons most happily to raigne over us upon the throne of their auncestors for which they render unto him from the bottome of their hearts their humblest thanks and praises doe truely firmely assuredly and in the sincerity of their hearts thinke and doe hereby recognize acknowledge and declare that King James the Second haveing abdicated the government and their Majestyes having accepted the crowne and royall dignity as aforesaid their said Majestyes did become were are and of right ought to be by the lawes of the realme our soveraigne liege lord and lady King and Queene of England France and Ireland and the dominions thereunto belonging in and to whose princely persons the royall state crowne and dignity of the said realmes with all honours stiles titles regalities prerogatives powers jurisdictions and authorities to the same belonging and appertaining are most fully and rightfully and intirely invested and incorporated united and annexed.

And for preventing all questions and divisions in this realme by reason of any pretended titles to the crowne and for preserveing a certainty in the succession thereof in and upon which the unity peace tranquillity and safety of this nation doth under God wholly consist and depend the said lords spirituall and temporall and commons doe beseech their Majestyes that it may be enacted established and declared that the crowne and regall government of the said kingdoms and dominions with all and singular the premisses thereunto belonging and appertaining shall bee and continue to their said Majestyes and the survivour of them dureing their lives and the life of the survivour of them and that the entire perfect and full exercise of the regall power and government be onely in and executed by his Majestie in the names of both their Majestyes dureing their joynt lives and after their deceases the said crowne and premisses shall be and remaine to the heires of the body of her Majestie and for default of such issue to her royall Highnesse the Princess Anne of Denmarke and the heires of her body and for default of such issue to the heires of the body of his said Majestie And thereunto the said lords spirituall and temporall and commons doe in the name of all the people aforesaid most humbly and faithfully submitt themselves their heires and posterities for ever and doe faithfully promise that they will stand to maintaine and defend their said Majesties and alsoe the limitation and succession of the crowne herein specified and contained to the utmost of their powers with their lives and estates against all persons whatsoever that shall attempt any thing to the contrary.

And whereas it hath beene found by experience that it is inconsistent with the safety and welfare of this protestant kingdome to be governed by a popish prince the said lords spirtuall and temporall and commons doe further pray that it may be enacted that all and every person and persons that is are or shall be reconciled to or shall hold communion with the see or church of Rome or shall professe the popish religion shall be excluded and be for ever uncapeable to inherit possesse or enjoy the crowne and government of this realme and Ireland and the dominions thereunto belonging or any part of the same or to have use or exercise any regall power authoritie or jurisdiction within the same And in all and every such case or cases the people of these realmes shall be and are hereby absolved of their allegiance and the said crowne and government shall from time to time descend to and be enjoyed by such person or persons being protestants as should have inherited and enjoyed the same in case the said person or persons soe reconciled holding communion or professing as aforesaid were naturally dead.

And that every King and Queene of this realme who at any time hereafter shall come to and succeede in the imperiall crowne of this kingdome shall on the first day of the meeting of the first Parlyament next after his or her comeing to the crowne sitting in his or her throne in the House of Peeres in the presence of the lords and commons therein assembled or at his or her coronation before such person or persons who shall administer the coronation oath to him or her at the time of his or her takeing the said oath (which shall first happen) make subscribe and audibly repeate the declaration mentioned in the Statute made in the thirtyeth yeare of the raigne of King Charles the Second entituled An Act for the more effectuall preserveing the Kings person and government by disableing papists from sitting in either House of Parlyament.

But if it shall happen that such King or Queene upon his or her succession to the crowne of this realme shall be under the age of twelve yeares then every such King or Queene shall make subscribe and audibly repeate the said declaration at his or her coronation or the first day of the meeting of the first Parlyament as aforesaid which shall first happen after such King or Queene shall have attained the said age of twelve years. All which their Majestyes are contented and pleased shall be declared enacted and established by authoritie of this present Parliament and shall stand remaine and be the law of this realme for ever And the same are by their said Majesties by and with the advice and consent of the lords spirituall and temporall and commons in Parlyament assembled and by the authoritie of the same declared enacted and established accordingly.

2   Non obstantes made void

Noe dispensation by non obstante of or to any statute or any part thereof shall be allowed but the same shall be held void and of noe effect except a dispensation be allowed of in such statute.

THE ACT OF SETTLEMENT (1700)
(12 & 13 Will. 3, c. 2)

An Act for the further Limitation of the Crown and better securing the Rights and Liberties of the Subject

1   The Princess Sophia, Electress and Duchess dowager of Hanover, daughter of the late Queen of Bohemia, daughter of King James the First, to inherit after the King and the Princess Anne, in default of issue of the said princess and his Majesty, respectively; and the heirs of her body, being protestants

That the most excellent Princess Sophia Electress and Dutchess dowager of Hanover daughter of the most excellent Princess Elizabeth late Queen of Bohemia daughter of our late sovereign lord King James the First of happy memory be and is hereby declared to be the next in succession in the protestant line to the imperiall crown and dignity of the said realms of England France and Ireland with the dominions and territories thereunto belonging after his Majesty and the Princess Ann of Denmark and in default of issue of the said Princess Ann and of his Majesty respectively and that from and after the deceases of his said Majesty our own soveriegn lord and of her royall Highness the Princess Ann of Denmark and for default of issue of the said Princess Ann and of his Majesty respectively the crown and regall government of the said kingdoms of England France and Ireland and of the dominions thereunto belonging with the royall state and dignity of the said realms and all honours stiles titles regalities prerogatives powers jurisdictions and authorities to the same belonging and appertaining shall be remain and continue to the said most excellent Princess Sophia and the heirs of her body being protestants And thereunto the said lords spirituall and temporall and commons shall and will in the name of all the people of this realm most humbly and faithfully submitt themselves their heirs and posterities and do faithfully promise that after the deceases of his Majesty and her royall Highness and the failure of the heirs of their respective bodies to stand to maintain and defend the said Princess Sophia and the heirs of her body being protestants according to the limitation and succession of the crown in this Act specified and contained to the utmost of their powers with their lives and estates against all persons whatsoever that shall attempt any thing to the contrary.

2   The persons inheritable by this Act, holding communion with the church of Rome, incapacitated as by the former Act; to take the oath at their coronation

Provided always and it is hereby enacted that all and every person and persons who shall or may take or inherit the said crown by vertue of the limitation of this present Act and is are or shall be reconciled to or shall hold communion with the see or church of Rome or shall profess the popish religion shall be subject to such incapacities as in such case or cases are by the said recited Act provided enacted and established. And that every King and Queen of this realm who shall come to and succeed in the imperiall crown of this kingdom by vertue of this Act shall have the coronation oath administered to him her or them at their respective coronations according to the Act of Parliament made in the first year of the reign of his Majesty and the said late Queen Mary intituled An Act for establishing the coronation oath and shall make subscribe and repeat the declaration in the Act first above recited mentioned or referred to in the manner and form thereby prescribed.

3   Further provisions for securing the religions, laws, and liberties of these realms

And whereas it is requisite and necessary that some further provision be made for securing our religion laws and liberties from and after the death of his Majesty and the Princess Ann of Denmark and in default of issue of the body of the said princess and of his Majesty respectively Be it enacted by the Kings most excellent Majesty by and with the advice and consent of the lords spirituall and temporall and commons in Parliament and by the authority of the same

That whosoever shall hereafter come to the possession of this crown shall joyn in communion with the Church of England as by law established

That in case the crown and imperiall dignity of this realm shall hereafter come to any person not being a native of this kingdom of England this nation be not obliged to ingage in any warr for the defence of any dominions or territories which do not belong to the crown of England without the consent of Parliament.

That no pardon under the great seal of England be pleadable to an impeachment by the commons in Parliament.

4   The laws and statutes of the realm confirmed

And whereas the laws of England are the birthright of the people thereof and all the Kings and Queens who shall ascend the throne of this realm ought to administer the government of the same according to the said laws and all their officers and ministers ought to serve them respectively according to the same The said lords spirituall and temporall and commons do therefore further humbly pray that all the laws and statutes of this realm for securing the established religion and the rights and liberties of the people thereof and all other laws and statutes of the same now in force may be ratified and confirmed And the same are by his Majesty by and with the advice and consent of the said lords spirituall and temporall and commons and by authority of the same ratified and confirmed accordingly.

UNION WITH SCOTLAND ACT 1706
(6 Anne, c. 11)

An Act for an Union of the Two Kingdoms of England and Scotland

Article I

That the two kingdoms of England and Scotland shall upon the first day of May which shall be in the year one thousand seven hundred and seven and for ever after be united into one kingdom by the name of Great Britain and that the ensigns armorial of the said United Kingdom be such as her Majesty shall appoint and the crosses of St. George and St. Andrew be conjoyned in such manner as Her Majesty shall think fit and used in all flags banners standards and ensigns both at sea and land.

Article II

That the succession to the monarchy of the United Kingdom of Great Britain and of the dominions thereto belonging after her most sacred Majesty and in default of issue of her Majesty be remain and continue to the most excellent Princess Sophia Electoress and Dutchess dowager of Hanover and the heirs of her body being protestants upon whom the crown of England is settled by an Act of Parliament made in England in the twelfth year of the reign of his late Majesty King William the Third intituled An Act for the further limitation of the crown and better securing the right and liberties of the subject And that all papists and persons marrying papists shall be excluded from and for ever incapable to inherit possess or enjoy the imperial crown of Great Britain and the dominions thereunto belonging or any part thereof and in every such case the crown and government shall from time to time descend to and be enjoyed by such person being a protestant as should have inherited and enjoyed the same in case such papist or person marrying a papist was naturally dead according to the provision for the descent of the crown of England made by another Act of Parliament in England in the first year of the reign of their late Majesties King William and Queen Mary intituled An Act declaring the rights and liberties of the subject and settling the succession of the crown.

Article III

That the United Kingdom of Great Britain be represented by one and the same Parliament to be stiled the Parliament of Great Britain.

Article IIII

That all the subjects of the United Kingdom of Great Britain shall from and after the union have full freedom and intercourse of trade and navigation to and from any port or place within the said United Kingdom and the dominions and plantations thereunto belonging and that there be a communication of all other rights privileges and advantages which do or may belong to the subjects of either kingdom except where it is otherwise expressly agreed in these articles.

Article VI

That all parts of the United Kingdom for ever from and after the union shall have the same allowances encouragements and drawbacks and be under the same prohibitions restrictions and regulations of trade and liable to the same customs and duties on import and export and that the allowances encouragements and drawbacks prohibitions restrictions and regulations of trade and the customs and duties on import and export settled in England when the union commences shall from and after the union take place throughout the whole United Kingdom.

Article XVIII

That the laws concerning regulation of trade customs and such excises to which Scotland is by virtue of this treaty to be liable be the same in Scotland from and after the union as in England and that all other laws in use within the kingdom of Scotland do after the union and notwithstanding thereof remain in the same force as before (except such as are contrary to or inconsistent with this treaty) but alterable by the Parliament of Great Britain with this difference betwixt the laws concerning publick right policy and civil government and those which concern private right that the laws which concern publick right policy and civil government may be made the same throughout the whole United Kingdom. But that no alteration be made in laws which concern private right except for evident utility of the subjects within Scotland

Article XXV

That all laws and statutes in either kingdom so far as they are contrary to or inconsistent with the terms of these articles or any of them shall from and after the union cease and become void and shall be so declared to be by the respective Parliaments of the said kingdoms.

As by the said articles of union ratified and approved by the said Act of Parliament of Scotland relation being thereunto had may appear.

OFFICIAL SECRETS ACT 1911
(1 & 2 Geo. 5, c. 28)

An Act to re-enact the Official Secrets Act 1889, with Amendments.   22 August 1911

1   Penalties for spying

(1)   If any person for any purpose prejudicial to the safety or interests of the State—

    (a)   approaches, inspects, passes over or is in the neighbourhood of, or enters any prohibited place within the meaning of this Act; or

    (b)   makes any sketch, plan, model, or note which is calculated to be or might be or is intended to be directly or indirectly useful to an enemy; or

    (c)   obtains, collects, records, or publishes, or communicates to any other person any secret official code word or pass word, or any sketch, plan, model, article, or note, or other document or information which is calculated to be or might be or is intended to be directly or indirectly useful to an enemy;

he shall be guilty of felony.

(2)   On a prosecution under this section, it shall not be necessary to show that the accused person was guilty of any particular act tending to show a purpose prejudicial to the safety or interests of the State, and, notwithstanding that no such act is proved against him, he may be convicted if, from the circumstances of the case, or his conduct, or his known character as proved, it appears that his purpose was a purpose prejudicial to the safety or interests of the State; and if any sketch, plan,

model, article, note, document, or information relating to or used in any prohibited place within the meaning of this Act, or anything in such a place or any secret official code word or pass word, is made, obtained, collected, recorded, published, or communicated by any person other than a person acting under lawful authority, it shall be deemed to have been made, obtained, collected, recorded, published or communicated for a purpose prejudicial to the safety or interests of the State unless the contrary is proved.

3 Definition of prohibited place

For the purposes of this Act, the expression "prohibited place" means—

(a)   any work of defence, arsenal, naval or air force establishment or station, factory, dockyard, mine, minefield, camp, ship, or aircraft belonging to or occupied by or on behalf of His Majesty, or any telegraph, telephone, wireless or signal station, or office so belonging or occupied, and any place belonging to or occupied by or on behalf of His Majesty and used for the purpose of building, repairing, making, or storing any munitions of war, or any sketches, plans, models, or documents relating thereto, or for the purpose of getting any metals, oil, or minerals of use in time of war;

(b)   any place not belonging to His Majesty where any munitions of war, or any sketches, models, plans or documents relating thereto, are being made, repaired, gotten or stored under contract with, or with any person on behalf of, His Majesty, or otherwise on behalf of His Majesty; and

(c)   any place belonging to or used for the purposes of His Majesty which is for the time being declared by order of a Secretary of State to be a prohibited place for the purposes of this section on the ground that information with respect thereto, or damage thereto, would be useful to an enemy; and

(d)   any railway, road, way, or channel, or other means of communication by land or water (including any works or structures being part thereof or connected therewith), or any place used for gas, water, or electricity works or other works for purposes of a public character, or any place where any munitions of war, or any sketches, models, plans or documents relating thereto, are being made, repaired, or stored otherwise than on behalf of His Majesty, which is for the time being declared by order or a Secretary of State to be a prohibited place for the purposes of this section, on the ground that information with respect thereto, or the destruction or obstruction thereof, or interference therewith, would be useful to an enemy.

9 Search warrants

(1)   If a justice of the peace is satisfied by information on oath that there is reasonable ground for suspecting that an offence under this Act has been or is about to be committed, he may grant a search warrant authorising any constable to enter at any time any premises or place named in the warrant, if necessary, by force, and to search the premises or place and every person found therein, and to seize any sketch, plan, model, article, note, or document, or anything of a like nature or anything which is evidence of an offence under this Act having been or being about to be committed, which he may find on the premises or place or on any such person, and with regard to or in connexion with which he has reasonable ground for suspecting that an offence under this Act has been or is about to be committed.

(2)   Where it appears to a superintendent of police that the case is one of great emergency and that in the interests of the State immediate action is necessary, he may by a written order under his hand give to any constable the like authority as may be given by the warrant of a justice under the section.

10 Extent of Act and place of trial of offence

(1)   This Act shall apply to all acts which are offences under this Act when committed in any part of His Majesty's dominions, or when committed by British officers or subjects elsewhere.

PARLIAMENT ACTS 1911 AND 1949
(1 & 2 Geo. 5, c. 13)

An Act to make provision with respect to the powers of the House of Lords in relation of the House of Commons, and to limit the duration of Parliament.   18 August 1911

1   Powers of House of Lords as to Money Bills

(1)   If a Money Bill, having been passed by the House of Commons, and sent up to the House of Lords at least one month before the end of the session, is not passed by the House of Lords without amendment within one month after it is so sent up to that House, the Bill shall, unless the House of Commons direct to the contrary, be presented to His Majesty and become an Act of Parliament on the Royal Assent being signified, notwithstanding that the House of Lords have not consented to the Bill.

(2)   A Money Bill means a Public Bill which in the opinion of the Speaker of the House of Commons contains only provisions dealing with all or any of the following subjects, namely, the imposition, repeal, remission, alteration, or regulation of taxation; the imposition for the payment of debt or other financial purposes of charges on the Consolidated Fund, the National Loans Fund or on money provided by Parliament, or the variation or repeal of any such charges; supply; the appropriation, receipt, custody, issue or audit of accounts of public money; the raising or guarantee of any loan or the repayment thereof; or subordinate matters incidental to those subjects or any of them. In this subsection the expressions "taxation", "public money" and "loan" respectively do not include any taxation, money, or loan raised by local authorities or bodies for local purposes.

(3)   There shall be endorsed on every Money Bill when it is sent up to the House of Lords and when it is presented to His Majesty for assent the certificate of the Speaker of the House of Commons signed by him that it is a Money Bill. Before giving his certificate, the Speaker shall consult, if practicable, two members to be appointed from the Chairmen's Panel at the beginning of each Session by the Committee of Selection.

2   Restriction of the powers of the House of Lords as to Bills other than Money Bills

(1)   If any Public Bill (other than a Money Bill or a Bill containing any provision to extend the maximum duration of Parliament beyond five years) is passed by the House of Commons in two successive sessions (whether of the same Parliament or not), and, having been sent up to the House of Lords at least one month before the end of the session, is rejected by the House of Lords in each of those sessions, that Bill shall, on its rejection for the second time by the House of Lords, unless the House of Commons direct to the contrary, be presented to His Majesty and become an Act of Parliament on the Royal Assent being signified thereto, notwithstanding that the House of Lords have not consented to the Bill:

Provided that this provision shall not take effect unless one year has elapsed between the date of the second reading in the first of those sessions of the Bill in the House of Commons and the date on which it passes the House of Commons in the second of those sessions.

(2)   When a Bill is presented to His Majesty for assent in pursuance of the provisions of this section, there shall be endorsed on the Bill the certificate of the Speaker of the House of Commons signed by him that the provisions of this section have been duly complied with.

(3)   A Bill shall be deemed to be rejected by the House of Lords if it is not passed by the House of Lords either without amendment or with such amendments only as may be agreed to by both Houses.

(4)   A Bill shall be deemed to be the same Bill as a former Bill sent up to the House of Lords in the preceding session if, when it is sent up to the House of Lords, it is identical with the former Bill or contains only such alterations as are certified by the Speaker of the House of Commons to be necessary owing to the time which has

elapsed since the date of the former Bill, or to represent any amendments which have been made by the House of Lords in the former Bill in the preceding sesion, and any amendments which are certified by the Speaker to have been made by the House of Lords in the second session and agreed to by the House of Commons shall be inserted in the Bill as presented for Royal Assent in pursuance of this section:

Provided that the House of Commons may, if they think fit, on the passage of such a Bill through the House in the second session, suggest any further amendments without inserting the amendments in the Bill, and any such suggested amendments shall be considered by the House of Lords, and, if agreed to by that House, shall be treated as amendments made by the House of Lords and agreed to by the House of Commons; but the exercise of this power by the House of Commons shall not affect the operation of this section in the event of the Bill being rejected by the House of Lords.

3 Certificate of Speaker

Any certificate of the Speaker of the House of Commons given under this Act shall be conclusive for all purposes, and shall not be questioned in any court of law.

4 Enacting words

(1) In every Bill presented to His Majesty under the preceding provisions of this Act, the words of enactment shall be as follows, that is to say:—

"Be it enacted by the King's most Excellent Majesty, by and with the advice and consent of the Commons in this present Parliament assembled, in accordance with the provisions of the Parliament Acts 1911 and 1949, and by authority of the same, as follows."

(2) Any alteration of a Bill necessary to give effect to this section shall not be deemed to be an amendment of the Bill.

5 Provisional Order Bills excluded

In this Act the expression "Public Bill" does not include any Bill for confirming a Provisional Order.

6 Saving for existing rights and privileges of the House of Commons

Nothing in this Act shall diminish or qualify the existing rights and privileges of the House of Commons.

OFFICIAL SECRETS ACT 1920
(10 & 11 Geo. 5, c. 75)

An Act to amend the Official Secrets Act 1911.   23 December 1920

1 Unauthorised use of uniforms; falsification of reports, forgery, personation, and false documents

(1) If any person for the purpose of gaining admission, or of assisting any other person to gain admission, to a prohibited place, within the meaning of the Official Secrets Act 1911 (hereinafter referred to as "the principal Act"), or for any other purpose prejudicial to the safety or interests of the State within the meaning of the said Act—

(a) uses or wears, without lawful authority, any naval, military, air-force, police, or other official uniform, or any uniform so nearly resembling the same as to be calculated to deceive, or falsely represents himself to be a person who is or has been entitled to use or wear any such uniform; or

(b) orally, or in writing in any declaration or application, or in any document signed by him or on his behalf, knowingly makes or connives at the making of any false statement or any omission; or

(c) tampers with any passport or any naval, military, air-force, police, or official pass, permit, certificate, licence, or other document of a similar character (hereinafter in this section referred to as an official document), or has in his possession any forged, altered, or irregular official document; or

(d)   personates, or falsely represents himself to be a person holding, or in the employment of a person holding office under His Majesty, or to be or not to be a person to whom an official document or secret official code word or pass word has been duly issued or communicated, or with intent to obtain an official document, secret official code word or pass word, whether for himself or any other person, knowingly makes any false statement; or

(e)   uses, or has in his possession or under his control, without the authority of the Government Department or the authority concerned, any die, seal, or stamp of or belonging to, or used, made or provided by any Government Department, or by any diplomatic, naval, military, or air force authority appointed by or acting under the authority of His Majesty, or any die, seal or stamp so nearly resembling any such die, seal or stamp as to be calculated to deceive, or counterfeits any such die, seal or stamp, or uses, or has in his possession, or under his control, any such counterfeited die, seal or stamp;

he shall be guilty of a misdemeanour.

(2)   If any person—

(a)   retains for any purpose prejudicial to the safety or interests of the State any official document, whether or not completed or issued for use, when he has no right to retain it, or when it is contrary to his duty to retain it, or fails to comply with any directions issued by any Government Department or any person authorised by such department with regard to the return or disposal thereof; or

(b)   allows any other person to have possession of any official document issued for his use alone, or communicates any secret official code word or pass word so issued, or, without lawful authority or excuse, has in his possession any official document or secret official code word or pass word issued for the use of some person other than himself, or on obtaining possession of any official document by finding or otherwise, neglects or fails to restore it to the person or authority by whom or for whose use it was issued, or to a police constable; or

(c)   without lawful authority or excuse, manufactures or sells, or has in his possession for sale any such die, seal or stamp as aforesaid;

he shall be guilty of a misdemeanour.

(3)   In the case of any prosecution under this section involving the proof of a purpose prejudicial to the safety or interests of the State, subsection (2) of section one of the principal Act shall apply in like manner as it applies to prosecutions under that section.

6   Duty of giving information as to commission of offences

(1)   Where a chief officer of police is satisfied that there is reasonable ground for suspecting that an offence under section one of the principal Act has been committed and for believing that any person is able to furnish information as to the offence or suspected offence, he may apply to a Secretary of State for permission to exercise the powers conferred by this subsection and, if such permission is granted, he may authorise a superintendent of police, or any police officer not below the rank of inspector, to require the person believed to be able to furnish information to give any information in his power relating to the offence or suspected offence, and, if so required and on tender of his reasonable expenses, to attend at such reasonable time and place as may be specified by the superintendent or other officer; and if a person required in pursuance of such an authorisation to give information, or to attend as aforesaid, fails to comply with any such requirement or knowingly gives false information, he shall be guilty of a misdemeanour.

(2)   Where a chief officer of police has reasonable grounds to believe that the case is one of great emergency and that in the interest of the State immediate action is necessary, he may exercise the powers conferred by the last foregoing subsection without applying for or being granted the permission of a Secretary of State, but if he does so shall forthwith report the circumstances to the Secretary of State.

(3)   References in this section to a chief officer of police shall be construed as including references to any other officer of police expressly authorised by a chief officer of police to act on his behalf for the purposes of this section when by reason of illness, absence or other cause he is unable to do so.

THE STATUTE OF WESTMINSTER 1931
(22 & 23 Geo. 5, c. 4)

An Act to give effect to certain resolutions passed by Imperial Conferences held in the years 1926 and 1930.   11 December 1931

1   Meaning of "Dominion" in this Act

In this Act the expression "Dominion" means any of the following Dominions, that is to say, the Dominion of Canada, the Commonwealth of Australia, the Dominion of New Zealand, the Irish Free State and Newfoundland.

2   Validity of laws made by Parliament of a Dominion

(1)   The Colonial Laws Validity Act 1865 shall not apply to any law made after the commencement of this Act by the Parliament of a Dominion.

(2)   No law and no provision of any law made after the commencement of this Act by the Parliament of a Dominion shall be void or inoperative on the ground that it is repugnant to the law of England, or to the provisions of any existing or future Act of Parliament of the United Kingdom, or to any order, rule or regulation made under any such Act, and the powers of the Parliament of a Dominion shall include the power to repeal or amend any such Act, order, rule or regulation in so far as the same is part of the law of the Dominion.

3   Power of Parliament of Dominion to legislate extra-territorally

It is hereby declared and enacted that the Parliament of a Dominion has full power to make laws having extra-territorial operation.

4   Parliament of United Kingdom not to legislate for Dominion except by consent

No Act of Parliament of the United Kingdom passed after the commencement of this Act shall extend, or be deemed to extend, to a Dominion as part of the law of that Dominion unless it is expressly declared in that Act that that Dominion has requested, and consented to, the enactment thereof.

PUBLIC ORDER ACT 1936
(1 Edw. 8 & 1 Geo. 6, c. 6)

An Act to prohibit the wearing of uniforms in connection with political objects and the maintenance by private persons of associations of military or similar character; and to make further provision for the preservation of public order on the occasion of public processions and meetings and in public places.   18 December 1936

1   Prohibition of uniforms in connection with political objects

(1)   Subject as hereinafter provided, any person who in any public place or at any public meeting wears uniform signifying his association with any political organisation or with the promotion of any political object shall be guilty of an offence:

Provided that, if the chief officer of police is satisfied that the wearing of any such uniform as aforesaid on any ceremonial, anniversary, or other special occasion will not be likely to involve risk of public disorder, he may, with the consent of a Secretary of State, by order permit the wearing of such uniform on that occasion either absolutely or subject to such conditions as may be specified in the order.

(2)   Where any person is charged before any court with an offence under this section, no further proceedings in respect thereof shall be taken against him without the consent of the Attorney-General except such as are authorised by section 6 of the Prosecution of Offences Act 1979 so, however, that if that person is remanded in custody he shall, after the expiration of a period of eight days from the date on which he was so remanded, be entitled to be released on bail without

sureties unless within that period the Attorney-General has consented to such further proceedings as aforesaid.

2 Prohibition of quasi-military organisations

(1) If the members or adherents of any association of persons, whether incorporated or not, are—

(a) organised or trained or equipped for the purpose of enabling them to be employed in usurping the functions of the police or of the armed forces of the Crown; or

(b) organised and trained or organised and equipped either for the purpose of enabling them to be employed for the use or display of physical force in promoting any political object, or in such manner as to arouse reasonable apprehension that they are organised and either trained or equipped for that purpose;

then any person who takes part in the control or management of the association, or in so organising or training as aforesaid any members or adherents thereof, shall be guilty of an offence under this section:

Provided that in any proceedings against a person charged with the offence of taking part in the control or management of such an association as aforesaid it shall be a defence to that charge to prove that he neither consented to nor connived at the organisation, training, or equipment of members or adherents of the association in contravention of the provisions of this section.

(5) If a judge of the High Court is satisfied by information on oath that there is reasonable ground for suspecting that an offence under this section has been committed, and that evidence of the commission thereof is to be found at any premises or place specified in the information, he may, on an application made by an officer of police of a rank not lower than that of inspector, grant a search warrant authorising any such officer as aforesaid named in the warrant together with any other persons named in the warrant and any other officers of police to enter the premises or place at any time within three months from the date of the warrant, if necessary by force, and to search the premises or place and every person found therein, and to seize anything found on the premises or place or on any such person which the officer has reasonable ground for suspecting to be evidence of the commission of such an offence as aforesaid:

Provided that no woman shall, in pursuance of a warrant issued under this subsection, be searched except by a woman.

(6) Nothing in this section shall be construed as prohibiting the employment of a reasonable number of persons as stewards to assist in the preservation of order at any public meeting held upon private premises, or the making of arrangements for that purpose or the instruction of the persons to be so employed in their lawful duties as such stewards, or their being furnished with badges or other distinguishing signs.

STATUTORY INSTRUMENTS ACT 1946
(9 & 10 Geo. 6, c. 36)

An Act to repeal the Rules Publication Act, 1893, and to make further provision as to the instruments by which statutory powers to make orders, rules, regulations and other subordinate legislation are exercised. 26 March 1946

1 Definition of "Statutory Instrument"

(1) Where by this Act or any Act passed after the commencement of this Act power to make, confirm or approve orders, rules, regulations or other subordinate legislation is conferred on His Majesty in Council or on any Minister of the Crown then, if the power is expressed—

(a) in the case of a power conferred on His Majesty, to be exercisable by Order in Council;

(b)   in the case of a power conferred on a Minister of the Crown, to be exercisable by statutory instrument,

any document by which that power is exercised shall be known as a "statutory instrument" and the provisions of this Act shall apply thereto accordingly.

(1A)   Where by any Act power to make, confirm or approve orders, rules, regulations or other subordinate legislation is conferred on the Welsh Ministers and the power is expressed to be exercisable by statutory instrument, any document by which that power is exercised shall be known as a "statutory instrument" and the provisions of this Act shall apply to it accordingly.

(2)   Whereby any Act passed before the commencement of this Act power to make statutory rules within the meaning of the Rules Publication Act, 1893, was conferred on any rule-making authority within the meaning of that Act, any document by which that power is exercised after the commencement of this Act shall, save as is otherwise provided by regulations made under this Act, be known as a "statutory instrument" and the provisions of this Act shall apply thereto accordingly.

2   Numbering, printing, publication and citation

(1)   Immediately after the making of any statutory instrument, it shall be sent to the King's printer of Acts of Parliament and numbered in accordance with regulations made under this Act, and except in such cases as may be provided by any Act passed after the commencement of this Act or prescribed by regulations made under this Act, copies thereof shall as soon as possible be printed and sold by or under the authority of the King's printer of Acts of Parliament.

(2)   Any statutory instrument may, without prejudice to any other mode of citation, be cited by the number given to it in accordance with the provisions of this section, and the calendar year.

3   Supplementary provisions as to publication

(1)   Regulations made for the purposes of this Act shall make provision for the publication by His Majesty's Stationery Office of lists showing the date upon which every statutory instrument printed and sold by or under the authority of the King's printer of Acts of Parliament was first issued by or under the authority of that office; and in any legal proceedings a copy of any list so published shall be received in evidence as a true copy, and an entry therein shall be conclusive evidence of the date on which any statutory instrument was first issued by or under the authority of His Majesty's Stationery Office.

(2)   In any proceedings against any person for an offence consisting of a contravention of any such statutory instrument, it shall be a defence to prove that the instrument had not been issued by or under the authority of His Majesty's Stationery Office at the date of the alleged contravention unless it is proved that at that date reasonable steps had been taken for the purpose of bringing the purport of the instrument to the notice of the public, or of persons likely to be affected by it, or of the person charged.

(3)   Save as therein otherwise expressly provided, nothing in this section shall affect any enactment or rule of law relating to the time at which any statutory instrument comes into operation.

4   Statutory instruments which are required to be laid before Parliament

(1)   Where by this Act or any Act passed after the commencement of this Act any statutory instrument is required to be laid before Parliament after being made, a copy of the instrument shall be laid before each House of Parliament and, subject as hereinafter provided, shall be so laid before the instrument comes into operation:

Provided that if it is essential that any such instrument should come into operation before copies thereof can be so laid as aforesaid, the instrument may be made so as to come into operation before it has been so laid; and where any statutory instrument comes into operation before it is laid before Parliament, notification shall forthwith be sent to the Speaker of the House of Commons and the Speaker of the House of Lords drawing attention to the fact that copies of the instrument have yet to be laid before Parliament and explaining why such copies were not so laid before the instrument came into operation.

(2)   Every copy of any such statutory instrument sold by or under the authority of the King's printer of Acts of Parliament shall bear on the face thereof—

(a)   a statement showing the date on which the statutory instrument came or will come into operation; and

(b)   either a statement showing the date on which copies thereof were laid before Parliament or a statement that such copies are to be laid before Parliament.

5   Statutory instruments which are subject to annulment by resolution of either House of Parliament

(1)   Where by this Act or any Act passed after the commencement of this Act, it is provided that any statutory instrument shall be subject to annulment in pursuance of resolution of either House of Parliament, the instrument shall be laid before Parliament after being made and the provisions of the last foregoing section shall apply thereto accordingly, and if either House, within the period of forty days beginning with the day on which a copy thereof is laid before it, resolves that an Address be presented to His Majesty praying that the instrument be annulled, no further proceedings shall be taken thereunder after the date of the resolution, and His Majesty may by Order in Council revoke the instrument, so, however, that any such resolution and revocation shall be without prejudice to the validity of anything previously done under the instrument or to the making of a new statutory instrument.

6   Statutory instruments of which drafts are to be laid before Parliament

(1)   Where by this Act or any Act passed after the commencement of this Act it is provided that a draft of any statutory instrument shall be laid before Parliament, but the Act does not prohibit the making of the instrument without the approval of Parliament, then, in the case of an Order in Council the draft shall not be submitted to His Majesty in Council, and in any other case the statutory instrument shall not be made, until after the expiration of a period of forty days beginning with the day on which a copy of the draft is laid before each House of Parliament, or, if such copies are laid on different days, with the later of the two days, and if within that period either House resolves that the draft be not submitted to His Majesty or that the statutory instrument be not made, as the case may be, no further proceedings shall be taken thereon, but without prejudice to the laying before Parliament of a new draft.

CROWN PROCEEDINGS ACT 1947
(10 & 11 Geo. 6, c. 44)

An Act to amend the law relating to the civil liabilities and rights of the Crown and to civil proceedings by and against the Crown, to amend the law relating to the civil liabilities of persons other than the Crown in certain cases involving the affairs or property of the Crown, and for purposes connected with the matters aforesaid.   [31 July 1947]

PART I
SUBSTANTIVE LAW

1   Right to sue the Crown

Where any person has a claim against the Crown after the commencement of this Act, and, if this Act had not been passed, the claim might have been enforced, subject to the grant of His Majesty's fiat, by petition of right, or might have been enforced by a proceeding provided by any stautory provision repealed by this Act, then, subject to the provisions of this Act, the claim may be enforced as of right, and without the fiat of His Majesty, by proceedings taken against the Crown for that purpose in accordance with the provisions of this Act.

2   Liability of the Crown in tort

(1)   Subject to the provisions of this Act, the Crown shall be subject to all those liabilities in tort to which, if it were a private person of full age and capacity, it would be subject—

     (a)   in respect of torts committed by its servants or agents;

     (b)   in respect of any breach of those duties which a person owes to his servants or agents at common law by reason of being their employer; and

     (c)   in respect of any breach of the duties attaching at common law to the ownership, occupation, possession or control of property:

Provided that no proceedings shall lie against the Crown by virtue of paragraph (a) of this subsection in respect of any act or omission of a servant or agent of the Crown unless the act or omission would apart from the provisions of this Act have given rise to a cause of action in tort against that servant or agent or his estate.

(2)   Where the Crown is bound by a statutory duty which is binding also upon persons other than the Crown and its officers, then, subject to the provisions of this Act, the Crown shall, in respect of a failure to comply with that duty, be subject to all those liabilities in tort (if any) to which it would be so subject if it were a private person of full age and capacity.

(3)   Where any functions are conferred or imposed upon an officer of the Crown as such either by any rule of the common law or by statute, and that officer commits a tort while performing or purporting to perform those functions, the liabilities of the Crown in respect of the tort shall be such as they would have been if those functions had been conferred or imposed solely by virtue of instructions lawfully given by the Crown.

(4)   Any enactment which negatives or limits the amount of the liability of any Government department, part of the Scottish Administration or officer of the Crown in respect of any tort committed by that department, part or officer shall, in the case of proceedings against the Crown under this section in respect of a tort committed by that department, part or officer, apply in relation to the Crown as it would have applied in relation to that department, part or officer if the proceedings against the Crown had been proceedings against that department, part or officer.

(5)   No proceedings shall lie against the Crown by virtue of this section in respect of anything done or omitted to be done by any person while discharging or purporting to discharge any responsibilities of a judicial nature vested in him, or any responsibilities which he has in connection with the execution of judicial process.

(6)   No proceedings shall lie against the Crown by virtue of this section in respect of any act, neglect or default of any officer of the Crown, unless that officer has been directly or indirectly appointed by the Crown and was at the material time paid in respect of his duties as an officer of the Crown wholly out of the Consolidated Fund of the United Kingdom, moneys provided by Parliament, the Scottish Consolidated Fund or any other Fund certified by the Treasury for the purposes of this subsection or was at the material time holding an office in respect of which the Treasury certify that the holder thereof would normally be so paid.

4   Application of law as to indemnity, contribution, joint and several tort-feasors, and contributory negligence

(1)   Where the Crown is subject to any liability by virtue of this Part of this Act, the law relating to indemnity and contribution shall be enforceable by or against the Crown in respect of the liability to which it is so subject as if the Crown were a private person of full age and capacity.

(3)   Without prejudice to the general effect of section one of this Act, the Law Reform (Contributory Negligence) Act 1945 (which amends the law relating to contributory negligence) shall bind the Crown.

11   Saving in respect of acts done under prerogative and statutory powers

(1)   Nothing in Part I of this Act shall extinguish or abridge any powers or authorities which, if this Act had not been passed, would have been exercisable by virtue of the prerogative of the Crown, or any powers or authorities conferred on the Crown by any statute, and, in particular, nothing in the said Part I shall extinguish or abridge any powers or authorities exercisable by the Crown, whether in time of peace or of war, for the purpose of the defence of the realm or of training, or maintaining the efficiency of, any of the armed forces of the Crown.

(2)   Where in any proceedings under this Act it is material to determine whether anything was properly done or omitted to be done in the exercise of the prerogative of the Crown, a Secretary of State may, if satisfied that the act or omission was necessary for any such purpose as is mentioned in the last preceding subsection, issue a certificate to the effect that the act or omission was necessary for that purpose; and the certificate shall, in those precedings, be conclusive as to the matter so certified.

PART II
JURISDICTION AND PROCEDURE

17   Parties to proceedings

(1)   The Minister for the Civil Service shall publish a list specifying the several Government departments which are authorised departments for the purposes of this Act, and the name and address for service of the person who is, or is acting for the purposes of this Act as, the solicitor for each such department, and may from time to time amend or vary the said list.

Any document purporting to be a copy of a list published under this section and purporting to be printed under the superintendence or the authority of His Majesty's Stationery Office shall in any legal proceedings be received as evidence for the purpose of establishing what departments are authorised departments for the purposes of this Act, and what person is, or is acting for the purposes of this Act as, the solicitor for any such department.

(2)   Civil proceedings by the Crown may be instituted either by an authorised Government department in its own name, whether that department was or was not at the commencement of this Act authorised to sue, or by the Attorney General.

(3)   Civil proceedings against the Crown shall be instituted against the appropriate authorised Government department, or, if none of the authorised Government departments is appropriate or the person instituting the proceedings has any reasonable doubt whether any and if so which of those departments is appropriate, against the Attorney General.

21   Nature of relief

(1)   In any civil proceedings by or against the Crown the court shall, subject to the provisions of this Act, have power to make all such orders as it has power to make in proceedings between subjects, and otherwise to give such appropriate relief as the case may require:

Provided that: —

(a)   where in any proceedings against the Crown any such relief is sought as might in proceedings between subjects be granted by way of injunction or specific performance, the court shall not grant an injunction or make an order for specific performance, but may in lieu thereof make an order declaratory of the rights of the parties; and

(b)   in any proceedings against the Crown for the recovery of land or other property the court shall not make an order for the recovery of the land or the delivery of the property, but may in lieu thereof make an order declaring that the plaintiff is entitled as against the Crown to the land or property or to the possession thereof.

(2)   The court shall not in any civil proceedings grant any injunction or make any order against an officer of the Crown if the effect of granting the injunction or making the order would be to give any relief against the Crown which could not have been obtained in proceedings against the Crown.

PART IV
MISCELLANEOUS AND SUPPLEMENTAL

40   Savings

(1)   Nothing in this Act shall apply to proceedings by or against, or authorise proceedings in tort to be brought against, His Majesty in His private capacity.

LIFE PEERAGES ACT 1958
(6 & 7 Eliz. 2, c. 21)

An Act to make provision for the creation of life peerages carrying the right to sit and vote in the House of Lords.   [30 April 1958]

1   Power to create life peerages carrying right to sit in the House of Lords

(1)   Her Majesty shall have power by letters patent to confer on any person a peerage for life having the incidents specified in subsection (2) of this section.

(2)   A peerage conferred under this section shall, during the life of the person on whom it is conferred, entitle him—

(a)   to rank as a baron under such style as may be appointed by the letters patent; and

(b)   subject to subsection (4) of this section, to receive writs of summons to attend the House of Lords and sit and vote therein accordingly,

and shall expire on his death.

(3)   A life peerage may be conferred under this section on a woman.

(4)   Nothing in this section shall enable any person to receive a writ of summons to attend the House of Lords, or to sit and vote in that House, at any time when disqualified therefor by law.

OBSCENE PUBLICATIONS ACT 1959
(7 & 8 Eliz. 2, c. 66)

An Act to amend the law relating to the publication of obscene matter; to provide for the protection of literature; and to strengthen the law concerning pornography.   [29 July 1959]

1   Test of obscenity

(1)   For the purposes of this Act an article shall be deemed to be obscene if its effect or (where the article comprises two or more distinct items) the effect of any one of its items is, if taken as a whole, such as to tend to deprave and corrupt persons who are likely, having regard to all relevant circumstances, to read, see or hear the matter contained or embodied in it.

(2)   In this Act "article" means any description of article containing or embodying matter to be read or looked at or both, any sound record, and any film or other record of a picture or pictures.

(3)   For the purposes of this Act a person publishes an article who—

(a)   distributes, circulates, sells, lets on hire, gives, or lends it, or who offers it for sale or for letting on hire; or

(b)   in the case of an article containing or embodying matter to be looked at or a record, shows, plays or projects it, or, where the matter is data stored electronically, transmits that data.

(4)   For the purposes of this Act a person also publishes an article to the extent that any matter recorded on it is included by him in a programme included in a programme service.

(5)   Where the inclusion of any matter in a programme so included would, if that matter were recorded matter, constitute the publication of an obscene article for the purposes of this Act by virtue of subsection (4) above, this Act shall have effect in relation to the inclusion of that matter in that programme as if it were recorded matter.

(6)   In this section "programme" and "programme service" have the same meaning as in the Broadcasting Act 1990.

2   Prohibition of publication of obscene matter

(1)   Subject as hereinafter provided, any person who, whether for gain or not, publishes an obscene article or who has an obscene article for publication for gain (whether gain to himself or gain to another) shall be liable—

(a) on summary conviction to a fine not exceeding the prescribed sum or to imprisonment for a term not exceeding six months;

(b) on conviction on indictment to a fine or to imprisonment for a term not exceeding five years or both.

(3) A prosecution for an offence against this section shall not be commenced more than two years after the commission of the offence.

(3A) Proceedings for an offence under this section shall not be instituted except by or with the consent of the Director of Public Prosecutions in any case where the article in question is a moving picture film of a width of not less than sixteen millimetres and the relevant publication or the only other publication which followed or could reasonably have been expected to follow from the relevant publication took place or (as the case may be) was to take place in the course of an exhibition of a film; and in this subsection "the relevant publication" means—

(a) in the case any proceedings under this section for publishing an obscene article, the publication in respect of which the defendant would be charged if the proceedings were brought; and

(b) in the case of any proceedings under this section for having an obscene article for publication for gain, the publication which, if the proceedings were brought, the defendant would be alleged to have had in contemplation.

(4) A person publishing an article shall not be proceeded against for an offence at common law consisting of the publication of any matter contained or embodied in the article where it is of the essence of the offence that the matter is obscene.

(4A) Without prejudice to subsection (4) above, a person shall not be proceeded against for an offence at common law—

(a) in respect of an exhibition of a film or anything said or done in the course of an exhibition of a film, where it is of the essence of the common law offence that the exhibition or, as the case may be, what was said or done was obscene, indecent, offensive, disgusting or injurious to morality; or

(b) in respect of an agreement to give an exhibition of a film or to cause anything to be said or done in the course of such an exhibition where the common law offence consists of conspiring to corrupt public morals or to do any act contrary to public morals or decency.

(5) A person shall not be convicted of an offence against this section if he proves that he had not examined the article in respect of which he is charged and had no reasonable cause to suspect that it was such that his publication of it would make him liable to be convicted of an offence against this section.

(6) In any proceedings against a person under this section the question whether an article is obscene shall be determined without regard to any publication by another person unless it could reasonably have been expected that the publication by the other person would follow from publication by the person charged.

(7) In this section "exhibition of a film" has the meaning given in paragraph 15 of Schedule 1 to the Licensing Act 2003.

3 Powers of search and seizure

(1) If a justice of the peace is satisfied by information on oath that there is reasonable ground for suspecting that, in any premises, or on any stall or vehicle, being premises or a stall or vehicle specified in the information, obscene articles are, or are from time to time, kept for publication for gain, the justice may issue a warrant under his hand empowering any constable to enter (if need be by force) and search the premises, or to search the stall or vehicle and to seize and remove any articles found therein or thereon which the constable has reason to believe to be obscene articles and to be kept for publication for gain.

(2) A warrant under the foregoing subsection shall, if any obscene articles are seized under the warrant, also empower the seizure and removal of any documents found in the premises or, as the case may be, on the stall or vehicle which relate to a trade or business carried on at the premises or from the stall or vehicle.

4 Defence of public good

(1) Subject to subsection (1A) of this section a person shall not be convicted of an offence against section two of this Act, and an order for forfeiture shall not be made under the

foregoing section, if it is proved that publication of the article in question is justified as being for the public good on the ground that it is in the interests of science, literature, art or learning, or of other objects of general concern.

(1A) Subsection (1) of this section shall not apply where the article in question is a moving picture film or soundtrack, but—

(a)   a person shall not be convicted of an offence against section 2 of this Act in relation to any such film or soundtrack, and

(b)   an order for forfeiture of any such film or soundtrack shall not be made under section 3 of this Act,

if it is proved that publication of the film or soundtrack is justified as being for the public good on the ground that it is in the interests of drama, opera, ballet or any other art, or of literature or learning.

(2)   It is hereby declared that the opinion of experts as to the literary, artistic, scientific or other merits of an article may be admitted in any proceedings under this Act either to establish or to negative the said ground.

(3)   In this section "moving picture soundtrack" means any sound record designed for playing with a moving picture film, whether incorporated with the film or not.

PARLIAMENTARY COMMISSIONER ACT 1967
(1967, c. 13)

An Act to make provision for the appointment and functions of a Parliamentary Commissioner for the investigation of administrative action taken on behalf of the Crown, and for purposes connected therewith.   [22 March 1967]

The Parliamentary Commissioner for Administration

1   Appointment and tenure of office

(1)   For the purpose of conducting investigations in accordance with the following provisions of this Act there shall be appointed a Commissioner, to be known as the Parliamentary Commissioner for Administration.

(2)   Her Majesty may by Letters Patent from time to time appoint a person to be the Commissioner.

(2A) A person appointed to be the Commissioner shall hold office until the end of the period for which he is appointed.

(3)   A person appointed to be the Commissioner may—

(a)   be relieved of office by Her Majesty at his own request, or

(b)   be removed from office by Her Majesty on the ground of misbehaviour, in consequence of Addresses from both Houses of Parliament.

(3A) Her Majesty may declare the office of Commissioner to have been vacated if satisfied that the person appointed to be the Commissioner is incapable for medical reasons—

(a)   of performing the duties of his office; and

(b)   of requesting to be relieved of it.

(3B) A person appointed to be the Commissioner is not eligible for re-appointment.

3   Administrative provisions

(1)   The Commissioner may appoint such officers as he may determine with the approval of the Treasury as to numbers and conditions of service.

4   Departments etc. subject to investigation

(1)   Subject to the provisions of this section and to the notes contained in Schedule 2 to this Act, this Act applies to the government departments, corporations and unincorporated bodies listed in that Schedule; and references in this Act to an authority to which this Act applies are references to any such corporation or body.

(2)   Her Majesty may by Order in Council amend Schedule 2 to this Act by the alteration of any entry or note, the removal of any entry or note or the insertion of any additional entry or note.

(3) An Order in Council may only insert an entry if—
    (a) it relates—
        (i) to a government department; or
        (ii) to a corporation or body whose functions are exercised on behalf of the Crown; or
    (b) it relates to a corporation or body—
        (i) which is established by virtue of Her Majesty's prerogative or by an Act of Parliament or an Order in Council or order made under an Act of Parliament or which is established in any other way by a Minister of the Crown in his capacity as a Minister or by a government department;
        (ii) at least half of whose revenues derive directly from money provided by Parliament, a levy authorised by an enactment, a fee or charge of any other description so authorised or more than one of those sources; and
        (iii) which is wholly or partly constituted by appointment made by Her Majesty or a Minister of the Crown or government department.

(3A) No entry shall be made if the result of making it would be that the Parliamentary Commissioner could investigate action which can be investigated by the Public Services Ombudsman for Wales under the Public Services Ombudsman (Wales) Act 2005.

(3B) No entry shall be made in respect of—
    (a) the Scottish Administration or any part of it;
    (b) any Scottish public authority with mixed functions or no reserved functions within the meaning of the Scotland Act 1998; or
    (c) the Scottish Parliamentary Corporate Body.

(4) No entry shall be made in respect of a corporation or body whose sole activity is, or whose main activities are, included among the activities specified in subsection (5) below.

(5) The activities mentioned in subsection (4) above are—
    (a) the provision of education, or the provision of training otherwise than under the Industrial Training Act 1982;
    (b) the development of curricula, the conduct of examinations or the validation of educational courses;
    (c) the control of entry to any profession or the regulation of the conduct of members of any profession;
    (d) the investigation of complaints by members of the public regarding the actions of any person or body, or the supervision or review of such investigations or of steps taken following them.

(6) No entry shall be made in respect of a corporation or body operating in an exclusively or predominantly commercial manner or a corporation carrying on under national ownership an industry or undertaking or part of an industry or undertaking.

(7) Any statutory instrument made by virtue of this section shall be subject to annulment in pursuance of a resolution of either House of Parliament.

5 Matters subject to investigation

(1) Subject to the provisions of this section, the Commissioner may investigate any action taken by or on behalf of a government department or other authority to which this Act applies, being action taken in the exercise of administrative functions of that department or authority, in any case where—
    (a) a written complaint is duly made to a member of the House of Commons by a member of the public who claims to have sustained injustice in consequence of maladministration in connection with the action so taken; and
    (b) the complaint is referred to the Commissioner, with the consent of the person who made it, by a member of that House with a request to conduct an investigation thereon.

(1A) Subsection (1C) of this section applies if—
    (a) a written complaint is duly made to a member of the House of Commons by a member of the public who claims that a person has failed to perform a relevant duty owed by him to the member of the public, and

(b)   the complaint is referred to the Commissioner, with the consent of the person who made it, by a member of the House of Commons with a request to conduct an investigation into it.

(1B) For the purposes of subsection (1A) of this section a relevant duty is a duty imposed by any of these—

(a)   a code of practice issued under section 32 of the Domestic Violence, Crime and Victims Act 2004 (code of practice for victims), or

(b)   sections 35 to 44 of that Act (duties of local probation boards in connection with victims of sexual or violent offences).

(1C) If this subsection applies, the Commissioner may investigate the complaint.

(2)   Except as hereinafter provided, the Commissioner shall not conduct an investigation under this Act in respect of any of the following matters, that is to say—

(a)   any action in respect of which the person aggrieved has or had a right of appeal, reference or review to or before a tribunal constituted by or under any enactment or by virtue of Her Majesty's prerogative;

(b)   any action in respect of which the person aggrieved has or had a remedy by way of proceedings in any court of law:

Provided that the Commissioner may conduct an investigation notwithstanding that the person aggrieved has or had such a right or remedy if satisfied that in the particular circumstances it is not reasonable to expect him to resort or have resorted to it.

(2A) Subsection (2)(a) of this section shall have effect in relation to the right of a person to make a complaint of unlawful discrimination under the Fair Employment and Treatment (Northern Ireland) Order 1998 as if it were such a right of appeal, reference or review as is mentioned in that subsection.

(3)   Without prejudice to subsection (2) of this section, the Commisioner shall not conduct an investigation under subsection (1) of this section in respect of any such action or matter as is described in Schedule 3 to this Act.

(4)   Her Majesty may by Order in Council amend the said Schedule 3 so as to exclude from the provisions of that Schedule such actions or matters as may be described in the Order; and any statutory instrument made by virtue of this subsection shall be subject to annulment in pursuance of a resolution of either House of Parliament.

(4A) Without prejudice to subsection (2) of this section, the Commissioner shall not conduct an investigation pursuant to a complaint under subsection (1A) of this section in respect of—

(a)   action taken by or with the authority of the Secretary of State for the purposes of protecting the security of the State, including action so taken with respect to passports, or

(b)   any action or matter described in any of paragraphs 1 to 4 and 6A to 11 of Schedule 3 to this Act.

(5)   In determining whether to initiate, continue or discontinue an investigation under this Act, the Commissioner shall, subject to the foregoing provisions of this section, act in accordance with his own discretion; and any question whether a complaint is duly made under this Act shall be determined by the Commissioner.

(5A) For the purposes of this section, administrative functions of a government department to which this Act applies include functions exercised by the department on behalf of the Scottish Ministers by virtue of section 93 of the Scotland Act 1998.

(5B) The Commissioner shall not conduct an investigation under this Act in respect of any action concerning Scotland and not relating to reserved matters which is taken by or on behalf of a cross-border public authority within the meaning of the Scotland Act 1998.

(6)   For the purposes of this section, administrative functions exercised by any person appointed by the Lord Chancellor as a member of the administrative staff of any court or tribunal shall be taken to be administrative functions of the Ministry of Justice or, in Northern Ireland, of the Northern Ireland Court Service.

6   Provisions relating to complaints

(1)   A complaint under this Act may be made by any individual, or by any body of persons whether incorporated or not, not being—

(a)   a local authority or other authority or body constituted for purposes of the public service or of local government or for the purposes of carrying on under national ownership any industry or undertaking or part of an industry or undertaking;

(b)   any other authority or body within subsection (1A) below.

(1A) An authority or body is within this subsection if—

(a)   its members are appointed by—

(i)   Her Majesty;

(ii)   any Minister of the Crown;

(iii)   any government department;

(iv)   the Scottish Ministers;

(v)   the First Minister; or

(vi)   the Lord Advocate, or

(b)   its revenues consist wholly or mainly of—

(i)   money provided by Parliament; or

(ii)   sums payable out of the Scottish Consolidated Fund (directly or indirectly).

(2)   Where the person by whom a complaint might have been made under the foregoing provisions of this Act has died or is for any reason unable to act for himself, the complaint may be made by his personal representative or by a member of his family or other individual suitable to represent him; but except as aforesaid a complaint shall not be entertained under this Act unless made by the person aggrieved himself.

(3)   A complaint shall not be entertained under this Act unless it is made to a member of the House of Commons not later than twelve months from the day on which the person aggrieved first had notice of the matters alleged in the complaint; but the Commissioner may conduct an investigation pursuant to a complaint not made within that period if he considers that there are special circumstances which make it proper to do so.

(4)   Except as provided in subsection (5) below a complaint shall not be entertained under this Act unless the person aggrieved is resident in the United Kingdom (or, if he is dead, was so resident at the time of his death) or the complaint relates to action taken in relation to him while he was present in the United Kingdom or on an installation in a designated area within the meaning of the Continental Shelf Act 1964 or on a ship registered in the United Kingdom or an aircraft so registered, or in relation to rights or obligations which accrued or arose in the United Kingdom or on such an installation, ship or aircraft.

(5)   A complaint may be entertained under this Act in circumstances not falling within subsection (4) above where—

(a)   the complaint relates to action taken in any country or territory outside the United Kingdom by an officer (not being an honorary consular officer) in the exercise of a consular function on behalf of the Government of the United Kingdom; and

(b)   the person aggrieved is a citizen of the United Kingdom and Colonies who, under section 2 of the Immigration Act 1971, has the right of abode in the United Kingdom.

7   Procedure in respect of investigations

(1)   Where the Commissioner proposes to conduct an investigation pursuant to a complaint under section 5(1) of this Act, he shall afford to the principal officer of the department or authority concerned, and to any person who is alleged in the complaint to have taken or authorised the action complained of, an opportunity to comment on any allegations contained in the complaint.

(1A) Where the Commissioner proposes to conduct an investigation pursuant to a complaint under section 5(1A) of this Act, he shall give the person to whom the complaint relates an opportunity to comment on any allegations contained in the complaint.

(2)   Every investigation under this Act shall be conducted in private, but except as aforesaid the procedure for conducting an investigation shall be such as the Commissioner considers appropriate in the circumstances of the case; and without prejudice to the generality of the foregoing provision the Commissioner may obtain information from such persons and in such manner, and make such inquiries, as he thinks fit, and may determine whether any person may be represented, by counsel or solicitor or otherwise, in the investigation.

8   Evidence

(1)   For the purposes of an investigation under section 5(1) of this Act the Commissioner may require any Minister, officer or member of the department or authority concerned

or any other person who in his opinion is able to furnish information or produce documents relevant to the investigation to furnish any such information or produce any such document.

(1A) For the purposes of an investigation pursuant to a complaint under section 5(1A) of this Act the Commissioner may require any person who in his opinion is able to furnish information or produce documents relevant to the investigation to furnish any such information or produce any such document.

(2) For the purposes of any investigation under this Act the Commissioner shall have the same powers as the Court in respect of the attendance and examination of witnesses (including the administration of oaths or affirmations and the examination of witnesses abroad) and in respect of the production of documents.

(3) No obligation to maintain secrecy or other restriction upon the disclosure of information obtained by or furnished to persons in Her Majesty's service, whether imposed by any enactment or by any rule of law, shall apply to the disclosure of information for the purposes of an investigation under this Act; and the Crown shall not be entitled in relation to any such investigation to any such privilege in respect of the production of documents or the giving of evidence as is allowed by law in legal proceedings.

(4) No person shall be required or authorised by virtue of this Act to furnish any information or answer any question relating to proceedings of the Cabinet or of any committee of the Cabinet or to produce so much of any document as relates to such proceedings; and for the purposes of this subsection a certificate issued by the Secretary of the Cabinet with the approval of the Prime Minister and certifying that any information, question, document or part of a document so relates shall be conclusive.

9   Obstruction and contempt

(1) If any person without lawful excuse obstructs the Commissioner or any officer of the Commissioner in the performance of his functions under this Act, or is guilty of any act or omission in relation to any investigation under this Act which, if that investigation were a proceeding in the Court, would constitute contempt of court, the Commissioner may certify the offence to the Court.

(2) Where an offence is certified under this section, the Court may inquire into the matter and, after hearing any witnesses who may be produced against or on behalf of the person charged with the offence, and after hearing any statement that may be offered in defence, deal with him in any manner in which the court could deal with him if he had committed the like offence in relation to the Court.

10   Reports by Commissioner

(1) In any case where the Commissioner conducts an investigation under this Act or decides not to conduct such an investigation, he shall send to the member of the House of Commons by whom the request for investigation was made (or if he is no longer a member of that House, to such member of that House as the Commissioner thinks appropriate) a report of the results of the investigation or, as the case may be, a statement of his reasons for not conducting an investigation.

(2) In any case where the Commissioner conducts an investigation under section 5(1) of this Act, he shall also send a report of the results of the investigation to the principal officer of the department or authority concerned and to any other person who is alleged in the relevant complaint to have taken or authorised the action complained of.

(2A) In any case where the Commissioner conducts an investigation pursuant to a complaint under section 5(1A) of this Act, he shall also send a report of the results of the investigation to the person to whom the complaint relates.

(3) If, after conducting an investigation under section 5(1) of this Act, it appears to the Commissioner that injustice has been caused to the person aggrieved in consequence of maladministration and that the injustice has not been, or will not be, remedied, he may, if he thinks fit, lay before each House of Parliament a special report upon the case.

(3A) If, after conducting an investigation pursuant to a complaint under section 5(1A) of this Act, it appears to the Commissioner that—

(a) the person to whom the complaint relates has failed to perform a relevant duty owed by him to the person aggrieved, and

(b)   the failure has not been, or will not be, remedied,

the Commissioner may, if he thinks fit, lay before each House of Parliament a special report upon the case.

(3B) For the purposes of subsection (3A) of this section "relevant duty" has the meaning given by section 5(1B) of this Act.

(4)   The Commissioner shall annually lay before each House of Parliament a general report on the performance of his functions under this Act and may from time to time lay before each House of Parliament such other reports with respect to those functions as he thinks fit.

(5)   For the purposes of the law of defamation, any such publication as is hereinafter mentioned shall be absolutely privileged.

Supplemental

12   Interpretation

(3)   It is hereby declared that nothing in this Act authorises or requires the Commissioner to question the merits of a decision taken without maladministration by a government department or other authority in the exercise of a discretion vested in that department or authority.

SCHEDULE 3
MATTERS NOT SUBJECT TO INVESTIGATION

1.   Action taken in matters certified by a Secretary of State or other Minister of the Crown to affect relations or dealings between the Government of the United Kingdom and any other Government or any international organisation of States or Governments.

2.   (1)   Action taken, in any country or territory outside the United Kingdom, by or on behalf of any officer representing or acting under the authority of Her Majesty in respect of the United Kingdom, or any other officer of the Government of the United Kingdom other than,

(a)   action which is taken by an officer (not being an honorary consular officer) in the exercise of a consular function on behalf of the Government of the United Kingdom;

(b)   action which is taken by an officer within a control zone or supplementary control zone; or

(c)   action which is taken by a British sea-fishery officer.

3.   Action taken in connection with the administration of the goverment of any country or territory outside the United Kingdom which forms part of Her Majesty's dominions or in which Her Majesty has jurisdiction.

4.   Action taken by the Secretary of State under the Extradition Act 2003.

5.   Action taken by or with the authority of the Secretary of State for the purposes of investigating crime or of protecting the security of the State, including action so taken with respect to passports.

6.   The commencement or conduct of civil or criminal proceedings before any court of law in the United Kingdom, of Service law proceedings (as defined by section 324(5) of the Armed Forces Act 2006) (anywhere), or of proceedings before any international court or tribunal.

6A.   Action taken by any person appointed by the Lord Chancellor as a member of the administrative staff of any court or tribunal, so far as that action is taken at the direction, or on the authority (whether express or implied) of any person acting in a judicial capacity or as a member of the tribunal.

6B.   (1)   Action taken by any member of the administrative staff of a relevant tribunal so far as that action is taken at the direction, or on the authority (whether express or implied), of any person acting in his capacity as a member of the tribunal.

(2)   In this paragraph, "relevant tribunal" has the meaning given by section 5(8) of this Act.

7.   Any exercise of the prerogative of mercy or of the power of a Secretary of State to make a reference in respect of any person to the High Court of Justiciary or the Courts Martial Appeal Court.

8.   (1)   Action taken on behalf of the Secretary of State by a local health authority, the National Health Service Commissioning Board, a clinical commissioning board or a Special Health Authority.

9.   Action taken in matters relating to contractual or other commercial transactions, whether within the United Kingdom or elsewhere, being transactions of a government department or authority to which this Act applies or of any such authority or body as is mentioned in paragraph (a) or (b) of subsection (1) of section 6 of this Act and not being transactions for or relating to—
   (a) the acquisition of land compulsorily or in circumstances in which it could be acquired compulsorily;
   (b) the disposal as surplus of land acquired compulsorily or in such circumstances as aforesaid.

10.   (1) Action taken in respect of appointments or removals, pay, discipline, superannuation or other personnel matters, in relation to—
   (a) service in any of the armed forces of the Crown, including reserve and auxiliary and cadet forces;
   (b) service in any office or employment under the Crown or under any authority to which this Act applies; or
   (c) service in any office or employment, or under any contract for services, in respect of which power to take action, or to determine or approve the action to be taken, in such matters is vested in Her Majesty, any Minister of the Crown or any such authority as aforesaid.

   (1A) Sub-paragraph (1)(a) shall not apply to any action which is taken by the Secretary of State in connection with the provision of any allowance, grant, supplement or benefit under—
   (a) the Naval, Military and Air Forces etc (Disablement and Death) Service Pensions Order 2006; or
   (b) the Armed Forces and Reserved Forces (Compensation Scheme) Order 2011.

   (2) Sub-paragraph (1)(c) above shall not apply to any action (not otherwise excluded from investigation by this Schedule) which is taken by the Secretary of State in connection with—
   (a) the provision of information relating to the terms and conditions of any employment covered by an agreement entered into by him under section 12(1) of the Overseas Development and Cooperation Act 1980 or pursuant to the exercise of his powers under Part 1 of the International Development Act 2002; or
   (b) the provision of any allowance, grant or supplement or any benefit (other than those relating to superannuation) arising from the designation of any person in accordance with such an agreement.

EUROPEAN COMMUNITIES ACT 1972
(1972, c. 68)

An Act to make provision in connection with the enlargement of the European Communities to include the United Kingdom, together with (for certain purposes) the Channel Islands, the Isle of Man and Gibraltar.   [17 October 1972]

PART I
GENERAL PROVISIONS

1   Short title and interpretation

   (2) In this Act—
         "the EU" means the European Union, being the Union established by the Treaty on European Union signed at Maastricht on 7th February 1992 (as amended by any later Treaty);
         "the Communities" means the European Economic Community, the European Coal and Steel Community and the European Atomic Energy Community;
         "the Treaties" or "the EU Treaties" means, subject to subsection (3) below, the pre-accession treaties, that is to say, those described in Part I of Schedule 1 to this Act, taken with—
         . . .

and any expression defined in Schedule 1 to this Act has the meaning there given to it.

(3)   If Her Majesty by Order in Council declares that a treaty specified in the Order is to be regarded as one of the EU Treaties as herein defined, the Order shall be conclusive that it is to be so regarded; but a treaty entered into by the United Kingdom after the 22nd January 1972, other than a pre-accession treaty to which the United Kingdom accedes on terms settled on or before that date, shall not be so regarded unless it is so specified, nor be so specified unless a draft of the Order in Council has been approved by resolution of each House of Parliament.

(4)   For purposes of subsections (2) and (3) above, "treaty" includes any international agreement, and any protocol or annex to a treaty or international agreement.

2   General implementation of Treaties

(1)   All such rights, powers, liabilities, obligations and restrictions from time to time created or arising by or under the Treaties, and all such remedies and procedures from time to time provided for by or under the Treaties, as in accordance with the Treaties are without further enactment to be given legal effect or used in the United Kingdom shall be recognised and available in law, and be enforced, allowed and followed accordingly; and the expression "enforceable EU right" and similar expressions shall be read as referring to one to which this subsection applies.

(2)   Subject to Schedule 2 to this Act, at any time after its passing Her Majesty may by Order in Council, and any designated Minister or department may by order, rules, regulations or scheme, make provision—

(a)   for the purpose of implementing any EU obligation of the United Kingdom, or enabling any such obligation to be implemented, or of enabling any rights enjoyed or to be enjoyed by the United Kingdom under or by virtue of the Treaties to be exercised; or

(b)   for the purpose of dealing with matters arising out of or related to any such obligation or rights or the coming into force, or the operation from time to time, of subsection (1) above;

and in the exercise of any statutory power or duty, including any power to give directions or to legislate by means of orders, rules, regulations or other subordinate instrument, the person entrusted with the power or duty may have regard to the objects of the EU and to any such obligation or rights as aforesaid.

In this subsection "designated Minister or Department" means such Minister of the Crown or government department as may from time to time be designated by Order in Council in relation to any matter or for any purpose, but subject to such restrictions or conditions (if any) as may be specified by the Order in Council.

(4)   The provision that may be made under subsection (2) above includes, subject to Schedule 2 to this Act, any such provision (of any such extent) as might be made by Act of Parliament, and any enactment passed or to be passed, other than one contained in this Part of this Act, shall be construed and have effect subject to the foregoing provisions of this section; but, except as may be provided by any Act passed after this Act, Schedule 2 shall have effect in connection with the powers conferred by this and the following sections of this Act to make Orders in Council or orders, rules, regulations or schemes.

3   Decisions on, and proof of, Treaties and Community instruments, etc.

(1)   For the purposes of all legal proceedings any question as to the meaning or effect of any of the Treaties, or as to the validity, meaning or effect of any EU instrument, shall be treated as a question of law (and, if not referred to the European Court, be for determination as such in accordance with the principles laid down by and any relevant decision of the European Court).

(2)   Judicial notice shall be taken of the Treaties, of the Official Journal of the European Union and of any decision of, or expression of opinion by, the European Court on any such question as aforesaid; and the Official Journal shall be admissible as evidence of any instrument or other act thereby communicated of the EU or of any EU institution.

LOCAL GOVERNMENT ACT 1972
(1972, c. 70)

An Act to make provision with respect to local government and the functions of local authorities in England and Wales; to amend Part II of the Transport Act 1968; to confer rights of appeal in respect of decisions relating to licences under the Home Counties (Music and Dancing) Licensing Act 1926; to make further provision with respect to magistrates' courts committees; to abolish certain inferior courts of record; and for connected purposes.   [26 October 1972]

PART VA
ACCESS TO MEETINGS AND DOCUMENTS OF CERTAIN AUTHORITIES, COMMITTEES AND SUB-COMMITEES

100A   Admission to meetings of principal councils

(1)   A meeting of a principal council shall be open to the public except to the extent that they are excluded (whether during the whole or part of the proceedings) under subsection (2) below or by resolution under subsection (4) below.

(2)   The public shall be excluded from a meeting of a principal council during an item of business whenever it is likely, in view of the nature of the business to be transacted or the nature of the proceedings, that, if members of the public were present during that item, confidential information would be disclosed to them in breach of the obligation of confidence; and nothing in this Part shall be taken to authorise or require the disclosure of confidential information in breach of the obligation of confidence.

(3)   For the purposes of subsection (2) above, "confidential information" means—

     (a)   information furnished to the council by a Government department upon terms (however expressed) which forbid the disclosure of the information to the public; and

     (b)   information the disclosure of which to the public is prohibited by or under any enactment or by the order of a court;

and, in either case, the reference to the obligation of confidence is to be construed accordingly.

(4)   A principal council may by resolution exclude the public from a meeting during an item of business whenever it is likely, in view of the nature of the business to be transacted or the nature of the proceedings, that if members of the public were present during that item there would be disclosure to them of exempt information, as defined in section 100I below.

(5A)   Where the public are excluded from a meeting of a principal council in England under subsection (2) or (4), the council may also prevent any person from reporting on the meeting using methods—

     (a)   which can be used without that person's presence at the meeting, and

     (b)   which enable persons not present at the meeting to see or hear the proceedings at the meeting as it takes place or later.

(7)   Subject to subsection (7A) nothing in this section shall require a principal council to permit the taking of photographs of any proceedings, or the use of any means to enable persons not present to see or hear any proceedings (whether at the time or later), or the making of any oral report on any proceedings as they take place.

(7A)   While a meeting of a principal council in England is open to the public, any person attending is to be permitted to report on the meeting.

(7B)   Subsection (7A) does not require a principal council in England to permit oral reporting or oral commentary on a meeting as it takes place if the person reporting or providing the commentary is present at the meeting.

(7C)   A person attending a meeting of a principal council in England for the purpose of reporting on the meeting must, so far as practicable, be afforded reasonable facilities for doing so.

(7D)   Subsection (7C) applies in place of subsection (6)(c) in the case of a principal council in England.

(7E) Any person who attends a meeting of a principal council in England for the purpose of reporting on the meeting may use any communication method, including the internet, to publish, post or otherwise share the results of the person's reporting activities.

(7F) Publication and dissemination may take place at the time of the meeting or occur after the meeting.

(8) This section is without prejudice to any power of exclusion to suppress or prevent disorderly conduct or other misbehaviour at a meeting.

(9) In this section "reporting" means—

(a) filming, photographing or making an audio recording of proceedings at a meeting,

(b) using any other means for enabling persons not present to see or hear proceedings at a meeting as it takes place or later, or

(c) reporting or providing commentary on proceedings at a meeting, orally or in writing, so that the report or commentary is available as the meeting takes place or later to persons not present.

100B Access to agenda and connected reports

(1) Copies of the agenda for a meeting of a principal council and, subject to subsection (2) below, copies of any report for the meeting shall be open to inspection by members of the public at the offices of the council in accordance with subsection (3) below.

(2) If the proper officer thinks fit, there may be excluded from the copies of reports provided in pursuance of subsection (1) above the whole of any report which, or any part which, relates only to items during which, in his opinion, the meeting is likely not to be open to the public.

(3) Any document which is required by subsection (1) above to be open to inspection shall be so open at least five clear days before the meeting, except that—

(a) where the meeting is convened at shorter notice, the copies of the agenda and reports shall be open to inspection from the time the meeting is convened, and

(b) where an item is added to an agenda copies of which are open to inspection by the public, copies of the item (or of the revised agenda), and the copies of any report for the meeting relating to the item, shall be open to inspection from the time the item is added to the agenda;

but nothing in this subsection requires copies of any agenda, item or report to be open to inspection by the public until copies are available to members of the council.

(4) An item of business may not be considered at a meeting of a principal council unless either—

(a) a copy of the agenda including the item (or a copy of the item) is open to inspection by members of the public in pursuance of subsection (1) above for at least five clear days before the meeting or, where the meeting is convened at shorter notice, from the time the meeting is convened; or

(b) by reason of special circumstances, which shall be specified in the minutes, the chairman of the meeting is of the opinion that the item should be considered at the meeting as a matter of urgency.

100C Inspection of minutes and other documents after meetings

(1) After a meeting of a principal council the following documents shall be open to inspection by members of the public at the offices of the council until the expiration of the period of six years beginning with the date of the meeting, namely—

(a) the minutes, or a copy of the minutes, of the meeting, excluding so much of the minutes of proceedings during which the meeting was not open to the public as discloses exempt information;

(b) where applicable, a summary under subsection (2) below;

(c) a copy of the agenda for the meeting; and

(d) a copy of so much of any report for the meeting as relates to any item during which the meeting was open to the public.

100D Inspection of background papers

(1) Subject, in the case of section 100C(1), to subsection (2) below, if and so long as copies of the whole or part of a report for a meeting of a principal council are

required by section 100B(1) or 100C(1) above to be open to inspection by members of the public—

    (a)   those copies shall each include a copy of a list compiled by the proper officer, of the background papers for the report or the part of the report; and

    (b)   at least one copy of each of the documents included in that list shall also be open to inspection at the offices of the council.

  (2)   Subsection (1) above does not require a copy of any document included in the list, to be open to inspection after the expiration of the period of four years beginning with the date of the meeting.

100E Application to committees and sub-committees

  (1)   Sections 100A to 100D above shall apply in relation to a committee or sub-committee of a principal council as they apply in relation to a principal council.

  (1A) But in section 100A, subsections (5A), (7A) to (7F) and (9) do not apply to a committee which is appointed or established jointly by one or more principal councils in England and one or more principal councils in Wales, or a sub-committee of such a committee.

100G Principal councils to publish additional information

  (1)   A principal council shall maintain a register stating—

    (a)   the name and address of every member of the council for the time being together with, in the case of a councillor, the ward or division which he represents; and

    (b)   in respect of every committee or sub-committee of the council—

        (i)   the members of the council who are members of the committee or sub-committee or who are entitled, in accordance with any standing orders relating to the committee or sub-committee, to speak at its meetings or any of them;

        (ii)   the name and address of every other person who is a member of the committee or sub-committee or who is entitled, in accordance with any standing orders relating to the committee or sub-committee, to speak at its meetings or any of them otherwise than in the capacity of an officer of the council; and

        (iii)   the functions in relation to the committee or sub-committee of every person falling within sub-paragraph (i) above who is not a member of the committee or sub-committee and of every person falling within sub-paragraph (ii) above.

  (2)   A principal council shall maintain a list—

    (a)   specifying those powers of the council which, for the time being, are exercisable from time to time by officers of the council in pursuance of arrangements made under this Act or any other enactment for their discharge by those officers; and

    (b)   stating the title of the officer by whom each of the powers so specified is for the time being so exercisable;

but this subsection does not require a power to be specified in the list if the arrangements for its discharge by the officer are made for a specified period not exceeding six months.

PART VI
DISCHARGE OF FUNCTIONS

101 Arrangements for discharge of functions by local authorities

  (1)   Subject to any express provision contained in this Act or any Act passed after this Act, a local authority may arrange for the discharge of any of their functions—

    (a)   by a committee, a sub-committee or an officer of the authority; or

    (b)   by any other local authority.

  (1A) A local authority may not under subsection (1)(b) above arrange for the discharge of any of their functions by another local authority if, or to the extent that, that function is also a function of the other local authority and is the responsibility of the other authority's executive.

  (1B) Arrangements made under subsection (1)(b) above by a local authority ("the first authority") with respect to the discharge of any of their functions shall cease to have effect with respect to that function if, or to the extent that,—

(a) the first authority are operating or begin to operate executive arrangements, and that function becomes the responsibility of the executive of that authority; or

(b) the authority with whom the arrangements are made ("the second authority") are operating or begin to operate executive arrangements, that function is also a function of the second authority and that function becomes the responsibility of the second authority's executive.

(1C) Subsections (1A) and (1B) above do not affect arrangements made by virtue of section 9EA or 19 of the Local Government Act 2000 (discharge of functions of and by another authority).

(2) Where by virtue of this section any functions of a local authority may be discharged by a committee of theirs, then, unless the local authority otherwise direct, the committee may arrange for the discharge of any of those functions by a sub-committee or an officer of the authority and where by virtue of this section any functions of a local authority may be discharged by a sub-committee of the authority, then, unless the local authority or the committee otherwise direct, the sub-committee may arrange for the discharge of any of those functions by an officer of the authority.

(3) Where arrangements are in force under this section for the discharge of any functions of a local authority by another local authority, then, subject to the terms of the arrangements, that other authority may arrange for the discharge of those functions by a committee, sub-committee or officer of theirs and subsection (2) above shall apply in relation to those functions as it applies in relation to the functions of that other authority.

(4) Any arrangements made by a local authority or committee under this section for the discharge of any functions by a committee, sub-committee, officer or local authority shall not prevent the authority or committee by whom the arrangements are made from exercising those functions.

(5) Two or more local authorities may discharge any of their functions jointly and, where arrangements are in force for them to do so,—

(a) they may also arrange for the discharge of those functions by a joint committee of theirs or by an officer of one of them and subsection (2) above shall apply in relation to those functions as it applies in relation to the functions of the individual authorities; and

(b) any enactment relating to those functions or the authorities by whom or the areas in respect of which they are to be discharged shall have effect subject to all necessary modifications in its application in relation to those functions and the authorities by whom and the areas in respect of which (whether in pursuance of the arrangements or otherwise) they are to be discharged.

(5A) Arrangements made under subsection (5) above by two or more local authorities with respect to the discharge of any of their functions shall cease to have effect with respect to that function if, or to the extent that, the function becomes the responsibility of an executive of any of the authorities.

(5B) Subsection (5A) above does not affect arrangements made by virtue of section 9EB or 20 of the Local Government Act 2000 (joint exercise of functions).

(5C) Arrangements under subsection (5) by two or more local authorities with respect to the discharge of any of their functions cease to have effect with respect to that function if, or to the extent that, the function becomes a general function of a mayor for the area of a combined authority.

(5D) Subsection (5C) does not prevent arrangements under subsection (5) being entered into in respect of that function by virtue of section 107E of the Local Democracy, Economic Development and Construction Act 2009 (joint exercise of general functions).

(5E) In subsection (5C), "general functions" has the meaning given in section 107D(2) of that Act.

(6) A local authority's functions with respect to levying, or issuing a precept for, a rate shall be discharged only by the authority.

PART VII
MISCELLANEOUS POWERS OF LOCAL AUTHORITIES

111   Subsidiary powers of local authorities

(1)   Without prejudice to any powers exercisable apart from this section but subject to the provisions of this Act and any other enactment passed before or after this Act, a local authority shall have power to do anything (whether or not involving the expenditure, borrowing or lending of money or the acquisition or disposal of any property or rights) which is calculated to facilitate, or is conducive or incidental to, the discharge of any of their functions.

(2)   For the purposes of this section, transacting the business of a parish or community meeting or any other parish or community business shall be treated as a function of the parish or community council.

(3)   A local authority shall not by virtue of this section raise money, whether by means of rates, precepts or borrowing, or lend money except in accordance with the enactments relating to those matters respectively.

(4)   In this section "local authority" includes the Common Council.

PART XI
GENERAL PROVISIONS AS TO LOCAL AUTHORITIES

Legal proceedings

222   Power of local authorities to prosecute or defend legal proceedings

(1)   Where a local authority consider it expedient for the promotion or protection of the interests of the inhabitants of their area—

(a)   they may prosecute or defend or appear in any legal proceedings and, in the case of civil proceedings, may institute them in their own name, and

(b)   they may, in their own name, make representations in the interests of the inhabitants at any public inquiry held by or on behalf of any Minister or public body under any enactment.

(2)   In this section "local authority" includes the Common Council and the London Fire and Emergency Planning Authority.

Byelaws

235   Power of councils to make byelaws for good rule and government and suppression of nuisances

(1)   The council of a district and the council of a London borough may make byelaws for the good rule and government of the whole or any part of the district principal or borough, as the case may be, and for the prevention and suppression of nuisances therein.

(2)   The confirming authority in relation to byelaws made under this section shall be the Secretary of State.

(3)   Byelaws shall not be made under this section for any purpose as respects any area if provision for that purpose as respects that area is made by, or is or may be made under, any other enactment.

SCHEDULE 12A

PART 1
DESCRIPTIONS OF EXEMPT INFORMATION: ENGLAND

1.   Information relating to any individual.
2.   Information which is likely to reveal the identity of an individual.
3.   Information relating to the financial or business affairs of any particular person (including the authority holding that information).

4.   Information relating to any consultations or negotiations, or contemplated consultations or negotiations, in connection with any labour relations matter arising between the authority or a Minister of the Crown and employees of, or office holders under, the authority.

5.   Information in respect of which a claim to legal professional privilege could be maintained in legal proceedings.

6.   Information which reveals that the authority proposes—
        (a)   to give under any enactment a notice under or by virtue of which requirements are imposed on a person; or
        (b)   to make an order or direction under any enactment.

7.   Information relating to any action taken or to be taken in connection with the prevention, investigation or prosecution of crime.

PART 4
DESCRIPTIONS OF EXEMPT INFORMATION: WALES

12.   Information relating to a particular individual.
13.   Information which is likely to reveal the identity of an individual.
14.   Information relating to the financial or business affairs of any particular person (including the authority holding that information).
15.   Information relating to any consultations or negotiations, or contemplated consultations or negotiations, in connection with any labour relations matter arising between the authority or a Minister of the Crown and employees of, or office holders under, the authority.
16.   Information in respect of which a claim to legal professional privilege could be maintained in legal proceedings.
17.   Information which reveals that the authority proposes—
        (a)   to give under any enactment a notice under or by virtue of which requirements are imposed on a person; or
        (b)   to make an order or direction under any enactment.
18.   Information relating to any action taken or to be taken in connection with the prevention, investigation or prosecution of crime

LOCAL GOVERNMENT ACT 1974
(1974, c. 7)

An Act to make further provision, in relation to England and Wales, with respect to the payment of grants to local authorities, rating and valuation, borrowing and lending by local authorities and the classification of highways; to extend the powers of the Countryside Commission to give financial assistance; to provide for the establishment of Commissions for the investigation of administrative action taken by or on behalf of local and other authorities; to restrict certain grants under the Transport Act 1968; to provide for the removal or relaxation of certain statutory controls affecting local government activities; to make provision in relation to the collection of sums by local authorities on behalf of water authorities; to amend section 259(3) of the Local Government Act 1972 and to make certain minor amendments of or consequential on that Act; and for connected purposes.   [8 February 1974]

PART III
LOCAL GOVERNMENT ADMINISTRATION

23   The Commission for Local Administration
        (1)   For the purpose of conducting investigations in accordance with this Part and Part 3A of this Act, there shall be—
               (a)   a body of commissioners to be known as the Commission for Local Administration in England,
               but the Commission may include persons appointed to act as advisers, not exceeding the number appointed to conduct investigations.

(2)   The Parliamentary Commissioner shall be a member of the Commission.

(3)   In the following provisions of this Part of this Act the expression "Local Commissioner" means a person, other than the Parliamentary Commissioner or an advisory member, who is a member of the Commission.

(4)   Appointments to the office of Commissioner shall be made by Her Majesty on the recommendation of the Secretary of State.

(5)   A Commissioner's appointment may be a full-time or part-time appointment and, with the Commissioner's consent, the terms of the appointment may be varied as to whether it is full-time or part-time.

(5A) A Commissioner must be appointed for a period of not more than 7 years.

(6)   A Commissioner may be relieved of office by Her Majesty at his own request or may be removed from office by Her Majesty on grounds of incapacity or misbehaviour.

(6A) A person appointed to be a Commissioner is not eligible for re-appointment.

(7)   The Secretary of State shall designate two of the Local Commissioners for England as chairman and vice-chairman respectively of the Commission for Local Administration in England.

(8A) The Commission must—
    (a)   divide the matters which may be investigated under this Part of the Act into such categories as they consider appropriate, and
    (b)   allocate, or make arrangements for allocating, responsibility for each category of matter to one or more of the Local Commissioners.

(10) The Commission—
    (a)   shall make arrangements for Local Commissioners to deal with matters for which they do not have responsibility pursuant to subsection 8A, and
    (b)   shall publish information about the procedures for making complaints under this Part of this Act.

25   Authorities subject to investigation

(1)   This Part of this Act applies to the following authorities—
    (a)   any local authority;
    (aaa) the Greater London Authority;
    (ab) a National Park Authority for a National Park in England;
    (b)   any joint board the constituent authorities of which are all local authorities;
    (bb) any development corporation established for the purposes of a new town;
    (bd) any urban development corporation established by an order under section 135 of the Local Government, Planning and Land Act 1980 for an urban development area in England;
    (bda) a Mayoral development corporation;
    (be) any housing action trust established under Part III of the Housing Act 1988 for an urban development area in England;
    (bf) the Homes and Communities Agency;
    (bg) a fire and rescue authority in England constituted by a scheme under section 2 of the Fire and Rescue Services Act 2004 or a scheme to which section 4 of that Act applies;
    (c)   any joint authority established by Part IV of the Local Government Act 1985;
    (cza) the London Fire and Emergency Planning Authority;
    (ca) any police and crime commissioner;
    (caa) the Mayor's Office for Policing and Crime;
    (cc) Transport for London;
    (ce) any economical prosperity board established under section 88 of the Local Democracy, Economic Development and Construction Act 2009;
    (cf) any combined authority established under section 103 of that Act;
    (d)   in relation to the flood defence functions of the Environment Agency, within the meaning of the Water Resources Act 1991, the Environment Agency and any Regional Flood and Coastal Committee for an area wholly or partly in England; and
    (e)   the London Transport Users' Committee.

(2)   Her Majesty may by Order in Council provide that this Part of this Act shall also apply, subject to any modifications or exceptions specified in the Order, to any authority specified in the Order, being an authority which is established by or under an Act of Parliament, and which has power to levy a rate, or to issue a precept.

(4)   Any reference to an authority to which this Part of this Act applies includes a reference—

(a)   to the members and officers of that authority, and

(b)   to a committee or sub-committee of that authority (including a joint committee or joint sub-committee on which the authority are represented),

and (for the avoidance of doubt) subsections (4ZA) to (5) apply for the purposes of this subsection.

(4ZA) Any reference to an authority to which this Part of this Act applies also includes, in the case of a local authority operating executive arrangements, the executive.

(4A) Any reference to an authority to which this Part of this Act applies also includes, in the case of the Greater London Authority, a reference to each of the following—

(a)   the London Assembly;

(5)   Any reference to an authority to which this Part of this Act applies also includes a reference to—

(c)   an admission appeal panel constituted by the authority in accordance with regulations under section 94(5) or 95(3) of the School Standards and Framework Act 1998, and

(d)   the governing body of any community, foundation or voluntary school maintained by the authority so far as acting in connection with the admission of pupils to the school or otherwise performing any of their functions under Chapter I of Part III of that Act, and

(e)   an exclusion review panel constituted by the authority in accordance with regulations under section 51A of the Education Act 2002.

(6)   Subsection (7) has effect where an authority to which this Part of this Act applies exercise a function entirely or partly by means of an arrangement with another person.

(7)   For the purposes of this Part of this Act, action taken by or on behalf of the other person in carrying out the arrangement shall be treated as action taken—

(a)   on behalf of the authority, and

(b)   in the exercise of the authority's function.

(8)   Subsection (7) does not have effect where, by virtue of another enactment, the action would be treated as action taken by the authority.

26   Matters subject to investigation

(1)   For the purpose of section 24A(1)(b), in relation to an authority to which this part of this Act applies, the following matters are subject to investigation by a Local Commissioner under this Part of this Act—

(a)   alleged or apparent maladministration in connection with the exercise of the authority's administrative functions;

(b)   an alleged or apparent failure in a service which it was the authority's function to provide;

(c)   an alleged or apparent failure to provide such a service;

(d)   an alleged or apparent failure in a service provided by the authority in pursuance of arrangements under section 7A of the National Health Service Act 2006;

(e)   an alleged or apparent failure to provide a service in pursuance of such arrangements.

(1A) Subsection (1) is subject to the following provisions of this section.

(5)   Before proceeding to investigate a matter, a Local Commissioner shall satisfy himself that—

(a)   the matter has been brought, by or on behalf of the person affected, to the notice of the authority to which it relates and that that authority has been afforded a reasonable opportunity to investigate the matter and to respond; or

(b)   in the particular circumstances, it is not reasonable to expect the matter to be brought to the notice of that authority or for that authority to be afforded a reasonable opportunity to investigate the matter and to respond.

(6)   A Local Commissioner shall not conduct an investigation under this Part of this Act in respect of any of the following matters, that is to say, —
(a)   any action in respect of which the person affected has or had a right of appeal, reference or review to or before a tribunal constituted by or under any enactment;
(b)   any action in respect of which in the person affected has or had a right of appeal to a Minister of the Crown; or
(c)   any action in respect of which the person affected has or had a remedy by way of proceedings in any court of law:
Provided that a Local Commissioner may conduct an investigation notwithstanding the existence of such a right or remedy if satisfied that in the particular circumstances it is not reasonable to expect the person affected to resort or have resorted to it.

(6A) A Local Commissioner shall not conduct an investigation under this Part of this Act in respect of any action taken by or on behalf of an authority in the exercise of any of the authority's functions otherwise than in relation to England.

(7)   A Local Commissioner shall not conduct an investigation in respect of any action which in his opinion affects all or most of the inhabitants of the following areas —
(aa) where the matter relates to a National Park Authority, the area of the Park for which it is such an authority;
(ba) where the matter relates to the Homes and Communities Agency, any designated area within the meaning of Part I of the Housing and Regeneration Act 2008;
(c)   in any other case, the area of the authority concerned.

(8)   Without prejudice to the preceding provisions of this section, a Local Commissioner shall not conduct an investigation under this Part of this Act in respect of any such action or matter as is described in Schedule 5 to this Act.

(9)   Her Majesty may by Order in Council amend the said Schedule 5 so as to add to or to exclude from the provisions of that Schedule (as it has effect for the time being) such actions or matters as may be described in the Order; and any Order made by virtue of this subsection shall be subject to annulment in pursuance of a resolution of either House of Parliament.

26A   Who can complain

(1)   Under this Part of this Act, a complaint about a matter may only be made —
(a)   by a member of the public who claims to have sustained injustice in consequence of the matter,
(b)   by a person authorised in writing by such a member of the public to act on his behalf, or
(c)   in accordance with subsection (2).

(2)   Where a member of the public by whom a complaint about a matter might have been made under this Part of this Act has died or is otherwise unable to authorise a person to act on his behalf, the complaint may be made —
(a)   by a personal representative (if any), or
(b)   by a peron who appears to a Local Commissioner to be suitable to represent him.

28   Procedure in respect of investigations

(1)   Where a Local Commissioner proposes to investigate a matter under this Part of this Act, he shall afford to the authority concerned, and to any person who is alleged in the complaint (if any), or who otherwise appears to the Local Commissioner, to have taken or authorised the action which would be the subject of the investigation, an opportunity to comment on the matter.

(2)   Every investigation under this Part of the Act shall be conducted in private, but except as aforesaid the procedure for conducting an investigation shall be such as the Local Commissioner considers appropriate in the circumstances of the case; and without prejudice to the generality of the preceding provision —
(a)   the Local Commissioner may, as well as adopting different procedure for different cases, adopt different procedure for cases of different descriptions; and
(b)   the Local Commissioner may obtain information from such persons and in such manner, and make such inquiries as he thinks fit, and may determine whether any person may be represented (by counsel or solicitor or otherwise) in the investigation.

(4)   The conduct of an investigation under this Part of this Act shall not affect any action taken by the authority concerned or any other person, or any power or duty of the authority concerned or any other person to take further action with respect to any matters subject to the investigation.

(5)   The differential procedure authorised by subsection (2)(a) includes (in particular) procedure for cases of a particular description that is expected to be faster than that for at least some other cases.

29   Investigations: further provisions

(1)   For the purposes of an investigation under this Part of this Act a Local Commissioner may require any member or officer of the authority concerned, or any other person who in his opinion is able to furnish information or produce documents relevant to the investigation, to furnish any such information or produce any such documents.

(2)   For the purposes of any such investigation a Local Commissioner shall have the same powers as the High Court in respect of the attendance and examination of witnesses, and in respect of the production of documents.

(3)   A Local Commissioner may, under subsection (1) above, require any person to furnish information concerning communications between the authority concerned and any Government department, or to produce any correspondence or other documents forming part of any such written communications.

(4)   No obligation to maintain secrecy or other restriction upon the disclosure of information obtained by or furnished to persons in Her Majesty's service, whether imposed by any enactment or by any rule of law, shall apply to the disclosure of information in accordance with subsection (3) above; and where that subsection applies the Crown shall not be entitled to any such privilege in respect of the production of documents or the giving of evidence as is allowed by law in legal proceedings.

30   Reports on investigations

(1)   If a Local Commissioner completes an investigation of a matter under this Part of this Act, he shall prepare a report of the results of the investigation and send a copy to each of the persons concerned (subject to subsection (1B)).

(1A)   A Local Commissioner may include in a report on a matter under subsection (1) any recommendations that he could include in a further report on the matter by virtue of section 31(2A) to (2BA).

(1B)   If, after the investigation of a matter is completed, the Local Commissioner decides—
(a)   that he is satisfied with action which the authority concerned have taken or propose to take, and
(b)   that it is not appropriate to prepare and send a copy of a report under subsection (1),
he may instead prepare a statement of his reasons for the decision and send a copy to each of the persons concerned.

(4)   Subject to the provisions of subsection (7) below, the authority concerned shall for a period of three weeks make copies of the report available for inspection by the public without charge at all reasonable hours at one or more of their offices; and any person shall be entitled to take copies of, or extracts from, the report when so made available.

(4A)   Subject to subsection (7) below, the authority concerned shall supply a copy of the report to any person on request if he pays such charge as the authority may reasonably require.

(5)   Not later than two weeks after the report is received by the authority concerned, the proper officer of the authority shall give public notice, by advertisement in the newspapers and such other ways as appear to him appropriate, that copies of the report will be available as provided by subsections (4) and (4A) above, and shall specify the date, being a date not more than one week after the public notice is first given from which the period of three weeks will begin.

(7)   The Local Commissioner may, if he thinks fit after taking into account the public interest as well as the interests of the complainant (if any) and of other persons, direct that a report specified in the direction shall not be subject to the provisions of subsections (4), (4A) and (5) above.

31   **Reports on investigations: further provisions**

(1)   This section applies where a Local Commissioner reports that there has been—
   - (a)   maladministration in connection with the exercise of the authority's administrative functions,
   - (b)   a failure in a service which it was the function of an authority to provide, or
   - (c)   a failure to provide such a service.

(2)   The report shall be laid before the authority concerned and it shall be the duty of that authority to consider the report and, within the period of three months beginning with the date on which they received the report, or such longer period as the Local Commissioner may agree in writing, to notify the Local Commissioner of the action which the authority have taken or propose to take.

(2A) If the Local Commissioner—
   - (a)   does not receive the notification required by subsection (2) above within the period allowed by or under that subsection; or
   - (b)   is not satisfied with the action which the authority concerned have taken; or
   - (c)   does not within a period of three months beginning with the end of the period so allowed or such longer period as the Local Commissioners may agree in writing, receive confirmation from the authority concerned that they have taken action, as proposed, to the satisfaction of the Local Commissioner,

   he shall make a further report setting out those facts and making recommendations.

(2B) Where the report relates to maladministration, those recommendations are recommendations with respect to action which, in the Local Commissioner's opinion, the authority concerned should take—
   - (a)   to remedy any injustice sustained by the person affected in consequence of the maladministration, and
   - (b)   to prevent injustice being caused in the future in consequence of similar maladministration in connection with the exercise of the authority's administrative functions.

(2C) Section 30 above, with any necessary modifications, and subsection (2) above shall apply to a report under subsection (2A) above as they apply to a report under that section.

(2D) If the Local Commissioner—
   - (a)   does not receive the notification required by subsection (2) above as applied by subsection (2C) above within the period allowed by or under that subsection or is satisfied before the period allowed by that subsection has expired that the authority concerned have decided to take no action, or
   - (b)   is not satisfied with the action which the authority concerned have taken or propose to take, or
   - (c)   does not within a period of three months beginning with the end of the period allowed by or under subsection (2) above as applied by subsection (2C) above, or such longer period as the Local Commissioner may agree in writing, receive confirmation from the authority concerned that they have taken action, as proposed, to the satisfaction of the Local Commissioner,

   he may, by notice to the authority, require them to arrange for a statement to be published in accordance with subsections (2E) and (2F) below.

(2E) The statement referred to in subsection (2D) above is a statement, in such form as the authority concerned and the Local Commissioner may agree, consisting of—
   - (a)   details of any action recommended by the Local Commissioner in his further report which the authority have not taken;
   - (b)   such supporting material as the Local Commissioner may require; and
   - (c)   if the authority so require, a statement of the reasons for their having taken no action on, or not the action recommended in, the report.

(2F) The requirements for the publication of the statement are that—
   - (a)   publication shall be in any two editions within a fortnight of a newspaper circulating in the area of the authority agreed with the Local Commissioner or, in default of agreement, nominated by him; and
   - (b)   publication in the first such edition shall be arranged for the earliest practicable date.

(2G) If the authority concerned—
    (a)   fail to arrange for the publication of the statement in accordance with subsections (2E) and (2F) above, or
    (b)   are unable, within the period of one month beginning with the date on which they received the notice under subsection (2D) above, or such longer period as the Local Commissioner may agree in writing, to agree with the Local Commissioner the form of the statement to be published,

the Local Commissioner shall arrange for such a statement as is mentioned in subsection (2E) above to be published in any two editions within a fortnight of a newspaper circulating within the authority's area.

(2H) The authority concerned shall reimburse the Commission on demand any reasonable expenses incurred by the Local Commissioner in performing his duty under subsection (2G) above.

(3) In any case where—
    (a)   a report is laid before an authority under subsection (2) or (2C) above, and
    (b)   on consideration of the report, it appears to the authority that a payment should be made to, or some other benefit should be provided for, a person who has suffered injustice in consequence of the maladministration or failure to which the report relates,

the authority may incur such expenditure as appears to them to be appropriate in making such a payment or providing such a benefit.

(4) Where the authority concerned is the Greater London Authority, any functions exercisable under this section by or in relation to the Authority shall be exercisable by or in relation to the Mayor and the Assembly acting jointly on behalf of the Authority, and references to the authority concerned (other than references to a member of the authority concerned) shall be construed accordingly.

34 Interpretation of Part III

(3) It is hereby declared that nothing in this Part of this Act authorises or requires a Local Commissioner to question the merits of a decision taken without maladministration by an authority in the exercise of a discretion vested in that authority.

SCHEDULE 5
MATTERS NOT SUBJECT TO INVESTIGATION

1.   The commencement or conduct of civil or criminal proceedings before any court of law.

2.   Action taken by or on behalf of any local policing body in connection with the investigation or prevention of crime.

3.   (1)   Action taken in matters relating to contractual or other commercial transactions of any authority to which Part 3 of this Act applies relating to—
        (a)   the operation of public passenger transport;
        (b)   the carrying on of a dock or harbour undertaking;
        (c)   the provision of entertainment;
        (d)   the provision and operation of industrial establishments;
        (e)   the provision and operation of markets.

    (2)   Sub-paragraph (1) does not include transactions for or relating to—
        (a)   the acquisition or disposal of land;
        (b)   the acquisition or disposal of moorings which are not moorings provided in connection with a dock or harbour undertaking.

    (3)   Sub-paragraph (1)(a) does not include action taken by or on behalf of the London Transport Users Committee in operating a procedure for examining complaints or reviewing decisions.

    (4)   Sub-paragraph (1)(e) does not include transactions relating to—
        (a)   the grant, renewal or revocation of a licence to occupy a pitch or stall in a fair or market, or
        (b)   the attachment of any condition to such a licence.

4.   Action taken in respect of appointments or removals, pay, discipline, superannuation or other personnel matters.

5.   (2)   Any action concerning—
           (a)   the giving of instruction, whether secular or religious, or
           (b)   conduct, curriculum, internal organisation, management or discipline in any school or other educational establishment maintained by the authority, except so far as relating to special educational needs (within the meaning given by section 579(1) of the Education Act 1996).

5A.   Action which—
           (a)   is taken by or on behalf of a local authority in its capacity as a registered provider of social housing, and
           (b)   is action in connection with its housing activities so far as they relate to the provision or management of social housing (and here "social housing" has the same meaning as in Part 2 of the Housing and Regeneration Act 2008).

5B.   In the case of a local authority which is a registered provider of social housing, action taken by or on behalf of the authority in connection with the management of dwellings owned by the authority and let on a long lease (and here "long lease" has the meaning given by section 59(3) of the Landlord and Tenant Act 1987).

6.   Any action taken by or on behalf of an authority mentioned in section 25(1)(ba) or (bb) of this Act which is—
           (a)   action in connection with functions in relation to social housing (and here "social housing" has the same meaning as in Part 2 of the Housing and Regeneration Act 2008), or
           (b)   action in connection with functions in relation to anything other than housing.

7.   Action taken by or on behalf of an authority mentioned in section 25(1)(bd) of this Act which is not action in connection with functions in relation to town and country planning.

8.   Action taken by or on behalf of the Homes and Communities Agency which is not action in connection with functions in relation to town and country planning.

HOUSE OF COMMONS DISQUALIFICATION ACT 1975
(1975, c. 24)

An Act to consolidate certain enactments relating to disqualification for membership of the House of Commons.   [8 May 1975]

1   Disqualification of holders of certain offices and places

(1)   Subject to the provisions of this Act, a person is disqualified for membership of the House of Commons who for the time being—
     (za)   is a Lord Spiritual;
     (a)   holds any of the judicial offices specified in Part I of Schedule 1 to this Act;
     (b)   is employed in the civil service of the Crown, whether in an established capacity or not, and whether for the whole or part of his time;
     (c)   is a member of any of the regular armed forces of the Crown;
     (d)   is a member of any police force maintained by a local policing body or police authority;
     (e)   is a member of the legislature of any country or territory outside the Commonwealth (other than Ireland); or
     (f)   holds any office described in Part II or Part III of Schedule 1.

(4)   Except as provided by this Act, a person shall not be disqualified for membership of the House of Commons by reason of his holding an office or place of profit under the Crown or any other office or place; and a person shall not be disqualified for appointment to or for holding any office or place by reason of his being a member of that House.

2   Ministerial offices

(1)   Not more than ninety-five persons being the holders of offices specified in Schedule 2 to this Act (in this section referred to as Ministerial offices) shall be entitled to sit and vote in the House of Commons at any one time.

(2)   If at any time the number of members of the House of Commons who are holders of Ministerial offices exceeds the number entitled to sit and vote in that House under subsection (1) above, none except any who were both members of that House and holders of Ministerial offices before the excess occurred shall sit or vote therein until the number has been reduced, by death, resignation or otherwise, to the number entitled to sit and vote as aforesaid.

(3)   A person holding a Ministerial office is not disqualified by this Act by reason of any office held by him ex officio as the holder of that Ministerial office.

5   Power to amend Schedule 1

(1)   If at any time it is resolved by the House of Commons that Schedule 1 to this Act be amended, whether by the addition or omission of any office or the removal of any office from one Part of the Schedule to another, or by altering the description of any office specified therein, Her Majesty may by Order in Council amend that Schedule accordingly.

6   Effects of disqualification and provision for relief

(1)   Subject to any order made by the House of Commons under this section,—

(a)   if any person disqualified by this Act for membership of that House, or for membership for a particular constituency, is elected as a member of that House, or as a member for that constituency, as the case may be, his election shall be void; and

(b)   if any person being a member of that House becomes disqualified by this Act for membership for the constituency for which he is sitting, his seat shall be vacated.

(2)   If, in a case falling or alleged to fall within subsection (1) above, it appears to the House of Commons that the grounds of disqualification or alleged disqualification under this Act which subsisted or arose at the material time have been removed, and that it is otherwise proper so to do, that House may by order direct that any such disqualification incurred on those grounds at that time shall be disregarded for the purposes of this section.

7   Jurisdiction of Privy Council as to disqualification

(1)   Any person who claims that a person purporting to be a member of the House of Commons is disqualified by this Act, or has been so disqualified at any time since his election, may apply to Her Majesty in Council, in accordance with such rules as Her Majesty in Council may prescribe, for a declaration to that effect.

(2)   Section 3 of the Judicial Committee Act 1833 (reference to the Judicial Committee of the Privy Council of appeals to Her Majesty in Council) shall apply to any application under this section as it applies to an appeal to Her Majesty in Council from a court.

8   Relaxation of obligation to accept office

(1)   No person being a member of the House of Commons, or for the time being nominated as a candidate for election to that House, shall be required to accept any office or place by virtue of which he would be disqualified by this Act for membership of that House, or for membership of that House for the constituency for which he is sitting or is a candidate.

(2)   This section does not affect any obligation to serve in the armed forces of the Crown, whether imposed by an enactment or otherwise.

SCHEDULE 2
MINISTERIAL OFFICE

Prime Minister and First Lord of the Treasury.
Lord President of the Council.
Lord Privy Seal.
Chancellor of the Duchy of Lancaster.
Paymaster General.
Secretary of State.
Chancellor of the Exchequer.
President of the Board of Trade.
Minister of State.

Chief Secretary to the Treasury.
Minister in charge of a public department of Her Majesty's Government in the United Kingdom (if not within the other provisions of this Schedule).
Attorney General.
Solicitor General.
Advocate General for Scotland.
Parliamentary Secretary to the Treasury.
Financial Secretary to the Treasury.
Parliamentary Secretary in a Government Department other than the Treasury, or not in a department.
Junior Lord of the Treasury.
Treasurer of Her Majesty's Household.
Comptroller of Her Majesty's Household.
Vice-Chamberlain of Her Majesty's Household.
Assistant Government Whip.

MINISTERIAL AND OTHER SALARIES ACT 1975
(1975, c. 27)

An Act to consolidate the enactments relating to the salaries of Ministers and Opposition Leaders and Chief Whips and to other matters connected therewith.   [8 May 1975]

1   Salaries

    (1)   Subject to the provisions of this Act—
        (a)   there shall be paid to the holder of any Ministerial office specified in Schedule 1 to this Act such salary as is provided for by that Schedule; and
        (b)   there shall be paid to the Leaders and Whips of the Opposition such salaries as are provided for by Schedule 2 to this Act.

    (2)   There shall be paid to the Lord Chancellor a salary (which shall be charged on and paid out of the Consolidated Fund of the United Kingdom) of—
        (a)   £68,827, where the Lord Chancellor is a member of the House of Commons;
        (b)   otherwise, £101,038.

    (3)   There shall be paid to the Speaker of the House of Commons a salary (which shall be charged on and paid out of the Consolidated Fund of the United Kingdom) of £75,766 a year; and on a dissolution of Parliament the Speaker of the House of Commons at the time of the dissolution shall for this purpose be deemed to remain Speaker until a Speaker is chosen by the New Parliament.

   (3A) There shall be paid to the Speaker of the House of Lords a salary (which shall be paid out of money provided by Parliament) of £101,038 a year.

    (5)   A person to whom any salary is payable under subsection (1) above shall be entitled to receive only one such salary, but if he is the holder of two or more offices in respect of which a salary is so payable and there is a difference between the salaries payable in respect of those offices, the office in respect of which a salary is payable to him shall be that in respect of which the highest salary is payable.

    (6)   Where a person who holds office as Lord Chancellor (and to whom a salary is accordingly payable under subsection (2)) is also the holder of one or more other offices in respect of which a salary is payable under this section, he shall only be entitled to one of those salaries.

    (7)   If, in the case of a person mentioned in subsection (6), there is a difference between the salaries payable in respect of the offices held by him, the office in respect of which a salary is payable to him shall be that in respect of which the highest salary is payable.

2   Opposition Leaders and Whips

    (1)   In this Act "Leader of the Opposition" means, in relation to either House of Parliament, that Member of that House who is for the time being the Leader in that House of the party in opposition to Her Majesty's Government having the greatest numerical strength in the House of Commons; and "Chief Opposition

Whip" means, in relation to either House of Parliament, the person for the time being nominated as such by the Leader of the Opposition in that House; and "Assistant Opposition Whip", in relation to the House of Commons, means a person for the time being nominated as such, and to be paid as such, by the Leader of the Opposition in the House of Commons.

(2) If any doubt arises as to which is or was at any material time the party in opposition to Her Majesty's Government having the greatest numerical strength in the House of Commons, or as to who is or was at any material time the leader in that House of such a party, the question shall be decided for the purposes of this Act by the Speaker of the House of Commons, and his decision, certified in writing under his hand, shall be final and conclusive.

(3) If any doubt arises as to who is or was at any material time the Leader in the House of Lords of the said party, the question shall be decided for the purposes of this Act by the Speaker of the House of Lords, and his decision, certified in writing under his hand, shall be final and conclusive.

4 Interpretation

(1) In this Act—

"Junior Lord of the Treasury" means any Lord Commissioner of the Treasury other than the First Lord and the Chancellor of the Exchequer;

"Minister of State" and "Parliamentary Secretary" have the same meanings as in the House of Commons Disqualification Act 1975.

HIGHWAYS ACT 1980
(1980, c. 66)

An Act to consolidate the Highways Acts 1959 to 1971 and related enactments with amendments to give effect to recommendations of the Law Commission. [13 November 1980]

Obstruction of highways and streets

137 Penalty for wilful obstruction

(1) If a person, without lawful authority or excuse, in any way wilfully obstructs the free passage along a highway he is guilty of an offence and liable to a fine not exceeding level 3 on the standard scale.

SENIOR COURTS ACT 1981
(1981, c. 54)

An Act to consolidate with amendments the Supreme Court of Judicature (Consolidation) Act 1925 and other enactments relating to the Senior Courts in England and Wales and the administration of justice therein; to repeal certain obsolete or unnecessary enactments so relating; to amend Part VIII of the Mental Health Act 1959, the Courts-Martial (Appeals) Act 1968, the Arbitration Act 1979 and the law relating to county courts; and for connected purposes. [28 July 1981]

PART I
CONSTITUTION OF SENIOR COURTS

The Senior Courts

1 The Senior Courts

(1) The Senior Courts of England and Wales shall consist of the Court of Appeal, the High Court of Justice and the Crown Court, each having such jurisdiction as is conferred on it by or under this or any other Act.

The Court of Appeal

2   The Court of Appeal

(1)   The Court of Appeal shall consist of—
     (a)   ex-officio judges, and
     (b)   ordinary judges, of whom the maximum full-time equivalent number is 38.

(2)   The following shall be ex-officio judges of the Court of Appeal—
     (b)   any person who was Lord Chancellor before 12 June 2003;
     (c)   any judge of the Supreme Court who at the date of his appointment was, or was qualified for appointment as, an ordinary judge of the Court of Appeal or held an office within paragraphs (d) to (g);
     (d)   the Lord Chief Justice;
     (e)   the Master of the Rolls;
     (f)   the President of the Queen's Bench Division;
     (g)   the President of the Family Division; and
     (h)   the Chancellor of the High Court;
   but a person within paragraph (b) or (c) shall not be required to sit and act as a judge of the Court of Appeal unless at the request of the Lord Chief Justice he consents to do so.

(2A)   The Lord Chief Justice may nominate a judicial officer holder (as defined in section 109(4) of the Constitutional Reform Act 2005) to exercise his function under subsection (2) of making requests to persons within paragraphs (b) and (c) of that subsection.

(3)   An ordinary judge of the Court of Appeal (including the vice-president, if any, of either division) shall be styled "Lord Justice of Appeal" or "Lady Justice of Appeal".

(4)   Her Majesty may by Order in Council from time to time amend subsection (1) so as to increase or further increase the maximum number of ordinary judges of the Court of Appeal.

(4A)   It is for the Lord Chancellor to recommend to Her Majesty the making of an Order under subsection (4).

(5)   No recommendation shall be made to Her Majesty in Council to make an Order under subsection (4) unless a draft of the Order has been laid before Parliament and approved by resolution of each House of Parliament.

(6)   The Court of Appeal shall be taken to be duly constituted notwithstanding any vacancy in the office of Lord Chief Justice, Master of the Rolls, President of the Queen's Bench Division, President of the Family Division or Chancellor of the High Court.

(7)   For the purposes of this section the full-time equivalent number of ordinary judges is to be calculated by taking the number of full-time ordinary judges and adding, for each ordinary judge who is not a full-time ordinary judge, such fraction as is reasonable.

3   Divisions of Court of Appeal

(1)   There shall be two divisions of the Court of Appeal, namely the criminal division and the civil division.

(2)   The Lord Chief Justice shall be president of the criminal division of the Court of Appeal and the Master of the Rolls shall be president of the civil division of that Court.

The High Court

4   The High Court

(1)   The High Court shall consist of—
     (b)   the Lord Chief Justice;
     (ba)   the President of the Queen's Bench Division;
     (c)   the President of the Family Division;
     (d)   the Chancellor of the High Court;
     (dd)   the Senior Presiding Judge;
     (ddd) the vice-president of the Queen's Bench Division; and
     (e)   the puisne judges of that court, of whom the maximum full-time equivalent number is 108.

(2)   The puisne judges of the High Court shall be styled "Justices of the High Court".

(3)   All the judges of the High Court shall, except where this Act expressly provides otherwise, have in all respects equal power, authority and jurisdiction.

5   Divisions of High Court

(1)   There shall be three divisions of the High Court namely—

(a)   the Chancery Division, consisting of the Chancellor of the High Court, who shall be president thereof, and such of the puisne judges as are for the time being attached thereto in accordance with this section;

(b)   the Queen's Bench Division, consisting of the Lord Chief Justice, the President of the Queen's Bench Division, the vice-president of the Queen's Bench Division, and such of the puisne judges as are for the time being so attached thereto; and

(c)   the Family Division, consisting of the President of the Family Division and such of the puisne judges as are for the time being so attached thereto.

The Crown Court

8   The Crown Court

(1)   The jurisdiction of the Crown Court shall be exercisable by—

(a)   any judge of the High Court; or

(b)   any Circuit judge, Recorder or District Judge (Magistrates' Courts); or

(c)   subject to and in accordance with the provisions of sections 74 and 75(2), a judge of the High Court, Circuit judge or Recorder sitting with not more than four justices of the peace,

and any such persons when exercising the jurisdiction of the Crown Court shall be judges of the Crown Court.

(1A)   The jurisdiction of the Crown Court exercisable by a qualifying judge advocate by virtue of subsection (1) is the jurisdiction of the Court in relation to any criminal cause or matter other than an appeal from a youth court.

(2)   A justice of the peace is not disqualified from acting as a judge of the Crown Court merely because the proceedings are not at a place within the local justice area to which he is assigned or because the proceedings are not related to that area in any other way.

(3)   When the Crown Court sits in the City of London it shall be known as the Central Criminal Court; and the Lord Mayor of the City and any Alderman of the City shall be entitled to sit as judges of the Central Criminal Court with any judge of the High Court, Circuit judge, Recorder or District Judge (Magistrates' Courts).

10   Appointment of judges of Senior Courts

(1)   Whenever the office of Lord Chief Justice, Master of the Rolls, President of the Queen's Bench Division, President of the Family Division or Chancellor of the High Court is vacant, Her Majesty may on the recommendation of the Lord Chancellor by letters patent appoint a qualified person to that office.

(2)   Subject to the limits on full-time equivalent numbers for the time being imposed by sections 2(1) and 4(1), Her Majesty may on the recommendation of the Lord Chancellor from time to time by letters patent appoint qualified persons as Lords Justices of Appeal or as puisne judges of the High Court.

(3)   No person shall be qualified for appointment—

(a)   as Lord Chief Justice, Master of the Rolls, President of the Queen's Bench Division, President of the Family Division or Chancellor of the High Court, unless he is qualified for appointment as a Lord Justice of Appeal or is a judge of the Court of Appeal;

(b)   as a Lord Justice of Appeal, unless—

(i)   he satisfies the judicial appointment eligibility condition on a 7-year basis; or

(ii)   he is a judge of the High Court; or

(c)   as a puisne judge of the High Court, unless—

(i)   he satisfies the judicial appointment eligibility condition on a 7-year basis; or

(ii)   he is a Circuit Judge who has held that office for at least 2 years.

(4)   A person appointed—

(a)   to any of the offices mentioned in subsection (1);

(b)   as a Lord Justice of Appeal;
(c)   as a puisne judge of the High Court;
shall take the required oaths as soon as may be after accepting office.

11   Tenure of office of judges of Senior Courts

(1)   This section applies to the office of any judge of the Senior Courts.
(2)   A person appointed to an office to which this section applies shall vacate it on the day on which he attains the age of seventy years unless by virtue of this section he has ceased to hold it before then.
(3)   A person appointed to an office to which this section applies shall hold that office during good behaviour, subject to a power of removal by Her Majesty on an address presented to Her by both Houses of Parliament.
(3A)   It is for the Lord Chancellor to recommend to Her Majesty the exercise of the power of removal under subsection (3).
(7)   A person who holds an office to which this section applies may at any time resign it by giving the Lord Chancellor notice in writing to that effect.
(8)   The Lord Chancellor, if satisfied by means of a medical certificate that a person holding an office to which this section applies—
(a)   is disabled by permanent infirmity from the performance of the duties of his office; and
(b)   is for the time being incapacitated from resigning his office,
may, subject to subsection (9), by instrument under his hand declare that person's office to have been vacated; and the instrument shall have the like effect for all purposes as if that person had on the date of the instrument resigned his office.
(9)   A declaration under subsection (8) with respect to a person shall be of no effect unless it is made—
(a)   in the case of any of the Lord Chief Justice, the Master of the Rolls, the President of the Queen's Bench Division, the President of the Family Division and the Chancellor of the High Court, with the concurrence of two others of them;
(b)   in the case of a Lord Justice of Appeal, with the concurrence of the Master of the Rolls;
(c)   in the case of a puisne judge of any Division of the High Court, with the concurrence of the senior judge of that Division.

12   Salaries etc. of judges of Senior Courts

(1)   Subject to subsections (2) and (3), there shall be paid to judges of the Senior Courts such salaries as may be determined by the Lord Chancellor with the concurrence of the Minister for the Civil Service.
(2)   Until otherwise determined under this section, there shall be paid to the judges mentioned in subsection (1) the same salaries as at the commencement of this Act.
(3)   Any salary payable under this section may be increased, but not reduced, by a determination or further determination under this section.

PART II
JURISDICTION

The Court of Appeal

15   General jurisdiction of Court of Appeal

(1)   The Court of Appeal shall be a superior court of record.
(2)   Subject to the provisions of this Act, there shall be exercisable by the Court of Appeal—
(a)   all such jurisdiction (whether civil or criminal) as is conferred on it by this or any other Act; and
(b)   all such other jurisdiction (whether civil or criminal) as was exercisable by it immediately before the commencement of this Act.
(3)   For all purposes of or incidental to—
(a)   the hearing and determination of any appeal to the civil division of the Court of Appeal; and

(b)   the amendment, execution and enforcement of any judgment or order made on such an appeal,

the Court of Appeal shall have all the authority and jurisdiction of the court or tribunal from which the appeal was brought.

(4)   It is hereby declared that any provision in this or any other Act which authorises or requires the taking of any steps for the execution or enforcement of a judgment or order of the High Court applies in relation to a judgment or order of the civil division of the Court of Appeal as it applies in relation to a judgment or order of the High Court.

16   Appeals from High Court

(1)   Subject as otherwise provided by this or any other Act (and in particular to the provision in section 13(2)(a) of the Administration of Justice Act 1969 excluding appeals to the Court of Appeal in cases where leave to appeal from the High Court directly to the Supreme Court is granted under Part II of that Act), or as provided by any order made by the Lord Chancellor under section 56(1) of the Access to Justice Act 1999, the Court of Appeal shall have jurisdiction to hear and determine appeals from any judgment or order of the High Court.

(2)   An appeal from a judgment or order of the High Court when acting as a prize court shall not be to the Court of Appeal, but shall be to Her Majesty in Council in accordance with the Prize Acts 1864 to 1944.

18   Restrictions on appeals to Court of Appeal

(1)   No appeal shall lie to the Court of Appeal—

(a)   except as provided by the Administration of Justice Act 1960, from any judgment of the High Court in any criminal cause or matter;

(b)   from any order of the High Court or any other court or tribunal allowing an extension of time for appealing from a judgment or order;

(c)   from any order, judgment or decision of the High Court or any other court or tribunal which, by virtue of any provision (however expressed) of this or any other Act, is final;

(d)   from a decree absolute of *divorce or* nullity of marriage, by a party who, having had time and opportunity to appeal from the decree nisi on which that decree was founded, has not appealed from the decree nisi;

(dd)   *from a divorce order;*

(fa)   from a dissolution order, nullity order or presumption of death order under Chapter 2 of Part 2 of the Civil Partnership Act 2004 that has been made final, by a party who, having had time and opportunity to appeal from the conditional order on which that final order was founded, has not appealed from the conditional order;

(g)   except as provided by Part I of the Arbitration Act 1996, from any decision of the High Court under that Part;

The High Court

General jurisdiction

19   General jurisdiction

(1)   The High Court shall be a superior court of record.

(2)   Subject to the provisions of this Act, there shall be exercisable by the High Court—

(a)   all such jurisdiction (whether civil or criminal) as is conferred on it by this or any other Act; and

(b)   all such other jurisdiction (whether civil or criminal) as was exercisable by it immediately before the commencement of this Act (including jurisdiction conferred on a judge of the High Court by any statutory provision).

28   Appeals from Crown Court and inferior courts

(1)   Subject to subsection (2), any order, judgment or other decision of the Crown Court may be questioned by any party to the proceedings, on the ground that it is wrong in law or is in excess of jurisdiction, by applying to the Crown Court to have a case stated by that court for the opinion of the High Court.

(2)   Subsection (1) shall not apply to—

    (a)   a judgment or other decision of the Crown Court relating to trial on indictment; or

    (b)   any decision of that court under the Local Government (Miscellaneous Provisions) Act 1982 which, by any provision of any of those Acts, is to be final.

(3)   Subject to the provisions of this Act and to rules of court, the High Court shall, in accordance with section 19(2), have jurisdiction to hear and determine—

    (a)   any application, or any appeal (whether by way of case stated or otherwise), which it has power to hear and determine under or by virtue of this or any other Act; and

    (b)   all such other appeals as it had jurisdiction to hear and determine immediately before the commencement of this Act.

(4)   In subsection (2)(a) the reference to a decision of the Crown Court relating to trial on indictment does not include a decision relating to a requirement to make a payment under regulations under section 23 or 24 of the Legal Aid, Sentencing and Punishment of Offenders Act 2012.

28A Proceedings on case stated by magistrates' court or Crown Court

(1)   This section applies where a case is stated for the opinion of the High Court—

    (a)   by a magistrates' court under section 111 of the Magistrates' Courts Act 1980; or

    (b)   by the Crown Court under section 28(1) of this Act.

(2)   The High Court may, if it thinks fit, cause the case to be sent back for amendment and, where it does so, the case shall be amended accordingly.

(3)   The High Court shall hear and determine the question arising on the case (or the case as amended) and shall—

    (a)   reverse, affirm or amend the determination in respect of which the case has been stated; or

    (b)   remit the matter to the magistrates' court, or the Crown Court, with the opinion of the High Court,

and may make such other order in relation to the matter (including as to costs) as it thinks fit.

(4)   Except as provided by the Administration of Justice Act 1960 (right of appeal to Supreme Court in criminal cases), a decision of the High Court under this section is final.

Other particular fields of jurisdiction

29 Mandatory, prohibiting and quashing orders

(1)   The orders of mandamus, prohibition and certiorari shall be known instead as mandatory, prohibiting and quashing orders respectively.

(1A)   The High Court shall have jurisdiction to make mandatory, prohibiting and quashing orders in those classes of case in which, immediately before 1st May 2004, it had jurisdiction to make orders of mandamus, prohibition and certiorari respectively.

(2)   Every such order shall be final, subject to any right of appeal therefrom.

(3)   In relation to the jurisdiction of the Crown Court, other than its jurisdiction in matters relating to trial on indictment, the High Court shall have all such jurisdiction to make mandatory, prohibiting or quashing orders as the High Court possesses in relation to the jurisdiction of an inferior court.

(3A)   The High Court shall have no jurisdiction to make mandatory, prohibiting or quashing orders in relation to the jurisdiction of a Court Martial in matters relating to—

    (a)   trial by the Court Martial for an offence, or

    (b)   appeals from the Service Civilian Court;

(4)   The power of the High Court under any enactment to require justices of the peace or a judge or officer of a county court to do any act relating to the duties of their respective offices, or to require a magistrates' court to state a case for the opinion of the High Court, in any case where the High Court formerly had by virtue of any enactment jurisdiction to make a rule absolute, or an order, for any of those purposes, shall be exercisable by mandatory order.

(5)   In any statutory provision—
    (a)   references to mandamus or to a writ or order of mandamus shall be read as references to a mandatory order;
    (b)   references to prohibition or to a writ or order of prohibition shall be read as references to a prohibiting order;
    (c)   references to certiorari or to a writ or order of certiorari shall be read as references to a quashing order; and
    (d)   references to the issue or award of a writ of mandamus, prohibition or certiorari shall be read as references to the making of the corresponding mandatory, prohibiting or quashing order.

(6)   In subsection (3) the reference to the Crown Court's jurisdiction in matters relating to trial on indictment does not include its jurisdiction relating to requirements to make payments under regulations under section 23 or 24 of the Legal Aid, Sentencing and Punishment of Offenders Act 2012.

31   Application for judicial review

(1)   An application to the High Court for one or more of the following forms of relief, namely—
    (a)   a mandatory, prohibiting or quashing order;
    (b)   a declaration or injunction under subsection (2); or
    (c)   an injunction under section 30 restraining a person not entitled to do so from acting in an office to which that section applies,
shall be made in accordance with rules of court by a procedure to be known as an application for judicial review.

(2)   A declaration may be made or an injunction granted under this subsection in any case where an application for judicial review, seeking that relief, has been made and the High Court considers that, having regard to—
    (a)   the nature of the matters in respect of which relief may be granted by mandatory, prohibiting or quashing orders;
    (b)   the nature of the persons and bodies against whom relief may be granted by such orders; and
    (c)   all the circumstances of the case,
it would be just and convenient for the declaration to be made or for the injunction to be granted, as the case may be.

(2A)   The High Court—
    (a)   must refuse to grant relief on an application for judicial review, and
    (b)   may not make an award under subsection (4) on such an application,
if it appears to the court to be highly likely that the outcome for the applicant would not have been substantially different if the conduct complained of had not occurred.

(2B)   The court may disregard the requirements in subsection (2A)(a) and (b) if it considers that it is appropriate to do so for reasons of exceptional public interest.

(2C)   If the court grants relief or makes an award in reliance on subsection (2B), the court must certify that the condition in subsection (2B) is satisfied.

(3)   No application for judicial review shall be made unless the leave of the High Court has been obtained in accordance with rules of court; and the court shall not grant leave to make such an application unless it considers that the applicant has a sufficient interest in the matter to which the application relates.

(3C)   When considering whether to grant leave to make an application for judicial review, the High Court—
    (a)   may of its own motion consider whether the outcome for the applicant would have been substantially different if the conduct complained of had not occurred, and
    (b)   must consider that question if the defendant asks it to do so.

(3D)   If, on considering that question, it appears to the High Court to be highly likely that the outcome for the applicant would not have been substantially different, the court must refuse to grant leave.

(3E)   The court may disregard the requirement in subsection (3D) if it considers that it is appropriate to do so for reasons of exceptional public interest.

(3F) If the court grants leave in reliance on subsection (3E), the court must certify that the condition in subsection (3E) is satisfied.

(4)   On an application for judicial review the High Court may award to the applicant damages, restitution or the recovery of a sum due if—

(a)   the application includes a claim for such an award arising from any matter to which the application relates; and

(b)   the court is satisfied that such an award would have been made if the claim had been made in an action begun by the applicant at the time of making the application.

(5)   If, on an application for judicial review, the High Court quashes the decision to which the application relates, it may in addition—

(a)   remit the matter to the court, tribunal or authority which made the decision, with a direction to reconsider the matter and reach a decision in accordance with the findings of the High Court, or

(b)   substitute its own decision for the decision in question.

(5A) But the power conferred by subsection (5)(b) is exercisable only if—

(a)   the decision in question was made by a court or tribunal,

(b)   the decision is quashed on the ground that there has been an error of law, and

(c)   without the error, there would have been only one decision which the court or tribunal could have reached.

(5B) Unless the High Court otherwise directs, a decision substituted by it under subsection (5)(b) has effect as if it were a decision of the relevant court or tribunal.

(6)   Where the High Court considers that there has been undue delay in making an application for judicial review, the court may refuse to grant—

(a)   leave for the making of the application; or

(b)   any relief sought on the application,

if it considers that the granting of the relief sought would be likely to cause substantial hardship to, or substantially prejudice the rights of, any person or would be detrimental to good administration.

(7)   Subsection (6) is without prejudice to any enactment or rule of court which has the effect of limiting the time within which an application for judicial review may be made.

(8)   In this section "the conduct complained of", in relation to an application for judicial review, means the conduct (or alleged conduct) of the defendant that the applicant claims justifies the High Court in granting relief.

POLICE AND CRIMINAL EVIDENCE ACT (PACE) 1984
(1984, c. 60)

An Act to make further provision in relation to the powers and duties of the police, persons in police detention, criminal evidence, police discipline and complaints against the police; to provide for arrangements for obtaining the views of the community on policing and for a rank of deputy chief constable; to amend the law relating to the Police Federations and Police Forces and Police Cadets in Scotland; and for connected purposes.   [31 October 1984]

PART I
POWERS TO STOP AND SEARCH

1   Power of constable to stop and search persons, vehicles etc.

(1)   A constable may exercise any power conferred by this section—

(a)   in any place to which at the time when he proposes to exercise the power the public or any section of the public has access, on payment or otherwise, as of right or by virtue of express or implied permission; or

(b)   in any other place to which people have ready access at the time when he proposes to exercise the power but which is not a dwelling.

(2) Subject to subsection (3) to (5) below, a constable—
    (a) may search—
        (i) any person or vehicle;
        (ii) anything which is in or on a vehicle,
    for stolen or prohibited articles, any article to which subsection (8A) below applies or any firework to which subsection (8B) below applies; and
    (b) may detain a person or vehicle for the purpose of such a search.
(3) This section does not give a constable power to search a person or vehicle or anything in or on a vehicle unless he has reasonable grounds for suspecting that he will find stolen or prohibited articles, any article to which subsection (8A) below applies, or any firework to which subsection (8B) below applies.
(4) If a person is in a garden or yard occupied with and used for the purposes of a dwelling or on other land so occupied and used, a constable may not search him in the exercise of the power conferred by this section unless the constable has reasonable grounds for believing—
    (a) that he does not reside in the dwelling; and
    (b) that he is not in the place in question with the express or implied permission of a person who resides in the dwelling.
(5) If a vehicle is in a garden or yard occupied with and used for the purposes of a dwelling or on other land so occupied and used, a constable may not search the vehicle or anything in or on it in the exercise of the power conferred by this section unless he has reasonable grounds for believing—
    (a) that the person in charge of the vehicle does not reside in the dwelling; and
    (b) that the vehicle is not in the place in question with the express or implied permission of a person who resides in the dwelling.
(6) If in the course of such a search a constable discovers an article which he has reasonable grounds for suspecting to be a stolen or prohibited article, an article to which subsection (8A) below applies or a firework to which subsection (8B) below applies, he may seize it.
(7) An article is prohibited for the purposes of this Part of this Act if it is—
    (a) an offensive weapon; or
    (b) an article—
        (i) made or adapted for use in the course of or in connection with an offence to which this sub-paragraph applies; or
        (ii) intended by the person having it with him for such use by him or by some other person.
(8) The offences to which subsection (7)(b)(i) above applies are—
    (a) burglary;
    (b) theft;
    (c) offences under section 12 of the Theft Act 1968 (taking motor vehicle or other conveyance without authority);
    (d) fraud (contrary to section 1 of the Fraud Act 2006); and
    (e) offences under section 1 of the Criminal Damage Act 1971 (destroying or damaging property).
(8A) This subsection applies to any article in relation to which a person has committed, or is committing or is going to commit an offence under section 139 *or 139AA* of the Criminal Justice Act 1988.
(8B) This subsection applies to any firework which a person possesses in contravention of a prohibition imposed by fireworks regulations.
(8C) In this section—
    (a) "firework" shall be construed in accordance with the definition of "fireworks" in section 1(1) of the Fireworks Act 2003; and
    (b) "fireworks regulations" has the same meaning as in that Act.
(9) In this Part of this Act "offensive weapon" means any article—
    (a) made or adapted for use for causing injury to persons; or
    (b) intended by the person having it with him for such use by him or by some other person.

2   Provisions relating to search under section 1 and other powers

(1)   A constable who detains a person or vehicle in the exercise—

    (a)   of the power conferred by section 1 above; or

    (b)   of any other power—

       (i)   to search a person without first arresting him; or

       (ii)   to search a vehicle without making an arrest,

need not conduct a search if it appears to him subsequently—

       (i)   that no search is required; or

       (ii)   that a search is impracticable.

(2)   If a constable contemplates a search, other than a search of an unattended vehicle, in the exercise—

    (a)   of the power conferred by section 1 above; or

    (b)   of any other power, except the power conferred by section 6 below and the power conferred by section 27(2) of the Aviation Security Act 1982—

       (i)   to search a person without first arresting him; or

       (ii)   to search a vehicle without making an arrest,

it shall be his duty, subject to subsection (4) below, to take reasonable steps before he commences the search to bring to the attention of the appropriate person—

       (i)   if the constable is not in uniform, documentary evidence that he is a constable; and

       (ii)   whether he is in uniform or not, the matters specified in subsection (3) below;

and the constable shall not commence the search until he has performed that duty.

(3)   The matters referred to in subsection (2)(ii) above are—

    (a)   the constable's name and the name of the police station to which he is attached;

    (b)   the object of the proposed search;

    (c)   the constable's grounds for proposing to make it; and

    (d)   the effect of section 3(7) or (8) below, as may be appropriate.

(4)   A constable need not bring the effect of section 3(7) or (8) below to the attention of the appropriate person if it appears to the constable that it will not be practicable to make the record in section 3(1) below.

(5)   In this section "the appropriate person" means—

    (a)   if the constable proposes to search a person, that person; and

    (b)   if he proposes to search a vehicle, or anything in or on a vehicle, the person in charge of the vehicle.

(6)   On completing a search of an unattended vehicle or anything in or on such a vehicle in the exercise of any such power as is mentioned in subsection (2) above a constable shall leave a notice—

    (a)   stating that he has searched it;

    (b)   giving the name of the police station to which he is attached;

    (c)   stating that an application for compensation for any damage caused by the search may be made to that police station; and

    (d)   stating the effect of section 3(8) below.

(7)   The constable shall leave the notice inside the vehicle unless it is not reasonably practicable to do so without damaging the vehicle.

(8)   The time for which a person or vehicle may be detained for the purposes of such a search is such time as is reasonably required to permit a search to be carried out either at the place where the person or vehicle was first detained or nearby.

(9)   Neither the power conferred by section 1 above nor any other power to detain and search a person without first arresting him or to detain and search a vehicle without making an arrest is to be construed—

    (a)   as authorising a constable to require a person to remove any of his clothing in public other than an outer coat, jacket or gloves; or

    (b)   as authorising a constable not in uniform to stop a vehicle.

3   Duty to make records concerning searches

(1)   Where a constable has carried out a search in the exercise of any such power as is mentioned in section 2(1) above, other than a search—

    (a)   under section 6 below; or

    (b)   under section 27(2) of the Aviation Security Act 1982,

a record of the search shall be made in writing unless it is not practicable to do so.

(2)   If a record of a search is required to be made by subsection (1) above—

    (a)   in a case where the search results in a person being arrested and taken to a police station, the constable shall secure that the record is made as part of the person's custody record;

    (b)   in any other case, the constable shall make the record on the spot, or, if that is not practicable, as soon as practicable after the completion of the search.

(6)   The record of a search of a person or a vehicle—

    (a)   shall state—

        (i)   the object of the search;

        (ii)   the grounds for making it;

        (iii)   the date and time when it was made;

        (iv)   the place where it was made;

        (v)   except in the case of a search of an unattended vehicle, the ethnic origins of the person searched or the person in charge of the vehicle searched (as the case may be); and

    (b)   shall identify the constable who carried out the search.

(6A)   The requirement in subsection (6)(a)(v) above for a record to state a person's ethnic origins is a requirement to state—

    (a)   the ethnic origins of the person as described by the person, and

    (b)   if different, the ethnic origins of the person as perceived by the constable.

(7)   If a record of a search of a person has been made under this section, the person who was searched shall be entitled to a copy of the record if he asks for one before the end of the period specified in subsection (9) below.

(8)   If—

    (a)   the owner of a vehicle which has been searched or the person who was in charge of the vehicle at the time when it was searched asks for a copy of the record of the search before the end of the period specified in subsection (9) below; and

    (b)   a record of the search of the vehicle has been made under this section,

the person who made the request shall be entitled to a copy.

(9)   The period mentioned in subsections (7) and (8) above is the period of 3 months beginning with the date on which the search was made.

(10)   The requirements imposed by this section with regard to records of searches of vehicles shall apply also to records of searches of vessels, aircraft and hovercraft.

4   Road checks

(1)   This section shall have effect in relation to the conduct of road checks by police officers for the purpose of ascertaining whether a vehicle is carrying—

    (a)   a person who has committed an offence other than a road traffic offence or a vehicle excise offence;

    (b)   a person who is a witness to such an offence;

    (c)   a person intending to commit such an offence; or

    (d)   a person who is unlawfully at large.

(2)   For the purposes of this section a road check consists of the exercise in a locality of the power conferred by section 163 of the Road Traffic Act 1988 in such a way as to stop during the period for which its exercise in that way in that locality continues all vehicles or vehicles selected by any criterion.

(3)   Subject to subsection (5) below, there may only be such a road check if a police officer of the rank of superintendent or above authorises it in writing.

(4)   An officer may only authorise a road check under subsection (3) above—

    (a)   for the purpose specified in subsection (1)(a) above, if he has reasonable grounds—

        (i)   for believing that the offence is an indictable offence; and

        (ii)   for suspecting that the person is, or is about to be, in the locality in which vehicles would be stopped if the road check were authorised;

    (b)   for the purpose specified in subsection (1)(b) above, if he has reasonable grounds for believing that the offence is an indictable offence;

(c)   for the purpose specified in subsection (1)(c) above, if he has reasonable grounds—
    (i)   for believing that the offence would be an indictable offence; and
    (ii)   for suspecting that the person is, or is about to be, in the locality in which vehicles would be stopped if the road check were authorised;

(d)   for the purpose specified in subsection (1)(d) above, if he has reasonable grounds for suspecting that the person is, or is about to be, in that locality.

(5)   An officer below the rank of superintendent may authorise such a road check if it appears to him that it is required as a matter of urgency for one of the purposes specified in subsection (1) above.

(6)   If an authorisation is given under subsection (5) above, it shall be the duty of the officer who gives it—
(a)   to make a written record of the time at which he gives it; and
(b)   to cause an officer of the rank of superintendent or above to be informed that it has been given.

(15)   Where a vehicle is stopped in a road check, the person in charge of the vehicle at the time when it is stopped shall be entitled to obtain a written statement of the purpose of the road check if he applies for such a statement not later than the end of the period of twelve months from the day on which the vehicle was stopped.

(16)   Nothing in this section affects the exercise by police officers of any power to stop vehicles for purposes other than those specified in subsection (1) above.

PART II
POWERS OF ENTRY, SEARCH AND SEIZURE

Search warrants

8   Power of justice of the peace to authorise entry and search of premises

(1)   If on an application made by a constable a justice of the peace is satisfied that there are reasonable grounds for believing—
(a)   that an indictable offence has been committed; and
(b)   that there is material on premises mentioned in subsection (1A) below which is likely to be of substantial value (whether by itself or together with other material) to the investigation of the offence; and
(c)   that the material is likely to be relevant evidence; and
(d)   that it does not consist of or include items subject to legal privilege, excluded material or special procedure material; and
(e)   that any of the conditions specified in subsection (3) below applies in relation to each set of premises specified in the application,
he may issue a warrant authorising a constable to enter and search the premises.

(1A)   The premises referred to in subsection (1)(b) above are—
(a)   one or more sets of premises specified in the application (in which case the application is for a "specific premises warrant"); or
(b)   any premises occupied or controlled by a person specified in the application, including such sets of premises as are so specified (in which case the application is for an "all premises warrant").

(1B)   If the application is for an all premises warrant, the justice of the peace must also be satisfied—
(a)   that because of the particulars of the offence referred to in paragraph (a) of subsection (1) above, there are reasonable grounds for believing that it is necessary to search premises occupied or controlled by the person in question which are not specified in the application in order to find the material referred to in paragraph (b) of that subsection; and
(b)   that it is not reasonably practicable to specify in the application all the premises which he occupies or controls and which might need to be searched.

(1C)   The warrant may authorise entry to and search of premises on more than one occasion if, on the application, the justice of the peace is satisfied that it is necessary to authorise multiple entries in order to achieve the purpose for which he issues the warrant.

(1D) If it authorises multiple entries, the number of entries authorised may be unlimited, or limited to a maximum.

(2) A constable may seize and retain anything for which a search has been authorised under subsection (1) above.

(3) The conditions mentioned in subsection (1)(e) above are—

    (a) that it is not practicable to communicate with any person entitled to grant entry to the premises;

    (b) that it is practicable to communicate with a person entitled to grant entry to the premises but it is not practicable to communicate with any person entitled to grant access to the evidence;

    (c) that entry to the premises will not be granted unless a warrant is produced;

    (d) that the purpose of a search may be frustrated or seriously prejudiced unless a constable arriving at the premises can secure immediate entry to them.

(4) In this Act "relevant evidence", in relation to an offence, means anything that would be admissible in evidence at a trial for the offence.

(5) The power to issue a warrant conferred by this section is in addition to any such power otherwise conferred.

9 Special provisions as to access

(1) A constable may obtain access to excluded material or special procedure material for the purposes of a criminal investigation by making an application under Schedule 1 below and in accordance with that Schedule.

(2) Any Act (including a local Act) passed before this Act under which a search of premises for the purposes of a criminal investigation could be authorised by the issue of a warrant to a constable shall cease to have effect so far as it relates to the authorisation of searches—

    (a) for items subject to legal privilege; or

    (b) for excluded material; or

    (c) for special procedure material consisting of documents or records other than documents.

10 Meaning of "items subject to legal privilege"

(1) Subject to subsection (2) below, in this Act "items subject to legal privilege"means—

    (a) communications between a professional legal adviser and his client or any person representing his client made in connection with the giving of legal advice to the client;

    (b) communications between a professional legal adviser and his client or any person representing his client or between such an adviser or his client or any such representative and any other person made in connection with or in contemplation of legal proceedings and for the purposes of such proceedings; and

    (c) items enclosed with or referred to in such communications and made—

        (i) in connection with the giving of legal advice; or

        (ii) in connection with or in contemplation of legal proceedings and for the purposes of such proceedings,

when they are in the possession of a person who is entitled to possession of them.

(2) Items held with the intention of furthering a criminal purpose are not items subject to legal privilege.

11 Meaning of "excluded material"

(1) Subject to the following provisions of this section, in this Act "excluded material" means—

    (a) personal records which a person has acquired or created in the course of any trade, business, profession or other occupation or for the purposes of any paid or unpaid office and which he holds in confidence;

    (b) human tissue or tissue fluid which has been taken for the purposes of diagnosis or medical treatment and which a person holds in confidence;

    (c) journalistic material which a person holds in confidence and which consists—

        (i) of documents; or

        (ii) of records other than documents.

(2) A person holds material other than journalistic material in confidence for the purposes of this section if he holds it subject —
    (a) to an express or implied undertaking to hold it in confidence; or
    (b) to a restriction on disclosure or an obligation of secrecy contained in any enactment, including an enactment contained in an Act passed after this Act.

(3) A person holds journalistic material in confidence for the purposes of this section if —
    (a) he holds it subject to such an undertaking, restriction or obligation; and
    (b) it has been continuously held (by one or more persons) subject to such an undertaking, restriction or obligation since it was first acquired or created for the purposes of journalism.

12   Meaning of "personal records"

In this Part of this Act "personal records" means documentary and other records concerning an individual (whether living or dead) who can be identified from them and relating —
    (a) to his physical or mental health;
    (b) to spiritual counselling or assistance given or to be given to him; or
    (c) to counselling or assistance given or to be given to him, for the purposes of his personal welfare, by any voluntary organisation or by any individual who —
        (i) by reason of his office or occupation has responsibilities for his personal welfare; or
        (ii) by reason of an order of a court has responsibilities for his supervision.

13   Meaning of "journalistic material"

(1) Subject to subsection (2) below, in this Act "journalistic material" means material acquired or created for the purposes of journalism.

(2) Material is only journalistic material for the purposes of this Act if it is in the possession of a person who acquired or created it for the purposes of journalism.

(3) A person who receives material from someone who intends that the recipient shall use it for the purposes of journalism is to be taken to have acquired it for those purposes.

14   Meaning of "special procedure material"

(1) In this Act "special procedure material" means —
    (a) material to which subsection (2) below applies; and
    (b) journalistic material, other than excluded material.

(2) Subject to the following provisions of this section, this subsection applies to material, other than items subject to legal privilege and excluded material, in the possession of a person who —
    (a) acquired or created it in the course of any trade, business, profession or other occupation or for the purposes of any paid or unpaid office; and
    (b) holds it subject —
        (i) to an express or implied undertaking to hold it in confidence; or
        (ii) to a restriction or obligation such as is mentioned in section 11(2)(b) above.

15   Search warrants — safeguards

(1) This section and section 16 below have effect in relation to the issue to constables under any enactment, including an enactment contained in an Act passed after this Act, of warrants to enter and search premises; and an entry on or search of premises under a warrant is unlawful unless it complies with this section and section 16 below.

(2) Where a constable applies for any such warrant, it shall be his duty —
    (a) to state —
        (i) the ground on which he makes the application;
        (ii) the enactment under which the warrant would be issued; and
        (iii) if the application is for a warrant authorising entry and search on more than one occasion, the ground on which he applies for such a warrant, and whether he seeks a warrant authorising an unlimited number of entries, or (if not) the maximum number of entries desired;
    (b) to specify the matters set out in subsection 2A below; and
    (c) to identify, so far as is practicable, the articles or persons to be sought.

(2A) The matters which must be specified pursuant to subsection (2)(b) above are—
    (a)   if the application relates to one or more sets of premises specified in the application, each set of premises which it is desired to enter and search;
    (b)   if the application relates to any premises occupied or controlled by a person specified in the application—
        (i)   as many sets of premises which it is desired to enter and search as it is reasonably practicable to specify;
        (ii)   the person who is in occupation or control of those premises and any others which it is desired to enter and search;
        (iii)   why it is necessary to search more premises than those specified under sub-paragraph (i); and
        (iv)   why it is not reasonably practicable to specify all the premises which it is desired to enter and search.

(3)   An application for such a warrant shall be made ex parte and supported by an information in writing.

(4)   The constable shall answer on oath any question that the justice of the peace or judge hearing the application asks him.

(5)   A warrant shall authorise an entry on one occasion only unless specified that it authorises multiple entries.

(5A) If it specifies that it authorises multiple entries, it must also specify whether the number of entries authorised is unlimited, or limited to a specified maximum.

(6)   A warrant—
    (a)   shall specify—
        (i)   the name of the person who applies for it;
        (ii)   the date on which it is issued;
        (iii)   the enactment under which it is issued; and
        (iv)   each set of premises to be searched, or (in the case of an all premises warrant) the person who is in occupation or control of premises to be searched, together with any premises under his occupation or control which can be specified and which are to be searched; and
    (b)   shall identify, so far as is practicable, the articles or persons to be sought.

16   Execution of warrants

(1)   A warrant to enter and search premises may be executed by any constable.

(2)   Such a warrant may authorise persons to accompany any constable who is executing it.

(2A) A person so authorised has the same powers as the constable whom he accompanies in respect of—
    (a)   the execution of the warrant, and
    (b)   the seizure of anything to which the warrant relates.

(2B) But he may exercise those powers only in the company, and under the supervision, of a constable.

(3)   Entry and search under a warrant must be within three months from the date of its issue.

(3A) If the warrant is an all premises warrant, no premises which are not specified in it may be entered or searched unless a police officer of at least the rank of inspector has in writing authorised them to be entered.

(3B) No premises may be entered or searched for the second or any subsequent time under a warrant which authorises multiple entries unless a police officer of at least the rank of inspector has in writing authorised that entry to those premises.

(4)   Entry and search under a warrant must be at a reasonable hour unless it appears to the constable executing it that the purpose of a search may be frustrated on an entry at a reasonable hour.

(5)   Where the occupier of premises which are to be entered and searched is present at the time when a constable seeks to execute a warrant to enter and search them, the constable—
    (a)   shall identify himself to the occupier and, if not in uniform, shall produce to him documentary evidence that he is a constable;
    (b)   shall produce the warrant to him; and
    (c)   shall supply him with a copy of it.

(6)   Where—
    (a)   the occupier of such premises is not present at the time when a constable seeks to execute such a warrant; but
    (b)   some other person who appears to the constable to be in charge of the premises is present,
    subsection (5) above shall have effect as if any reference to the occupier were a reference to that other person.

(7)   If there is no person present who appears to the constable to be in charge of the premises, he shall leave a copy of the warrant in a prominent place on the premises.

(8)   A search under a warrant may only be a search to the extent required for the purpose for which the warrant was issued.

(9)   A constable executing a warrant shall make an endorsement on it stating—
    (a)   whether the articles or persons sought were found; and
    (b)   whether any articles were seized, other than articles which were sought, and
    unless the warrant is a warrant specifying one set of premises only, he shall do so separately in respect of each set of premises entered and searched, which he shall in each case state in the endorsement.

Entry and search without search warrant

17   Entry for purpose of arrest etc.

(1)   Subject to the following provisions of this section, and without prejudice to any other enactment, a constable may enter and search any premises for the purpose—
    (a)   of executing—
        (i)   a warrant of arrest issued in connection with or arising out of criminal proceedings; or
        (ii)   a warrant of commitment issued under section 76 of the Magistrates' Courts Act 1980;
    (b)   of arresting a person for an indictable offence;
    (c)   of arresting a person for an offence under—
        (i)   section 1 (prohibition of uniforms in connection with political objects) ... of the Public Order Act 1936;
        (ii)   any enactment contained in sections 6 to 8 or 10 of the Criminal Law Act 1977 (offences relating to entering and remaining on property);
        (iii)   section 4 of the Public Order Act 1986 (fear or provocation of violence); or
        (iiia)   section 4 (driving etc. when under influence of drink or drugs) or 163 (failure to stop when required to do so by constable in uniform) of the Road Traffic Act 1988;
        (iiib)   section 27 of the Transport and Works Act 1992 (which relates to offences involving drink or drugs);
        (iv)   section 76 of the Criminal Justice and Public Order Act 1994 (failure to comply with an interim possession order);
        (v)   any of sections 4, 5, 6(1) and (2), 7 and 8(1) and (2) of the Animal Welfare Act 2006 (offences relating to the prevention of harm to animals);
        (vi)   section 144 of the Legal Aid, Sentencing and Punishment of Offenders Act 2012 (squatting in a residential building);
    (ca)   of arresting, in pursuance of section 32(1A) of the Children and Young Persons Act 1969, any child or young person who has been remanded to local authority accommodation or youth detention accommodation under section 91 of the Legal Aid, Sentencing and Punishment of Offenders Act 2012;
    (caa)   of arresting a person for an offence to which section 61 of the Animal Health Act 1981 applies;
    (cb)   of recapturing any person who is, or is deemed for any purpose to be, unlawfully at large while liable to be detained—
        (i)   in a prison, remand centre, young offender institution, secure training centre, or secure college;
        (ii)   in pursuance of section 92 of the Powers of Criminal Courts (Sentencing) Act 2000 (dealing with children and young persons guilty of grave crimes), in any other place;

    (d)   of recapturing any person whatever who is unlawfully at large and whom he is pursuing; or

    (e)   of saving life or limb or preventing serious damage to property.

(2)   Except for the purpose specified in paragraph (e) of subsection (1) above, the powers of entry and search conferred by this section—

    (a)   are only exercisable if the constable has reasonable grounds for believing that the person whom he is seeking is on the premises; and

    (b)   are limited, in relation to premises consisting of two or more separate dwellings, to powers to enter and search—

        (i)   any parts of the premises which the occupiers of any dwelling comprised in the premises use in common with the occupiers of any other such dwelling; and

        (ii)   any such dwelling in which the constable has reasonable grounds for believing that the person whom he is seeking may be.

(3)   The powers of entry and search conferred by this section are only exercisable for the purposes specified in subsection (1)(c)(ii), (iv) or (vi) above by a constable in uniform.

(4)   The power of search conferred by this section is only a power to search to the extent that is reasonably required for the purpose for which the power of entry is exercised.

(5)   Subject to subsection (6) below, all the rules of common law under which a constable has power to enter premises without a warrant are hereby abolished.

(6)   Nothing in subsection (5) above affects any power of entry to deal with or prevent a breach of the peace.

18 Entry and search after arrest

(1)   Subject to the following provisions of this section, a constable may enter and search any premises occupied or controlled by a person who is under arrest for an indictable offence, if he has reasonable grounds for suspecting that there is on the premises evidence, other than items subject to legal privilege, that relates—

    (a)   to that offence; or

    (b)   to some other indictable offence which is connected with or similar to that offence.

(2)   A constable may seize and retain anything for which he may search under subsection (1) above.

(3)   The power to search conferred by subsection (1) above is only a power to search to the extent that is reasonably required for the purpose of discovering such evidence.

(4)   Subject to subsection (5) below, the powers conferred by this section may not be exercised unless an officer of the rank of inspector or above has authorised them in writing.

(5)   A constable may conduct a search under subsection (1)—

    (a)   before the person is taken to a police station or released on bail under section 30A, and

    (b)   without obtaining an authorisation under subsection (4),

    if the condition in subsection (5A) is satisfied.

(5A)   The condition is that the presence of the person at a place (other than a police station) is necessary for the effective investigation of the offence.

(6)   If a constable conducts a search by virtue of subsection (5) above, he shall inform an officer of the rank of inspector or above that he has made the search as soon as practicable after he has made it.

(7)   An officer who—

    (a)   authorises a search; or

    (b)   is informed of a search under subsection (6) above, shall make a record in writing—

        (i)   of the grounds for the search; and

        (ii)   of the nature of the evidence that was sought.

(8)   If the person who was in occupation or control of the premises at the time of the search is in police detention at the time the record is to be made, the officer shall make the record as part of his custody record.

Seizure etc.

19   General power of seizure etc.

(1)   The powers conferred by subsections (2), (3) and (4) below are exercisable by a constable who is lawfully on any premises.

(2)   The constable may seize anything which is on the premises if he has reasonable grounds for believing—
   (a)   that it has been obtained in consequence of the commission of an offence; and
   (b)   that it is necessary to seize it in order to prevent it being concealed, lost, damaged, altered or destroyed.

(3)   The constable may seize anything which is on the premises if he has reasonable grounds for believing—
   (a)   that it is evidence in relation to an offence which he is investigating or any other offence; and
   (b)   that it is necessary to seize it in order to prevent the evidence being concealed, lost, altered or destroyed.

(4)   The constable may require any information which is stored in any electronic form and is accessible from the premises to be produced in a form in which it can be taken away and in which it is visible and legible or which can readily be produced in a visible and legible form if he has reasonable grounds for believing—
   (a)   that—
      (i)   it is evidence in relation to an offence which he is investigating or any other offence; or
      (ii)   it has been obtained in consequence of the commission of an offence; and
   (b)   that it is necessary to do so in order to prevent it being concealed, lost, tampered with or destroyed.

(5)   The powers conferred by this section are in addition to any power otherwise conferred.

(6)   No power of seizure conferred on a constable under any enactment (including an enactment contained in an Act passed after this Act) is to be taken to authorise the seizure of an item which the constable exercising the power has reasonable grounds for believing to be subject to legal privilege.

20   Extension of powers of seizure to computerised information

(1)   Every power of seizure which is conferred by an enactment to which this section applies on a constable who has entered premises in the exercise of a power conferred by an enactment shall be construed as including a power to require any information stored in any electronic form and accessible from the premises to be produced in a form in which it can be taken away and in which it is visible and legible or from which it can readily be produced in a visible and legible form.

(2)   This section applies—
   (a)   to any enactment contained in an Act passed before this Act;
   (b)   to sections 8 and 18 above;
   (c)   to paragraph 13 of Schedule 1 to this Act; and
   (d)   to any enactment contained in an Act passed after this Act.

21   Access and copying

(1)   A constable who seizes anything in the exercise of a power conferred by any enactment, including an enactment contained in an Act passed after this Act, shall, if so requested by a person showing himself—
   (a)   to be the occupier of premises on which it was seized; or
   (b)   to have had custody or control of it immediately before the seizure,
   provide that person with a record of what he seized.

(2)   The officer shall provide the record within a reasonable time from the making of the request for it.

(3)   Subject to subsection (8) below, if a request for permission to be granted access to anything which—
   (a)   has been seized by a constable; and
   (b)   is retained by the police for the purpose of investigating an offence,

is made to the officer in charge of the investigation by a person who had custody or control of the thing immediately before it was so seized or by someone acting on behalf of such a person, the officer shall allow the person who made the request access to it under the supervision of a constable.

(4) Subject to subsection (8) below, if a request for a photograph or copy of any such thing is made to the officer in charge of the investigation by a person who had custody or control of the thing immediately before it was so seized, or by someone acting on behalf of such a person, the officer shall—

(a) allow the person who made the rquest access to it under the supervision of a constable for the purpose of photographing or copying it; or

(b) photograph or copy it, or cause it to be photographed or copied.

(5) A constable may also photograph or copy, or have photographed or copied, anything which he has power to seize, without a request being made under subsection (4) above.

(6) Where anything is photographed or copied under subsection (4)(b) above, the photograph or copy shall be supplied to the person who made the request.

(7) The photograph or copy shall be so supplied within a reasonable time from the making of the request.

(8) There is no duty under this section to grant access to, or to supply a photograph or copy of, anything if the officer in charge of the investigation for the purposes of which it was seized has reasonable grounds for believing that to do so would prejudice—

(a) that investigation;

(b) the investigation of an offence other than the offence for the purposes of investigating which the thing was seized; or

(c) any criminal proceedings which may be brought as a result of—

(i) the investigation of which he is in charge; or

(ii) any such investigation as is mentioned in paragraph (b) above.

(9) The references to a constable in subsections (1), (2), (3)(a) and (5) include a person authorised under section 16(2) to accompany a constable executing a warrant.

22 Retention

(1) Subject to subsection (4) below, anything which has been seized by a constable or taken away by a constable following a requirement made by virtue of section 19 or 20 above may be retained so long as is necessary in all the circumstances.

(2) Without prejudice to the generality of subsection (1) above—

(a) anything seized for the purposes of a criminal investigation may be retained, except as provided by subsection (4) below—

(i) for use as evidence at a trial for an offence; or

(ii) for forensic examination or for investigation in connection with an offence; and

(b) anything may be retained in order to establish its lawful owner, where there are reasonable grounds for believing that it has been obtained in consequence of the commission of an offence.

(3) Nothing seized on the ground that it may be used—

(a) to cause physical injury to any person;

(b) to damage property;

(c) to interfere with evidence; or

(d) to assist in escape from police detention or lawful custody,

may be retained when the person from whom it was seized is no longer in police detention or the custody of a court or is in the custody of a court but has been released on bail.

(4) Nothing may be retained for either of the purposes mentioned in subsection (2)(a) above if a photograph or copy would be sufficient for that purpose.

23 Meaning of "premises" etc.

In this Act—

"premises" includes any place and, in particular, includes—

(a) any vehicle, vessel, aircraft or hovercraft;

(b) any offshore installation;

(ba) any renewable energy installation;

(c) any tent or moveable structure.

PART III

ARREST

24   Arrest without warrant: constables

(1)   A constable may arrest without a warrant—

    (a)   anyone who is about to commit an offence;

    (b)   anyone who is in the act of committing an offence;

    (c)   anyone whom he has reasonable grounds for suspecting to be about to commit an offence;

    (d)   anyone whom he has reasonable grounds for suspecting to be committing an offence.

(2)   If a constable has reasonable grounds for suspecting that an offence has been committed, he may arrest without a warrant anyone whom he has reasonable grounds to suspect of being guilty of it.

(3)   If an offence has been committed, a constable may arrest without a warrant—

    (a)   anyone who is guilty of the offence;

    (b)   anyone whom he has reasonable grounds for suspecting to be guilty of it.

(4)   But the power of summary arrest conferred by subsection (1), (2) or (3) is exercisable only if the constable has reasonable grounds for believing that for any of the reasons mentioned in subsection (5) it is necessary to arrest the person in question.

(5)   The reasons are—

    (a)   to enable the name of the person in question to be ascertained (in the case where the constable does not know, and cannot readily ascertain, the person's name, or has reasonable grounds for doubting whether a name given by the person as his name is his real name);

    (b)   correspondingly as regards the person's address;

    (c)   to prevent the person in question—

        (i)   causing physical injury to himself or any other person;

        (ii)   suffering physical injury;

        (iii)   causing loss of or damage to property;

        (iv)   committing an offence against public decency (subject to subsection (6));

        or

        (v)   causing an unlawful obstruction of the highway;

    (d)   to protect a child or other vulnerable person from the person in question;

    (e)   to allow the prompt and effective investigation of the offence or of the conduct of the person in question;

    (f)   to prevent any prosecution for the offence from being hindered by the disappearance of the person in question.

(6)   Subsection (5)(c)(iv) applies only where members of the public going about their normal business cannot reasonably be expected to avoid the person in question.

24A   Arrest without warrant: other persons

(1)   A person other than a constable may arrest without a warrant—

    (a)   anyone who is in the act of committing an indictable offence;

    (b)   anyone whom he has reasonable grounds for suspecting to be committing an indictable offence.

(2)   Where an indictable offence has been committed, a person other than a constable may arrest without a warrant—

    (a)   anyone who is guilty of the offence;

    (b)   anyone whom he has reasonable grounds for suspecting to be guilty of it.

(3)   But the power of summary arrest conferred by subsection (1) or (2) is exercisable only if—

    (a)   the person making the arrest has reasonable grounds for believing that for any of the reasons mentioned in subsection (4) it is necessary to arrest the person in question; and

    (b)   it appears to the person making the arrest that it is not reasonably practicable for a constable to make it instead.

(4)   The reasons are to prevent the person in question—
    (a)   causing physical injury to himself or any other person;
    (b)   suffering physical injury;
    (c)   causing loss of or damage to property; or
    (d)   making off before a constable can assume responsibility for him.

(5)   This section does not apply in relation to an offence under Part 3 or 3A of the Public Order Act 1986.

26 Repeal of statutory powers of arrest without warrant or order

(1)   Subject to subsection (2) below, so much of any Act (including a local Act) passed before this Act as enables a constable—
    (a)   to arrest a person for an offence without a warrant; or
    (b)   to arrest a person otherwise than for an offence without a warrant or an order of a court,
shall cease to have effect.

(2)   Nothing in subsection (1) above affects the enactments specified in Schedule 2 to this Act.

28 Information to be given on arrest

(1)   Subject to subsection (5) below, where a person is arrested, otherwise than by being informed that he is under arrest, the arrest is not lawful unless the person arrested is informed that he is under arrest as soon as is practicable after his arrest.

(2)   Where a person is arrested by a constable, subsection (1) above applies regardless of whether the fact of the arrest is obvious.

(3)   Subject to subsection (5) below, no arrest is lawful unless the person arrested is informed of the ground for the arrest at the time of, or as soon as is practicable after, the arrest.

(4)   Where a person is arrested by a constable, subsection (3) above applies regardless of whether the ground for the arrest is obvious.

(5)   Nothing in this section is to be taken to require a person to be informed—
    (a)   that he is under arrest; or
    (b)   of the ground for the arrest,
if it was not reasonably practicable for him to be so informed by reason of his having escaped from arrest before the information could be given.

29 Voluntary attendance at police station etc.

Where for the purpose of assisting with an investigation a person attends voluntarily at a police station or at any other place where a constable is present or accompanies a constable to a police station or any such other place without having been arrested—
(a)   he shall be entitled to leave at will unless he is placed under arrest;
(b)   he shall be informed at once that he is under arrest if a decision is taken by a constable to prevent him from leaving at will.

30 Arrest elsewhere than at police station

(1)   Subsection (1A) applies where a person is, at any place other than a police station—
    (a)   arrested by a constable for an offence, or
    (b)   taken into custody by a constable after being arrested for an offence by a person other than a constable.

(1A) The person must be taken by a constable to a police station as soon as practicable after the arrest.

(1B) Subsection (1A) has effect subject to section 30A (release on bail) and subsection (7) (release without bail).

(2)   Subject to subsections (3) and (5) below, the police station to which an arrested person is taken under subsection (1A) above shall be a designated police station.

(6)   If the first police station to which an arrested person is taken after his arrest is not a designated police station, he shall be taken to a designated police station not more than six hours after his arrival at the first police station unless he is released previously.

(7)   A person arrested by a constable at any place other than a police station must be released without bail if the condition in subsection (7A) is satisfied.

(7A) The condition is that, at any time before the person arrested reaches a police station, a constable is satisfied that there are no grounds for keeping him under arrest or releasing him on bail under section 30A.

(10) Nothing in subsection (1A) or in section 30A prevents a constable delaying taking a person to a police station or releasing him on bail if the condition in subsection (10A) is satisfied.

(10A) The condition is that the presence of the person at a place (other than a police station) is necessary in order to carry out such investigations as it is reasonable to carry out immediately.

(11) Where there is any such delay the reasons for the delay must be recorded when the person first arrives at the police station or (as the case may be) is released on bail.

30A Bail elsewhere than at police station

(1) A constable may release on bail a person who is arrested or taken into custody in the circumstances mentioned in section 30(1).

(2) A person may be released on bail under subsection (1) at any time before he arrives at a police station.

(3) A person released on bail under subsection (1) must be required to attend a police station.

(3A) Where a constable releases a person on bail under subsection (1)—
   (a) no recognizance for the person's surrender to custody shall be taken from the person,
   (b) no security for the person's surrender to custody shall be taken from the person or from anyone else on the person's behalf,
   (c) the person shall not be required to provide a surety or sureties for his surrender to custody, and
   (d) no requirement to reside in a bail hostel may be imposed as a condition of bail.

(3B) Subject to subsection (3A), where a constable releases a person on bail under subsection (1) the constable may impose, as conditions of the bail, such requirements as appear to the constable to be necessary—
   (a) to secure that the person surrenders to custody,
   (b) to secure that the person does not commit an offence while on bail,
   (c) to secure that the person does not interfere with witnesses or otherwise obstruct the course of justice, whether in relation to himself or any other person, or
   (d) for the person's own protection or, if the person is under the age of 17, for the person's own welfare or in the person's own interests.

(4) Where a person is released on bail under subsection (1), a requirement may be imposed on the person as a condition of bail only under the preceding provisions of this section.

(5) The police station which the person is required to attend may be any police station.

30B Bail under section 30A: notices

(1) Where a constable grants bail to a person under section 30A, he must give that person a notice in writing before he is released.

(2) The notice must state—
   (a) the offence for which he was arrested, and
   (b) the ground on which he was arrested.

(3) The notice must inform him that he is required to attend a police station.

(4) It may also specify the police station which he is required to attend and the time when he is required to attend.

(4A) If the person is granted bail subject to conditions under section 30A(3B), the notice also—
   (a) must specify the requirements imposed by those conditions,
   (b) must explain the opportunities under sections 30CA(1) and 30CB(1) for variation of those conditions, and
   (c) if it does not specify the police station at which the person is required to attend, must specify a police station at which the person may make a request under section 30CA(1)(b).

(5)   If the notice does not include the information mentioned in subsection (4), the person must subsequently be given a further notice in writing which contains that information.

(6)   The person may be required to attend a different police station from that specified in the notice under subsection (1) or (5) or to attend at a different time.

(7)   He must be given notice in writing of any such change as is mentioned in subsection (6) but more than one such notice may be given to him.

30D   Failure to answer to bail under section 30A

(1)   A constable may arrest without a warrant a person who—

(a)   has been released on bail under section 30A subject to a requirement to attend a specified police station, but

(b)   fails to attend the police station at the specified time.

(2A)   A person who has been released on bail under section 30A may be arrested without a warrant by a constable if the constable has reasonable grounds for suspecting that a person has broken any of the conditions of bail.

31   Arrest for further offence

Where—

(a)   a person—

(i)   has been arrested for an offence; and

(ii)   is at a police station in consequence of that arrest; and

(b)   it appears to a constable that, if he were released from that arrest, he would be liable to arrest for some other offence,

he shall be arrested for that other offence.

32   Search upon arrest

(1)   A constable may search an arrested person, in any case where the person to be searched has been arrested at a place other than a police station, if the constable has reasonable grounds for believing that the arrested person may present a danger to himself or others.

(2)   Subject to subsections (3) to (5) below, a constable shall also have power in any such case—

(a)   to search the arrested person for anything—

(i)   which he might use to assist him to escape from lawful custody; or

(ii)   which might be evidence relating to an offence; and

(b)   if the offence for which he has been arrested is an indictable offence, to enter and search any premises in which he was when arrested or immediately before he was arrested for evidence relating to the offence.

(3)   The power to search conferred by subsection (2) above is only a power to search to the extent that is reasonably required for the purpose of discovering any such thing or any such evidence.

(4)   The powers conferred by this section to search a person are not to be construed as authorising a constable to require a person to remove any of his clothing in public other than an outer coat, jacket or gloves but they do authorise a search of a person's mouth.

(5)   A constable may not search a person in the exercise of the power conferred by subsection (2)(a) above unless he has reasonable grounds for believing that the person to be searched may have concealed on him anything for which a search is permitted under that paragraph.

(6)   A constable may not search premises in the exercise of the power conferred by subsection (2)(b) above unless he has reasonable grounds for believing that there is evidence for which a search is permitted under that paragraph on the premises.

(7)   In so far as the power of search conferred by subsection (2)(b) above relates to premises consisting of two or more separate dwellings, it is limited to a power to search—

(a)   any dwelling in which the arrest took place or in which the person arrested was immediately before his arrest; and

(b)   any parts of the premises which the occupier of any such dwelling uses in common with the occupiers of any other dwellings comprised in the premises.

(8)   A constable searching a person in the exercise of the power conferred by subsection (1) above may seize and retain anything he finds, if he has reasonable grounds for believing that the person searched might use it to cause physical injury to himself or to any other person.

(9)   A constable searching a person in the exercise of the power conferred by subsection (2)(a) above may seize and retain anything he finds, other than an item subject to legal privilege, if he has reasonable grounds for believing—
   (a)   that he might use it to assist him to escape from lawful custody; or
   (b)   that it is evidence of an offence or has been obtained in consequence of the commission of an offence.

(10) Nothing in this section shall be taken to affect the power conferred by section 43 of the Terrorism Act 2000.

PART IV
DETENTION

Detention — conditions and duration

34   Limitations on police detention

(1)   A person arrested for an offence shall not be kept in police detention except in accordance with the provisions of this Part of this Act.

(2)   Subject to subsection (3) below, if at any time a custody officer—
   (a)   becomes aware, in relation to any person in police detention, that the grounds for the detention of that person have ceased to apply; and
   (b)   is not aware of any other grounds on which the continued detention of that person could be justified under the provisions of this Part of this Act,
   it shall be the duty of the custody officer, subject to subsection (4) below, to order his immediate release from custody.

(3)   No person in police detention shall be released except on the authority of a custody officer at the police station where his detention was authorised or, if it was authorised at more than one station, a custody officer at the station where it was last authorised.

(4)   A person who appears to the custody officer to have been unlawfully at large when he was arrested is not to be released under subsection (2) above.

(5)   A person whose release is ordered under subsection (2) above shall be released without bail unless it appears to the custody officer—
   (a)   that there is need for further investigation of any matter in connection with which he was detained at any time during his period of his detention; or
   (b)   that, in respect of any such matter, proceedings may be taken against him or he may be given a youth caution under section 662A of the Crime and Disorder Act 1998.

35   Designated police stations

(1)   The chief officer of police for each police area shall designate the police stations in his area which, subject to sections 30(3) and (5), 30A(5) and 30D(2) above, are to be the stations in that area to be used for the purpose of detention arrested persons.

(2)   A chief officer's duty under subsection (1) above is to designate police stations appearing to him to provide enough accommodation for that purpose.

(3)   Without prejudice to section 12 of the Interpretation Act 1978 (continuity of duties) a chief officer—
   (a)   may designate a station which was not previously designated;

(4)   In this Act "designated police station" means a police station designated under this section.

36   Custody officers at police stations

(1)   One or more custody officers shall be appointed for each designated police station.

(2)   A custody officer for a police station designated under section 35(1) above shall be appointed—
   (a)   by the chief officer of police for the area in which the designated police station is situated; or

(b)   by such other police officer as the chief officer of police for that area may direct.

(3)   No officer may be appointed a custody officer unless the officer is of at least the rank of sergeant.

(4)   An officer of any rank may perform the functions of a custody officer at a designated police station if a custody officer is not readily available to perform them.

(5)   Subject to the following provisions of this section and to section 39(2) below, none of the functions of a custody officer in relation to a person shall be performed by an officer who at the time when the function falls to be performed is involved in the investigation of an offence for which that person is in police detention at that time.

37   Duties of custody officer before charge

(1)   Where—
    (a)   a person is arrested for an offence—
        (i)   without a warrant; or
        (ii)   under a warrant not endorsed for bail,
    the custody officer at each police station where he is detained after his arrest shall determine whether he has before him sufficient evidence to charge that person with the offence for which he was arrested and may detain him at the police station for such period as is necessary to enable him to do so.

(2)   If the custody officer determines that he does not have such evidence before him, the person arrested shall be released either on bail or without bail, unless the custody officer has reasonable grounds for believing that his detention without being charged is necessary to secure or preserve evidence relating to an offence for which he is under arrest or to obtain such evidence by questioning him.

(3)   If the custody officer has reasonable grounds for so believing, he may authorise the person arrested to be kept in police detention.

(4)   Where a custody officer authorises a person who has not been charged to be kept in police detention, he shall, as soon as is practicable, make a written record of the grounds for the detention.

(5)   Subject to subsection (6) below, the written record shall be made in the presence of the person arrested who shall at that time be informed by the custody officer of the grounds for his detention.

(6)   Subsection (5) above shall not apply where the person arrested is, at the time when the written record is made—
    (a)   incapable of understanding what is said to him;
    (b)   violent or likely to become violent; or
    (c)   in urgent need of medical attention.

(7)   Subject to section 41(7) below, if the custody officer determines that he has before him sufficient evidence to charge the person arrested with the offence for which he was arrested, the person arrested—
    (a)   shall be—
        (i)   released without charge and on bail; or
        (ii)   kept in police detention,
        for the purpose of enabling the Director of Public Prosecutions to make a decision under section 37B below,
    (b)   shall be released without charge and on bail but not for that purpose,
    (c)   shall be released without charge and without bail, or
    (d)   shall be charged.

(7A) The decision as to how a person is to be dealt with under subsection (7) above shall be that of the custody officer.

(7B) Where a person is dealt with under subsection (7)(a) above, it shall be the duty of the custody officer to inform him that he is being released or (as the case may be) detained, to enable the Director of Public Prosecutions to make a decision under section 37B below.

(9)   If the person arrested is not in a fit state to be dealt with under subsection (7) above, he may be kept in police detention until he is.

(10) The duty imposed on the custody officer under subsection (1) above shall be carried out by him as soon as practicable after the person arrested arrives at the police station or, in the case of a person arrested at the police station, as soon as practicable after the arrest.

(15) In this Part of this Act—

"arrested juvenile" means a person arrested with or without a warrant who appears to be under the age of 18.

38   Duties of custody officer after charge

(1) Where a person arrested for an offence otherwise than under a warrant endorsed for bail is charged with an offence, the custody officer shall, subject to section 25 of the Criminal Justice and Public Order Act 1994, order his release from police detention, either on bail or without bail, unless—

(a)   if the person arrested is not an arrested juvenile—

   (i)   his name or address cannot be ascertained or the custody officer has reasonable grounds for doubting whether a name or address furnished by him as his name or address is his real name or address;

   (ii)   the custody officer has reasonable grounds for believing that the person arrested will fail to appear in court to answer to bail;

   (iii) in the case of a person arrested for an imprisonable offence, the custody officer has reasonable grounds for believing that the detention of the person arrested is necessary to prevent him from committing an offence;

   (iiia) in a case of where a sample may be taken from the person under section 63B below, the custody officer has reasonable grounds for believing that the detention of the person is necessary to enable the sample to be taken from him;

   (iv)   in the case of a person arrested for an offence which is not an imprisonable offence, the custody officer has reasonable grounds for believing that the detention of the person arrested is necessary to prevent him from causing physical injury to any other person or from causing loss of or damage to property;

   (v)   the custody officer has reasonable grounds for believing that the detention of the person arrested is necessary to prevent him from interfering with the administration of justice or with the investigation of offences or of a particular offence; or

   (vi)   the custody officer has reasonable grounds for believing that the detention of the person arrested is necessary for his own protection;

(b)   if he is an arrested juvenile—

   (i)   any of the requirements of paragraph (a) above is satisfied but in the case of paragraph (a)(iiia) above, only if the arrested juvenile has attained the minimum age; or

   (ii)   the custody officer has reasonable grounds for believing that he ought to be detained in his own interests.

(c)   the offence with which the person is charged is murder.

(2) If the release of a person arrested is not required by subsection (1) above, the custody officer may authorise him to be kept in police detention but may not authorise a person to be kept in police detention by virtue of subsection (1)(a)(iiia) after the end of the period of six hours beginning when he was charged with the offence.

(3) Where a custody officer authorises a person who has been charged to be kept in police detention, he shall, as soon as practicable, make a written record of the grounds for the detention.

(4) Subject to subsection (5) below, the written record shall be made in the presence of the person charged who shall at that time be informed by the custody officer of the grounds for his detention.

(5) Subsection (4) above shall not apply where the person charged is, at the time when the written record is made—

(a)   incapable of understanding what is said to him;

(b)   violent or likely to become violent; or

(c)   in urgent need of medical attention.

(6)   Where a custody officer authorises an arrested juvenile to be kept in police detention under subsection (1) above, the custody officer shall, unless he certifies—

    (a)   that, by reason of such circumstances as are specified in the certificate, it is impracticable for him to do so; or

    (b)   in the case of an arrested juvenile who has attained the age of 12 years, that no secure accommodation is available and that keeping him in other local authority accommodation would not be adequate to protect the public from serious harm from him,

secure that the arrested juvenile is moved to local authority accommodation.

(6B) Where an arrested juvenile is moved to local authority accommodation under subsection 6 above, it shall be lawful for any person acting on behalf of the authority to detain him.

39   Responsibilities in relation to persons detained

(1)   Subject to subsection (2) and (4) below, it shall be the duty of the custody officer at a police station to ensure—

    (a)   that all persons in police detention at that station are treated in accordance with this Act and any code of practice issued under it and relating to the treatment of persons in police detention; and

    (b)   that all matters relating to such persons which are required by this Act or by such codes of practice to be recorded are recorded in the custody records relating to such persons.

(6)   Where—

    (a)   an officer of higher rank than the custody officer gives directions relating to a person in police detention; and

    (b)   the directions are at variance—

        (i)   with any decision made or action taken by the custody officer in the performance of a duty imposed on him under this Part of this Act; or

        (ii)   with any decision or action which would be for the directions have been made or taken by him in the performance of such a duty,

the custody officer shall refer the matter at once to an officer of the rank of superintendent or above who is responsible for the police station for which the custody officer is acting as custody officer.

40   Review of police detention

(1)   Reviews of the detention of each person in police detention in connection with the investigation of an offence shall be carried out periodically in accordance with the following provisions of this section—

    (a)   in the case of a person who has been arrested and charged, by the custody officer; and

    (b)   in the case of a person who has been arrested but not charged, by an officer of at least the rank of inspector who has not been directly involved in the investigation.

(2)   The officer to whom it falls to carry out a review is referred to in this section as a "review officer".

(3)   Subject to subsection (4) below—

    (a)   the first review shall be not later than six hours after the detention was first authorised;

    (b)   the second review shall be not later than nine hours after the first;

    (c)   subsequent reviews shall be at intervals of not more than nine hours.

(4)   A review may be postponed—

    (a)   if, having regard to all the circumstances prevailing at the latest time for it specified in subsection (3) above, it is not practicable to carry out the review at that time;

    (b)   without prejudice to the generality of paragraph (a) above—

        (i)   if at that time the person in detention is being questioned by a police officer and the review officer is satisfied that an interruption of the questioning for the purpose of carrying out the review would prejudice the investigation in connection with which he is being questioned; or

        (ii)   if at that time no review officer is readily available.

(5)   If a review is postponed under subsection (4) above it shall be carried out as soon as practicable after the latest time specified for it in subsection (3) above.

(6)   If a review is carried out after postponement under subsection (4) above, the fact that it was so carried out shall not affect any requirement of this section as to the time at which any subsequent review is to be carried out.

(7)   The review officer shall record the reasons for any postponement of a review in the custody record.

(8)   Subject to subsection (9) below, where the person whose detention is under review has not been charged before the time of the review, section 37(1) to (6) above shall have effect in relation to him, but with the modifications specified in subsection (8A).

(8A)   The modifications are—
    (a)   the substitution of references to the person whose detention is under review for references to the person arrested;
    (b)   the substitution of references to the review officer for references to the custody officer; and
    (c)   in subsection (6), the insertion of the following paragraph after paragraph (a)—
    "(aa) asleep;"

(9)   Where a person has been kept in police detention by virtue of section 37(9) or 37D(5) above, section 37(1) to (6) shall not have effect in relation to him but it shall be the duty of the review officer to determine whether he is yet in a fit state.

(10)   Where the person whose detention is under review has been charged before the time of the review, section 38(1) to (6B) above shall have effect in relation to him, with the modifications specified in subsection 10A.

(10A)The modifications are—
    (a)   the substitution of a reference to the person whose detention is under review for any reference to the person arrested or to the person charged; and
    (b)   in subsection (5), the insertion of the following paragraph after paragraph (a)—
    "(aa) asleep;".

(11)   Where—
    (a)   an officer of higher rank than the review officer gives directions relating to a person in police detention; and
    (b)   the directions are at variance—
        (i)   with any decision made or action taken by the review officer in the performance of a duty imposed on him under this Part of this Act; or
        (ii)   with any decision or action which would but for the directions have been made or taken by him in the performance of such a duty,
    the review officer shall refer the matter at once to an officer of the rank of superintendent or above who is responsible for the police station for which the review officer is acting as review officer in connection with the detention.

(12)   Before determining whether to authorise a person's continued detention the review officer shall give—
    (a)   that person (unless he is asleep); or
    (b)   any solicitor representing him who is available at the time of the review,
    an opportunity to make representations to him about the detention.

40A   Use of telephone for review under s. 40

(1)   A review under section 40(1)(b) may be carried out by means of a discussion, conducted by telephone, with one or more persons at the police station where the arrested person is held.

(2)   But subsection (1) does not apply if—
    (a)   the review is of a kind authorised by regulations under section 45A to be carried out using video-conferencing facilities; and
    (b)   it is reasonably practicable to carry it out in accordance with those regulations.

(3)   Where any review is carried out under this section by an officer who is not present at the station where the arrested person is held—
    (a)   any obligation of that officer to make a record in connection with the carrying out of the review shall have effect as an obligation to cause another officer to make the record;
    (b)   any requirement for the record to be made in the presence of the arrested person shall apply to the making of that record by that other officer; and

    (c)   the requirements under section 40(12) and (13) above for—
        (i)   the arrested person, or
        (ii)   a solicitor representing him,
        to be given any opportunity to make representations (whether in writing or orally) to that officer shall have effect as a requirement for that person, or such a solicitor, to be given an opportunity to make representations in a manner authorised by subsection (4) below.

(4)   Representations are made in a manner authorised by this subsection—
    (a)   in a case where facilities exist for the immediate transmission of written representations to the officer carrying out the review, if they are made either—
        (i)   orally by telephone to that officer; or
        (ii)   in writing to that officer by means of those facilities; and
    (b)   in any other case, if they are made orally by telephone to that officer.

(5)   In this section "video-conferencing facilities" has the same meaning as in section 45A below.

41   Limits on period of detention without charge

(1)   Subject to the following provisions of this section and to sections 42 and 43 below, a person shall not be kept in police detention for more than 24 hours without being charged.

(2)   The time from which the period of detention of a person is to be calculated (in this Act referred to as "the relevant time")—
    (a)   in the case of a person to whom this paragraph applies, shall be—
        (i)   the time at which that person arrives at the relevant police station; or
        (ii)   the time 24 hours after the time of that person's arrest,
        whichever is the earlier;
    (b)   in the case of a person arrested outside England and Wales, shall be—
        (i)   the time at which that person arrives at the first police station to which he is taken in the police area in England or Wales in which the offence for which he was arrested is being investigated; or
        (ii)   the time 24 hours after the time of that person's entry into England and Wales,
        whichever is the earlier;
    (c)   in the case of a person who—
        (i)   attends voluntarily at a police station; or
        (ii)   accompanies a constable to a police station without having been arrested, and is arrested at the police station, the time of his arrest;
    (ca)   in the case of a person who attends a police station to answer to bail granted under section 30A, the time when he arrives at the police station;
    (d)   in any other case except where subsection (5) below applies shall be the time at which the person arrested arrives at the first police station to which he is taken after his arrest.

(7)   Subject to subsection (8) below, a person who at the expiry of 24 hours after the relevant time is in police detention and has not been charged shall be released at that time either on bail or without bail.

(8)   Subsection (7) above does not apply to a person whose detention for more than 24 hours after the relevant time has been authorised or is otherwise permitted in accordance with section 42 or 43 below.

(9)   A person released under subsection (7) above shall not be re-arrested without a warrant for the offence for which he was previously arrested unless new evidence justifying a further arrest has come to light since his release; but this subsection does not prevent an arrest under section 46A below.

42   Authorisation of continued detention

(1)   Where a police officer of the rank of superintendent or above who is responsible for the police station at which a person is detained has reasonable grounds for believing that—
    (a)   the detention of that person without charge is necessary to secure or preserve evidence relating to an offence for which he is under arrest or to obtain such evidence by questioning him;

(b)   an offence for which he is under arrest is an indictable offence; and

(c)   the investigation is being conducted diligently and expeditiously,

he may authorise the keeping of that person in police detention for a period expiring at or before 36 hours after the relevant time.

(2)   Where an officer such as is mentioned in subsection (1) above has authorised the keeping of a person in police detention for a period expiring less than 36 hours after the relevant time, such an officer may authorise the keeping of that person in police detention for a further period expiring not more than 36 hours after that time if the conditions specified in subsection (1) above are still satisfied when he gives the authorisation.

(3)   If it is proposed to transfer a person in police detention to another police area, the officer determining whether or not to authorise keeping him in detention under subsection (1) above shall have regard to the distance and the time the journey would take.

(4)   No authorisation under subsection (1) above shall be given in respect of any person—

(a)   more than 24 hours after the relevant time; or

(b)   before the second review of his detention under section 40 above has been carried out.

(5)   Where an officer authorises the keeping of a person in police detention under subsection (1) above, it shall be his duty—

(a)   to inform that person of the grounds for his continued detention; and

(b)   to record the grounds in that person's custody record.

(6)   Before determining whether to authorise the keeping of a person in detention under subsection (1) or (2) above, an officer shall give—

(a)   that person; or

(b)   any solicitor representing him who is available at the time when it falls to the officer to determine whether to give the authorisation,

an opportunity to make representations to him about the detention.

(9)   Where—

(a)   an officer authorises the keeping of a person in detention under subsection (1) above; and

(b)   at the time of the authorisation he has not yet exercised a right conferred on him by section 56 or 58 below,

the officer—

(i)   shall inform him of that right;

(ii)   shall decide whether he should be permitted to exercise it;

(iii)   shall record the decision in his custody record; and

(iv)   if the decision is to refuse to permit the exercise of the right, shall also record the grounds for the decision in that record.

(10)   Where an officer has authorised the keeping of a person who has not been charged in detention under subsection (1) or (2) above, he shall be released from detention, either on bail or without bail, not later than 36 hours after the relevant time, unless—

(a)   he has been charged with an offence; or

(b)   his continued detention is authorised or otherwise permitted in accordance with section 43 below.

(11)   A person released under subsection (10) above shall not be re-arrested without a warrant for the offence for which he was previously arrested unless new evidence justifying a further arrest has come to light since his release; but this subsection does not prevent an arrest under section 46A below.

43   Warrants of further detention

(1)   Where, on an application on oath made by a constable and supported by an information, a magistrate's court is satisfied that there are reasonable grounds for believing that the further detention of the person to whom the application relates is justified, it may issue a warrant of further detention authorising the keeping of that person in police detention.

(2)   A court may not hear an application for a warrant of further detention unless the person to whom the application relates—

(a)   has been furnished with a copy of the information; and

(b)   has been brought before the court for the hearing.

(3)   The person to whom the application relates shall be entitled to be legally represented at the hearing and, if he is not so represented but wishes to be so represented—
    (a)   the court shall adjourn the hearing to enable him to obtain representation; and
    (b)   he may be kept in police detention during the adjournment.

(4)   A person's further detention is only justified for the purposes of this section or section 44 below if—
    (a)   his detention without charge is necessary to secure or preserve evidence relating to an offence for which he is under arrest or to obtain such evidence by questioning him;
    (b)   an offence for which he is under arrest is an indictable offence; and
    (c)   the investigation is being conducted diligently and expeditiously.

(5)   Subject to subsection (7) below, an application for a warrant of further detention may be made—
    (a)   at any time before the expiry of 36 hours after the relevant time; or
    (b)   in a case where—
        (i)   it is not practicable for the magistrates' court to which the application will be made to sit at the expiry of 36 hours after the relevant time; but
        (ii)   the court will sit during the 6 hours following the end of that period,
    at any time before the expiry of the said 6 hours.

(6)   In a case to which subsection (5)(b) above applies—
    (a)   the person to whom the application relates may be kept in police detention until the application is heard; and
    (b)   the custody officer shall make a note in that person's custody record—
        (i)   of the fact that he was kept in police detention for more than 36 hours after the relevant time; and
        (ii)   of the reason why he was so kept.

(7)   If—
    (a)   an application for a warrant of further detention is made after the expiry of 36 hours after the relevant time; and
    (b)   it appears to the magistrates' court that it would have been reasonable for the police to make it before the expiry of that period,
    the court shall dismiss the application.

(8)   Where on an application such as is mentioned in subsection (1) above a magistrates' court is not satisfied that there are reasonable grounds for believing that the further detention of the person to whom the application relates is justified, it shall be its duty—
    (a)   to refuse the application; or
    (b)   to adjourn the hearing of it until a time not later than 36 hours after the relevant time.

(9)   The person to whom the application relates may be kept in police detention during the adjournment.

(10)   A warrant of further detention shall—
    (a)   state the time at which it is issued;
    (b)   authorise the keeping in police detention of the person to whom it relates for the period stated in it.

(11)   Subject to subsection (12) below, the period stated in a warrant of further detention shall be such period as the magistrates' court thinks fit, having regard to the evidence before it.

(12)   The period shall not be longer than 36 hours.

(14)   Any information submitted in support of an application under this section shall state—
    (a)   the nature of the offence for which the person to whom the application relates has been arrested;
    (b)   the general nature of the evidence on which that person was arrested;
    (c)   what inquiries relating to the offence have been made by the police and what further inquiries are proposed by them;
    (d)   the reasons for believing the continued detention of that person to be necessary for the purposes of such further inquiries.

(15)   Where an application under this section is refused, the person to whom the application relates shall forthwith be charged or, subject to subsection (16) below, released, either on bail or without bail.

(16) A person need not be released under subsection (15) above—
    (a)   before the expiry of 24 hours after the relevant time; or
    (b)   before the expiry of any longer period for which his continued detention is or has been authorised under section 42 above.

(17) Where an application under this section is refused, no further application shall be made under this section in respect of the person to whom the refusal relates, unless supported by evidence which has come to light since the refusal.

(18) Where a warrant of further detention is issued, the person to whom it relates shall be released from police detention, either on bail or without bail, upon or before the expiry of the warrant unless he is charged.

(19) A person released under subsection (18) above shall not be re-arrested without a warrant for the offence for which he was previously arrested unless new evidence justifying a further arrest has come to light since his release; but this subsection does not prevent an arrest under section 46A below.

44   Extension of warrants of further detention

(1) On an application on oath made by a constable and supported by an information a magistrates' court may extend a warrant of further detention issued under section 43 above if it is satisfied that there are reasonable grounds for believing that the further detention of the person to whom the application relates is justified.

(2) Subject to subsection (3) below, the period for which a warrant of further detention may be extended shall be such period as the court thinks fit, having regard to the evidence before it.

(3) The period shall not—
    (a)   be longer than 36 hours; or
    (b)   end later than 96 hours after the relevant time.

(4) Where a warrant of further detention has been extended under subsection (1) above, or further extended under this subsection, for a period ending before 96 hours after the relevant time, on an application such as is mentioned in that subsection a magistrates' court may further extend the warrant if it is satisfied as there mentioned; and subsections (2) and (3) above apply to such further extensions as they apply to extensions under subsection (1) above.

(5) A warrant of further detention shall, if extended or further extended under this section, be endorsed with a note of the period of the extension.

(6) Subsections (2), (3), and (14) of section 43 above shall apply to an application made under this section as they apply to an application made under that section.

45   Detention before charge — supplementary

(2) Any reference in this Part of this Act to a period of time or a time of day is to be treated as approximate only.

45A   Use of video-conferencing facilities for decisions about detention

(1) Subject to the following provisions of this section, the Secretary of State may by regulations provide that, in the case of an arrested person who is held in a police station, some or all of the functions mentioned in subsection (2) may be performed (notwithstanding anything in the preceding provisions of this Part) by an officer who—
    (a)   is not present in that police station; but
    (b)   has access to the use of video-conferencing facilities that enable him to communicate with persons in that station.

(2) Those functions are—
    (a)   the functions in relation to an arrested person taken to, or answering to bail at, a police station that is not a designated police station which, in the case of an arrested person taken to a station that is a designated police station, are functions of a custody officer under section 37, 38 or 40 above; and
    (b)   the function of carrying out a review under section 40(1)(b) above (review, by an officer of at least the rank of inspector, of the detention of person arrested but not charged).

(3) Regulations under this section shall specify the use to be made in the performance of the functions mentioned in subsection (2) above of the facilities mentioned in subsection (1) above.

Detention — miscellaneous

46 Detention after charge

(1) Where a person—
  (a) is charged with an offence; and
  (b) after being charged—
    (i) is kept in police detention; or
    (ii) is detained by a local authority in pursuance of arrangements made under section 38(6) above,
  he shall be brought before a magistrates' court in accordance with the provisions of this section.

(2) If he is to be brought before a magistrates' court in the local justice area in which the police station at which he was charged is situated, he shall be brought before such a court as soon as is practicable and in any event not later than the first sitting after he is charged with the offence.

(3) If no magistrates' court in that area is due to sit either on the day on which he is charged or on the next day, the custody officer for the police station at which he was charged shall inform the designated officer for the area that there is a person in the area to whom subsection (2) above applies.

(4) If the person charged is to be brought before a magistrates' court in a local justice area other than that in which the police station at which he was charged is situated, he shall be removed to that area as soon as is practicable and brought before such a court as soon as is practicable after this arrival in the area and in any event not later than the first sitting of a magistrates' court in that area after this arrival in the area.

(5) If no magistrates' court in that area is due to sit either on the day on which he arrives in the area or on the next day—
  (a) he shall be taken to a police station in the area; and
  (b) the custody officer at that station shall inform the designated officer for the area that there is a person in the area to whom subsection (4) applies.

(6) Subject to subsection (8) below, where the designated officer for a local justice area has been informed—
  (a) under subsection (3) above that there is a person in the area to whom subsection (2) above applies; or
  (b) under subsection (5) above that there is a person in the area to whom subsection (4) above applies,
  the designated officer shall arrange for a magistrates' court to sit not later than the day next following the relevant day.

(7) In this section "the relevant day" —
  (a) in relation to a person who is to be brought before a magistrates' court in the local justice area in which the police station at which he was charged is situated, means the day on which he was charged; and
  (b) in relation to a person who is to be brought before a magistrates' court in any other local justice area, means the day on which he arrives in the area.

(8) Where the day next following the relevant day is Christmas Day, Good Friday or a Sunday, the duty of the designated officer under subsection (6) above is a duty to arrange for a magistrates' court to sit not later than the first day after the relevant day which is not one of those days.

46A Power of arrest for failure to answer to police bail

(1) A constable may arrest without a warrant any person who, having been released on bail under this Part of this Act subject to a duty to attend at a police station, fails to attend at that police station at the time appointed for him to do so.

(1ZA) The reference in subsection (1) to a person who fails to attend at a police station at the time appointed for him to do so includes a reference to a person who—
  (a) attends at a police station to answer to bail granted subject to the duty mentioned in section 47(3)(b), but
  (b) leaves the police station at any time before the beginning of proceedings in relation to a live link direction under section 57C of the Crime and Disorder Act 1998 in relation to him.

(1ZB) The reference in subsection (1) to a person who fails to attend at a police station at the time appointed for the person to do so includes a reference to a person who—

    (a)   attends at a police station to answer to bail granted subject to the duty mentioned in section 47(3)(b), but

    (b)   refuses to be searched under section 54B.

(1A)   A person who has been released on bail under section 37, 37C(2)(b) or 37(CA)(2)(b) above may be arrested without warrant by a constable if the constable has reasonable grounds for suspecting that the person has broken any of the conditions of bail.

(2)   A person who is arrested under this section shall be taken to the police station appointed as the place at which he is to surrender to custody as soon as practicable after the arrest.

(3)   For the purposes of—

    (a)   section 30 above (subject to the obligation in subsection (2) above), and

    (b)   section 31 above,

an arrest under the section shall be treated as an arrest for an offence.

47   Bail after arrest

(1)   Subject to the following provisions of this section, a release on bail of a person under this Part of this Act shall be a release on bail granted in accordance with sections 3, 3A, 5 and 5A of the Bail Act 1976 as they apply to bail granted by a constable.

(1A)   The normal powers to impose conditions of bail shall be available to him where a custody officer releases a person on bail under section 37 above or section 38(1) above (including that subsection as applied by section 40(10) above) but not in any other cases.

In this subsection "the normal powers to impose conditions of bail" has the meaning given in section 3(6) of the Bail Act 1976.

(2)   Nothing in the Bail Act 1976 shall prevent the re-arrest without warrant of a person released on bail subject to a duty to attend at a police station if new evidence justifying a further arrest has come to light since his release.

PART V

QUESTIONING AND TREATMENT OF PERSONS BY POLICE

53   Abolition of certain powers of constables to search persons

(1)   Subject to subsection (2) below, there shall cease to have effect any Act (including a local Act) passed before this Act in so far as it authorises—

    (a)   any search by a constable of a person in police detention at a police station; or

    (b)   an intimate search of a person by a constable;

and any rule of common law which authorises a search such as is mentioned in paragraph (a) or (b) above is abolished.

54   Search of detained persons

(1)   The custody officer at a police station shall ascertain everything which a person has with him when he is—

    (a)   brought to the station after being arrested elsewhere or after being committed to custody by an order or sentence of a court; or

    (b)   arrested at the station or detained there as a person falling within section 34(7), under section 37 above or as a person to whom section 46ZA(4) or (5) applies.

(2)   The custody officer may record or cause to be recorded all or any of the things which he ascertains under subsection (1).

(2A)   In the case of an arrested person, any such record may be made as part of his custody record.

(3)   Subject to subsection (4) below, a custody officer may seize and retain any such thing or cause any such thing to be seized and retained.

(4)   Clothes and personal effects may only be seized if the custody officer—

    (a)   believes that the person from whom they are seized may use them—

        (i)   to cause physical injury to himself or any other person;

        (ii)   to damage property;

        (iii)   to interfere with evidence; or

        (iv)   to assist him to escape; or

    (b)   has reasonable grounds for believing that they may be evidence relating to an offence.

(5)   Where anything is seized, the person from whom it is seized shall be told the reason for the seizure unless he is—

    (a)   violent or likely to become violent; or

    (b)   incapable of understanding what is said to him.

(6)   Subject to subsection (7) below, a person may be searched if the custody officer considers it necessary to enable him to carry out his duty under subsection (1) above and to the extent that the custody officer considers necessary for that purpose.

(6A) A person who is in custody at a police station or is in police detention otherwise than at a police station may at any time be searched in order to ascertain whether he has with him anything which he could use for any of the purposes specified in subsection (4)(a) above.

(6B) Subject to subsection (6C) below, a constable may seize and retain, or cause to be seized and retained, anything found on such a search.

(6C) A constable may only seize clothes and personal effects in the circumstances specified in subsection (4) above.

(7)   An intimate search may not be conducted under this section.

(8)   A search under this section shall be carried out by a constable.

(9)   The constable carrying out a search shall be of the same sex as the person searched.

54A   Searches and examination to ascertain identity

(1)   If an officer of at least the rank of inspector authorises it, a person who is detained in a police station may be searched or examined, or both—

    (a)   for the purpose of ascertaining whether he has any mark that would tend to identify him as a person involved in the commission of an offence; or

    (b)   for the purpose of facilitating the ascertainment of his identity.

(2)   An officer may only give an authorisation under subsection (1) for the purpose mentioned in paragraph (a) of that subsection if—

    (a)   the appropriate consent to a search or examination that would reveal whether the mark in question exists has been withheld; or

    (b)   it is not practicable to obtain such consent.

(3)   An officer may only give an authorisation under subsection (1) in a case in which subsection (2) does not apply if—

    (a)   the person in question has refused to identify himself; or

    (b)   the officer has reasonable grounds for suspecting that that person is not who he claims to be.

(4)   An officer may give an authorisation under subsection (1) orally or in writing but, if he gives it orally, he shall confirm it in writing as soon as is practicable.

(7)   A person may not under this section carry out a search or examination of a person of the opposite sex or take a photograph of any part of the body of a person of the opposite sex.

(8)   An intimate search may not be carried out under this section.

(9)   A photograph taken under this section—

    (a)   may be used by, or disclosed to, any person for any purpose related to the prevention or detection of crime, the investigation of an offence or the conduct of a prosecution; and

    (b)   after being so used or disclosed, may be retained but may not be used or disclosed except for a purpose so related.

(11) In this section—

    (a)   references to ascertaining a person's identity include references to showing that he is not a particular person; and

    (b)   references to taking a photograph include references to using any process by means of which a visual image may be produced, and references to photographing a person shall be construed accordingly.

(12) In this section "mark" includes features and injuries; and a mark is an identifying mark for the purposes of this section if its existence in any person's case facilitates the ascertainment of his identity or his identification as a person involved in the commission of an offence.

(13) Nothing in this section applies to a person arrested under an extradition arrest power.

54C   Power to retain articles seized

(1) Except as provided by subsections (2) and (3), a constable may retain a thing seized under section 54B until the time when the person from whom it was seized leaves the police station.

(2) A constable may retain a thing seized under section 54B in order to establish its lawful owner, where there are reasonable grounds for believing that it has been obtained in consequence of the commission of an offence.

(3) If a thing seized under section 54B may be evidence of, or in relation to, an offence, a constable may retain it—
  (a)   for use as evidence at a trial for an offence; or
  (b)   for forensic examination or for investigation in connection with an offence.

(4) Nothing may be retained for either of the purposes mentioned in subsection (3) if a photograph or copy would be sufficient for that purpose.

(5) Nothing in this section affects any power of a court to make an order under section 1 of the Police (Property) Act 1897.

(6) The references in this section to anything seized under section 54B include anything seized by a person to whom paragraph 27A of Schedule 4 to the Police Reform Act 2002 applies.

55   Intimate searches

(1) Subject to the following provisions of this section, if an officer of at least the rank of inspector has reasonable grounds for believing—
  (a)   that a person who has been arrested and is in police detention may have concealed on him anything which—
    (i)   he could use to cause physical injury to himself or others; and
    (ii)   he might so use while he is in police detention or in the custody of a court; or
  (b)   that such a person—
    (i)   may have a Class A drug concealed on him; and
    (ii)   was in possession of it with the appropriate criminal intention before his arrest,
  he may authorise an intimate search of that person.

(2) An officer may not authorise an intimate search of a person for anything unless he has reasonable grounds for believing that it cannot be found without his being intimately searched.

(3) An officer may give an authorisation under subsection (1) above orally or in writing but, if he gives it orally, he shall confirm it in writing as soon as is practicable.

(3A) A drug offence search shall not be carried out unless the appropriate consent is given in writing.

(4) An intimate search which is only a drug offence search shall be by way of examination by a suitably qualified person.

(5) Except as provided by subsection (4) above, an intimate search shall be by way of examination by a suitably qualified person unless an officer of at least the rank of inspector considers that this is not practicable.

(6) An intimate search which is not carried out as mentioned in subsection (5) above shall be carried out by a constable.

(7) A constable may not carry out an intimate search of a person of the opposite sex.

(8) No intimate search may be carried out except—
  (a)   at a police station;
  (b)   at a hospital;
  (c)   at a registered medical practitioner's surgery; or
  (d)   at some other place used for medical purposes.

(9)   An intimate search which is only a drug offence search may not be carried out at a police station.

(10)   If an intimate search of a person is carried out, the custody record relating to him shall state—

(a)   which parts of his body were searched; and

(b)   why they were searched.

(12)   This custody officer at a police station may seize and retain anything which is found on an intimate search of a person, or cause any such thing to be seized and retained—

(a)   if he believes that the person from whom it is seized may use it—

(i)   to cause physical injury to himself or any other person;

(ii)   to damage property;

(iii)   to interfere with evidence; or

(iv)   to assist him to escape; or

(b)   if he has reasonable grounds for believing that it may be evidence relating to an offence.

(13)   Where anything is seized under this section, the person from whom it is seized shall be told the reason for the seizure unless he is—

(a)   violent or likely to become violent; or

(b)   incapable of understanding what is said to him.

56   Right to have someone informed when arrested

(1)   Where a person has been arrested and is being held in custody in a police station or other premises, he shall be entitled, if he so requests, to have one friend or relative or other person who is known to him or who is likely to take an interest in his welfare told, as soon as is practicable except to the extent that delay is permitted by this section, that he has been arrested and is being detained there.

(2)   Delay is only permitted—

(a)   in the case of a person who is in police detention for an indictable offence; and

(b)   if an officer of at least the rank of inspector authorises it.

(3)   In any case the person in custody must be permitted to exercise the right conferred by subsection (1) above within 36 hours from the relevant time as defined in section 41(2) above.

(4)   An officer may give an authorisation under subsection (2) above orally or in writing but, if he gives it orally, he shall confirm it in writing as soon as is practicable.

(5)   Subject to subsection (5A) below an officer may only authorise delay where he has reasonable grounds for believing that telling the named person of the arrest—

(a)   will lead to interference with or harm to evidence connected with an indictable offence or interference with or physical injury to other persons; or

(b)   will lead to the alerting of other persons suspected of having committed such an offence but not yet arrested for it; or

(c)   will hinder the recovery of any property obtained as a result of such an offence.

(5A)   An officer may also authorise delay where he has reasonable grounds for believing that—

(a)   the person detained for the indictable offence has benefited from his criminal conduct, and

(b)   the recovery of the value of the property constituting the benefit will be hindered by telling the named person of the arrest.

(5B)   For the purposes of subsection (5A) above the question whether a person has benefited from his criminal conduct is to be decided in accordance with Part 2 of the Proceeds of Crime Act 2002.

(6)   If a delay is authorised—

(a)   the detained person shall be told the reason for it; and

(b)   the reason shall be noted on his custody record.

(7)   The duties imposed by subsection (6) above shall be performed as soon as is practicable.

(8)   The rights conferred by this section on a person detained at a police station or other premises are exercisable whenever he is transferred from one place to another; and this section applies to each subsequent occasion on which they are exercisable as it applies to the first such occasion.

(9)   There may be no further delay in permitting the exercise of the right conferred by subsection (1) above once the reason for authorising delay ceases to subsist.

(10) Nothing in this section applies to a person arrested or detained under the terrorism provisions.

58   Access to legal advice

(1)   A person arrested and held in custody in a police station or other premises shall be entitled, if he so requests, to consult a solicitor privately at any time.

(2)   Subject to subsection (3) below, a request under subsection (1) above and the time at which it was made shall be recorded in the custody record.

(3)   Such a request need not be recorded in the custody record of a person who makes it at a time while he is at a court after being charged with an offence.

(4)   If a person makes such a request, he must be permitted to consult a solicitor as soon as is practicable except to the extent that delay is permitted by this section.

(5)   In any case he must be permitted to consult a solicitor within 36 hours from the relevant time, as defined in section 41(2) above.

(6)   Delay in compliance with a request is only permitted—
      (a)   in the case of a person who is in police detention for an indictable offence; and
      (b)   if an officer of at least the rank of superintendent authorises it.

(7)   An officer may give an authorisation under subsection (6) above orally or in writing but, if he gives it orally, he shall confirm it in writing as soon as is practicable.

(8)   Subject to subsection (8A) below an officer may only authorise delay where he has reasonable grounds for believing that the exercise of the right conferred by subsection (1) above at the time when the person detained desires to exercise it—
      (a)   will lead to interference with or harm to evidence connected with an indictable offence or interference with or physical injury to other persons; or
      (b)   will lead to the alerting of other persons suspected of having committed such an offence but not yet arrested for it; or
      (c)   will hinder the recovery of any property obtained as a result of such an offence.

(8A) An officer may also authorise delay where he has reasonable grounds for believing that—
      (a)   the person detained for the indictable offence has benefited from his criminal conduct, and
      (b)   the recovery of the value of the property constituting the benefit will be hindered by the exercise of the right conferred by subsection (1) above.

(8B) For the purposes of subsection (8A) above the question whether a person has benefited from his criminal conduct is to be decided in accordance with Part 2 of the Proceeds of Crime Act 2002.

(9)   If delay is authorised—
      (a)   the detained person shall be told the reason for it; and
      (b)   the reason shall be noted on his custody record.

(10) The duties imposed by subsection (9) above shall be performed as soon as is practicable.

(11) There may be no further delay in permitting the exercise of the right conferred by subsection (1) above once the reason for authorising delay ceases to subsist.

(12) Nothing in this section applies to a person arrested or detained under the terrorism provisions.

60   Tape-recording of interviews

(1)   It shall be the duty of the Secretary of State—
      (a)   to issue a code of practice in connection with the tape-recording of interviews of persons suspected of the commission of criminal offences which are held by police officers at police stations; and
      (b)   to make an order requiring the tape-recording of interviews of persons suspected of the commission of criminal offences, or of such descriptions of criminal offences as may be specified in the order, which are so held, in accordance with the code as it has effect for the time being.

(2)   An order under subsection (1) above shall be made by statutory instrument and shall be subject to annulment in pursuance of a resolution of either House of Parliament.

60A Visual recording of interviews

(1) The Secretary of State shall have power—

   (a) to issue a code of practice for the visual recording of interviews held by police officers at police stations; and

   (b) to make an order requiring the visual recording of interviews so held, and requiring the visual recording to be in accordance with the code for the time being in force under this section.

(2) A requirement imposed by an order under this section may be imposed in relation to such cases or police stations in such areas, or both, as may be specified or described in the order.

(3) An order under subsection (1) above shall be made by statutory instrument and shall be subject to annulment in pursuance of a resolution of either House of Parliament.

61 Fingerprinting

(1) Except as provided by this section no person's fingerprints may be taken without the appropriate consent.

(2) Consent to the taking of a person's fingerprints must be in writing if it is given at a time when he is at a police station.

(3) The fingerprints of a person detained at a police station may be taken without the appropriate consent if—

   (a) he is detained in consequence of his arrest for a recordable offence; and

   (b) he has not had his fingerprints taken in the course of the investigation of the offence by the police.

(3A) Where a person mentioned in paragraph (a) of subsection (3) or (4) has already had his fingerprints taken in the course of the investigation of the offence by the police, that fact shall be disregarded for the purposes of that subsection if—

   (a) the fingerprints taken on the previous occasion do not constitute a complete set of his fingerprints; or

   (b) some or all of the fingerprints taken on the previous occasion are not of sufficient quality to allow satisfactory analysis, comparison or matching (whether in the case in question or generally).

(4) The fingerprints of a person detained at a police station may be taken without the appropriate consent if—

   (a) he has been charged with a recordable offence or informed that he will be reported for such an offence; and

   (b) he has not had his fingerprints taken in the course of the investigation of the offence by the police.

(4A) The fingerprints of a person who has answered to bail at a court or police station may be taken without the appropriate consent at the court or station if—

   (a) the court, or

   (b) an officer of at least the rank of inspector,

   authorises them to be taken.

(4B) A court or officer may only give an authorisation under subsection (4A) if—

   (a) the person who has answered to bail has answered to it for a person whose fingerprints were taken on a previous occasion and there are reasonable grounds for believing that he is not the same person; or

   (b) the person who has answered to bail claims to be a different person from a person whose fingerprints were taken on a previous occasion.

(5) An officer may give an authorisation under subsection (4A) above orally or in writing but, if he gives it orally, he will confirm it in writing as soon as is practicable.

(5A) The fingerprints of a person may be taken without the appropriate consent if (before or after the coming into force of this subsection) he has been arrested for a recordable offence and released and—

   (a) in the case of a person who is on bail, he has not had his fingerprints taken in the course of the investigation of the offence by the police; or

   (b) in any case, he has had his fingerprints taken in the course of that investigation but

      (i) subsection (3A)(a) or (b) above applies, or

      (ii) subsection (5C) below applies.

(5B) The fingerprints of a person not detained at a police station may be taken without the appropriate consent if (before or after the coming into force of this subsection) he has been charged with a recordable offence or informed that he will be reported for such an offence and—

    (a)   he has not had his fingerprints taken in the course of the investigation of the offence by the police; or

    (b)   he has had his fingerprints taken in the course of that investigation but

        (i)   subsection (3A)(a) or (b) above applies, or

        (ii)   subsection (5C) below applies.

(5C) This subsection applies where—

    (a)   the investigation was discontinued but subsequently resumed, and

    (b)   before the resumption of the investigation the fingerprints were destroyed pursuant to section 63D(3) below.

(6) Subject to this section, the fingerprints of a person may be taken without the appropriate consent if (before or after the coming into force of this subsection)—

    (a)   he has been convicted of a recordable offence, or

    (b)   he has been given a caution in respect of a recordable offence which, at the time of the caution, he has admitted, and

either of the conditions mentioned in subsection (6ZA) below is met.

(6ZA)The conditions referred to in subsection (6) above are—

    (a)   the person has not had his fingerprints taken since he was convicted or cautioned;

    (b)   he has had his fingerprints taken since then but subsection (3A)(a) or (b) above applies.

(6ZB) Fingerprints may only be taken as specified in subsection (6) above with the authorisation of an officer of at least the rank of inspector.

(6ZC) An officer may only give an authorisation under subsection (6ZB) above if the officer is satisfied that taking the fingerprints is necessary to assist in the prevention or detection of crime.

(6A) A constable may take a person's fingerprints without the appropriate consent if—

    (a)   the constable reasonably suspects that the person is committing or attempting to commit an offence, or has committed or attempted to commit an offence; and

    (b)   either of the two conditions mentioned in subsection (6B) is met.

(6B) The conditions are that—

    (a)   the name of the person is unknown to, and cannot be readily ascertained by, the constable;

    (b)   the constable has reasonable grounds for doubting whether a name furnished by the person as his name is his real name.

(6C) The taking of fingerprints by virtue of subsection (6A) or (6BA) does not count for any of the purposes of this Act as taking them in the course of the investigation of an offence by the police.

(6D) Subject to this section, the fingerprints of a person may be taken without the appropriate consent if—

    (a)   under the law in force in a country or territory outside England and Wales the person has been convicted of an offence under that law (whether before or after the coming into force of this subsection and whether or not he has been punished for it);

    (b)   the act constituting the offence would constitute a qualifying offence if done in England and Wales (whether or not it constituted such an offence when the person was convicted); and

    (c)   either of the conditions mentioned in subsection (6E) below is met.

(6E) The conditions referred to in subsection (6D)(c) above are—

    (a)   the person has not had his fingerprints taken on a previous occasion under subsection (6D) above;

    (b)   he has had his fingerprints taken on a previous occasion under that subsection but subsection (3A)(a) or (b) above applies.

(6F) Fingerprints may only be taken as specified in subsection (6D) above with the authorisation of an officer of at least the rank of inspector.

(6G) An officer may only give an authorisation under subsection (6F) above if the officer is satisfied that taking the fingerprints is necessary to assist in the prevention or detection of crime.

(7) Where a person's fingerprints are taken without the appropriate consent by virtue of any power conferred by this section—

(a) before the fingerprints are taken, the person shall be informed of—

(i) the reason for taking the fingerprints;

(ii) the power by virtue of which they are taken; and

(iii) in a case where the authorisation of the court or an officer is required for the exercise of the power, the fact that the authorisation has been given; and

(b) those matters shall be recorded as soon as practicable after the fingerprints are taken.

(7A) If a person's fingerprints are taken at a police station, or by virtue of subsection (4A), (6A) at a place other than a police station, whether with or without the appropriate consent—

(a) before the fingerprints are taken, an officer shall inform him that they may be the subject of a speculative search; and

(b) the fact that the person has been informed of this possibility shall be recorded as soon as is practicable after the fingerprints have been taken.

(8) If he is detained at a police station when the fingerprints are taken, the matters referred to in subsection (7)(a)(i) to (iii) above and, in the case falling within subsection (7A) above, the fact referred to in paragraph (b) of that subsection shall be recorded on his custody record.

(8B) Any power under this section to take the fingerprints of a person without the appropriate consent, if not otherwise specified to be exercisable by a constable, shall be exercisable by a constable.

(9) Nothing in this section—

(a) affects any power conferred by paragraph 18(2) of Schedule 2 to the Immigration Act 1971; or

(b) applies to a person arrested or detained under the terrorism provisions.

(10) Nothing in this section applies to a person arrested under an extradition arrest power.

62 Intimate samples

(1) Subject to section 63B below, an intimate sample may be taken from a person in police detention only—

(a) if a police officer of at least the rank of inspector authorises it to be taken; and

(b) if the appropriate consent is given.

(1A) An intimate sample may be taken from a person who is not in police detention but from whom, in the course of the investigation of an offence, two or more non-intimate samples suitable for the same means of analysis have been taken which have proved insufficient—

(a) if a police officer of at least the rank of inspector authorises it to be taken; and

(b) if the appropriate consent is given.

(2) An officer may only give an authorisation under subsection (1) or (1A) above if he has reasonable grounds—

(a) for suspecting the involvement of the person from whom the sample is to be taken in a recordable offence; and

(b) for believing that the sample will tend to confirm or disprove his involvement.

(2A) An intimate sample may be taken from a person where—

(a) two or more non-intimate samples suitable for the same means of analysis have been taken from the person under section 63(3E) below (persons convicted of offences outside England and Wales etc) but have proved insufficient;

(b) a police officer of at least the rank of inspector authorises it to be taken; and

(c) the appropriate consent is given.

(2B)   An officer may only give an authorisation under subsection (2A) above if the officer is satisfied that taking the sample is necessary to assist in the prevention or detection of crime.

(3)   An officer may give an authorisation under subsection (1) or (1A) or (2A) above orally or in writing but, if he gives it orally, he shall confirm it in writing as soon as is practicable.

(4)   The appropriate consent must be given in writing.

(5)   Before an intimate sample is taken from a person, an officer shall inform him of the following—

     (a)   the reason for taking the sample;

     (b)   the fact that authorisation has been given and the provision of this section under which it has been given; and

     (c)   if the sample was taken at a police station, the fact that the sample may be the subject of a speculative search.

(6)   The reason referred to in subsection (5)(a) above must include, except in a case where the sample is taken under subsection (2A) above, a statement of the nature of the offence in which it is suspected that the person has been involved.

(7)   After an intimate sample has been taken from a person, the following shall be recorded as soon as practicable—

     (a)   the matters referred to in subsection (5)(a) and (b) above;

     (b)   if the sample was taken at a police station, the fact that the person has been informed as specified in subsection (5)(c) above; and

     (c)   the fact that the appropriate consent was given.

(8)   If an intimate sample is taken from a person detained at a police station, the matters required to be recorded by subsection (7) above shall be recorded in his custody record.

(9)   In the case of an intimate sample which is a dental impression, the sample may be taken from a person only by a registered dentist.

(9A)   In the case of any other form of intimate sample, except in the case of a sample of urine, the sample may be taken from a person only by—

     (a)   a registered medical practitioner; or

     (b)   a registered health care professional.

(10)   Where the appropriate consent to the taking of an intimate sample from a person was refused without good cause, in any proceedings against that person for an offence—

     (a)   the court, in determining—

         (ii)   whether there is a case to answer; and

     (aa)   a judge, in deciding whether to grant an application made by the accused under paragraph 2 of Schedule 3 to the Crime and Disorder Act 1998 (applications for dismissal); and

     (b)   the court or jury, in determining whether that person is guilty of the offence charged,

   may draw such inferences from the refusal as appear proper.

(11)   Nothing in this section applies to the taking of a specimen for the purposes of any of the provisions of sections 4 to 11 of the Road Traffic Act 1988 or of sections 26 to 38 of the Transport and Works Act 1992.

(12)   Nothing in this section applies to a person arrested or detained under the terrorism provisions; and subsection (1A) shall not apply where the non-intimate samples mentioned in that subsection were taken under paragraph 10 of Schedule 8 to the Terrorism Act 2000.

63   Other samples

(1)   Except as provided by this section, a non-intimate sample may not be taken from a person without the appropriate consent.

(2)   Consent to the taking of a non-intimate sample must be given in writing.

(2A)   A non-intimate sample may be taken from a person without the appropriate consent if two conditions are satisfied.

(2B)   The first is that the person is in police detention in consequence of his arrest for a recordable offence.

(2C) The second is that—
- (a)   he has not had a non-intimate sample of the same type and from the same part of the body taken in the course of the investigation of the offence by the police, or
- (b)   he has had such a sample taken but it proved insufficient.

(3)   A non-intimate sample may be taken from a person without the appropriate consent if—
- (a)   he is being held in custody by the police on the authority of a court; and
- (b)   an officer of at least the rank of inspector authorises it to be taken without the appropriate consent.

(3ZA) A non-intimate sample may be taken from a person without the appropriate consent if (before or after the coming into force of this subsection) he has been arrested for a recordable offence and released and—
- (a)   in the case of a person who is on bail, he has not had a non-intimate sample of the same type and from the same part of the body taken from him in the course of the investigation of the offence by the police; or
- (b)   in any case, he has had a non-intimate sample taken from him in the course of that investigation but—
  - (i)   it was not suitable for the same means of analysis, or
  - (ii)   it proved insufficient, or
  - (iii)   subsection (3AA) below applies.

(3A)   A non-intimate sample may be taken from a person (whether or not he is in police detention or held in custody by the police on the authority of a court) without the appropriate consent if he has been charged with a recordable offence or informed that he will be reported for such an offence and—
- (a)   he has not had a non-intimate sample taken from him in the course of the investigation of the offence by the police; or
- (b)   he has had a non-intimate sample taken from him in the course of that investigation but—
  - (i)   it was not suitable for the same means of analysis, or
  - (ii)   it proved insufficient, or
  - (iii)   subsection (3AA) below applies; or
- (c)   he has had a non-intimate sample taken from him in the course of that investigation and—
  - (i)   the sample has been destroyed pursuant to section 64ZA below or any other enactment, and
  - (ii)   it is disputed, in relation to any proceedings relating to the offence, whether a DNA profile relevant to the proceedings is derived from the sample.

(3AA) This subsection applies where the investigation was discontinued but subsequently resumed, and before the resumption of the investigation—
- (a)   any DNA profile derived from the sample was destroyed pursuant to section 63D(3) below, and
- (b)   the sample itself was destroyed pursuant to section 63R(4), (5) or (12) below.

(3B)   Subject to this section, a non-intimate sample may be taken from a person without the appropriate consent if (before or after the coming into force of this subsection)—
- (a)   he has been convicted of a recordable offence, or
- (b)   he has been given a caution in respect of a recordable offence which, at the time of the caution, he has admitted, and

either of the conditions mentioned in subsection (3BA) below is met.

(3BA) The conditions referred to in subsection (3B) above are—
- (a)   a non-intimate sample has not been taken from the person since he was convicted or cautioned;
- (b)   such a sample has been taken from him since then but—
  - (i)   it was not suitable for the same means of analysis, or
  - (ii)   it proved insufficient.

(3BB) A non-intimate sample may only be taken as specified in subsection (3B) above with the authorisation of an officer of at least the rank of inspector.

(3BC)An officer may only give an authorisation under subsection (3BB) above if the officer is satisfied that taking the sample is necessary to assist in the prevention or detection of crime.

(3C) A non-intimate sample may also be taken from a person without the appropriate consent if he is a person to whom section 2 of the Criminal Evidence (Amendment) Act 1997 applies (persons detained following acquittal on grounds of insanity or finding of unfitness to plead).

(4) An officer may only give an authorisation under subsection (3) above if he has reasonable grounds—

    (a)   for suspecting the involvement of the person from whom the sample is to be taken in a recordable offence; and

    (b)   for believing that the sample will tend to confirm or disprove his involvement.

(5) An officer may give an authorisation under subsection (3) above orally or in writing but, if he gives it orally, he shall confirm it in writing as soon as is practicable.

(5A) An officer shall not give an authorisation under subsection (3) above for the taking from any person of a non-intimate sample consisting of a skin impression if—

    (a)   a skin impression of the same part of the body has already been taken from that person in the course of the investigation of the offence; and

    (b)   the impression previously taken is not one that has proved insufficient.

(6) Where a non-intimate sample is taken from a person without the appropriate consent by virtue of any power conferred by this section—

    (a)   before the sample is taken, an officer shall inform him of—

        (i)   the reason for taking the sample;

        (ii)   the power by virtue of which it is taken; and

        (iii)   in a case where the authorisation of an officer is required for the exercise of the power, the fact that the authorisation has been given; and

    (b)   those matters shall be recorded as soon as practicable after the sample is taken.

(7) The reason referred to in subsection (6)(a)(i) above must include, except in a case where the non-intimate sample is taken under subsection (3B) or (3E) above, a statement of the nature of the offence in which it is suspected that the person has been involved.

(8B) If a non-intimate sample is taken from a person at a police station, whether with or without the appropriate consent—

    (a)   before the sample is taken, an officer shall inform him that it may be the subject of a speculative search; and

    (b)   the fact that the person has been informed of this possibility shall be recorded as soon as practicable after the sample has been taken.

(9) If a non-intimate sample is taken from a person detained at a police station, the matters required to be recorded by subsection (6) or (8B) above shall be recorded in his custody record.

(9ZA)The power to take a non-intimate sample from a person without the appropriate consent shall be exercisable by any constable.

(9A) Subsection (3B) above shall not apply to—

    (a)   any person convicted before 10th April 1995 unless he is a person to whom section 1 of the Criminal Evidence (Amendment) Act 1997 applies (persons imprisoned or detained by virtue of pre-existing conviction for sexual offence etc); or

    (b)   a person given a caution before 10th April 1995.

(10) Nothing in this section applies to a person arrested or detained under the terrorism provisions.

(11) Nothing in this section applies to a person arrested under an extradition arrest power.

63B   Testing for presence of Class A drugs

(1) A sample of urine or a non-intimate sample may be taken from a person in police detention for the purpose of ascertaining whether he has any specified Class A drug in his body if—

    (a)   either the arrest condition or the charge condition is met;

(b)　both the age condition and the request condition are met; and

(c)　the notification condition is met in relation to the arrest condition, the charge condition or the age condition (as the case may be).

(1A)　The arrest condition is that the person concerned has been arrested for an offence but has not been charged with that offence and either—

(a)　the offence is a trigger offence; or

(b)　a police officer of at least the rank of inspector has reasonable grounds for suspecting that the misuse by that person of a specified Class A drug caused or contributed to the offence and has authorised the sample to be taken.

(2)　The charge condition is either—

(a)　that the person concerned has been charged with a trigger offence; or

(b)　that the person concerned has been charged with an offence and a police officer of at least the rank of inspector, who has reasonable grounds for suspecting that the misuse by that person of any specified Class A drug caused or contributed to the offence, has authorised the sample to be taken.

(3)　The age condition is—

(a)　if the arrest condition is met, that the person concerned has attained the age of 18;

(b)　if the charge condition is met, that he has attained the age of 14.

(4)　The request condition is that a police officer has requested the person concerned to give the sample.

(4A)　The notification condition is that—

(a)　the relevant chief officer has been notified by the Secretary of State that appropriate arrangements have been made for the police area as a whole, or for the particular police station, in which the person is in police detention, and

(b)　the notice has not been withdrawn.

(4B)　For the purposes of subsection (4A) above, appropriate arrangements are arrangements for the taking of samples under this section from whichever of the following is specified in the notification—

(a)　persons in respect of whom the arrest condition is met;

(b)　persons in respect of whom the charge condition is met;

(c)　persons who have not attained the age of 18.

(5)　Before requesting the person concerned to give a sample, an officer must—

(a)　warn him that if, when so requested, he fails without good cause to do so he may be liable to prosecution, and

(b)　in a case within subsection (1A)(b) or (2)(b) above, inform him of the giving of the authorisation and of the grounds in question.

64A　Photographing of suspects etc.

(1)　A person who is detained at a police station may be photographed—

(a)　with the appropriate consent; or

(b)　if the appropriate consent is withheld or it is not practicable to obtain it, without it.

(2)　A person proposing to take a photograph of any person under this section—

(a)　may, for the purpose of doing so, require the removal of any item or substance worn on or over the whole or any part of the head or face of the person to be photographed; and

(b)　if the requirement is not complied with, may remove the item or substance himself.

(4)　A photograph taken under this section—

(a)　may be used by, or disclosed to, any person for any purpose related to the prevention or detection of crime, the investigation of an offence or the conduct of a prosecution or the enforcement of a sentence; and

(b)　after being so used or disclosed, may be retained but may not be used or disclosed except for a purpose so related.

65　Part V—supplementary

(1)　In this Part of this Act—

"analysis", in relation to a skin impression, includes comparison and matching;

"appropriate consent" means—

(a)　　in relation to a person who has attained the age of 17 years, the consent of that person;

(b)　　in relation to a person who has not attained that age but has attained the age of 14 years, the consent of that person and his parent or guardian; and

(c)　　in relation to a person who has not attained the age of 14 years, the consent of his parent or guardian;

"DNA profile" means any information derived from a DNA sample;

"DNA sample" means any material that has come from a human body and consists of or includes human cells;

"control order" has the same meaning as in the Prevention of Terrorism Act 2005;

"extradition arrest power" means any of the following—

(a)　　a Part 1 warrant (within the meaning given by the Extradition Act 2003) in respect of which a certificate under section 2 of that Act has been issued;

(b)　　section 5 of that Act;

(c)　　a warrant issued under section 71 of that Act;

(d)　　a provisional warrant (within the meaning given by that Act).

"fingerprints", in relation to any person, means a record (in any form and produced by any method) of the skin pattern and other physical characteristics or features of—

(a)　　any of that person's fingers; or

(b)　　either of his palms;

"intimate sample" means—

(a)　　a sample of blood, semen or any other tissue fluid, urine or pubic hair;

(b)　　a dental impression;

(c)　　a swab taken from any part of a person's genitals (including pubic hair) or from a person's body orifice other than the mouth;

"intimate search" means a search which consists of the physical examination of a person's body orifices other than the mouth;

"non-intimate sample" means—

(a)　　a sample of hair other than pubic hair;

(b)　　a sample taken from a nail or from under a nail;

(c)　　a swab taken from any part of a person's body other than a part from which a swab taken would be an intimate sample;

(d)　　saliva;

(e)　　a skin impression;

"offence", in relation to any country or territory outside England and Wales, includes an act punishable under the law of that country or territory, however it is described;

"registered dentist" has the same meaning as in the Dentists Act 1984;

"registered health care professional" means a person (other than a medical practitioner) who is—

(a)　　a registered nurse; or

(b)　　a registered member of a health care profession which is designated for the purposes of this paragraph by an order made by the Secretary of State;

"skin impression", in relation to any person, means any record (other than a fingerprint) which is a record "in any form and produced by any method) of the skin pattern and other physical characteristics or features of the whole or any part of his foot or of any other part of his body;

"speculative search", in relation to a person's fingerprints or samples, means such a check against other fingerprints or samples or against information derived from other samples as is referred to in section 63A(1) above;

"sufficient" and "insufficient", in relation to a sample, means (subject to subsection (2) below) sufficient or insufficient (in point of quantity or quality) for the purpose of enabling information to be produced by the means of analysis used or to be used in relation to the sample;

"the terrorism provisions" means section 41 of the Terrorism Act 2000, and any provision of Schedule 7 to that Act conferring a power of detention;

"terrorism" has the meaning given in section 1 of that Act; and

"terrorist investigation" has the meaning given by section 32 of that Act.

(1A) A health care profession is any profession mentioned in section 60(2) of the Health Act 1999 other than the profession of practising medicine and the profession of nursing.

(1B) An order under subsection (1) shall be made by statutory instrument and shall be subject to annulment in pursuance of a resolution of either House of Parliament.

(2) References in this Part of this Act to a sample's proving insufficient include references to where, as a consequence of—

(a) the loss, destruction or contamination of the whole or any part of the sample,

(b) any damage to the whole or a part of the sample, or

(c) the use of the whole or a part of the sample for an analysis which produced no results or which produced results some or all of which must be regarded, in the circumstances, as unreliable,

the sample has become unavailable or insufficient for the purpose of enabling information, or information of a particular description, to be obtained by means of analysis of the sample.

PART VI
CODES OF PRACTICE — GENERAL

66 Codes of practice

(1) The Secretary of State shall issue codes of practice in connection with—

(a) the exercise by police officers of statutory powers—

(i) to search a person without first arresting him;

(ii) to search a vehicle without making an arrest; or

(iii) to arrest a person;

(b) the detention, treatment, questioning and indication of persons by police officers;

(c) searches of premises by police officers; and

(d) the seizure of property found by police officers on persons or premises.

(2) Codes shall (in particular) include provisions in connection with the exercise by police officers of powers under section 63B, above.

67 Codes of practice — supplementary

(1) In this section, "code" means a code of practice under section 60, 60A or 66.

(2) The Secretary of State may at any time revise the whole or any part of a code.

(3) A code may be made, or revised, so as to—

(a) apply only in relation to one or more specified areas,

(b) have effect only for a specified period,

(c) apply only in relation to specified offences or descriptions of offender.

(4) Before issuing a code, or any revision of a code, the Secretary of State must consult—

(a) such persons as appear to the Secretary of State to represent the views of police and crime commissioners,

(aa) the Mayor's Office for Policing and Crime,

(ab) the Common Council of the City of London,

(b) the Association of Chief Police Officers of England, Wales and Northern Ireland,

(c) the General Council of the Bar,

(d) the Law Society of England and Wales,

(e) the Institute of Legal Executives, and

(f) such other persons as he thinks fit.

(5) A code, or a revision of a code, does not come into operation until the Secretary of State by order so provides.

(6) The power conferred by subsection (5) is exercisable by statutory instrument.

(7) An order bringing a code into operation may not be made unless a draft of the order has been laid before Parliament and approved by a resolution of each House.

(7A) An order bringing a revision of a code into operation must be laid before Parliament if the order has been made without a draft having been so laid and approved by a resolution of each House.

(7B) When an order or draft of an order is laid, the code or revision of a code to which it relates must also be laid.

(10) A failure on the part—

(a)   of a police officer to comply with any provision of a code;

(b)   of any person other than a police officer who is charged with the duty of investigating offences or charging offenders to have regard to any relevant provision of a code in the discharge of the duty, or

(c)   of a person designated under section 38 or 39 or accredited under section 41 of the Police Reform Act 2002 to have regard to any relevant provision of such a code in the exercise or performance of the powers and duties conferred or imposed on him by that designation or accreditation,

shall not of itself render him liable to any criminal or civil proceedings.

(11) In all criminal and civil proceedings any such code shall be admissible in evidence; and if any provision of a code appears to the court or tribunal conducting the proceedings to be relevant to any question arising in the proceedings it shall be taken into account in determining that question.

PART VIII
EVIDENCE IN CRIMINAL PROCEEDINGS — GENERAL

Confessions

76   Confessions

(1)   In any proceedings a confession made by an accused person may be given in evidence against him in so far as it is relevant to any matter in issue in the proceedings and is not excluded by the court in pursuance of this section.

(2)   If, in any proceedings where the prosecution proposes to give in evidence a confession made by an accused person, it is represented to the court that the confession was or may have been obtained—

(a)   by oppression of the person who made it; or

(b)   in consequence of anything said or done which was likely, in the circumstances existing at the time, to render unreliable any confession which might be made by him in consequence thereof,

the court shall not allow the confession to be given in evidence against him except in so far as the prosecution proves to the court beyond reasonable doubt that the confession (notwithstanding that it may be true) was not obtained as aforesaid.

(3)   In any proceedings where the prosecution proposes to give in evidence a confession made by an accused person, the court may of its own motion require the prosecution, as a condition of allowing it to do so, to prove that the confession was not obtained as mentioned in subsection (2) above.

(4)   The fact that a confession is wholly or partly excluded in pursuance of this section shall not affect the admissibility in evidence—

(a)   of any facts discovered as a result of the confession; or

(b)   where the confession is relevant as showing that the accused speaks, writes or expresses himself in a particular way, of so much of the confession as is necessary to show that he does so.

(5)   Evidence that a fact to which this subsection applies was discovered as a result of a statement made by an accused person shall not be admissible unless evidence of how it was discovered is given by him or on his behalf.

(6)   Subsection (5) above applies—

(a)   to any fact discovered as a result of a confession which is wholly excluded in pursuance of this section; and

(b)   to any fact discovered as a result of a confession which is partly so excluded, if that fact is discovered as a result of the excluded part of the confession.

(7)   Nothing in Part VII of this Act shall prejudice the admissibility of a confession made by an accused person.

(8)   In this section "oppression" includes torture, inhuman or degrading treatment, and the use or threat of violence (whether or not amounting to torture).

76A   Confessions may be given in evidence for co-accused

(1)   In any proceedings a confession made by an accused person may be given in evidence for another person charged in the same proceedings (a co-accused) in so far as it is relevant to any matter in issue in the proceedings and is not excluded by the court in pursuance of this section.

(2)   If, in any proceedings where a co-accused proposes to give in evidence a confession made by an accused person, it is represented to the court that the confession was or may have been obtained—

(a)   by oppression of the person who made it; or

(b)   in consequence of anything said or done which was likely, in the circumstances existing at the time, to render unreliable any confession which might be made by him in consequence thereof,

the court shall not allow the confession to be given in evidence for the co-accused except in so far as it is proved to the court on the balance of probabilities that the confession (notwithstanding that it may be true) was not so obtained.

(3)   Before allowing a confession made by an accused person to be given in evidence for a co-accused in any proceedings, the court may of its own motion require the fact that the confession was not obtained as mentioned in subsection (2) above to be proved in the proceedings on the balance of probabilities.

(4)   The fact that a confession is wholly or partly excluded in pursuance of this section shall not affect the admissibility in evidence—

(a)   of any facts discovered as a result of the confession; or

(b)   where the confession is relevant as showing that the accused speaks, writes or expresses himself in a particular way, of so much of the confession as is necessary to show that he does so.

77   Confessions by mentally handicapped persons

(1)   Without prejudice to the general duty of the court at a trial on indictment with a jury to direct the jury on any matter on which it appears to the court appropriate to do so, where at such a trial—

(a)   the case against the accused depends wholly or substantially on a confession by him; and

(b)   the court is satisfied—

(i)   that he is mentally handicapped; and

(ii)   that the confession was not made in the presence of an independent person,

the court shall warn the jury that there is special need for caution before convicting the accused in reliance on the confession, and shall explain that the need arises because of the circumstances mentioned in paragraphs (a) and (b) above.

(2)   In any case where at the summary trial of a person for an offence it appears to the court that a warning under subsection (1) above would be required if the trial were on indictment with a jury, the court shall treat the case as one in which there is a special need for caution before convicting the accused on his confession.

Miscellaneous

78   Exclusion of unfair evidence

(1)   In any proceedings the court may refuse to allow evidence on which the prosecution proposes to rely to be given if it appears to the court that, having regard to all the circumstances, including the circumstances in which the evidence was obtained, the admission of the evidence would have such an adverse effect on the fairness of the proceedings that the court ought not to admit it.

(2)   Nothing in this section shall prejudice any rule of law requiring a court to exclude evidence.

PART VIII
SUPPLEMENTARY

82   Part VIII — interpretation

(1)   In this Part of this Act—
"confession" includes any statement wholly or partly adverse to the person who made it, whether made to a person in authority or not and whether made in words or otherwise;

(3)   Nothing in this Part of this Act shall prejudice any power of a court to exclude evidence (whether by preventing questions from being put or otherwise) at its discretion.

PART XI
MISCELLANEOUS AND SUPPLEMENTARY

117   Power of constable to use reasonable force

Where any provision of this Act—

(a)   confers a power on a constable; and

(b)   does not provide that the power may only be exercised with the consent of some person, other than a police officer,

the officer may use reasonable force, if necessary, in the exercise of the power.

PUBLIC ORDER ACT 1986
(1986, c. 64)

An Act to abolish the common law offences of riot, rout, unlawful assembly and affray and certain statutory offences relating to public order; to create new offences relating to public order; to control public processions and assemblies; to control the stirring up of racial hatred; to provide for the exclusion of certain offenders from sporting events; to create a new offence relating to the contamination of or interference with goods; to confer power to direct certain trespassers to leave land; to amend section 7 of the Conspiracy and Protection of Property Act 1875, section 1 of the Prevention of Crime Act 1953, Part V of the Criminal Justice (Scotland) Act 1980 and the Sporting Events (Control of Alcohol etc.) Act 1985; to repeal certain obsolete or unnecessary enactments; and for connected purposes.   [7 November 1986]

PART I
NEW OFFENCES

1   Riot

(1)   Where 12 or more persons who are present together use or threaten unlawful violence for a common purpose and the conduct of them (taken together) is such as would cause a person of reasonable firmness present at the scene to fear for his personal safety, each of the persons using unlawful violence for the common purpose is guilty of riot.

(2)   It is immaterial whether or not the 12 or more use or threaten unlawful violence simultaneously.

(3)   The common purpose may be inferred from conduct.

(4)   No person of reasonable firmness need actually be, or be likely to be, present at the scene.

(5)   Riot may be committed in private as well as in public places.

(6)   A person guilty of riot is liable on conviction on indictment to imprisonment for a term not exceeding ten years or a fine or both.

2　Violent disorder

(1)　Where 3 or more persons who are present together use or threaten unlawful violence and the conduct of them (taken together) is such as would cause a person of reasonable firmness present at the scene to fear for his personal safety, each of the persons using or threatening unlawful violence is guilty of violent disorder.

(2)　It is immaterial whether or not the 3 or more use or threaten unlawful violence simultaneously.

(3)　No person of reasonable firmness need actually be, or be likely to be, present at the scene.

(4)　Violent disorder may be committed in private as well as in public places.

(5)　A person guilty of violent disorder is liable on conviction on indictment to imprisonment for a term not exceeding 5 years or a fine or both, or on summary conviction to imprisonment for a term not exceeding 6 months or a fine not exceeding the statutory maximum or both.

3　Affray

(1)　A person is guilty of affray if he uses or threatens unlawful violence towards another and his conduct is such as would cause a person of reasonable firmness present at the scene to fear for his personal safety.

(2)　Where 2 or more persons use or threaten the unlawful violence, it is the conduct of them taken together that must be considered for the purposes of subsection (1).

(3)　For the purposes of this section a threat cannot be made by the use of words alone.

(4)　No person of reasonable firmness need actually be, or be likely to be, present at the scene.

(5)　Affray may be committed in private as well as in public places.

(7)　A person guilty of affray is liable on conviction on indictment to imprisonment for a term not exceeding 3 years or a fine or both, or on summary conviction to imprisonment for a term not exceeding 6 months or a fine not exceeding the statutory maximum or both.

4　Fear or provocation of violence

(1)　A person is guilty of an offence if he—

(a)　uses towards another person threatening, abusive or insulting words or behaviour, or

(b)　distributes or displays to another person any writing, sign or other visible representation which is threatening, abusive or insulting,

with intent to cause that person to believe that immediate unlawful violence will be used against him or another by any person, or to provoke the immediate use of unlawful violence by that person or another, or whereby that person is likely to believe that such violence will be used or it is likely that such violence will be provoked.

(2)　An offence under this section may be committed in a public or a private place, except that no offence is committed where the words or behaviour are used, or the writing, sign or other visible representation is distributed or displayed, by a person inside a dwelling and the other person is also inside that or another dwelling.

(4)　A person guilty of an offence under this section is liable on summary conviction to imprisonment for a term not exceeding 6 months or a fine not exceeding level 5 on the standard scale or both.

4A　Intentional harassment, alarm or distress

(1)　A person is guilty of an offence if, with intent to cause a person harassment, alarm or distress, he—

(a)　uses threatening, abusive or insulting words or behaviour, or disorderly behaviour, or

(b)　displays any writing, sign or other visible representation which is threatening, abusive or insulting,

thereby causing that or another person harassment, alarm or distress.

(2)　An offence under this section may be committed in a public or a private place, except that no offence is committed where the words or behaviour are used, or the writing, sign or other visible representation is displayed, by a person inside a dwelling and the person who is harassed, alarmed or distressed is also inside that or another dwelling.

(3)   It is a defence for the accused to prove—

    (a)   that he was inside a dwelling and had no reason to believe that the words or behaviour used, or the writing, sign or other visible representation displayed, would be heard or seen by a person outside that or any other dwelling, or

    (b)   that his conduct was reasonable.

(5)   A person guilty of an offence under this section is liable on summary conviction to imprisonment for a term not exceeding 6 months or a fine not exceeding level 5 on the standard scale or both.

5   Harassment, alarm or distress

(1)   A person is guilty of an offence if he—

    (a)   uses threatening or abusive words or behaviour, or disorderly behaviour, or

    (b)   displays any writing, sign or other visible representation which is threatening or abusive,

within the hearing or sight of a person likely to be caused harassment, alarm or distress thereby.

(2)   An offence under this section may be committed in a public or a private place, except that no offence is committed where the words or behaviour are used, or the writing, sign or other visible representation is displayed, by a person inside a dwelling and the other person is also inside that or another dwelling.

(3)   It is a defence for the accused to prove—

    (a)   that he had no reason to believe that there was any person within hearing or sight who was likely to be caused harassment, alarm or distress, or

    (b)   that he was inside a dwelling and had no reason to believe that the words or behaviour used, or the writing, sign or other visible representation displayed, would be heard or seen by a person outside that or any other dwelling, or

    (c)   that his conduct was reasonable.

(6)   A person guilty of an offence under this section is liable on summary conviction to a fine not exceeding level 3 on the standard scale.

6   Mental element: miscellaneous

(1)   A person is guilty of riot only if he intends to use violence or is aware that his conduct may be violent.

(2)   A person is guilty of violent disorder or affray only if he intends to use or threaten violence or is aware that his conduct may be violent or threaten violence.

(3)   A person is guilty of an offence under section 4 only if he intends his words or behaviour, or the writing, sign or other visible representation, to be threatening, abusive or insulting, or is aware that it may be threatening, abusive or insulting.

(4)   A person is guilty of an offence under section 5 only if he intends his words or behaviour, or the writing, sign or other visible representation, to be threatening or abusive, or is aware that it may be threatening or abusive or (as the case may be) he intends his behaviour to be or is aware that it may be disorderly.

(5)   For the purposes of this section a person whose awareness is impaired by intoxication shall be taken to be aware of that of which he would be aware if not intoxicated, unless he shows either that his intoxication was not self-induced or that it was caused solely by the taking or administration of a substance in the course of medical treatment.

(6)   In subsection (5) "intoxication" means any intoxication, whether caused by drink, drugs or other means, or by a combination of means.

(7)   Subsections (1) and (2) do not affect the determination for the purposes of riot or violent disorder of the number of persons who use or threaten violence.

7   Procedure: miscellaneous

(1)   No prosecution for an offence of riot or incitement to riot may be instituted except by or with the consent of the Director of Public Prosecutions.

8   Interpretation

In this Part—

    "dwelling" means any structure or part of a structure occupied as a person's home or as other living accommodation (whether the occupation is separate or shared with

others) but does not include any part not so occupied, and for this purpose "structure" includes a tent, caravan, vehicle, vessel or other temporary or movable structure;
"violence" means any violent conduct, so that—

(a) except in the context of affray, it includes violent conduct towards property as well as violent conduct towards persons, and

(b) it is not restricted to conduct causing or intended to cause injury or damage but includes any other violent conduct (for example, throwing at or towards a person a missile of a kind capable of causing injury which does not hit or falls short).

9   Offences abolished

(1) The common law offences of riot, rout, unlawful assembly and affray are abolished.

PART II
PROCESSIONS AND ASSEMBLIES

11   Advance notice of public processions

(1) Written notice shall be given in accordance with this section of any proposal to hold a public procession intended—

(a) to demonstrate support for or opposition to the views or actions of any person or body of persons,

(b) to publicise a cause or campaign, or

(c) to mark or commemorate an event,

unless it is not reasonably practicable to give any advance notice of the procession.

(2) Subsection (1) does not apply where the procession is one commonly or customarily held in the police area (or areas) in which it is proposed to be held or is a funeral procession organised by a funeral director acting in the normal course of his business.

(3) The notice must specify the date when it is intended to hold the procession, the time when it is intended to start it, its proposed route, and the name and address of the person (or of one of the persons) proposing to organise it.

(4) Notice must be delivered to a police station—

(a) in the police area in which it is proposed the procession will start, or

(b) where it is proposed the procession will start in Scotland and cross into England, in the first police area in England on the proposed route.

(5) If delivered not less than 6 clear days before the date when the procession is intended to be held, the notice may be delivered by post by the recorded delivery service; but section 7 of the Interpretation Act 1978 (under which a document sent by post is deemed to have been served when posted and to have been delivered in the ordinary course of post) does not apply.

(6) If not delivered in accordance with subsection (5), the notice must be delivered by hand not less than 6 clear days before the date when the procession is intended to be held or, if that is not reasonably practicable, as soon as delivery is reasonably practicable.

(7) Where a public procession is held, each of the persons organising it is guilty of an offence if—

(a) the requirements of this section as to notice have not been satisfied, or

(b) the date when it is held, the time when it starts, or its route, differs from the date, time or route specified in the notice.

(8) It is a defence for the accused to prove that he did not know of, and neither suspected nor had reason to suspect, the failure to satisfy the requirements or (as the case may be) the difference of date, time or route.

(9) To the extent that an alleged offence turns on a difference of date, time or route, it is a defence for the accused to prove that the difference arose from circumstances beyond his control or from something done with the agreement of a police officer or by his direction.

(10) A person guilty of an offence under subsection (7) is liable on summary conviction to a fine not exceeding level 3 on the standard scale.

12   Imposing conditions on public processions

(1)   If the senior police officer, having regard to the time or place at which and the circumstances in which any public procession is being held or is intended to be held and to its route or proposed route, reasonably believes that—

(a)   it may result in serious public disorder, serious damage to property or serious disruption to the life of the community, or

(b)   the purpose of the persons organising it is the intimidation of others with a view to compelling them not to do an act they have a right to do, or to do an act they have a right not to do,

he may give directions imposing on the persons organising or taking part in the procession such conditions as appear to him necessary to prevent such disorder, damage, disruption or intimidation, including conditions as to the route of the procession or prohibiting it from entering any public place specified in the directions.

(2)   In subsection (1) "the senior police officer" means—

(a)   in relation to a procession being held, or to a procession intended to be held in a case where persons are assembling with a view to taking part in it, the most senior in rank of the police officers present at the scene, and

(b)   in relation to a procession intended to be held in a case where paragraph (a) does not apply, the chief officer of police.

(3)   A direction given by a chief officer of police by virtue of subsection (2)(b) shall be given in writing.

(4)   A person who organises a public procession and knowingly fails to comply with a condition imposed under this section is guilty of an offence, but it is a defence for him to prove that the failure arose from circumstances beyond his control.

(5)   A person who takes part in a public procession and knowingly fails to comply with a condition imposed under this section is guilty of an offence, but it is a defence for him to prove that the failure arose from circumstances beyond his control.

(6)   A person who incites another to commit an offence under subsection (5) is guilty of an offence.

(8)   A person guilty of an offence under subsection (4) is liable on summary conviction to imprisonment for a term not exceeding 3 months [*51 weeks*] or a fine not exceeding level 4 on the standard scale or both.

(9)   A person guilty of an offence under subsection (5) is liable on summary conviction to a fine not exceeding level 3 on the standard scale.

(10) A person guilty of an offence under subsection (6) is liable on summary conviction to imprisonment for a term not exceeding 3 months [*51 weeks*] or a fine not exceeding level 4 on the standard scale or both.

13   Prohibiting public processions

(1)   If at any time the chief officer of police reasonably believes that, because of particular circumstances existing in any district or part of a district, the powers under section 12 will not be sufficient to prevent the holding of public processions in that district or part from resulting in serious public disorder, he shall apply to the council of the district for an order prohibiting for such period not exceeding 3 months as may be specified in the application the holding of all public processions (or of any class of public procession so specified) in the district or part concerned.

(2)   On receiving such an application, a council may with the consent of the Secretary of State make an order either in the terms of the application or with such modifications as may be approved by the Secretary of State.

(3)   Subsection (1) does not apply in the City of London or the metropolitan police district.

(4)   If at any time the Commissioner of Police for the City of London or the Commissioner of Police of the Metropolis reasonably believes that, because of particular circumstances existing in his police area or part of it, the powers under section 12 will not be sufficient to prevent the holding of public processions in that area or part from resulting in serious public disorder, he may with the consent of the Secretary of State make an order prohibiting for such period not exceeding 3 months as may be specified in the order the holding of all public processions (or of any class of public procession so specified) in the area or part concerned.

(5) An order made under this section may be revoked or varied by a subsequent order made in the same way, that is, in accordance with subsections (1) and (2) or subsection (4), as the case may be.

(6) An order under this section shall, if not made in writing, be recorded in writing as soon as practicable after being made.

(7) A person who organises a public procession the holding of which he knows is prohibited by virtue of an order under this section is guilty of an offence.

(8) A person who takes part in a public procession the holding of which he knows is prohibited by virtue of an order under this section is guilty of an offence.

(9) A person who incites another to commit an offence under subsection (8) is guilty of an offence.

(11) A person guilty of an offence under subsection (7) is liable on summary conviction to imprisonment for a term not exceeding 3 months [*51 weeks*] or a fine not exceeding level 4 on the standard scale or both.

(12) A person guilty of an offence under subsection (8) is liable on summary conviction to a fine not exceeding level 3 on the standard scale.

(13) A person guilty of an offence under subsection (9) is liable on summary conviction to imprisonment for a term not exceeding 3 months [*51 weeks*] or a fine not exceeding level 4 on the standard scale or both.

14 Imposing conditions on public assemblies

(1) If the senior police officer, having regard to the time or place at which and the circumstances in which any public assembly is being held or is intended to be held, reasonably believes that—

(a) it may result in serious public disorder, serious damage to property or serious disruption to the life of the community, or

(b) the purpose of the persons organising it is the intimidation of others with a view to compelling them not to do an act they have a right to do, or to do an act they have a right not to do,

he may give directions imposing on the persons organising or taking part in the assembly such conditions as to the place at which the assembly may be (or continue to be) held, its maximum duration, or the maximum number of persons who may constitute it, as appear to him necessary to prevent such disorder, damage, disruption or intimidation.

(2) In subsection (1) "the senior police officer" means—

(a) in relation to an assembly being held, the most senior in rank of the police officers present at the scene, and

(b) in relation to an assembly intended to be held, the chief officer of police.

(3) A direction given by a chief officer of police by virtue of subsection (2)(b) shall be given in writing.

(4) A person who organises a public assembly and knowingly fails to comply with a condition imposed under this section is guilty of an offence, but it is a defence for him to prove that the failure arose from circumstances beyond his control.

(5) A person who takes part in a public assembly and knowingly fails to comply with a condition imposed under this section is guilty of an offence, but it is a defence for him to prove that the failure arose from circumstances beyond his control.

(6) A person who incites another to commit an offence under subsection (5) is guilty of an offence.

(8) A person guilty of an offence under subsection (4) is liable on summary conviction to imprisonment for a term not exceeding 3 months [*51 weeks*] or a fine not exceeding level 4 on the standard scale or both.

(9) A person guilty of an offence under subsection (5) is liable on summary conviction to a fine not exceeding level 3 on the standard scale.

(10) A person guilty of an offence under subsection (6) is liable on summary conviction to imprisonment for a term not exceeding 3 months [*51 weeks*] or a fine not exceeding level 4 on the standard scale or both.

14A   Prohibiting trespassory assemblies

(1)   If at any time the chief officer of police reasonably believes that an assembly is intended to be held in any district at a place on land to which the public has no right of access or only a limited right of access and that the assembly—

(a)   is likely to be held without the permission of the occupier of the land or to conduct itself in such a way as to exceed the limits of any permission of his or the limits of the public's right of access, and

(b)   may result—

(i)   in serious disruption to the life of the community, or

(ii)   where the land, or a building or monument on it, is of historical, architectural, archaeological or scientific importance, in significant damage to the land, building or monument,

he may apply to the council of the district for an order prohibiting for a specified period the holding of all trespassory assemblies in the district or a part of it, as specified.

(2)   On receiving such an application, a council may—

(a)   in England and Wales, with the consent of the Secretary of State make an order either in the terms of the application or with such modifications as may be approved by the Secretary of State; or

(b)   in Scotland, make an order in the terms of the application.

(3)   Subsection (1) does not apply in the City of London or the metropolitan police district.

(4)   If at any time the Commissioner of Police for the City of London or the Commissioner of Police of the Metropolis reasonably believes that an assembly is intended to be held at a place on land to which the public has no right of access or only a limited right of access in his police area and that the assembly—

(a)   is likely to be held without the permission of the occupier of the land or to conduct itself in such a way as to exceed the limits of any permission of his or the limits of the public's right of access, and

(b)   may result—

(i)   in serious disruption to the life of the community, or

(ii)   where the land, or a building or monument on it, is of historical, architectural, archaeological or scientific importance, in significant damage to the land, building or monument,

he may with the consent of the Secretary of State make an order prohibiting for a specified period the holding of all trespassory assemblies in this area or a part of it, as specified.

(5)   An order prohibiting the holding of trespassory assemblies operates to prohibit any assembly which—

(a)   is held on land to which the public has no right of access or only a limited right of access, and

(b)   takes place in the prohibited circumstances, that is to say, without the permission of the occupier of the land or so as to exceed the limits of any permission of his or the limits of the public as right of access.

(6)   No order under this section shall prohibit the holding of assemblies for a period exceeding 4 days or in an area exceeding an area represented by a circle with a radius of 5 miles from a specified centre.

(7)   An order made under this section may be revoked or varied by a subsequent order made in the same way, that is, in accordance with subsection (1) and (2) or subsection (4), as the case may be.

(8)   Any order under this section shall, if not made in writing, be recorded in writing as soon as practicable after being made.

(9)   In this section and sections 14B and 14C—

"assembly" means an assembly of 20 or more persons;

"land", means land in the open air;

"limited", in relation to a right of access by the public to land, means that their use of it is restricted to use for a particular purpose (as in the case of a highway or road) or is subject to other restrictions;

"occupier" means—

(a)   in England and Wales, the person entitled to possession of the land by virtue of an estate or interest held by him; or

(b)   in Scotland, the person lawfully entitled to natural possession of the land,
and in subsection (1) and (4) includes the person reasonably believed by the authority
applying for or making the order to be the occupier;
"public" includes a section of the public; and
"specified" means specified in an order under this section.

14B   Offences in connection with trespassory assemblies and arrest therefor

(1)   A person who organises an assembly the holding of which he knows is prohibited by
an order under section 14A is guilty of an offence.

(2)   A person who takes part in an assembly which he knows is prohibited by an order
under section 14A is guilty of an offence.

(3)   In England and Wales, a person who incites another to commit an offence under
subsection (2) is guilty of an offence.

14C   Stopping persons from proceeding to trespassory assemblies

(1)   If a constable in uniform reasonably believes that a person is on his way to an
assembly within the area to which an order under section 14A applies which the
constable reasonably believes is likely to be an assembly which is prohibited by that
order, he may, subject to subsection (2) below—
(a)   stop that person, and
(b)   direct him not to proceed in the direction of the assembly.

(2)   The power conferred by subsection (1) may only be exercised within the area to which
the order applies.

(3)   A person who fails to comply with a direction under subsection (1) which he knows
has been given to him is guilty of an offence.

(5)   A person guilty of an offence under subsection (3) is liable on summary conviction to
a fine not exceeding level 3 on the standard scale.

15   Delegation

(1)   The chief officer of police may delegate, to such extent and subject to such conditions
as he may specify, any of his functions under sections 12 to 14A to an assistant chief
constable; and references in those subsections to the person delegating shall be
construed accordingly.

(2)   Subsection (1) shall have effect in the City of London and the metropolitan police
district as if "an assistant chief constable" read "an assistant commissioner of police".

16   Interpretation

In this Part—
"public assembly" means an assembly of 2 or more persons in a public place which
is wholly or partly open to the air;
"public place" means—
(a)   any highway, or in Scotland any road within the meaning of the Roads (Scotland)
Act 1984, and
(b)   any place to which at the material time the public or any section of the public
has access, on payment or otherwise, as of right or by virtue of express or
implied permission;
"public procession" means a procession in a public place.

PART III
RACIAL HATRED

Meaning of "racial hatred"

17   Meaning of "racial hatred"

In this Part "racial hatred" means hatred against a group of persons defined by reference to
colour, race, nationality (including citizenship) or ethnic or national origins.

Acts intended or likely to stir up racial hatred

18   Use of words or behaviour or display of written material

(1)   A person who uses threatening, abusive or insulting words or behaviour, or displays any written material which is threatening, abusive or insulting, is guilty of an offence if—

(a)   he intends thereby to stir up racial hatred, or

(b)   having regard to all the circumstances racial hatred is likely to be stirred up thereby.

(2)   An offence under this section may be committed in a public or a private place, except that no offence is committed where the words or behaviour are used, or the written material is displayed, by a person inside a dwelling and are not heard or seen except by other persons in that or another dwelling.

(4)   In proceedings for an offence under this section it is a defence for the accused to prove that he was inside a dwelling and had no reason to believe that the words or behaviour used, or the written material displayed, would be heard or seen by a person outside that or any other dwelling.

(5)   A person who is not shown to have intended to stir up racial hatred is not guilty of an offence under this section if he did not intend his words or behaviour, or the written material, to be, and was not aware that it might be, threatening, abusive or insulting.

(6)   This section does not apply to words or behaviour used, or written material displayed, solely for the purpose of being included in a programme service.

19   Publishing or distributing written material

(1)   A person who publishes or distributes written material which is threatening, abusive or insulting is guilty of an offence if—

(a)   he intends thereby to stir up racial hatred, or

(b)   having regard to all the circumstances racial hatred is likely to be stirred up thereby.

(2)   In proceedings for an offence under this section it is a defence for an accused who is not shown to have intended to stir up racial hatred to prove that he was not aware of the content of the material and did not suspect, and had no reason to suspect, that it was threatening, abusive or insulting.

(3)   References in this Part to the publication or distribution of written material are to its publication or distribution to the public or a section of the public.

20   Public performance of play

(1)   If a public performance of a play is given which involves the use of threatening, abusive or insulting words or behaviour, any person who presents or directs the performance is guilty of an offence if—

(a)   he intends thereby to stir up racial hatred, or

(b)   having regard to all the circumstances (and, in particular, taking the performance as a whole) racial hatred is likely to be stirred up thereby.

21   Distributing, showing or playing a recording

(1)   A person who distributes, or shows or plays, a recording of visual images or sounds which are threatening, abusive or insulting is guilty of an offence if—

(a)   he intends thereby to stir up racial hatred, or

(b)   having regard to all the circumstances racial hatred is likely to be stirred up thereby.

(2)   In this Part "recording" means any record from which visual images or sounds may, by any means, be reproduced; and references to the distribution, showing or playing of a recording are to its distribution, showing or playing to the public or a section of the public.

(3)   In proceedings for an offence under this section it is a defence for an accused who is not shown to have intended to stir up racial hatred to prove that he was not aware of the content of the recording and did not suspect, and had no reason to suspect, that it was threatening, abusive or insulting.

(4)   This section does not apply to the showing or playing of a recording solely for the purpose of enabling the recording to be included in a programme service.

22   Broadcasting or including programme in cable programme service

(1)   If a programme involving threatening, abusive or insulting visual images or sounds is included in a programme service, each of the persons mentioned in subsection (2) is guilty of an offence if—

(a)   he intends thereby to stir up racial hatred, or

(b)   having regard to all the circumstances racial hatred is likely to be stirred up thereby.

(2)   The persons are—

(a)   the person providing the programme service,

(b)   any person by whom the programme is produced or directed, and

(c)   any person by whom offending words or behaviour are used.

Racially inflammatory material

23   Possession of racially inflammatory material

(1)   A person who has in his possession written material which is threatening, abusive or insulting, or a recording of visual images or sounds which are threatening, abusive or insulting, with a view to—

(a)   in the case of written material, its being displayed, published, distributed, broadcast or included in a cable programme service, whether by himself or another, or

(b)   in the case of a recording, its being distributed, shown, played, or included in a cable programme service, whether by himself or another,

is guilty of an offence if he intends racial hatred to be stirred up thereby or, having regard to all the circumstances, racial hatred is likely to be stirred up thereby.

(2)   For this purpose regard shall be had to such display, publication, distribution, showing, playing, or inclusion in a programme service as he has, or it may reasonably be inferred that he has, in view.

(3)   In proceedings for an offence under this section it is a defence for an accused who is not shown to have intended to stir up racial hatred to prove that he was not aware of the content of the written material or recording and did not suspect, and had no reason to suspect, that it was threatening, abusive or insulting.

24   Powers of entry and search

(1)   If in England and Wales a justice of the peace is satisfied by information on oath laid by a constable that there are reasonable grounds for suspecting that a person has possession of written material or a recording in contravention of section 23, the justice may issue a warrant under his hand authorising any constable to enter and search the premises where it is suspected the material or recording is situated.

(2)   If in Scotland a sheriff or justice of the peace is satisfied by evidence on oath that there are reasonable grounds for suspecting that a person has possession of written material or a recording in contravention of section 23, the sheriff or justice may issue a warrant authorising any constable to enter and search the premises where it is suspected the material or recording is situated.

(3)   A constable entering or searching premises in pursuance of a warrant issued under this section may use reasonable force if necessary.

Supplementary provisions

26   Savings for reports of parliamentary or judicial proceedings

(1)   Nothing in this Part applies to a fair and accurate report of proceedings in Parliament or the Scottish Parliament or in the National Assembly for Wales.

(2)   Nothing in this Part applies to a fair and accurate report of proceedings publicly heard before a court or tribunal exercising judicial authority where the report is published contemporaneously with the proceedings or, if it is not reasonably practicable or would be unlawful to publish a report of them contemporaneously, as soon as publication is reasonably practicable and lawful.

27   Procedure and punishment

(1)   No proceedings for an offence under this Part may be instituted in England and Wales except by or with the consent of the Attorney General.

(2)   For the purposes of the rules in England and Wales against charging more than one offence in the same count or information, each of sections 18 to 23 creates one offence.

(3)   A person guilty of an offence under this Part is liable—

(a)   on conviction on indictment to imprisonment for a term not exceeding seven years or a fine or both;

(b)   on summary conviction to imprisonment for a term not exceeding six months or a fine not exceeding the statutory maximum or both.

40   Amendments repeals and savings

(4)   Nothing in this Act affects the common law powers in England and Wales to deal with or prevent a breach of the peace.

(5)   As respects Scotland, nothing in this Act affects any power of a constable under any rule of law.

OFFICIAL SECRETS ACT 1989
(1989, c. 6)

An Act to replace section 2 of the Official Secrets Act 1911 by provisions protecting more limited classes of official information.   [11 May 1989]

1   Security and intelligence

(1)   A person who is or has been—

(a)   a member of the security and intelligence services; or

(b)   a person notified that he is subject to the provisions of this subsection,

is guilty of an offence if without lawful authority he discloses any information, document or other article relating to security or intelligence which is or has been in his possession by virtue of his position as a member of any of those services or in the course of his work while the notification is or was in force.

(2)   The reference in subsection (1) above to disclosing information relating to security or intelligence includes a reference to making any statement which purports to be a disclosure of such information or is intended to be taken by those to whom it is addressed as being such a disclosure.

(3)   A person who is or has been a Crown servant or government contractor is guilty of an offence if without lawful authority he makes a damaging disclosure of any information, document or other article relating to security or intelligence which is or has been in his possession by virtue of his position as such but otherwise than as mentioned in subsection (1) above.

(4)   For the purposes of subsection (3) above a disclosure is damaging if—

(a)   it causes damage to the work of, or of any part of, the security and intelligence services; or

(b)   it is of information or a document or other article which is such that its unauthorised disclosure would be likely to cause such damage or which falls within a class or description of information, documents or articles the unauthorised disclosure of which would be likely to have that effect.

(5)   It is a defence for a person charged with an offence under this section to prove that at the time of the alleged offence he did not know, and had no reasonable cause to believe, that the information, document or article in question related to security or intelligence or, in the case of an offence under subsection (3), that the disclosure would be damaging within the meaning of that subsection.

(6) Notification that a person is subject to subsection (1) above shall be effected by a notice in writing served on him by a Minister of the Crown; and such a notice may be served if, in the Minister's opinion, the work undertaken by the person in question is or includes work connected with the security and intelligence services and its nature is such that the interests of national security require that he should be subject to the provisions of that subsection.

(7) Subject to subsection (8) below, a notification for the purposes of subsection (1) above shall be in force for the period of five years beginning with the day on which it is served but may be renewed by further notices under subsection (6) above for periods of five years at a time.

(8) A notification for the purposes of subsection (1) above may at any time be revoked by a further notice in writing served by the Minister on the person concerned; and the Minister shall serve such a further notice as soon as, in his opinion, the work undertaken by that person ceases to be such as is mentioned in subsection (6) above.

(9) In this section "security or intelligence" means the work of, or in support of, the security and intelligence services or any part of them, and references to information relating to security or intelligence include references to information held or transmitted by those services or by persons in support of, or of any part of, them.

2 Defence

(1) A person who is or has been a Crown servant or government contractor is guilty of an offence if without lawful authority he makes a damaging disclosure of any information, document or other article relating to defence which is or has been in his possession by virtue of his position as such.

(2) For the purposes of subsection (1) above a disclosure is damaging if—
   (a) it damages the capability of, or of any part of, the armed forces of the Crown to carry out their tasks or leads to loss of life or injury to members of those forces or serious damage to the equipment or installations of those forces; or
   (b) otherwise than as mentioned in paragraph (a) above, it endangers the interests of the United Kingdom abroad, seriously obstructs the promotion or protection by the United Kingdom of those interests or endangers the safety of British citizens abroad; or
   (c) it is of information or of a document or article which is such that its unauthorised disclosure would be likely to have any of those effects.

(3) It is a defence for a person charged with an offence under this section to prove that at the time of the alleged offence he did not know, and had no reasonable cause to believe, that the information, document or article in question related to defence or that its disclosure would be damaging within the meaning of subsection (1) above.

(4) In this section "defence" means—
   (a) the size, shape, organisation, logistics, order of battle, deployment, operations, state of readiness and training of the armed forces of the Crown;
   (b) the weapons, stores or other equipment of those forces and the invention, development, production and operation of such equipment and research relating to it;
   (c) defence policy and strategy and military planning and intelligence;
   (d) plans and measures for the maintenance of essential supplies and services that are or would be needed in time of war.

3 International relations

(1) A person who is or has been a Crown servant or government contractor is guilty of an offence if without lawful authority he makes a damaging disclosure of—
   (a) any information, document or other article relating to international relations; or
   (b) any confidential information, document or other article which was obtained from a State other than the United Kingdom or an international organisation,
   being information or a document or article which is or has been in his possession by virtue of his position as a Crown servant or government contractor.

(2) For the purposes of subsection (1) above a disclosure is damaging if—
   (a) it endangers the interests of the United Kingdom abroad, seriously obstructs the promotion or protection by the United Kingdom of those interests or endangers the safety of British citizens abroad; or

(b) it is of information or of a document or article which is such that its unauthorised disclosure would be likely to have any of those effects.

(3) In the case of information or a document or article within subsection (1)(b) above—
(a) the fact that it is confidential, or
(b) its nature or contents,
may be sufficient to establish for the purposes of subsection (2)(b) above that the information, document or article is such that its unauthorised disclosure would be likely to have any of the effects there mentioned.

(4) It is a defence for a person charged with an offence under this section to prove that at the time of the alleged offence he did not know, and had no reasonable cause to believe, that the information, document or article in question was such as is mentioned in subsection (1) above or that its disclosure would be damaging within the meaning of that subsection.

(5) In this section "international relations" means the relations between States, between international organisations or between one or more States and one or more such organisations and includes any matter relating to a State other than the United Kingdom or to an international organisation which is capable of affecting the relations of the United Kingdom with another State or with an international organisation.

(6) For the purposes of this section any information, document or article obtained from a State or organisation is confidential at any time while the terms on which it was obtained require it to be held in confidence or while the circumstances in which it was obtained make it reasonable for the State or organisation to expect that it would be so held.

4 Crime and special investigation powers

(1) A person who is or has been a Crown servant or government contractor is guilty of an offence if without lawful authority he discloses any information, document or other article to which this section applies and which is or has been in his possession by virtue of his position as such.

(2) This section applies to any information, document or other article—
(a) the disclosure of which—
(i) results in the commission of an offence; or
(ii) facilitates an escape from legal custody or the doing of any other act prejudicial to the safekeeping of persons in legal custody; or
(iii) impedes the prevention or detection of offences or the apprehension or prosecution of suspected offenders; or
(b) which is such that its unauthorised disclosure would be likely to have any of those effects.

(3) This section also applies to—
(a) any information obtained by reason of the interception of any communication in obedience to a warrant issued under section 2 of the Interception of Communications Act 1985, or under the authority of an interception warrant under Section 5 of the Regulation of Investigatory Powers Act 2000, any information relating to the obtaining of information by reason of any such interception and any document or other article which is or has been used or held for use in, or has been obtained by reason of, any such interception; and
(b) any information obtained by reason of action authorised by a warrant issued under section 3 of the Security Service Act 1989 or under section 5 of the Intelligence Services Act 1994 or by an authorisation given under section 7 of that Act, any information relating to the obtaining of information by reason of any such action and any document or other article which is or has been used or held for use in, or has been obtained by reason of, any such action.

(4) It is a defence for a person charged with an offence under this section in respect of a disclosure falling within subsection (2)(a) above to prove that at the time of the alleged offence he did not know, and had no reasonable cause to believe, that the disclosure would have any of the effects there mentioned.

(5) It is a defence for a person charged with an offence under this section in respect of any other disclosure to prove that at the time of the alleged offence he did not know,

and had no reasonable cause to believe, that the information, document or article in question was information or a document or article to which this section applies.

(6) In this section "legal custody" includes detention in pursuance of any enactment or any instrument made under an enactment.

5 Information resulting from unauthorised disclosures or entrusted in confidence

(1) Subsection (2) below applies where—

   (a) any information, document or other article protected against disclosure by the foregoing provisions of this Act has come into a person's possession as a result of having been—

      (i) disclosed (whether to him or another) by a Crown servant or government contractor without lawful authority; or

      (ii) entrusted to him by a Crown servant or government contractor on terms requiring it to be held in confidence or in circumstances in which the Crown servant or government contractor could reasonably expect that it would be so held; or

      (iii) disclosed (whether to him or another) without lawful authority by a person to whom it was entrusted as mentioned in sub-paragraph (ii) above; and

   (b) the disclosure without lawful authority of the information, document or article by the person into whose possession it has come is not an offence under any of those provisions.

(2) Subject to subsections (3) and (4) below, the person into whose possession the information, document or article has come is guilty of an offence if he discloses it without lawful authority knowing, or having reasonable cause to believe, that it is protected against disclosure by the foregoing provisions of this Act and that it has come into his possession as mentioned in subsection (1) above.

(3) In the case of information or a document or article protected against disclosure by sections 1 to 3 above, a person does not commit an offence under subsection (2) above unless—

   (a) the disclosure by him is damaging; and

   (b) he makes it knowing, or having reasonable cause to believe, that it would be damaging;

and the question whether a disclosure is damaging shall be determined for the purposes of this subsection as it would be in relation to a disclosure of that information, document or article by a Crown servant in contravention of section 1(3), 2(1) or 3(1) above.

(4) A person does not commit an offence under subsection (2) above in respect of information or a document or other article which has come into his possession as a result of having been disclosed—

   (a) as mentioned in subsection (1)(a)(i) above by a government contractor; or

   (b) as mentioned in subsection (1)(a)(iii) above,

unless that disclosure was by a British citizen or took place in the United Kingdom, in any of the Channel Islands or in the Isle of Man or a colony.

(5) For the purposes of this section information or a document or article is protected against disclosure by the foregoing provisions of this Act if—

   (a) it relates to security or intelligence, defence or international relations within the meaning of section 1, 2 or 3 above or is such as is mentioned in section 3(1)(b) above; or

   (b) it is information or a document or article to which section 4 above applies;

and information or a document or article is protected against disclosure by sections 1 to 3 above if it falls within paragraph (a) above.

(6) A person is guilty of an offence if without lawful authority he discloses any information, document or other article which he knows, or has reasonable cause to believe, to have come into his possession as a result of a contravention of section 1 of the Official Secrets Act 1911.

6   Information entrusted in confidence to other States or international organisations

(1) This section applies where—

    (a)   any information, document or other article which—

        (i)   relates to security or intelligence, defence or international relations; and

        (ii)   has been communicated in confidence by or on behalf of the United Kingdom to another State or to an international organisation,

        has come into a person's possession as a result of having been disclosed (whether to him or another) without the authority of that State or organisation or, in the case of an organisation, of a member of it; and

    (b)   the disclosure without lawful authority of the information, document or article by the person into whose possession it has come is not an offence under any of the foregoing provisions of this Act.

(2) Subject to subsection (3) below, the person into whose possession the information, document or article has come is guilty of an offence if he makes a damaging disclosure of it knowing, or having reasonable cause to believe, that it is such as is mentioned in subsection (1) above, that it has come into his possession as there mentioned and that its disclosure would be damaging.

(3) A person does not commit an offence under subsection (2) above if the information, document or article is disclosed by him with lawful authority or has previously been made available to the public with the authority of the State or organisation concerned or, in the case of an organisation, of a member of it.

(4) For the purposes of this section "security or intelligence", "defence" and "international relations" have the same meaning as in sections 1, 2 and 3 above and the question whether a disclosure is damaging shall be determined as it would be in relation to a disclosure of the information, document or article in question by a Crown servant in contravention of section 1(3), 2(1) and 3(1) above.

(5) For the purposes of this section information or a document or article is communicated in confidence if it is communicated on terms requiring it to be held in confidence or in circumstances in which the person communicating it could reasonably expect that it would be so held.

7   Authorised disclosures

(1) For the purposes of this Act a disclosure by—

    (a)   a Crown servant; or

    (b)   a person, not being a Crown servant or government contractor, in whose case a notification for the purposes of section 1(1) above is in force,

is made with lawful authority if, and only if, it is made in accordance with his official duty.

(2) For the purposes of this Act a disclosure by a government contractor is made with lawful authority if, and only if, it is made—

    (a)   in accordance with an official authorisation; or

    (b)   for the purposes of the functions by virtue of which he is a government contractor and without contravening an official restriction.

(3) For the purposes of this Act a disclosure made by any other person is made with lawful authority if, and only if, it is made—

    (a)   to a Crown servant for the purposes of his functions as such; or

    (b)   in accordance with an official authorisation.

(4) It is a defence for a person charged with an offence under any of the foregoing provisions of this Act to prove that at the time of the alleged offence he believed that he had lawful authority to make the disclosure in question and had no reasonable cause to believe otherwise.

(5) In this section "official authorisation" and "official restriction" mean, subject to subsection (6) below, an authorisation or restriction duly given or imposed by a Crown servant or government contractor or by or on behalf of a prescribed body or a body of a prescribed class.

(6) In relation to section 6 above "official authorisation" includes an authorisation duly given by or on behalf of the State or organisation concerned or, in the case of an organisation, a member of it.

8 Safeguarding of information

(1) Where a Crown servant or government contractor, by virtue of his position as such, has in his possession or under his control any document or other article which it would be an offence under any of the foregoing provisions of this Act for him to disclose without lawful authority he is guilty of an offence if—
   (a) being a Crown servant, he retains the document or article contrary to his official duty; or
   (b) being a government contractor, he fails to comply with an official direction for the return or disposal of the document or article,
   or if he fails to take such care to prevent the unauthorised disclosure of the document or article as a person in his position may reasonably be expected to take.

(2) It is a defence for a Crown servant charged with an offence under subsection (1) (a) above to prove that at the time of the alleged offence he believed that he was acting in accordance with his official duty and had no reasonable cause to believe otherwise.

(3) In subsections (1) and (2) above references to a Crown servant include any person, not being a Crown servant or government contractor, in whose case a notification for the purposes of section 1(1) above is in force.

(4) Where a person has in his possession or under his control any document or other article which it would be an offence under section 5 above for him to disclose without lawful authority, he is guilty of an offence if—
   (a) he fails to comply with an official direction for its return or disposal; or
   (b) where he obtained it from a Crown servant or government contractor on terms requiring it to be held in confidence or in circumstances in which that servant or contractor could reasonably expect that it would be so held, he fails to take such care to prevent its unauthorised disclosure as a person in his position may reasonably be expected to take.

(5) Where a person has in his possession or under his control any document or other article which it would be an offence under section 6 above for him to disclose without lawful authority, he is guilty of an offence if he fails to comply with an official direction for its return or disposal.

(6) A person is guilty of an offence if he discloses any official information, document or other article which can be used for the purpose of obtaining access to any information, document or other article protected against disclosure by the foregoing provisions of this Act and the circumstances in which it is disclosed are such that it would be reasonable to expect that it might be used for that purpose without authority.

(7) For the purposes of subsection (6) above a person discloses information or a document or article which is official if—
   (a) he has or has had it in his possession by virtue of his position as a Crown servant or government contractor; or
   (b) he knows or has reasonable cause to believe that a Crown servant or government contractor has or has had it in his possession by virtue of his position as such.

(8) Subsection (5) of section 5 above applies for the purposes of subsection (6) above as it applies for the purposes of that section.

(9) In this section "official direction" means a direction duly given by a Crown servant or government contractor or by or on behalf of a prescribed body or a body of a prescribed class.

9 Prosecutions

(1) Subject to subsection (2) below, no prosecution for an offence under this Act shall be instituted in England and Wales or in Northern Ireland except by or with the consent of the Attorney General or, as the case may be, the Advocate General for Northern Ireland.

(2)   Subsection (1) above does not apply to an offence in respect of any such information, document or article as is mentioned in section 4(2) above but no prosecution for such an offence shall be instituted in England and Wales or in Northern Ireland except by or with the consent of the Director of Public Prosecutions or, as the case may be, the Director of Public Prosecutions for Northern Ireland.

10   Penalties

(1)   A person guilty of an offence under any provision of this Act other than section 8(1), (4) or (5) shall be liable—
    (a)   on conviction on indictment, to imprisonment for a term not exceeding two years or a fine or both;
    (b)   on summary conviction, to imprisonment for a term not exceeding six months or a fine not exceeding the statutory maximum or both.

(2)   A person guilty of an offence under section 8(1), (4) or (5) above shall be liable on summary conviction to imprisonment for a term not exceeding three months or a fine not exceeding level 5 on the standard scale or both.

12   "Crown servant" and "government contractor"

(1)   In this Act "Crown servant" means—
    (a)   a Minister of the Crown;
    (aa)   a member of the Scottish Government or a junior Scottish Minister;
    (ab)   The First Minister for Wales, a Welsh Minister appointed under section 48 of the Government of Wales Act 2006, the Counsel General to the Welsh Assembly Government or a Deputy Welsh Minister;
    (c)   any person employed in the civil service of the Crown, including Her Majesty's Diplomatic Service, Her Majesty's Overseas Civil Service, the civil service of Northern Ireland and the Northern Ireland Court Service;
    (d)   any member of the naval, military or air forces of the Crown, including any person employed by an association established for the purposes of Part XI of the Reserve Forces Act 1980;
    (e)   any constable and any other person employed or appointed in or for the purposes of any police force (including the Police Service of Northern Ireland and the Police Service of Northern Ireland Reserve) or an NCA special (within the meaning of Part 1 of the Crime and Courts Act 2013);
    (f)   any person who is a member or employee of a prescribed body or a body of a prescribed class and either is prescribed for the purposes of this paragraph or belongs to a prescribed class of members or employees of any such body;
    (g)   any person who is the holder of a prescribed office or who is an employee of such a holder and either is prescribed for the purposes of this paragraph or belongs to a prescribed class of such employees.

(2)   In this Act "government contractor" means, subject to subsection (3) below, any person who is not a Crown servant but who provides, or is employed in the provision of, goods or services—
    (a)   for the purposes of any Minister or person mentioned in paragraph (a), (ab) or (b) of subsection (1) above, or any office-holder in the Scottish Administration, of any of the services, forces or bodies mentioned in that subsection or of the holder of any office prescribed under that subsection; or
    (b)   under an agreement or arrangement certified by the Secretary of State as being one to which the government of a State other than the United Kingdom or an international organisation is a party or which is subordinate to, or made for the purposes of implementing, any such agreement or arrangement.

13   Other interpretation provisions

(1)   In this Act—
"disclose" and "disclosure" , in relation to a document or other article, include parting with possession of it;
"international organisation" means, subject to subsections (2) and (3) below, an organisation of which only States are members and includes a reference to any organ of such an organisation;

"prescribed" means prescribed by an order made by the Secretary of State;

"State" includes the government of a State and any organ of its government and references to a State other than the United Kingdom include references to any territory outside the United Kingdom.

(2) In section 12(2)(b) above the reference to an international organisation includes a reference to any such organisation whether or not one of which only States are members and includes a commercial organisation.

(3) In determining for the purposes of subsection (1) above whether only States are members of an organisation, any member which is itself an organisation of which only States are members, or which is an organ of such an organisation, shall be treated as a State.

SECURITY SERVICE ACT 1989
(1989, c. 5)

An Act to place the Security Service on a statutory basis; to enable certain actions to be taken on the authority of warrants issued by the Secretary of State, with provision for the issue of such warrants to be kept under review by a Commissioner; to establish a procedure for the investigation by a Tribunal or, in some cases, by the Commissioner of complaints about the Service; and for connected purposes. [27 April 1989]

1 The Security Service

(1) There shall continue to be a Security Service (in this Act referred to as "the Service") under the authority of the Secretary of State.

(2) The function of the Service shall be the protection of national security and, in particular, its protection against threats from espionage, terrorism and sabotage, from the activities of agents of foreign powers and from actions intended to overthrow or undermine parliamentary democracy by political, industrial or violent means.

(3) It shall also be the function of the Service to safeguard the economic well-being of the United Kingdom against threats posed by the actions or intentions of persons outside the British Islands.

(4) It shall also be the function of the Service to act in support of the activities of police forces, the Serious Organised Crime Agency and other law enforcement agencies in the prevention and detection of serious crime.

2 The Director-General

(1) The operations of the Service shall continue to be under the control of a Director-General appointed by the Secretary of State.

(2) The Director-General shall be responsible for the efficiency of the Service and it shall be his duty to ensure—

(a) that there are arrangements for securing that no information is obtained by the Service except so far as necessary for the proper discharge of its functions or disclosed by it except so far as necessary for that purpose or for the purpose of the prevention or detection of serious crime or for the purpose of any criminal proceedings; and

(b) that the Service does not take any action to further the interests of any political party; and

(c) that there are arrangements, agreed with the Director General of the Serious Organised Crime Agency, for co-ordinating the activities of the Service in pursuance of section 1(4) of this Act with the activities of police forces, the Serious Organised Crime Agency and other law enforcement agencies.

(4) The Director-General shall make an annual report on the work of the Service to the Prime Minister and the Secretary of State and may at any time report to either of them on any matter relating to its work.

INTELLIGENCE SERVICES ACT 1994
(1994, c. 33)

An Act to make provision about the Secret Intelligence Service and the Government Communications Headquarters, including provision for the issue of warrants and authorisations enabling certain actions to be taken and for the issue of such warrants and authorisations to be kept under review; to make further provision about warrants issued on applications by the Security Service; to establish a procedure for the investigation of complaints about the Secret Intelligence Service and the Government Communications Headquarters; to make provision for the establishment of an Intelligence and Security Committee to scrutinise all three of those bodies; and for connected purposes.   [26 May 1994]

The Secret Intelligence Service

1   The Secret Intelligence Service

    (1)   There shall continue to be a Secret Intelligence Service (in this Act referred to as "the Intelligence Service") under the authority of the Secretary of State; and, subject to subsection (2) below, its functions shall be—

        (a)   to obtain and provide information relating to the actions or intentions of persons outside the British Islands; and

        (b)   to perform other tasks relating to the actions or intentions of such persons.

    (2)   The functions of the Intelligence Service shall be exercisable only—

        (a)   in the interests of national security, with particular reference to the defence and foreign policies of Her Majesty's Government in the United Kingdom; or

        (b)   in the interests of the economic well-being of the United Kingdom; or

        (c)   in support of the prevention or detection of serious crime.

2   The Chief of the Intelligence Service

    (1)   The operations of the Intelligence Service shall continue to be under the control of a Chief of that Service appointed by the Secretary of State.

    (2)   The Chief of the Intelligence Service shall be responsible for the efficiency of that Service and it shall be his duty to ensure—

        (a)   that there are arrangements for securing that no information is obtained by the Intelligence Service except so far as necessary for the proper discharge of its functions and that no information is disclosed by it except so far as necessary—

            (i)   for that purpose;

            (ii)   in the interests of national security;

            (iii)   for the purpose of the prevention or detection of serious crime; or

            (iv)   for the purpose of any criminal proceedings; and

        (b)   that the Intelligence Service does not take any action to further the interests of any United Kingdom political party.

    (3)   Without prejudice to the generality of subsection (2)(a) above, the disclosure of information shall be regarded as necessary for the proper discharge of the functions of the Intelligence Service if it consists of—

        (a)   the disclosure of records subject to and in accordance with the Public Records Act 1958; or

        (b)   the disclosure, subject to and in accordance with arrangements approved by the Secretary of State, of information to the Comptroller and Auditor General for the purposes of his functions.

    (4)   The Chief of the Intelligence Service shall make an annual report on the work of the Intelligence Service to the Prime Minister and the Secretary of State and may at any time report to either of them on any matter relating to its work.

GCHQ

3   The Government Communications Headquarters

    (1)   There shall continue to be a Government Communications Headquarters under the authority of the Secretary of State; and, subject to subsection (2) below, its functions shall be—

(a) to monitor, make use of or interfere with electromagnetic, acoustic and other emissions and any equipment producing such emissions and to obtain and provide information derived from or related to such emissions or equipment and from encrypted material; and

(b) to provide advice and assistance about—

   (i) languages, including terminology used for technical matters, and

   (ii) cryptography and other matters relating to the protection of information and other material,

to the armed forces of the Crown, to Her Majesty's Government in the United Kingdom or to a Northern Ireland Department or, in such cases as it considers appropriate, to other organisations or persons, or to the general public, in the United Kingdom or elsewhere.

(2) The functions referred to in subsection (1)(a) above shall be exercisable only—

(a) in the interests of national security, with particular reference to the defence and foreign policies of Her Majesty's Government in the United Kingdom; or

(b) in the interests of the economic well-being of the United Kingdom in relation to the actions or intentions of persons outside the British Islands; or

(c) in support of the prevention or detection of serious crime.

(3) In this Act the expression "GCHQ" refers to the Government Communications Headquarters and to any unit or part of a unit of the armed forces of the Crown which is for the time being required by the Secretary of State to assist the Government Communications Headquarters in carrying out its functions.

4 The Director of GCHQ

(1) The operations of GCHQ shall continue to be under the control of a Director appointed by the Secretary of State.

(2) The Director shall be responsible for the efficiency of GCHQ and it shall be his duty to ensure—

(a) that there are arrangements for securing that no information is obtained by GCHQ except so far as necessary for the proper discharge of its functions and that no information is disclosed by it except so far as necessary for that purpose or for the purpose of any criminal proceedings; and

(b) that GCHQ does not take any action to further the interests of any United Kingdom political party.

(3) Without prejudice to the generality of subsection (2)(a) above, the disclosure of information shall be regarded as necessary for the proper discharge of the functions of GCHQ if it consists of—

(a) the disclosure of records subject to and in accordance with the Public Records Act 1958; or

(b) the disclosure, subject to and in accordance with arrangements approved by the Secretary of State, of information to the Comptroller and Auditor General for the purposes of his functions.

(4) The Director shall make an annual report on the work of GCHQ to the Prime Minister and the Secretary of State and may at any time report to either of them on any matter relating to its work.

Authorisation of certain actions

5 Warrants: general

(1) No entry on or interference with property or with wireless telegraphy shall be unlawful if it is authorised by a warrant issued by the Secretary of State under this section.

(2) The Secretary of State may, on an application made by the Security Service, the Intelligence Service or GCHQ, issue a warrant under this section authorising the taking, of such action as is specified in the warrant in respect of any property so specified or in respect of wireless telegraphy so specified if the Secretary of State—

(a) thinks it necessary for the action to be taken for the purpose of assisting, as the case may be,—

   (i) the Security Service in carrying out any of its functions under the 1989 Act; or

        (ii)   the Intelligence Service in carrying out any of its functions under section 1 above; or

        (iii)   GCHQ in carrying out any function which falls within section 3(1)(a) above; and

   (b)   is satisfied that the taking of the action is proportionate to what the action seeks to achieve;

   (c)   is satisfied that satisfactory arrangements are in force under section 2(2)(a) of the 1989 Act (duties of the Director-General of the Security Service), section 2(2)(a) above or section 4(2)(a) above with respect to the disclosure of information obtained by virtue of this section and that any information obtained under the warrant will be subject to those arrangements.

(2A)   The matters to be taken into account in considering whether the requirements of subsection (2)(a) and (b) are satisfied in the case of any warrant shall include whether what it is thought necessary to achieve by the conduct authorised by the warrant could reasonably be achieved by other means.

(3A)   A warrant issued on the application of the Security Service for the purposes of the exercise of their function under section 1(4) of the Security Service Act 1989, or on the application of the Intelligence Service or GCHQ for the purposes of the exercise of their functions by virtue of section 1(2)(c) or 3(2)(c), may not relate to property in the British Islands unless it authorises the taking of action in relation to conduct within subsection (3B) below.

(3B)   Conduct is within this subsection if it constitutes (or, if it took place in the United Kingdom, would constitute) one or more offences, and either—

   (a)   it involves the use of violence, results in substantial financial gain or is conduct by a large number of persons in pursuit of a common purpose; or

   (b)   the offence or one of the offences is an offence for which a person who has attained the age of twenty-one and has no previous convictions could reasonably be expected to be sentenced to imprisonment for a term of three years or more.

(4)   Subject to subsection (5) below, the Security Service may make an application under subsection (2) above for a warrant to be issued authorising that Service (or a person acting on its behalf) to take such action as is specified in the warrant on behalf of the Intelligence Service or GCHQ and, where such a warrant is issued, the functions of the Security Service shall include the carrying out of the action so specified, whether or not it would otherwise be within its functions.

(5)   The Security Service may not make an application for a warrant by virtue of subsection (4) above except where the action proposed to be authorised by the warrant—

   (a)   is action in respect of which the Intelligence Service or, as the case may be, GCHQ could make such an application; and

   (b)   is to be taken otherwise than in support of the prevention or detection of serious crime.

6   Warrants: procedure and duration, etc.

(1)   A warrant shall not be issued except—

   (a)   under the hand of the Secretary of State or, in the case of a warrant by the Scottish Ministers (by virtue of provision made under section 63 of the Scotland Act 1998), a member of the Scottish Executive; or

   (b)   in an urgent case where the Secretary of State has expressly authorised its issue and a statement of that fact is endorsed on it, under the hand of a senior official;

Supplementary

11   Interpretation and consequential amendments

(1)   In this Act—

   (a)   "the 1989 Act" means the Security Service Act 1989;

   (c)   "Minister of the Crown" has the same meaning as in the Ministers of the Crown Act 1975;

   (d)   "senior official" has the same meaning as in the Regulation of Investigatory Powers Act 2000;

(e) "wireless telegraphy" has the same meaning as in the Wireless Telegraphy Act 1949 and, in relation to wireless telegraphy, "interfere" has the same meaning as in that Act;

(f) "working day" means any day other than a Saturday, a Sunday, Christmas Day, Good Friday or a day which is a bank holiday under the Banking and Financial Dealings Act 1971 in any part of the United Kingdom.

CRIMINAL JUSTICE AND PUBLIC ORDER ACT 1994
(1994, c. 33)

An Act to make further provision in relation to criminal justice (including employment in the prison service); to amend or extend the criminal law and powers for preventing crime and enforcing that law; to amend the Video Recordings Act 1984; and for purposes connected with those purposes.

[3 November 1994]

Note: Sections 60, 61 and 68 will be amended when the Criminal Justice Act 2003, Sch 26 comes into force.

PART IV
POLICE POWERS

Powers of police to stop and search

60 Powers to stop and search in anticipation of, or after, violence

(1) If a police officer of or above the rank of inspector reasonably believes—

(a) that incidents involving serious violence may take place in any locality in his police area, and that it is expedient to give an authorisation under this section to prevent their occurrence,

(aa) that—

(i) an incident involving serious violence has taken place in England and Wales in his police area;

(ii) a dangerous instrument or offensive weapon used in the incident is being carried in any locality in his police area by a person; and

(iii) it is expedient to give an authorisation under this section to find the instrument or weapon; or

(b) that persons are carrying dangerous instruments or offensive weapons in any locality in his police area without good reason,

he may give an authorisation that the powers conferred by this section are to be exercisable at any place within that locality for a specified period not exceeding 24 hours.

(3) If it appears to an officer of or above the rank of superintendent that it is expedient to do so, having regard to offences which have, or are reasonably suspected to have, been committed in connection with any activity falling within the authorisation, he may direct that the authorisation shall continue in being for a further 24 hours.

(3A) If an inspector gives an authorisation under subsection (1) he must, as soon as it is practicable to do so, cause an officer of or above the rank of superintendent to be informed.

(4) This section confers on any constable in uniform power—

(a) to stop any pedestrian and search him or anything carried by him for offensive weapons or dangerous instruments;

(b) to stop any vehicle and search the vehicle, its driver and any passenger for offensive weapons or dangerous instruments.

(5) A constable may, in the exercise of the powers conferred by subsection (4) above, stop any person or vehicle and make any search he thinks fit whether or not he has any grounds for suspecting that the person or vehicle is carrying weapons or articles of that kind.

(6)   If in the course of a search under this section a constable discovers a dangerous instrument or an article which he has reasonable grounds for suspecting to be an offensive weapon, he may seize it.

(7)   This section applies (with the necessary modifications) to ships, aircraft and hovercraft as it applies to vehicles.

(8)   A person who fails—
(a)   to stop, or to stop a vehicle;
when required to do so by a constable in the exercise of his powers under this section shall be liable on summary conviction to imprisonment for a term not exceeding one month or to a fine not exceeding level 3 on the standard scale or both.

(9)   Subject to section 9ZA, any authorisation under this section shall be in writing signed by the officer giving it and shall specify the grounds on which it is given and the locality in which and the period during which the powers conferred by this section are exercisable and a direction under subsection (3) above shall also be given in writing or, where that is not practicable, recorded in writing as soon as it is practicable to do so.

(9ZA) An authorisation under subsection (1)(aa) need not be given in writing where it is not practicable to do so but any oral authorisation must state the matters which would otherwise have to be specified under subsection (9) and must be recorded in writing as soon as it us practicable to do so.

(10)   Where a vehicle is stopped by a constable under this section, the driver shall be entitled to obtain a written statement that the vehicle was stopped under the powers conferred by this section if he applies for such a statement not later than the end of the period of twelve months from the day on which the vehicle was stopped and similarly as respects a pedestrian who is stopped and searched under this section.

(10A) A person who is searched by a constable under this section shall be entitled to obtain a written statement that he was searched under the powers conferred by this section if he applies for such a statement not later than the end of the period of twelve months from the day on which he was searched.

(11)   In this section—
"dangerous instruments" means instruments which have a blade or are sharply pointed;
"offensive weapon" has the meaning given by section 1(9) of the Police and Criminal Evidence Act 1984; and
"vehicle" includes a caravan as defined in section 29(1) of the Caravan Sites and Control of Development Act 1960.

(11A) For the purpose of this section, a person carries a dangerous instrument or an offensive weapon if he has it in his possession.

(12)   The powers conferred by this section are in addition to and not in derogation of, any power otherwise conferred.

PART V
PUBLIC ORDER: COLLECTIVE TRESPASS OR NUISANCE ON LAND

Powers to remove trespassers on land

61   Power to remove trespassers on land

(1)   If the senior police officer present at the scene reasonably believes that two or more persons are trespassing on land and are present there with the common purpose of residing there for any period, that reasonable steps have been taken by or on behalf of the occupier to ask them to leave and—
(a)   that any of those persons has caused damage to the land or to property on the land or used threatening, abusive or insulting words or behaviour towards the occupier, a member of his family or an employee or agent of his, or
(b)   that those persons have between them six or more vehicles on the land, he may direct those persons, or any of them, to leave the land and to remove any vehicles or other property they have with them on the land.

(2) Where the persons in question are reasonably believed by the senior police officer to be persons who were not originally trespassers but have become trespassers on the land, the officer must reasonably believe that the other conditions specified in subsection (1) are satisfied after those persons became trespassers before he can exercise the power conferred by that subsection.

(3) A direction under subsection (1) above, if not communicated to the persons referred to in subsection (1) by the police officer giving the direction, may be communicated to them by any constable at the scene.

(4) If a person knowing that a direction under subsection (1) above has been given which applies to him—

(a) fails to leave the land as soon as reasonably practicable, or

(b) having left again enters the land as a trespasser within the period of three months beginning with the day on which the direction was given,

he commits an offence and is liable on summary conviction to imprisonment for a term not exceeding three months [*51 weeks*] or a fine not exceeding level 4 on the standard scale, or both.

(6) In proceedings for an offence under this section it is a defence for the accused to show—

(a) that he was not trespassing on the land, or

(b) that he had a reasonable excuse for failing to leave the land as soon as reasonably practicable or, as the case may be, for again entering the land as a trespasser.

(7) In its application in England and Wales to common land this section has effect as if in the preceding subsections of it—

(a) references to trespassing or trespassers were references to acts and persons doing acts which constitute either a trespass as against the occupier or an infringement of the commoners' rights; and

(b) references to "the occupier" included the commoners or any of them or, in the case of common land to which the public has access, the local authority as well as any commoner.

(8) Subsection (7) above does not—

(a) require action by more than one occupier; or

(b) constitute persons trespassers as against any commoner or the local authority if they are permitted to be there by the other occupier.

(9) In this section—

"common land" means—

(a) land registered as common land in a register of common land kept under Part 1 of the Commons Act 2006; and

(b) land to which Part 1 of the Act does not apply and which is subject to rights of common as defined in that Act;

"land" does not include—

(a) buildings other than—

(i) agricultural buildings within the meaning of, in England and Wales, paragraphs 3 to 8 of Schedule 5 to the Local Government Finance Act 1988 or, in Scotland, section 7(2) of the Valuation and Rating (Scotland) Act 1956, or

(ii) scheduled monuments within the meaning of the Ancient Monuments and Archaeological Areas Act 1979;

(b) land forming part of—

(i) a highway unless it is a footpath, bridleway or byway open to all traffic within the meaning of Part III of the Wildlife and Countryside Act 1981, is a restricted byway within the meaning of Part II of the Countryside and Rights of Way Act 2000 or is a cycle track under the Highways Act 1980 or the Cycle Tracks Act 1984; or

(ii) a road within the meaning of the Roads (Scotland) Act 1984 unless it falls within the definitions in section 151(2)(a)(ii) or (b) (footpaths and cycle tracks) of that Act or is a bridleway within the meaning of section 47 of the Countryside (Scotland) Act 1967;

"occupier" (and in subsection (8) "the other occupier") means—

(a) in England and Wales, the person entitled to possession of the land by virtue of an estate or interest held by him; and

(b) in Scotland, the person lawfully entitled to natural possession of the land;

"property", in relation to damage to property on land, means—

(a) in England and Wales, property within the meaning of section 10(1) of the Criminal Damage Act 1971; and

(b) in Scotland, either—

(i)   heritable property other than land; or

(ii) corporeal moveable property, and

"damage" includes the deposit of any substance capable of polluting the land;

"trespass" means, in the application of this section—

(a) in England and Wales, subject to the extensions effected by subsection (7) above, trespass as against the occupier of the land;

(b) in Scotland, entering, or as the case may be remaining on, land without lawful authority and without the occupier's consent; and

"trespassing" and "trespasser" shall be construed accordingly;

and a person may be regarded for the purposes of this section as having a purpose of residing in a place notwithstanding that he has a home elsewhere.

62   Supplementary powers of seizure

(1) If a direction has been given under section 61 and a constable reasonably suspects that any person to whom the direction applies has, without reasonable excuse—

(a) failed to remove any vehicle on the land which appears to the constable to belong to him or to be in his possession or under his control; or

(b) entered the land as a trespasser with a vehicle within the period of three months beginning with the day on which the direction was given, the constable may seize and remove that vehicle.

(2) In this section, "trespasser" and "vehicle" have the same meaning as in section 61.

Powers in relation to raves

63   Powers to remove persons attending or preparing for a rave

(1) This section applies to a gathering on land in the open air of 20 or more persons (whether or not trespassers) at which amplified music is played during the night (with or without intermissions) and is such as, by reason of its loudness and duration and the time at which it is played, is likely to cause serious distress to the inhabitants of the locality; and for this purpose—

(a) such a gathering continues during intermissions in the music and, where the gathering extends over several days, throughout the period during which amplified music is played at night (with or without intermissions); and

(b) "music" includes sounds wholly or predominantly characterised by the emission of a succession of repetitive beats.

(1A) This section also applies to a gathering if—

(a) it is a gathering on land of 20 or more persons who are trespassing on the land; and

(b) it would be a gathering of a kind mentioned in subsection (1) above if it took place on land in the open air.

(2) If, as respects any land, a police officer of at least the rank of superintendent reasonably believes that—

(a) two or more persons are making preparations for the holding there of a gathering to which this section applies,

(b) ten or more persons are waiting for such a gathering to begin there, or

(c) ten or more persons are attending such a gathering which is in progress,

he may give a direction that those persons and any other persons who come to prepare or wait for or to attend the gathering are to leave the land and remove any vehicles or other property which they have with them on the land.

(3) A direction under subsection (2) above, if not communicated to the persons referred to in subsection (2) by the police officer giving the direction, may be communicated to them by any constable at the scene.

(4)   Persons shall be treated as having had a direction under subsection (2) above communicated to them if reasonable steps have been taken to bring it to their attention.

(5)   A direction under subsection (2) above does not apply to an exempt person.

(6)   If a person knowing that a direction has been given which applies to him—
       (a)   fails to leave the land as soon as reasonably practicable, or
       (b)   having left again enters the land within the period of 7 days beginning with the day on which the direction was given,
       he commits an offence and is liable on summary conviction to imprisonment for a term not exceeding three months [*51 weeks*] or a fine not exceeding level 4 on the standard scale, or both.

(7)   In proceedings for an offence under subsection 6 above it is a defence for the accused to show that he had a reasonable excuse for failing to leave the land as soon as reasonably practicable or, as the case may be, for again entering the land.

(7A)   A person commits an offence if—
       (a)   he knows that a direction under subsection (2) above has been given which applies to him, and
       (b)   he makes preparations for or attends a gathering to which this section applies within the period of 24 hours starting when the direction was given.

(7B)   A person guilty of an offence under subsection (7A) above is liable on summary conviction to imprisonment for a term not exceeding three months [*51 weeks*] or a fine not exceeding level 4 on the standard scale, or both.

64   Supplementary powers of entry and seizure

(1)   If a police officer of at least the rank of superintendent reasonably believes that circumstances exist in relation to any land which would justify the giving of a direction under section 63 in relation to a gathering to which that section applies he may authorise any constable to enter the land for any of the purposes specified in subsection (2) below.

(2)   Those purposes are—
       (a)   to ascertain whether such circumstances exist; and
       (b)   to exercise any power conferred on a constable by section 63 or subsection (4) below.

(3)   A constable who is so authorised to enter land for any purpose may enter the land without a warrant.

(4)   If a direction has been given under section 63 and a constable reasonably suspects that any person to whom the direction applies has, without reasonable excuse—
       (a)   failed to remove any vehicle or sound equipment on the land which appears to the constable to belong to him or to be in his possession or under his control; or
       (b)   entered the land as a trespasser with a vehicle or sound equipment within the period of 7 days beginning with the day on which the direction was given,
       the constable may seize and remove that vehicle or sound equipment.

(5)   Subsection (4) above does not authorise the seizure of any vehicle or sound equipment of an exempt person.

68   Offence of aggravated trespass

(1)   A person commits the offence of aggravated trespass if he trespasses on land and, in relation to any lawful activity which persons are engaging in or are about to engage in on that or adjoining land does there anything which is intended by him to have the effect—
       (a)   of intimidating those persons or any of them so as to deter them or any of them from engaging in that activity,
       (b)   of obstructing that activity, or
       (c)   of disrupting that activity.

(1A)   The reference in subsection (1) above to trespassing includes, in Scotland, the exercise of access rights (within the meaning of the Land Reform (Scotland) Act 2003) up to the point when they cease to be exercisable by virtue of the commission of the offence under that subsection.

(2)   Activity on any occasion on the part of a person or persons on land is "lawful" for the purposes of this section if he or they may engage in the activity on the land on that occasion without committing an offence or trespassing on the land.

(3)   A person guilty of an offence under this section is liable on summary conviction to imprisonment for a term not exceeding *three months* [*51 weeks*] or a fine not exceeding level 4 on the standard scale, or both.

(5)   In this section "land" does not include—

(a)   the highways and roads excluded from the application of section 61 by paragraph (b) of the definition of "land" in subsection (9) of that section; or

(b)   a road within the meaning of the Roads (Northern Ireland) Order 1993.

POLICE ACT 1996
(1996, c. 16)

An Act to consolidate the Police Act 1964, Part IX of the Police and Criminal Evidence Act 1984, Chapter I of Part I of the Police and Magistrates' Courts Act 1994 and certain other enactments relating to the police.   [22 May 1996]

PART IV
COMPLAINTS, DISCIPLINARY PROCEEDINGS ETC.

CHAPTER II
DISCIPLINARY AND OTHER PROCEEDINGS

88   Liability for wrongful acts of constables

(1)   The chief officer of police for a police area shall be liable in respect of any unlawful conduct of constables under his direction and control in the performance or purported performance of their functions in like manner as a master is liable in respect of any unlawful conduct of his servants in the course of their employment, and accordingly shall in the case of a tort be treated for all purposes as a joint tortfeasor.

(2)   There shall be paid out of the police fund—

(a)   any damages or costs awarded against the chief officer of police in any proceedings brought against him by virtue of this section and any costs incurred by him in any such proceedings so far as not recovered by him in the proceedings; and

(b)   any sum required in connection with the settlement of any claim made against the chief officer of police by virtue of this section, if the settlement is approved by the local policing body.

(3)   Any proceedings in respect of a claim made by virtue of this section shall be brought against the chief officer of police for the time being or, in the case of a vacancy in that office, against the person for the time being performing the functions of the chief officer of police; and references in subsections (1) and (2) to the chief officer of police shall be construed accordingly.

(4)   A local policing body may, in such cases and to such extent as appear to it to be appropriate, pay out of the police fund—

(a)   any damages or costs awarded against a person to whom this subsection applies in proceedings for any unlawful conduct of that person,

(b)   any costs incurred and not recovered by such a person in such proceedings, and

(c)   any sum required in connection with the settlement of a claim that has or might have given rise to such proceedings.

(5)   Subsection (4) applies to a person who is—

(a)   a member of the police force maintained by the local policing body,

(b)   a constable for the time being required to serve with that force by virtue of section 24 or 98 of this Act, or

(c)   a special constable appointed for the local policing body's police area.

PART V
MISCELLANEOUS AND GENERAL

Offences

89   Assaults on constables

(1)   Any person who assaults a constable in the execution of his duty, or a person assisting a constable in the execution of his duty, shall be guilty of an offence and liable on summary conviction to imprisonment for a term not exceeding six months or to a fine not exceeding level 5 on the standard scale, or to both.

(2)   Any person who resists or wilfully obstructs a constable in the execution of his duty, or a person assisting a constable in the execution of his duty, shall be guilty of an offence and liable on summary conviction to imprisonment for a term not exceeding one month [*51 weeks*] or to a fine not exceeding level 3 on the standard scale, or to both.

(3)   This section also applies to a constable who is a member of the Police Service of Scotland or Northern Ireland when he is executing a warrant, or otherwise acting in England and Wales, by virtue of any enactment conferring powers on him in England and Wales.

Note: Section 89 will be amended when the Criminal Justice Act 2003, Sch 26 comes into force.

90   Impersonation, etc.

(1)   Any person who with intent to deceive impersonates a member of a police force or special constable, or makes any statement or does any act calculated falsely to suggest that he is such a member or constable, shall be guilty of an offence and liable on summary conviction to imprisonment for a term not exceeding six months or to a fine not exceeding level 5 on the standard scale, or to both.

(2)   Any person who, not being a constable, wears any article of police uniform in circumstances where it gives him an appearance so nearly resembling that of a member of a police force as to be calculated to deceive shall be guilty of an offence and liable on summary conviction to a fine not exceeding level 3 on the standard scale.

(3)   Any person who, not being a member of a police force or special constable, has in his possession any article of police uniform shall, unless he proves that he obtained possession of that article lawfully and has possession of it for a lawful purpose, be guilty of an offence and liable on summary conviction to a fine not exceeding level 1 on the standard scale.

(4)   In this section—

(a)   "article of police uniform" means any article of uniform or any distinctive badge or mark or document of identification usually issued to members of police forces or special constables, or anything having the appearance of such an article, badge, mark or document, and

(b)   "special constable" means a special constable appointed for a police area.

POLICE ACT 1997
(1997, c. 50)

An Act to make provision for the National Criminal Intelligence Service and the National Crime Squad; to make provision about entry on and interference with property and with wireless telegraphy in the course of the prevention or detection of serious crime; to make provision for the Police Information Technology Organisation; to provide for the issue of certificates about criminal records; to make provision about the administration and organisation of the police; to repeal certain enactments about rehabilitation of offenders; and for connected purposes.   [21 March 1997]

PART III
AUTHORISATION OF ACTION IN RESPECT OF PROPERTY

Authorisations

93   Authorisations to interfere with property etc.

(1)   Where subsection (2) applies, an authorising officer may authorise—

    (a)   the taking of such action, in respect of such property in the relevant area, as he may specify,

    (ab)   the taking of such action falling within subsection (1A) in respect of property outside the relevant area, as he may specify, or

    (b)   the taking of such action in the relevant area as he may specify, in respect of wireless telegraphy.

(1A)   The action falling within this subsection is action for maintaining or retrieving any equipment, apparatus or device the placing or use of which in the relevant area has been authorised under this Part or Part II of the Regulation of Investigatory Powers Act 2000 or under any enactment contained in or made under an Act of the Scottish Parliament which makes provision equivalent to that made by Part II of that Act of 2000.

(1B)   Subsection (1) applies where the authorising officer is a National Crime Agency officer giving an authorisation on an application made by virtue of subsection (3)(b)(i), an officer of Revenue and Customs, an immigration officer or the chair of the Competition and Markets Authority with the omission of—

    (a)   the words "in the relevant area" in each place where they occur; and

    (b)   paragraph (ab).

(2)   This subsection applies where the authorising officer believes—

    (a)   that it is necessary for the action specified to be taken for the purpose of preventing or detecting serious crime, and

    (b)   that the taking of the action is proportionate to what the action seeks to achieve.

(2A)   Subsection (2) applies where the authorising officer is the Chief Constable or the Deputy Chief Constable of the Police Service of Northern Ireland as if the reference in subsection (2)(a) to preventing or detecting serious crime included a reference to the interests of national security.

(2AA)   Where the authorising officer is the chair of the Competition and Markets Authority, the only purpose falling within subsection (2)(a) is the purpose of preventing or detecting an offence under section 188 of the Enterprise Act 2002.

(2B)   The matters to be taken into account in considering whether the requirements of subsection (2) are satisfied in the case of any authorisation shall include whether what it is thought necessary to achieve by the authorised action could reasonably be achieved by other means.

(3)   An authorising officer shall not give an authorisation under this section except on an application made—

    (za)   if the authorising officer is within subsection (5)(a) to (c)—

        (i)   by a member of the officer's police force;

        (ii)   in a case where the chief officer of police of that force ("the authorising force") has made an agreement under section 22A of the Police Act 1996 with the chief officer of police of one or more other police forces, by a member of a collaborative force; or

        (iii)   in a case where the chief officer of police of the authorising force has made an agreement under that section with the Director General of the National Crime Agency, by a National Crime Agency officer (but see subsection (3AA));

    (zb)   if the authorising officer is within subsection (5)(d), by a constable of the Police Service of Scotland;

    (a)   if the authorising officer is within subsection (5)(e) to (ea) or (ee), by a member of his police force,

    (aa)   if the authorising officer is within subsection (5)(eb) to (ed), by a member, as the case may be, of the Royal Navy Police, the Royal Military Police or the Royal Air Force Police,

(b)   if the authorising officer is within subsection (5)(f)—
- (i)   by a National Crime Agency officer or
- (ii)   in a case where the Director General of the National Crime Agency has made an agreement under section 22A of the Police Act 1996 with the chief officer of police of one or more police forces, by a member of a collaborative force;

(d)   if the authorising officer is within subsection (5)(h), by an officer of Revenue and Customs,

(da) if the authorising officer is within subsection (5)(ha), by an immigration officer;

(e)   if the authorising officer is within subsection (5)(i), by an officer of the Competition and Markets Authority, or

(ea) if the authorising officer is within subsection (5)(ia), by a staff officer of the Police Investigations and Review Commissioner.

(3A) For the purposes of subsection (3)(za)(ii)—
- (a)   a police force is a collaborative force if—
  - (i)   its chief officer of police is a party to the agreement mentioned in that provision; and
  - (ii)   its members are permitted by the terms of the agreement to make applications for authorisations under this section to the authorising officer of the authorising force; and
- (b)   a reference to a police force is to the following—
  - (i)   any police force maintained under section 2 of the Police Act 1996 (police forces in England and Wales outside London);
  - (ii)   the metropolitan police force; and
  - (iii) the City of London police force.

(3AA) A National Crime Agency officer may make an application by virtue of subsection (3)(za)(iii) only if permitted by the terms of the agreement mentioned in that provision to make applications for authorisations under this section to the authorising officer of the authorising force.

(3AB) For the purposes of subsection (3)(b), a police force is a collaborative force if—
- (a)   its chief officer of police is a party to the agreement mentioned in that provision, and
- (b)   its members are permitted by the terms of the agreement to make applications for authorisations under this section to the authorising officer mentioned in that provision.

Paragraph (b) of subsection (3A) applies for the purposes of this subsection.

(3ZA) An authorisation under this section may be given by the authorising officer within subsection (5)(ia) only where it relates to the taking of action in pursuance of paragraph (b)(i) of section 33A of the Police, Public Order and Criminal Justice (Scotland) Act 2006.

(4)   For the purposes of subsection (2), conduct which constitutes one or more offences shall be regarded as serious crime if, and only if,—
- (a)   it involves the use of violence, results in substantial financial gain or is conduct by a large number of persons in pursuit of a common purpose, or
- (b)   the offence or one of the offences is an offence for which a person who has attained the age of twenty-one (*eighteen in relation to England and Wales*) and has no previous convictions could reasonably be expected to be sentenced to imprisonment for a term of three years or more,

and, where the authorising officer is within subsection (5)(h), the conduct relates to an assigned matter within the meaning of section 1(1) of the Customs and Excise Management Act 1979 or, where the authorising officer is within subsection (5)(ha), any of the offences is an immigration or nationality offence.

(5)   In this section "authorising officer" means—
- (a)   the chief constable of a police force maintained under section 2 of the Police Act 1996 (maintenance of police forces for areas in England and Wales except London);
- (b)   the Commissioner, or an Assistant Commissioner, of Police of the Metropolis;
- (c)   the Commissioner of Police for the City of London;

(d)   the chief constable of the Police Service of Scotland, or any deputy chief constable or assistant chief constable of the Police Service of Scotland who is designated for the purposes of this paragraph by the chief constable;

(e)   the Chief Constable or a Deputy Chief Constable of the Police Service of Northern Ireland;

(ea)   the Chief Constable of the Ministry of Defence Police;

(eb)   the Provost Marshal of the Royal Navy Police;

(ec)   the Provost Marshal of the Royal Military Police;

(ed)   the Provost Marshal of the Royal Air Force Police;

(ee)   the Chief Constable of the British Transport Police;

(f)   the Director General of the National Crime Agency, or any other National Crime Agency officer who is designated for the purposes of this paragraph by that Director General;

(h)   an officer of Revenue and Customs is a senior official within the meaning of the Regulation of Investigatory Powers Act 2000 and who is designated for the purposes of this paragraph by the Commissioners of Her Majesty's Revenue and Customs;

(ha)   an immigration officer who is a senior official within the meaning of the Regulation of Investigatory Powers Act 2000 and who is designated for the purposes of this paragraph by the Secretary of State;

(i)   the chair of the Competition and Markets Authority;

(ia)   the Police Investigations and Review Commissioner;

(7)   The powers conferred by, or by virtue of, this section are additional to any other powers which a person has as a constable either at common law or under or by virtue of any other enactment and are not to be taken to affect any of those other powers.

Note: Section 93 will be amended when the Criminal Justice and Court Services Act 2000, Sch 7 comes into force.

95   Authorisations: form and duration etc.

(1)   An authorisation shall be in writing, except that in an urgent case an authorisation (other than one given by virtue of section 94) may be given orally.

(2)   An authorisation shall, unless renewed under subsection (3), cease to have effect—

    (a)   if given orally or by virtue of section 94, at the end of the period of 72 hours beginning with the time when it took effect;

    (b)   in any other case, at the end of the period of three months beginning with the day on which it took effect.

(3)   If at any time before an authorisation would cease to have effect the authorising officer who gave the authorisation, or in whose absence it was given, considers it necessary for the authorisation to continue to have effect for the purpose for which it was issued, he may, in writing, renew it for a period of three months beginning with the day on which it would cease to have effect.

(4)   A person shall cancel an authorisation given by him if satisfied that the authorisation is one in relation to which the requirement of paragraphs (a) to (b) of section 93(2) are no longer satisfied.

96   Notification of authorisations etc.

(1)   Where a person gives, renews or cancels an authorisation, he shall, as soon as is reasonably practicable and in accordance with arrangements made by the Chief Commissioner, give notice in writing that he has done so to a Commissioner appointed under section 91(1)(b).

(2)   Subject to subsection (3), a notice under this section shall specify such matters as the Secretary of State may by order prescribe.

(3)   A notice under this section of the giving or renewal of an authorisation shall specify—

    (a)   whether section 97 applies to the authorisation or renewal, and

    (b)   where that section does not apply by virtue of subsection (3) of that section, the grounds on which the case is believed to be one of urgency.

(4)   Where a notice is given to a Commissioner under this section, he shall, as soon as is reasonably practicable, scrutinise the notice.

Authorisations requiring approval

97 Authorisations requiring approval

(1) An authorisation to which this section applies shall not take effect until—
    (a) it has been approved in accordance with this section by a Commissioner appointed under section 91(1)(b), and
    (b) the person who gave the authorisation has been notified under subsection (4).
(2) Subject to subsection (3), this section applies to an authorisation if, at the time it is given, the person who gives it believes—
    (a) that any of the property specified in the authorisation—
        (i) is used wholly or mainly as a dwelling or as a bedroom in a hotel, or
        (ii) constitutes office premises, or
    (b) that the action authorised by it is likely to result in any person acquiring knowledge of—
        (i) matters subject to legal privilege,
        (ii) confidential personal information, or
        (iii) confidential journalistic material.
(3) This section does not apply to an authorisation where the person who gives it believes that the case is one of urgency.
(4) Where a Commissioner receives a notice under section 96 which specifies that this section applies to the authorisation, he shall as soon as is reasonably practicable—
    (a) decide whether to approve the authorisation or refuse approval, and
    (b) give written notice of his decision to the person who gave the authorisation.
(5) A Commissioner shall approve an authorisation if, and only if, he is satisfied that there are reasonable grounds for believing the matters specified in section 93(2).

98 Matters subject to legal privilege

(1) Subject to subsection (5) below, in section 97 "matters subject to legal privilege" means matters to which subsection (2), (3) or (4) below applies.
(2) This subsection applies to communications between a professional legal adviser and—
    (a) his client, or
    (b) any person representing his client,
which are made in connection with the giving of legal advice to the client.
(3) This subsection applies to communications—
    (a) between a professional legal adviser and his client or any person representing his client, or
    (b) between a professional legal adviser or his client or any such representative and any other person,
which are made in connection with or in contemplation of legal proceedings and for the purposes of such proceedings.
(4) This subsection applies to items enclosed with or referred to in communications of the kind mentioned in subsection (2) or (3) and made—
    (a) in connection with the giving of legal advice, or
    (b) in connection with or in contemplation of legal proceedings and for the purposes of such proceedings.
(5) For the purposes of section 97—
    (a) communications and items are not matters subject to legal privilege when they are in the possession of a person who is not entitled to possession of them, and
    (b) communications and items held, or oral communications made, with the intention of furthering a criminal purpose are not matters subject to legal privilege.

99 Confidential personal information

(1) In section 97 "confidential personal information" means—
    (a) personal information which a person has acquired or created in the course of any trade, business, profession or other occupation or for the purposes of any paid or unpaid office, and which he holds in confidence, and
    (b) communications as a result of which personal information—
        (i) is acquired or created as mentioned in paragraph (a), and
        (ii) is held in confidence.

(2)   For the purposes of this section "personal information" means information concerning an individual (whether living or dead) who can be identified from it and relating—
    (a)   to his physical or mental health, or
    (b)   to spiritual counselling or assistance given or to be given to him.

(3)   A person holds information in confidence for the purposes of this section if he holds it subject—
    (a)   to an express or implied undertaking to hold it in confidence, or
    (b)   to a restriction on disclosure or an obligation of secrecy contained in any enactment (including an enactment contained in an Act passed after this Act).

100   Confidential journalistic material

(1)   In section 97 "confidential journalistic material" means—
    (a)   material acquired or created for the purposes of journalism which—
        (i)   is in the possession of persons who acquired or created it for those purposes,
        (ii)   is held subject to an undertaking, restriction or obligation of the kind mentioned in section 99(3), and
        (iii)   has been continuously held (by one or more persons) subject to such an undertaking, restriction or obligation since it was first acquired or created for the purposes of journalism, and
    (b)   communications as a result of which information is acquired for the purposes of journalism and held as mentioned in paragraph (a)(ii).

(2)   For the purposes of subsection (1), a person who receives material, or acquires information, from someone who intends that the recipient shall use it for the purposes of journalism is to be taken to have acquired it for those purposes.

103   Quashing of authorisations etc.

(1)   Where, at any time, a Commissioner appointed under section 91(1)(b) is satisfied that, at the time an authorisation was given or renewed, there were no reasonable grounds for believing the matters specified in section 93(2), he may quash the authorisation or, as the case may be, renewal.

(2)   Where, in the case of an authorisation or renewal to which section 97 does not apply, a Commissioner appointed under section 91(1)(b) is at any time satisfied that, at the time the authorisation was given or, as the case may be, renewed,—
    (a)   there were reasonable grounds for believing any of the matters specified in subsection (2) of section 97, and
    (b)   there were no reasonable grounds for believing the case to be one of urgency for the purposes of subsection (3) of that section,
he may quash the authorisation or, as the case may be, renewal.

(3)   Where a Commissioner quashes an authorisation or renewal under subsection (1) or (2), he may order the destruction of any records relating to information obtained by virtue of the authorisation (or, in the case of a renewal, relating wholly or partly to information so obtained after the renewal) other than records required for pending criminal or civil proceedings.

Appeals

104   Appeals by authorising officers

(1)   An authorising officer who gives an authorisation, or in whose absence it is given, may, within the prescribed period, appeal to the Chief Commissioner against—
    (a)   any refusal to approve the authorisation or any renewal of it under section 97;
    (b)   any decision to quash the authorisation, or any renewal of it, under subsection (1) of section 103;
    (c)   any decision to quash the authorisation, or any renewal of it, under subsection (2) of that section;
    (d)   any decision to cancel the authorisation under subsection (4) of that section;
    (e)   any decision to order the destruction of records under subsection (5) of that section;
    (f)   any refusal to make an order under subsection (6) of that section;

(2) In subsection (1), "the prescribed period" means the period of seven days beginning with the day on which the refusal, decision or, as the case may be, determination appealed against is reported to the authorising officer.

(3) In determining an appeal within subsection (1)(a), the Chief Commissioner shall, if he is satisfied that there are reasonable grounds for believing the matters specified in section 93(2), allow the appeal and direct the Commissioner to approve the authorisation or renewal under that section.

General

107 Supplementary provisions relating to Commissioners

(1) The Chief Commissioner shall keep under review the performance of functions under this Part.

(2) The Chief Commissioner shall make an annual report on the matters with which he is concerned to the Prime Minister and to the Scottish Ministers and may at any time report to him or them (as the case may require) on anything relating to any of those matters.

(3) The Prime Minister shall lay before each House of Parliament a copy of each annual report made by the Chief Commissioner under subsection (2) together with a statement as to whether any matter has been excluded from that copy in pursuance of subsection (4) below.

(3A) The Scottish Ministers shall lay before the Scottish Parliament a copy of each annual report made by the Chief Commissioner under subsection (2), together with a statement as to whether any matter has been excluded from that copy in pursuance of subsection (4) below.

(4) The Prime Minister may exclude a matter from the copy of a report as laid before each House of Parliament, if it appears to him, after consultation with the Chief Commissioner and the Scottish Ministers, that the publication of that matter in the report would be prejudicial to any of the purposes for which authorisations may be given or granted under this Part of this Act or Part II of the Regulation of Investigatory Powers Act 2000 or under any enactment contained in or made under an act of the Scottish Parliament which makes provision equivalent to that made by Part II of that Act of 2000 or to the discharge of—

(a) the functions of any local policing body or the Scottish Police Authority,

(b) the functions of the National Crime Agency,

(bza) the functions of the Police Investigations and Review Commissioner under section 33A(b)(i) of the Police Public Order and Criminal Justice (Scotland) Act 2006,

(c) the duties of the Commissioners for Her Majesty's Revenue and Customs, or

(d) the functions of the Secretary of State relating to immigration.

HUMAN RIGHTS ACT 1998
(1998, c. 42)

An Act to give further effect to rights and freedoms guaranteed under the European Convention on Human Rights; to make provision with respect to holders of certain judicial offices who become judges of the European Court of Human Rights; and for connected purposes. [9 November 1998]

Introduction

1 The Convention Rights

(1) In this Act "the Convention rights" means the rights and fundamental freedoms set out in—

(a) Articles 2 to 12 and 14 of the Convention,

(b) Articles 1 to 3 of the First Protocol, and

(c) Article 1 of the Thirteenth Protocol,

as read with Articles 16 to 18 of the Convention.

(2)   Those Articles are to have effect for the purposes of this Act subject to any designated derogation or reservation (as to which see sections 14 and 15).

(3)   The Articles are set out in Schedule 1.

(4)   The Secretary of State may by order make such amendments to this Act as he considers appropriate to reflect the effect, in relation to the United Kingdom, of a protocol.

(5)   In subsection (4) "protocol" means a protocol to the Convention—

    (a)   which the United Kingdom has ratified; or

    (b)   which the United Kingdom has signed with a view to ratification.

(6)   No amendment may be made by an order under subsection (4) so as to come into force before the protocol concerned is in force in relation to the United Kingdom.

2   Interpretation of Convention rights

(1)   A court or tribunal determining a question which has arisen in connection with a Convention right must take into account any—

    (a)   judgment, decision, declaration or advisory opinion of the European Court of Human Rights,

    (b)   opinion of the Commission given in a report adopted under Article 31 of the Convention,

    (c)   decision of the Commission in connection with Article 26 or 27(2) of the Convention, or

    (d)   decision of the Committee of Ministers taken under Article 46 of the Convention, whenever made or given, so far as, in the opinion of the court or tribunal, it is relevant to the proceedings in which that question has arisen.

(2)   Evidence of any judgment, decision, declaration or opinion of which account may have to be taken under this section is to be given in proceedings before any court or tribunal in such manner as may be provided by rules.

(3)   In this section "rules" means rules of court or, in the case of proceedings before a tribunal, rules made for the purposes of this section—

    (a)   by the Lord Chancellor or the Secretary of State, in relation to any proceedings outside Scotland;

    (b)   by the Secretary of State, in relation to proceedings in Scotland; or

    (c)   by a Northern Ireland department, in relation to proceedings before a tribunal in Northern Ireland—

        (i)   which deals with transferred matters; and

        (ii)   for which no rules made under paragraph (a) are in force.

Legislation

3   Interpretation of legislation

(1)   So far as it is possible to do so, primary legislation and subordinate legislation must be read and given effect in a way which is compatible with the Convention rights.

(2)   This section—

    (a)   applies to primary legislation and subordinate legislation whenever enacted;

    (b)   does not affect the validity, continuing operation or enforcement of any incompatible primary legislation; and

    (c)   does not affect the validity, continuing operation or enforcement of any incompatible subordinate legislation if (disregarding any possibility of revocation) primary legislation prevents removal of the incompatibility.

4   Declaration of incompatibility

(1)   Subsection (2) applies in any proceedings in which a court determines whether a provision of primary legislation is compatible with a Convention right.

(2)   If the court is satisfied that the provision is incompatible with a Convention right, it may make a declaration of that incompatibility.

(3)   Subsection (4) applies in any proceedings in which a court determines whether a provision of subordinate legislation, made in the exercise of a power conferred by primary legislation, is compatible with a Convention right.

(4)   If the court is satisfied—
    (a)   that the provision is incompatible with a Convention right, and
    (b)   that (disregarding any possibility of revocation) the primary legislation concerned prevents removal of the incompatibility,
    it may make a declaration of that incompatibility.

(5)   In this section "court" means—
    (a)   the Supreme Court;
    (b)   the Judicial Committee of the Privy Council;
    (c)   the Court Martial Appeal Court;
    (d)   in Scotland, the High Court of Justiciary sitting otherwise than as a trial court or the Court of Session;
    (e)   in England and Wales or Northern Ireland, the High Court or the Court of Appeal;
    (f)   the Court of Protection, in any matter being dealt with by the President of the Family Division, the Chancellor of the High Court or a puisne judge of the High Court.

(6)   A declaration under this section ("a declaration of incompatibility")—
    (a)   does not affect the validity, continuing operation or enforcement of the provision in respect of which it is given; and
    (b)   is not binding on the parties to the proceedings in which it is made.

5   Right of Crown to intervene

(1)   Where a court is considering whether to make a declaration of incompatibility, the Crown is entitled to notice in accordance with rules of court.

(2)   In any case to which subsection (1) applies—
    (a)   a Minister of the Crown (or a person nominated by him),
    (b)   a member of the Scottish Executive,
    (c)   a Northern Ireland Minister,
    (d)   a Northern Ireland department,
    is entitled, on giving notice in accordance with rules of court, to be joined as a party to the proceedings.

(3)   Notice under subsection (2) may be given at any time during the proceedings.

(4)   A person who has been made a party to criminal proceedings (other than in Scotland) as the result of a notice under subsection (2) may, with leave, appeal to the Supreme Court against any declaration of incompatibility made in the proceedings.

(5)   In subsection (4)—
    "criminal proceedings" includes all proceedings before the Court Martial Appeal Court; and
    "leave" means leave granted by the court making the declaration of incompatibility or by the Supreme Court.

Public authorities

6   Acts of public authorities

(1)   It is unlawful for a public authority to act in a way which is incompatible with a Convention right.

(2)   Subsection (1) does not apply to an act if—
    (a)   as the result of one or more provisions of primary legislation, the authority could not have acted differently; or
    (b)   in the case of one or more provisions of, or made under, primary legislation which cannot be read or given effect in a way which is compatible with the Convention rights, the authority was acting so as to give effect to or enforce those provisions.

(3)   In this section "public authority" includes—
    (a)   a court or tribunal, and
    (b)   any person certain of whose functions are functions of a public nature,
    but does not include either House of Parliament or a person exercising functions in connection with proceedings in Parliament.

(5)   In relation to a particular act, a person is not a public authority by virtue only of subsection (3)(b) if the nature of the act is private.

(6)   "An act" includes a failure to act but does not include a failure to—

      (a)   introduce in, or lay before, Parliament a proposal for legislation; or

      (b)   make any primary legislation or remedial order.

7   Proceedings

(1)   A person who claims that a public authority has acted (or proposes to act) in a way which is made unlawful by section 6(1) may—

      (a)   bring proceedings against the authority under this Act in the appropriate court or tribunal, or

      (b)   rely on the Convention right or rights concerned in any legal proceedings,

but only if he is (or would be) a victim of the unlawful act.

(2)   In subsection (1)(a) "appropriate court or tribunal" means such court or tribunal as may be determined in accordance with rules; and proceedings against an authority include a counterclaim or similar proceeding.

(3)   If the proceedings are brought on an application for judicial review, the applicant is to be taken to have a sufficient interest in relation to the unlawful act only if he is, or would be, a victim of that act.

(4)   If the proceedings are made by way of a petition for judicial review in Scotland, the applicant shall be taken to have title and interest to sue in relation to the unlawful act only if he is, or would be, a victim of that act.

(5)   Proceedings under subsection (1)(a) must be brought before the end of—

      (a)   the period of one year beginning with the date on which the act complained of took place; or

      (b)   such longer period as the court or tribunal considers equitable having regard to all the circumstances,

but that is subject to any rule imposing a stricter time limit in relation to the procedure in question.

(6)   In subsection (1)(b) "legal proceedings" includes—

      (a)   proceedings brought by or at the instigation of a public authority; and

      (b)   an appeal against the decision of a court or tribunal.

(7)   For the purposes of this section, a person is a victim of an unlawful act only if he would be a victim for the purposes of Article 34 of the Convention if proceedings were brought in the European Court of Human Rights in respect of that act.

(8)   Nothing in this Act creates a criminal offence.

8   Judicial remedies

(1)   In relation to any act (or proposed act) of a public authority which the court finds is (or would be) unlawful, it may grant such relief or remedy, or make such order, within its powers as it considers just and appropriate.

(2)   But damages may be awarded only by a court which has power to award damages, or to order the payment of compensation, in civil proceedings.

(3)   No award of damages is to be made unless, taking account of all the circumstances of the case, including—

      (a)   any other relief or remedy granted, or order made, in relation to the act in question (by that or any other court), and

      (b)   the consequences of any decision (of that or any other court) in respect of that act,

the court is satisfied that the award is necessary to afford just satisfaction to the person in whose favour it is made.

(4)   In determining—

      (a)   whether to award damages, or

      (b)   the amount of an award,

the court must take into account the principles applied by the European Court of Human Rights in relation to the award of compensation under Article 41 of the Convention.

9   Judicial acts

(1)   Proceedings under section 7(1)(a) in respect of a judicial act may be brought only—

      (a)   by exercising a right of appeal;

(b)   on an application (in Scotland a petition) for judicial review; or

(c)   in such other forum as may be prescribed by rules.

(2)   That does not affect any rule of law which prevents a court from being the subject of judicial review.

(3)   In proceedings under this Act in respect of a judicial act done in good faith, damages may not be awarded otherwise than to compensate a person to the extent required by Article 5(5) of the Convention.

(4)   An award of damages permitted by subsection (3) is to be made against the Crown; but no award may be made unless the appropriate person, if not a party to the proceedings, is joined.

(5)   In this section—

"appropriate person" means the Minister responsible for the court concerned, or a person or government department nominated by him;

"court" includes a tribunal;

"judge" includes a member of a tribunal, a justice of the peace (or, in Northern Ireland, a lay magistrate) and a clerk or other officer entitled to exercise the jurisdiction of a court;

"judicial act" means a judicial act of a court and includes an act done on the instructions, or on behalf, of a judge; and

"rules" has the same meaning as in section 7(9).

Remedial action

10   Power to take remedial action

(1)   This section applies if—

(a)   a provision of legislation has been declared under section 4 to be incompatible with a Convention right and, if an appeal lies—

(i)   all persons who may appeal have stated in writing that they do not intend to do so;

(ii)   the time for bringing an appeal has expired and no appeal has been brought within that time; or

(iii)   an appeal brought within that time has been determined or abandoned; or

(b)   it appears to a Minister of the Crown or Her Majesty in Council that, having regard to a finding of the European Court of Human Rights made after the coming into force of this section in proceedings against the United Kingdom, a provision of legislation is incompatible with an obligation of the United Kingdom arising from the Convention.

(2)   If a Minister of the Crown considers that there are compelling reasons for proceeding under this section, he may by order make such amendments to the legislation as he considers necessary to remove the incompatibility.

(3)   If, in the case of subordinate legislation, a Minister of the Crown considers—

(a)   that it is necessary to amend the primary legislation under which the subordinate legislation in question was made, in order to enable the incompatibility to be removed, and

(b)   that there are compelling reasons for proceeding under this section,

he may by order make such amendments to the primary legislation as he considers necessary.

(4)   This section also applies where the provision in question is in subordinate legislation and has been quashed, or declared invalid, by reason of incompatibility with a Convention right and the Minister proposes to proceed under paragraph 2(b) of Schedule 2.

Other rights and proceedings

11   Safeguard for existing human rights

A person's reliance on a Convention right does not restrict—

(a)   any other right or freedom conferred on him by or under any law having effect in any part of the United Kingdom; or

(b)   his right to make any claim or bring any proceedings which he could make or bring apart from sections 7 to 9.

12   Freedom of expression

(1)   This section applies if a court is considering whether to grant any relief which, if granted, might affect the exercise of the Convention right to freedom of expression.

(2)   If the person against whom the application for relief is made ("the respondent") is neither present nor represented, no such relief is to be granted unless the court is satisfied—

(a)   that the applicant has taken all practicable steps to notify the respondent; or

(b)   that there are compelling reasons why the respondent should not be notified.

(3)   No such relief is to be granted so as to restrain publication before trial unless the court is satisfied that the applicant is likely to establish that publication should not be allowed.

(4)   The court must have particular regard to the importance of the Convention right to freedom of expression and, where the proceedings relate to material which the respondent claims, or which appears to the court, to be journalistic, literary or artistic material (or to conduct connected with such material), to—

(a)   the extent to which—

(i)   the material has, or is about to, become available to the public; or

(ii)   it is, or would be, in the public interest for the material to be published;

(b)   any relevant privacy code.

(5)   In this section—

"court" includes a tribunal; and

"relief" includes any remedy or order (other than in criminal proceedings).

13   Freedom of thought, conscience and religion

(1)   If a court's determination of any question arising under this Act might affect the exercise by a religious organisation (itself or its members collectively) of the Convention right to freedom of thought, conscience and religion, it must have particular regard to the importance of that right.

(2)   In this section "court" includes a tribunal.

Derogations and reservations

14   Derogations

(1)   In this Act "designated derogation" means any derogation by the United Kingdom from an Article of the Convention, or of any protocol to the Convention, which is designated for the purposes of this Act in an order made by the Secretary of State.

(3)   If a designated derogation is amended or replaced it ceases to be a designated derogation.

(4)   But subsection (3) does not prevent the Secretary of State from exercising his power under subsection (1) to make a fresh designation order in respect of the Article concerned.

(6)   A designation order may be made in anticipation of the making by the United Kingdom of a proposed derogation.

15   Reservations

(1)   In this Act "designated reservation" means—

(a)   the United Kingdom's reservation to Article 2 of the First Protocol to the Convention; and

(b)   any other reservation by the United Kingdom to an Article of the Convention, or of any protocol to the Convention, which is designated for the purposes of this Act in an order made by the Secretary of State.

(2)   The text of the reservation referred to in subsection (1)(a) is set out in Part II of Schedule 3.

(3)   If a designated reservation is withdrawn wholly or in part it ceases to be a designated reservation.

(4) But subsection (3) does not prevent the Secretary of State from exercising his power under subsection (1)(b) to make a fresh designation order in respect of the Article concerned.

(5) The Secretary of State must by order make such amendments to this Act as he considers appropriate to reflect—
    (a) any designation order; or
    (b) the effect of subsection (3).

16 Period for which designated derogations have effect

(1) If it has not already been withdrawn by the United Kingdom, a designated derogation ceases to have effect for the purposes of this Act at the end of the period of five years beginning with the date on which the order designating it was made.

(2) At any time before the period—
    (a) fixed by subsection (1), or
    (b) extended by an order under this subsection,
comes to an end, the Secretary of State may by order extend it by a further period of five years.

(3) An order under section 14(1) ceases to have effect at the end of the period for consideration, unless a resolution has been passed by each House approving the order.

(4) Subsection (3) does not affect—
    (a) anything done in reliance on the order; or
    (b) the power to make a fresh order under section 14(1).

Parliamentary procedure

19 Statements of compatibility

(1) A Minister of the Crown in charge of a Bill in either House of Parliament must, before Second Reading of the Bill—
    (a) make a statement to the effect that in his view the provisions of the Bill are compatible with the Convention rights ("a statement of compatibility"); or
    (b) make a statement to the effect that although he is unable to make a statement of compatibility the government nevertheless wishes the House to proceed with the Bill.

(2) The statement must be in writing and be published in such manner as the Minister making it considers appropriate.

Supplemental

20 Orders etc. under this Act

(1) Any power of a Minister of the Crown to make an order under this Act is exercisable by statutory instrument.

SCHEDULE 2
REMEDIAL ORDERS

Orders

1. (1) A remedial order may—
    (a) contain such incidental, supplemental, consequential or transitional provision as the person making it considers appropriate;
    (b) be made so as to have effect from a date earlier than that on which it is made;
    (c) make provision for the delegation of specific functions;
    (d) make different provision for different cases.

  (2) The power conferred by sub-paragraph (1)(a) includes—
    (a) power to amend primary legislation (including primary legislation other than that which contains the incompatible provision); and
    (b) power to amend or revoke subordinate legislation (including subordinate legislation other than that which contains the incompatible provision).

(3)   A remedial order may be made so as to have the same extent as the legislation which it affects.

(4)   No person is to be guilty of an offence solely as a result of the retrospective effect of a remedial order.

Procedure

2.   No remedial order may be made unless—

(a)   a draft of the order has been approved by a resolution of each House of Parliament made after the end of the period of 60 days beginning with the day on which the draft was laid; or

(b)   it is declared in the order that it appears to the person making it that, because of the urgency of the matter, it is necessary to make the order without a draft being so approved.

Calculating periods

6.   In calculating any period for the purposes of this Schedule, no account is to be taken of any time during which—

(a)   Parliament is dissolved or prorogued; or

(b)   both Houses are adjourned for more than four days.

7.   (1)   This paragraph applies in relation to—

(a)   any remedial order made, and any draft of such an order proposed to be made,—

(i)   by the Scottish Ministers; or

(ii)   within devolved competence (within the meaning of the Scotland Act 1998) by Her Majesty in Council; and

(b)   any document or statement to be laid in connection with such an order (or proposed order).

(2)   This Schedule has effect in relation to any such order (or proposed order), document or statement subject to the following modifications.

(3)   Any reference to Parliament, each House of Parliament or both Houses of Parliament shall be construed as a reference to the Scottish Parliament.

(4)   Paragraph 6 does not apply and instead, in calculating any period for the purposes of this Schedule, no account is to be taken of any time during which the Scottish Parliament is dissolved or is in recess for more than four days.

SCOTLAND ACT 1998
(1998, c. 46)

An Act to provide for the establishment of a Scottish Parliament and Administration and other changes in the government of Scotland; to provide for changes in the constitution and functions of certain public authorities; to provide for the variation of the basic rate of income tax in relation to income of Scottish taxpayers in accordance with a resolution of the Scottish Parliament; to amend the law about parliamentary constituencies in Scotland; and for connected purposes.

[19 November 1998]

PART I
THE SCOTTISH PARLIAMENT

The Scottish Parliament

1   The Scottish Parliament

(1)   There shall be a Scottish Parliament.

(2)   One member of the Parliament shall be returned for each constituency (under the simple majority system) at an election held in the constituency.

(3) Members of the Parliament for each region shall be returned at a general election under the additional member system of proportional representation provided for in this part and vacancies among such members shall be filled in accordance with this Part.

(4) The validity of any proceedings of the Parliament is not affected by any vacancy in its membership.

(5) Schedule 1 (which makes provision for the constituencies and regions for the purposes of this Act and the number of regional members) shall have effect.

General elections

2 Ordinary general elections

(1) The day on which the poll at the first ordinary general election for membership of the Parliament shall be held, and the day, time and place for the meeting of the Parliament following that poll, shall be appointed by order made by the Secretary of State.

(2) The poll at subsequent ordinary general elections shall be held on the first Thursday in May in the fourth calendar year following that in which the previous ordinary general election was held, unless the day.
   (a) subsection (2A) prevents the poll being held on that day, or
   (b) the day of the poll is determined by a proclamation under subsection (5).

(2A) The poll shall not be held on the same date as the date of the poll at—
   (a) a parliamentary general election (other than an early parliamentary general election), or
   (b) a European parliamentary general election.

(2B) Where subsection (2A) prevents the poll being held on the day specified in subsection (2), the poll shall be held on such day, subject to subsection (2A), as the Scottish Ministers may by order specify, unless the day of the poll is determined by a proclamation under subsection (5) as modified by subsection (5ZA).

(3) If the poll is to be held on the first Thursday in May, or on the day specified by an order under subsection (2B) the Parliament—
   (a) is dissolved by virtue of this section at the beginning of the minimum period which ends with that day, and
   (b) shall meet within the period of seven days beginning immediately after the day of the poll.

(4) In subsection (3), "the minimum period" means the period determined in accordance with an order under section 12(1).

(5) Subject to subsection (2A), if the Presiding Officer proposes a day for the holding of the poll which is not more than one month earlier, nor more than one month later, than the first Thursday in May, Her Majesty may by proclamation under the Scottish Seal—
   (a) dissolve the Parliament,
   (b) require the poll at the election to be held on the day proposed, and
   (c) require the Parliament to meet within the period of seven days beginning immediately after the day of the poll.

(5ZA) Where a day is specified by order under subsection (2B), subsection (5) applies as if the reference to the first Thursday in May were a reference to that day.

(5A) If, under this section as modified by virtue of an Act of the Scottish Parliament, the poll at an ordinary general election would, apart from subsection (5), be held on a day other than that provided by subsection (2) as originally enacted—
   (a) references in subsections (3) and (5) to the first Thursday in May are to be read as references to that other day (if it is not the first Thursday in May), and
   (b) subsection (5B) applies to any day proposed under subsection (5).

(5B) The day proposed must not be the same as the day of the poll at—
   (a) a parliamentary general election, other than an early parliamentary general election,
   (b) a European parliamentary general election, or
   (c) an ordinary local election.

(5C) In subsection (5B) "ordinary local election" has the meaning given by section 43(1C) of the Representation of the People Act 1983.

(6)   In this Act "the Scottish Seal" means Her Majesty's Seal appointed by the Treaty of Union to be kept and used in Scotland in place of the Great Seal of Scotland.

Presiding Officer and administration

19   Presiding Officer

(1)   The Parliament shall, following a general election, elect from among its members a Presiding Officer and two deputies.

(1A) The Parliament must do so—

    (a)   before it conducts any other proceedings, except the taking by its members of the oath of allegiance (see section 84), and

    (b)   in any event, within the period of 14 days beginning immediately after the day of the poll at the election.

(1B) The Parliament may, at any time, elect from among its members one or more additional deputies.

(2)   A person elected Presiding Officer or deputy shall hold office until the conclusion of the next election for Presiding Officer under subsection (1) unless he previously resigns, ceases to be a member of the Parliament otherwise than by virtue of a dissolution or is removed from office by resolution of the Parliament.

(2A) But standing orders may make provision for additional deputies to hold office for a shorter time than provided by subsection (2).

(3)   If the Presiding Officer or a deputy elected under subsection (1) ceases to hold office before the Parliament is dissolved, the Parliament shall elect another from among its members to fill his place.

(4)   The Presiding Officer's functions may be exercised by a deputy if the office of Presiding Officer is vacant or the Presiding Officer is for any reason unable to act.

(5)   The Presiding Officer may (subject to standing orders) authorise any deputy to exercise functions on his behalf.

(6)   Standing orders may include provision as to the participation (including voting) of the Presiding Officer and deputies in the proceedings of the Parliament.

(7)   The validity of any act of the Presiding Officer or a deputy is not affected by any defect in his election.

Proceedings etc.

22   Standing orders

(1)   The proceedings of the Parliament shall be regulated by standing orders.

Legislation

28   Acts of the Scottish Parliament

(1)   Subject to section 29, the Parliament may make laws, to be known as Acts of the Scottish Parliament.

(2)   Proposed Acts of the Scottish Parliament shall be known as Bills; and a Bill shall become an Act of the Scottish Parliament when it has been passed by the Parliament and has received Royal Assent.

(3)   A Bill receives Royal Assent at the beginning of the day on which Letters Patent under the Scottish Seal signed with Her Majesty's own hand signifying Her Assent are recorded in the Register of the Great Seal.

(4)   The date of Royal Assent shall be written on the Act of the Scottish Parliament by the Clerk, and shall form part of the Act.

(5)   The validity of an Act of the Scottish Parliament is not affected by any invalidity in the proceedings of the Parliament leading to its enactment.

(6)   Every Act of the Scottish Parliament shall be judicially noticed.

(7)   This section does not affect the power of the Parliament of the United Kingdom to make laws for Scotland.

(8)   But it is recognised that the Parliament of the United Kingdom will not normally legislate with regard to devolved matters without the consent of the Scottish Parliament.

29 Legislative competence

(1)   An Act of the Scottish Parliament is not law so far as any provision of the Act is outside the legislative competence of the Parliament.

(2)   A provision is outside the competence so far as any of the following paragraphs apply—

    (a)   it would form part of the law of a country or territory other than Scotland, or confer or remove functions exercisable otherwise than in or as regards Scotland,

    (b)   it relates to reserved matters,

    (c)   it is in breach of the restrictions in Schedule 4.

    (d)   it is incompatible with any of the Convention rights or with EU law,

    (e)   it would remove the Lord Advocate from his position as head of the systems of criminal prosecution and investigation of deaths in Scotland.

(3)   For the purposes of this section, the question whether a provision of an Act of the Scottish Parliament relates to a reserved matter is to be determined, subject to subsection (4), by reference to the purpose of the provision, having regard (among other things) to its effect in all the circumstances.

(4)   A provision which—

    (a)   would otherwise not relate to reserved matters, but

    (b)   makes modifications of Scots private law, or Scots criminal law, as it applies to reserved matters,

    is to be treated as relating to reserved matters unless the purpose of the provision is to make he law in question apply consistently to reserved matters and otherwise.

(5)   Subsection (1) is subject to section 30(6).

30 Legislative competence: supplementary

(1)   Schedule 5 (which defines reserved matters) shall have effect.

Other provisions

37 Acts of Union

The Union with Scotland Act 1706 and the Union with England Act 1707 have effect subject to this Act.

PART II
THE SCOTTISH ADMINISTRATION

Ministers and their staff

44 The Scottish Executive

(1)   There shall be a Scottish Government, whose members shall be—

    (a)   the First Minister,

    (b)   such Ministers as the First Minister may appoint under section 47, and

    (c)   the Lord Advocate and the Solicitor General for Scotland.

(2)   The members of the Scottish Government are referred to collectively as the Scottish Ministers.

(3)   A person who holds a Ministerial office may not be appointed a member of the Scottish Government; and if a member of the Scottish Government is appointed to a Ministerial office he shall cease to hold office as a member of the Scottish Government.

(4)   In subsection (3), references to a member of the Scottish Government include a junior Scottish Minister and "Ministerial office" has the same meaning as in section 2 of the House of Commons Disqualification Act 1975.

45 The First Minister

(1)   The First Minister shall be appointed by Her Majesty from among the members of the Parliament and shall hold office at Her Majesty's pleasure.

(2)   The First Minister may at any time tender his resignation to Her Majesty and shall do so if the Parliament resolves that the Scottish Government no longer enjoys the confidence of the Parliament.

(3)   The First Minister shall cease to hold office if a person is appointed in his place.

(4)   If the office of First Minister is vacant or he is for any reason unable to act, the functions exercisable by him shall be exercisable by a person designated by the Presiding Officer.

(5)   A person shall be so designated only if—

(a)   he is a member of the Parliament, or

(b)   if the Parliament has been dissolved, he is a person who ceased to be a member by virtue of the dissolution.

(6)   Functions exercisable by a person by virtue of subsection (5)(a) shall continue to be exercisable by him even if the Parliament is dissolved.

(7)   The First Minister shall be the Keeper of the Scottish Seal.

46   Choice of the First Minister

(1)   If one of the following events occurs, the Parliament shall within the period allowed nominate one of its members for appointment as First Minister.

(2)   The events are—

(a)   the holding of a poll at a general election,

(b)   the First Minister tendering his resignation to Her Majesty,

(c)   the office of First Minister becoming vacant (otherwise than in consequence of his so tendering his resignation),

(d)   the First Minister ceasing to be a member of the Parliament otherwise than by virtue of a dissolution.

(3)   The period allowed is the period of 28 days which begins with the day on which the event in question occurs; but—

(a)   if another of those events occurs within the period allowed, that period shall be extended (subject to paragraph (b)) so that it ends with the period of 28 days beginning with the day on which that other event occurred, and

(b)   the period shall end if the Parliament passes a resolution under section 3(1)(a) or when Her Majesty appoints a person as First Minister.

(4)   The Presiding Officer shall recommend to Her Majesty the appointment of any member of the Parliament who is nominated by the Parliament under this section.

47   Ministers

(1)   The First Minister may, with the approval of Her Majesty, appoint Ministers from among the members of the Parliament.

48   The Scottish Law Officers

(1)   It is for the First Minister to recommend to Her Majesty the appointment or removal of a person as Lord Advocate or Solicitor General for Scotland; but he shall not do so without the agreement of the Parliament.

Ministerial functions

53   General transfer of functions

(1)   The functions mentioned in subsection (2) shall, so far as they are exercisable within devolved competence, be exercisable by the Scottish Ministers instead of by a Minister of the Crown.

(2)   Those functions are—

(a)   those of Her Majesty's prerogative and other executive functions which are exercisable on behalf of Her Majesty by a Minister of the Crown,

(b)   other functions conferred on a Minister of the Crown by a prerogative instrument, and

(c)   functions conferred on a Minister of the Crown by any pre-commencement enactment,

but do not include any retained functions of the Lord Advocate.

54   Devolved competence

(1)   References in this Act to the exercise of a function being within or outside devolved competence are to be read in accordance with this section.

(2) It is outside devolved competence—

   (a) to make any provision by subordinate legislation which would be outside the legislative competence of the Parliament if it were included in an Act of the Scottish Parliament, or

   (b) to confirm or approve any subordinate legislation containing such provision.

(3) In the case of any function other than a function of making, confirming or approving subordinate legislation, it is outside devolved competence to exercise the function (or exercise it in any way) so far as a provision of an Act of the Scottish Parliament conferring the function (or, as the case may be, conferring it so as to be exercisable in that way) would be outside the legislative competence of the Parliament.

57 EU law and Convention rights

(1) Despite the transfer to the Scottish Ministers by virtue of section 53 of functions in relation to observing and implementing obligations under EU law, any function of a minister of the Crown in relation to any matter shall continue to be exercisable by him as regards Scotland for the purposes specified in section 2(2) of the European Communities Act 1972.

(2) A member of the Scottish Government has no power to make any subordinate legislation, or to do any other act, so far as the legislation or act is incompatible with any of the Convention rights or with EU law.

(3) Subsection (2) does not apply to an act of the Lord Advocate—

   (a) in prosecuting any offence, or

   (b) in his capacity as head of the systems of criminal prosecution and investigation of deaths in Scotland.

63A Permanence of the Scottish Parliament and Scottish Government

(1) The Scottish Parliament and the Scottish Government are a permanent part of the United Kingdom's constitutional arrangements.

(2) The purpose of this section is, with due regard to the other provisions of this Act, to signify the commitment of the Parliament and Government of the United Kingdom to the Scottish Parliament and the Scottish Government.

(3) In view of that commitment it is declared that the Scottish Parliament and the Scottish Government are not to be abolished except on the basis of a decision of the people of Scotland voting in a referendum.

Juridical

98 Devolution issues

Schedule 6 (which makes provision in relation to devolution issues) shall have effect.

100 Human rights

(1) This Act does not enable a person—

   (a) to bring any proceedings in a court or tribunal on the ground that an act is incompatible with the Convention rights, or

   (b) to rely on any of the Convention rights in any such proceedings,

unless he would be a victim for the purposes of Article 34 of the Convention (within the meaning of the Human Rights Act 1998) if proceedings in respect of the act were brought in the European Court of Human Rights.

(2) Subsection (1) does not apply to the Lord Advocate, the Advocate General, the Attorney General, the Advocate General for Northern Ireland or the Attorney General for Northern Ireland.

(3) This Act does not enable a court or tribunal to award any damages in respect of an act which is incompatible with any of the Convention rights which it could not award if section 8(3) and (4) of the Human Rights Act 1998 applied.

(3A) Subsection (3B) applies to any proceedings brought by virtue of this Act against the Scottish Ministers or a member of the Scottish Government in a court or tribunal on the ground that an act of the Scottish Ministers or a member of the Scottish Government is incompatible with the Convention rights.

(3B) Proceedings to which this subsection applies must be brought before the end of—
    (a)   the period of one year beginning with the date on which the act complained of took place, or
    (b)   such longer period as the court or tribunal considers equitable having regard to all the circumstances,
but that is subject to any rule imposing a stricter time limit in relation to the procedure in question.

(3C) Subsection (3B) does not apply to proceedings brought by the Lord Advocate, the Advocate General, the Attorney General, the Attorney General for Northern Ireland or the Advocate General for Northern Ireland.

(3D) In subsections (3A) and (3B) "act" does not include the making of any legislation but it does include any other act or failure to act (including a failure to make legislation).

(3E) In subsection (3B) "rule" has the same meaning as it has in section 7(5) of the Human Rights Act 1998.

(4)   Subject to subsection (3D), in this section "act" means—
    (a)   making any legislation,
    (b)   any other act or failure to act, if it is the act or failure of a member of the Scottish Government.

NORTHERN IRELAND ACT 1998
(1998, c. 47)

Note: See also Northern Ireland Act 2009 (2009, c. 3) for more information.

An Act to make new provision for the government of Northern Ireland for the purpose of implementing the agreement reached at multi-party talks on Northern Ireland set out in Command Paper 3883.   [19 November 1998]

PART I
PRELIMINARY

1   Status of Northern Ireland

(1)   It is hereby declared that Northern Ireland in its entirety remains part of the United Kingdom and shall not cease to be so without the consent of a majority of the people of Northern Ireland voting in a poll held for the purposes of this section in accordance with Schedule 1.

(2)   But if the wish expressed by a majority in such a poll is that Northern Ireland should cease to be part of the United Kingdom and form part of a united Ireland the Secretary of State shall lay before Parliament such proposals to give effect to that wish as may be agreed between Her Majesty's Government in the United Kingdom and the Government of Ireland.

PART II
LEGISLATIVE POWERS

General

5   Acts of the Northern Ireland Assembly

(1)   Subject to sections 6 to 8, the Assembly may make laws, to be known as Acts.

(2)   A Bill shall become an Act when it has been passed by the Assembly and has received Royal Assent.

(3)   A Bill receives Royal Assent at the beginning of the day on which Letters Patent under the Great Seal of Northern Ireland signed with Her Majesty's own hand signifying Her Assent are notified to the Presiding Officer.

(4) The date of Royal Assent shall be written on the Act by the Presiding Officer, and shall form part of the Act.

(5) The validity of any proceedings leading to the enactment of an Act of the Assembly shall not be called into question in any legal proceedings.

(6) This section does not affect the power of the Parliament of the United Kingdom to make laws for Northern Ireland, but an Act of the Assembly may modify any provision made by or under an Act of Parliament in so far as it is part of the law of Northern Ireland.

6 Legislative competence

(1) A provision of an Act is not law if it is outside the legislative competence of the Assembly.

(2) A provision is outside that competence if any of the following paragraphs apply—

    (a) it would form part of the law of a country or territory other than Northern Ireland, or confer or remove functions exercisable otherwise than in or as regards Northern Ireland;

    (b) it deals with an excepted matter and is not ancillary to other provisions (whether in the Act or previously enacted) dealing with reserved or transferred matters;

    (c) it is incompatible with any of the Convention rights;

    (d) it is incompatible with EU law;

    (e) it discriminates against any person or class of person on the ground of religious belief or political opinion;

    (f) it modifies an enactment in breach of section 7.

(3) For the purposes of this Act, a provision is ancillary to other provisions if it is a provision—

    (a) which provides for the enforcement of those other provisions or is otherwise necessary or expedient for making those other provisions effective; or

    (b) which is otherwise incidental to, or consequential on, those provisions;

and references in this Act to provisions previously enacted are references to provisions contained in, or in any instrument made under, other Northern Ireland legislation or an Act of Parliament.

(4) Her Majesty may by Order in Council specify functions which are to be treated, for such purposes of this Act as may be specified, as being, or as not being, functions which are exercisable in or as regards Northern Ireland.

(5) No recommendation shall be made to Her Majesty to make an Order in Council under subsection (4) unless a draft of the Order has been laid before and approved by resolution of each House of Parliament.

7 Entrenched enactments

(1) Subject to subsection (2), the following enactments shall not be modified by an Act of the Assembly or subordinate legislation made, confirmed or approved by a Minister or Northern Ireland department—

    (a) the European Communities Act 1972;

    (b) the Human Rights Act 1998;

    (c) section 43(1) to (6) and (8), section 67, sections 84 to 86B, section 95(3) and (4) and section 98; and

    (d) section 1 and section 84 of the Justice (Northern Ireland) Act 2002.

(2) Subsection (1) does not prevent an Act of the Assembly or subordinate legislation modifying section 3(3) or (4) or 11(1) of the European Communities Act 1972.

(3) In this Act "Minister", unless the context otherwise requires, means the First Minister, the deputy First Minister or a Northern Ireland Minister.

7A Cross-community support required for Bill altering size of Assembly

(1) The Assembly shall not pass a relevant Bill without cross-community support.

(2) In this section—

"pass", in relation to a Bill, means pass at the stage in the Assembly's proceedings at which the Bill falls finally to be passed or rejected;

"relevant Bill" means a Bill containing a provision which deals with a matter falling within a description specified in paragraph 7A of Schedule 3 (size of Assembly).

PART III
EXECUTIVE AUTHORITIES

Authorities

16A Appointment of First Minister, deputy First Minister and Northern Ireland Ministers following Assembly election

(1)   This section applies where an Assembly is elected under section 31 or 32.

(2)   All Northern Ireland Ministers shall cease to hold office.

(3)   Within a period of seven days beginning with the first meeting of the Assembly—

    (a)   the offices of First Minister and deputy First Minister shall be filled by applying subsections (4) to (7); and

    (b)   the Ministerial offices to be held by Northern Ireland Ministers (other than the relevant Ministerial office (within the meaning of Part IA of Schedule 4A)) shall be filled by applying section 18(2) to (6).

(4)   The nominating officer of the largest political party of the largest political designation shall nominate a member of the Assembly to be the First Minister.

(5)   The nominating officer of the largest political party of the second largest political designation shall nominate a member of the Assembly to be the deputy First Minister.

(6)   If the persons nominated do not take up office within a period specified in standing orders, further nominations shall be made under subsections (4) and (5).

(7)   Subsections (4) to (6) shall be applied as many times as may be necessary to secure that the offices of First Minister and deputy First Minister are filled.

(8)   But no person may take up office as First Minister, deputy First Minister or Northern Ireland Minister by virtue of this section after the end of the period mentioned in subsection (3) (see further section 32(3)).

(9)   The persons nominated under subsections (4) and (5) shall not take up office until each of them has affirmed the terms of the pledge of office.

(10)   Subject to the provisions of this Part, the First Minister and the deputy First Minister shall hold office until immediately before those offices are next filled by virtue of this section.

(11)   The holder of the office of First Minister or deputy First Minister may by notice in writing to the Presiding Officer designate a Northern Ireland Minister to exercise the functions of that office—

    (a)   during any absence or incapacity of the holder; or

    (b)   during any vacancy in that office arising otherwise than under section 16B(2),

    but a person shall not have power to act by virtue of paragraph (a) for a continuous period exceeding six weeks.

(12)   This section shall be construed in accordance with, and is subject to, section 16C.

23 Prerogative and executive powers

(1)   The executive power in Northern Ireland shall continue to be vested in Her Majesty.

24 EU law, Convention rights etc.

(1)   A Minister or Northern Ireland department has no power to make, confirm or approve any subordinate legislation, or to do any act, so far as the legislation or act—

    (a)   is incompatible with any of the Convention rights;

    (b)   is incompatible with EU law;

    (c)   discriminates against a person or class of person on the ground of religious belief or political opinion;

    (d)   in the case of an act, aids or incites another person to discriminate against a person or class of person on that ground; or

    (e)   in the case of legislation, modifies an enactment in breach of section 7.

25 Excepted and reserved matters

(1)   If any subordinate legislation made, confirmed or approved by, a Minister or Northern Ireland department contains a provision dealing with an excepted or reserved matter, the Secretary of State may by order revoke the legislation.

(2)   An order made under subsection (1) shall recite the reasons for revoking the legislation and may make provision having retrospective effect.

26   International obligations

(1)   If the Secretary of State considers that any action proposed to be taken by a Minister or Northern Ireland department would be incompatible with any international obligations, with the interests of defence or national security or with the protection of public safety or public order, he may by order direct that the proposed action shall not be taken.

PART IV
THE NORTHERN IRELAND ASSEMBLY

Presiding Officer and Commission

39   Presiding Officer

(1)   Each Assembly shall as its first business elect from among its members a Presiding Officer and deputies.

40   Commission

(1)   There shall be a body corporate, to be known as the Northern Ireland Assembly Commission ("the Commission"), to perform—
(a)   the functions conferred on the Commission by virtue of any enactment; and
(b)   any functions conferred on the Commission by resolution of the Assembly.

PART VII
HUMAN RIGHTS AND EQUAL OPPORTUNITIES

Human rights

68   The Northern Ireland Human Rights Commission

(1)   There shall be a body corporate to be known as the Northern Ireland Human Rights Commission.
(2)   The Commission shall consist of a Chief Commissioner and other Commissioners appointed by the Secretary of State.
(3)   In making appointments under this section, the Secretary of State shall as far as practicable secure that the Commissioners, as a group, are representative of the community in Northern Ireland.
(4)   Schedule 7 (which makes supplementary provision about the Commission) shall have effect.

69   The Commission's functions

(1)   The Commission shall keep under review the adequacy and effectiveness in Northern Ireland of law and practice relating to the protection of human rights.
(2)   The Commission shall, before the end of the period of two years beginning with the commencement of this section, make to the Secretary of State such recommendations as it thinks fit for improving—
(a)   its effectiveness;
(b)   the adequacy and effectiveness of the functions conferred on it by this Part; and
(c)   the adequacy and effectiveness of the provisions of this Part relating to it.
(3)   The Commission shall advise the Secretary of State and the Executive Committee of the Assembly of legislative and other measures which ought to be taken to protect human rights—
(a)   as soon as reasonably practicable after receipt of a general or specific request for advice; and
(b)   on such other occasions as the Commission thinks appropriate.
(4)   The Commission shall advise the Assembly whether a Bill is compatible with human rights—
(a)   as soon as reasonably practicable after receipt of a request for advice; and
(b)   on such other occasions as the Commission thinks appropriate.
(5)   The Commission may—
(a)   give assistance to individuals in accordance with section 70; and
(b)   bring proceedings involving law or practice relating to the protection of human rights.

(6) The Commission shall promote understanding and awareness of the importance of human rights in Northern Ireland; and for this purpose it may undertake, commission or provide financial or other assistance for—
   (a) research; and
   (b) educational activities.

(7) The Secretary of State shall request the Commission to provide advice of the kind referred to in paragraph 4 of the Human Rights section of the Belfast Agreement.

(8) For the purpose of exercising its functions under this section the Commission may conduct such investigations as it considers necessary or expedient.

(8A) The Commission shall publish a report of its finding on an investigation.

(9) The Commission may decide to publish its advice and the outcome of its research.

(10) The Commission shall do all that it can to ensure the establishment of the committee referred to in paragraph 10 of that section of that Agreement.

(11) In this section—
   (a) a reference to the Assembly includes a reference to a committee of the Assembly;
   (b) "human rights" includes the Convention rights.

71   Restrictions on application of rights

(1) Nothing in section 6(2)(c), 24(1)(a) shall enable a person—
   (a) to bring any proceedings in a court or tribunal on the aground that any legislation or act is incompatible with the Convention rights; or
   (b) to rely on any of the Convention rights in any such proceedings,
   unless he would be a victim for the purposes of article 34 of the Convention if proceedings in respect of the legislation or act were brought in the European Court of Human Rights.

(2) Subsection (1) does not apply to the Attorney General, the Advocate General for Northern Ireland, the Attorney General for Northern Ireland, the Advocate General for Scotland or the Lord Advocate.

(2A) Subsection (1) does not apply to the Commission.

(2B) In relation to the Commission's instituting, or intervening in, human rights proceedings—
   (a) the Commission need not be a victim or potential victim of the unlawful act to which the proceedings relate,
   (b) section 7(3) and (4) of the Human Rights Act 1998 (breach of Convention rights: sufficient interest, &c.) shall not apply,
   (c) the Commission may act only if there is or would be one or more victims of the unlawful act, and
   (d) no award of damages may be made to the Commission (whether or not the exception in section 8(3) of that Act applies).

(2C) For the purposes of subsection (2B)—
   (a) "human rights proceedings" means proceedings which rely (wholly or partly) on—
      (i) section 7(1)(b) of the Human Rights Act 1998, or
      (ii) section 69(5)(b) of this Act, and
   (b) an expression used in subsection (2B) and in section 7 of the Human Rights Act 1998 has the same meaning in subsection (2B) as in section 7.

(3) Section 6(2)(c)—
   (a) does not apply to a provision of an Act of the Assembly if the passing of the Act is, by virtue of subsection (2) of section 6 of the Human Rights Act 1998, not unlawful under subsection (1) of that section; and
   (b) does not enable a court or tribunal to award in respect of the passing of an Act of the Assembly any damages which it could not award on finding the passing of the Act unlawful under that subsection.

(4) Section 24(1)(a)—
   (a) does not apply to an act which, by virtue of subsection (2) of section 6 of the Human Rights Act 1998, is not unlawful under subsection (1) of that section; and

(b)   does not enable a court or tribunal to award in respect of an act any damages
       which it could not award on finding the act unlawful under that subsection.

(5)   In this section "the Convention" has the same meaning as in the Human Rights Act
       1998.

PART VIII
MISCELLANEOUS

80   Legislative power to remedy ultra vires acts

(1)   The Secretary of State may by order make such provision as he considers necessary
       or expedient in consequence of—
       (a)   any provision of an Act of the Assembly which is not, or may not be, within the
              legislative competence of the Assembly; or
       (b)   any purported exercise by a Minister or Northern Ireland department of his or its
              functions which is not, or may not be, a valid exercise of those functions.

(2)   An order under this section may—
       (a)   make provision having retrospective effect;
       (b)   make consequential or supplementary provision, including provision amending
              or repealing any Northern Ireland legislation, or any instrument made under
              such legislation;
       (c)   make transitional or saving provision.

83   Interpretation of Acts of the Assembly etc.

(1)   This section applies where—
       (a)   any provision of an Act of the Assembly, or of a Bill for such an Act, could be
              read either—
              (i)   in such a way as to be within the legislative competence of the Assembly;
                     or
              (ii)   in such a way as to be outside that competence; or
       (b)   any provision of subordinate legislation made, confirmed or approved, or
              purporting to be made, confirmed or approved, by a Northern Ireland authority
              could be read either—
              (i)   in such a way as not to be invalid by reason of section 24 or, as the case
                     may be, section 76; or
              (ii)   in such a way as to be invalid by reason of that section.

(2)   The provision shall be read in the way which makes it within that competence or, as
       the case may be, does not make it invalid by reason of that section, and shall have
       effect accordingly.

(3)   In this section "Northern Ireland authority" means a Minister, a Northern Ireland
       department or a public authority (within the meaning of section 76) carrying out
       functions relating to Northern Ireland.

HOUSE OF LORDS ACT 1999
(1999, c. 34)

*An Act to restrict membership of the House of Lords by virtue of a hereditary peerage; to make
related provision about disqualifications for voting at elections to and for membership of the House
of Commons; and for connected purposes.*   [11 November 1999]

1   Exclusion of hereditary peers

No-one shall be a member of the House of Lords by virtue of a hereditary peerage.

2   Exception from section 1

(1)   Section 1 shall not apply in relation to anyone excepted from it by or in accordance
       with Standing Orders of the House.

(2)   At any time 90 people shall be excepted from section 1; but anyone excepted as holder of the office of Earl Marshal, or as performing the office of Lord Great Chamberlain, shall not count towards that limit.

(3)   Once excepted from section 1, a person shall continue to be so throughout his life (until an Act of Parliament provides to the contrary).

(4)   Standing Orders shall make provision for filling vacancies among the people excepted from section 1; and in any case where—

    (a)   the vacancy arises on a death occurring after the end of the first Session of the next Parliament after that in which this Act is passed, and

    (b)   the deceased person was excepted in consequence of an election,

that provision shall require the holding of a by-election.

(5)   A person may be excepted from section 1 by or in accordance with Standing Orders made in anticipation of the enactment or commencement of this section.

(6)   Any question whether a person is excepted from section 1 shall be decided by the Clerk of the Parliaments, whose certificate shall be conclusive.

3   Removal of disqualifications in relation to the House of Commons

(1)   The holder of a hereditary peerage shall not be disqualified by virtue of that peerage for—

    (a)   voting at elections to the House of Commons, or

    (b)   being, or being elected as, a member of that House.

(2)   Subsection (1) shall not apply in relation to anyone excepted from section 1 by virtue of section 2.

6   Interpretation and short title

(1)   In this Act "hereditary peerage" includes the principality of Wales and the earldom of Chester.

FREEDOM OF INFORMATION ACT 2000
(2000, c. 36)

An Act to make provision for the disclosure of information held by public authorities or by persons providing services for them and to amend the Data Protection Act 1998 and the Public Records Act 1958; and for connected purposes.   [30 November 2000]

PART I
ACCESS TO INFORMATION HELD BY PUBLIC AUTHORITIES

Right to information

1   General right of access to information held by public authorities

(1)   Any person making a request for information to a public authority is entitled—

    (a)   to be informed in writing by the public authority whether it holds information of the description specified in the request, and

    (b)   if that is the case, to have that information communicated to him.

(2)   Subsection (1) has effect subject to the following provisions of this section and to the provisions of sections 2, 9, 12 and 14.

(3)   Where a public authority—

    (a)   reasonably requires further information in order to identify and locate the information requested, and

    (b)   has informed the applicant of that requirement,

the authority is not obliged to comply with subsection (1) unless it is supplied with that further information.

(4)   The information—

    (a)   in respect of which the applicant is to be informed under subsection (1)(a), or

    (b)   which is to be communicated under subsection (1)(b),

is the information in question held at the time when the request is received, except that account may be taken of any amendment or deletion made between that time and the time when the information is to be communicated under subsection (1)(b), being an amendment or deletion that would have been made regardless of the receipt of the request.

(5) A public authority is to be taken to have complied with subsection (1)(a) in relation to any information if it has communicated the information to the applicant in accordance with subsection (1)(b).

(6) In this Act, the duty of a public authority to comply with subsection (1)(a) is referred to as "the duty to confirm or deny".

2 Effect of the exemptions in Part II

(1) Where any provision of Part II states that the duty to confirm or deny does not arise in relation to any information, the effect of the provision is that where either—
  (a) the provision confers absolute exemption, or
  (b) in all the circumstances of the case, the public interest in maintaining the exclusion of the duty to confirm or deny outweighs the public interest in disclosing whether the public authority holds the information,
  section 1(1)(a) does not apply.

(2) In respect of any information which is exempt information by virtue of any provision of Part II, section 1(1)(b) does not apply if or to the extent that—
  (a) the information is exempt information by virtue of a provision conferring absolute exemption, or
  (b) in all the circumstances of the case, the public interest in maintaining the exemption outweighs the public interest in disclosing the information.

(3) For the purposes of this section, the following provisions of Part II (and no others) are to be regarded as conferring absolute exemption—
  (a) section 21,
  (b) section 23,
  (c) section 32,
  (d) section 34,
  (e) section 36 so far as relating to information held by the House of Commons or the House of Lords,
  (ea) in section 37, paragraphs (a) to (ab) of subsection (1), and subsection (2) so far as relating to those paragraphs,
  (f) in section 40—
    (i) subsection (1), and
    (ii) subsection (2) so far as relating to cases where the first condition referred to in that subsection is satisfied by virtue of subsection (3)(a)(i) or (b) of that section,
  (g) section 41, and
  (h) section 44.

3 Public authorities

(1) In this Act "public authority" means—
  (a) subject to section 4(4), any body which, any other person who, or the holder of any office which—
    (i) is listed in Schedule 1, or
    (ii) is designated by order under section 5, or
  (b) a publicly-owned company as defined by section 6.

(2) For the purposes of this Act, information is held by a public authority if—
  (a) it is held by the authority, otherwise than on behalf of another person, or
  (b) it is held by another person on behalf of the authority.

6 Publicly-owned companies

(1) A company is a "publicly-owned company" for the purposes of section 3(1)(b) if—
  (a) it is wholly owned by the Crown,
  (b) it is wholly owned by the wider public sector, or
  (c) it is wholly owned by the Crown and the wider public sector.

8   Request for information

(1)   In this Act any reference to a "request for information" is a reference to such a request which—

(a)   is in writing,

(b)   states the name of the applicant and an address for correspondence, and

(c)   describes the information requested.

(2)   For the purposes of subsection (1)(a), a request is to be treated as made in writing where the text of the request—

(a)   is transmitted by electronic means,

(b)   is received in legible form, and

(c)   is capable of being used for subsequent reference.

9   Fees

(1)   A public authority to whom a request for information is made may, within the period for complying with section 1(1), give the applicant a notice in writing (in this Act referred to as a "fees notice") stating that a fee of an amount specified in the notice is to be charged by the authority for complying with section 1(1).

(2)   Where a fees notice has been given to the applicant, the public authority is not obliged to comply with section 1(1) unless the fee is paid within the period of three months beginning with the day on which the fees notice is given to the applicant.

(3)   Subject to subsection (5), any fee under this section must be determined by the public authority in accordance with regulations made by the Secretary of State.

10   Time for compliance with request

(1)   Subject to subsections (2) and (3), a public authority must comply with section 1(1) promptly and in any event not later than the twentieth working day following the date of receipt.

(2)   Where the authority has given a fees notice to the applicant and the fee is paid in accordance with section 9(2), the working days in the period beginning with the day on which the fees notice is given to the applicant and ending with the day on which the fee is received by the authority are to be disregarded in calculating for the purposes of subsection (1) the twentieth working day following the date of receipt.

11   Means by which communication to be made

(1)   Where, on making his request for information, the applicant expresses a preference for communication by any one or more of the following means, namely—

(a)   the provision to the applicant of a copy of the information in permanent form or in another form acceptable to the applicant,

(b)   the provision to the applicant of a reasonable opportunity to inspect a record containing the information, and

(c)   the provision to the applicant of a digest or summary of the information in permanent form or in another form acceptable to the applicant,

the public authority shall so far as reasonably practicable give effect to that preference.

(1A) Where—

(a)   an applicant makes a request for information to a public authority in respect of information that is, or forms part of, a dataset held by the public authority, and

(b)   on making the request for information, the applicant expresses a preference for communication by means of the provision to the applicant of a copy of the information in electronic form,

the public authority must, so far as reasonably practicable, provide the information to the applicant in an electronic form which is capable of re-use.

(2)   In determining for the purposes of this section whether it is reasonably practicable to communicate information by particular means, the public authority may have regard to all the circumstances, including the cost of doing so.

(3)   Where the public authority determines that it is not reasonably practicable to comply with any preference expressed by the applicant in making his request, the authority shall notify the applicant of the reasons for its determination.

(4)   Subject to subsections (1) and (1A), a public authority may comply with a request by communicating information by any means which are reasonable in the circumstances.

(5)   In this Act "dataset" means information comprising a collection of information held in electronic form where all or most of the information in the collection—
    (a)   has been obtained or recorded for the purpose of providing a public authority with information in connection with the provision of a service by the authority or the carrying out of any other function of the authority,
    (b)   is factual information which—
        (i)   is not the product of analysis or interpretation other than calculation, and
        (ii)   is not an official statistic (within the meaning given by section 6(1) of the Statistics and Registration Service Act 2007), and
    (c)   remains presented in a way that (except for the purpose of forming part of the collection) has not been organised, adapted or otherwise materially altered since it was obtained or recorded.

11A   Release of datasets for re-use

(1)   This section applies where—
    (a)   a person makes a request for information to a public authority in respect of information that is, or forms part of, a dataset held by the authority,
    (b)   any of the dataset or part of a dataset so requested is a relevant copyright work,
    (c)   the public authority is the only owner of the relevant copyright work, and
    (d)   the public authority is communicating the relevant copyright work to the applicant in accordance with this Act.

(1A) But if the whole of the relevant copyright work is a document to which the Re-use of Public Sector Information Regulations 2015 apply, this section does not apply to the relevant copyright work.

(1B) If part of the relevant copyright work is a document to which those Regulations apply—
    (a)   this section does not apply to that part, but
    (b)   this section does apply to the part to which the Regulations do not apply (and references in the following provisions of this section to the relevant copyright work are to be read as references to that part).

(2)   When communicating the relevant copyright work to the applicant, the public authority must make the relevant copyright work available for re-use by the applicant in accordance with the terms of the specified licence.

(3)   The public authority may exercise any power that it has by virtue of regulations under section 11B to charge a fee in connection with making the relevant copyright work available for re-use in accordance with subsection (2).

(4)   Nothing in this section or section 11B prevents a public authority which is subject to a duty under subsection (2) from exercising any power that it has by or under an enactment other than this Act to charge a fee in connection with making the relevant copyright work available for re-use.

(5)   Where a public authority intends to charge a fee (whether in accordance with regulations under section 11B or as mentioned in subsection (4)) in connection with making a relevant copyright work available for re-use by an applicant, the authority must give the applicant a notice in writing (in this section referred to as a "re-use fee notice") stating that a fee of an amount specified in, or determined in accordance with, the notice is to be charged by the authority in connection with complying with subsection (2).

(6)   Where a re-use fee notice has been given to the applicant, the public authority is not obliged to comply with subsection (2) while any part of the fee which is required to be paid is unpaid.

(7)   Where a public authority intends to charge a fee as mentioned in subsection (4), the re-use fee notice may be combined with any other notice which is to be given under the power which enables the fee to be charged.

(8)   In this section—
"copyright owner" has the meaning given by Part 1 of the Copyright, Designs and Patents Act 1988 (see section 173 of that Act);
"copyright work" has the meaning given by Part 1 of the Act of 1988 (see section 1(2) of that Act);

"database" has the meaning given by section 3A of the Act of 1988;

"database right" has the same meaning as in Part 3 of the Copyright and Rights in Databases Regulations 1997 (SI 1997/3032);

"owner", in relation to a relevant copyright work, means—

(a)   the copyright owner, or

(b)   the owner of the database right in the database;

"relevant copyright work" means—

(a)   a copyright work, or

(b)   a database subject to a database right,

but excludes a relevant Crown work or a relevant Parliamentary work;

"relevant Crown work" means—

(a)   a copyright work in relation to which the Crown is the copyright owner, or

(b)   a database in relation to which the Crown is the owner of the database right;

"relevant Parliamentary work" means—

(a)   a copyright work in relation to which the House of Commons or the House of Lords is the copyright owner, or

(b)   a database in relation to which the House of Commons or the House of Lords is the owner of the database right;

"the specified licence" is the licence specified by the Minister for the Cabinet Office in a code of practice issued under section 45, and the Minister for the Cabinet Office may specify different licences for different purposes.

12   Exemption where cost of compliance exceeds appropriate limit

(1)   Section 1(1) does not oblige a public authority to comply with a request for information if the authority estimates that the cost of complying with the request would exceed the appropriate limit.

(2)   Subsection (1) does not exempt the public authority from its obligation to comply with paragraph (a) of section 1(1) unless the estimated cost of complying with that paragraph alone would exceed the appropriate limit.

(3)   In subsections (1) and (2) "the appropriate limit" means such amount as may be prescribed, and different amounts may be prescribed in relation to different cases.

(4)   The Minister for the Cabinet Office may by regulations provide that, in such circumstances as may be prescribed, where two or more requests for information are made to a public authority—

(a)   by one person, or

(b)   by different persons who appear to the public authority to be acting in concert or in pursuance of a campaign,

the estimated cost of complying with any of the requests is to be taken to be the estimated total cost of complying with all of them.

(5)   The Minister for the Cabinet Office may by regulations make provision for the purposes of this section as to the costs to be estimated and as to the manner in which they are to be estimated.

14   Vexatious or repeated requests

(1)   Section 1(1) does not oblige a public authority to comply with a request for information if the request is vexatious.

(2)   Where a public authority has previously complied with a request for information which was made by any person, it is not obliged to comply with a subsequent identical or substantially similar request from that person unless a reasonable interval has elapsed between compliance with the previous request and the making of the current request.

16   Duty to provide advice and assistance

(1)   It shall be the duty of a public authority to provide advice and assistance, so far as it would be reasonable to expect the authority to do so, to persons who propose to make, or have made, requests for information to it.

(2)   Any public authority which, in relation to the provision of advice or assistance in any case, conforms with the code of practice under section 45 is to be taken to comply with the duly imposed by subsection (1) in relation to that case.

Refusal of request

17 Refusal of request

(1) A public authority which, in relation to any request for information, is to any extent relying on a claim that any provision of Part II relating to the duty to confirm or deny is relevant to the request or on a claim that information is exempt information must, within the time for complying with section 1(1), give the applicant a notice which—

   (a) states that fact,

   (b) specifies the exemption in question, and

   (c) states (if that would not otherwise be apparent) why the exemption applies.

(3) A public authority which, in relation to any request for information, is to any extent relying on a claim that subsection (1)(b) or (2)(b) of section 2 applies must, either in the notice under subsection (1) or in a separate notice given within such time as is reasonable in the circumstances, state the reasons for claiming—

   (a) that, in all the circumstances of the case, the public interest in maintaining the exclusion of the duty to confirm or deny outweighs the public interest in disclosing whether the authority holds the information, or

   (b) that, in all the circumstances of the case, the public interest in maintaining the exemption outweighs the public interest in disclosing the information.

(4) A public authority is not obliged to make a statement under subsection (1)(c) or (3) if, or to the extent that, the statement would involve the disclosure of information which would itself be exempt information.

(5) A public authority which, in relation to any request for information, is relying on a claim that section 12 or 14 applies must, within the time for complying with section 1(1), give the applicant a notice stating that fact.

The Information Commissioner and the Information Tribunal

18 The Information Commissioner

(1) The Data Protection Commissioner shall be known instead as the Information Commissioner.

(3) In this Act—

   (a) the Information Commissioner is referred to as "the Commissioner".

Publication schemes

19 Publication schemes

(1) It shall be the duty of every public authority—

   (a) to adopt and maintain a scheme which relates to the publication of information by the authority and is approved by the Commissioner (in this Act referred to as a "publication scheme"),

   (b) to publish information in accordance with its publication scheme, and

   (c) from time to time to review its publication scheme.

(2) A publication scheme must—

   (a) specify classes of information which the public authority publishes or intends to publish,

   (b) specify the manner in which information of each class is, or is intended to be, published, and

   (c) specify whether the material is, or is intended to be, available to the public free of charge or on payment.

(2A) A publication scheme must, in particular, include a requirement for the public authority concerned—

   (a) to publish—

      (i) any dataset held by the authority in relation to which a person makes a request for information to the authority, and

      (ii) any up-dated version held by the authority of such a dataset,

      unless the authority is satisfied that it is not appropriate for the dataset to be published,

    (b)   where reasonably practicable, to publish any dataset the authority publishes by virtue of paragraph (a) in an electronic form which is capable of re-use,

    (c)   subject to subsections (2AA) and (2AB) where any information in a dataset published by virtue of paragraph (a) is a relevant copyright work in relation to which the authority is the only owner, to make the information available for re-use in accordance with the terms of the specified licence.

(2AA) If the whole of the relevant copyright work is a document to which the Re-use of Public Sector Information Regulations 2015 apply, subsections (2A)(c) and (2B) to (2F) do not apply to the relevant copyright work.

(2AB) If part of the relevant copyright work is a document to which those Regulations apply—

    (a)   subsections (2A)(c) and (2B) to (2F) do not apply to that part, but

    (b)   those provisions do apply to the part to which the Regulations do not apply (and references in the following provisions of this section to the relevant copyright work are to be read as references to that part).

(2B) The public authority may exercise any power that it has by virtue of regulations under section 11B to charge a fee in connection with making the relevant copyright work available for re-use in accordance with a requirement imposed by virtue of subsection (2A)(c).

(2C) Nothing in this section or section 11B prevents a public authority which is subject to such a requirement from exercising any power that it has by or under an enactment other than this Act to charge a fee in connection with making the relevant copyright work available for re-use.

(2D) Where a public authority intends to charge a fee (whether in accordance with regulations under section 11B or as mentioned in subsection (2C)) in connection with making a relevant copyright work available for re-use by an applicant, the authority must give the applicant a notice in writing (in this section referred to as a "re-use fee notice") stating that a fee of an amount specified in, or determined in accordance with, the notice is to be charged by the authority in connection with complying with the requirement imposed by virtue of subsection (2A)(c).

(2E) Where a re-use fee notice has been given to the applicant, the public authority is not obliged to comply with the requirement imposed by virtue of subsection (2A)(c) while any part of the fee which is required to be paid is unpaid.

(2F) Where a public authority intends to charge a fee as mentioned in subsection (2C), the re-use fee notice may be combined with any other notice which is to be given under the power which enables the fee to be charged.

(3)   In adopting or reviewing a publication scheme, a public authority shall have regard to the public interest—

    (a)   in allowing public access to information held by the authority, and

    (b)   in the publication of reasons for decisions made by the authority.

(4)   A public authority shall publish its publication scheme in such manner as it thinks fit.

(5)   The Commissioner may, when approving a scheme, provide that his approval is to expire at the end of a specified period.

(6)   Where the Commissioner has approved the publication scheme of any public authority, he may at any time give notice to the public authority revoking his approval of the scheme as from the end of the period of six months beginning with the day on which the notice is given.

(7)   Where the Commissioner—

    (a)   refuses to approve a proposed publication scheme, or

    (b)   revokes his approval of a publication scheme,

he must give the public authority a statement of his reasons for doing so.

(8)   In this section—

"copyright owner" has the meaning given by Part 1 of the Copyright, Designs and Patents Act 1988 (see section 173 of that Act);

"copyright work" has the meaning given by Part 1 of the Act of 1988 (see section 1(2) of that Act);

"database" has the meaning given by section 3A of the Act of 1988;

"database right" has the same meaning as in Part 3 of the Copyright and Rights in Databases Regulations 1997;

"owner", in relation to a relevant copyright work, means—

(a)   the copyright owner, or

(b)   the owner of the database right in the database;

"relevant copyright work" means—

(a)   a copyright work, or

(b)   a database subject to a database right,

but excludes a relevant Crown work or a relevant Parliamentary work;

"relevant Crown work" means—

(a)   a copyright work in relation to which the Crown is the copyright owner, or

(b)   a database in relation to which the Crown is the owner of the database right;

"relevant Parliamentary work" means—

(a)   a copyright work in relation to which the House of Commons or the House of Lords is the copyright owner, or

(b)   a database in relation to which the House of Commons or the House of Lords is the owner of the database right;

"the specified licence" has the meaning given by section 11A(8).

20   Model publication schemes

(1)   The Commissioner may from time to time approve, in relation to public authorities falling within particular classes, model publication schemes prepared by him or by other persons.

(2)   Where a public authority falling within the class to which an approved model scheme relates adopts such a scheme without modification, no further approval of the Commissioner is required so long as the model scheme remains approved; and where such an authority adopts such a scheme with modifications, the approval of the Commissioner is required only in relation to the modifications.

PART II
EXEMPT INFORMATION

21   Information accessible to applicant by other means

(1)   Information which is reasonably accessible to the applicant otherwise than under section 1 is exempt information.

(2)   For the purposes of subsection (1)—

(a)   information may be reasonably accessible to the applicant even though it is accessible only on payment, and

(b)   information is to be taken to be reasonably accessible to the applicant if it is information which the public authority or any other person is obliged by or under any enactment to communicate (otherwise than by making the information available for inspection) to members of the public on request, whether free of charge or on payment.

(3)   For the purposes of subsection (1), information which is held by a public authority and does not fall within subsection (2)(b) is not to be regarded as reasonably accessible to the applicant merely because the information is available from the public authority itself on request, unless the information is made available in accordance with the authority's publication scheme and any payment required is specified in, or determined in accordance with, the scheme.

22   Information intended for future publication

(1)   Information is exempt information if—

(a)   the information is held by the public authority with a view to its publication, by the authority or any other person, at some future date (whether determined or not),

(b)   the information was already held with a view to such publication at the time when the request for information was made, and

(c)   it is reasonable in all the circumstances that the information should be withheld from disclosure until the date referred to in paragraph (a).

(2)   The duty to confirm or deny does not arise if, or to the extent that, compliance with section 1(1)(a) would involve the disclosure of any information (whether or, not already recorded) which falls within subsection (1).

22A   Research

(1)   Information obtained in the course of, or derived from, a programme of research is exempt information if—
    (a)   the programme is continuing with a view to the publication, by a public authority or any other person, of a report of the research (whether or not including a statement of that information), and
    (b)   disclosure of the information under this Act before the date of publication would, or would be likely to, prejudice—
        (i)   the programme,
        (ii)   the interests of any individual participating in the programme,
        (iii)   the interests of the authority which holds the information, or
        (iv)   the interests of the authority mentioned in paragraph (a) (if it is a different authority from that which holds the information).
(2)   The duty to confirm or deny does not arise in relation to information which is (or if it were held by the public authority would be) exempt information by virtue of subsection (1) if, or to the extent that, compliance with section I(l)(a) would, or would be likely to, prejudice any of the matters mentioned in subsection (1)(b).

23   Information supplied by, or relating to, bodies dealing with security matters

(1)   Information held by a public authority is exempt information if it was directly or indirectly supplied to the public authority by, or relates to, any of the bodies specified in subsection (3).
(2)   A certificate signed by a Minister of the Crown certifying that the information to which it applies was directly or indirectly supplied by, or relates to, any of the bodies specified in subsection (3) shall, subject to section 60, be conclusive evidence of that fact.
(3)   The bodies referred to in subsections (1) and (2) are—
    (a)   the Security Service,
    (b)   the Secret Intelligence Service,
    (c)   the Government Communications Headquarters,
    (d)   the special forces,
    (e)   the Tribunal established under section 65 of the Regulation of Investigatory Powers Act 2000,
    (f)   the Tribunal established under section 7 of the Interception of Communications Act 1985,
    (g)   the Tribunal established under section 5 of the Security Service Act 1989,
    (h)   the Tribunal established under section 9 of the Intelligence Services Act 1994,
    (i)   the Security Vetting Appeals Panel,
    (j)   the Security Commission,
    (k)   the National Criminal Intelligence Service,
    (l)   the Service Authority for the National Criminal Intelligence Service,
    (m)   the Serious Organised Crime Agency,
    (n)   the National Crime Agency, and
    (o)   the Intelligence and Security Committee of Parliament.

24   National security

(1)   Information which does not fall within section 23(1) is exempt information if exemption from section 1(1)(b) is required for the purpose of safeguarding national security.
(2)   The duty to confirm or deny does not arise if, or to the extent that, exemption from section 1(1)(a) is required for the purpose of safeguarding national security.
(3)   A certificate signed by a Minister of the Crown certifying that exemption from section 1(1)(b), or from section 1(1)(a) and (b), is, or at any time was, required for the purpose of safeguarding national security shall, subject to section 60, be conclusive evidence of that fact.

(4)   A certificate under subsection (3) may identify the information to which it applies by means of a general description and may be expressed to have prospective effect.

26   Defence

(1)   Information is exempt information if its disclosure under this Act would, or would be likely to, prejudice—
 (a)   the defence of the British Islands or of any colony, or
 (b)   the capability, effectiveness or security of any relevant forces.
(2)   In subsection (1)(b) "relevant forces" means—
 (a)   the armed forces of the Crown, and
 (b)   any forces co-operating with those forces,
 or any part of any of those forces.
(3)   The duty to confirm or deny does not arise if, or to the extent that, compliance with section 1(1)(a) would, or would be likely to, prejudice any of the matters mentioned in subsection (1).

27   International relations

(1)   Information is exempt information if its disclosure under this Act would, or would be likely to, prejudice—
 (a)   relations between the United Kingdom and any other State,
 (b)   relations between the United Kingdom and any international organisation or international court,
 (c)   the interests of the United Kingdom abroad, or
 (d)   the promotion or protection by the United Kingdom of its interests abroad.
(2)   Information is also exempt information if it is confidential information obtained from a State other than the United Kingdom or from an international organisation or international court.
(3)   For the purposes of this section, any information obtained from a State, organisation or court is confidential at any time while the terms on which it was obtained require it to be held in confidence or while the circumstances in which it was obtained make it reasonable for the State, organisation or court to expect that it will be so held.
(4)   The duty to confirm or deny does not arise if, or to the extent that, compliance with section 1(1)(a)—
 (a)   would, or would be likely to, prejudice any of the matters mentioned in subsection (1), or
 (b)   would involve the disclosure of any information (whether or not already recorded) which is confidential information obtained from a State other than the United Kingdom or from an international organisation or international court.

28   Relations within the United Kingdom

(1)   Information is exempt information if its disclosure under this Act would, or would be likely to, prejudice relations between any administration in the United Kingdom and any other such administration.
(2)   In subsection (1) "administration in the United Kingdom" means—
 (a)   the government of the United Kingdom,
 (b)   the Scottish Administration,
 (c)   the Executive Committee of the Northern Ireland Assembly, or
 (d)   the Welsh Assembly Government.
(3)   The duty to confirm or deny does not arise if, or to the extent that, compliance with section 1(1)(a) would, or would be likely to, prejudice any of the matters mentioned in subsection (1).

29   The economy

(1)   Information is exempt information if its disclosure under this Act would, or would be likely to, prejudice—
 (a)   the economic interests of the United Kingdom or of any part of the United Kingdom, or
 (b)   the financial interests of any administration in the United Kingdom, as defined by section 28(2).

(2)   The duty to confirm or deny does not arise if, or to the extent that, compliance with section 1(1)(a) would, or would be likely to, prejudice any of the matters mentioned in subsection (1).

30   Investigations and proceedings conducted by public authorities

(1)   Information held by a public authority is exempt information if it has at any time been held by the authority for the purposes of—

(a)   any investigation which the public authority has a duty to conduct with a view to it being ascertained—

(i)   whether a person should be charged with an offence, or

(ii)   whether a person charged with an offence is guilty of it,

(b)   any investigation which is conducted by the authority and in the circumstances may lead to a decision by the authority to institute criminal proceedings which the authority has power to conduct, or

(c)   any criminal proceedings which the authority has power to conduct.

(2)   Information held by a public authority is exempt information if—

(a)   it was obtained or recorded by the authority for the purposes of its functions relating to—

(i)   investigations falling within subsection (1)(a) or (b),

(ii)   criminal proceedings which the authority has power to conduct,

(iii)   investigations (other than investigations falling within subsection (1) (a) or (b)) which are conducted by the authority for any of the purposes specified in section 31(2) and either by virtue of Her Majesty's prerogative or by virtue of powers conferred by or under any enactment, or

(iv)   civil proceedings which are brought by or on behalf of the authority and arise out of such investigations, and

(b)   it relates to the obtaining of information from confidential sources.

(3)   The duty to confirm or deny does not arise in relation to information which is (or if it were held by the public authority would be) exempt information by virtue of subsection (1) or (2).

31   Law enforcement

(1)   Information which is not exempt information by virtue of section 30 is exempt information if its disclosure under this Act would, or would be likely to, prejudice—

(a)   the prevention or detection of crime,

(b)   the apprehension or prosecution of offenders,

(c)   the administration of justice,

(d)   the assessment or collection of any tax or duty or of any imposition of a similar nature,

(e)   the operation of the immigration controls,

(f)   the maintenance of security and good order in prisons or in other institutions where persons are lawfully detained,

(g)   the exercise by any public authority of its functions for any of the purposes specified in subsection (2),

(h)   any civil proceedings which are brought by or on behalf of a public authority and arise out of an investigation conducted, for any of the purposes specified in subsection (2), by or on behalf of the authority by virtue of Her Majesty's prerogative or by virtue of powers conferred by or under an enactment, or

(i)   any inquiry held under the Fatal Accidents and Sudden Deaths Inquiries (Scotland) Act 1976 to the extent that the inquiry arises out of an investigation conducted, for any of the purposes specified in subsection (2), by or on behalf of the authority by virtue of Her Majesty's prerogative or by virtue of powers conferred by or under an enactment.

(2)   The purposes referred to in subsection (1)(g) to (i) are—

(a)   the purpose of ascertaining whether any person has failed to comply with the law,

(b)   the purpose of ascertaining whether any person is responsible for any conduct which is improper,

(c)   the purpose of ascertaining whether circumstances which would justify regulatory action in pursuance of any enactment exist or may arise,

(d)   the purpose of ascertaining a person's fitness or competence in relation to the management of bodies corporate or in relation to any profession or other activity which he is, or seeks to become, authorised to carry on,

(e)   the purpose of ascertaining the cause of an accident,

(f)   the purpose of protecting charities against misconduct or mismanagement (whether by trustees or other persons) in their administration,

(g)   the purpose of protecting the property of charities from loss or misapplication,

(h)   the purpose of recovering the property of charities,

(i)   the purpose of securing the health, safety and welfare of persons at work, and

(j)   the purpose of protecting persons other than persons at work against risk to health or safety arising out of or in connection with the actions of persons at work.

(3)   The duty to confirm or deny does not arise if, or to the extent that, compliance with section 1(1)(a) would, or would be likely to, prejudice any of the matters mentioned in subsection (1).

32   Court records, etc.

(1)   Information held by a public authority is exempt information if it is held only by virtue of being contained in—

(a)   any document filed with, or otherwise placed in the custody of, a court for the purposes of proceedings in a particular cause or matter,

(b)   any document served upon, or by, a public authority for the purposes of proceedings in a particular cause or matter, or

(c)   any document created by—

(i)   a court, or

(ii)   a member of the administrative staff of a court,

for the purposes of proceedings in a particular cause or matter.

33   Audit functions

(1)   This section applies to any public authority which has functions in relation to—

(a)   the audit of the accounts of other public authorities, or

(b)   the examination of the economy, efficiency and effectiveness with which other public authorities use their resources in discharging their functions.

(2)   Information held by a public authority to which this section applies is exempt information if its disclosure would, or would be likely to, prejudice the exercise of any of the authority's functions in relation to any of the matters referred to in subsection (1).

(3)   The duty to confirm or deny does not arise in relation to a public authority to which this section applies if, or to the extent that, compliance with section 1(1)(a) would, or would be likely to, prejudice the exercise of any of the authority's functions in relation to any of the matters referred to in subsection (1).

34   Parliamentary privilege

(1)   Information is exempt information if exemption from section 1(1)(b) is required for the purpose of avoiding an infringement of the privileges of either House of Parliament.

(2)   The duty to confirm or deny does not apply if, or to the extent that, exemption from section 1(1)(a) is required for the purpose of avoiding an infringement of the privileges of either House of Parliament.

(3)   A certificate signed by the appropriate authority certifying that exemption from section 1(1)(b), or from section 1(1)(a) and (b), is, or at any time was, required for the purpose of avoiding an infringement of the privileges of either House of Parliament shall be conclusive evidence of that fact.

(4)   In subsection (3) "the appropriate authority" means—

(a)   in relation to the House of Commons, the Speaker of that House, and

(b)   in relation to the House of Lords, the Clerk of the Parliaments.

35   Formulation of government policy, etc.

(1)   Information held by a government department or by the Welsh Assembly Government is exempt information if it relates to—

(a)   the formulation or development of government policy,

(b)   Ministerial communications,

(c)   the provision of advice by any of the Law Officers or any request for the provision of such advice, or

(d)   the operation of any Ministerial private office.

(2)   Once a decision as to government policy has been taken, any statistical information used to provide an informed background to the taking of the decision is not to be regarded—

(a)   for the purposes of subsection (1)(a), as relating to the formulation or development of government policy, or

(b)   for the purposes of subsection (1)(b), as relating to Ministerial communications.

(3)   The duty to confirm or deny does not arise in relation to information which is (or if it were held by the public authority would be) exempt information by virtue of subsection (1).

(4)   In making any determination required by section 2(1)(b) or (2)(b) in relation to information which is exempt information by virtue of subsection (1)(a), regard shall be had to the particular public interest in the disclosure of factual information which has been used, or is intended to be used, to provide informed background to decision-taking.

36   Prejudice to effective conduct of public affairs

(1)   This section applies to—

(a)   information which is held by a government department or by the Welsh Assembly Government and is not exempt information by virtue of section 35, and

(b)   information which is held by any other public authority.

(2)   Information to which this section applies is exempt information if, in the reasonable opinion of a qualified person, disclosure of the information under this Act—

(a)   would, or would be likely to, prejudice—

(i)   the maintenance of the convention of the collective responsibility of Ministers of the Crown, or

(ii)   the work of the Executive Committee of the Northern Ireland Assembly, or

(iii)   the work of the Cabinet of the Welsh Assembly Government,

(b)   would, or would be likely to, inhibit—

(i)   the free and frank provision of advice, or

(ii)   the free and frank exchange of views for the purposes of deliberation, or

(c)   would otherwise prejudice, or would be likely otherwise to prejudice, the effective conduct of public affairs.

(3)   The duty to confirm or deny does not arise in relation to information to which this section applies (or would apply if held by the public authority) if, or to the extent that, in the reasonable opinion of a qualified person, compliance with section 1(1)(a) would, or would be likely to, have any of the effects mentioned in subsection (2).

(4)   In relation to statistical information, subsections (2) and (3) shall have effect with the omission of the words "in the reasonable opinion of a qualified person".

(5)   In subsections (2) and (3) "qualified person" —

(a)   in relation to information held by a government department in the charge of a Minister of the Crown, means any Minister of the Crown,

(b)   in relation to information held by a Northern Ireland department, means the Northern Ireland Minister in charge of the department,

(c)   in relation to information held by any other government department, means the commissioners or other person in charge of that department,

(d)   in relation to information held by the House of Commons, means the Speaker of that House,

(e)   in relation to information held by the House of Lords, means the Clerk of the Parliaments,

(f)   in relation to information held by the Northern Ireland Assembly, means the Presiding Officer,

(g)   in relation to information held by the Welsh Assembly Government, means the Welsh Ministers or the Counsel General to the Welsh Assembly Government,

(ga)   in relation to information held by the National Assembly for Wales, means the Presiding Officer of the National Assembly for Wales, (gb) in relation to information held by any Welsh public authority (other than one referred to in section 83(1)(b)(ii) (subsidiary of the Assembly Commission), the Auditor General for Wales, the Wales Audit Office or the Public Services Ombudsman for Wales), means—

    (i) the public authority, or

    (ii) any officer or employee of the authority authorised by the Welsh Ministers or the Counsel General to the Welsh Assembly Government,

(gc) in relation to information held by a Welsh public authority referred to in section 83(1)(b)(ii), means—

    (i) the public authority, or

    (ii) any officer or employee of the authority authorised by the Presiding Officer of the National Assembly for Wales,

(i) in relation to information held by the National Audit Office or the Comptroller and Auditor General, means the Comptroller and Auditor General,

(j) in relation to information held by the Northern Ireland Audit Office, means the Comptroller and Auditor General for Northern Ireland,

(k) in relation to information held by the Auditor General for Wales or the Wales Audit Office, means the Auditor General for Wales,

(ka) in relation to information held by the Public Services Ombudsman for Wales, means the Public Services Ombudsman for Wales,

(l) in relation to information held by any Northern Ireland public authority other than the Northern Ireland Audit Office, means—

    (i) the public authority, or

    (ii) any officer or employee of the authority authorised by the First Minister and deputy First Minister in Northern Ireland acting jointly,

(m) in relation to information held by the Greater London Authority, means the Mayor of London,

(n) in relation to information held by a functional body within the meaning of the Greater London Authority Act 1999, means the chairman of that functional body, and

(o) in relation to information held by any public authority not falling within any of paragraphs (a) to (n), means—

    (i) a Minister of the Crown,

    (ii) the public authority, if authorised for the purposes of this section by a Minister of the Crown, or

    (iii) any officer or employee of the public authority who is authorised for the purposes of this section by a Minister of the Crown.

37 Communications with Her Majesty, etc. and honours

(1) Information is exempt information if it relates to—

    (a) communications with the Sovereign,

    (aa) communications with the heir to, or the person who is for the time being second in line of succession to, the Throne,

    (ab) communications with a person who has subsequently acceded to the Throne or become heir to, or second in line to, the Throne,

    (ac) communications with other members of the Royal Family (other than communications which fall within any of paragraphs (a) to (ab) because they are made or received on behalf of a person falling within any of those paragraphs), and

    (ad) communications with the Royal Household (other than communications which fall within any of paragraphs (a) to (ac) because they are made or received on behalf of a person falling within any of those paragraphs), or

    (b) the conferring by the Crown of any honour or dignity.

(2) The duty to confirm or deny does not arise in relation to information which is (or if it were held by the public authority would be) exempt information by virtue of subsection (1).

38   Health and safety

(1)   Information is exempt information if its disclosure under this Act would, or would be likely to—

    (a)   endanger the physical or mental health of any individual, or
    (b)   endanger the safety of any individual.

(2)   The duty to confirm or deny does not arise if, or to the extent that, compliance with section 1(1)(a) would, or would be likely to, have either of the effects mentioned in subsection (1).

39   Environmental information

(1)   Information is exempt information if the public authority holding it—

    (a)   is obliged by environmental information regulations to make the information available to the public in accordance with the regulations, or
    (b)   would be so obliged but for any exemption contained in the regulations.

(1A)   In subsection (1) "environmental information regulations" means—

    (a)   regulations made under section 74, or
    (b)   regulations made under section 2(2) of the European Communities Act 1972 for the purpose of implementing any EU obligation relating to public access to, and the dissemination of, information on the environment.

(2)   The duty to confirm or deny does not arise in relation to information which is (or if it were held by the public authority would be) exempt information by virtue of subsection (1).

(3)   Subsection (1)(a) does not limit the generality of section 21(1).

40   Personal information

(1)   Any information to which a request for information relates is exempt information if it constitutes personal data of which the applicant is the data subject.

(2)   Any information to which a request for information relates is also exempt information if—

    (a)   it constitutes personal data which do not fall within subsection (1), and
    (b)   either the first or the second condition below is satisfied.

(3)   The first condition is—

    (a)   in a case where the information falls within any of paragraphs (a) to (d) of the definition of "data" in section 1(1) of the Data Protection Act 1998, that the disclosure of the information to a member of the public otherwise than under this Act would contravene—
        (i)   any of the data protection principles, or
        (ii)   section 10 of that Act (right to prevent processing likely to cause damage or distress), and
    (b)   in any other case, that the disclosure of the information to a member of the public otherwise than under this Act would contravene any of the data protection principles if the exemptions in section 33A(1) of the Data Protection Act 1998 (which relate to manual data held by public authorities) were disregarded.

(4)   The second condition is that by virtue of any provision of Part IV of the Data Protection Act 1998 the information is exempt from section 7(1)(c) of that Act (data subject's right of access to personal data).

(5)   The duty to confirm or deny—

    (a)   does not arise in relation to information which is (or if it were held by the public authority would be) exempt information by virtue of subsection (1), and
    (b)   does not arise in relation to other information if or to the extent that either—
        (i)   the giving to a member of the public of the confirmation or denial that would have to be given to comply with section 1(1)(a) would (apart from this Act) contravene any of the data protection principles or section 10 of the Data Protection Act 1998 or would do so if the exemptions in section 33A(1) of that Act were disregarded, or
        (ii)   by virtue of any provision of Part IV of the Data Protection Act 1998 the information is exempt from section 7(1)(a) of that Act (data subject's right to be informed whether personal data being processed).

(6) In determining for the purposes of this section whether anything done before 24th October 2007 would contravene any of the data protection principles, the exemptions in Part III of Schedule 8 to the Data Protection Act 1998 shall be disregarded.

(7) In this section—

"the data protection principles" means the principles set out in Part I of Schedule 1 to the Data Protection Act 1998, as read subject to Part II of that Schedule and section 27(1) of that Act;

"data subject" has the same meaning as in section 1(1) of that Act;

"personal data" has the same meaning as in section 1(1) of that Act.

41 Information provided in confidence

(1) Information is exempt information if—

    (a) it was obtained by the public authority from any other person (including another public authority), and

    (b) the disclosure of the information to the public (otherwise than under this Act) by the public authority holding it would constitute a breach of confidence actionable by that or any other person.

(2) The duty to confirm or deny does not arise if, or to the extent that, the confirmation or denial that would have to be given to comply with section 1(1)(a) would (apart from this Act) constitute an actionable breach of confidence.

42 Legal professional privilege

(1) Information in respect of which a claim to legal professional privilege or, in Scotland, to confidentiality of communications could be maintained in legal proceedings is exempt information.

(2) The duty to confirm or deny does not arise if, or to the extent that, compliance with section 1(1)(a) would involve the disclosure of any information (whether or not already recorded) in respect of which such a claim could be maintained in legal proceedings.

43 Commercial interests

(1) Information is exempt information if it constitutes a trade secret.

(2) Information is exempt information if its disclosure under this Act would, or would be likely to, prejudice the commercial interests of any person (including the public authority holding it).

(3) The duty to confirm or deny does not arise if, or to the extent that, compliance with section 1(1)(a) would, or would be likely to, prejudice the interests mentioned in subsection (2).

44 Prohibitions on disclosure

(1) Information is exempt information if its disclosure (otherwise than under this Act) by the public authority holding it—

    (a) is prohibited by or under any enactment,

    (b) is incompatible with any EU obligation, or

    (c) would constitute or be punishable as a contempt of court.

(2) The duty to confirm or deny does not arise if the confirmation or denial that would have to be given to comply with section 1(1)(a) would (apart from this Act) fall within any of paragraphs (a) to (c) of subsection (1).

PART III
GENERAL FUNCTIONS OF MINISTER FOR THE CABINET OFFICE, SECRETARY OF STATE AND INFORMATION COMMISSIONER

45 Issue of code of practice by the Minister for the Cabinet Office

(1) The Minister for the Cabinet Office shall issue, and may from time to time revise, a code of practice providing guidance to public authorities as to the practice which it would, in his opinion, be desirable for them to follow in connection with the discharge of the authorities' functions under Part I.

(2) The code of practice must, in particular, include provision relating to—

    (a) the provision of advice and assistance by public authorities to persons who propose to make, or have made, requests for information to them,

(b)   the transfer of requests by one public authority to another public authority by which the information requested is or may be held,

(c)   consultation with persons to whom the information requested relates or persons whose interests are likely to be affected by the disclosure of information,

(d)   the inclusion in contracts entered into by public authorities of terms relating to the disclosure of information, and

(da)   the disclosure by public authorities of datasets held by them,

(e)   the provision by public authorities of procedures for dealing with complaints about the handling by them of requests for information.

(2A) Provision of the kind mentioned in subsection (2)(da) may, in particular, include provision relating to—

(a)   the giving of permission for datasets to be re-used,

(b)   the disclosure of datasets in an electronic form which is capable of re-use,

(c)   the making of datasets available for re-use in accordance with the terms of a licence,

(d)   other matters relating to the making of datasets available for re-use,

(e)   standards applicable to public authorities in connection with the disclosure of datasets.

(3)   Any code under this section may make different provision for different public authorities.

(4)   Before issuing or revising any code under this section, the Minister for the Cabinet Office shall consult the Commissioner.

(5)   The Secretary of State shall lay before each House of Parliament any code or revised code made under this section.

47   General functions of Commissioner

(1)   It shall be the duty of the Commissioner to promote the following of good practice by public authorities and, in particular, so to perform his functions under this Act as to promote the observance by public authorities of—

(a)   the requirements of this Act, and

(b)   the provisions of the codes of practice under sections 45 and 46.

(2)   The Commissioner shall arrange for the dissemination in such form and manner as he considers appropriate of such information as it may appear to him expedient to give to the public—

(a)   about the operation of this Act,

(b)   about good practice, and

(c)   about other matters within the scope of his functions under this Act, and may give advice to any person as to any of those matters.

(3)   The Commissioner may, with the consent of any public authority, assess whether that authority is following good practice.

49   Reports to be laid before Parliament

(1)   The Commissioner shall lay annually before each House of Parliament a general report on the exercise of his functions under this Act.

(2)   The Commissioner may from time to time lay before each House of Parliament such other reports with respect to those functions as he thinks fit.

PART IV
ENFORCEMENT

50   Application for decision by Commissioner

(1)   Any person (in this section referred to as "the complainant") may apply to the Commissioner for a decision whether, in any specified respect, a request for information made by the complainant to a public authority has been dealt with in accordance with the requirements of Part I.

(2)   On receiving an application under this section, the Commissioner shall make a decision unless it appears to him—

(a)   that the complainant has not exhausted any complaints procedure which is provided by the public authority in conformity with the code of practice under section 45,

(b)   that there has been undue delay in making the application,

(c)   that the application is frivolous or vexatious, or

(d)   that the application has been withdrawn or abandoned.

(3)   Where the Commissioner has received an application under this section, he shall either—

(a)   notify the complainant that he has not made any decision under this section as a result of the application and of his grounds for not doing so, or

(b)   serve notice of his decision (in this Act referred to as a "decision notice") on the complainant and the public authority.

(4)   Where the Commissioner decides that a public authority—

(a)   has failed to communicate information, or to provide confirmation or denial, in a case where it is required to do so by section 1(1), or

(b)   has failed to comply with any of the requirements of sections 11 and 17, the decision notice must specify the steps which must be taken by the authority for complying with that requirement and the period within which they must be taken.

(5)   A decision notice must contain particulars of the right of appeal conferred by section 57.

PART IV
ENFORCEMENT

53.   Exception from duty to comply with decision notice or enforcement notice

(1)   This section applies to a decision notice or enforcement notice which—

(a)   is served on—

(i)   a government department,

(ii)   the Welsh Government, or

(iii)   any public authority designated for the purposes of this section by an order made by the Minister for the Cabinet Office, and

(b)   relates to a failure, in respect of one or more requests for information—

(i)   to comply with section 1(1)(a) in respect of information which falls within any provision of Part II stating that the duty to confirm or deny does not arise, or

(ii)   to comply with section 1(1)(b) in respect of exempt information.

(2)   A decision notice or enforcement notice to which this section applies shall cease to have effect if, not later than the twentieth working day following the effective date, the accountable person in relation to that authority gives the Commissioner a certificate signed by him stating that he has on reasonable grounds formed the opinion that, in respect of the request or requests concerned, there was no failure falling within subsection (1)(b).

(3)   Where the accountable person gives a certificate to the Commissioner under subsection (2) he shall as soon as practicable thereafter lay a copy of the certificate before—

(a)   each House of Parliament,

(b)   the Northern Ireland Assembly, in any case where the certificate relates to a decision notice or enforcement notice which has been served on a Northern Ireland department or any Northern Ireland public authority, or

(c)   the National Assembly for Wales, in any case where the certificate relates to a decision notice or enforcement notice which has been served on—

(i)   the Welsh Government,

(ii)   the National Assembly for Wales, or

(iii)   any Welsh public authority.

(4)   In subsection (2) "the effective date", in relation to a decision notice or enforcement notice, means—

(a)   the day on which the notice was given to the public authority, or

(b)   where an appeal under section 57 is brought, the day on which that appeal (or any further appeal arising out of it) is determined or withdrawn.

(5)   Before making an order under subsection (1)(a)(iii), the Minister for the Cabinet Office shall—

(a)   if the order relates to a Welsh public authority, consult the Welsh Ministers,

(aa)   if the order relates to the National Assembly for Wales, consult the Presiding Officer of that Assembly,

(b)   if the order relates to the Northern Ireland Assembly, consult the Presiding Officer of that Assembly, and

(c)   if the order relates to a Northern Ireland public authority, consult the First Minister and deputy First Minister in Northern Ireland.

(6)   Where the accountable person gives a certificate to the Commissioner under subsection (2) in relation to a decision notice, the accountable person shall, on doing so or as soon as reasonably practicable after doing so, inform the person who is the complainant for the purposes of section 50 of the reasons for his opinion.

(7)   The accountable person is not obliged to provide information under subsection (6) if, or to the extent that, compliance with that subsection would involve the disclosure of exempt information.

(8)   In this section "the accountable person"—

(a)   in relation to a Northern Ireland department or any Northern Ireland public authority, means the First Minister and deputy First Minister in Northern Ireland acting jointly,

(b)   in relation the Welsh Government, the National Assembly for Wales or any Welsh public authority, means the First Minister for Wales, and

(c)   in relation to any other public authority, means—

(i)   a Minister of the Crown who is a member of the Cabinet, or

(ii)   the Attorney General, the Advocate General for Scotland or the Attorney General for Northern Ireland.

(9)   In this section "working day" has the same meaning as in section 10.

TERRORISM ACT 2000
(2000, c. 11)

An Act to make provision about terrorism; and to make temporary provision for Northern Ireland about the prosecution and punishment of certain offences, the preservation of peace and the maintenance of order.   [20 July 2000]

PART I
INTRODUCTORY

1   Terrorism: interpretation

(1)   In this Act "terrorism" means the use or threat of action where—

(a)   the action falls within subsection (2),

(b)   the use or threat is designed to influence the government or an international governmental organisation or to intimidate the public or a section of the public, and

(c)   the use or threat is made for the purpose of advancing a political, religious, racial or ideological cause.

(2)   Action falls within this subsection if it—

(a)   involves serious violence against a person,

(b)   involves serious damage to property,

(c)   endangers a person's life, other than that of the person committing the action,

(d)   creates a serious risk to the health or safety of the public or a section of the public, or

(e)   is designed seriously to interfere with or seriously to disrupt an electronic system.

(3)   The use or threat of action falling within subsection (2) which involves the use of firearms or explosives is terrorism whether or not subsection (1)(b) is satisfied.

(4)   In this section—

    (a)   "action" includes action outside the United Kingdom,

    (b)   a reference to any person or to property is a reference to any person, or to property, wherever situated,

    (c)   a reference to the public includes a reference to the public of a country other than the United Kingdom, and

    (d)   "the government" means the government of the United Kingdom, of a Part of the United Kingdom or of a country other than the United Kingdom.

(5)   In this Act a reference to action taken for the purposes of terrorism includes a reference to action taken for the benefit of a proscribed organisation.

PART II
PROSCRIBED ORGANISATIONS

Procedure

3   Proscription

(1)   For the purposes of this Act an organisation is proscribed if—

    (a)   it is listed in Schedule 2, or

    (b)   it operates under the same name as an organisation listed in that Schedule.

(2)   Subsection (1)(b) shall not apply in relation to an organisation listed in Schedule 2 if its entry is the subject of a note in that Schedule.

(3)   The Secretary of State may by order—

    (a)   add an organisation to Schedule 2;

    (b)   remove an organisation from that Schedule;

    (c)   amend that Schedule in some other way.

(4)   The Secretary of State may exercise his power under subsection (3)(a) in respect of an organisation only if he believes that it is concerned in terrorism.

(5)   For the purposes of subsection (4) an organisation is concerned in terrorism if it—

    (a)   commits or participates in acts of terrorism,

    (b)   prepares for terrorism,

    (c)   promotes or encourages terrorism, or

    (d)   is otherwise concerned in terrorism.

(5A)   The cases in which an organisation promotes or encourages terrorism for the purposes of subsection (5)(c) include any case in which activities of the organisation—

    (a)   include the unlawful glorification of the commission or preparation (whether in the past, in the future or generally) of acts of terrorism; or

    (b)   are carried out in a manner that ensures that the organisation is associated with statements containing any such glorification.

(5B)   The glorification of any conduct is unlawful for the purposes of subsection (5A) if there are persons who may become aware of it who could reasonably be expected to infer that what is being glorified, is being glorified as—

    (a)   conduct that should be emulated in existing circumstances, or

    (b)   conduct that is illustrative of a type of conduct that should be so emulated.

(5C)   In this section—

'glorification' includes any form of praise or celebration, and cognate expressions are to be construed accordingly;

'statement' includes a communication without words consisting of sounds or images or both.

(6)   Where the Secretary of State believes—

    (a)   that an organisation listed in Schedule 2 is operating wholly or partly under a name that is not specified in that Schedule (whether as well as or instead of under the specified name), or

    (b)   that an organisation that is operating under a name that is not so specified is otherwise for all practical purposes the same as an organisation so listed, he may, by order, provide that the name that is not specified in that Schedule is to be treated as another name for the listed organisation.

(7) Where an order under subsection (6) provides for a name to be treated as another name for an organisation, this Act shall have effect in relation to acts occurring while—

(a) the order is in force, and

(b) the organisation continues to be listed in Schedule 2,

as if the organisation were listed in that Schedule under the other name, as well as under the name specified in the Schedule.

(8) The Secretary of State may at any time by order revoke an order under subsection (6) or otherwise provide for a name specified in such an order to cease to be treated as a name for a particular organisation.

(9) Nothing in subsections (6) to (8) prevents any liability from being established in any proceedings by proof that an organisation is the same as an organisation listed in Schedule 2, even though it is or was operating under a name specified neither in Schedule 2 nor in an order under subsection (6).

4　Deproscription: application

(1) An application may be made to the Secretary of State for an order under section 3(3) or (8)—

(a) removing an organisation from Schedule 2, or

(b) providing for a name to cease to be treated as a name for an organisation listed in that Schedule.

(2) An application may be made by—

(a) the organisation, or

(b) any person affected by the organisation's proscription or by the treatment of the name as a name for the organisation.

(3) The Secretary of State shall make regulations prescribing the procedure for applications under this section.

(4) The regulations shall, in particular—

(a) require the Secretary of State to determine an application within a specified period of time, and

(b) require an application to state the grounds on which it is made.

5　Deproscription: appeal

(1) There shall be a commission, to be known as the Proscribed Organisations Appeal Commission.

(2) Where an application under section 4 has been refused, the applicant may appeal to the Commission.

(3) The Commission shall allow an appeal against a refusal to deproscribe an organisation or to provide for a name to cease to be treated as a name for an organisation if it considers that the decision to refuse was flawed when considered in the light of the principles applicable on an application for judicial review.

(4) Where the Commission allows an appeal under this section, it may make an order under this subsection.

(5) Where an order is made under subsection (4) in respect of an appeal against a refusal to deproscribe an organisation the Secretary of State shall as soon as is reasonably practicable—

(a) lay before Parliament, in accordance with section 123(4), the draft of an order under section 3(3)(b) removing the organisation from the list in Schedule 2, or

(b) make an order removing the organisation from the list in Schedule 2 in pursuance of section 123(5).

(5A) Where an order is made under subsection (4) in respect of an appeal against a refusal to provide for a name to cease to be treated as a name for an organisation, the Secretary of State shall, as soon as is reasonably practicable, make an order under section 3(8) providing that the name in question is to cease to be so treated in relation to that organisation.

(6) Schedule 3 (constitution of the Commission and procedure) shall have effect.

6   Further appeal

(1)   A party to an appeal under section 5 which the, Proscribed Organisations Appeal Commission has determined may bring a further appeal on a question of law to—

   (a)   the Court of Appeal, if the first appeal was heard in England and Wales,

   (b)   the Court of Session, if the first appeal was heard in Scotland, or

   (c)   the Court of Appeal in Northern Ireland, if the first appeal was heard in Northern Ireland.

(2)   An appeal under subsection (1) may be brought only with the permission—

   (a)   of the Commission, or

   (b)   where the Commission refuses permission, of the court to which the appeal would be brought.

(3)   An order under section 5(4) shall not require the Secretary of State to take any action until the final determination or disposal of an appeal under this section (including any appeal to the Supreme Court).

Offences

11   Membership

(1)   A person commits an offence if he belongs or professes to belong to a proscribed organisation.

(2)   It is a defence for a person charged with an offence under subsection (1) to prove—

   (a)   that the organisation was not proscribed on the last (or only) occasion on which he became a member or began to profess to be a member, and

   (b)   that he has not taken part in the activities of the organisation at any time while it was proscribed.

(3)   A person guilty of an offence under this section shall be liable—

   (a)   on conviction on indictment, to imprisonment for a term not exceeding ten years, to a fine or to both, or

   (b)   on summary conviction, to imprisonment for a term not exceeding six months, to a fine not exceeding the statutory maximum or to both.

12   Support

(1)   A person commits an offence if—

   (a)   he invites support for a proscribed organisation, and

   (b)   the support is not, or is not restricted to, the provision of money or other property (within the meaning of section 15).

(2)   A person commits an offence if he arranges, manages or assists in arranging or managing a meeting which he knows is—

   (a)   to support a proscribed organisation,

   (b)   to further the activities of a proscribed organisation, or

   (c)   to be addressed by a person who belongs or professes to belong to a proscribed organisation.

(3)   A person commits an offence if he addresses a meeting and the purpose of his address is to encourage support for a proscribed organisation or to further its activities.

(4)   Where a person is charged with an offence under subsection (2)(c) in respect of a private meeting it is a defence for him to prove that he had no reasonable cause to believe that the address mentioned in subsection (2)(c) would support a proscribed organisation or further its activities.

(5)   In subsections (2) to (4)—

   (a)   "meeting" means a meeting of three or more persons, whether or not the public are admitted, and

   (b)   a meeting is private if the public are not admitted.

(6)   A person guilty of an offence under this section shall be liable—

   (a)   on conviction on indictment, to imprisonment for a term not exceeding ten years, to a fine or to both, or

   (b)   on summary conviction, to imprisonment for a term not exceeding six months, to a fine not exceeding the statutory maximum or to both.

13   Uniform

(1)   A person in a public place commits an offence if he—

     (a)   wears an item of clothing, or

     (b)   wears, carries or displays an article,

in such a way or in such circumstances as to arouse reasonable suspicion that he is a member or supporter of a proscribed organisation.

(2)   A constable in Scotland may arrest a person without a warrant if he has reasonable grounds to suspect that the person is guilty of an offence under this section.

(3)   A person guilty of an offence under this section shall be liable on summary conviction to—

     (a)   imprisonment for a term not exceeding six months,

     (b)   a fine not exceeding level 5 on the standard scale, or

     (c)   both.

PART III
TERRORIST PROPERTY

Offences

15   Fund-raising

(1)   A person commits an offence if he—

     (a)   invites another to provide money or other property, and

     (b)   intends that it should be used, or has reasonable cause to suspect that it may be used, for the purposes of terrorism.

(2)   A person commits an offence if he—

     (a)   receives money or other property, and

     (b)   intends that it should be used, or has reasonable cause to suspect that it may be used, for the purposes of terrorism.

(3)   A person commits an offence if he—

     (a)   provides money or other property, and

     (b)   knows or has reasonable cause to suspect that it will or may be used for the purposes of terrorism.

(4)   In this section a reference to the provision of money or other property is a reference to its being given, lent or otherwise made available, whether or not for consideration.

19   Disclosure of information: duty

(1)   This section applies where a person—

     (a)   believes or suspects that another person has committed an offence under any of sections 15 to 18, and

     (b)   bases his belief or suspicion on information which comes to his attention—

         (i)   in the course of a trade, profession or business, or

         (ii)   in the course of his employment (whether or not in the course of a trade, profession or business).

(1A)   But this section does not apply if the information came to the person in the course of a business in the regulated sector.

(2)   The person commits an offence if he does not disclose to a constable as soon as is reasonably practicable—

     (a)   his belief or suspicion, and

     (b)   the information on which it is based.

(3)   It is a defence for a person charged with an offence under subsection (2) to prove that he had a reasonable excuse for not making the disclosure.

(4)   Where—

     (a)   a person is in employment,

     (b)   his employer has established a procedure for the making of disclosures of the matters specified in subsection (2), and

     (c)   he is charged with an offence under that subsection,

it is a defence for him to prove that he disclosed the matters specified in that subsection in accordance with the procedure.

(5)   Subsection (2) does not require disclosure by a professional legal adviser of—

     (a)   information which he obtains in privileged circumstances, or

     (b)   a belief or suspicion based on information which he obtains in privileged circumstances.

(6)   For the purpose of subsection (5) information is obtained by an adviser in privileged circumstances if it comes to him, otherwise than with a view to furthering a criminal purpose—
(a)   from a client or a client's representative, in connection with the provision of legal advice by the adviser to the client,
(b)   from a person seeking legal advice from the adviser, or from the person's representative, or
(c)   from any person, for the purpose of actual or contemplated legal proceedings.

22   Penalties

A person guilty of an offence under any of sections 15 to 18 shall be liable—
(a)   on conviction on indictment, to imprisonment for a term not exceeding 14 years, to a fine or to both, or
(b)   on summary conviction, to imprisonment for a term not exceeding six months, to a fine not exceeding the statutory maximum or to both.

Forfeiture

23   Forfeiture: terrorist property offences

(1)   The court by or before which a person is convicted of an offence under any of sections 15 to 18 may make a forfeiture order in accordance with the provisions of this section.

PART V
COUNTER-TERRORIST POWERS

Suspected terrorists

40   Terrorist: interpretation

(1)   In this Part "terrorist" means a person who—
(a)   has committed an offence under any of sections 11, 12, 15 to 18, 54 and 56 to 63, or
(b)   is or has been concerned in the commission, preparation or instigation of acts of terrorism.
(2)   The reference in subsection (1)(b) to a person who has been concerned in the commission, preparation or instigation of acts of terrorism includes a reference to a person who has been, whether before or after the passing of this Act, concerned in the commission, preparation or instigation of acts of terrorism within the meaning given by section 1.

41   Arrest without warrant

(1)   A constable may arrest without a warrant a person whom he reasonably suspects to be a terrorist.
(2)   Where a person is arrested under this section the provisions of Schedule 8 (detention: treatment, review and extension) shall apply.
(3)   Subject to subsections (4) to (7), a person detained under this section shall (unless detained under any other power) be released not later than the end of the period of 48 hours beginning—
(a)   with the time of his arrest under this section, or
(b)   if he was being detained under Schedule 7 when he was arrested under this section, with the time when his examination under that Schedule began.
(4)   If on a review of a person's detention under Part II of Schedule 8 the review officer does not authorise continued detention, the person shall (unless detained in accordance with subsection (5) or (6) or under any other power) be released.
(5)   Where a police officer intends to make an application for a warrant under paragraph 29 of Schedule 8 extending a person's detention, the person may be detained pending the making of the application.
(6)   Where an application has been made under paragraph 29 or 36 of Schedule 8 in respect of a person's detention, he may be detained pending the conclusion of proceedings on the application.
(7)   Where an application under paragraph 29 or 36 of Schedule 8 is granted in respect of a person's detention, he may be detained, subject to paragraph 37 of that Schedule, during the period specified in the warrant.

(8)   The refusal of an application in respect of a person's detention under paragraph 29 or 36 of Schedule 8 shall not prevent his continued detention in accordance with this section.

(9)   A person who has the powers of a constable in one Part of the United Kingdom may exercise the power under subsection (1) in any Part of the United Kingdom.

42   Search of premises

(1)   A justice of the peace may on the application of a constable issue a warrant in relation to specified premises if he is satisfied that there are reasonable grounds for suspecting that a person whom the constable reasonably suspects to be a person falling within section 40(1)(b) is to be found there.

(2)   A warrant under this section shall authorise any constable to enter and search the specified premises for the purpose of arresting the person referred to in subsection (1) under section 41.

(3)   In the application of subsection (1) to Scotland—
(a)   "justice of the peace" includes the sheriff, and
(b)   the justice of the peace or sheriff can be satisfied as mentioned in that subsection only by having heard evidence on oath.

43   Search of persons

(1)   A constable may stop and search a person whom he reasonably suspects to be a terrorist to discover whether he has in his possession anything which may constitute evidence that he is a terrorist.

(2)   A constable may search a person arrested under section 41 to discover whether he has in his possession anything which may constitute evidence that he is a terrorist.

(4)   A constable may seize and retain anything which he discovers in the course of a search of a person under subsection (1) or (2) and which he reasonably suspects may constitute evidence that the person is a terrorist.

(4A) Subsection (4B) applies if a constable, in exercising the power under subsection (1) to stop a person whom the constable reasonably suspects to be a terrorist, stops a vehicle (see section 116(2)).

(4B) The constable—
(a)   may search the vehicle and anything in or on it to discover whether there is anything which may constitute evidence that the person concerned is a terrorist, and
(b)   may seize and retain anything which the constable—
(i)   discovers in the course of such a search, and
(ii)   reasonably suspects may constitute evidence that the person is a terrorist.

(4C) Nothing in subsection (4B) confers a power to search any person but the power to search in that subsection is in addition to the power in subsection (1) to search a person whom the constable reasonably suspects to be a terrorist.

(5)   A person who has the powers of a constable in one Part of the United Kingdom may exercise a power under this section in any Part of the United Kingdom.

43A   Search of vehicles

(1)   Subsection (2) applies if a constable reasonably suspects that a vehicle is being used for the purposes of terrorism.

(2)   The constable may stop and search—
(a)   the vehicle;
(b)   the driver of the vehicle;
(c)   a passenger in the vehicle;
(d)   anything in or on the vehicle or carried by the driver or a passenger;
to discover whether there is anything which may constitute evidence that the vehicle is being used for the purposes of terrorism.

(3)   A constable may seize and retain anything which the constable—
(a)   discovers in the course of a search under this section, and
(b)   reasonably suspects may constitute evidence that the vehicle is being used for the purposes of terrorism.

(4)   A person who has the powers of a constable in one Part of the United Kingdom may exercise a power under this section in any Part of the United Kingdom.

(5)   In this section "driver", in relation to an aircraft, hovercraft or vessel, means the captain, pilot or other person with control of the aircraft, hovercraft or vessel or any member of its crew and, in relation to a train, includes any member of its crew.

Powers to stop and search in specified locations

47A   Searches in specified areas or places

(1)   A senior police officer may give an authorisation under subsection (2) or (3) in relation to a specified area or place if the officer—
   (a)   reasonably suspects that an act of terrorism will take place; and
   (b)   reasonably considers that—
      (i)   the authorisation is necessary to prevent such an act;
      (ii)   the specified area or place is no greater than is necessary to prevent such an act; and
      (iii)   the duration of the authorisation is no longer than is necessary to prevent such an act.

(2)   An authorisation under this subsection authorises any constable in uniform to stop a vehicle in the specified area or place and to search—
   (a)   the vehicle;
   (b)   the driver of the vehicle;
   (c)   a passenger in the vehicle;
   (d)   anything in or on the vehicle or carried by the driver or a passenger.

(3)   An authorisation under this subsection authorises any constable in uniform to stop a pedestrian in the specified area or place and to search—
   (a)   the pedestrian;
   (b)   anything carried by the pedestrian.

(4)   A constable in uniform may exercise the power conferred by an authorisation under subsection (2) or (3) only for the purpose of discovering whether there is anything which may constitute evidence that the vehicle concerned is being used for the purposes of terrorism or (as the case may be) that the person concerned is a person falling within section 40(1)(b).

(5)   But the power conferred by such an authorisation may be exercised whether or not the constable reasonably suspects that there is such evidence.

(6)   A constable may seize and retain anything which the constable—
   (a)   discovers in the course of a search under such an authorisation; and
   (b)   reasonably suspects may constitute evidence that the vehicle concerned is being used for the purposes of terrorism or (as the case may be) that the person concerned is a person falling within section 40(1)(b).

(7)   Schedule 6B (which makes supplementary provision about authorisations under this section) has effect.

(8)   In this section—
   "driver" has the meaning given by section 43A(5);
   "senior police officer" has the same meaning as in Schedule 6B (see paragraph 14(1) and (2) of that Schedule);
   "specified" means specified in an authorisation.

Code of practice relating to sections 43, 43A and 47A

47AA   Code of practice relating to sections 43, 43A and 47A

(1)   The Secretary of State must prepare a code of practice containing guidance about—
   (a)   the exercise of the powers conferred by sections 43 and 43A,
   (b)   the exercise of the powers to give an authorisation under section 47A(2) or (3),
   (c)   the exercise of the powers conferred by such an authorisation and section 47A(6), and
   (d)   such other matters in connection with the exercise of any of the powers mentioned in paragraphs (a) to (c) as the Secretary of State considers appropriate.

(2)   Such a code may make different provision for different purposes.

(3)   In the course of preparing such a code, the Secretary of State must consult the Lord Advocate and such other persons as the Secretary of State considers appropriate.

47AE Effect of code

   (1)   A constable must have regard to the search powers code when exercising any powers to which the code relates.

   (2)   A failure on the part of a constable to act in accordance with any provision of the search powers code does not of itself make that person liable to criminal or civil proceedings.

   (3)   The search powers code is admissible in evidence in any such proceedings.

   (4)   A court or tribunal may, in particular, take into account a failure by a constable to have regard to the search powers code in determining a question in any such proceedings.

   (5)   The references in this section to a constable include, in relation to any functions exercisable by a person by virtue of paragraph 16 of Schedule 2A to the Police (Northern Ireland) Act 2003 (search powers in specified areas or places for community support officers), references to that person.

   (6)   In this section "the search powers code" means the code of practice issued under section 47AB (2) (as altered or replaced from time to time).

Inciting terrorism overseas

59 England and Wales

   (1)   A person commits an offence if—

      (a)   he incites another person to commit an act of terrorism wholly or partly outside the United Kingdom, and

      (b)   the act would, if committed in England and Wales, constitute one of the offences listed in subsection (2).

   (2)   Those offences are—

      (a)   murder,

      (b)   an offence under section 18 of the Offences against the Person Act 1861 (wounding with intent),

      (c)   an offence under section 23 or 24 of that Act (poison),

      (d)   an offence under section 28 or 29 of that Act (explosions), and

      (e)   an offence under section 1(2) of the Criminal Damage Act 1971 (endangering life by damaging property).

   (3)   A person guilty of an offence under this section shall be liable to any penalty to which he would be liable on conviction of the offence listed in subsection (2) which corresponds to the act which he incites.

   (4)   For the purposes of subsection (1) it is immaterial whether or not the person incited is in the United Kingdom at the time of the incitement.

   (5)   Nothing in this section imposes criminal liability on any person acting on behalf of, or holding office under, the Crown.

Terrorist bombing and finance offences

62 Terrorist bombing: jurisdiction

   (1)   If—

      (a)   a person does anything outside the United Kingdom as an act of terrorism or for the purposes of terrorism, and

      (b)   his action would have constituted the commission of one of the offences listed in subsection (2) if it had been done in the United Kingdom,

    he shall be guilty of the offence.

   (2)   The offences referred to in subsection (1)(b) are—

      (a)   an offence under section 2, 3 or 5 of the Explosive Substances Act 1883 (causing explosions, &c.),

      (b)   an offence under section 1 of the Biological Weapons Act 1974 (biological weapons), and

      (c)   an offence under section 2 of the Chemical Weapons Act 1996 (chemical weapons).

PART VIII
GENERAL

114 Police powers

(1) A power conferred by virtue of this Act on a constable—
  (a) is additional to powers which he has at common law or by virtue of any other enactment, and
  (b) shall not be taken to affect those powers.

(2) A constable may if necessary use reasonable force for the purpose of exercising a power conferred on him by virtue of this Act (apart from paragraphs 2 and 3 of Schedule 7).

(3) Where anything is seized by a constable under a power conferred by virtue of this Act, it may (unless the contrary intention appears) be retained for so long as is necessary in all the circumstances.

116 Powers to stop and search

(1) A power to search premises conferred by virtue of this Act shall be taken to include power to search a container.

(2) A power conferred by virtue of this Act to stop a person includes power to stop a vehicle (other than an aircraft which is airborne).

(3) A person commits an offence if he fails to stop a vehicle when required to do so by virtue of this section.

(4) A person guilty of an offence under subsection (3) shall be liable on summary conviction to—
  (a) imprisonment for a term not exceeding six months,
  (b) a fine not exceeding level 5 on the standard scale, or
  (c) both.

SCHEDULE 2
PROSCRIBED ORGANISATIONS

The Irish Republican Army.
Cumann na mBan.
Fianna na hEireann.
The Red Hand Commando.
Saor Eire.
The Ulster Freedom Fighters.
The Ulster Volunteer Force.
The Irish National Liberation Army.
The Irish People's Liberation Organisation.
The Ulster Defence Association.
The Loyalist Volunteer Force.
The Continuity Army Council.
The Orange Volunteers.
The Red Hand Defenders.
Al-Qa'ida
Egyptian Islamic Jihad
Al-Gama'at al-Islamiya
Armed Islamic Group (Groupe Islamique Armée) (GIA)
Salafist Group for Call and Combat (Groupe Salafiste pour la Prédication et le Combat) (GSPC)
Babbar Khalsa
Harakat Mujahideen
Jaish e Mohammed
Lashkar e Tayyaba
Liberation Tigers of Tamil Eelam (LTTE)
The military wing of Hizballah, including the Jihad Council and all units reporting to it (including the Hizballah External Security Organisation)
Hamas-Izz al-Din al-Qassem Brigades
Palestinian Islamic Jihad—Shaqaqi

Abu Nidal Organisation
Islamic Army of Aden
Kurdistan Workers' Party (Partiya Karkeren Kurdistan) (PKK)
Revolutionary Peoples' Liberation Party—Front (Devrimci Halk Kurtulus Partisi-Cephesi) (DHKP-C)
Basque Homeland and Liberty (Euskadi ta Askatasuna) (ETA)
17 November Revolutionary Organisation (N17)
Abu Sayyaf Group
Asbat Al-Ansar
Islamic Movement of Uzbekistan
Jemaah Islamiyah
Al Ittihad Al Islamia
Ansar al Islam
Ansar al Sunna
Groupe Islamique Combattant Marocain
Harakat-ul-Jihad-ul-Islami
Harakat-ul-Jihad-ul-Islami (Bangladesh)
Harakat-ul-Mujahideen/Alami
Hezb-e Islami Gulbuddin
Islamic Jihad Union
Jamaat ul-Furquan
Jundallah
Khuddam ul-Islam
Lashkar-e Jhangvi
Libyan Islamic Fighting Group
Sipah-e Sahaba Pakistan
Al-Ghurabaa
The Saved Sect
Baluchistan Liberation Army
Teyrebaz Azadiye Kurdistan
Jammat-ul Mujahadeen Bangladesh
Tehrik Nefaz-e-Shariat Muhammadi
Al Shabaab
Tehrik-e Taliban Pakistan
Indian Mujahideen
Ansarul Muslimina Fi Biladis Sudan (Vanguard for the protection of Muslims in Black Africa) (Ansaru)
Jama'atu Ahli Sunna Lidda Awati Wal Jihad (Boko Haram)
Minbar Ansar Deen (Ansar Al Sharia UK)
Imarat Kavkaz (Caucasus Emirate)
Ansar Bayt al-Maqdis (Ansar Jerusalem)
Al Murabitun
Ansar al Sharia – Tunisia
Islamic State of Iraq and the Levant (Islamic State of Iraq and al-Sham) (Dawat al Islamiya fi Iraq wa al Sham (DAISh))
Turkiye Halk Kurtulus Partisi-Cephesi (Turkish People's Liberation Party) (The Hasty Ones) (Mukavamet Suriye)
Kateeba al-Kawthar (Ajnad al-sham) (Junud ar-Rahman al Muhajireen)
Abdallah Azzam Brigades, including the Ziyad al-Jarrah Battalions
Popular Front for the Liberation of Palestine—General Command
Ansar al-Sharia-Benghazi (Partisans of Islamic Law)
Ajnad Misr (Soldiers of Egypt)
Jaysh al Khalifatu Islamiya (Army of the Islamic Caliphate) (Majahideen of the Caucasus and the Levant)
Jund Al-Aqsa (Soldiers of Al-Aqsa)
Jund al Khalifa-Algeria (Soldiers of the Caliphate in Algeria)
Jamaat ul-Ahrar
The Haqqani Network
Global Islamic Media Front (including GIMF Bangla Team (Ansarullah Bangla Team) (Ansar-al Islam))
Mujahedeen Indonesia Timur (East Indonesia Mujahedeen)

Turkestan Islamic Party (East Turkestan Islamic Party) (East Turkestan Islamic Movement) (East Turkestan Jihadist Movement) (Hizb al-Islami al-Turkistani)
Jamaah Anshorut Daulah
National Action

SCHEDULE 3
THE PROSCRIBED ORGANISATIONS APPEAL COMMISSION

Constitution and administration

1. (1) The Commission shall consist of members appointed by the Lord Chancellor.
    (2) The Lord Chancellor shall appoint one of the members as chairman.
    (3) A member shall hold and vacate office in accordance with terms of his appointment.
    (4) A member may resign at any time by notice in writing to the Lord Chancellor.

Procedure

4. (1) The Commission shall sit at such times and in such places as the Lord Chancellor may direct after consulting the following—
        (a) the Lord Chief Justice of England and Wales;
        (b) the Lord President of the Court of Session;
        (c) the Lord Chief Justice of Northern Ireland.
    (2) The Commission may sit in two or more divisions.
    (3) At each sitting of the Commission—
        (a) three members shall attend,
        (b) one of the members shall be a person who holds or has held high judicial office (within the meaning of Part 3 of the Constitutional Reform Act 2005) or is or has been a member of the Judicial Committee of the Privy Council, and
        (c) the chairman or another member nominated by him shall preside and report the Commission's decision.
5. (1) The Lord Chancellor may make rules—
        (a) regulating the exercise of the right of appeal to the Commission;
        (b) prescribing practice and procedure to be followed in relation to proceedings before the Commission;
        (c) providing for proceedings before the Commission to be determined without an oral hearing in specified circumstances;
        (d) making provision about evidence in proceedings before the Commission (including provision about the burden of proof and admissibility of evidence);
        (e) making provision about proof of the Commission's decisions.
    (2) In making the rules the Lord Chancellor shall, in particular, have regard to the need to secure—
        (a) that decisions which are the subject of appeals are properly reviewed, and
        (b) that information is not disclosed contrary to the public interest.

SCHEDULE 6
FINANCIAL INFORMATION

Orders

1. (1) Where an order has been made under this paragraph in relation to a terrorist investigation, a constable named in the order may require a financial institution to which the order applies to provide customer information for the purposes of the investigation.
    (1A) The order may provide that it applies to—
        (a) all financial institutions,
        (b) a particular description, or particular descriptions, of financial institutions, or
        (c) a particular financial institution or particular financial institutions.
    (2) The information shall be provided—
        (a) in such manner and within such time as the constable may specify, and
        (b) notwithstanding any restriction on the disclosure of information imposed by statute or otherwise.

(3)   An institution which fails to comply with a requirement under this paragraph shall be guilty of an offence.

(4)   It is a defence for an institution charged with an offence under sub-paragraph (3) to prove—

   (a)   that the information required was not in the institution's possession, or

   (b)   that it was not reasonably practicable for the institution to comply with the requirement.

(5)   An institution guilty of an offence under sub-paragraph (3) shall be liable on summary conviction to a fine not exceeding level 5 on the standard scale.

Procedure

2.   An order under paragraph 1 may be made only on the application of—

   (a)   in England and Wales or Northern Ireland, a police officer of at least the rank of superintendent, or

   (b)   in Scotland, the procurator fiscal.

3.   An order under paragraph 1 may be made only by—

   (a)   in England and Wales, a Circuit judge, or a District Judge (Magistrates' Courts),

   (b)   in Scotland, the sheriff, or

   (c)   in Northern Ireland, a Crown Court judge.

4.   (1)   Criminal Procedure Rules may make provision about the procedure for an application under paragraph 1.

   (2)   The High Court of Justiciary may, by Act of Adjournal, make provision about the procedure for an application under paragraph 1.

   (3)   Crown Court rules may make provision about the procedure for an application under paragraph 1.

Criteria for making order

5.   An order under paragraph 1 may be made only if the person making it is satisfied that—

   (a)   the order is sought for the purposes of a terrorist investigation,

   (b)   the tracing of terrorist property is desirable for the purposes of the investigation, and

   (c)   the order will enhance the effectiveness of the investigation.

SCHEDULE 8
DETENTION

Extensions of warrants

36.   (1)   Each of the following—

   (a)   in England and Wales, a Crown Prosecutor,

   (b)   in Scotland, the Lord Advocate or a procurator fiscal,

   (c)   in Northern Ireland, the Director of Public Prosecutions for Northern Ireland,

   (d)   in any part of the United Kingdom, a police officer of at least the rank of superintendent,

   may apply for the extension or further extension of the period specified in a warrant of further detention.

(1A) The person to whom an application under sub-paragraph (1) may be made is a judicial authority.

(2)   Where the period specified is extended, the warrant shall be endorsed with a note stating the new specified period.

(3)   Subject to sub-paragraph (3AA), the period by which the specified period is extended or further extended shall be the period which—

   (a)   begins with the time specified in sub-paragraph (3A); and

   (b)   ends with whichever is the earlier of—

      (i)   the end of the period of seven days beginning with that time; and

      (ii)   the end of the period of 14 days beginning with the relevant time.

(3A) The time referred to in sub-paragraph (3)(a) is—

   (a)   in the case of a warrant specifying a period which has not previously been extended under this paragraph, the end of the period specified in the warrant, and

(b)   in any other case, the end of the period for which the period specified in the warrant was last extended under this paragraph.

(3AA) A judicial authority may extend or further extend the period specified in a warrant by a shorter period than is required by sub-paragraph (3) if—

(a)   the application for the extension is an application for an extension by a period that is shorter than is so required; or

(b)   the judicial authority is satisfied that there are circumstances that would make it inappropriate for the period of the extension to be as long as the period so required.

(3B) In this paragraph "the relevant time", in relation to a person, means—

(a)   the time of his arrest under section 41, or

(b)   if he was being detained under Schedule 7 when he was arrested under section 41, the time when his examination under that Schedule began.

(4)   Paragraphs 30(3) and 31 to 34 shall apply to an application under this paragraph as they apply to an application for a warrant of further detention.

(5)   A judicial authority may adjourn the hearing of an application under sub-paragraph (1) only if the hearing is adjourned to a date before the expiry of the period specified in the warrant.

(6)   Sub-paragraph (5) shall not apply to an adjournment under paragraph 33(2).

CRIMINAL JUSTICE AND POLICE ACT 2001
(2001, c. 16)

An Act to make provision for combatting crime and disorder; to make provision about the disclosure of information relating to criminal matters and about powers of search and seizure; to amend the Police and Criminal Evidence Act 1984, the Police and Criminal Evidence (Northern Ireland) Order 1989 and the Terrorism Act 2000; to make provision about the police, the National Criminal Intelligence Service and the National Crime Squad; to make provision about the powers of the courts in relation to criminal matters; and for connected purposes.   [11 May 2001]

PART 2
POWERS OF SEIZURE

Additional powers of seizure

50   Additional powers of seizure from premises

(1)   Where—

(a)   a person who is lawfully on any premises finds anything on those premises that he has reasonable grounds for believing may be or may contain something for which he is authorised to search on those premises,

(b)   a power of seizure to which this section applies or the power conferred by subsection (2) would entitle him, if he found it, to seize whatever it is that he has grounds for believing that thing to be or to contain, and

(c)   in all the circumstances, it is not reasonably practicable for it to be determined, on those premises—

(i)   whether what he has found is something that he is entitled to seize, or

(ii)   the extent to which what he has found contains something that he is entitled to seize,

that person's powers of seizure shall include power under this section to seize so much of what he has found as it is necessary to remove from the premises to enable that to be determined.

(2)   Where—

(a)   a person who is lawfully on any premises finds anything on those premises ("the seizable property") which he would be entitled to seize but for its being comprised in something else that he has (apart from this subsection) no power to seize,

(b)   the power under which that person would have power to seize the seizable property is a power to which this section applies, and

(c)   in all the circumstances it is not reasonably practicable for the seizable property to be separated, on those premises, from that in which it is comprised,

that person's powers of seizure shall include power under this section to seize both the seizable property and that from which it is not reasonably practicable to separate it.

(3)   The factors to be taken into account in considering, for the purposes of this section, whether or not it is reasonably practicable on particular premises for something to be determined, or for something to be separated from something else, shall be confined to the following—

(a)   how long it would take to carry out the determination or separation on those premises;

(b)   the number of persons that would be required to carry out that determination or separation on those premises within a reasonable period;

(c)   whether the determination or separation would (or would if carried out on those premises) involve damage to property;

(d)   the apparatus or equipment that it would be necessary or appropriate to use for the carrying out of the determination or separation; and

(e)   in the case of separation, whether the separation—

(i)   would be likely, or

(ii)   if carried out by the only means that are reasonably practicable on those premises, would be likely,

to prejudice the use of some or all of the separated seizable property for a purpose for which something seized under the power in question is capable of being used.

(5)   This section applies to each of the powers of seizure specified in Part 1 of Schedule 1.

51   Additional powers of seizure from the person

(1)   Where—

(a)   a person carrying out a lawful search of any person finds something that he has reasonable grounds for believing may be or may contain something for which he is authorised to search,

(b)   a power of seizure to which this section applies or the power conferred by subsection (2) would entitle him, if he found it, to seize whatever it is that he has grounds for believing that thing to be or to contain, and

(c)   in all the circumstances it is not reasonably practicable for it to be determined, at the time and place of the search—

(i)   whether what he has found is something that he is entitled to seize, or

(ii)   the extent to which what he has found contains something that he is entitled to seize,

that person's powers of seizure shall include power under this section to seize so much of what he has found as it is necessary to remove from that place to enable that to be determined.

(2)   Where—

(a)   a person carrying out a lawful search of any person finds something ("the seizable property") which he would be entitled to seize but for its being comprised in something else that he has (apart from this subsection) no power to seize,

(b)   the power under which that person would have power to seize the seizable property is a power to which this section applies, and

(c)   in all the circumstances it is not reasonably practicable for the seizable property to be separated, at the time and place of the search, from that in which it is comprised,

that person's powers of seizure shall include power under this section to seize both the seizable property and that from which it is not reasonably practicable to separate it.

(3)   The factors to be taken into account in considering, for the purposes of this section, whether or not it is reasonably practicable, at the time and place of a search, for

something to be determined, or for something to be separated from something else, shall be confined to the following—

(a) how long it would take to carry out the determination or separation at that time and place;

(b) the number of persons that would be required to carry out that determination or separation at that time and place within a reasonable period;

(c) whether the determination or separation would (or would if carried out at that time and place) involve damage to property;

(d) the apparatus or equipment that it would be necessary or appropriate to use for the carrying out of the determination or separation; and

(e) in the case of separation, whether the separation—

   (i) would be likely, or

   (ii) if carried out by the only means that are reasonably practicable at that time and place, would be likely,

to prejudice the use of some or all of the separated seizable property for a purpose for which something seized under the power in question is capable of being used.

(4) Section 19(6) of the 1984 Act and Article 21(6) of the Police and Criminal Evidence (Northern Ireland) Order 1989 (powers of seizure not to include power to seize anything a person has reasonable grounds for believing is legally privileged) shall not apply to the power of seizure conferred by subsection (2).

(5) This section applies to each of the powers of seizure specified in Part 2 of Schedule 1.

52 Notice of exercise of power under s. 50 or 51

(1) Where a person exercises a power of seizure conferred by section 50, it shall (subject to subsections (2) and (3)) be his duty, on doing so, to give to the occupier of the premises a written notice—

(a) specifying what has been seized in reliance on the powers conferred by that section;

(b) specifying the grounds on which those powers have been exercised;

(c) setting out the effect of sections 59 to 61;

(d) specifying the name and address of the person to whom notice of an application under section 59(2) to the appropriate judicial authority in respect of any of the seized property must be given; and

(e) specifying the name and address of the person to whom an application may be made to be allowed to attend the initial examination required by any arrangements made for the purposes of section 53(2).

(2) Where it appears to the person exercising on any premises a power of seizure conferred by section 50—

(a) that the occupier of the premises is not present on the premises at the time of the exercise of the power, but

(b) that there is some other person present on the premises who is in charge of the premises,

subsection (1) of this section shall have effect as if it required the notice under that subsection to be given to that other person.

(3) Where it appears to the person exercising a power of seizure conferred by section 50 that there is no one present on the premises to whom he may give a notice for the purposes of complying with subsection (1) of this section, he shall, before leaving the premises, instead of complying with that subsection, attach a notice such as is mentioned in that subsection in a prominent place to the premises.

(4) Where a person exercises a power of seizure conferred by section 51 it shall be his duty, on doing so, to give a written notice to the person from whom the seizure is made—

(a) specifying what has been seized in reliance on the powers conferred by that section;

(b) specifying the grounds on which those powers have been exercised;

(c) setting out the effect of sections 59 to 61;

(d)   specifying the name and address of the person to whom notice of any application under section 59(2) to the appropriate judicial authority in respect of any of the seized property must be given; and

(e)   specifying the name and address of the person to whom an application may be made to be allowed to attend the initial examination required by any arrangements made for the purposes of section 53(2).

Return or retention of seized property

53   Examination and return of property seized under s. 50 or 51

(1)   This section applies where anything has been seized under a power conferred by section 50 or 51.

(2)   It shall be the duty of the person for the time being in possession of the seized property in consequence of the exercise of that power to secure that there are arrangements in force which (subject to section 61) ensure—

(a)   that an initial examination of the property is carried out as soon as reasonably practicable after the seizure;

(b)   that that examination is confined to whatever is necessary for determining how much of the property falls within subsection (3);

(c)   that anything which is found, on that examination, not to fall within subsection (3) is separated from the rest of the seized property and is returned as soon as reasonably practicable after the examination of all the seized property has been completed; and

(d)   that, until the initial examination of all the seized property has been completed and anything which does not fall within subsection (3) has been returned, the seized property is kept separate from anything seized under any other power.

(3)   The seized property falls within this subsection to the extent only—

(a)   that it is property for which the person seizing it had power to search when he made the seizure but is not property the return of which is required by section 54;

(b)   that it is property the retention of which is authorised by section 56; or

(c)   that it is something which, in all the circumstances, it will not be reasonably practicable, following the examination, to separate from property falling within paragraph (a) or (b).

(4)   In determining for the purposes of this section the earliest practicable time for the carrying out of an initial examination of the seized property, due regard shall be had to the desirability of allowing the person from whom it was seized, or a person with an interest in that property, an opportunity of being present or (if he chooses) of being represented at the examination.

(5)   In this section, references to whether or not it is reasonably practicable to separate part of the seized property from the rest of it are references to whether or not it is reasonably practicable to do so without prejudicing the use of the rest of that property, or a part of it, for purposes for which (disregarding the part to be separated) the use of the whole or of a part of the rest of the property, if retained, would be lawful.

54   Obligation to return items subject to legal privilege

(1)   If, at any time after a seizure of anything has been made in exercise of a power of seizure to which this section applies—

(a)   it appears to the person for the time being having possession of the seized property in consequence of the seizure that the property—

(i)   is an item subject to legal privilege, or

(ii)   has such an item comprised in it,

and

(b)   in a case where the item is comprised in something else which has been lawfully seized, it is not comprised in property falling within subsection (2),

it shall be the duty of that person to secure that the item is returned as soon as reasonably practicable after the seizure.

(2)   Property in which an item subject to legal privilege is comprised falls within this subsection if—

(a) the whole or a part of the rest of the property is property falling within subsection (3) or property the retention of which is authorised by section 56; and

(b) in all the circumstances, it is not reasonably practicable for that item to be separated from the rest of that property (or, as the case may be, from that part of it) without prejudicing the use of the rest of that property, or that part of it, for purposes for which (disregarding that item) its use, if retained, would be lawful.

(3) Property falls within this subsection to the extent that it is property for which the person seizing it had power to search when he made the seizure, but is not property which is required to be returned under this section or section 55.

(4) This section applies—

(a) to the powers of seizure conferred by sections 50 and 51;

(b) to each of the powers of seizure specified in Parts 1 and 2 of Schedule 1; and

(c) to any power of seizure (not falling within paragraph (a) or (b)) conferred on a constable by or under any enactment, including an enactment passed after this Act.

56 Property seized by constables etc.

(1) The retention of—

(a) property seized on any premises by a constable who was lawfully on the premises,

(b) property seized on any premises by a relevant person who was on the premises accompanied by a constable, and

(c) property seized by a constable carrying out a lawful search of any person,

is authorised by this section if the property falls within subsection (2) or (3).

(2) Property falls within this subsection to the extent that there are reasonable grounds for believing—

(a) that it is property obtained in consequence of the commission of an offence; and

(b) that it is necessary for it to be retained in order to prevent its being concealed, lost, damaged, altered or destroyed.

(3) Property falls within this subsection to the extent that there are reasonable grounds for believing—

(a) that it is evidence in relation to any offence; and

(b) that it is necessary for it to be retained in order to prevent its being concealed, lost, altered or destroyed.

(4) Nothing in this section authorises the retention (except in pursuance of section 54(2)) of anything at any time when its return is required by section 54.

(4A) Subsection (1)(a) includes property seized on any premises—

(a) by a person authorised under section 16(2) of the 1984 Act to accompany a constable executing a warrant, or

(b) by a person accompanying a constable under section 2(6) of the Criminal Justice Act 1987 in the execution of a warrant under section 2(4) of that Act.

58 Person to whom seized property is to be returned

(1) Where—

(a) anything has been seized in exercise of any power of seizure, and

(b) there is an obligation under this Part for the whole or any part of the seized property to be returned,

the obligation to return it shall (subject to the following provisions of this section) be an obligation to return it to the person from whom it was seized.

(2) Where—

(a) any person is obliged under this Part to return anything that has been seized to the person from whom it was seized, and

(b) the person under that obligation is satisfied that some other person has a better right to that thing than the person from whom it was seized,

his duty to return it shall, instead, be a duty to return it to that other person or, as the case may be, to the person appearing to him to have the best right to the thing in question.

(3)   Where different persons claim to be entitled to the return of anything that is required to be returned under this Part, that thing may be retained for as long as is reasonably necessary for the determination in accordance with subsection (2) of the person to whom it must be returned.

(4)   References in this Part to the person from whom something has been seized, in relation to a case in which the power of seizure was exercisable by reason of that thing's having been found on any premises, are references to the occupier of the premises at the time of the seizure.

Remedies and safeguards

59   Application to the appropriate judicial authority

(1)   This section applies where anything has been seized in exercise, or purported exercise, of a relevant power of seizure.

(2)   Any person with a relevant interest in the seized property may apply to the appropriate judicial authority, on one or more of the grounds mentioned in subsection (3), for the return of the whole or a part of the seized property.

(3)   Those grounds are—
     (a)   that there was no power to make the seizure;
     (b)   that the seized property is or contains an item subject to legal privilege that is not comprised in property falling within section 54(2);
     (c)   that the seized property is or contains any excluded material or special procedure material which—
         (i)   has been seized under a power to which section 55 applies;
         (ii)   is not comprised in property falling within section 55(2) or (3); and
         (iii)   is not property the retention of which is authorised by section 56;
     (d)   that the seized property is or contains something seized under section 50 or 51 which does not fall within section 53(3);
     and subsections (5) and (6) of section 55 shall apply for the purposes of paragraph (c) as they apply for the purposes of that section.

(4)   Subject to subsection (6), the appropriate judicial authority, on an application under subsection (2), shall—
     (a)   if satisfied as to any of the matters mentioned in subsection (3), order the return of so much of the seized property as is property in relation to which the authority is so satisfied; and
     (b)   to the extent that that authority is not so satisfied, dismiss the application.

(5)   The appropriate judicial authority—
     (a)   on an application under subsection (2),
     (b)   on an application made by the person for the time being having possession of anything in consequence of its seizure under a relevant power of seizure, or
     (c)   on an application made—
         (i)   by a person with a relevant interest in anything seized under section 50 or 51, and
         (ii)   on the grounds that the requirements of section 53(2) have not been or are not being complied with,
     may give such directions as the authority thinks fit as to the examination, retention, separation or return of the whole or any part of the seized property.

(6)   On any application under this section, the appropriate judicial authority may authorise the retention of any property which—
     (a)   has been seized in exercise, or purported exercise, of a relevant power of seizure, and
     (b)   would otherwise fall to be returned,
     if that authority is satisfied that the retention of the property is justified on grounds falling within subsection (7).

(7)   Those grounds are that (if the property were returned) it would immediately become appropriate—
     (a)   to issue, on the application of the person who is in possession of the property at the time of the application under this section, a warrant in pursuance of which, or of the exercise of which, it would be lawful to seize the property; or

    (b)   to make an order under—

        (i)   paragraph 4 of Schedule 1 to the 1984 Act,

        (ii)   paragraph 4 of Schedule 1 to the Police and Criminal Evidence (Northern Ireland) Order 1989,

        (iii)   section 20BA of the Taxes Management Act 1970, or

        (iv)   paragraph 5 of Schedule 5 to the Terrorism Act 2000,

under which the property would fall to be delivered up or produced to the person mentioned in paragraph (a).

(8)   Where any property which has been seized in exercise, or purported exercise, of a relevant power of seizure has parts ("part A" and "part B") comprised in it such that—

    (a)   it would be inappropriate, if the property were returned, to take any action such as is mentioned in subsection (7) in relation to part A,

    (b)   it would (or would but for the facts mentioned in paragraph (a)) be appropriate, if the property were returned, to take such action in relation to part B, and

    (c)   in all the circumstances, it is not reasonably practicable to separate part A from part B without prejudicing the use of part B for purposes for which it is lawful to use property seized under the power in question,

the facts mentioned in paragraph (a) shall not be taken into account by the appropriate judicial authority in deciding whether the retention of the property is justified on grounds falling within subsection (7).

61   The duty to secure

(1)   The duty to secure that arises under this section is a duty of the person for the time being having possession, in consequence of the seizure, of the seized property to secure that arrangements are in force that ensure that the seized property (without being returned) is not, at any time after the giving of the notice of the application under section 60(1), either—

    (a)   examined or copied, or

    (b)   put to any use to which its seizure would, apart from this subsection, entitle it to be put,

except with the consent of the applicant or in accordance with the directions of the appropriate judicial authority.

(2)   Subsection (1) shall not have effect in relation to any time after the withdrawal of the application to which the notice relates.

Construction of Part 2

63   Copies

(1)   Subject to subsection (3)—

    (a)   in this Part, "seize" includes "take a copy of", and cognate expressions shall be construed accordingly;

    (b)   this Part shall apply as if any copy taken under any power to which any provision of this Part applies were the original of that of which it is a copy; and

    (c)   for the purposes of this Part, except sections 50 and 51, the powers mentioned in subsection (2) (which are powers to obtain hard copies etc. of information which is stored in electronic form) shall be treated as powers of seizure, and references to seizure and to seized property shall be construed accordingly.

ANTI-TERRORISM, CRIME AND SECURITY ACT 2001
(2001, c. 24)

An Act to amend the Terrorism Act 2000; to make further provision about terrorism and security; to provide for the freezing of assets; to make provision about immigration and asylum; to amend or extend the criminal law and powers for preventing crime and enforcing that law; to make provision about the control of pathogens and toxins; to provide for the retention of communications data; to provide for implementation of Title VI of the Treaty on European Union; and for connected purposes.   [14 December 2001]

PART 1
TERRORIST PROPERTY

1   Forfeiture of terrorist cash

(1)   Schedule 1 (which makes provision for enabling cash which—

(a)   is intended to be used for the purposes of terrorism,

(b)   consists of resources of an organisation which is a proscribed organisation, or

(c)   is, or represents, property obtained through terrorism,

to be forfeited in civil proceedings before a magistrates' court or (in Scotland) the sheriff) is to have effect.

(2)   The powers conferred by Schedule 1 are exercisable in relation to any cash whether or not any proceedings have been brought for an offence in connection with the cash.

PART 2
FREEZING ORDERS

Orders

4   Power to make order

(1)   The Treasury may make a freezing order if the following two conditions are satisfied.

(2)   The first condition is that the Treasury reasonably believe that—

(a)   action to the detriment of the United Kingdom's economy (or part of it) has been or is likely to be taken by a person or persons, or

(b)   action constituting a threat to the life or property of one or more nationals of the United Kingdom or residents of the United Kingdom has been or is likely to be taken by a person or persons.

(3)   If one person is believed to have taken or to be likely to take the action the second condition is that the person is—

(a)   the government of a country or territory outside the United Kingdom, or

(b)   a resident of a country or territory outside the United Kingdom.

(4)   If two or more persons are believed to have taken or to be likely to take the action the second condition is that each of them falls within paragraph (a) or (b) of subsection (3); and different persons may fall within different paragraphs.

5   Contents of order

(1)   A freezing order is an order which prohibits persons from making funds available to or for the benefit of a person or persons specified in the order.

(2)   The order must provide that these are the persons who are prohibited—

(a)   all persons in the United Kingdom, and

(b)   all persons elsewhere who are nationals of the United Kingdom or are bodies incorporated under the law of any part of the United Kingdom or are Scottish partnerships.

(3)   The order may specify the following (and only the following) as the person or persons to whom or for whose benefit funds are not to be made available—

(a)   the person or persons reasonably believed by the Treasury to have taken or to be likely to take the action referred to in section 4;

(b)   any person the Treasury reasonably believe has provided or is likely to provide assistance (directly or indirectly) to that person or any of those persons.

(4)   A person may be specified under subsection (3) by—

(a)   being named in the order, or

(b)   falling within a description of persons set out in the order.

(5)   The description must be such that a reasonable person would know whether he fell within it.

(6)   Funds are financial assets and economic benefits of any kind.

Orders: procedure etc.

10   Procedure for making freezing orders

(1)   A power to make a freezing order is exercisable by statutory instrument.

(2) A freezing order—
  (a) must be laid before Parliament after being made;
  (b) ceases to have effect at the end of the relevant period unless before the end of that period the order is approved by a resolution of each House of Parliament (but without that affecting anything done under the order or the power to make a new order).
(3) The relevant period is a period of 28 days starting with the day on which the order is made.
(4) In calculating the relevant period no account is to be taken of any time during which Parliament is dissolved or prorogued or during which both Houses are adjourned for more than 4 days.
(5) If the Treasury propose to make a freezing order in the belief that the condition in section 4(2)(b) is satisfied, they must not make the order unless they consult the Secretary of State.

POLICE REFORM ACT 2002
(2002, c. 30)

An Act to make new provision about the supervision, administration, functions and conduct of police forces, police officers and other persons serving with, or carrying out functions in relation to, the police; to amend police powers and to provide for the exercise of police powers by persons who are not police officers; to amend the law relating to anti-social behaviour orders; to amend the law relating to sex offender orders; and for connected purposes. [24 July 2002]

PART 2
COMPLAINTS AND MISCONDUCT

The Independent Police Complaints Commission

9   The Independent Police Complaints Commission
(1) There shall be a body corporate to be known as the Independent Police Complaints Commission (in this Part referred to as "the Commission").
(2) The Commission shall consist of—
  (a) a chairman appointed by Her Majesty; and
  (b) not less than five other members appointed by the Secretary of State.
(3) A person shall not be appointed as the chairman of the Commission, or as another member of the Commission, if—
  (a) he holds or has held office as a constable in any part of the United Kingdom;
  (b) he is or has been under the direction and control of a chief officer or of any person holding an equivalent office in Scotland or Northern Ireland;
  (c) he is a person in relation to whom a designation under section 39 is or has been in force;
  (d) he is a person in relation to whom an accreditation under section 41 or 41A is or has been in force;
  (da) he has been the chairman or a member of, or a member of the staff of, the Serious Organised Crime Agency;
  (db) he has been—
    (i) the chairman or chief executive of, or
    (ii) another member of, or
    (iii) another member of the staff of,
    the National Policing Improvement Agency.
  (dc) the person is, or has been, a National Crime Agency officer;
  (e) he has been a member of the National Criminal Intelligence Service or the National Crime Squad; or

(f)   he is or has at any time been a member of a body of constables which at the time of his membership is or was a body of constables in relation to which any procedures are or were in force by virtue of an agreement or order under—

(i)   section 26 of this Act; or

(ii)   section 78 of the 1996 Act or section 96 of the 1984 Act (which made provision corresponding to that made by section 26 of this Act).

(4)   An appointment made in contravention of subsection (3) shall have no effect.

(5)   The Commission shall not—

(a)   be regarded as the servant or agent of the Crown; or

(b)   enjoy any status, privilege or immunity of the Crown;

and the Commission's property shall not be regarded as property of, or property held on behalf of, the Crown.

(6)   Schedule 2 (which makes further provision in relation to the Commission) shall have effect.

(7)   The Police Complaints Authority shall cease to exist on such day as the Secretary of State may by order appoint.

10   General functions of the Commission

(1)   The functions of the Commission shall be—

(a)   to secure the maintenance by the Commission itself, and by local policing bodies and chief officers, of suitable arrangements with respect to the matters mentioned in subsection (2);

(b)   to keep under review all arrangements maintained with respect to those matters;

(c)   to secure that arrangements maintained with respect to those matters comply with the requirements of the following provisions of this Part, are efficient and effective and contain and manifest an appropriate degree of independence;

(d)   to secure that public confidence is established and maintained in the existence of suitable arrangements with respect to those matters and with the operation of the arrangements that are in fact maintained with respect to those matters;

(e)   to make such recommendations, and to give such advice, for the modification of the arrangements maintained with respect to those matters, and also of police practice in relation to other matters, as appear, from the carrying out by the Commission of its other functions, to be necessary or desirable;

(f)   to such extent as it may be required to do so by regulations made by the Secretary of State, to carry out functions in relation to bodies of constables maintained otherwise than by local policing bodies which broadly correspond to those conferred on the Commission in relation to police forces by the preceding paragraphs of this subsection; and

(g)   to carry out functions in relation to the National Crime Agency which correspond to those conferred on the Commission in relation to police forces by paragraph (e) of this subsection;

(ga)   to carry out such corresponding functions in relation to officers of the Gangmasters and Labour Abuse Authority in their capacity as labour abuse prevention officers (see section 114B of the Police and Criminal Evidence Act 1984 (PACE powers for labour abuse prevention officers)).

(2)   Those matters are—

(a)   the handling of complaints made about the conduct of persons serving with the police;

(b)   the recording of matters from which it appears that there may have been conduct by such persons which constitutes or involves the commission of a criminal offence or behaviour justifying disciplinary proceedings;

(ba)   the recording of matters from which it appears that a person has died or suffered serious injury during, or following, contact with a person serving with the police;

(c)   the manner in which any such complaints or any such matters as are mentioned in paragraph (b) or (ba) are investigated or otherwise handled and dealt with.

(3)   The Commission shall also have the functions which are conferred on it by—

(b)   any agreement or order under section 26 of this Act (other bodies of constables);

(bc)   any regulations under section 26C of this Act (the National Crime Agency);

(bd)   any regulations under section 26D of this Act (labour abuse prevention officers);

    (c)   any regulations under section 39 of this Act (police powers for contracted-out staff); or

    (d)   any regulations or arrangements relating to disciplinary or similar proceedings against persons serving with the police, or against members of any body of constables maintained otherwise than by a local policing body.

(4)   It shall be the duty of the Commission—

    (a)   to exercise the powers and perform the duties conferred on it by the following provisions of this Part in the manner that it considers best calculated for the purpose of securing the proper carrying out of its functions under subsections (1) and (3); and

    (b)   to secure that arrangements exist which are conducive to, and facilitate, the reporting of misconduct by persons in relation to whose conduct the Commission has functions.

(5)   It shall also be the duty of the Commission—

    (a)   to enter into arrangements with the chief inspector of constabulary for the purpose of securing co-operation, in the carrying out of their respective functions, between the Commission and the inspectors of constabulary; and

    (b)   to provide those inspectors with all such assistance and co-operation as may be required by those arrangements, or as otherwise appears to the Commission to be appropriate, for facilitating the carrying out by those inspectors of their functions.

(6)   Subject to the other provisions of this Part, the Commission may do anything which appears to it to be calculated to facilitate, or is incidental or conducive to, the carrying out of its functions.

(7)   The Commission may, in connection with the making of any recommendation or the giving of any advice to any person for the purpose of carrying out—

    (a)   its function under subsection (1)(e),

    (b)   any corresponding function conferred on it by virtue of subsection (1)(f), or

    (c)   its function under subsection (1)(g) or (h),

impose any such charge on that person for anything done by the Commission for the purposes of, or in connection with, the carrying out of that function as it thinks fit.

11   Reports to the Secretary of State

(1)   As soon as practicable after the end of each of its financial years, the Commission shall make a report to the Secretary of State on the carrying out of its functions during that year.

(2)   The Commission shall also make such reports to the Secretary of State about matters relating generally to the carrying out of its functions as he may, from time to time, require.

(3)   The Commission may, from time to time, make such other reports to the Secretary of State as it considers appropriate for drawing his attention to matters which—

    (a)   have come to the Commission's notice; and

    (b)   are matters that it considers should be drawn to his attention by reason of their gravity or of other exceptional circumstances.

(4)   The Commission shall prepare such reports containing advice and recommendations as it thinks appropriate for the purpose of carrying out—

    (a)   its function under subsection (1)(e) of section 10; or

    (b)   any corresponding function conferred on it by virtue of subsection (1)(f) of that section.

(5)   Where the Secretary of State receives any report under this section, he shall—

    (a)   in the case of every annual report under subsection (1), and

    (b)   in the case of any other report, if and to the extent that he considers it appropriate to do so,

lay a copy of the report before Parliament and cause the report to be published.

(6)   The Commission shall send a copy of every annual report under subsection (1)—

    (a)   to every local policing body;

    (d)   to every authority that is maintaining a body of constables in relation to which any procedures are for the time being in force by virtue of any agreement or order under section 26 or by virtue of subsection (9) of that section, and

    (f)   to the National Crime Agency.

(7)   The Commission shall send a copy of every report under subsection (3)—

      (a)   to any local policing body that appears to the Commission to be concerned; and

      (b)   to the chief officer of police of any police force that appears to it to be concerned.

(8)   Where a report under subsection (3) relates to the National Crime Agency, the Commission shall send a copy of that report to the Agency.

(9)   Where a report under subsection (3) relates to a body of constables maintained by an authority other than a local policing body, the Commission shall send a copy of that report—

      (a)   to that authority; and

      (b)   to the person having the direction and control of that body of constables.

(10)   The Commission shall send a copy of every report under subsection (4) to—

      (a)   the Secretary of State;

      (b)   every local policing body;

      (c)   every chief officer;

      (f)   every authority that is maintaining a body of constables in relation to which any procedures are for the time being in force by virtue of any agreement or order under section 26 or by virtue of subsection (9) of that section;

      (g)   every person who has the direction and control of such a body of constables; and

      (i)   the National Crime Agency.

(11)   The Commission shall send a copy of every report made or prepared by it under subsection (3) or (4) to such of the persons (in addition to those specified in the preceding subsections) who—

      (a)   are referred to in the report, or

      (b)   appear to the Commission otherwise to have a particular interest in its contents,

as the Commission thinks fit.

Application of Part 2

12   Complaints, matters and persons to which Part 2 applies

(1)   In this Part references to a complaint are references (subject to the following provisions of this section) to any complaint about the conduct of a person serving with the police which is made (whether in writing or otherwise) by—

      (a)   a member of the public who claims to be the person in relation to whom the conduct took place;

      (b)   a member of the public not falling within paragraph (a) who claims to have been adversely affected by the conduct;

      (c)   a member of the public who claims to have witnessed the conduct;

      (d)   a person acting on behalf of a person falling within any of paragraphs (a) to (c).

(2)   In this Part "conduct matter" means (subject to the following provisions of this section, section 28A and any regulations made under it, and any regulations made by virtue of section 23(2)(d)) any matter which is not and has not been the subject of a complaint but in the case of which there is an indication (whether from the circumstances or otherwise) that a person serving with the police may have—

      (a)   committed a criminal offence; or

      (b)   behaved in a manner which would justify the bringing of disciplinary proceedings.

(2A)   In this Part "death or serious injury matter" (or "DSI matter" for short) means (subject to section 28A and any regulations made under it) any circumstances (other than those which are or have been the subject of a complaint or which amount to a conduct matter)—

      (a)   in or in consequence of which a person has died or has sustained serious injury; and

      (b)   in relation to which the requirements of either subsection (2B) or subsection (2C) are satisfied.

(2B)   The requirements of this subsection are that at the time of the death or serious injury the person—

      (a)   had been arrested by a person serving with the police and had not been released from that arrest; or

(b)   was otherwise detained in the custody of a person serving with the police.

(2C) The requirements of this subsection are that—

    (a)   at or before the time of the death or serious injury the person had contact (of whatever kind, and whether direct or indirect) with a person serving with the police who was acting in the execution of his duties; and

    (b)   there is an indication that the contact may have caused (whether directly or indirectly) or contributed to the death or serious injury.

(2D) In subsection (2A) the reference to a person includes a person serving with the police, but in relation to such a person "contact" in subsection (2C) does not include contact that he has whilst acting in the execution of his duties.

(3)   The complaints that are complaints for the purposes of this Part by virtue of subsection (1)(b) do not, except in a case falling within subsection (4), include any made by or on behalf of a person who claims to have been adversely affected as a consequence only of having seen or heard the conduct, or any of the alleged effects of the conduct.

(4)   A case falls within this subsection if—

    (a)   it was only because the person in question was physically present, or sufficiently nearby, when the conduct took place or the effects occurred that he was able to see or hear the conduct or its effects; or

    (b)   the adverse effect is attributable to, or was aggravated by, the fact that the person in relation to whom the conduct took place was already known to the person claiming to have suffered the adverse effect.

(5)   For the purposes of this section a person shall be taken to have witnessed conduct if, and only if—

    (a)   he acquired his knowledge of that conduct in a manner which would make him a competent witness capable of giving admissible evidence of that conduct in criminal proceedings; or

    (b)   he has in his possession or under his control anything which would in any such proceedings constitute admissible evidence of that conduct.

(6)   For the purposes of this Part a person falling within subsection 1(a) to (c) to shall not be taken to have authorised another person to act on his behalf unless—

    (a)   that other person is for the time being designated for the purposes of this Part by the Commission as a person through whom complaints may be made, or he is of a description of persons so designated; or

    (b)   the other person has been given, and is able to produce, the written consent to his so acting of the person on whose behalf he acts.

(7)   For the purposes of this Part, a person is serving with the police if—

    (a)   he is a member of a police force;

    (aa) he is a civilian employee of a police force;

    (b)   he is an employee of the Common Council of the City of London who is under the direction and control of a chief officer; or

    (c)   he is a special constable who is under the direction and control of a chief officer.

(8)   The Secretary of State may make regulations providing that, for the purposes of this Part and of any regulations made under this Part—

    (a)   a contractor,

    (b)   a sub-contractor of a contractor, or

    (c)   an employee of a contractor or a sub-contractor,

is to be treated as a person serving with the police.

(9)   Regulations under subsection (8) may make modifications to this Part, and to any regulations made under this Part, in its application to those persons.

(10) In subsection (8) "contractor" means a person who has entered into a contract with a local policing body or a chief officer to provide services to a chief officer.

Handling of complaints, conduct matters and DSI matters etc.

13   Handling of complaints, conduct matters and DSI matters etc.

Schedule 3 (which makes provision for the handling of complaints, conduct matters and DSI matters and for the carrying out of investigations) shall have effect.

Co-operation, assistance and information

15   General duties of local policing bodies, chief officers and inspectors

(1)   It shall be the duty of—

    (a)   every local policing body maintaining a police force,

    (b)   the chief officer of police of every police force, and

    (c)   every inspector of constabulary carrying out any of his functions in relation to a police force,

to ensure that it or he is kept informed, in relation to that force, about all matters falling within subsection (2).

(1A)   It shall be the duty of the National Crime Agency to ensure that it is kept informed, in relation to the Agency, about all matters falling within subsection (2).

(2)   Those matters are—

    (a)   matters with respect to which any provision of this Part has effect;

    (b)   anything which is done under or for the purposes of any such provision; and

    (c)   any obligations to act or refrain from acting that have arisen by or under this Part but have not yet been complied with, or have been contravened.

(2A)   Subsection (2B) applies in a case where it appears to a local policing body that—

    (a)   an obligation to act or refrain from acting has arisen by or under this Part,

    (b)   that obligation is an obligation of the chief officer of police of the police force which is maintained by the local policing body, and

    (c)   the chief officer has not yet complied with that obligation, or has contravened it.

(2B)   The local policing body may direct the chief officer to take such steps as the local policing body thinks appropriate.

(2C)   The chief officer must comply with any direction given under subsection (2B).

(3)   Where—

    (a)   a local policing body maintaining any police force requires the chief officer of that force or of any other force to provide a member of his force for appointment under paragraph 16, 17 or 18 of Schedule 3,

    (b)   the chief officer of police of any police force requires the chief officer of police of any other police force to provide a member of that other force for appointment under any of those paragraphs, or

    (c)   a local policing body or chief officer requires the Director General of the National Crime Agency to provide a National Crime Agency officer for appointment under any of those paragraphs,

it shall be the duty of the chief officer to whom the requirement is addressed or of the Director General to comply with it.

(4)   It shall be the duty of—

    (a)   every local policing body maintaining a police force,

    (b)   the chief officer of police of every police force, and

    (c)   the National Crime Agency

to provide the Commission and every member of the Commission's staff with all such assistance as the Commission or that member of staff may reasonably require for the purposes of, or in connection with, the carrying out of any investigation by the Commission under this Part.

(5)   It shall be the duty of—

    (a)   every local policing body maintaining a police force,

    (b)   the chief officer of police of every police force, and

    (c)   the National Crime Agency

to ensure that a person appointed under paragraph 16, 17 or 18 of Schedule 3 to carry out an investigation is given all such assistance and co-operation in the carrying out of that investigation as that person may reasonably require

(6)   The duties imposed by subsections (4) and (5) on a local policing body maintaining a police force and on the chief officer of such a force and on the National Crime Agency have effect—

    (a)   irrespective of whether the investigation relates to the conduct of a person who is or has been a member of that force or a National Crime Agency officer; and

(b)   irrespective of who has the person appointed to carry out the investigation under his direction and control;

but a chief officer of a third force may be required to give assistance and co-operation under subsection (5) only with the approval of the chief officer of the force to which the person who requires it belongs.

(7)   In subsection (6) "third force", in relation to an investigation, means a police force other than—

    (a)   the force to which the person carrying out the investigation belongs; or

    (b)   the force to which the person whose conduct is under investigation belonged at the time of the conduct;

17   Provision of information to the Commission

(1)   It shall be the duty of—

    (a)   every local policing body, and

    (b)   every chief officer,

at such times, in such circumstances and in accordance with such other requirements as may be set out in regulations made by the Secretary of State, to provide the Commission with all such information and documents as may be specified or described in regulations so made.

(2)   It shall also be the duty of every local policing body and of every chief officer—

    (a)   to provide the Commission with all such other information and documents specified or described in a notification given by the Commission to that body or chief officer, and

    (b)   to produce or deliver up to the Commission all such evidence and other things so specified or described,

as appear to the Commission to be required by it for the purposes of the carrying out of any of its functions.

(3)   Anything falling to be provided, produced or delivered up by any person in pursuance of a requirement imposed under subsection (2) must be provided, produced or delivered up in such form, in such manner and within such period as may be specified in—

    (a)   the notification imposing the requirement; or

    (b)   in any subsequent notification given by the Commission to that person for the purposes of this subsection.

(4)   Nothing in this section shall require a local policing body or chief officer—

    (a)   to provide the Commission with any information or document, or to produce or deliver up any other thing, before the earliest time at which it is practicable for that body or chief officer to do so; or

    (b)   to provide, produce or deliver up anything at all in a case in which it never becomes practicable for that body or chief officer to do so.

(5)   A requirement imposed by any regulations or notification under this section may authorise or require information or documents to which it relates to be provided to the Commission electronically.

18   Inspections of police premises on behalf of the Commission

(1)   Where—

    (a)   the Commission requires—

        (i)   a local policing body maintaining any police force, or

        (ii)   the chief officer of police of any such force,

to allow a person nominated for the purpose by the Commission to have access to any premises occupied for the purposes of that force and to documents and other things on those premises, and

    (b)   the requirement is imposed for any of the purposes mentioned in subsection (2),

it shall be the duty of the body or, as the case may be, of the chief officer to secure that the required access is allowed to the nominated person.

(2)   Those purposes are—

    (a)   the purposes of any examination by the Commission of the efficiency and effectiveness of the arrangements made by the force in question for handling complaints or dealing with recordable conduct matters or DSI matters;

      (b)   the purposes of any investigation by the Commission under this Part or of any investigation carried out under its supervision or management.

(3)   A requirement imposed under this section for the purposes mentioned in subsection (2)(a) must be notified to the body or chief officer at least 48 hours before the time at which access is required.

(4)   Where—

      (a)   a requirement imposed under this section for the purposes mentioned in subsection (2)(a) requires access to any premises, document or thing to be allowed to any person, but

      (b)   there are reasonable grounds for not allowing that person to have the required access at the time at which he seeks to have it,

the obligation to secure that the required access is allowed shall have effect as an obligation to secure that the access is allowed to that person at the earliest practicable time after there cease to be any such grounds as that person may specify.

(5)   The provisions of this section are in addition to, and without prejudice to—

      (a)   the rights of entry, search and seizure that are or may be conferred on—

          (i)   a person designated for the purposes of paragraph 19 of Schedule 3, or

          (ii)   any person who otherwise acts on behalf of the Commission,

      in his capacity as a constable or as a person with the powers and privileges of a constable; or

      (b)   the obligations of local policing bodies and chief officers under sections 15 and 17.

19   Use of investigatory powers by or on behalf of the Commission

(1)   The Secretary of State may by order make such provision as he thinks appropriate for the purpose of authorising—

      (a)   the use of directed and intrusive surveillance, and

      (b)   the conduct and use of covert human intelligence sources,

for the purposes of, or for purposes connected with, the carrying out of the Commission's functions.

(2)   An order under this section may, for the purposes of or in connection with any such provision as is mentioned in subsection (1), provide for—

      (a)   Parts 2 and 4 the Regulation of Investigatory Powers Act 2000 (surveillance and covert human intelligence sources and scrutiny of investigatory powers), and

      (b)   Part 3 of the 1997 Act (authorisations in respect of property),

to have effect with such modifications as may be specified in the order.

(3)   The Secretary of State shall not make an order containing (with or without any other provision) any provision authorised by this section unless a draft of that order has been laid before Parliament and approved by a resolution of each House.

(4)   Expressions used in this section and in Part 2 of the Regulation of Investigatory Powers Act 2000 have the same meanings in this section as in that Part.

20   Duty to keep the complainant informed

(1)   In any case in which there is an investigation of a complaint in accordance with the provisions of Schedule 3—

      (a)   by the Commission, or

      (b)   under its management,

it shall be the duty of the Commission to provide the complainant with all such information as will keep him properly informed, while the investigation is being carried out and subsequently, of all the matters mentioned in subsection (4).

(2)   In any case in which there is an investigation of a complaint in accordance with the provisions of Schedule 3—

      (a)   by the appropriate authority on its own behalf, or

      (b)   under the supervision of the Commission,

it shall be the duty of the appropriate authority to provide the complainant with all such information as will keep him properly informed, while the investigation is being carried out and subsequently, of all the matters mentioned in subsection (4).

(3)   Where subsection (2) applies, it shall be the duty of the Commission to give the appropriate authority all such directions as it considers appropriate for securing

that that authority complies with its duty under that subsection; and it shall be the duty of the appropriate authority to comply with any direction given to it under this subsection.

(4) The matters of which the complainant must be kept properly informed are—

(a) the progress of the investigation;

(b) any provisional findings of the person carrying out the investigation;

(c) whether any report has been submitted under paragraph 22 of Schedule 3;

(d) the action (if any) that is taken in respect of the matters dealt with in any such report; and

(e) the outcome of any such action.

(5) The duties imposed by this section on the Commission and the appropriate authority in relation to any complaint shall be performed in such manner, and shall have effect subject to such exceptions, as may be provided for by regulations made by the Secretary of State.

(6) The Secretary of State shall not by regulations provide for any exceptions from the duties imposed by this section except so far as he considers it necessary to do so for the purpose of—

(a) preventing the premature or inappropriate disclosure of information that is relevant to, or may be used in, any actual or prospective criminal proceedings;

(b) preventing the disclosure of information in any circumstances in which it has been determined in accordance with the regulations that its non-disclosure—

(i) is in the interests of national security;

(ii) is for the purposes of the prevention or detection of crime, or the apprehension or prosecution of offenders;

(iii) is required on proportionality grounds; or

(iv) is otherwise necessary in the public interest.

(7) The non-disclosure of information is required on proportionality grounds if its disclosure would cause, directly or indirectly, an adverse effect which would be disproportionate to the benefits arising from its disclosure.

(8) Regulations under this section may include provision framed by reference to the opinion of, or a determination by, the Commission or any local policing body or chief officer.

(9) It shall be the duty of a person appointed to carry out an investigation under this Part to provide the Commission or, as the case may be, the appropriate authority with all such information as the Commission or that authority may reasonably require for the purpose of performing its duty under this section.

21 Duty to provide information for other persons

(1) A person has an interest in being kept properly informed about the handling of a complaint or recordable conduct matter or DSI matter if—

(a) it appears to the Commission or to an appropriate authority that he is a person falling within subsection (2) or (2A); and

(b) that person has indicated that he consents to the provision of information to him in accordance with this section and that consent has not been withdrawn.

(2) A person falls within this subsection if (in the case of a complaint or recordable conduct matter)—

(a) he is a relative of a person whose death is the alleged result from the conduct complained of or to which the recordable conduct matter relates;

(b) he is a relative of a person whose serious injury is the alleged result from that conduct and that person is incapable of making a complaint;

(c) he himself has suffered serious injury as the alleged result of that conduct.

(2A) A person falls within this subsection if (in the case of a DSI matter)—

(a) he is a relative of the person who has died;

(b) he is a relative of the person who has suffered serious injury and that person is incapable of making a complaint;

(c) he himself is the person who has suffered serious injury.

(3) A person who does not fall within subsection (2) or (2A) has an interest in being kept properly informed about the handling of a complaint or recordable conduct matter or DSI matter if—

(a)   the Commission or an appropriate authority considers that he has an interest in the handling of the complaint or recordable conduct matter or DSI matter which is sufficient to make it appropriate for information to be provided to him in accordance with this section; and

(b)   he has indicated that he consents to the provision of information to him in accordance with this section.

(4)   In relation to a complaint, this section confers no rights on the complainant.

(5)   A person who has an interest in being kept properly informed about the handling of a complaint or conduct matter or DSI matter is referred to in this section as an "interested person".

(6)   In any case in which there is an investigation of the complaint or recordable conduct matter or DSI matter in accordance with the provisions of Schedule 3—

(a)   by the Commission, or

(b)   under its management,

it shall be the duty of the Commission to provide the interested person with all such information as will keep him properly informed, while the investigation is being carried out and subsequently, of all the matters mentioned in subsection (9).

(7)   In any case in which there is an investigation of the complaint or recordable conduct matter or DSI matter in accordance with the provisions of Schedule 3—

(a)   by the appropriate authority on its own behalf, or

(b)   under the supervision of the Commission,

it shall be the duty of the appropriate authority to provide the interested person with all such information as will keep him properly informed, while the investigation is being carried out and subsequently, of all the matters mentioned in subsection (9).

(8)   Where subsection (7) applies, it shall be the duty of the Commission to give the appropriate authority all such directions as it considers appropriate for securing that that authority complies with its duty under that subsection; and it shall be the duty of the appropriate authority to comply with any direction given to it under this subsection.

(9)   The matters of which the interested person must be kept properly informed are—

(a)   the progress of the investigation;

(b)   any provisional findings of the person carrying out the investigation;

(ba)   whether the Commission or the appropriate authority has made a determination under paragraph 21A of Schedule 3;

(c)   whether any report has been submitted under paragraph 22 or 24A of Schedule 3;

(d)   the action (if any) that is taken in respect of the matters dealt with in any such report; and

(e)   the outcome of any such action.

(10)   The duties imposed by this section on the Commission and the appropriate authority in relation to any complaint or recordable conduct matter or DSI matter shall be performed in such manner, and shall have effect subject to such exceptions, as may be provided for by regulations made by the Secretary of State.

(11)   Subsections (6) to (9) of section 20 apply for the purposes of this section as they apply for the purposes of that section.

(12)   In this section "relative" means a person of a description prescribed in regulations made by the Secretary of State.

Guidance and regulations

22   Power of the Commission to issue guidance

(1)   The Commission may issue guidance—

(a)   to local policing bodies,

(b)   to chief officers, and

(c)   to persons who are serving with the police otherwise than as chief officers,

concerning the exercise or performance, by the persons to whom the guidance is issued, of any of the powers or duties specified in subsection (2).

(2)   Those powers and duties are—

(a)   those that are conferred or imposed by or under this Part; and

      (b)   those that are otherwise conferred or imposed but relate to—
          (i)   the handling of complaints;
          (ii)   the means by which recordable conduct matters or DSI matters are dealt with; or
          (iii) the detection or deterrence of misconduct by persons serving with the police.

(3)   Before issuing any guidance under this section, the Commission shall consult with—
      (a)   such persons as appear to the Commission to represent the views of police and crime commissioners;
      (aa) the Mayor's Office for Policing and Crime;
      (ab) the Common Council;
      (b)   the Association of Chief Police Officers; and
      (c)   such other persons as it thinks fit.

(4)   The approval of the Secretary of State shall be required for the issue by the Commission of any guidance under this section.

(5)   Without prejudice to the generality of the preceding provisions of this section, the guidance that may be issued under this section includes—
      (a)   guidance about the handling of complaints which have not yet been recorded and about dealing with recordable conduct matters or DSI matters that have not been recorded;
      (b)   guidance about the procedure to be followed by the appropriate authority when recording a complaint or any recordable conduct matter or DSI matter;
      (c)   guidance about—
          (i)   how to decide whether a complaint is suitable for being subjected to local resolution;
      (d)   guidance about how to protect the scene of an incident or alleged incident which—
          (i)   is or may become the subject-matter of a complaint; or
          (ii)   is or may involve a recordable conduct matter or DSI matter;
      (e)   guidance about the circumstances in which it is appropriate (where it is lawful to do so)—
          (i)   to disclose to any person, or to publish, any information about an investigation of a complaint or conduct matter or DSI matter; or
          (ii)   to provide any person with, or to publish, any report or other document relating to such an investigation;
      (f)   guidance about the matters to be included in a memorandum under paragraph 23 or 25 of Schedule 3 and about the manner in which, and the place at which, such a memorandum is to be delivered to the Commission.

(6)   Nothing in this section shall authorise the issuing of any guidance about a particular case.

(7)   It shall be the duty of every person to whom any guidance under this section is issued to have regard to that guidance in exercising or performing the powers and duties to which the guidance relates.

(8)   A failure by a person to whom guidance under this section is issued to have regard to the guidance shall be admissible in evidence in any disciplinary proceedings or on any appeal from a decision taken in any such proceedings.

Interpretation of Part 2

29   Interpretation of Part 2

(1)   In this Part—
      "the appropriate authority"—
      (a)   in relation to a person serving with the police or in relation to any complaint, conduct matter or investigation relating to the conduct of such a person, means—
          (i)   if that person is the chief officer or an acting chief officer, the local police body for the area of the police force of which he is a member; and
          (ii)   if he is not the chief officer or an acting chief officer, the chief officer under whose direction and control he is; and

(b)   in relation to a death or serious injury matter, means—
- (i)   if the relevant officer is the chief officer or an acting chief officer, the local police body for the area of the police force of which he is a member; and
- (ii)   if he is not the chief officer or an acting chief officer, the chief officer under whose direction and control he is,

and, for the purposes of this definition, "acting chief officer" means a person exercising or performing functions of a chief constable in accordance with section 41 of the Police Reform and Social Responsibility Act 2011; a person exercising powers or duties of the Commissioner of Police of the Metropolis in accordance with section 44 or 45(4) of that Act; or a person exercising duties of the Commissioner of Police for the City of London in accordance with section 25 of the City of London Police Act 1839.

"chief officer" means the chief officer of police of any police force;

"the Commission" has the meaning given by section 9(1);

"complainant" shall be construed in accordance with subsection (2);

"complaint" has the meaning given by section 12;

"conduct" includes acts, omissions, statements and decisions (whether actual, alleged or inferred);

"conduct matter" has the meaning given by section 12;

"death or serious injury matter" and "DSI matter" have the meaning given in section 12;

"disciplinary proceedings" means—

(a)   in relation to a member of a police force or a special constable, proceedings under any regulations made by virtue of section 50 or 51 of the 1996 Act and identified as disciplinary proceedings by those regulations; and

(h)   in relation to a person serving with the police who is not a member of a police force or a special constable, proceedings identified as such by regulations made by the Secretary of State for the purposes of this Part;

"document" means anything in which information of any description is recorded;

"information" includes estimates and projections, and statistical analyses;

"local resolution", in relation to a complaint, means the handling of that complaint in accordance with a procedure which—

(a)   does not involve a formal investigation; and

(b)   is laid down by regulations under paragraph 8 of Schedule 3 for complaints which it has been decided, in accordance with paragraph 6 of that Schedule, to subject to local resolution;

"person complained against", in relation to a complaint, means the person whose conduct is the subject-matter of the complaint;

"recordable conduct matter" means (subject to any regulations under section 23(2)(d))—

(a)   a conduct matter that is required to be recorded by the appropriate authority under paragraph 10 or 11 of Schedule 3 or has been so recorded; or

(aa)   a conduct matter that is required to be recorded by the appropriate authority under section 28A(8) or has been so recorded;

"relevant force", in relation to the appropriate authority, means—

(a)   if that authority is a local policing body, the police force which the body is responsible for maintaining; and

(b)   if that authority is the chief officer of police of a police force, his force;

"serious injury" means a fracture, a deep cut, a deep laceration or an injury causing damage to an internal organ or the impairment of any bodily function;

"serving with the police", in relation to any person, shall be construed in accordance with section 12(7) to (10).

(1A) In this Part "the relevant officer", in relation to a DSI matter, means the person serving with the police (within the meaning of section 12(7))—

(a)   who arrested the person who has died or suffered serious injury,

(b)   in whose custody that person was at the time of the death or serious injury, or

(c)   with whom that person had the contact in question;

and where there is more than one such person it means, subject to subsection (1B), the one who so dealt with him last before the death or serious injury occurred.

(1B) Where it cannot be determined which of two or more persons serving with the police dealt with a person last before a death or serious injury occurred, the relevant officer is the most senior of them.

(2) References in this Part, in relation to anything which is or purports to be a complaint, to the complainant are references —

    (a) except in the case of anything which is or purports to be a complaint falling within section 12(1)(d), to the person by whom the complaint or purported complaint was made; and

    (b) in that case, to the person on whose behalf the complaint or purported complaint was made;

but where any person is acting on another's behalf for the purposes of any complaint or purported complaint, anything that is to be or may be done under this Part by or in relation to the complainant may be done, instead, by or in relation to the person acting on the complainant's behalf.

(3) Subject to subsection (4), references in this Part, in relation to any conduct or anything purporting to be a complaint about any conduct, to a member of the public include references to any person falling within any of the following paragraphs (whether at the time of the conduct or at any subsequent time) —

    (a) a person serving with the police;

    (ca) a member of the National Crime Agency; or

    (d) a person engaged on relevant service, within the meaning of section 97(1)(a) or (d) of the 1996 Act (temporary service of various kinds).

(4) In this Part references, in relation to any conduct or to anything purporting to be a complaint about any conduct, to a member of the public do not include references to —

    (a) a person who, at the time when the conduct is supposed to have taken place, was under the direction and control of the same chief officer as the person whose conduct it was; or

    (b) a person who —

        (i) at the time when the conduct is supposed to have taken place, in relation to him, or

        (ii) at the time when he is supposed to have been adversely affected by it, or to have witnessed it,

was on duty in his capacity as a person falling within subsection (3)(a) to (d).

(5) For the purposes of this Part a person is adversely affected if he suffers any form of loss or damage, distress or inconvenience, if he is put in danger or if he is otherwise unduly put at risk of being adversely affected.

(6) References in this Part to the investigation of any complaint or matter by the appropriate authority on its own behalf, under the supervision of the Commission, under the management of the Commission or by the Commission itself shall be construed as references to its investigation in accordance with paragraph 16, 17, 18 or, as the case may be, 19 of Schedule 3.

(7) The Commissioner of Police for the City of London shall be treated for the purposes of this Part as if he were a member of the City of London police force.

PART 4

POLICE POWERS ETC.

CHAPTER 1

EXERCISE OF POLICE POWERS ETC. BY CIVILIANS

38   **Police powers for civilian staff**

(1) The chief officer of police of any police force may designate a relevant employee as an officer of one or more of the descriptions specified in subsection (2).

(2) The description of officers are as follows —

    (a) community support officer;

    (b) investigating officer;

   (c)   detention officer;
   (d)   escort officer;
(4)   A chief officer of police shall not designate a person under this section unless he is satisfied that that person—
   (a)   is a suitable person to carry out the functions for the purposes of which he is designated;
   (b)   is capable of effectively carrying out those functions; and
   (c)   has received adequate training in the carrying out of those functions and in the exercise and performance of the powers and duties to be conferred or imposed on him by virtue of the designation.
(5)   A person designated under this section shall have the powers and duties conferred or imposed on him by the designation.
(5A) A person designated under this section as a community support officer shall also have the standard powers and duties of a community support officer (see section 38A(2)).
(5B) The reference in subsection (4)(c) to the powers and duties to be conferred or imposed on a person by virtue of his designation, so far as it is a reference to the standard powers and duties of a community support officer, is a reference to the powers and duties that at the time of the person's designation are the standard powers and duties of a community support officer.
(6)   Powers and duties may be conferred or imposed on a designated person by means only of the application to him by his designation of provisions of the applicable Part of Schedule 4 that are to apply to the designated person; and for this purpose the applicable Part of that Schedule is—
   (a)   in the case of a person designated as a community support officer, Part 1;
   (b)   in the case of a person designated as an investigating officer, Part 2;
   (c)   in the case of a person designated as a detention officer, Part 3; and
   (d)   in the case of a person designated as an escort officer, Part 4.
(6A) Subsection (6) has effect subject to subsection (5A) and (8).
(7)   A relevant employee authorised or required to do anything by virtue of a designation under this section—
   (a)   shall not be authorised or required by virtue of that designation to engage in any conduct otherwise than in the course of that employment; and
   (b)   shall be so authorised or required subject to such restrictions and conditions (if any) as may be specified in his designation.
(8)   Where any power exercisable by any person in reliance on his designation under this section is a power which, in the case of its exercise by a constable, includes or is supplemented by a power to use reasonable force, any person exercising that power in reliance on that designation shall have the same entitlement as a constable to use reasonable force.
(9)   Where any power exercisable by any person in reliance on his designation under this section includes power to use force to enter any premises, that power shall not be exercisable by that person except—
   (a)   in the company, and under the supervision, of a constable; or
   (b)   for the purpose of saving life or limb or preventing serious damage to property.
(11) In this section "relevant employee" means—
   (a)   in the case of—
      (i)   a police force maintained for a police area in accordance with section 2 of the Police Act 1996, or
      (ii)   the police force maintained for the metropolitan police district in accordance with section 5A of that Act,
      a member of the civilian staff of that police force (within the meaning of Part 1 of the Police Reform and Social Responsibility Act 2011);
   (b)   in the case of any other police force, a person who—
      (i)   is employed by the police authority maintaining that force, and
      (ii)   is under the direction and control of the chief officer making a designation under subsection (1).

38A Standard powers and duties of community support officers

(1) The Secretary of State may by order provide for provisions of Part 1 of Schedule 4 to apply to every person who under section 38 is designated as a community support officer.

(2) The powers and duties conferred or imposed by the provisions for the time being applied under subsection (1) are to be known as the standard powers and duties of a community support officer.

(3) Before making an order under subsection (1), the Secretary of State shall consult with—

   (a) such persons as appear to the Secretary of State to represent the views of police and crime commissioners;

   (ab) the Mayor's Office for Policing and Crime;

   (ac) the Common Council of the City of London; and

   (b) the Association of Chief Police Officers.

(4) The Secretary of State shall not make an order containing (with or without any other provision) any provision authorised by subsection (1) unless a draft of that order has been laid before Parliament and approved by a resolution of each House.

(5) A provision of Part 1 of Schedule 4 may be applied to a person concurrently by an order under subsection (1) and a designation under section 38.

(6) If an order under subsection (1) confers or imposes additional powers and duties on a person who is under the direction and control of a chief officer of police of a police force, that chief officer must ensure that the person receives adequate training in the exercise and performance of the additional powers and duties.

38B Police powers for civilian employees under collaboration agreements

(1) The chief officer of police of a police force (the "assisted force") may designate a person ("C") who—

   (a) is a civilian employee of another police force (the "assisting force"),

   (b) is designated under section 38 by the chief officer of police of the assisting police force (the "section 38 designation"), and

   (c) is permitted, under relevant police collaboration provision, to discharge powers and duties specified in that provision for the purposes of the assisted force.

(2) The designation under subsection (1) (the "collaboration designation") must designate C as an officer of one or more of the descriptions specified in section 38(2).

(3) The collaboration designation may designate C as an officer of a particular description specified in section 38(2) only if the section 38 designation designates C as an officer of that description.

(4) C shall have the powers and duties conferred or imposed on C by the collaboration designation.

(5) A power or duty may be conferred or imposed on C by the collaboration designation only if C is permitted, under the relevant police collaboration provision, to discharge that power or duty for the purposes of the assisted force.

(6) C shall not be authorised or required by virtue of the collaboration designation to engage in any conduct otherwise than in the course of discharging a power or duty conferred or imposed on C by the collaboration designation.

(7) The collaboration designation must specify the restrictions and conditions to which C is subject in the discharge of the powers and duties conferred or imposed by the collaboration designation.

(8) Those restrictions and conditions must include the restrictions and conditions specified in the relevant police collaboration provision.

(9) C is authorised or required to discharge any power or duty conferred or imposed by the collaboration designation subject to the restrictions and conditions specified in the collaboration designation.

(10) References in this section to the discharge of functions by civilian employees of the assisting force for the purposes of the assisted force have the same meaning as in section 23B of the Police Act 1996.

(11) In this section—

"civilian employee" has the meaning given by section 23I of the Police Act 1996;

"relevant police collaboration provision" means provision, contained in a collaboration agreement under section 22A of the Police Act 1996, which is of the kind referred to in section 23AA of that Act.

39   Police powers for contracted-out staff

(1) This section applies if a local policing body has entered into a contract with a person ("the contractor") for the provision of services relating to the detention or escort of persons who have been arrested or are otherwise in custody.

(2) The chief officer of police of the police force maintained by that local policing body may designate any person who is an employee of the contractor as either or both of the following—

    (a)   a detention officer; or

    (b)   an escort officer.

(3) A person designated under this section shall have the powers and duties conferred or imposed on him by the designation.

(4) A chief officer of police shall not designate a person under this section unless he is satisfied that that person—

    (a)   is a suitable person to carry out the functions for the purposes of which he is designated;

    (b)   is capable of effectively carrying out those functions; and

    (c)   has received adequate training in the carrying out of those functions and in the exercise and performance of the powers and duties to be conferred on him by virtue of the designation.

(5) A chief officer of police shall not designate a person under this section unless he is satisfied that the contractor is a fit and proper person to supervise the carrying out of the functions for the purposes of which that person is designated.

(6) Powers and duties may be conferred or imposed on a designated person by means only of the application to him by his designation of provisions of the applicable Part of Schedule 4 that are to apply to the designated person; and for this purpose the applicable Part of that Schedule is—

    (a)   in the case of a person designated as a detention officer, Part 3; and

    (b)   in the case of a person designated as an escort officer, Part 4.

(7) An employee of the contractor authorised or required to do anything by virtue of a designation under this section—

    (a)   shall not be authorised or required by virtue of that designation to engage in any conduct otherwise than in the course of that employment; and

    (b)   shall be so authorised or required subject to such restrictions and conditions (if any) as may be specified in his designation.

(8) Where any power exercisable by any person in reliance on his designation under this section is a power which, in the case of its exercise by a constable, includes or is supplemented by a power to use reasonable force, any person exercising that power in reliance on that designation shall have the same entitlement as a constable to use reasonable force.

(12) A designation under this section, unless it is previously withdrawn or ceases to have effect in accordance with subsection (13), shall remain in force for such period as may be specified in the designation; but it may be renewed at any time with effect from the time when it would otherwise expire.

(13) A designation under this section shall cease to have effect—

    (a)   if the designated person ceases to be an employee of the contractor; or

    (b)   if the contract between the local policing body and the contractor is terminated or expires.

40   Community safety accreditation schemes

(1) The chief officer of police of any police force may, if he considers that it is appropriate to do so for the purposes specified in subsection (3), establish and maintain a scheme ("a community safety accreditation scheme").

(2) A community safety accreditation scheme is a scheme for the exercise in the chief officer's police area by persons accredited by him under section 41 of the powers conferred by their accreditations under that section.

(3) Those purposes are—
(a) contributing to community safety and security; and
(b) in co-operation with the police force for the area, combatting crime and disorder, public nuisance and other forms of anti-social behaviour.

(4) Before establishing a community safety accreditation scheme for his police area, a chief officer of any police force (other than the Commissioner of Police of the Metropolis) must consult with—
(a) the local policing body maintaining that force, and
(b) every local authority any part of whose area lies within the police area.

(5) Before establishing a community safety accreditation scheme for the metropolitan police district, the Commissioner of Police of the Metropolis must consult with—
(a) the Mayor's Office for Policing and Crime;
(b) the Mayor of London; and
(c) every local authority any part of whose area lies within the metropolitan police district.

(6) In subsections (4)(b) and (5)(c) "local authority" means—
(a) in relation to England, a district council, a London borough council, the Common Council of the City of London or the Council of the Isles of Scilly; and
(b) in relation to Wales, a county council or a county borough council.

(7) Every police and crime plan under section 5 or 6 of the Police Reform and Social Responsibility Act 2011 which is issued after the commencement of this section must set out—
(a) whether a community safety accreditation scheme is maintained for the police area in question;
(b) if not, whether there is any proposal to establish such a scheme for that area during the period to which the plan relates;
(c) particulars of any such proposal or of any proposal to modify during that period any community safety accreditation scheme that is already maintained for that area;
(d) the extent (if any) of any arrangements for provisions specified in Schedule 4 to be applied to designated persons employed by the local policing body; and
(e) the respects in which any community safety accreditation scheme that is maintained or proposed will be supplementing those arrangements during the period to which the plan relates.

(8) A community safety accreditation scheme must contain provision for the making of arrangements with employers who—
(a) are carrying on business in the police area in question, or
(b) are carrying on business in relation to the whole or any part of that area or in relation to places situated within it,
for those employers to supervise the carrying out by their employees of the community safety functions for the purposes of which powers are conferred on those employees by means of accreditations under section 41.

(9) It shall be the duty of a chief officer of police who establishes and maintains a community safety accreditation scheme to ensure that the employers of the persons on whom powers are conferred by the grant of accreditations under section 41 have established and maintain satisfactory arrangements for handling complaints relating to the carrying out by those persons of the functions for the purposes of which the powers are conferred.

42 Supplementary provisions relating to designations and accreditations

(A1) A person who exercises or performs any power or duty in relation to any person in reliance on his designation under section 28 as a community support officer, or who purports to do so, shall produce to that person evidence of his designation, if requested to do so.

Learning Resources Centre
Middlesbrough College
Dock Street
Middlesbrough
TS2 1AD

(B1) A person who exercises or performs any non-standard power or non-standard duty in relation to any person in reliance on his designation under section 38 as a community support officer, or who purports to do so, shall produce to that person evidence that the power or duty has been conferred or imposed on him, if requested to do so.

(C1) For the purposes of subsection (B1), a power or duty is "non-standard" if it is not one of the standard powers and duties of a community support officer.

(1) A person who exercises or performs any power or duty in relation to any person in reliance on his designation under section 38, 38B or 39 or his accreditation under section 41 or 41A, or who purports to do so, shall produce that designation or accreditation to that person, if requested to do so.

(1A) Subsection (1) does not apply to a person who exercises or performs any power or duty in reliance on his designation under section 38 as a community support officer, or who purports to do so.

(2) A power exercisable by any person in reliance on his designation by a chief officer of police under section 38 or 39 or his accreditation under section 41 shall, subject to subsection (2A), be exercisable only by a person wearing such uniform as may be—

    (a) determined or approved for the purposes of this Chapter by the chief officer of police who granted the designation or accreditation; and

    (b) identified or described in the designation or accreditation;

and, in the case of an accredited person, such a power shall be exercisable only if he is also wearing such badge as may be specified for the purposes of this subsection by the Secretary of State, and is wearing it in such manner, or in such place, as may be so specified.

(2ZA) A power exercisable by any person in reliance on a designation under section 38B by the chief officer of police of the assisted force shall, subject to subsection (2A), be exercisable only by a person wearing such uniform as may be—

    (a) determined or approved for the purposes of this Chapter by the chief officer of police of the assisting police force; and

    (b) identified or described in the designation.

In this subsection, "assisted force" and "assisting force" have the same meanings as in section 38B.

(2A) A police officer of or above the rank of inspector may direct a particular investigating officer not to wear a uniform for the purposes of a particular operation; and if he so directs, subsection (2) or (2ZA) shall not apply in relation to that investigating officer for the purposes of that operation.

(2B) In subsection (2A), "investigating officer" means a person designated as an investigating officer under section 38 (in relation to subsection (2)) or section 38B (in relation to subsection (2ZA)) by the chief officer of police of the same force as the officer giving the direction.

(3) A chief officer of police who has granted a designation or accreditation to any person under section 38, 38B, 39 or 41 or an accreditation to any weights and measures inspector under section 41A may at any time, by notice to the designated or accredited person or the accredited inspector, modify or withdraw that designation or accreditation.

(5) Where any person's designation under section 39 is modified or withdrawn, the chief officer giving notice of the modification or withdrawal shall send a copy of the notice to the contractor responsible for supervising that person in the carrying out of the functions for the purposes of which the designation was granted.

(6) Where any person's accreditation under section 41 is modified or withdrawn, the chief officer giving notice of the modification or withdrawal shall send a copy of the notice to the employer responsible for supervising that person in the carrying out of the functions for the purposes of which the accreditation was granted.

(6A) Where the accreditation of a weights and measures inspector under section 41A is modified or withdrawn, the chief officer giving notice of the modification or withdrawal shall send a copy of the notice to the local weights and measures authority by which the inspector was appointed.

(7) For the purposes of determining liability for the unlawful conduct of employees of a chief officer of police or local policing body, conduct by such an employee in reliance

or purported reliance on a designation under section 38 shall be taken to be conduct in the course of his employment by the chief officer of police or local policing body; and, in the case of a tort, that authority shall fall to be treated as a joint tortfeasor accordingly.

(7A) For the purposes of determining liability for the unlawful conduct of a civilian employee of a police force (within the meaning of section 38B), conduct by such an employee in reliance or purported reliance on a designation under section 38B shall be taken to be conduct in the course of the employee's employment by the employer; and, in the case of a tort, that employer shall fall to be treated as a joint tortfeasor accordingly.

(9) For the purposes of determining liability for the unlawful conduct of employees of a contractor (within the meaning of section 39), conduct by such an employee in reliance or purported reliance on a designation under that section shall be taken to be conduct in the course of his employment by that contractor; and, in the case of a tort, that contractor shall fall to be treated as a joint tortfeasor accordingly.

(10) For the purposes of determining liability for the unlawful conduct of employees of a person with whom a chief officer of police has entered into any arrangements for the purposes of a community safety accreditation scheme, conduct by such an employee in reliance or purported reliance on an accreditation under section 41 shall be taken to be conduct in the course of his employment by that employer; and, in the case of a tort, that employer shall fall to be treated as a joint tortfeasor accordingly.

46   Offences against designated and accredited persons etc.

(2) Any person who resists or wilfully obstructs—
   (a)   a designated person in the execution of his duty,
   (b)   an accredited person in the execution of his duty,
   (ba)   an accredited inspector in the exercise of his duty, or
   (c)   a person assisting a designated or accredited person or an accredited inspector in the execution of his duty,

is guilty of an offence and shall be liable, on summary conviction, to imprisonment for a term not exceeding one month [*51 weeks*] or to a fine not exceeding level 3 on the standard scale, or to both.

(4) In this section references to the execution by a designated person, accredited person or an accredited inspector of his duty are references to his exercising any power or performing any duty which is his by virtue of his designation or accreditation.

(5) References in this section to a designated person are to—
   (a)   a designated person within the meaning given by section 47(1), and
   (b)   a person in relation to whom a designation under section 38B is for the time being in force.

47   Interpretation of Chapter 1

(1) In this Chapter—

"accredited inspector" means a weights and measures inspector in relation to whom an accreditation under section 41A is for the time being in force;

"accredited person" means a person in relation to whom an accreditation under section 41 is for the time being in force;

"community safety functions" means any functions the carrying out of which would be facilitated by the ability to exercise one or more of the powers mentioned in Schedule 5;

"conduct" includes omissions and statements;

"designated person" means a person in relation to whom a designation under section 38 or 39 is for the time being in force;

(2) In this Chapter—
   (a)   references to carrying on business include references to carrying out functions under any enactment; and
   (b)   references to the employees of a person carrying on business include references to persons holding office under a person, and references to employers shall be construed accordingly.

CHAPTER 2
PROVISIONS MODIFYING AND SUPPLEMENTING POLICE POWERS

Power to require name and address

50   Persons acting in an anti-social manner

(1)   If a constable in uniform has reason to believe that a person has been acting, or is acting, in an anti-social manner, he may require that person to give his name and address to the constable.

(1A) In subsection (1) "anti-social behaviour" has the meaning given by section 2 of the Anti-social Behaviour, Crime and Policing Act 2014 (ignoring subsection (2) of that section).

(2)   Any person who—
   (a)   fails to give his name and address when required to do so under subsection (1), or
   (b)   gives a false or inaccurate name or address in response to a requirement under that subsection, is guilty of an offence and shall be liable, on summary conviction, to a fine not exceeding level 3 on the standard scale.

Persons in police detention

51   Independent custody visitors for places of detention

(1)   Every local policing body shall—
   (a)   make arrangements for detainees to be visited by persons appointed under the arrangements ("independent custody visitors"); and
   (b)   keep those arrangements under review and from time to time revise them as they think fit.

(1A) Every local policing body must ensure—
   (a)   that the arrangements made by it require independent custody visitors to prepare and submit to it a report of any visit made under the arrangements to a suspected terrorist detainee, and
   (b)   that a copy of any report submitted under paragraph (a) is given to the person appointed under section 36(1) of the Terrorism Act 2006 (independent reviewer of terrorism legislation).

(2)   The arrangements must secure that the persons appointed under the arrangements are independent of both—
   (a)   the local policing body; and
   (b)   the chief officer of police of the police force maintained by that body.

(3)   The arrangements may confer on independent custody visitors such powers as the local policing body considers necessary to enable them to carry out their functions under the arrangements and may, in particular, confer on them powers—
   (a)   to require access to be given to each police station;
   (b)   to examine records relating to the detention of persons there;
   (ba)   in relation to suspected terrorist detainees, to listen to the audio recordings and view the video recordings (with or without sound) of interviews with those detainees which have taken place during their detention there and which were conducted by a constable;
   (c)   to meet detainees there for the purposes of a discussion about their treatment and conditions while detained; and
   (d)   to inspect the facilities there including in particular, cell accommodation, washing and toilet facilities and the facilities for the provision of food.

(3A) The arrangements may include provision for access to the whole or part of an audio or video recording of an interview of the kind mentioned in subsection (3)(ba) to be denied to independent custody visitors if—
   (a)   it appears to an officer of or above the rank of inspector that there are grounds for denying access at the time it is requested;
   (b)   the grounds are grounds specified for the purposes of paragraph (a) in the arrangements; and
   (c)   the procedural requirements imposed by the arrangements in relation to a denial of access to such recordings are complied with.

(3B) Grounds are not to be specified in any arrangements for the purposes of subsection (3A)(a) unless they are grounds for the time being set out for the purposes of this subsection in the code of practice issued by the Secretary of State under subsection (6).

(4) The arrangements may include provision for access to a detainee to be denied to independent custody visitors if—

(a) it appears to an officer of or above the rank of inspector that there are grounds for denying access at the time it is requested;

(b) the grounds are grounds specified for the purposes of paragraph (a) in the arrangements; and

(c) the procedural requirements imposed by the arrangements in relation to a denial of access are complied with.

(5) Grounds shall not be specified in any arrangements for the purposes of subsection (4)(a) unless they are grounds for the time being set out for the purposes of this subsection in the code of practice issued by the Secretary of State under subsection (6).

(6) The Secretary of State shall issue, and may from time to time revise, a code of practice as to the carrying out by local policing bodies and independent custody visitors of their functions under the arrangements.

(7) Before issuing or revising a code of practice under this section, the Secretary of State shall consult with—

(a) such persons as appear to the Secretary of State to represent the views of police and crime commissioners;

(aa) the Mayor's Office for Policing and Crime;

(ab) the Common Council of the City of London; and

(b) the Association of Chief Police Officers; and

(c) such other persons as he thinks fit.

(8) The Secretary of State shall lay any code of practice issued by him under this section, and any revisions of any such code, before Parliament.

(9) Local policing bodies and independent custody visitors shall have regard to the code of practice for the time being in force under subsection (6) in the carrying out of their functions under the preceding provisions of this section.

(10) In this section—

"detainee", in relation to arrangements made under this section, means a person detained in a police station in the police area of the local policing body;

"suspected terrorist detainee" means a detainee detained under section 41 of the Terrorism Act 2000.

Seizure of motor vehicles

59   Vehicles used in manner causing alarm, distress or annoyance

(1) Where a constable in uniform has reasonable grounds for believing that a motor vehicle is being used on any occasion in a manner which—

(a) contravenes section 3 or 34 of the Road Traffic Act 1988 (careless and inconsiderate driving and prohibition of off-road driving), and

(b) is causing, or is likely to cause, alarm, distress or annoyance to members of the public, he shall have the powers set out in subsection (3).

(2) A constable in uniform shall also have the powers set out in subsection (3) where he has reasonable grounds for believing that a motor vehicle has been used on any occasion in a manner falling within subsection (1).

(3) Those powers are—

(a) power, if the motor vehicle is moving, to order the person driving it to stop the vehicle;

(b) power to seize and remove the motor vehicle;

(c) power, for the purposes of exercising a power falling within paragraph (a) or (b), to enter any premises on which he has reasonable grounds for believing the motor vehicle to be;

(d) power to use reasonable force, if necessary, in the exercise of any power conferred by any of paragraphs to (a) to (c).

(4) A constable shall not seize a motor vehicle in the exercise of the powers conferred on him by this section unless—

    (a) he has warned the person appearing to him to be the person whose use falls within subsection (1) that he will seize it, if that use continues or is repeated; and

    (b) it appears to him that the use has continued or been repeated after the warning.

(5) Subsection (4) does not require a warning to be given by a constable on any occasion on which he would otherwise have the power to seize a motor vehicle under this section if—

    (a) the circumstances make it impracticable for him to give the warning;

    (b) the constable has already on that occasion given a warning under that subsection in respect of any use of that motor vehicle or of another motor vehicle by that person or any other person;

    (c) the constable has reasonable grounds for believing that such a warning has been given on that occasion otherwise than by him; or

    (d) the constable has reasonable grounds for believing that the person whose use of that motor vehicle on that occasion would justify the seizure is a person to whom a warning under that subsection has been given (whether or not by that constable or in respect the same vehicle or the same or a similar use) on a previous occasion in the previous twelve months.

(6) A person who fails to comply with an order under subsection (3)(a) is guilty of an offence and shall be liable, on summary conviction, to a fine not exceeding level 3 on the standard scale.

(7) Subsection (3)(c) does not authorise entry into a private dwelling house.

(8) The powers conferred on a constable by this section shall be exercisable only at a time when regulations under section 60 are in force.

(9) In this section—

"driving" has the same meaning as in the Road Traffic Act 1988;

"motor vehicle" means any mechanically propelled vehicle, whether or not it is intended or adapted for use on roads; and

"private dwelling house" does not include any garage or other structure occupied with the dwelling house, or any land appurtenant to the dwelling house.

60   Retention etc. of vehicles seized under section 59

(1) The Secretary of State may by regulations make provision as to—

    (a) the removal and retention of motor vehicles seized under section 59; and

    (b) the release or disposal of such motor vehicles.

(2) Regulations under subsection (1) may, in particular, make provision—

    (a) for the giving of notice of the seizure of a motor vehicle under section 59 to a person who is the owner of that vehicle or who, in accordance with the regulations, appears to be its owner;

    (b) for the procedure by which a person who claims to be the owner of a motor vehicle seized under section 59 may seek to have it released;

    (c) for requiring the payment of fees, charges or costs in relation to the removal and retention of such a motor vehicle and to any application for its release;

    (d) as to the circumstances in which a motor vehicle seized under section 59 may be disposed of:

    (e) as to the destination—

        (i) of any fees or charges payable in accordance with the regulations; and

        (ii) of the proceeds (if any) arising from the disposal of a motor vehicle seized under section 59;

    (f) for the delivery to a local authority, in circumstances prescribed by or determined in accordance with the regulations, of any motor vehicle seized under section 59.

(3) Regulations under subsection (1) must provide that a person who would otherwise be liable to pay any fee or charge under the regulations shall not be liable to pay it if—

    (a) the use by reference to which the motor vehicle in question was seized was not a use by him; and

    (b) he did not know of the use of the vehicle in the manner which led to its seizure, had not consented to its use in that manner and could not, by the taking of reasonable steps, have prevented its use in that manner.

(4)   In this section—
"local authority"—
    (a)   in relation to England, means the council of a county, metropolitan district or London borough, the Common Council of the City of London or Transport for London; and
    (b)   in relation to Wales, means the council of a county or county borough; "motor vehicle" has the same meaning as in section 59.

CONSTITUTIONAL REFORM ACT 2005
(2005, c. 4)

An Act to make provision for modifying the office of Lord Chancellor, and to make provision relating to the functions of that office; to establish a Supreme Court of the United Kingdom, and to abolish the appellate jurisdiction of the House of Lords; to make provision about the jurisdiction of the Judicial Committee of the Privy Council and the judicial functions of the President of the Council; to make other provision about the judiciary, their appointment and discipline; and for connected purposes. [24 March 2005]

PART 1
THE RULE OF LAW

1   The rule of law
This Act does not adversely affect—
    (a)   the existing constitutional principle of the rule of law, or
    (b)   the Lord Chancellor's existing constitutional role in relation to that principle.

PART 2
ARRANGEMENTS TO MODIFY THE OFFICE OF LORD CHANCELLOR

Qualifications for office of Lord Chancellor

2   Lord Chancellor to be qualified by experience
(1)   A person may not be recommended for appointment as Lord Chancellor unless he appears to the Prime Minister to be qualified by experience.
(2)   The Prime Minister may take into account any of these—
    (a)   experience as a Minister of the Crown;
    (b)   experience as a member of either House of Parliament;
    (c)   experience as a qualifying practitioner;
    (d)   experience as a teacher of law in a university;
    (e)   other experience that the Prime Minister considers relevant.
(3)   In this section "qualifying practitioner" means any of these—
    (a)   a person who has a Senior Courts qualification, within the meaning of section 71 of the Courts and Legal Services Act 1990;
    (b)   an advocate in Scotland or a solicitor entitled to appear in the Court of Session and the High Court of Justiciary;
    (c)   a member of the Bar of Northern Ireland or a solicitor of the Court of Judicature of Northern Ireland.

Continued judicial independence

3   Guarantee of continued judicial independence
(1)   The Lord Chancellor, other Ministers of the Crown and all with responsibility for matters relating to the judiciary or otherwise to the administration of justice must uphold the continued independence of the judiciary.
(2)   Subsection (1) does not impose any duty which it would be within the legislative competence of the Scottish Parliament to impose.

(3)   A person is not subject to the duty imposed by subsection (1) if he is subject to the duty imposed by section 1(1) of the Justice (Northern Ireland) Act 2002.

(4)   The following particular duties are imposed for the purpose of upholding that independence.

(5)   The Lord Chancellor and other Ministers of the Crown must not seek to influence particular judicial decisions through any special access to the judiciary.

(6)   The Lord Chancellor must have regard to—
    (a)   the need to defend that independence;
    (b)   the need for the judiciary to have the support necessary to enable them to exercise their functions;
    (c)   the need for the public interest in regard to matters relating to the judiciary or otherwise to the administration of justice to be properly represented in decisions affecting those matters.

(7)   In this section "the judiciary" includes the judiciary of any of the following—
    (a)   the Supreme Court;
    (b)   any other court established under the law of any part of the United Kingdom;
    (c)   any international court.

Representations by senior judges

5   Representations to Parliament

(AI)   The President of the Supreme Court may lay before Parliament written representations on matters that appear to the President to be matters of importance relating to the Supreme Court or to the jurisdiction it exercises.

(1)   The chief justice of any part of the United Kingdom may lay before Parliament written representations on matters that appear to him to be matters of importance relating to the judiciary, or otherwise to the administration of justice, in that part of the United Kingdom.

(2)   In relation to Scotland the matters mentioned in subsections (A1) and (1) do not include matters within the legislative competence of the Scottish Parliament, unless they are matters to which a Bill for an Act of Parliament relates.

(3)   In relation to Northern Ireland the matters mentioned in subsections (A1) and (1) do not include transferred matters within the legislative competence of the Northern Ireland Assembly, unless they are matters to which a Bill for an Act of Parliament relates.

Judiciary and courts in England and Wales

7   President of the Courts of England and Wales

(1)   The Lord Chief Justice holds the office of President of the Courts of England and Wales and is Head of the Judiciary of England and Wales.

(2)   As President of the Courts of England and Wales he is responsible—
    (a)   for representing the views of the judiciary of England and Wales to Parliament, to the Lord Chancellor and to Ministers of the Crown generally;
    (b)   for the maintenance of appropriate arrangements for the welfare, training and guidance of the judiciary of England and Wales within the resources made available by the Lord Chancellor;
    (c)   for the maintenance of appropriate arrangements for the deployment of the judiciary of England and Wales and the allocation of work within courts.

(3)   The President of the Courts of England and Wales is president of the courts listed in subsection (4) and is entitled to sit in any of those courts.

(4)   The courts are—
the Court of Appeal
the High Court
the Crown Court
the family court
the county court
the magistrates' courts.

8   Head and Deputy Head of Criminal Justice

(1)   There is to be a Head of Criminal Justice.

(2)   The Head of Criminal Justice is—

(a)   the Lord Chief Justice, or

(b)   if the Lord Chief Justice appoints another person, that person.

(3)   The Lord Chief Justice may appoint a person to be Deputy Head of Criminal Justice.

(4)   The Lord Chief Justice must not appoint a person under subsection (2)(b) or (3) unless these conditions are met—

(a)   the Lord Chief Justice has consulted the Lord Chancellor;

(b)   the person to be appointed is a judge of the Court of Appeal.

(5)   A person appointed under subsection (2)(b) or (3) holds the office to which he is appointed in accordance with the terms of his appointment.

14   Transfer of appointment functions to Her Majesty

Schedule 3 provides for—

(a)   Her Majesty instead of the Lord Chancellor to make appointments to certain offices, and

(b)   the modification of enactments relating to those offices.

15   Other functions of the Lord Chancellor and organisation of the courts

(1)   Schedule 4 provides for—

(a)   the transfer of functions to or from the Lord Chancellor,

(b)   the modification of other functions of the Lord Chancellor,

(c)   the modification of enactments relating to those functions, and

(d)   the modification of enactments relating to the organisation of the courts.

Speakership of the House of Lords

18   Speakership of the House of Lords

Schedule 6 contains amendments relating to the Speakership of the House of Lords.

PART 3
THE SUPREME COURT

The Supreme Court

23   The Supreme Court

(1)   There is to be a Supreme Court of the United Kingdom.

(2)   The Court consists of the persons appointed as its judges by Her Majesty by letters patent, but no appointment may cause the full-time equivalent number of judges of the Court at any time to be more than 12.

(3)   Her Majesty may from time to time by Order in Council amend subsection (2) so as to increase or further increase the maximum full-time equivalent number of judges of the Court.

(4)   No recommendation may be made to Her Majesty in Council to make an Order under subsection (3) unless a draft of the Order has been laid before and approved by resolution of each House of Parliament.

(5)   Her Majesty may by letters patent appoint one of the judges to be President and one to be Deputy President of the Court.

(6)   The judges other than the President and Deputy President are to be styled "Justices of the Supreme Court".

(7)   The Court is to be taken to be duly constituted despite any vacancy in the office of President or Deputy President.

(8)   For the purposes of this section, the full-time equivalent number of judges of the Court is to be calculated by taking the number of full-time judges and adding, for each judge who is not a full-time judge, such fraction as is reasonable.

24   First members of the Court

On the commencement of section 23—

(a)   the persons who immediately before that commencement are Lords of Appeal in Ordinary become judges of the Supreme Court,

(b)   the person who immediately before that commencement is the senior Lord of Appeal in Ordinary becomes the President of the Court, and

(c)   the person who immediately before that commencement is the second senior Lord of Appeal in Ordinary becomes the Deputy President of the Court.

Appointment of judges

25   Qualification for appointment

(1)   A person is not qualified to be appointed a judge of the Supreme Court unless he has (at any time)—

(a)   held high judicial office for a period of at least 2 years, or

(b)   satisfied the judicial-appointment eligibility on a 15-year basis, or

(c)   been a qualifying practitioner for a period of at least 15 years.

26   Selection of members of the Court

(1)   This section applies to a recommendation for an appointment to one of the following offices—

(a)   judge of the Supreme Court;

(b)   President of the Court;

(c)   Deputy President of the Court.

(2)   A recommendation may be made only by the Prime Minister.

(3)   The Prime Minister—

(a)   must recommend any person who is selected as a result of the convening of a selection commission under this section;

(b)   may not recommend any other person.

(4)   Where a person who is not a judge of the Court is recommended for appointment as President or Deputy President, the recommendation must also recommend the person for appointment as a judge.

(5)   If there is a vacancy in the office of President of the Court or in the office of Deputy President of the Court, or it appears to him that there will soon be such a vacancy, the Lord Chancellor must convene a selection commission for the selection of a person to be recommended.

(5A)   If—

(a)   the full-time equivalent number of judges of the Court is less than the maximum specified in section 23(2), or it appears to the Lord Chancellor that the full-time equivalent number of judges of the Court will soon be less than that maximum, and

(b)   the Lord Chancellor, or the senior judge of the Court, after consulting the other considers it desirable that a recommendation be made for an appointment to the office of judge of the Court,

the Lord Chancellor must convene a selection commission for the selection of a person to be recommended.

(5B)   In subsection (5A)(b) "the senior judge of the Court" means—

(a)   the President of the Court, or

(b)   if there is no President, the Deputy President, or

(c)   if there is no President and no Deputy President, the senior ordinary judge.

27   Selection process

(1)   The commission must—

(a)   determine the selection process to be applied by it,

(b)   apply the selection process, and

(c)   make a selection accordingly.

(1A)   The commission must have an odd number of members not less than five.

(1B)   The members of the commission must include—

(a)   at least one who is non-legally-qualified,

(b)   at least one judge of the Court,

(c)   at least one member of the Judicial Appointments Commission,

(d)   at least one member of the Judicial Appointments Board for Scotland, and

(e)   at least one member of the Northern Ireland Judicial Appointments Commission,

and more than one of the requirements may be met by the same person's membership of the commission.

(1C)   If the commission is convened for the selection of a person to be recommended for appointment as President of the Court—

(a)   its members may not include the President of the Court, and

(b)   it is to be chaired by one of its non-legally-qualified members.

(1D)   If the commission is convened for the selection of a person to be recommended for appointment as Deputy President of the Court, its members may not include the Deputy President of the Court.

(4)   Subsections (5) to (10) apply to any selection under this section or regulations under section 27A.

(5)   Selection must be on merit.

(5A)   Where two persons are of equal merit—

(a)   section 159 of the Equality Act 2010 (positive action: recruitment etc) does not apply in relation to choosing between them, but

(b)   Part 5 of that Act (public appointments etc) does not prevent the commission from preferring one of them over the other for the purpose of increasing diversity within the group of persons who are the judges of the Court.

(6)   A person may be selected only if he meets the requirements of section 25.

(7)   A person may not be selected if he is a member of the commission.

(8)   In making selections for the appointment of judges of the Court the commission must ensure that between them the judges will have knowledge of, and experience of practice in, the law of each part of the United Kingdom.

(9)   The commission must have regard to any guidance given by the Lord Chancellor as to matters to be taken into account (subject to any other provision of this Act) in making a selection.

(10)   Any selection must be of one person only.

(11)   For the purposes of this section a person is non-legally-qualified if the person—

(a)   does not hold, and has never held, any of the offices listed in Schedule 1 to the House of Commons Disqualification Act 1975 (judicial offices disqualifying for membership of the House of Commons), and

(b)   is not practising or employed as a lawyer, and never has practised or been employed as a lawyer.

27A   Regulations about selection process

(1)   The Lord Chancellor must by regulations made with the agreement of the senior judge of the Supreme Court—

(a)   make further provision about membership of selection commissions convened under section 26,

(b)   make further provision about the process that is to be applied in any case where a selection commission is required to be convened under section 26, and

(c)   secure that, in every such case, there will come a point in the process when a selection has to be accepted, either unconditionally or subject only to matters such as the selected person's willingness and availability, by or on behalf of the Lord Chancellor.

(2)   The regulations may in particular—

(a)   provide for process additional to the selection process applied by a selection commission under section 27(1), including post-acceptance process;

(b)   make provision as to things that are, or as to things that are not, to be done by a selection commission—

(i)   as part of the selection process applied by it under section 27(1), or

(ii)   in determining what that process is to be;

(c)   provide for the Lord Chancellor to be entitled to require a selection commission to reconsider a selection under section 27(1) or any subsequent selection;

(d)   provide for the Lord Chancellor to be entitled to reject a selection under section 27(1) or any subsequent selection;

(e)   give other functions to the Lord Chancellor;
(f)   provide for particular action to be taken by a selection commission after it has complied with section 27;
(g)   provide for the dissolution of a selection commission;
(h)   provide for section 16(2)(a) or (b) not to apply in relation to functions of the Lord Chief Justice—
    (i)   as a member of a selection commission (including functions of chairing a selection commission), or
    (ii)   in relation to the nomination or appointment of members of a selection commission;
(i)   provide for a person to cease to be a member of a selection commission where a requirement about the commission's members ceases to be met by the person's membership of the commission;
(j)   provide for a person to become a member of a selection commission already convened where another person ceases to be a member of the commission or where a requirement about the commission's members ceases to be met by another person's membership of the commission;
(k)   provide for payment to a member of a selection commission of amounts by way of allowances or expenses;
(l)   make provision as to what amounts to practice or employment as a lawyer for the purposes of section 27(11)(b).

(3)   Before making regulations under this section the Lord Chancellor must consult—
    (a)   the First Minister in Scotland,
    (b)   the Northern Ireland Judicial Appointments Commission,
    (c)   the First Minister for Wales,
    (d)   the Lord President of the Court of Session,
    (e)   the Lord Chief Justice of Northern Ireland, and
    (f)   the Lord Chief Justice of England and Wales.

(4)   Regulations under this section—
    (a)   may make different provision for different purposes;
    (b)   may make transitory, transitional or saving provision.

(5)   In this section "the senior judge", in relation to the Court, has the meaning given by section 26(5B).

27B   Selection guidance: supplementary

(1)   Before issuing any selection guidance the Lord Chancellor must—
    (a)   consult the senior judge of the Supreme Court;
    (b)   after doing so, lay a draft of the proposed guidance before each House of Parliament.

(2)   If the draft is approved by a resolution of each House of Parliament within the 40-day period the Lord Chancellor must issue the guidance in the form of the draft.

(3)   In any other case the Lord Chancellor must take no further steps in relation to the proposed guidance.

(4)   Subsection (3) does not prevent a new draft of the proposed guidance from being laid before each House of Parliament after consultation with the senior judge of the Court.

(5)   Selection guidance comes into force on such date as the Lord Chancellor may appoint by order.

(6)   Where selection guidance is in force, the Lord Chancellor may revoke the guidance only by—
    (a)   new selection guidance issued in accordance with the previous provisions of this section, or
    (b)   an order made after consulting the senior judge of the Court.

(7)   In this section—
    "40-day period" in relation to the draft of any proposed selection guidance means—
    (a)   if the draft is laid before one House on a day later than the day on which it is laid before the other House, the period of 40 days beginning with the later day, and
    (b)   in any other case, the period of 40 days beginning with the day on which the draft is laid before each House,
    no account being taken of any period during which Parliament is dissolved or prorogued or during which both Houses are adjourned for more than 4 days;

"the senior judge", in relation to the Court, has the meaning given by section 26(5B);
"selection guidance" means guidance mentioned in section 27(9).

33 Tenure

A judge of the Supreme Court holds that office during good behaviour, but may be removed from it on the address of both Houses of Parliament.

34 Salaries and allowances

(1) A judge of the Supreme Court is entitled to a salary.

(5) Salaries payable under this section are to be charged on and paid out of the Consolidated Fund of the United Kingdom.

41 Relation to other courts etc

(1) Nothing in this Part is to affect the distinctions between the separate legal systems of the parts of the United Kingdom.

(2) A decision of the Supreme Court on appeal from a court of any part of the United Kingdom, other than a decision on a devolution matter, is to be regarded as the decision of a court of that part of the United Kingdom.

(3) A decision of the Supreme Court on a devolution matter—
   (a) is not binding on that Court when making such a decision;
   (b) otherwise, is binding in all legal proceedings.

PART 4
JUDICIAL APPOINTMENTS AND DISCIPLINE

CHAPTER 1
COMMISSION AND OMBUDSMAN

61 The Judicial Appointments Commission

(1) There is to be a body corporate called the Judicial Appointments Commission.

62 Judicial Appointments and Conduct Ombudsman

(1) There is to be a Judicial Appointments and Conduct Ombudsman.

CHAPTER 2
APPOINTMENTS

General provisions

63 Merit and good character

(1) Subsections (2) to (4) apply to any selection under this Part by the Commission or a selection panel ("the selecting body").

(2) Selection must be solely on merit.

(3) A person must not be selected unless the selecting body is satisfied that he is of good character.

(4) Neither "solely" in subsection (2), nor Part 5 of the Equality Act 2010 (public appointments etc), prevents the selecting body, where two persons are of equal merit, from preferring one of them over the other for the purpose of increasing diversity within—
   (a) the group of persons who hold offices for which there is selection under this Part, or
   (b) a sub-group of that group.

64 Encouragement of diversity

(1) The Commission, in performing its functions under this Part, must have regard to the need to encourage diversity in the range of persons available for selection for appointments.

(2) This section is subject to section 63.

65   Guidance about procedures

(1)   The Lord Chancellor may issue guidance about procedures for the performance by the Commission or a selection panel of its functions of—

(a)   identifying persons willing to be considered for selection under this Part, and

(b)   assessing such persons for the purposes of selection.

(2)   The guidance may, among other things, relate to consultation or other steps in determining such procedures.

(3)   The purposes for which guidance may be issued under this section include the encouragement of diversity in the range of persons available for selection.

Lord Chief Justice and Heads of Division

67   Selection of Lord Chief Justice and Heads of Division

(1)   Sections 68 to 70 apply to a recommendation for an appointment to one of the following offices—

(a)   Lord Chief Justice;

(b)   Master of the Rolls;

(c)   President of the Queen's Bench Division;

(d)   President of the Family Division;

(e)   Chancellor of the High Court.

(2)   Any such recommendation must be made in accordance with those sections and section 94C and regulations made under it.

70   Selection process

(1)   On receiving a request the Commission must appoint a selection panel.

(1A)   The panel must have an odd number of members not less than five.

(1B)   The members of the panel must include—

(a)   at least two who are non-legally-qualified,

(b)   at least two judicial members, and

(c)   at least two members of the Commission,

and contributions to meeting more than one of the requirements may be made by the same person's membership of the panel.

(1C)   The members of the panel may not include the current holder of the office for which a selection is to be made.

(1D)   If the panel is convened for the selection of a person to be recommended for appointment as Lord Chief Justice, it is to be chaired by one of its non-legally-qualified members.

(2)   The panel must—

(a)   determine the selection process to be applied by it,

(b)   apply the selection process, and

(c)   make a selection accordingly.

(3)   One person only must be selected for each recommendation to which a request relates.

(4)   Subsection (3) applies to selection under this section and to selection under regulations under section 94C.

(6)   A selection panel is a committee of the Commission.

SCHEDULE 12   **Section 61**

THE JUDICIAL APPOINTMENTS COMMISSION

PART 1

THE COMMISSIONERS

The Commissioners

1.   The Commission consists of—

(a)   a chairman, and

(b)   such number of other Commissioners as the Lord Chancellor may specify by regulations made with the agreement of the Lord Chief Justice,

appointed by Her Majesty on the recommendation of the Lord Chancellor.

2.   (1)   The chairman must be a lay member.

3.   A person must not be appointed as a Commissioner if he is employed in the civil service of the State.

3A.   The number of Commissioners who are holders of judicial office must be less than the number of Commissioners (including the chairman) who are not holders of judicial office.

3B.   (1)   The Lord Chancellor may, by regulations made with the agreement of the Lord Chief Justice, make provision about the composition of the Commission.

      (2)   The power to make regulations under this paragraph is to be exercised so as to ensure that the Commission's members include—

          (a)   holders of judicial office,

          (b)   persons practising or employed as lawyers, and

          (c)   lay members.

      (3)   Regulations under this paragraph may (in particular)—

          (a)   make provision about the number, maximum number or minimum number of Commissioners of a particular description;

          (b)   make provision about eligibility for appointment as a Commissioner, eligibility for appointment as the chairman or eligibility for appointment as a Commissioner of a particular description.

3C.   The Lord Chancellor may by regulations made with the agreement of the Lord Chief Justice—

      (a)   define "lay member", in relation to the Commission, for the purposes of this Part of this Act;

      (b)   define "holder of judicial office" for the purposes of paragraphs 3A, 3B(2)(a), 11 and 20(5).

SERIOUS ORGANISED CRIME AND POLICE ACT 2005
(2005, c. 15)

An Act to provide for the establishment and functions of the Serious Organised Crime Agency; to make provision about investigations, prosecutions, offenders and witnesses in criminal proceedings and the protection of persons involved in investigations or proceedings; to make further provision for combatting crime and disorder, including new provision about powers of arrest and search warrants and about parental compensation orders; to make further provision about the police and policing and persons supporting the police; to make provision for protecting certain organisations from interference with their activities; to make provision about criminal records.   [7 April 2005]

PART 2
INVESTIGATIONS, PROSECUTIONS, PROCEEDINGS AND PROCEEDS OF CRIME

CHAPTER 1
INVESTIGATORY POWERS OF DPP, ETC.

Introductory

60   Investigatory powers of DPP etc.

      (1)   This Chapter confers powers on—

          (a)   the Director of Public Prosecutions,

          (c)   the Lord Advocate, and

          (d)   the Director of Public Prosecutions for Northern Ireland,

      in relation to the giving of disclosure notices in connection with the investigation of offences to which this Chapter applies or in connection with a terrorist investigation.

      (2)   The Director of Public Prosecutions may, to such extent as he may determine, delegate the exercise of his powers under this Chapter to a Crown prosecutor.

      (4)   The Lord Advocate may, to such extent as he may determine, delegate the exercise of his powers under this Chapter to a procurator fiscal.

(4A) The Director of Public Prosecutions for Northern Ireland may, to such extent as he may determine, delegate the exercise of his powers under this Chapter to a Public Prosecutor.

(5) In this Chapter "the Investigating Authority" means—

    (a)   the Director of Public Prosecutions,

    (c)   the Lord Advocate, or

    (d)   the Director of Public Prosecutions for Northern Ireland.

(6) But, in circumstances where the powers of any of those persons are exercisable by any other person by virtue of subsection (2), (4) or (4A), references to "the Investigating Authority" accordingly include any such other person.

(7) In this Chapter "terrorist investigation" means an investigation of—

    (a)   the commission, preparation or instigation of acts of terrorism,

    (b)   any act or omission which appears to have been for the purposes of terrorism and which consists in or involves the commission, preparation or instigation of an offence, or

    (c)   the commission, preparation or instigation of an offence under the Terrorism Act 2000 or under Part 1 of the Terrorism Act 2006 other than an offence under section 1 or 2 of that Act.

61   Offences to which this Chapter applies

(1) This Chapter applies to the following offences—

    (a)   any offence listed in Schedule 2 to the Proceeds of Crime Act 2002 (lifestyle offences: England and Wales);

    (b)   any offence listed in Schedule 4 to that Act (lifestyle offences: Scotland);

    (ba)   any offence listed in Schedule 5 to that Act (lifestyle offences: Northern Ireland);

    (c)   any offence under sections 15 to 18 of the Terrorism Act 2000 (offences relating to fund-raising, money laundering etc.);

    (d)   any offence under section 170 of the Customs and Excise Management Act 1979 (fraudulent evasion of duty) or section 72 of the Value Added Tax Act 1994 (offences relating to VAT) which is a qualifying offence;

    (e)   any offence under section 17 of the Theft Act 1968 or section 17 of the Theft Act (Northern Ireland) 1969 (false accounting), or any offence at common law of cheating in relation to the public revenue, which is a qualifying offence;

    (f)   any offence under section 1 of the Criminal Attempts Act 1981 or Article 3 of the Criminal Attempts and Conspiracy (Northern Ireland) Order 1983, or in Scotland at common law, of attempting to commit any offence in paragraph (c) or any offence in paragraph (d) or (e) which is a qualifying offence;

    (g)   any offence under section 1 of the Criminal Law Act 1977 or Article 9 of the Criminal Attempts and Conspiracy (Northern Ireland) Order 1983, or in Scotland at common law, of conspiracy to commit any offence in paragraph (c) or any offence in paragraph (d) or (e) which is a qualifying offence.

    (h)   any offence under the Bribery Act 2010.

(2) For the purposes of subsection (1) an offence in paragraph (d) or (e) of that subsection is a qualifying offence if the Investigating Authority certifies that in his opinion—

    (a)   in the case of an offence in paragraph (d) or an offence of cheating the public revenue, the offence involved or would have involved a loss, or potential loss, to the public revenue of an amount not less than £5,000;

    (b)   in the case of an offence under section 17 of the Theft Act 1968, the offence involved or would have involved a loss or gain, or potential loss or gain, of an amount not less than £5,000.

(3) A document purporting to be a certificate under subsection (2) is to be received in evidence and treated as such a certificate unless the contrary is proved.

Disclosure notices

62   Disclosure notices

(1) If it appears to the Investigating Authority—

    (a)   that there are reasonable grounds for suspecting that an offence to which this Chapter applies has been committed,

     (b)   that any person has information (whether or not contained in a document) which relates to a matter relevant to the investigation of that offence, and

     (c)   that there are reasonable grounds for believing that information which may be provided by that person in compliance with a disclosure notice is likely to be of substantial value (whether or not by itself) to that investigation,

he may give, or authorise an appropriate person to give, a disclosure notice to that person.

(1A) If it appears to the Investigating Authority—

     (a)   that any person has information (whether or not contained in a document) which relates to a matter relevant to a terrorist investigation, and

     (b)   that there are reasonable grounds for believing that information which may be provided by that person in compliance with a disclosure notice is likely to be of substantial value (whether or not by itself) to that investigation,

he may give, or authorise an appropriate person to give, a disclosure notice to that person.

(2)   In this Chapter "appropriate person" means—

     (a)   a constable,

     (b)   a member of the staff of SOCA who is for the time being designated under section 43, or

     (c)   an officer of Revenue and Customs.

But in the application of this Chapter to Northern Ireland, this subsection has effect as if paragraph (b) were omitted.

(3)   In this Chapter "disclosure notice" means a notice in writing requiring the person to whom it is given to do all or any of the following things in accordance with the specified requirements, namely—

     (a)   answer questions with respect to any matter relevant to the investigation;

     (b)   provide information with respect to any such matter as is specified in the notice;

     (c)   produce such documents, or documents of such descriptions, relevant to the investigation as are specified in the notice.

(4)   In subsection (3) "the specified requirements" means such requirements specified in the disclosure notice as relate to—

     (a)   the time at or by which,

     (b)   the place at which, or

     (c)   the manner in which,

the person to whom the notice is given is to do any of the things mentioned in paragraphs (a) to (c) of that subsection; and those requirements may include a requirement to do any of those things at once.

(5)   A disclosure notice must be signed or counter-signed by the Investigating Authority.

(6)   This section has effect subject to section 64 (restrictions on requiring information etc.).

63   Production of documents

(1)   This section applies where a disclosure notice has been given under section 62.

(2)   An authorised person may—

     (a)   take copies of or extracts from any documents produced in compliance with the notice, and

     (b)   require the person producing them to provide an explanation of any of them.

(3)   Documents so produced may be retained for so long as the Investigating Authority considers that it is necessary to retain them (rather than copies of them) in connection with the investigation for the purposes of which the disclosure notice was given.

(4)   If the Investigating Authority has reasonable grounds for believing—

     (a)   that any such documents may have to be produced for the purposes of any legal proceedings, and

     (b)   that they might otherwise be unavailable for those purposes,

they may be retained until the proceedings are concluded.

(5)   If a person who is required by a disclosure notice to produce any documents does not produce the documents in compliance with the notice, an authorised person may require that person to state, to the best of his knowledge and belief, where they are.

(6)   In this section "authorised person" means any appropriate person who either—
(a)   is the person by whom the notice was given, or
(b)   is authorised by the Investigating Authority for the purposes of this section.
(7)   This section has effect subject to section 64 (restrictions on requiring information etc.).

64   Restrictions on requiring information etc.

(1)   A person may not be required under section 62 or 63—
(a)   to answer any privileged question,
(b)   to provide any privileged information, or
(c)   to produce any privileged document,
except that a lawyer may be required to provide the name and address of a client of his.
(8)   A person may not be required under section 62 or 63 to disclose any information or produce any document in respect of which he owes an obligation of confidence by virtue of carrying on any banking business, unless—
(a)   the person to whom the obligation of confidence is owed consents to the disclosure or production, or
(b)   the requirement is made by, or in accordance with a specific authorisation given by, the Investigating Authority.

65   Restrictions on use of statements

(1)   A statement made by a person in response to a requirement imposed under section 62 or 63 ("the relevant statement") may not be used in evidence against him in any criminal proceedings unless subsection (2) or (3) applies.
(2)   This subsection applies where the person is being prosecuted—
(a)   for an offence under section 67 of this Act, or
(b)   for an offence under section 5 of the Perjury Act 1911 (false statements made on oath otherwise than in judicial proceedings or made otherwise than on oath), or
(c)   for an offence under section 44(2) of the Criminal Law (Consolidation) (Scotland) Act 1995 (false statutory declarations and other false statements without oath) or at common law for an offence of attempting to pervert the course, or defeat the ends, of justice, or
(d)   for an offence under Article 10 of the Perjury (Northern Ireland) Order 1979 (false statements made otherwise than on oath).
(3)   This subsection applies where the person is being prosecuted for some other offence and—
(a)   the person, when giving evidence in the proceedings, makes a statement inconsistent with the relevant statement, and
(b)   in the proceedings evidence relating to the relevant statement is adduced, or a question about it is asked, by or on behalf of the person.

Enforcement

66   Power to enter and seize documents

(1)   A justice of the peace may issue a warrant under this section if, on an information on oath laid by the Investigating Authority, he is satisfied—
(a)   that any of the conditions mentioned in subsection (2) is met in relation to any documents of a description specified in the information, and
(b)   that the documents are on premises so specified.
(2)   The conditions are—
(a)   that a person has been required by a disclosure notice to produce the documents but has not done so;
(b)   that it is not practicable to give a disclosure notice requiring their production;
(c)   that giving such a notice might seriously prejudice the investigation of an offence to which this Chapter applies.
(3)   A warrant under this section is a warrant authorising an appropriate person named in it—
(a)   to enter and search the premises, using such force as is reasonably necessary;
(b)   to take possession of any documents appearing to be documents of a description specified in the information, or to take any other steps which

      appear to be necessary for preserving, or preventing interference with, any such documents;

(c)   in the case of any such documents consisting of information recorded otherwise than in legible form, to take possession of any computer disk or other electronic storage device which appears to contain the information in question, or to take any other steps which appear to be necessary for preserving, or preventing interference with, that information;

(d)   to take copies of or extracts from any documents or information falling within paragraph (b) or (c);

(e)   to require any person on the premises to provide an explanation of any such documents or information or to state where any such documents or information may be found;

(f)   to require any such person to give the appropriate person such assistance as he may reasonably require for the taking of copies or extracts as mentioned in paragraph (d).

(4)   A person executing a warrant under this section may take other persons with him, if it appears to him to be necessary to do so.

(5)   A warrant under this section must, if so required, be produced for inspection by the owner or occupier of the premises or anyone acting on his behalf.

(6)   If the premises are unoccupied or the occupier is temporarily absent, a person entering the premises under the authority of a warrant under this section must leave the premises as effectively secured against trespassers as he found them.

(7)   Where possession of any document or device is taken under this section—

(a)   the document may be retained for so long as the Investigating Authority considers that it is necessary to retain it (rather than a copy of it) in connection with the investigation for the purposes of which the warrant was sought, or

(b)   the device may be retained for so long as he considers that it is necessary to retain it in connection with that investigation,

as the case may be.

(8)   If the Investigating Authority has reasonable grounds for believing—

(a)   that any such document or device may have to be produced for the purposes of any legal proceedings, and

(b)   that it might otherwise be unavailable for those purposes,

it may be retained until the proceedings are concluded.

(9)   Nothing in this section authorises a person to take possession of, or make copies of or take extracts from, any document or information which, by virtue of section 64, could not be required to be produced or disclosed under section 62 or 63.

(10)   In the application of this section to Scotland—

(a)   subsection (1) has effect as if, for the words from the beginning to "satisfied—", there were substituted "A sheriff may issue a warrant under this section, on the application of a procurator fiscal, if he is satisfied—";

(b)   subsections (1)(a) and (3)(b) have effect as if, for "in the information", there were substituted "in the application"; and

(c)   subsections (4) to (6) do not have effect.

(11)   In the application of this section to Northern Ireland—

(a)   subsection (1) has effect as if, for the words from the beginning to "laid", there were substituted "A lay magistrate may issue a warrant under this section if, on complaint on oath made"; and

(b)   subsections (1)(a) and (3)(b) have effect as if, for "in the information", there were substituted "in the complaint".

67   Offences in connection with disclosure notices or search warrants

(1)   A person commits an offence if, without reasonable excuse, he fails to comply with any requirement imposed on him under section 62 or 63.

(2)   A person commits an offence if, in purported compliance with any requirement imposed on him under section 62 or 63—

(a)   he makes a statement which is false or misleading, and

(b)   he either knows that it is false or misleading or is reckless as to whether it is false or misleading.

"False or misleading" means false or misleading in a material particular.

(3)   A person commits an offence if he wilfully obstructs any person in the exercise of any rights conferred by a warrant under section 66.

(4)   A person guilty of an offence under subsection (1) or (3) is liable on summary conviction—
    (a)   to imprisonment for a term not exceeding 51 weeks, or
    (b)   to a fine not exceeding level 5 on the standard scale,
           or to both.

(5)   A person guilty of an offence under subsection (2) is liable—
    (a)   on conviction on indictment, to imprisonment for a term not exceeding two years or to a fine, or to both;
    (b)   on summary conviction, to imprisonment for a term not exceeding 12 months or to a fine not exceeding the statutory maximum, or to both.

(6)   In the application of this section to Scotland, the reference to 51 weeks in subsection (4)(a) is to be read as a reference to 12 months.

(7)   In the application of this section to Northern Ireland—
    (a)   the reference to 51 weeks in subsection (4)(a) is to be read as a reference to 6 months; and
    (b)   the reference to 12 months in subsection (5)(b) is to be read as a reference to 6 months.

Supplementary

69   Manner in which disclosure notice may be given

(1)   This section provides for the manner in which a disclosure notice may be given under section 62.

(2)   The notice may be given to a person by—
    (a)   delivering it to him,
    (b)   leaving it at his proper address,
    (c)   sending it by post to him at that address.

(3)   The notice may be given—
    (a)   in the case of a body corporate, to the secretary or clerk of that body;
    (b)   in the case of a partnership, to a partner or a person having the control or management of the partnership business;
    (c)   in the case of an unincorporated association (other than a partnership), to an officer of the association.

(4)   For the purposes of this section and section 7 of the Interpretation Act 1978 (service of documents by post) in its application to this section, the proper address of a person is his usual or last-known address (whether residential or otherwise), except that—
    (a)   in the case of a body corporate or its secretary or clerk, it is the address of the registered office of that body or its principal office in the United Kingdom,
    (b)   in the case of a partnership, a partner or a person having the control or management of the partnership business, it is that of the principal office of the partnership in the United Kingdom, and
    (c)   in the case of an unincorporated association (other than a partnership) or an officer of the association, it is that of the principal office of the association in the United Kingdom.

(5)   This section does not apply in Scotland.

PART 3
POLICE POWERS ETC.

Exclusion zones

112   Power to direct a person to leave a place

(1)   A constable may direct a person to leave a place if he believes, on reasonable grounds, that the person is in the place at a time when he would be prohibited from entering it by virtue of—
    (a)   an order to which subsection (2) applies, or
    (b)   a condition to which subsection (3) applies.

(2)   This subsection applies to an order which—
  (a)   was made, by virtue of any enactment, following the person's conviction of an offence, and
  (b)   prohibits the person from entering the place or from doing so during a period specified in the order.

(3)   This subsection applies to a condition which—
  (a)   was imposed, by virtue of any enactment, as a condition of the person's release from a prison in which he was serving a sentence of imprisonment following his conviction of an offence, and
  (b)   prohibits the person from entering the place or from doing so during a period specified in the condition.

(4)   A direction under this section may be given orally.

(5)   Any person who knowingly contravenes a direction given to him under this section is guilty of an offence and liable on summary conviction to imprisonment for a term not exceeding 51 weeks or to a fine not exceeding level 4 on the standard scale, or to both.

PART 4
PUBLIC ORDER AND CONDUCT IN PUBLIC PLACES ETC.

Trespass on designated site

128   Offence of trespassing on designated site

(1)   A person commits an offence if he enters, or is on, any protected site in England and Wales or Northern Ireland as a trespasser.

(1A)   In this section "protected site" means—
  (a)   a nuclear site; or
  (b)   a designated site.

(1B)   In this section "nuclear site" means—
  (a)   so much of any premises in respect of which a nuclear site licence (within the meaning of the Nuclear Installations Act 1965) is for the time being in force as lies within the outer perimeter of the protection provided for those premises; and
  (b)   so much of any other premises of which premises falling within paragraph (a) form a part as lies within that outer perimeter.

(1C)   For this purpose—
  (a)   the outer perimeter of the protection provided for any premises is the line of the outermost fences, walls or other obstacles provided or relied on for protecting those premises from intruders; and
  (b)   that line shall be determined on the assumption that every gate, door or other barrier across a way through a fence, wall or other obstacle is closed.

(2)   A "designated site" means a site—
  (a)   specified or described (in any way) in an order made by the Secretary of State, and
  (b)   designated for the purposes of this section by the order.

(3)   The Secretary of State may only designate a site for the purposes of this section if—
  (a)   it is comprised in Crown land; or
  (b)   it is comprised in land belonging to Her Majesty in Her private capacity or to the immediate heir to the Throne in his private capacity; or
  (c)   it appears to the Secretary of State that it is appropriate to designate the site in the interests of national security.

(4)   It is a defence for a person charged with an offence under this section to prove that he did not know, and had no reasonable cause to suspect, that the site in relation to which the offence is alleged to have been committed was a designated site.

(5)   A person guilty of an offence under this section is liable on summary conviction—
  (a)   to imprisonment for a term not exceeding 51 weeks, or
  (b)   to a fine not exceeding level 5 on the standard scale,
  or to both.

(6) No proceedings for an offence under this section may be instituted against any person—
  (a) in England and Wales, except by or with the consent of the Attorney General, or
  (b) in Northern Ireland, except by or with the consent of the Attorney General for Northern Ireland.

(7) For the purposes of this section a person who is on any protected site as a trespasser does not cease to be a trespasser by virtue of being allowed time to leave the site.

(8) In this section—
  (a) "site" means the whole or part of any building or buildings, or any land, or both;
  (b) "Crown land" means land in which there is a Crown interest or a Duchy interest.

(9) For this purpose—
  "Crown interest" means an interest belonging to Her Majesty in right of the Crown, and
  "Duchy interest" means an interest belonging to Her Majesty in right of the Duchy of Lancaster or belonging to the Duchy of Cornwall.

(10) In the application of this section to Northern Ireland, the reference to 51 weeks in subsection (5)(a) is to be read as a reference to 6 months.

131 Designated sites: access

(1) The following provisions do not apply to land in respect of which a designation order is in force—
  (a) section 2(1) of the Countryside and Rights of Way Act 2000 (rights of public in relation to access land),
  (b) Part III of the Countryside (Northern Ireland) Order 1983 (access to open country), and
  (c) section 1 of the Land Reform (Scotland) Act 2003 (access rights).

(2) The Secretary of State may take such steps as he considers appropriate to inform the public of the effect of any designation order, including, in particular, displaying notices on or near the site to which the order relates.

(3) But the Secretary of State may only—
  (a) display any such notice, or
  (b) take any other steps under subsection (2),
  in or on any building or land, if the appropriate person consents.

(4) The "appropriate person" is—
  (a) a person appearing to the Secretary of State to have a sufficient interest in the building or land to consent to the notice being displayed or the steps being taken, or
  (b) a person acting on behalf of such a person.

(5) In this section a "designation order" means—
  (a) in relation to England and Wales or Northern Ireland, an order under section 128,

EQUALITY ACT 2006
(2006, c. 3)

An Act to make provision for the establishment of the Commission for Equality and Human Rights; to dissolve the Equal Opportunities Commission, the Commission for Racial Equality and the Disability Rights Commission; to make provision about discrimination on grounds of religion or belief; to enable provision to be made about discrimination on grounds of sexual orientation; to impose duties relating to sex discrimination on persons performing public functions; to amend the Disability Discrimination Act 1995; and for connected purposes. [16 February 2006]

PART 1
THE COMMISSION FOR EQUALITY AND HUMAN RIGHTS

The Commission

1 Establishment

There shall be a body corporate known as the Commission for Equality and Human Rights.

3   General duty

The Commission shall exercise its functions under this Part with a view to encouraging and supporting the development of a society in which—

(a)   people's ability to achieve their potential is not limited by prejudice or discrimination,

(b)   there is respect for and protection of each individual's human rights,

(c)   there is respect for the dignity and worth of each individual,

(d)   each individual has an equal opportunity to participate in society, and

(e)   there is mutual respect between groups based on understanding and valuing of diversity and on shared respect for equality and human rights.

4   Strategic plan

(1)   The Commission shall prepare a plan showing—

(a)   activities or classes of activity to be undertaken by the Commission in pursuance of its functions under this Act,

(b)   an expected timetable for each activity or class, and

(c)   priorities for different activities or classes, or principles to be applied in determining priorities.

(2)   The Commission shall review the plan—

(a)   at least once during the period of three years beginning with its completion,

(b)   at least once during each period of three years beginning with the completion of a review, and

(c)   at such other times as the Commission thinks appropriate.

(3)   If the Commission thinks it appropriate as a result of a review, the Commission shall revise the plan.

(4)   The Commission shall send the plan and each revision to the Secretary of State, who shall lay a copy before Parliament.

(5)   The Commission shall publish the plan and each revision.

Duties

8   Equality and diversity

(1)   The Commission shall, by exercising the powers conferred by this Part—

(a)   promote understanding of the importance of equality and diversity,

(b)   encourage good practice in relation to equality and diversity,

(c)   promote equality of opportunity,

(d)   promote awareness and understanding of rights under the Equality Act 2010,

(e)   enforce that Act,

(f)   work towards the elimination of unlawful discrimination, and

(g)   work towards the elimination of unlawful harassment.

(2)   In subsection (1)—

"diversity" means the fact that individuals are different,

"equality" means equality between individuals, and

"unlawful" is to be construed in accordance with section 34.

(3)   In promoting equality of opportunity between disabled persons and others, the Commission may, in particular, promote the favourable treatment of disabled persons.

(4)   In this Part "disabled person" means a person who—

(a)   is a disabled person within the meaning of the Equality Act 2010, or

(b)   has been a disabled person within that meaning (whether or not at a time when that Act had effect).

9   Human rights

(1)   The Commission shall, by exercising the powers conferred by this Part—

(a)   promote understanding of the importance of human rights,

(b)   encourage good practice in relation to human rights,

(c)   promote awareness, understanding and protection of human rights, and

(d)   encourage public authorities to comply with section 6 of the Human Rights Act 1998 (compliance with Convention rights).

(2)   In this Part "human rights" means—

(a)   the Convention rights within the meaning given by section 1 of the Human Rights Act 1998, and

(b)   other human rights.

(3)   In determining what action to take in pursuance of this section the Commission shall have particular regard to the importance of exercising the powers conferred by this Part in relation to the Convention rights.

(4)   In fulfilling a duty under section 8 the Commission shall take account of any relevant human rights.

(5)   A reference in this Part (including this section) to human rights does not exclude any matter by reason only of its being a matter to which section 8 relates.

11   Monitoring the law

(1)   The Commission shall monitor the effectiveness of the equality and human rights enactments.

(2)   The Commission may—

     (a)   advise central government about the effectiveness of any of the equality and human rights enactments;

     (b)   recommend to central government the amendment, repeal, consolidation (with or without amendments) or replication (with or without amendments) of any of the equality and human rights enactments;

     (c)   advise central or devolved government about the effect of an enactment (including an enactment in or under an Act of the Scottish Parliament);

     (d)   advise central or devolved government about the likely effect of a proposed change of law.

(3)   In this section—

     (a)   "central government" means Her Majesty's Government,

     (b)   "devolved government" means—

         (i)   the Scottish Ministers, and

         (ii)   the Welsh Ministers, the First Minister for Wales and the Counsel General to the Welsh Assembly Government, and

     (c)   a reference to the equality and human rights enactments is a reference to the Human Rights Act 1998, this Act and the Equality Act 2010.

General powers

13   Information, advice, &c.

(1)   In pursuance of its duties under sections 8 and 9 the Commission may—

     (a)   publish or otherwise disseminate ideas or information;

     (b)   undertake research;

     (c)   provide education or training;

     (d)   give advice or guidance (whether about the effect or operation of an enactment or otherwise);

     (e)   arrange for a person to do anything within paragraphs (a) to (d);

     (f)   act jointly with, co-operate with or assist a person doing anything within paragraphs (a) to (d).

(2)   The reference to giving advice in subsection (1)(d) does not include a reference to preparing, or assisting in the preparation of, a document to be used for the purpose of legal proceedings.

Enforcement powers

20   Investigations

(1)   The Commission may investigate whether or not a person—

     (a)   has committed an unlawful act,

     (b)   has complied with a requirement imposed by an unlawful act notice under section 21, or

     (c)   has complied with an undertaking given under section 23.

(2)   The Commission may conduct an investigation under subsection (1)(a) only if it suspects that the person concerned may have committed an unlawful act.

(3)   A suspicion for the purposes of subsection (2) may (but need not) be based on the results of, or a matter arising during the course of, an inquiry under section 16.

(4)   Before settling a report of an investigation recording a finding that a person has committed an unlawful act or has failed to comply with a requirement or undertaking the Commission shall—
    (a)   send a draft of the report to the person,
    (b)   specify a period of at least 28 days during which he may make written representations about the draft, and
    (c)   consider any representations made.
(5)   Schedule 2 makes supplemental provision about investigations.

TERRORISM ACT 2006
(2006, c. 11)

An Act to make provision for and about offences relating to conduct carried out or capable of being carried out, for purposes connected with terrorism; to amend enactments relating to terrorism; and for connected purposes.   [30 March 2006]

PART 1
OFFENCES

Encouragement etc. of terrorism

1   Encouragement of terrorism

(1)   This section applies to a statement that is likely to be understood by some or all of the members of the public to whom it is published as a direct or indirect encouragement or other inducement to them to the commission, preparation or instigation of acts of terrorism or Convention offences.

(2)   A person commits an offence if—
    (a)   he publishes a statement to which this section applies or causes another to publish such a statement; and
    (b)   at the time he publishes it or causes it to be published, he—
        (i)   intends members of the public to be directly or indirectly encouraged or otherwise induced by the statement to commit, prepare or instigate acts of terrorism or Convention offences; or
        (ii)   is reckless as to whether members of the public will be directly or indirectly encouraged or otherwise induced by the statement to commit, prepare or instigate such acts or offences.

(3)   For the purposes of this section, the statements that are likely to be understood by members of the public as indirectly encouraging the commission or preparation of acts of terrorism or Convention offences include every statement which—
    (a)   glorifies the commission or preparation (whether in the past, in the future or generally) of such acts or offences; and
    (b)   is a statement from which those members of the public could reasonably be expected to infer that what is being glorified is being glorified as conduct that should be emulated by them in existing circumstances.

(4)   For the purposes of this section the questions how a statement is likely to be understood and what members of the public could reasonably be expected to infer from it must be determined having regard both—
    (a)   to the contents of the statement as a whole; and
    (b)   to the circumstances and manner of its publication.

(5)   It is irrelevant for the purposes of subsections (1) to (3)—
    (a)   whether anything mentioned in those subsections relates to the commission, preparation or instigation of one or more particular acts of terrorism or Convention offences, of acts of terrorism or Convention offences of a particular description or of acts of terrorism or Convention offences generally; and,
    (b)   whether any person is in fact encouraged or induced by the statement to commit, prepare or instigate any such act or offence.

(6)   In proceedings for an offence under this section against a person in whose case it is not proved that he intended the statement directly or indirectly to encourage or otherwise induce the commission, preparation or instigation of acts of terrorism or Convention offences, it is a defence for him to show—

     (a)   that the statement neither expressed his views nor had his endorsement (whether by virtue of section 3 or otherwise); and

     (b)   that it was clear, in all the circumstances of the statement's publication, that it did not express his views and (apart from the possibility of his having been given and failed to comply with a notice under subsection (3) of that section) did not have his endorsement.

(7)   A person guilty of an offence under this section shall be liable—

     (a)   on conviction on indictment, to imprisonment for a term not exceeding 7 years or to a fine, or to both;

     (b)   on summary conviction in England and Wales, to imprisonment for a term not exceeding 12 months or to a fine not exceeding the statutory maximum, or to both;

     (c)   on summary conviction in Scotland or Northern Ireland, to imprisonment for a term not exceeding 6 months or to a fine not exceeding the statutory maximum, or to both.

(8)   In relation to an offence committed before the commencement of section 154(1) of the Criminal Justice Act 2003, the reference in subsection (7)(b) to 12 months is to be read as a reference to 6 months.

2   Dissemination of terrorist publications

(1)   A person commits an offence if he engages in conduct falling within subsection (2) and, at the time he does so—

     (a)   he intends an effect of his conduct to be a direct or indirect encouragement or other inducement to the commission, preparation or instigation of acts of terrorism;

     (b)   he intends an effect of his conduct to be the provision of assistance in the commission or preparation of such acts; or

     (c)   he is reckless as to whether his conduct has an effect mentioned in paragraph (a) or (b).

(2)   For the purposes of this section a person engages in conduct falling within this subsection if he—

     (a)   distributes or circulates a terrorist publication;

     (b)   gives, sells or lends such a publication;

     (c)   offers such a publication for sale or loan;

     (d)   provides a service to others that enables them to obtain, read, listen to or look at such a publication, or to acquire it by means of a gift, sale or loan;

     (e)   transmits the contents of such a publication electronically; or

     (f)   has such a publication in his possession with a view to its becoming the subject of conduct falling within any of paragraphs (a) to (e).

(3)   For the purposes of this section a publication is a terrorist publication, in relation to conduct falling within subsection (2), if matter contained in it is likely—

     (a)   to be understood, by some or all of the persons to whom it is or may become available as a consequence of that conduct, as a direct or indirect encouragement or other inducement to them to the commission, preparation or instigation of acts of terrorism; or

     (b)   to be useful in the commission or preparation of such acts and to be understood, by some or all of those persons, as contained in the publication, or made available to them, wholly or mainly for the purpose of being so useful to them.

(4)   For the purposes of this section matter that is likely to be understood by a person as indirectly encouraging the commission or preparation of acts of terrorism includes any matter which—

     (a)   glorifies the commission or preparation (whether in the past, in the future or generally) of such acts; and

     (b)   is matter from which that person could reasonably be expected to infer that what is being glorified is being glorified as conduct that should be emulated by him in existing circumstances.

(5) For the purposes of this section the question whether a publication is a terrorist publication in relation to particular conduct must be determined—
    (a) as at the time of that conduct; and
    (b) having regard both to the contents of the publication as a whole and to the circumstances in which that conduct occurs.

(6) In subsection (1) references to the effect of a person's conduct in relation to a terrorist publication include references to an effect of the publication on one or more persons to whom it is or may become available as a consequence of that conduct.

(7) It is irrelevant for the purposes of this section whether anything mentioned in subsections (1) to (4) is in relation to the commission, preparation or instigation of one or more particular acts of terrorism, of acts of terrorism of a particular description or of acts of terrorism generally.

(8) For the purposes of this section it is also irrelevant, in relation to matter contained in any article whether any person—
    (a) is in fact encouraged or induced by that matter to commit, prepare or instigate acts of terrorism; or
    (b) in fact makes use of it in the commission or preparation of such acts.

(9) In proceedings for an offence under this section against a person in respect of conduct to which subsection (10) applies, it is a defence for him to show—
    (a) that the matter by reference to which the publication in question was a terrorist publication neither expressed his views nor had his endorsement (whether by virtue of section 3 or otherwise); and
    (b) that it was clear, in all the circumstances of the conduct, that that matter did not express his views and (apart from the possibility of his having been given and failed to comply with a notice under subsection (3) of that section) did not have his endorsement.

(10) This subsection applies to the conduct of a person to the extent that—
    (a) the publication to which his conduct related contained matter by reference to which it was a terrorist publication by virtue of subsection (3)(a); and
    (b) that person is not proved to have engaged in that conduct with the intention specified in subsection (1)(a).

(11) A person guilty of an offence under this section shall be liable—
    (a) on conviction on indictment, to imprisonment for a term not exceeding 7 years or to a fine, or to both;
    (b) on summary conviction in England and Wales, to imprisonment for a term not exceeding 12 months or to a fine not exceeding the statutory maximum, or to both;
    (c) on summary conviction in Scotland or Northern Ireland, to imprisonment for a term not exceeding 6 months or to a fine not exceeding the statutory maximum, or to both.

(12) In relation to an offence committed before the commencement of section 154(1) of the Criminal Justice Act 2003, the reference in subsection (11)(b) to 12 months is to be read as a reference to 6 months.

(13) In this section—
    "lend" includes let on hire, and "loan" is to be construed accordingly;
    "publication" means an article or record of any description that contains any of the following, or any combination of them—
    (a) matter to be read;
    (b) matter to be listened to;
    (c) matter to be looked at or watched.

3 Application of ss. 1 and 2 to internet activity etc.

(1) This section applies for the purposes of sections 1 and 2 in relation to cases where—
    (a) a statement is published or caused to be published in the course of, or in connection with, the provision or use of a service provided electronically; or
    (b) conduct falling within section 2(2) was in the course of, or in connection with, the provision or use of such a service.

(2)   The cases in which the statement, or the article or record to which the conduct relates, is to be regarded as having the endorsement of a person ("the relevant person") at any time include a case in which—

(a)   a constable has given him a notice under subsection (3);

(b)   that time falls more than 2 working days after the day on which the notice was given; and

(c)   the relevant person has failed, without reasonable excuse, to comply with the notice.

(3)   A notice under this subsection is a notice which—

(a)   declares that, in the opinion of the constable giving it, the statement or the article or record is unlawfully terrorism-related;

(b)   requires the relevant person to secure that the statement or the article or record, so far as it is so related, is not available to the public or is modified so as no longer to be so related;

(c)   warns the relevant person that a failure to comply with the notice within 2 working days will result in the statement, or the article or record, being regarded as having his endorsement; and

(d)   explains how, under subsection (4), he may become liable by virtue of the notice if the statement, or the article or record, becomes available to the public after he has complied with the notice.

(4)   Where—

(a)   a notice under subsection (3) has been given to the relevant person in respect of a statement, or an article or record, and he has complied with it, but

(b)   he subsequently publishes or causes to be published a statement which is, or is for all practical purposes, the same or to the same effect as the statement to which the notice related, or to matter contained in the article or record to which it related, (a "repeat statement");

the requirements of subsection (2)(a) to (c) shall be regarded as satisfied in the case of the repeat statement in relation to the times of its subsequent publication by the relevant person.

(5)   In proceedings against a person for an offence under section 1 or 2 the requirements of subsection (2)(a) to (c) are not, in his case, to be regarded as satisfied in relation to any time by virtue of subsection (4) if he shows that he—

(a)   has, before that time, taken every step he reasonably could to prevent a repeat statement from becoming available to the public and to ascertain whether it does; and

(b)   was, at that time, a person to whom subsection (6) applied.

(6)   This subsection applies to a person at any time when he—

(a)   is not aware of the publication of the repeat statement; or

(b)   having become aware of its publication, has taken every step that he reasonably could to secure that it either ceased to be available to the public or was modified as mentioned in subsection (3)(b).

(7)   For the purposes of this section a statement or an article or record is unlawfully terrorism-related if it constitutes, or if matter contained in the article or record constitutes—

(a)   something that is likely to be understood, by any one or more of the persons to whom it has or may become available, as a direct or indirect encouragement or other inducement to the commission, preparation or instigation of acts of terrorism or Convention offences; or

(b)   information which—

(i)   is likely to be useful to any one or more of those persons in the commission or preparation of such acts; and

(ii)   is in a form or context in which it is likely to be understood by any one or more of those persons as being wholly or mainly for the purpose of being so useful.

(8)   The reference in subsection (7) to something that is likely to be understood as an indirect encouragement to the commission or preparation of acts of terrorism or Convention offences includes anything which is likely to be understood as—

    (a)   the glorification of the commission or preparation (whether in the past, in the future or generally) of such acts or such offences; and

    (b)   a suggestion that what is being glorified is being glorified as conduct that should be emulated in existing circumstances.

(9)   In this section "working day" means any day other than—

    (a)   a Saturday or a Sunday;

    (b)   Christmas Day or Good Friday; or

    (c)   a day which is a bank holiday under the Banking and Financial Dealings Act 1971 in any part of the United Kingdom.

4   Giving of notices under s. 3

(1)   Except in a case to which any of subsections (2) to (4) applies, a notice under section 3(3) may be given to a person only—

    (a)   by delivering it to him in person; or

    (b)   by sending it to him, by means of a postal service providing for delivery to be recorded, at his last known address.

(2)   Such a notice may be given to a body corporate only—

    (a)   by delivering it to the secretary of that body in person; or

    (b)   by sending it to the appropriate person, by means of a postal service providing for delivery to be recorded, at the address of the registered or principal office of the body.

(3)   Such a notice may be given to a firm only—

    (a)   by delivering it to a partner of the firm in person;

    (b)   by so delivering it to a person having the control or management of the partnership business; or

    (c)   by sending it to the appropriate person, by means of a postal service providing for delivery to be recorded, at the address of the principal office of the partnership.

(4)   Such a notice may be given to an unincorporated body or association only—

    (a)   by delivering it to a member of its governing body in person; or

    (b)   by sending it to the appropriate person, by means of a postal service providing for delivery to be recorded, at the address of the principal office of the body or association.

(5)   In the case of—

    (a)   a company registered outside the United Kingdom,

    (b)   a firm carrying on business outside the United Kingdom, or

    (c)   an unincorporated body or association with offices outside the United Kingdom, the references in this section to its principal office include references to its principal office within the United Kingdom (if any).

(6)   In this section "the appropriate person" means—

    (a)   in the case of a body corporate, the body itself or its secretary;

    (b)   in the case of a firm, the firm itself or a partner of the firm or a person having the control or management of the partnership business; and

    (c)   in the case of an unincorporated body or association, the body or association itself or a member of its governing body.

(7)   For the purposes of section 3 the time at which a notice under subsection (3) of that section is to be regarded as given is—

    (a)   where it is delivered to a person, the time at which it is so delivered; and

    (b)   where it is sent by a postal service providing for delivery to be recorded, the time recorded as the time of its delivery.

(8)   In this section "secretary", in relation to a body corporate, means the secretary or other equivalent officer of the body.

Preparation of terrorist acts and terrorist training

5   Preparation of terrorist acts

(1)   A person commits an offence if, with the intention of—

    (a)   committing acts of terrorism, or

    (b)   assisting another to commit such acts,

he engages in any conduct in preparation for giving effect to his intention.

(2)   It is irrelevant for the purposes of subsection (1) whether the intention and preparations relate to one or more particular acts of terrorism, acts of terrorism of a particular description or acts of terrorism generally.

(3)   A person guilty of an offence under this section shall be liable, on conviction on indictment, to imprisonment for life.

6   Training for terrorism

(1)   A person commits an offence if—

     (a)   he provides instruction or training in any of the skills mentioned in subsection (3); and

     (b)   at the time he provides the instruction or training, he knows that a person receiving it intends to use the skills in which he is being instructed or trained—

         (i)   for or in connection with the commission or preparation of acts of terrorism or Convention offences; or

         (ii)   for assisting the commission or preparation by others of such acts or offences.

(2)   A person commits an offence if—

     (a)   he receives instruction or training in any of the skills mentioned in subsection (3); and

     (b)   at the time of the instruction or training, he intends to use the skills in which he is being instructed or trained—

         (i)   for or in connection with the commission or preparation of acts of terrorism or Convention offences; or

         (ii)   for assisting the commission or preparation by others of such acts or offences.

(3)   The skills are—

     (a)   the making, handling or use of a noxious substance, or of substances of a description of such substances;

     (b)   the use of any method or technique for doing anything else that is capable of being done for the purposes of terrorism, in connection with the commission or preparation of an act of terrorism or Convention offence or in connection with assisting the commission or preparation by another of such an act or offence; and

     (c)   the design or adaptation for the purposes of terrorism, or in connection with the commission or preparation of an act of terrorism or Convention offence, of any method or technique for doing anything.

(4)   It is irrelevant for the purposes of subsections (1) and (2)—

     (a)   whether any instruction or training that is provided is provided to one or more particular persons or generally;

     (b)   whether the acts or offences in relation to which a person intends to use skills in which he is instructed or trained consist of one or more particular acts of terrorism or Convention offences, acts of terrorism or Convention offences of a particular description or acts of terrorism or Convention offences generally; and

     (c)   whether assistance that a person intends to provide to others is intended to be provided to one or more particular persons or to one or more persons whose identities are not yet known.

(5)   A person guilty of an offence under this section shall be liable—

     (a)   on conviction on indictment, to imprisonment for life or to a fine, or to both;

     (b)   on summary conviction in England and Wales, to imprisonment for a term not exceeding 12 months or to a fine not exceeding the statutory maximum, or to both;

     (c)   on summary conviction in Scotland or Northern Ireland, to imprisonment for a term not exceeding 6 months or to a fine not exceeding the statutory maximum, or to both.

(6)   In relation to an offence committed before the commencement of section 154(1) of the Criminal Justice Act 2003, the reference in subsection (5)(b) to 12 months is to be read as a reference to 6 months.

(7)   In this section—
       "noxious substance" means—
       (a)   a dangerous substance within the meaning of Part 7 of the Anti-terrorism, Crime
              and Security Act 2001; or
       (b)   any other substance which is hazardous or noxious or which may be or become
              hazardous or noxious only in certain circumstances;
       "substance" includes any natural or artificial substance (whatever its origin or method
       of production and whether in solid or liquid form or in the form of a gas or vapour) and
       any mixture of substances.

7   Powers of forfeiture in respect of offences under s. 6

(1)   A court before which a person is convicted of an offence under section 6 may order
       the forfeiture of anything the court considers to have been in the person's possession
       for purposes connected with the offence.
(2)   Before making an order under subsection (1) in relation to anything the court must
       give an opportunity of being heard to any person (in addition to the convicted person)
       who claims to be the owner of that thing or otherwise to have an interest in it.
(3)   An order under subsection (1) may not be made so as to come into force at any time
       before there is no further possibility (disregarding any power to grant permission for
       the bringing of an appeal out of time) of the order's being varied or set aside on
       appeal.
(4)   Where a court makes an order under subsection (1), it may also make such other
       provision as appears to it to be necessary for giving effect to the forfeiture.
(5)   That provision may include, in particular, provision relating to the retention, handling,
       destruction or other disposal of what is forfeited.
(6)   Provision made by virtue of this section may be varied at any time by the court that
       made it.
(7)   The power of forfeiture under this section is in addition to any power of forfeiture
       under section 23A of the Terrorism Act 2000.

8   Attendance at a place used for terrorist training

(1)   A person commits an offence if—
       (a)   he attends at any place, whether in the United Kingdom or elsewhere;
       (b)   while he is at that place, instruction or training of the type mentioned in section
              6(1) of this Act or section 54(1) of the Terrorism Act 2000 (weapons training) is
              provided there;
       (c)   that instruction or training is provided there wholly or partly for purposes
              connected with the commission or preparation of acts of terrorism or Convention
              offences; and
       (d)   the requirements of subsection (2) are satisfied in relation to that person.
(2)   The requirements of this subsection are satisfied in relation to a person if—
       (a)   he knows or believes that instruction or training is being provided there wholly
              or partly for purposes connected with the commission or preparation of acts of
              terrorism or Convention offences; or
       (b)   a person attending at that place throughout the period of that person's
              attendance could not reasonably have failed to understand that instruction or
              training was being provided there wholly or partly for such purposes.
(3)   It is immaterial for the purposes of this section—
       (a)   whether the person concerned receives the instruction or training himself; and
       (b)   whether the instruction or training is provided for purposes connected with one
              or more particular acts of terrorism or Convention offences, acts of terrorism
              or Convention offences of a particular description or acts of terrorism or
              Convention offences generally.
(4)   A person guilty of an offence under this section shall be liable—
       (a)   on conviction on indictment, to imprisonment for or to a fine, or to both;
       (b)   on summary conviction in England and Wales, to imprisonment for a term not
              exceeding 12 months or to a fine not exceeding the statutory maximum, or to
              both;

(c)   on summary conviction in Scotland or Northern Ireland, to imprisonment for a term not exceeding 6 months or to a fine not exceeding the statutory maximum, or to both.

(5)   In relation to an offence committed before the commencement of section 154(1) of the Criminal Justice Act 2003, the reference in subsection (4)(b) to 12 months is to be read as a reference to 6 months.

(6)   References in this section to instruction or training being provided include references to its being made available.

Offences involving radioactive devices and materials and nuclear facilities and sites

9   Making and possession of devices or materials

(1)   A person commits an offence if—
    (a)   he makes or has in his possession a radioactive device, or
    (b)   he has in his possession radioactive material,
with the intention of using the device or material in the course of or in connection with the commission or preparation of an act of terrorism or for the purposes of terrorism, or of making it available to be so used.

(2)   It is irrelevant for the purposes of subsection (1) whether the act of terrorism to which an intention relates is a particular act of terrorism, an act of terrorism of a particular description or an act of terrorism generally.

(3)   A person guilty of an offence under this section shall be liable, on conviction on indictment, to imprisonment for life.

(4)   In this section—
"radioactive device" means—
    (a)   a nuclear weapon or other nuclear explosive device;
    (b)   a radioactive material dispersal device;
    (c)   a radiation-emitting device;
"radioactive material" means nuclear material or any other radioactive substance which—
    (a)   contains nuclides that undergo spontaneous disintegration in a process accompanied by the emission of one or more types of ionising radiation, such as alpha radiation, beta radiation, neutron particles or gamma rays; and
    (b)   is capable, owing to its radiological or fissile properties, of—
        (i)   causing serious bodily injury to a person;
        (ii)   causing serious damage to property;
        (iii)   endangering a person's life; or
        (iv)   creating a serious risk to the health or safety of the public.

(5)   In subsection (4)—
"device" includes any of the following, whether or not fixed to land, namely, machinery, equipment, appliances, tanks, containers, pipes and conduits;
"nuclear material" has the same meaning as in the Nuclear Material (Offences) Act 1983 (see section 6 of that Act).

10   Misuse of devices or material and misuse and damage of facilities

(1)   A person commits an offence if he uses—
    (a)   a radioactive device, or
    (b)   radioactive material,
in the course of or in connection with the commission of an act of terrorism or for the purposes of terrorism.

(2)   A person commits an offence if, in the course of or in connection with the commission of an act of terrorism or for the purposes of terrorism, he uses or damages a nuclear facility in a manner which—
    (a)   causes a release of radioactive material; or
    (b)   creates or increases a risk that such material will be released.

(3)   A person guilty of an offence under this section shall be liable, on conviction on indictment, to imprisonment for life.

(4)   In this section—
"nuclear facility" means—

(a)   a nuclear reactor, including a reactor installed in or on any transportation device for use as an energy source in order to propel it or for any other purpose; or

(b)   a plant or conveyance being used for the production, storage, processing or transport of radioactive material;

"radioactive device" and "radioactive material" have the same meanings as in section 9.

(5)   In subsection (4)—

"nuclear reactor" has the same meaning as in the Nuclear Installations Act 1965 (see section 26 of that Act);

"transportation device" means any vehicle or any space object (within the meaning of the Outer Space Act 1986).

11   Terrorist threats relating to devices, materials or facilities

(1)   A person commits an offence if, in the course of or in connection with the commission of an act of terrorism or for the purposes of terrorism—

(a)   he makes a demand—

(i)   for the supply to himself or to another of a radioactive device or of radioactive material;

(ii)   for a nuclear facility to be made available to himself or to another; or

(iii) for access to such a facility to be given to himself or to another;

(b)   he supports the demand with a threat that he or another will take action if the demand is not met; and

(c)   the circumstances and manner of the threat are such that it is reasonable for the person to whom it is made to assume that there is real risk that the threat will be carried out if the demand is not met.

(2)   A person also commits an offence if—

(a)   he makes a threat falling within subsection (3) in the course of or in connection with the commission of an act of terrorism or for the purposes of terrorism; and

(b)   the circumstances and manner of the threat are such that it is reasonable for the person to whom it is made to assume that there is real risk that the threat will be carried out, or would be carried out if demands made in association with the threat are not met.

(3)   A threat falls within this subsection if it is—

(a)   a threat to use radioactive material;

(b)   a threat to use a radioactive device; or

(c)   a threat to use or damage a nuclear facility in a manner that releases radioactive material or creates or increases a risk that such material will be released.

(4)   A person guilty of an offence under this section shall be liable, on conviction on indictment, to imprisonment for life.

(5)   In this section—

"nuclear facility" has the same meaning as in section 10;

"radioactive device" and "radioactive material" have the same meanings as in section 9.

17   Commission of offences abroad

(1)   If—

(a)   a person does anything outside the United Kingdom, and

(b)   his action, if done in a part of the United Kingdom, would constitute an offence falling within subsection (2),

he shall be guilty in that part of the United Kingdom of the offence.

(2)   The offences falling within this subsection are—

(a)   an offence under section 1 of this Act so far as it is committed in relation to any statement, in relation to which that section has effect by reason of its relevance to the commission, preparation or instigation of one or more Convention offences;

(b)   an offence under section 5 or 6 or any of sections 8 to 11 of this Act;

(c)   an offence under section 11(1) of the Terrorism Act 2000 (membership of proscribed organisations);

(d)   an offence under section 54 of that Act (weapons training);

(e)   conspiracy to commit an offence falling within this subsection;

(f)   inciting a person to commit such an offence;

(g)   attempting to commit such an offence;

(h)   aiding, abetting, counselling or procuring the commission of such an offence.

(3)   Subsection (1) applies irrespective of whether the person is a British citizen or, in the case of a company, a company incorporated in a part of the United Kingdom.

(4)   In the case of an offence falling within subsection (2) which is committed wholly or partly outside the United Kingdom—

(a)   proceedings for the offence may be taken at any place in the United Kingdom; and

(b)   the offence may for all incidental purposes be treated as having been committed at any such place.

18   Liability of company directors etc.

(1)   Where an offence under this Part is committed by a body corporate and is proved to have been committed with the consent or connivance of—

(a)   a director, manager, secretary or other similar officer of the body corporate, or

(b)   a person who was purporting to act in any such capacity, he (as well as the body corporate) is guilty of that offence and shall be liable to be proceeded against and punished accordingly.

(2)   Where an offence under this Part—

(a)   is committed by a Scottish firm, and

(b)   is proved to have been committed with the consent or connivance of a partner of the firm,

he (as well as the firm) is guilty of that offence and shall be liable to be proceeded against and punished accordingly.

(3)   In this section "director", in relation to a body corporate whose affairs are managed by its members, means a member of the body corporate.

19   Consents to prosecutions

(1)   Proceedings for an offence under this Part—

(a)   may be instituted in England and Wales only with the consent of the Director of Public Prosecutions;

(2)   But if it appears to the Director of Public Prosecutions or the Director of Public Prosecutions for Northern Ireland that an offence under this Part has been committed outside the United Kingdom or for a purpose wholly or partly connected with the affairs of a country other than the United Kingdom, his consent for the purposes of this section may be given only with the permission—

(a)   in the case of the Director of Public Prosecutions, of the Attorney General;

Interpretation of Part 1

20   Interpretation of Part 1

(1)   Expressions used in this Part and in the Terrorism Act 2000 have the same meanings in this Part as in that Act.

GOVERNMENT OF WALES ACT 2006
(2006, c. 32)

An Act to make provision about the government of Wales.   [25 July 2006]

PART A1
PERMANENCE OF THE ASSEMBLY AND WELSH GOVERNMENT

A1   Permanence of the Assembly and Welsh Government

(1)   The Assembly established by Part 1 and the Welsh Government established by Part 2 are a permanent part of the United Kingdom's constitutional arrangements.

(2)   The purpose of this section is, with due regard to the other provisions of this Act, to signify the commitment of the Parliament and Government of the United Kingdom to the Assembly and the Welsh Government.

(3)   In view of that commitment it is declared that the Assembly and the Welsh Government are not to be abolished except on the basis of a decision of the people of Wales voting in a referendum.

A2   Recognition of Welsh law

(1)   The law that applies in Wales includes a body of Welsh law made by the Assembly and the Welsh Ministers.

(2)   The purpose of this section is, with due regard to the other provisions of this Act, to recognise the ability of the Assembly and the Welsh Ministers to make law forming part of the law of England and Wales.

PART 1
NATIONAL ASSEMBLY FOR WALES

The Assembly

1   The Assembly

(1)   There is to be an Assembly for Wales to be known as the National Assembly for Wales or Cynulliad Cenedlaethol Cymru (referred to in this Act as "the Assembly").

(2)   The Assembly is to consist of—
   (a)   one member for each Assembly constituency (referred to in this Act as "Assembly constituency members"), and
   (b)   members for each Assembly electoral region (referred to in this Act as "Assembly regional members").

2   Assembly constituencies and electoral regions

(1)   The Assembly constituencies are the constituencies specified in the Parliamentary Constituencies and Assembly Electoral Regions (Wales) Order 2006 as amended by—
   (a)   the Parliamentary Constituencies and Assembly Electoral Regions (Wales) (Amendment) Order 2008, and
   (b)   any Order in Council under the Parliamentary Constituencies Act 1986 giving effect (with or without modifications) to a report falling within section 13(3) or (4) of the Parliamentary Voting System and Constituencies Act 2011.

(2)   There are five Assembly electoral regions.

(3)   The Assembly electoral regions are as specified in the Parliamentary Constituencies and Assembly Electoral Regions (Wales) Order 2006.

(4)   There are four seats for each Assembly electoral region.

General elections

3   Ordinary general elections

(1)   The poll at an ordinary general election is to be held on the first Thursday in May in the fifth calendar year following that in which the previous ordinary general election was held, unless provision is made for the day of the poll by an order under section 4 unless—
   (a)   subsection (1A) prevents the poll being held on that day, or
   (b)   the day of the poll is determined by a proclamation under section 4.

(1A) The poll is not to be held on the same date as the date of the poll at—
   (a)   a parliamentary general election (other than an early parliamentary general election), or
   (b)   a European Parliamentary general election.

(1B) Where subsection (1A) prevents the poll being held on the day specified in subsection (1), the poll is to be held on such day, subject to subsection (1A), as the Welsh Ministers may by order specify unless the day of the poll is determined by a proclamation under section 4(2) as modified by section 4(2A).

(2)   If the poll is to be held on the first Thursday in May or on the day specified by an order under subsection (1B), the Assembly —

        (a)   is dissolved by virtue of this section at the beginning of the minimum period which ends with that day, and

        (b)   must meet within the period of seven days beginning immediately after the day of the poll.

(3)   In subsection (2) "the minimum period" means the period determined in accordance with an order under section 13.

Duration of membership

14   Term of office of Assembly members

The term of office of an Assembly member —

(a)   begins when the Assembly member is declared to be returned, and

(b)   ends with the dissolution of the Assembly.

Proceedings etc.

35   Equality of treatment

(1)   The official languages of the Assembly are English and Welsh.

(1A) The official languages must, in the conduct of Assembly proceedings, be treated on a basis of equality.

(1B) All persons have the right to use either official language when participating in Assembly proceedings.

(1C) Reports of Assembly proceedings must, in the case of proceedings which fall within section 1(5)(a) (proceedings of the Assembly), contain a record of what was said, in the official language in which it was said, and also a full translation into the other official language.

(1D) Paragraph 8 of Schedule 2 makes provision about how the Assembly Commission must enable effect to be given to subsections (1) to (1C).

PART 2
WELSH ASSEMBLY GOVERNMENT

Government

45   Welsh Government

(1)   There is to be a Welsh Government, or Llywodraeth Cymru, whose members are —

        (a)   the First Minister or Prif Weinidog (see sections 46 and 47),

        (b)   the Welsh Ministers, or Gweinidogion Cymru, appointed under section 48,

        (c)   the Counsel General to the Welsh Government or Cwnsler Cyffredinol i Lywodraeth Cymru (see section 49) (referred to in this Act as "the Counsel General"), and

        (d)   the Deputy Welsh Ministers or Dirprwy Weinidogion Cymru (see section 50).

(2)   In this Act and in any other enactment or instrument the First Minister and the Welsh Ministers appointed under section 48 are referred to collectively as the Welsh Ministers.

Ministers, staff etc.

46   The First Minister

(1)   The First Minister is to be appointed by Her Majesty after nomination in accordance with section 47.

(2)   The First Minister holds office at Her Majesty's pleasure.

(3)   The First Minister may at any time tender resignation to Her Majesty and ceases to hold office as First Minister when it is accepted.

(5)   The functions of the First Minister are exercisable by a person designated by the Presiding Officer if—

(a)   the office of the First Minister is vacant,

(b)   the First Minister is for any reason unable to act, or

(c)   the First Minister has ceased to be an Assembly member otherwise than by a reason of a dissolution.

(8)   If a person is designated to exercise the functions of the First Minister, the designation continues to have effect even if the Assembly is dissolved.

47   Choice of First Minister

(1)   If one of the following events occurs, the Assembly must, before the end of the relevant period, nominate an Assembly member for appointment as First Minister.

(2)   The events are—

(a)   the holding of a poll at a general election,

(b)   the Assembly resolving that the Welsh Ministers no longer enjoy the confidence of the Assembly,

(c)   the First Minister tendering resignation to Her Majesty,

(d)   the First Minister dying or becoming permanently unable to act and to tender resignation, and

(e)   the First Minister ceasing to be an Assembly member otherwise than by reason of a dissolution.

(3)   The relevant period is the period of 28 days beginning with the day on which the event occurs;

(4)   The Presiding Officer must recommend to Her Majesty the appointment of the person nominated by the Assembly under subsection (1).

48   Welsh Ministers

(1)   The First Minister may, with the approval of Her Majesty, appoint Welsh Ministers from among the Assembly members.

(2)   A Welsh Minister appointed under this section holds office at Her Majesty's pleasure.

(3)   A Welsh Minister appointed under this section may be removed from office by the First Minister.

49   Counsel General

(1)   The Counsel General is to be appointed by Her Majesty on the recommendation of the First Minister.

50   Deputy Welsh Ministers

(1)   The First Minister may, with the approval of Her Majesty, appoint Deputy Welsh Ministers from among the Assembly members to assist the First Minister, a Welsh Minister appointed under section 48 or the Counsel General in the exercise of functions.

51   Limit on number of Ministers

(1)   No more than twelve persons are to hold a relevant Welsh Ministerial office at any time.

(2)   A relevant Welsh Ministerial office means the office of Welsh Minister appointed under section 48 or the office of Deputy Welsh Minister.

52   Staff

(1)   The Welsh Ministers may appoint persons to be members of the staff of the Welsh Government.

(2)   Service as a member of the staff of the Welsh Government is service in the civil service of the State.

Functions

59   Implementation of EU law

(1)   The power to designate a Minister of the Crown or government department under section 2(2) of the European Communities Act 1972 (c. 68) may be exercised to designate the Welsh Ministers.

60   Promotion etc. of well-being

(1)   The Welsh Ministers may do anything which they consider appropriate to achieve any one or more of the following objects—

   (a)   the promotion or improvement of the economic well-being of Wales,

   (b)   the promotion or improvement of the social well-being of Wales, and

   (c)   the promotion or improvement of the environmental well-being of Wales.

(2)   The power under subsection (1) may be exercised in relation to or for the benefit of—

   (a)   the whole or any part of Wales, or

   (b)   all or any persons resident or present in Wales.

(3)   The power under subsection (1) includes power to do anything in relation to or for the benefit of any area outside Wales, or all or any persons resident or present anywhere outside Wales, if the Welsh Ministers consider that it is likely to achieve one or more of the objects in that subsection.

(4)   The power under subsection (1) includes power—

   (a)   to enter into arrangements or agreements with any person,

   (b)   to co-operate with, or facilitate or co-ordinate the activities of, any person,

   (c)   to exercise on behalf of any person any functions of that person, and

   (d)   to provide staff, goods, services or accommodation to any person.

61   Support of culture etc.

The Welsh Ministers may do anything which they consider appropriate to support—

(a)   archaeological remains in Wales,

(b)   ancient monuments in Wales,

(c)   buildings and places of historical or architectural interest in Wales,

(d)   historic wrecks in Wales,

(e)   arts and crafts relating to Wales,

(f)   museums and galleries in Wales,

(g)   libraries in Wales,

(h)   archives and historical records relating to Wales,

(i)   cultural activities and projects relating to Wales,

(j)   sport and recreational activities relating to Wales, and

(k)   the Welsh language.

62   Representations about matters affecting Wales

The Welsh Ministers, the First Minister and the Counsel General may make appropriate representations about any matter affecting Wales.

64   Polls for ascertaining views of the public

(1)   The Welsh Ministers may hold a poll in an area consisting of Wales or any part (or parts) of Wales for the purpose of ascertaining the views of those polled about whether or how any of the functions of the Welsh Ministers (other than that under section 62) should be exercised.

(2)   The persons entitled to vote in a poll under this section are those who—

   (a)   would be entitled to vote as electors at a local government election in an electoral area wholly or partly included in the area in which the poll is held, and

   (b)   are registered in the register of local government electors at an address within the area in which the poll is held.

EU law, human rights and international obligations etc.

80   EU law

(1)   An EU obligation of the United Kingdom is also an obligation of the Welsh Ministers if and to the extent that the obligation could be implemented (or enabled to be implemented) or complied with by the exercise by the Welsh Ministers of any of their functions.

(2)   Subsection (1) does not apply in the case of an EU obligation of the United Kingdom if—

   (a)   it is an obligation to achieve a result defined by reference to a quantity (whether expressed as an amount, proportion or ratio or otherwise), and (b)　the quantity relates to the United Kingdom (or to an area including the United Kingdom or to an area consisting of a part of the United Kingdom which includes the whole or part of Wales or of the Welsh zone).

(3)　But if such an EU obligation could (to any extent) be implemented (or enabled to be implemented) or complied with by the exercise by the Welsh Ministers of any of their functions, a Minister of the Crown may by order provide for the achievement by the Welsh Ministers (in the exercise of their functions) of so much of the result to be achieved under the EU obligation as is specified in the order.

(7)　Where an order under subsection (3) is in force in relation to an EU obligation, to the extent that the EU obligation involves achieving what is specified in the order it is also an obligation of the Welsh Ministers (enforceable as if it were an obligation of the Welsh Ministers under subsection (1)).

(8)　The Welsh Ministers have no power—
(a)　to make, confirm or approve any subordinate legislation, or
(b)　to do any other act,
so far as the subordinate legislation or act is incompatible with EU law or an obligation under subsection (7).

81　Human rights

(1)　The Welsh Ministers have no power—
(a)　to make, confirm or approve any subordinate legislation, or
(b)　to do any other act,
so far as the subordinate legislation or act is incompatible with any of the Convention rights.

(2)　Subsection (1) does not enable a person—
(a)　to bring any proceedings in a court or tribunal, or
(b)　to rely on any of the Convention rights in any such proceedings,
in respect of an act unless that person would be a victim for the purposes of Article 34 of the Convention if proceedings were brought in the European Court of Human Rights in respect of that act.

(3)　Subsection (2) does not apply to the Attorney General, the Counsel General, the Advocate General for Scotland or the Attorney General for Northern Ireland.

(4)　Subsection (1)—
(a)　does not apply to an act which, by virtue of subsection (2) of section 6 of the Human Rights Act 1998, is not unlawful under subsection (1) of that section, and
(b)　does not enable a court or tribunal to award in respect of any act any damages which it could not award on finding the act unlawful under that subsection.

(6)　In subsection (2) "the Convention" has the same meaning as in the Human Rights Act 1998.

82　International obligations etc.

(1)　If the Secretary of State considers that any action proposed to be taken by the Welsh Ministers would be incompatible with any international obligation, the Secretary of State may by order direct that the proposed action is not to be taken.

90　Documents

(1)　A document is validly executed by the Welsh Ministers if it is executed by the First Minister or any Welsh Minister appointed under section 48.

(2)　The application of the seal of the Welsh Ministers is to be authenticated by the First Minister, any Welsh Minister appointed under section 48 or any person authorised by the Welsh Ministers (whether generally or specifically) for that purpose.

(3)　A document purporting to be—
(a)　duly executed under the seal of the Welsh Ministers, or
(b)　signed on behalf of the Welsh Ministers,
is to be received in evidence and, unless the contrary is proved, is to be taken to be so executed or signed.

PART 4
ACTS OF THE ASSEMBLY

Power

107 Acts of the Assembly

(1) The Assembly may make laws, to be known as Acts of the National Assembly for Wales or Deddfau Cynulliad Cenedlaethol Cymru (referred to in this Act as "Acts of the Assembly").

(2) Proposed Acts of the Assembly are to be known as Bills; and a Bill becomes an Act of the Assembly when it has been passed by the Assembly and has received Royal Assent.

108A Legislative competence

(1) An Act of the Assembly is not law so far as any provision of the Act is outside the Assembly's legislative competence.

(2) A provision is outside that competence so far as any of the following paragraphs apply—

    (a) it extends otherwise than only to England and Wales;

    (b) it applies otherwise than in relation to Wales or confers, imposes, modifies or removes (or gives power to confer, impose, modify or remove) functions exercisable otherwise than in relation to Wales;

    (c) it relates to reserved matters (see Schedule 7A);

    (d) it breaches any of the restrictions in Part 1 of Schedule 7B, having regard to any exception in Part 2 of that Schedule from those restrictions;

    (e) it is incompatible with the Convention rights or with EU law.

(3) But subsection (2)(b) does not apply to a provision that—

    (a) is ancillary to a provision of any Act of the Assembly or Assembly Measure or to a devolved provision of an Act of Parliament, and

    (b) has no greater effect otherwise than in relation to Wales, or in relation to functions exercisable otherwise than in relation to Wales, than is necessary to give effect to the purpose of that provision.

(4) For this purpose, a provision of an Act of Parliament is "devolved" if it would be within the Assembly's legislative competence if it were contained in an Act of the Assembly (ignoring any requirement for consent or consultation imposed under paragraph 8, 10 or 11 of Schedule 7B or otherwise).

(5) In determining what is necessary for the purposes of subsection (3), any power to make laws other than that of the Assembly is disregarded.

(6) The question whether a provision of an Act of the Assembly relates to a reserved matter is determined by reference to the purpose of the provision, having regard (among other things) to its effect in all the circumstances.

(7) For the purposes of this Act a provision is ancillary to another provision if it—

    (a) provides for the enforcement of the other provision or is otherwise appropriate for making that provision effective, or

    (b) is otherwise incidental to, or consequential on, that provision.

(2) For Schedule 7 to that Act (Acts of the Assembly) substitute—

    (a) the Schedule 7A set out in Schedule 1 to this Act, and

    (b) the Schedule 7B set out in Schedule 2 to this Act.

PART 6
MISCELLANEOUS AND SUPPLEMENTARY

156 English and Welsh texts of legislation

(1) The English and Welsh texts of—

    (a) any Assembly Measure or Act of the Assembly which is in both English and Welsh when it is enacted, or

    (b) any subordinate legislation which is in both English and Welsh when it is made,

are to be treated for all purposes as being of equal standing.

SERIOUS CRIME ACT 2007
(2007, c. 27)

An Act to make provision about serious crime prevention orders; to create offences in respect of the encouragement or assistance of crime; to enable information to be shared or processed to prevent fraud or for purposes relating to proceeds of crime; to enable data matching to be conducted both in relation to fraud and for other purposes; to amend the Proceeds of Crime Act 2002 in relation to certain investigations and in relation to accredited financial investigators, management receivers and enforcement receivers, cash recovery proceedings and search warrants; to extend stop and search powers in connection with incidents involving serious violence [30 October 2007]

PART 1
SERIOUS CRIME PREVENTION ORDERS

General

1   Serious crime prevention orders

(1)   The High Court in England and Wales may make an order if—
  (a)   it is satisfied that a person has been involved in serious crime (whether in England and Wales or elsewhere); and
  (b)   it has reasonable grounds to believe that the order would protect the public by preventing, restricting or disrupting involvement by the person in serious crime in England and Wales.

(1A) The appropriate court in Scotland may make an order if—
  (a)   it is satisfied that a person has been involved in serious crime (whether in Scotland or elsewhere); and
  (b)   it has reasonable grounds to believe that the order would protect the public by preventing, restricting or disrupting involvement by the person in serious crime in Scotland.

(3)   An order under this section may contain—
  (a)   such prohibitions, restrictions or requirements; and
  (b)   such other terms;
  as the court considers appropriate for the purpose of protecting the public by preventing, restricting or disrupting involvement by the person concerned in serious crime in England and Wales, Scotland or (as the case may be) Northern Ireland.

(4)   The powers of the court in respect of an order under this section are subject to sections 6 to 15 (safeguards).

(5)   In this Part—
  "appropriate court" means the Court of Session or sheriff;
  "serious crime prevention order" means—
  (a)   an order under this section;
  (b)   an order under section 19 (corresponding order of the Crown Court on conviction); or
  (c)   an order under section 22A (corresponding order of the High Court of Justiciary or sheriff on conviction).

(6)   For the purposes of this Part references to the person who is the subject of a serious crime prevention order are references to the person against whom the public are to be protected.

2   Involvement in serious crime: England and Wales orders

(1)   For the purposes of this Part, a person has been involved in serious crime in England and Wales if he—
  (a)   has committed a serious offence in England and Wales;
  (b)   has facilitated the commission by another person of a serious offence in England and Wales; or
  (c)   has conducted himself in a way that was likely to facilitate the commission by himself or another person of a serious offence in England and Wales (whether or not such an offence was committed).

(2)   In this Part "a serious offence in England and Wales" means an offence under the law of England and Wales which, at the time when the court is considering the application or matter in question—

     (a)   is specified, or falls within a description specified, in Part 1 of Schedule 1; or

     (b)   is one which, in the particular circumstances of the case, the court considers to be sufficiently serious to be treated for the purposes of the application or matter as if it were so specified.

(3)   For the purposes of this Part, involvement in serious crime in England and Wales is any one or more of the following—

     (a)   the commission of a serious offence in England and Wales;

     (b)   conduct which facilitates the commission by another person of a serious offence in England and Wales;

     (c)   conduct which is likely to facilitate the commission, by the person whose conduct it is or another person, of a serious offence in England and Wales (whether or not such an offence is committed).

(4)   For the purposes of section 1(1)(a), a person has been involved in serious crime elsewhere than in England and Wales if he—

     (a)   has committed a serious offence in a country outside England and Wales;

     (b)   has facilitated the commission by another person of a serious offence in a country outside England and Wales; or

     (c)   has conducted himself in a way that was likely to facilitate the commission by himself or another person of a serious offence in a country outside England and Wales (whether or not such an offence was committed).

(5)   In subsection (4) "a serious offence in a country outside England and Wales" means an offence under the law of a country outside England and Wales which, at the time when the court is considering the application or matter in question—

     (a)   would be an offence under the law of England and Wales if committed in or as regards England and Wales; and

     (b)   either—

         (i)   would be an offence which is specified, or falls within a description specified, in Part 1 of Schedule 1 if committed in or as regards England and Wales; or

         (ii)   is conduct which, in the particular circumstances of the case, the court considers to be sufficiently serious to be treated for the purposes of the application or matter as if it meets the test in sub-paragraph (i).

(6)   The test in subsection (4) is to be used instead of the tests in sections 2A(1) and 3(1) in deciding for the purposes of section 1(1)(a) whether a person has been involved in serious crime in Scotland or (as the case may be) Northern Ireland.

(7)   An act punishable under the law of a country outside the United Kingdom constitutes an offence under that law for the purposes of subsection (5), however it is described in that law.

4   Involvement in serious crime: supplementary

(1)   In considering for the purposes of this Part whether a person has committed a serious offence—

     (a)   the court must decide that the person has committed the offence if—

         (i)   he has been convicted of the offence; and

         (ii)   the conviction has not been quashed on appeal nor has the person been pardoned of the offence; but

     (b)   the court must not otherwise decide that the person has committed the offence.

(2)   In deciding for the purposes of this Part whether a person ("the respondent") facilitates the commission by another person of a serious offence, the court must ignore—

     (a)   any act that the respondent can show to be reasonable in the circumstances; and

     (b)   subject to this, his intentions, or any other aspect of his mental state, at the time.

(3)   In deciding for the purposes of this Part whether a person ("the respondent") conducts himself in a way that is likely to facilitate the commission by himself or another person of a serious offence (whether or not such an offence is committed), the court must ignore—

(a)	any act that the respondent can show to be reasonable in the circumstances; and

(b)	subject to this, his intentions, or any other aspect of his mental state, at the time.

(4)	The Secretary of State may by order amend Part 1 of Schedule 1.

(4A)	The Scottish Ministers may by order amend Part 1A of Schedule 1.

(4B)	The Scottish Ministers may not exercise the power conferred by subsection (4A) in relation to an offence which relates to a reserved matter (within the meaning of the Scotland Act 1998) without the consent of the Secretary of State.

(5)	The Department of Justice in Northern Ireland may by order amend Part 2 of Schedule 1.

## 5	Type of provision that may be made by orders

(1)	This section contains examples of the type of provision that may be made by a serious crime prevention order but it does not limit the type of provision that may be made by such an order.

(2)	Examples of prohibitions, restrictions or requirements that may be imposed by serious crime prevention orders in England and Wales, Scotland or Northern Ireland include prohibitions, restrictions or requirements in relation to places other than England and Wales, Scotland or (as the case may be) Northern Ireland.

(3)	Examples of prohibitions, restrictions or requirements that may be imposed on individuals (including partners in a partnership) by serious crime prevention orders include prohibitions or restrictions on, or requirements in relation to—

(a)	an individual's financial, property or business dealings or holdings;

(b)	an individual's working arrangements;

(c)	the means by which an individual communicates or associates with others, or the persons with whom he communicates or associates;

(d)	the premises to which an individual has access;

(e)	the use of any premises or item by an individual;

(f)	an individual's travel (whether within the United Kingdom, between the United Kingdom and other places or otherwise).

(4)	Examples of prohibitions, restrictions or requirements that may be imposed on bodies corporate, partnerships and unincorporated associations by serious crime prevention orders include prohibitions or restrictions on, or requirements in relation to—

(a)	financial, property or business dealings or holdings of such persons;

(b)	the types of agreements to which such persons may be a party;

(c)	the provision of goods or services by such persons;

(d)	the premises to which such persons have access;

(e)	the use of any premises or item by such persons;

(f)	the employment of staff by such persons.

(5)	Examples of requirements that may be imposed on any persons by serious crime prevention orders include—

(a)	a requirement on a person to answer questions, or provide information, specified or described in an order—

(i)	at a time, within a period or at a frequency;

(ii)	at a place;

(iii)	in a form and manner; and

(iv)	to a law enforcement officer or description of law enforcement officer; notified to the person by a law enforcement officer specified or described in the order;

(b)	a requirement on a person to produce documents specified or described in an order—

(i)	at a time, within a period or at a frequency;

(ii)	at a place;

(iii)	in a manner; and

(iv)	to a law enforcement officer or description of law enforcement officer; notified to the person by a law enforcement officer specified or described in the order.

(6)	The prohibitions, restrictions or requirements that may be imposed on individuals by serious crime prevention orders include prohibitions, restrictions or requirements in relation to an individual's private dwelling (including, for example, prohibitions or restrictions on, or requirements in relation to, where an individual may reside).

(7)   In this Part—
       "document" means anything in which information of any description is recorded (whether or not in legible form);
       "a law enforcement officer" means—
       (a)   a constable;
       (b)   a National Crime Agency officer who is for the time being designated under section 9 or 10 of the Crime and Courts Act 2013;
       (c)   an officer of Revenue and Customs; or
       (d)   a member of the Serious Fraud Office; and
       "premises" includes any land, vehicle, vessel, aircraft or hovercraft.
(8)   Any reference in this Part to the production of documents is, in the case of a document which contains information recorded otherwise than in legible form, a reference to the production of a copy of the information in legible form.

Extension of jurisdiction to Crown Court

19   Orders by Crown Court on conviction

(1)   Subsection (2) applies where the Crown Court in England and Wales is dealing with a person who—
       (a)   has been convicted by or before a magistrates' court of having committed a serious offence in England and Wales and has been committed to the Crown Court to be dealt with; or
       (b)   has been convicted by or before the Crown Court of having committed a serious offence in England and Wales.
(2)   The Crown Court may, in addition to dealing with the person in relation to the offence, make an order if it has reasonable grounds to believe that the order would protect the public by preventing, restricting or disrupting involvement by the person in serious crime in England and Wales.
(2A)   A court that makes an order by virtue of subsection (2) in the case of a person who is already the subject of a serious crime prevention order in England and Wales must discharge the existing order.
(5)   An order under this section may contain—
       (a)   such prohibitions, restrictions or requirements; and
       (b)   such other terms;
       as the court considers appropriate for the purpose of protecting the public by preventing, restricting or disrupting involvement by the person concerned in serious crime in England and Wales or (as the case may be) Northern Ireland.
(6)   The powers of the court in respect of an order under this section are subject to sections 6 to 15 (safeguards).
(7)   An order must not be made under this section except—
       (a)   in addition to a sentence imposed in respect of the offence concerned; or
       (b)   in addition to an order discharging the person conditionally.
(8)   An order under this section is also called a serious crime prevention order.

UK BORDERS ACT 2007
(2007, c. 30)

An Act to make provision about immigration and asylum; and for connected purposes.

[30 October 2007]

Detention at ports

1   Designated immigration officers

(1)   The Secretary of State may designate immigration officers for the purposes of section 2.
(2)   The Secretary of State may designate only officers who the Secretary of State thinks are—
       (a)   fit and proper for the purpose, and
       (b)   suitably trained.

(3) A designation—
    (a) may be permanent or for a specified period, and
    (b) may (in either case) be revoked.

2 Detention

(1) A designated immigration officer at a port in England, Wales or Northern Ireland may detain an individual if the immigration officer thinks that the individual—
    (a) may be liable to arrest by a constable under section 24(1), (2) or (3) of the Police and Criminal Evidence Act 1984 or Article 26(1), (2) or (3) of the Police and Criminal Evidence (Northern Ireland) Order 1989, or
    (b) is subject to a warrant for arrest.

(2) A designated immigration officer who detains an individual—
    (a) must arrange for a constable to attend as soon as is reasonably practicable,
    (b) may search the individual for, and retain, anything that might be used to assist escape or to cause physical injury to the individual or another person,
    (c) must retain anything found on a search which the immigration officer thinks may be evidence of the commission of an offence, and
    (d) must, when the constable arrives, deliver to the constable the individual and anything retained on a search.

(3) An individual may not be detained under this section for longer than three hours.

(4) A designated immigration officer may use reasonable force for the purpose of exercising a power under this section.

(5) Where an individual whom a designated immigration officer has detained or attempted to detain under this section leaves the port, a designated immigration officer may—
    (a) pursue the individual, and
    (b) return the individual to the port.

(6) Detention under this section shall be treated as detention under the Immigration Act 1971 for the purposes of Part 8 of the Immigration and Asylum Act 1999 (detained persons).

PARLIAMENTARY STANDARDS ACT 2009
(2009, c. 13)

An Act to make provision establishing a body corporate known as the Independent Parliamentary Standards Authority and an officer known as the Commissioner for Parliamentary Investigations; to make provision relating to salaries and allowances for members of the House of Commons and to their financial interests and conduct; and for connected purposes. [21 July 2009]

Independent Parliamentary Standards Authority etc

3 Independent Parliamentary Standards Authority etc

(1) There is to be a body corporate known as the Independent Parliamentary Standards Authority ("IPSA").

(2) Schedule 1 (which makes provision about the IPSA, and in particular provides for its administration functions to be carried out by its chief executive in accordance with paragraph 17 of that Schedule) has effect.

(3) There is to be an officer known as the Compliance Officer for the Independent Parliamentary Standards Authority ("the Compliance Officer").

(4) Schedule 2 (which makes provision about the Compliance Officer) has effect.

(5) There is to be a committee known as the Speaker's Committee for the Independent Parliamentary Standards Authority ("the Committee").

(6) Schedule 3 (which makes provision about the Committee) has effect.

3A General duties of the IPSA

(1) In carrying out its functions the IPSA must have regard to the principle that it should act in a way which is efficient, cost-effective and transparent.

(2) In carrying out its functions the IPSA must have regard to the principle that members of the House of Commons should be supported in efficiently, cost-effectively and transparently carrying out their Parliamentary functions.

Salaries and allowances for MPs

4 MPs' salaries

(1) Members of the House of Commons are to receive a salary for the relevant period.
(2) The salaries are to be paid by the IPSA.
(3) Salaries are to be paid on a monthly basis in arrears.
(4) The amounts of the salaries are to be determined by the IPSA (see section 4A).
(5) "Relevant period", in relation to a person who is a member of the House of Commons, means the period beginning with the day after the day of the poll for the parliamentary election at which the member was elected and ending with—
    (a) if the person is a member immediately before Parliament is dissolved, the day of the poll for the parliamentary general election which follows the dissolution;
    (b) otherwise, the day on which the person ceases to be a member.
(6) No payment of salary is to be made to a member before the member has made and subscribed the oath required by the Parliamentary Oaths Act 1866 (or the corresponding affirmation).
(7) The duty of the IPSA to pay a salary to a member is subject to anything done in relation to the member in the exercise of the disciplinary powers of the House of Commons.

4A Determination of MPs' salaries

(1) This section is about determinations under section 4(4).
(2) A determination may provide for higher salaries to be payable to members while holding an office or position specified for the purposes of this subsection in a resolution of the House of Commons.
(3) A determination by virtue of subsection (2) may make different provision for different offices or positions or different classes of member (and may include exceptions).
(4) A determination may include a formula or other mechanism for adjusting salaries from time to time.
(5) A determination (other than the first determination) may have retrospective effect.
(6) The IPSA must review the current determination (and make a new determination as appropriate)—
    (a) in the first year of each Parliament;
    (b) at any other time it considers appropriate.
(7) In reviewing a determination (and before making the first determination) the IPSA must consult—
    (a) the Review Body on Senior Salaries,
    (b) persons appearing to the IPSA to represent persons likely to be affected by the determination or the review,
    (c) the Minister for the Civil Service,
    (d) the Treasury, and
    (e) any other person the IPSA considers appropriate.
(8) After making a determination, the IPSA must publish in a way it considers appropriate—
    (a) the determination, and
    (b) a statement of how it arrived at the determination.
(9) If the IPSA reviews the current determination but decides not to make a new determination, it must publish in a way it considers appropriate a statement of how it arrived at that decision.
(10) The IPSA may delegate to the Review Body on Senior Salaries its function of reviewing a determination (but not its function of deciding whether or not to make a new determination).

5 MPs' allowances scheme

(1) The IPSA is to pay allowances to members of the House of Commons in accordance with the MPs' allowances scheme.
(2) In this Act "the MPs' allowances scheme" means the scheme prepared under this section as it is in effect for the time being.
(3) The IPSA must—
    (a) prepare the scheme;
    (b) review the scheme regularly and revise it as appropriate.

(4) In preparing or revising the scheme, the IPSA must consult—
   (a) the Speaker of the House of Commons,
   (b) the Committee on Standards in Public Life,
   (c) the Leader of the House of Commons,
   (d) any committee of the House of Commons nominated by the Speaker,
   (e) members of the House of Commons,
   (f) the Review Body on Senior Salaries,
   (g) Her Majesty's Revenue and Customs,
   (h) the Treasury, and
   (i) any other person the IPSA considers appropriate.
(5) The Speaker must lay the scheme (or revision) before the House of Commons.
(5A) When the scheme (or revision) is laid, the IPSA must publish in a way it considers appropriate—
   (a) the scheme (or revision), and
   (b) a statement of its reasons for adopting that scheme (or making that revision).
(6) The scheme (or revision) comes into effect on the date specified in the scheme (or revision).
(7) The scheme may, for example—
   (a) provide for allowances to be payable in respect of specified kinds of expenditure or in specified circumstances;
   (b) provide for allowances to be payable only on specified conditions (such as a condition that claims for allowances must be supported by documentary evidence);
   (c) impose limits on the amounts that may be paid.
(8) The scheme may provide for allowances to be payable in connection with a person's ceasing to be a member of the House of Commons; and in relation to any such allowances, references in this Act to a member of the House of Commons include a former member of that House.
(8A) Any duty of the IPSA to pay an allowance to a member is subject to anything done in relation to the member in the exercise of the disciplinary powers of the House of Commons.
(9) This section does not affect the provision of pensions for or in respect of persons with service as a member of the House of Commons (see Schedule 6 to the Constitutional Reform and Governance Act 2010).
(10) In section 3A(1) of the European Parliament (Pay and Pensions) Act 1979 (power to make order aligning MEPs' resettlement grants with MPs' resettlement grants), after "resolutions of the House of Commons" insert ", or a scheme under section 5 of the Parliamentary Standards Act 2009,".

6 Dealing with claims under the scheme

(1) No allowance is to be paid to a member of the House of Commons under the MPs' allowances scheme unless a claim for the allowance has been made to the IPSA.
(2) The claim must be made by the member (except where the scheme provides otherwise).
(3) On receipt of a claim, the IPSA must—
   (a) determine whether to allow or refuse the claim, and
   (b) if it is allowed, determine how much of the amount claimed is to be allowed and pay it accordingly.
(6) The MPs' allowances scheme may include—
   (a) further provision about how claims are to be dealt with;
   (b) provision for deducting amounts within subsection (6A) from allowances payable under the scheme or salaries payable under section 4;
   (c) provision about how such deductions, and deductions under paragraph 5 or 12 of Schedule 4, are to be made.
(6A) This subsection applies to amounts which a member (under section 9(8) or otherwise) has agreed to repay, in respect of amounts paid to the member under the MPs' allowances scheme that should not have been allowed.

(7) The scheme may provide for an allowance to which a member is entitled under the scheme to be paid to another person at the member's direction; and references in this Act to the payment of an allowance to a member are to be read accordingly.

(8) The IPSA must publish such information as it considers appropriate in respect of—
    (a) each claim made under or by virtue of this section, and
    (b) each payment of an allowance by the IPSA under or by virtue of this section.

(9) The IPSA must publish the information at times it considers appropriate and in a way it considers appropriate.

(10) The IPSA must determine procedures to be followed by the IPSA in relation to publication of the information, and in doing so must consult—
    (a) the Speaker of the House of Commons,
    (b) the Leader of the House of Commons,
    (c) the House of Commons Committee on Standards and Privileges,
    (d) the Compliance Officer, and
    (e) any other person the IPSA considers appropriate.

6A Review of IPSA's determination

(1) This section applies if—
    (a) the IPSA determines under section 6(3) that a claim is to be refused or that only part of the amount claimed is to be allowed, and
    (b) the member (after asking the IPSA to reconsider the determination and giving it a reasonable opportunity to do so) asks the Compliance Officer to review the determination (or any altered determination resulting from the IPSA's reconsideration).

(2) The Compliance Officer must—
    (a) consider whether the determination (or the altered determination) is the determination that should have been made, and
    (b) in light of that consideration, decide whether or not to confirm or alter it.

(3) The Compliance Officer must give the IPSA a statement of any decision under subsection (2)(b), and may include a statement of the Compliance Officer's findings about the way in which the IPSA has dealt with the claim.

(4) The IPSA must make any payments or adjustments necessary to give effect to the Compliance Officer's decision; but it must not do so until—
    (a) it is no longer possible for there to be a relevant appeal, and
    (b) all relevant appeals have been withdrawn or determined.

(5) A relevant appeal is—
    (a) an appeal under subsection (6) brought before the end of the period mentioned in subsection (7), or
    (b) a further appeal in relation to the Compliance Officer's decision which—
        (i)   is brought before the end of the usual period for bringing such an appeal, and
        (ii) is an appeal against the determination of an appeal which was itself a relevant appeal.

(6) The member may appeal to the First-tier Tribunal against a decision of the Compliance Officer under subsection (2)(b).

(7) The appeal must be brought before the end of the period of 28 days beginning with the day on which notice of the decision is sent to the member (unless the Tribunal directs that it may be brought after the end of that period).

(8) The appeal is by way of a rehearing.

(9) On an appeal under subsection (6) the Tribunal may—
    (a) allow the appeal in whole or in part, or
    (b) dismiss the appeal.

(10) If the Tribunal allows the appeal (in whole or in part) it may—
    (a) order the IPSA to make any payments or adjustments necessary to give effect to that decision;
    (b) make any other order it thinks fit.

(11) If the Tribunal dismisses the appeal it may make any other order it thinks fit.

(12) The Compliance Officer must notify the IPSA of the Tribunal's decision (and the result of any further appeal).

7 Information and guidance

(A1) The IPSA must—
  (a) prepare guidance for members of the House of Commons about making claims under the MPs' allowances scheme;
  (b) review the guidance regularly and revise it as appropriate;
  (c) publish the guidance in a way the IPSA considers appropriate;
  (d) provide to any member on request such further advice about making claims as the IPSA considers appropriate.

(1) The IPSA must provide to members of the House of Commons—
  (a) details of any general information or guidance about taxation issues published by HMRC that it considers they should be aware of, and
  (b) any other general information or guidance about taxation issues that it considers appropriate (consulting HMRC for this purpose as it considers appropriate).

(2) "Taxation issues" means—
  (a) issues about the taxation of salaries payable under section 4 and allowances payable under the MPs' allowances scheme, and
  (b) any other issues about taxation arising in connection with those salaries and allowances.

(3) "HMRC" means Her Majesty's Revenue and Customs.

9 Investigations

(1) The Compliance Officer may conduct an investigation if the Compliance Officer has reason to believe that a member of the House of Commons may have been paid an amount under the MPs' allowances scheme that should not have been allowed.

(2) An investigation may be conducted—
  (a) on the Compliance Officer's own initiative,
  (b) at the request of the IPSA,
  (c) at the request of the member, or
  (d) in response to a complaint by an individual.

(3) For the purposes of the investigation the member and the IPSA—
  (a) must provide the Compliance Officer with any information (including documents) the Compliance Officer reasonably requires, and
  (b) must do so within such period as the Compliance Officer reasonably requires.

(4) The Compliance Officer must, after giving the member and the IPSA an opportunity to make representations to the Compliance Officer, prepare a statement of the Compliance Officer's provisional findings.

(5) The Compliance Officer must, after giving the member and the IPSA an opportunity to make representations to the Compliance Officer about the provisional findings, prepare a statement of the Compliance Officer's findings (subject to subsection (7)).

(6) Provisional findings under subsection (4) and findings under subsection (5) may include—
  (a) a finding that the member failed to comply with subsection (3),
  (b) findings about the role of the IPSA in the matters under investigation, including findings that the member's being paid an amount under the MPs' allowances scheme that should not have been allowed was wholly or partly the IPSA's fault.

(7) If subsection (8) applies, the Compliance Officer need not make a finding under subsection (5) as to whether the member was paid an amount under the MPs' allowances scheme that should not have been allowed.

(8) This subsection applies if—
  (a) the member accepts a provisional finding that the member was paid an amount under the MPs' allowances scheme that should not have been allowed,
  (b) such other conditions as may be specified by the IPSA are, in the Compliance Officer's view, met in relation to the case, and

    (c)   the member agrees to repay to the IPSA, in such manner and within such period as the Compliance Officer considers reasonable, such amount as the Compliance Officer considers reasonable (and makes the repayment accordingly).

(9)   Before specifying conditions under subsection (8)(b) the IPSA must consult the persons listed in section 9A(6).

(10) References in this section (and section 9A) to a member of the House of Commons include a former member of that House.

9A   Procedures etc

(1)   The IPSA must determine procedures to be followed by the Compliance Officer in relation to investigations under section 9.

(2)   The procedures must in particular include provision about—
    (a)   complaints under section 9(2)(d),
    (b)   representations under section 9(4),
    (c)   representations under section 9(5), and
    (d)   the circumstances in which the Compliance Officer must publish the documents listed in subsection (4).

(3)   Provision under subsection (2)(b) must include provision giving the member who is the subject of the investigation—
    (a)   an opportunity to be heard in person, and
    (b)   an opportunity, where the Compliance Officer considers it appropriate, to call and examine witnesses.

(4)   The documents referred to in subsection (2)(d) are—
    (a)   statements of provisional findings under section 9(4),
    (b)   statements of findings under section 9(5), and
    (c)   agreements under section 9(8).

(5)   The IPSA must also determine procedures to be followed by the Compliance Officer as to the circumstances in which the Compliance Officer must publish—
    (a)   statements under section 6A(3), and
    (b)   penalty notices under paragraph 6 of Schedule 4.

(6)   Procedures under this section must be fair, and before determining procedures the IPSA must consult—
    (a)   the Speaker of the House of Commons,
    (b)   the Leader of the House of Commons,
    (c)   the House of Commons Committee on Standards and Privileges,
    (d)   the Compliance Officer, and
    (e)   any other person the IPSA considers appropriate

10   Offence of providing false or misleading information for allowances claims

(1)   A member of the House of Commons commits an offence if the member—
    (a)   makes a claim under the MPs' allowances scheme, and
    (b)   provides information for the purposes of the claim that the member knows to be false or misleading in a material respect.

(2)   A person guilty of an offence under subsection (1) is liable—
    (a)   on summary conviction, to imprisonment for a term not exceeding 12 months or to a fine not exceeding the statutory maximum or to both;
    (b)   on conviction on indictment, to imprisonment for a term not exceeding 12 months or to a fine or to both.

(3)   In the application of this section—
    (a)   in England and Wales, in relation to an offence committed before the commencement of section 154(1) of the Criminal Justice Act 2003 (c. 44), or
    (b)   in Northern Ireland,
the reference in subsection (2) (a) to 12 months is to be read as a reference to 6 months.

CONSTITUTIONAL REFORM AND GOVERNANCE ACT 2010
(2010, c. 25)

PART 2
RATIFICATION OF TREATIES

20 Treaties to be laid before Parliament before ratification

(1) Subject to what follows, a treaty is not to be ratified unless—
    (a) a Minister of the Crown has laid before Parliament a copy of the treaty,
    (b) the treaty has been published in a way that a Minister of the Crown thinks appropriate, and
    (c) period A has expired without either House having resolved, within period A, that the treaty should not be ratified.

(2) Period A is the period of 21 sitting days beginning with the first sitting day after the date on which the requirement in subsection (1)(a) is met.

(3) Subsections (4) to (6) apply if the House of Commons resolved as mentioned in subsection (1)(c) (whether or not the House of Lords also did so).

(4) The treaty may be ratified if—
    (a) a Minister of the Crown has laid before Parliament a statement indicating that the Minister is of the opinion that the treaty should nevertheless be ratified and explaining why, and
    (b) period B has expired without the House of Commons having resolved, within period B, that the treaty should not be ratified.

(5) Period B is the period of 21 sitting days beginning with the first sitting day after the date on which the requirement in subsection (4)(a) is met.

(6) A statement may be laid under subsection (4)(a) in relation to the treaty on more than one occasion.

(7) Subsection (8) applies if—
    (a) the House of Lords resolved as mentioned in subsection (1)(c), but
    (b) the House of Commons did not.

(8) The treaty may be ratified if a Minister of the Crown has laid before Parliament a statement indicating that the Minister is of the opinion that the treaty should nevertheless be ratified and explaining why.

(9) "Sitting day" means a day on which both Houses of Parliament sit.

21 Extension of 21 sitting day period

(1) A Minister of the Crown may, in relation to a treaty, extend the period mentioned in section 20(1)(c) by 21 sitting days or less.

(2) The Minister does that by laying before Parliament a statement—
    (a) indicating that the period is to be extended, and
    (b) setting out the length of the extension.

(3) The statement must be laid before the period would have expired without the extension.

(4) The Minister must publish the statement in a way the Minister thinks appropriate.

(5) The period may be extended more than once.

22 Section 20 not to apply in exceptional cases

(1) Section 20 does not apply to a treaty if a Minister of the Crown is of the opinion that, exceptionally, the treaty should be ratified without the requirements of that section having been met.

(2) But a treaty may not be ratified by virtue of subsection (1) after either House has resolved, as mentioned in section 20(1)(c), that the treaty should not be ratified.

(3) If a Minister determines that a treaty is to be ratified by virtue of subsection (1), the Minister must, either before or as soon as practicable after the treaty is ratified—
    (a) lay before Parliament a copy of the treaty,
    (b) arrange for the treaty to be published in a way that the Minister thinks appropriate, and
    (c) lay before Parliament a statement indicating that the Minister is of the opinion mentioned in subsection (1) and explaining why.

EUROPEAN UNION ACT 2011
(2011, c. 12)

An Act to make provision about treaties relating to the European Union and decisions made under them, including provision implementing the Protocol signed at Brussels on 23 June 2010 amending the Protocol (No. 36) on transitional provisions annexed to the Treaty on European Union, to the Treaty on the Functioning of the European Union and to the Treaty establishing the European Atomic Energy Community; and to make provision about the means by which directly applicable or directly effective European Union law has effect in the United Kingdom.   [19th July 2011]

PART 1
RESTRICTIONS ON TREATIES AND DECISIONS RELATING TO EU

Introductory

Restrictions relating to amendments of TEU or TFEU

2   Treaties amending or replacing TEU or TFEU

(1)   A treaty which amends or replaces TEU or TFEU is not to be ratified unless—
  (a)   a statement relating to the treaty was laid before Parliament in accordance with section 5,
  (b)   the treaty is approved by Act of Parliament, and
  (c)   the referendum condition or the exemption condition is met.

(2)   The referendum condition is that—
  (a)   the Act providing for the approval of the treaty provides that the provision approving the treaty is not to come into force until a referendum about whether the treaty should be ratified has been held throughout the United Kingdom or, where the treaty also affects Gibraltar, throughout the United Kingdom and Gibraltar,
  (b)   the referendum has been held, and
  (c)   the majority of those voting in the referendum are in favour of the ratification of the treaty.

(3)   The exemption condition is that the Act providing for the approval of the treaty states that the treaty does not fall within section 4.

5   Statement to be laid before Parliament

(1)   If a treaty amending TEU or TFEU is agreed in an inter-governmental conference, a Minister of the Crown must lay the required statement before Parliament before the end of the 2 months beginning with the date on which the treaty is agreed.

(2)   If an Article 48(6) decision is adopted by the European Council subject to its approval by the member States, a Minister of the Crown must lay the required statement before Parliament before the end of the 2 months beginning with the date on which the decision is adopted.

(3)   The required statement is a statement as to whether, in the Minister's opinion, the treaty or Article 48(6) decision falls within section 4.

(4)   If the Minister is of the opinion that an Article 48(6) decision falls within section 4 only because of provision of the kind mentioned in subsection (1)(i) or (j) of that section, the statement must indicate whether in the Minister's opinion the effect of that provision in relation to the United Kingdom is significant.

(5)   The statement must give reasons for the Minister's opinion under subsection (3) and, if relevant, subsection (4).

(6)   In relation to an Article 48(6) decision adopted by the European Council before the day on which this section comes into force ("the commencement date"), the condition in section 3(1)(a) is to be taken to be complied with if a statement under this section is laid before Parliament before the end of the 2 months beginning with the commencement date.

Restrictions relating to other decisions under TEU or TFEU

6   Decisions requiring approval by Act and by referendum

(1)   A Minister of the Crown may not vote in favour of or otherwise support a decision to which this subsection applies unless—
    (a)   the draft decision is approved by Act of Parliament, and
    (b)   the referendum condition is met.

(2)   Where the European Council has recommended to the member States the adoption of a decision under Article 42(2) of TEU in relation to a common EU defence, a Minister of the Crown may not notify the European Council that the decision is adopted by the United Kingdom unless—
    (a)   the decision is approved by Act of Parliament, and
    (b)   the referendum condition is met.

(3)   A Minister of the Crown may not give a notification under Article 4 of Protocol (No. 21) on the position of the United Kingdom and Ireland in respect of the area of freedom, security and justice annexed to TEU and TFEU which relates to participation by the United Kingdom in a European Public Prosecutor's Office or an extension of the powers of that Office unless—
    (a)   the notification has been approved by Act of Parliament, and
    (b)   the referendum condition is met.

(4)   The referendum condition is that set out in section 3(2), with references to a decision being read for the purposes of subsection (1) as references to a draft decision and for the purposes of subsection (3) as references to a notification.

(5)   The decisions to which subsection (1) applies are—
    (a)   a decision under the provision of Article 31(3) of TEU that permits the adoption of qualified majority voting;
    (b)   a decision under Article 48(7) of TEU which in relation to any provision listed in Schedule 1—
        (i)   adopts qualified majority voting, or
        (ii)   applies the ordinary legislative procedure in place of a special legislative procedure requiring the Council to act unanimously;
    (c)   a decision under Article 86(1) of TFEU involving participation by the United Kingdom in a European Public Prosecutor's Office;
    (d)   where the United Kingdom has become a participant in a European Public Prosecutor's Office, a decision under Article 86(4) of TFEU to extend the powers of that Office;
    (e)   a decision under Article 140(3) of TFEU which would make the euro the currency of the United Kingdom;
    (f)   a decision under the provision of Article 153(2) of TFEU (social policy) that permits the application of the ordinary legislative procedure in place of a special legislative procedure;
    (g)   a decision under the provision of Article 192(2) of TFEU (environment) that permits the application of the ordinary legislative procedure in place of a special legislative procedure;
    (h)   a decision under the provision of Article 312(2) of TFEU (EU finance) that permits the adoption of qualified majority voting;
    (i)   a decision under the provision of Article 333(1) of TFEU (enhanced co-operation) that permits the adoption of qualified majority voting, where the decision relates to a provision listed in Schedule 1 and the United Kingdom is a participant in the enhanced co-operation to which the decision relates;
    (j)   a decision under the provision of Article 333(2) of TFEU (enhanced co-operation) that permits the adoption of the ordinary legislative procedure in place of a special legislative procedure, where—
        (i)   the decision relates to a provision listed in Schedule 1,
        (ii)   the special legislative procedure requires the Council to act unanimously, and
        (iii)   the United Kingdom is a participant in the enhanced co-operation to which the decision relates;

(k)   a decision under Article 4 of the Schengen Protocol that removes any border control of the United Kingdom.

(6)   In subsection (5)(k) "the Schengen Protocol" means the Protocol (No. 19) on the Schengen *acquis* integrated into the framework of the European Union, annexed to TEU and TFEU.

7   Decisions requiring approval by Act

(1)   A Minister of the Crown may not confirm the approval by the United Kingdom of a decision to which this subsection applies unless the decision is approved by Act of Parliament.

(2)   The decisions to which subsection (1) applies are—
   (a)   a decision under the provision of Article 25 of TFEU that permits the adoption of provisions to strengthen or add to the rights listed in Article 20(2) of that Treaty (rights of citizens of the European Union);
   (b)   a decision under the provision of Article 223(1) of TFEU that permits the laying down of the provisions necessary for the election of the members of the European Parliament in accordance with that Article;
   (c)   a decision under the provision of Article 262 of TFEU that permits the conferring of jurisdiction on the Court of Justice of the European Union in disputes relating to the application of acts adopted on the basis of the EU Treaties which create European intellectual property rights;
   (d)   a decision under the third paragraph of Article 311 of TFEU to adopt a decision laying down provisions relating to the system of own resources of the European Union.

(3)   A Minister of the Crown may not vote in favour of or otherwise support a decision to which this subsection applies unless the draft decision is approved by Act of Parliament.

(4)   The decisions to which subsection (3) applies are—
   (a)   a decision under the provision of Article 17(5) of TEU that permits the alteration of the number of members of the European Commission;
   (b)   a decision under Article 48(7) of TEU which in relation to any provision not listed in Schedule 1—
      (i)   adopts qualified majority voting, or
      (ii)   applies the ordinary legislative procedure in place of a special legislative procedure requiring the Council to act unanimously;
   (c)   a decision under the provision of Article 64(3) of TFEU that permits the adoption of measures which constitute a step backwards in European Union law as regards the liberalisation of the movement of capital to or from third countries;
   (d)   a decision under the provision of Article 126(14) of TFEU that permits the adoption of provisions to replace the Protocol (No. 12) on the excessive deficit procedure annexed to TEU and TFEU;
   (e)   a decision under the provision of Article 333(1) of TFEU (enhanced co-operation) that permits the adoption of qualified majority voting, where the decision relates to a provision not listed in Schedule 1 and the United Kingdom is a participant in the enhanced co-operation to which the decision relates;
   (f)   a decision under the provision of Article 333(2) of TFEU (enhanced co-operation) that permits the adoption of the ordinary legislative procedure in place of a special legislative procedure, where—
      (i)   the decision relates to a provision not listed in Schedule 1,
      (ii)   the special legislative procedure requires the Council to act unanimously, and
      (iii)   the United Kingdom is a participant in the enhanced co-operation to which the decision relates.

8   Decisions under Article 352 of TFEU

(1)   A Minister of the Crown may not vote in favour of or otherwise support an Article 352 decision unless one of subsections (3) to (5) is complied with in relation to the draft decision.

(2)   An Article 352 decision is a decision under the provision of Article 352 of TFEU that permits the adoption of measures to attain one of the objectives set out in the EU Treaties (but for which those Treaties have not provided the necessary powers).

(3)   This subsection is complied with if a draft decision is approved by Act of Parliament.

(4)   This subsection is complied with if—

    (a)   in each House of Parliament a Minister of the Crown moves a motion that the House approves Her Majesty's Government's intention to support a specified draft decision and is of the opinion that the measure to which it relates is required as a matter of urgency, and

    (b)   each House agrees to the motion without amendment.

(5)   This subsection is complied with if a Minister of the Crown has laid before Parliament a statement specifying a draft decision and stating that in the opinion of the Minister the decision relates only to one or more exempt purposes.

(6)   The exempt purposes are—

    (a)   to make provision equivalent to that made by a measure previously adopted under Article 352 of TFEU, other than an excepted measure;

    (b)   to prolong or renew a measure previously adopted under that Article, other than an excepted measure;

    (c)   to extend a measure previously adopted under that Article to another member State or other country;

    (d)   to repeal existing measures adopted under that Article;

    (e)   to consolidate existing measures adopted under that Article without any change of substance.

(7)   In subsection (6)(a) and (b), "excepted measure" means a measure adopted after the commencement of this section and resulting from a decision in relation to which a Minister of the Crown had relied on compliance with subsection (4).

9   Approval required in connection with Title V of Part 3 of TFEU

(1)   A Minister of the Crown may not give a notification to which this subsection applies unless Parliamentary approval has been given in accordance with subsection (3).

(2)   Subsection (1) applies in relation to a notification under Article 3 of Protocol (No. 21) on the position of the United Kingdom and Ireland in respect of the area of freedom, security and justice annexed to TEU and TFEU (the "AFSJ Protocol") that the United Kingdom wishes to take part in the adoption and application of a measure proposed under any of the following—

    (a)   the provision of Article 81(3) of TFEU (family law) that permits the application of the ordinary legislative procedure in place of a special legislative procedure;

    (b)   the provision of Article 82(2)(d) of TFEU (criminal procedure) that permits the identification of further specific aspects of criminal procedure to which directives adopted under the ordinary legislative procedure may relate;

    (c)   the provision of Article 83(1) of TFEU (particularly serious crime with a cross-border dimension) that permits the identification of further areas of crime to which directives adopted under the ordinary legislative procedure may relate.

(3)   Parliamentary approval is given if—

    (a)   in each House of Parliament a Minister of the Crown moves a motion that the House approves Her Majesty's Government's intention to give a notification in respect of a specified measure, and

    (b)   each House agrees to the motion without amendment.

(4)   Despite any Parliamentary approval given for the purposes of subsection (1), a Minister may not vote in favour of or otherwise support a decision under a provision falling within any of paragraphs (a) to (c) of subsection (2) unless the draft decision is approved by Act of Parliament.

(5)   A Minister of the Crown may not give a notification under Article 4 of the AFSJ Protocol that the United Kingdom wishes to accept a measure to which this subsection applies unless the notification in respect of the measure has been approved by Act of Parliament.

(6)   The measures to which subsection (5) applies are—

    (a)   a measure adopted under a provision described in any of paragraphs (a) to (c) of subsection (2), or

    (b)   a measure established under Article 81(3), 82(2)(d) or 83(1) of TFEU by virtue of a previous decision adopted, without the participation of the United Kingdom, under a provision falling within any of those paragraphs.

10   Parliamentary control of certain decisions not requiring approval by Act

(1)   A Minister of the Crown may not vote in favour of or otherwise support a decision under any of the following unless Parliamentary approval has been given in accordance with this section—

   (a)   the provision of Article 56 of TFEU that permits the extension of the provisions of Chapter 3 of Title IV of Part 3 of that Treaty (free movement of services) to nationals of a third country;

   (b)   Article 129(3) of TFEU (amendment of provisions of the Statute of the European System of Central Banks or of the European Central Bank);

   (c)   the provision of Article 252 of TFEU that permits an increase in the number of Advocates-General;

   (d)   the provision of Article 257 of TFEU that permits the establishment of specialised courts attached to the General Court;

   (e)   the provision of Article 281 of TFEU that permits the amendment of the Statute of the Court of Justice of the European Union;

   (f)   the provision of Article 308 of TFEU that permits the amendment of the Statute of the European Investment Bank.

(2)   A Minister of the Crown may not vote in favour of or otherwise support a decision to which this subsection applies unless Parliamentary approval has been given in accordance with this section.

(3)   Subsection (2) applies to a decision under Article 48(7) of TEU which in relation to a provision of TFEU applies the ordinary legislative procedure in place of a special legislative procedure not requiring the Council to act unanimously.

(4)   A Minister of the Crown may not confirm the approval by the United Kingdom of a decision under Article 218(8) of TFEU for the accession of the European Union to the European Convention for the Protection of Human Rights and Fundamental Freedoms in accordance with Article 6(2) of TEU unless Parliamentary approval has been given in accordance with this section.

(5)   Parliamentary approval is given if—

   (a)   in each House of Parliament a Minister of the Crown moves a motion that the House approves Her Majesty's Government's intention to support the adoption of a specified draft decision, and

   (b)   each House agrees to the motion without amendment.

Further provisions about referendums held in pursuance of section 2, 3 or 6

11   Persons entitled to vote in referendum

(1)   The persons entitled to vote in any referendum held in pursuance of section 2, 3 or 6 are to be as follows—

   (a)   the persons who, on the date of the referendum, would be entitled to vote as an elector at a parliamentary election in a constituency in the United Kingdom;

   (b)   the persons who, on that date, are disqualified by reason of being peers from voting as electors in parliamentary elections but—

      (i)   would be entitled to vote as electors at a local government election in any electoral area in Great Britain,

      (ii)   would be entitled to vote as electors at a local election in any district electoral area in Northern Ireland, or

      (iii)   would be entitled to vote as electors at a European Parliamentary election in any electoral region by virtue of section 3 of the Representation of the People Act 1985 (peers resident outside the United Kingdom);

   (c)   if the referendum is also held in Gibraltar, the Commonwealth citizens who, on the date of the referendum, would be entitled to vote in Gibraltar at a European Parliamentary election in the combined electoral region in which Gibraltar is comprised.

(2)   In subsection (1)(b)(i) "local government election" includes a municipal election in the City of London (that is, an election to the office of mayor, alderman, common councilman or sheriff and also the election of any officer elected by the mayor, aldermen and liverymen in common hall).

PART 3
GENERAL

Status of EU law

18   Status of EU law dependent on continuing statutory basis

Directly applicable or directly effective EU law (that is, the rights, powers, liabilities, obligations, restrictions, remedies and procedures referred to in section 2(1) of the European Communities Act 1972) falls to be recognised and available in law in the United Kingdom only by virtue of that Act or where it is required to be recognised and available in law by virtue of any other Act.

POLICE REFORM AND SOCIAL RESPONSIBILITY ACT 2011
(2011, c. 13)

An Act to make provision for the prohibition of certain activities in Parliament Square.
[15th September 2011]

PART 3
PARLIAMENT SQUARE GARDEN AND SURROUNDING AREA

142   Controlled area of Parliament Square

(1)   For the purposes of this Part, the "controlled area of Parliament Square" means the area of land that is comprised in—
   (a)   the central garden of Parliament Square, and
   (b)   the footways that immediately adjoin the central garden of Parliament Square.

(2)   In subsection (1)—
"the central garden of Parliament Square" means the site in Parliament Square on which the Minister of Works was authorised by the Parliament Square (Improvements) Act 1949 to lay out the garden referred to in that Act as "the new central garden";
"footway" has the same meaning as in the Highways Act 1980 (see section 329(1) of that Act).

142A Other controlled areas in vicinity of the Palace of Westminster

(1)   For the purposes of this Part, the "Palace of Westminster controlled area" means the area of land in the City of Westminster that is comprised in—
   (a)   the highways in the postal district SW1 known as—
      (i)   Bridge Street,
      (ii)   St Margaret's Street, and
      (iii) Abingdon Street,
   (b)   so much of the highway in the postal district SW1 known as Great College Street as immediately adjoins Abingdon Street Garden,
   (c)   Old Palace Yard,
   (d)   Abingdon Street Garden (and its pathways), and
   (e)   Victoria Tower Gardens.

(2)   In subsection (1)—
"Abingdon Street Garden" means the garden constructed on the sites of properties formerly known as 18 to 28 (both inclusive) Abingdon Street, London, SW1, together with the garden surrounding the adjoining Jewel Tower and the lawn surrounding the King George V Memorial;
"highway" has the same meaning as in the Highways Act 1980 (see section 328 of that Act);
"Old Palace Yard" includes the King George V Memorial.

143   Prohibited activities in controlled area of Parliament Square or in Palace of Westminster controlled area

(1)   A constable or authorised officer who has reasonable grounds for believing that a person is doing, or is about to do, a prohibited activity may direct the person—

     (a)   to cease doing that activity, or

     (b)   (as the case may be) not to start doing that activity.

(2)   For the purposes of this Part, a "prohibited activity" is any of the following—

     (a)   operating any amplified noise equipment in the controlled area of Parliament Square or in the Palace of Westminster controlled area;

     (b)   erecting or keeping erected in the controlled area of Parliament Square—

         (i)   any tent, or

         (ii)   any other structure that is designed, or adapted, (solely or mainly) for the purpose of facilitating sleeping or staying in a place for any period;

     (c)   using any tent or other such structure in the controlled area of Parliament Square for the purpose of sleeping or staying in that area;

     (d)   placing or keeping in place in the controlled area of Parliament Square any sleeping equipment with a view to its use (whether or not by the person placing it or keeping it in place) for the purpose of sleeping overnight in that area;

     (e)   using any sleeping equipment in the controlled area of Parliament Square for the purpose of sleeping overnight in that area.

(3)   But an activity is not to be treated as a "prohibited activity" within subsection (2) if it is done—

     (a)   for police, fire and rescue authority or ambulance purposes,

     (b)   by or on behalf of a relevant authority, or

     (c)   by a person so far as authorised under section 147 to do it (authorisation for operation of amplified noise equipment).

(4)   In subsection (2)(a) "amplified noise equipment" means any device that is designed or adapted for amplifying sound, including (but not limited to)—

     (a)   loudspeakers, and

     (b)   loudhailers.

(5)   In subsection (3)(b) "relevant authority" means any of the following—

     (a)   a Minister of the Crown or a government department,

     (b)   the Greater London Authority, or

     (c)   Westminster City Council.

(6)   It is immaterial for the purposes of a prohibited activity—

     (a)   in the case of an activity within subsection (2)(b) or (c) of keeping a tent or similar structure erected or using a tent or similar structure, whether the tent or structure was first erected before or after the coming into force of this section;

     (b)   in the case of an activity within subsection (2)(d) or (e) of keeping in place any sleeping equipment or using any such equipment, whether the sleeping equipment was first placed before or after the coming into force of this section.

(7)   In this section "sleeping equipment" means any sleeping bag, mattress or other similar item designed, or adapted, (solely or mainly) for the purpose of facilitating sleeping in a place.

(8)   A person who fails without reasonable excuse to comply with a direction under subsection (1) commits an offence and is liable on summary conviction to a fine not exceeding level 5 on the standard scale.

144   Directions under section 143: further provision

(1)   A direction requiring a person to cease doing a prohibited activity may include a direction that the person does not start doing that activity again after having ceased it.

(2)   A direction requiring a person not to start doing a prohibited activity continues in force until—

     (a)   the end of such period beginning with the day on which the direction is given as may be specified by the constable or authorised officer giving the direction, or

     (b)   if no such period is specified, the end of the period of 90 days beginning with the day on which the direction is given.

(3)   A period specified under subsection (2)(a) may not be longer than 90 days.

(4)   A direction may be given to a person to cease operating, or not to start operating, any amplified noise equipment only if it appears to the constable or authorised officer giving the direction that the following condition is met.

(5)   The condition is that the person is operating, or is about to operate, the equipment in such a manner as to produce sound that other persons in or in the vicinity of the controlled area of Parliament Square, or the Palace of Westminster controlled area can hear or are likely to be able to hear.

(6)   A direction—
         (a)   may be given orally,
         (b)   may be given to any person individually or to two or more persons together, and
         (c)   may be withdrawn or varied by the person who gave it.

(7)   In this section—
         "amplified noise equipment" has the meaning given by section 143(4);
         "direction" means a direction given under section 143(1).

145   Power to seize property

(1)   A constable or authorised officer may seize and retain a prohibited item that is on any land in the controlled area of Parliament Square if it appears to that constable or officer that the item is being, or has been, used in connection with the commission of an offence under section 143 in that area.

(1A)   A constable or authorised officer may seize and retain a prohibited item that is on any land in the Palace of Westminster controlled area if it appears to that constable or officer that the item is being, or has been, used in connection with the commission of an offence under section 143 in that area.

(2)   A constable may seize and retain a prohibited item that is on any land outside of the controlled area of Parliament Square if it appears to the constable that the item has been used in connection with the commission of an offence under section 143 in that area.

(2A)   A constable may seize and retain a prohibited item that is on any land outside of the Palace of Westminster controlled area if it appears to the constable that the item has been used in connection with the commission of an offence under section 143 in that area.

(3)   A "prohibited item" is any item of a kind mentioned in section 143(2).

(4)   A constable may use reasonable force, if necessary, in exercising a power of seizure under this section.

(5)   An item seized under this section must be returned to the person from whom it was seized—
         (a)   no later than the end of the period of 28 days beginning with the day on which the item was seized, or
         (b)   if proceedings are commenced against the person for an offence under section 143 before the return of the item under paragraph (a), at the conclusion of those proceedings.

(6)   If it is not possible to return an item under subsection (5) because the name or address of the person from whom it was seized is not known—
         (a)   the item may be returned to any other person appearing to have rights in the property who has come forward to claim it, or
         (b)   if there is no such person, the item may be disposed of or destroyed at any time after the end of the period of 90 days beginning with the day on which the item was seized.

(7)   Subsections (5)(b) and (6) do not apply if a court makes an order under section 146(1)(a) for the forfeiture of the item.

(8)   The references in this section to an item that is "on" any land include references to an item that is in the possession of a person who is on any such land.

146   Power of court on conviction

(1)   The court may do either or both of the following on the conviction of a person ("P") of an offence under section 143—
         (a)   make an order providing for the forfeiture of any item of a kind mentioned in subsection (2) of that section that was used in the commission of the offence;
         (b)   make such other order as the court considers appropriate for the purpose of preventing P from engaging in any prohibited activity in a relevant area.

(2)   An order under subsection (1)(b) may (in particular) require P not to enter the controlled area of Parliament Square for such period as may be specified in the order.

(2A) In this section "relevant area" means an area consisting of either or both of the following areas—

(a)   the controlled area of Parliament Square, and

(b)   the Palace of Westminster controlled area.

(3)   Power of the court to make an order under this section is in addition to the court's power to impose a fine under section 143(8).

147   Authorisation for operation of amplified noise equipment

(1)   The responsible authority for any land in the controlled area of Parliament Square or the Palace of Westminster controlled area may authorise a person in accordance with this section to operate on that land (or any part of it) any amplified noise equipment (as defined by section 143(4)).

(2)   An application for authorisation must be made to the responsible authority by or on behalf of the person (or persons) seeking the authorisation.

(3)   The responsible authority may—

(a)   determine the form in which, and the manner in which, an application is to be made;

(b)   specify the information to be supplied in connection with an application;

(c)   require a fee to be paid for determining an application.

(4)   If an application is duly made to a responsible authority, the authority must—

(a)   determine the application, and

(b)   give notice in writing to the applicant of the authority's decision within the period of 21 days beginning with the day on which the authority receives the application.

(5)   The notice must specify—

(a)   the person (or persons) authorised (whether by name or description),

(b)   the kind of amplified noise equipment to which the authorisation applies,

(c)   the period to which the authorisation applies, and

(d)   any conditions to which the authorisation is subject.

(6)   The responsible authority may at any time—

(a)   withdraw an authorisation given to a person under this section, or

(b)   vary any condition to which an authorisation is subject.

(7)   Variation under subsection (6)(b) includes—

(a)   imposing a new condition,

(b)   removing an existing condition, or

(c)   altering any period to which a condition applies.

(8)   The exercise of a power under subsection (6) to withdraw an authorisation or to vary a condition is effected by the responsible authority giving notice in writing to the applicant.

148   Meaning of "authorised officer" and "responsible authority"

(1)   This section applies for the purposes of this Part.

(2)   "Authorised officer", in relation to any land in the controlled area of Parliament Square, or in relation to any land in the Palace of Westminster controlled area other than Royal Park land, means—

(a)   an employee of the responsible authority for that land who is authorised in writing by the authority for the purposes of this Part, and

(b)   any other person who, under arrangements made with the responsible authority (whether by that or any other person), is so authorised for the purposes of this Part.

(3)   "Responsible authority", in relation to any land in the controlled area of Parliament Square, means—

(a)   the Greater London Authority, for any land comprised in the central garden of Parliament Square (as defined by section 142(2)), and

(b)   Westminster City Council, for any other land.

(4)   "Responsible authority", in relation to any land in the Palace of Westminster controlled area, means—

(a)   the Secretary of State, for any land comprised in Royal Park land;

(b)   Westminster City Council, for any other land.

(5)   In this section "Royal Park land" means any land of a description specified in Schedule 1 to the Royal Parks and Other Open Spaces Regulations 1997 (SI 1997/1639), as that Schedule has effect on the day on which the Anti-social Behaviour, Crime and Policing Act 2014 is passed.

FIXED-TERM PARLIAMENTS ACT 2011
(2011, c. 14)

An Act to make provision about the dissolution of Parliament and the determination of polling days for parliamentary general elections; and for connected purposes.   [15th September 2011]

1   Polling days for parliamentary general elections

(2)   The polling day for the next parliamentary general election after the passing of this Act is to be 7 May 2015.

(3)   The polling day for each subsequent parliamentary general election is to be the first Thursday in May in the fifth calendar year following that in which the polling day for the previous parliamentary general election fell.

(4)   But, if the polling day for the previous parliamentary general election—
    (a)   was appointed under section 2(7), and
    (b)   in the calendar year in which it fell, fell before the first Thursday in May, subsection (3) has effect as if for "fifth" there were substituted "fourth".

(5)   The Prime Minister may by order made by statutory instrument provide that the polling day for a parliamentary general election in a specified calendar year is to be later than the day determined under subsection (2) or (3), but not more than two months later.

2   Early parliamentary general elections

(1)   An early parliamentary general election is to take place if—
    (a)   the House of Commons passes a motion in the form set out in subsection (2), and
    (b)   if the motion is passed on a division, the number of members who vote in favour of the motion is a number equal to or greater than two thirds of the number of seats in the House (including vacant seats).

(2)   The form of motion for the purposes of subsection (1)(a) is—
"That there shall be an early parliamentary general election."

(3)   An early parliamentary general election is also to take place if—
    (a)   the House of Commons passes a motion in the form set out in subsection (4), and
    (b)   the period of 14 days after the day on which that motion is passed ends without the House passing a motion in the form set out in subsection (5).

(4)   The form of motion for the purposes of subsection (3)(a) is—
"That this House has no confidence in Her Majesty's Government."

(5)   The form of motion for the purposes of subsection (3)(b) is—
"That this House has confidence in Her Majesty's Government."

TERRORISM PREVENTION AND INVESTIGATION MEASURES ACT 2011
(2011, c. 23)

An Act to make provision for the imposition of terrorism prevention and investigation measures.
[14th December 2011]

New regime to protect the public from terrorism

2   Imposition of terrorism prevention and investigation measures

(1)   The Secretary of State may by notice (a "TPIM notice") impose specified terrorism prevention and investigation measures on an individual if conditions A to E in section 3 are met.

(2)   In this Act "terrorism prevention and investigation measures" means requirements, restrictions and other provision which may be made in relation to an individual by virtue of Schedule 1 (terrorism prevention and investigation measures).

(3)   In this section and Part 1 of Schedule 1 "specified" means specified in the TPIM notice.

(4)   The Secretary of State must publish factors that he or she considers are appropriate to take into account when deciding whether to impose restrictions on an individual by virtue of paragraph 2 of Schedule 1 (travel measure).

3   Conditions A to E

(1)   Condition A is that the Secretary of State is satisfied, on the balance of probabilities, that the individual is, or has been, involved in terrorism-related activity (the "relevant activity").

(2)   Condition B is that some or all of the relevant activity is new terrorism-related activity.

(3)   Condition C is that the Secretary of State reasonably considers that it is necessary, for purposes connected with protecting members of the public from a risk of terrorism, for terrorism prevention and investigation measures to be imposed on the individual.

(4)   Condition D is that the Secretary of State reasonably considers that it is necessary, for purposes connected with preventing or restricting the individual's involvement in terrorism-related activity, for the specified terrorism prevention and investigation measures to be imposed on the individual.

(5)   Condition E is that—

    (a)   the court gives the Secretary of State permission under section 6, or

    (b)   the Secretary of State reasonably considers that the urgency of the case requires terrorism prevention and investigation measures to be imposed without obtaining such permission.

(6)   In this section "new terrorism-related activity" means—

    (a)   if no TPIM notice relating to the individual has ever been in force, terrorism-related activity occurring at any time (whether before or after the coming into force of this Act);

    (b)   if only one TPIM notice relating to the individual has ever been in force, terrorism-related activity occurring after that notice came into force; or

    (c)   if two or more TPIM notices relating to the individual have been in force, terrorism-related activity occurring after such a notice came into force most recently.

4   Involvement in terrorism-related activity

(1)   For the purposes of this Act, involvement in terrorism-related activity is any one or more of the following—

    (a)   the commission, preparation or instigation of acts of terrorism;

    (b)   conduct which facilitates the commission, preparation or instigation of such acts, or which is intended to do so;

    (c)   conduct which gives encouragement to the commission, preparation or instigation of such acts, or which is intended to do so;

    (d)   conduct which gives support or assistance to individuals who are known or believed by the individual concerned to be involved in conduct falling within paragraph (a);

and for the purposes of this Act it is immaterial whether the acts of terrorism in question are specific acts of terrorism or acts of terrorism in general.

(2)   For the purposes of this Act, it is immaterial whether an individual's involvement in terrorism-related activity occurs before or after the coming into force of this Act.

Two year limit on imposition of measures without new terrorism-related activity

5   Two year limit for TPIM notices

(1)   A TPIM notice—

    (a)   comes into force when the notice is served on the individual or, if later, at the time specified for this purpose in the notice; and

    (b)   is in force for the period of one year.

(2) The Secretary of State may by notice extend a TPIM notice for a period of one year beginning when the TPIM notice would otherwise expire.

(3) A TPIM notice—

    (a) may be extended under subsection (2) only if conditions A, C and D are met; and

    (b) may be so extended on only one occasion.

(4) This section is subject, in particular, to sections 13 (revocation and revival of TPIM notices) and 14 (replacement of TPIM notice that is quashed etc).

Court scrutiny of imposition of measures

6   Prior permission of the court

(1) This section applies if the Secretary of State—

    (a) makes the relevant decisions in relation to an individual, and

    (b) makes an application to the court for permission to impose measures on the individual.

(2) The application must set out a draft of the proposed TPIM notice.

(3) The function of the court on the application is—

    (a) to determine whether the relevant decisions of the Secretary of State are obviously flawed, and

    (b) to determine whether to give permission to impose measures on the individual and (where applicable) whether to exercise the power of direction under subsection (9).

(4) The court may consider the application—

    (a) in the absence of the individual;

    (b) without the individual having been notified of the application; and

    (c) without the individual having been given an opportunity (if the individual was aware of the application) of making any representations to the court.

(5) But that does not limit the matters about which rules of court may be made.

(6) In determining the application, the court must apply the principles applicable on an application for judicial review.

(7) In a case where the court determines that a decision of the Secretary of State that condition A, condition B, or condition C is met is obviously flawed, the court may not give permission under this section.

(8) In any other case, the court may give permission under this section.

(9) If the court determines that the Secretary of State's decision that condition D is met is obviously flawed, the court may (in addition to giving permission under subsection (8)) give directions to the Secretary of State in relation to the measures to be imposed on the individual.

(10) In this section "relevant decisions" means the decisions that the following conditions are met—

    (a) condition A;

    (b) condition B;

    (c) condition C; and

    (d) condition D.

8   Directions hearing

(1) This section applies if the court—

    (a) gives permission under section 6 for measures to be imposed on an individual, or

    (b) confirms under paragraph 4(3) of Schedule 2 (whether or not subject to paragraph 4(2) of that Schedule) a TPIM notice which imposes measures on an individual.

(2) The court must, at the hearing where it gives the permission or confirms the notice, give directions for a further hearing (a "directions hearing")—

    (a) which, unless the court otherwise directs (whether in those directions or subsequently), is to be held within the period of 7 days beginning with the relevant day, and

    (b) which the individual is to have the opportunity to attend.

(3) In a case where this section applies because the court gives permission under section 6, directions given under subsection (2) may not be served on the individual unless the TPIM notice has been served on that individual.

(4) At the directions hearing, the court must give directions for a further hearing (a "review hearing") in relation to the imposition of measures on the individual.

(5) Directions under subsection (4) must provide for the review hearing to be held as soon as reasonably practicable.

(6) In this section "relevant day" means—

   (a) in a case falling within subsection (1)(a), the day on which the TPIM notice imposing the measures is served on the individual;

   (b) in a case falling within subsection (1)(b), the day on which the court confirms the TPIM notice.

9   Review hearing

(1) On a review hearing held in compliance with directions under section 8(4), the function of the court is to review the decisions of the Secretary of State that the relevant conditions were met and continue to be met.

(2) In doing so, the court must apply the principles applicable on an application for judicial review.

(3) The court—

   (a) must discontinue the review hearing if the individual requests the court to do so; and

   (b) may discontinue the review hearing in any other circumstances.

(4) The court may not discontinue the review hearing in accordance with subsection (3)(b) without giving the Secretary of State and the individual the opportunity to make representations.

(5) The court has the following powers (and only those powers) on a review hearing—

   (a) power to quash the TPIM notice;

   (b) power to quash measures specified in the TPIM notice;

   (c) power to give directions to the Secretary of State for, or in relation to,—

      (i)   the revocation of the TPIM notice, or

      (ii) the variation of measures specified in the TPIM notice.

(6) If the court does not exercise any of its powers under subsection (5), the court must decide that the TPIM notice is to continue in force.

(7) If the court exercises a power under subsection (5)(b) or (c)(ii), the court must decide that the TPIM notice is to continue in force subject to that exercise of that power.

(8) In this section "relevant conditions" means—

   (a) condition A;

   (b) condition B;

   (c) condition C; and

   (d) condition D.

Consultation requirements

10   Criminal investigations into terrorism-related activity

(1) The Secretary of State must consult the chief officer of the appropriate police force about the matter mentioned in subsection (2) before—

   (a) making an application under section 6 for permission to impose measures on an individual, or

   (b) imposing measures on an individual in a case to which section 3(5)(b) applies (urgency of the case requires measures to be imposed without obtaining the permission of the court).

(2) The matter is whether there is evidence available that could realistically be used for the purposes of prosecuting the individual for an offence relating to terrorism.

(3) The "appropriate police force" means the police force—

   (a) that is investigating the commission of any such offence by the individual, or

   (b) by which it appears to the Secretary of State that the commission of any such offence by the individual would fall to be investigated.

(4)   If the Secretary of State serves a TPIM notice on an individual, the Secretary of State must inform the chief officer of the appropriate police force—

(a)   that the TPIM notice has been served, and

(b)   that the chief officer must act in accordance with the duty under subsection (5).

(5)   After being informed of the matters mentioned in subsection (4), the chief officer must—

(a)   secure that the investigation of the individual's conduct, with a view to a prosecution of the individual for an offence relating to terrorism, is kept under review throughout the period the TPIM notice is in force, and

(b)   report to the Secretary of State on the review carried out under paragraph (a).

(6)   The chief officer must consult the relevant prosecuting authority before responding to consultation under subsection (1).

(7)   The chief officer must also, to the extent that the chief officer considers it appropriate to do so, consult the relevant prosecuting authority in carrying out the duty under subsection (5)(a).

(8)   The "relevant prosecuting authority" is—

(a)   in the case of offences that would be likely to be prosecuted in England and Wales, the Director of Public Prosecutions;

(b)   in the case of offences that would be likely to be prosecuted in Scotland, the appropriate procurator fiscal;

(c)   in the case of offences that would be likely to be prosecuted in Northern Ireland, the Director of Public Prosecutions for Northern Ireland.

(9)   The duty to consult under subsection (1) or (6) may be satisfied by consultation that took place wholly or partly before the passing of this Act.

(10)   In this section—

"chief officer"—

(a)   in relation to a police force maintained for a police area in England and Wales, means the chief officer of police of that force;

(b)   in relation to the Police Service of Scotland, means the chief constable of that Service;

(c)   in relation to the Police Service of Northern Ireland, means the Chief Constable of that Service;

(d)   in relation to the Serious Organised Crime Agency, means the Director General of that Agency;

"police force" means—

(a)   a police force maintained for a police area in England and Wales;

(b)   the Police Service of Scotland;

(c)   the Police Service of Northern Ireland;

(d)   the National Crime Agency.

Review of ongoing necessity

11   Review of ongoing necessity

During the period that a TPIM notice is in force, the Secretary of State must keep under review whether conditions C and D are met.

Changes concerning TPIM notices

12   Variation of measures

(1)   The Secretary of State may by notice (a "variation notice") vary measures specified in a TPIM notice if—

(a)   the variation consists of the relaxation or removal of measures;

(b)   the variation is made with the consent of the individual; or

(c)   the Secretary of State reasonably considers that the variation is necessary for purposes connected with preventing or restricting the individual's involvement in terrorism-related activity.

(2)   The individual to whom a TPIM notice relates may make an application to the Secretary of State for the variation of measures specified in the TPIM notice.

(3)   The Secretary of State must consider an application made under subsection (2).

(4)   An application under subsection (2) must be made in writing.

(5)   The Secretary of State may by notice request the provision, within such period of time as the notice may specify, of further information from the individual in connection with an application under subsection (2).

(6)   The Secretary of State is not required to consider an application further unless any information requested under subsection (5) is provided in accordance with the notice mentioned in that subsection.

(7)   A variation under subsection (1) takes effect when the variation notice is served or, if later, at the time specified for this purpose in the variation notice.

(8)   The power under subsection (1) is exercisable whether or not an application has been made under subsection (2).

(9)   In a case where a TPIM notice—

    (a)   has expired without being extended under section 5(2), or

    (b)   has been revoked,

the power under subsection (1) may (in particular) be exercised in relation to the TPIM notice before any revival of the TPIM notice under section 13(6) so as to take effect at the time that the TPIM notice comes back into force on its revival.

(10)   In such a case, the question of whether condition D is met is to be determined for the purposes of section 13(6) by reference to the measures specified in the TPIM notice as they would be after the exercise of the power under subsection (1).

13   Revocation and revival of TPIM notices

(1)   The Secretary of State may by notice (a "revocation notice") revoke a TPIM notice at any time.

(2)   The revocation of a TPIM notice takes effect when the revocation notice is served or, if different, at the time specified for this purpose in the revocation notice.

(3)   The individual to whom a TPIM notice relates may make an application to the Secretary of State for the revocation of the TPIM notice.

(4)   The Secretary of State must consider an application made under subsection (3).

(5)   The power under subsection (1) is exercisable whether or not an application has been made under subsection (3).

(6)   The Secretary of State may by notice (a "revival notice") at any time revive a TPIM notice which—

    (a)   has expired without being extended under section 5(2), or

    (b)   has been revoked,if conditions A, C and D are met.

(7)   The power of revival may be exercised—

    (a)   under subsection (6) (a) or (b) whether or not the TPIM notice has previously been revoked and revived; and

    (b)   under subsection (6) (b) whether or not the TPIM notice has been extended under section 5(2).

(8)   But the power of revival under subsection (6) (b) may not be exercised to revive a TPIM notice which the Secretary of State was required to revoke by directions given by the court in TPIM proceedings.

(9)   A TPIM notice which is revived—

    (a)   comes back into force when the revival notice is served or, if later, at the time specified for this purpose in the revival notice; and

    (b)   is in force—

        (i)   for the period of one year (in a case where the revived notice had expired), or

        (ii)   for the period of time for which the TPIM notice would have continued in force if it had not been revoked (in a case where the revived notice had been revoked).

14   Replacement of TPIM notice that is quashed etc

(1)   This section applies if—

    (a)   a TPIM notice, the extension of a TPIM notice, or the revival of a TPIM notice, is quashed in TPIM proceedings, or

(b)   a TPIM notice is revoked by the Secretary of State in compliance with directions given by the court in TPIM proceedings.

(2)   The replacement TPIM notice is to be in force for the period of time for which the overturned notice would have continued in force but for the quashing or revocation.

(3)   The replacement TPIM notice may not be extended under section 5(2) if the overturned notice had been extended under section 5(2) (including where the extension is quashed).

(4)   Terrorism-related activity is to be treated as new terrorism-related activity in relation to the imposition of measures by the replacement TPIM notice if it was new terrorism-related activity in relation to the imposition of measures by the overturned notice.

(5)   Terrorism-related activity that occurs after the coming into force of the overturned notice does not cease to be new terrorism-related activity by virtue of the coming into force of the replacement TPIM notice.

(6)   Subsections (2) to (5) do not apply to the replacement notice if—
    (a)   some or all of the relevant activity (within the meaning of section 3) occurred after the overturned notice came into force, and
    (b)   the Secretary of State determines that those subsections should not apply to that notice.

(7)   In this section—
"new terrorism-related activity" has the same meaning as in section 3;
"overturned notice" means the TPIM notice to which the quashing or revocation referred to in subsection (1) relates;
"replacement TPIM notice" means the first TPIM notice to impose measures on the individual to whom the overturned notice relates after the quashing or revocation referred to in subsection (1).

15   Other provision relating to the quashing of TPIM notices etc

(1)   A power in TPIM proceedings to quash a TPIM notice, the extension of a TPIM notice, the revival of a TPIM notice, or measures specified in a TPIM notice, includes—
    (a)   in England and Wales or Northern Ireland, power to stay the quashing for a specified time, or pending an appeal or further appeal against the decision to quash; or
    (b)   in Scotland, power to determine that the quashing is of no effect for a specified time or pending such an appeal or further appeal.

(2)   A decision in TPIM proceedings to quash measures specified in a TPIM notice, or (except as provided in section 14) a decision in TPIM proceedings to quash, or to give directions to the Secretary of State in relation to, a TPIM notice, the extension of a TPIM notice, or the revival of a TPIM notice, does not prevent the Secretary of State—
    (a)   from exercising any power under this Act to impose measures (whether or not to the same or similar effect as measures to which the decision relates), or
    (b)   from relying, in whole or in part, on any matters for the purpose of so exercising such a power (whether or not the matters were relied on in exercising powers under this Act in relation to measures or the TPIM notice to which the decision relates).

(3)   Schedule 3 (appeals against convictions) has effect.

Appeals and court proceedings

16   Appeals

(1)   If the Secretary of State extends or revives a TPIM notice (see section 5(2) or 13(6))—
    (a)   the individual to whom the TPIM notice relates may appeal to the court against the extension or revival; and
    (b)   the function of the court on such an appeal is to review the Secretary of State's decisions that conditions A, C and D were met and continue to be met.

(2)   If the Secretary of State varies measures specified in a TPIM notice (and the variation does not consist of the relaxation or removal of measures) without the consent of the individual to whom the TPIM notice relates (see section 12(1)(c))—
    (a)   the individual may appeal to the court against the variation; and

      (b)   the function of the court on such an appeal is to review the Secretary of State's decisions that the variation was necessary, and continues to be necessary, for purposes connected with preventing or restricting involvement by the individual in terrorism-related activity.

(3)   If the individual to whom a TPIM notice relates makes an application to the Secretary of State for the variation of measures specified in the TPIM notice (see section 12(2))—

      (a)   the individual may appeal to the court against any decision by the Secretary of State on the application; and

      (b)   the function of the court on such an appeal is to review the Secretary of State's decisions that the measures to which the application relates were necessary, and continue to be necessary, for purposes connected with preventing or restricting involvement by the individual in terrorism-related activity.

(4)   If the individual to whom a TPIM notice relates makes an application to the Secretary of State for the revocation of the TPIM notice (see section 13(3))—

      (a)   the individual may appeal to the court against any decision by the Secretary of State on the application; and

      (b)   the function of the court on such an appeal is to review the Secretary of State's decisions that conditions A, C and D were met and continue to be met.

(5)   If the individual to whom a TPIM notice relates makes an application to the Secretary of State for permission—

      (a)   the individual may appeal to the court against any decision by the Secretary of State on the application (including any decision about conditions to which permission is subject); and

      (b)   the function of the court on such an appeal is to review the decision.

(6)   In determining the matters mentioned in subsections (1) to (5) the court must apply the principles applicable on an application for judicial review.

(7)   The only powers of the court on an appeal under this section are—

      (a)   power to quash the extension or revival of the TPIM notice;

      (b)   power to quash measures specified in the TPIM notice;

      (c)   power to give directions to the Secretary of State for, or in relation to,—

          (i)   the revocation of the TPIM notice, or

          (ii)   the variation of measures the TPIM notice specifies;

      (d)   power to give directions to the Secretary of State in relation to permission or conditions to which permission is subject.

(8)   If the court does not exercise any of its powers under subsection (7), it must dismiss the appeal.

(9)   In this section "permission" means permission for the purposes of measures specified in a TPIM notice (see, in particular, paragraph 13 of Schedule 1).

17   Jurisdiction in relation to decisions under this Act

(1)   TPIM decisions are not to be questioned in any legal proceedings other than—

      (a)   proceedings in the court; or

      (b)   proceedings on appeal from such proceedings.

(2)   The court is the appropriate tribunal for the purposes of section 7 of the Human Rights Act 1998 in relation to proceedings all or any part of which call a TPIM decision into question.

(3)   In this Act "TPIM decision" means—

      (a)   a decision made by the Secretary of State in exercise or performance of any power or duty under any of sections 2 to 15 or under Schedule 1 or 2;

      (b)   a decision made by the Secretary of State for the purposes of, or in connection with, the exercise or performance of any such power or duty;

      (c)   a decision by a constable to give a direction by virtue of paragraph 4 of Schedule 1 (movement directions measure) or paragraph 10(1)(b) of that Schedule (reporting measure);

      (d)   a decision by a person to give a direction by virtue of paragraph 12(2)(d) of Schedule 1 (monitoring measure).

18　Proceedings relating to measures

(1)　No appeal shall lie from any determination of the court in TPIM proceedings, except on a question of law.

(2)　No appeal by any person other than the Secretary of State shall lie from any determination—

(a)　on an application for permission under section 6; or

(b)　on a reference under Schedule 2.

20　Reviews of operation of Act

(1)　The Secretary of State must appoint a person to review the operation of this Act ("the independent reviewer").

(2)　In each calendar year the Independent reviewer must, by 31 January, inform the Secretary of State what (if any) reviews under this section the reviewer intends to carry out in that year.

Those reviews must be completed during that year or as soon as reasonably practicable after the end of it.

(4)　The independent reviewer must send to the Secretary of State a report on the outcome of each review carried out under subsection (2) as soon as reasonably practicable after completion of the review.

(5)　On receiving a report under subsection (4), the Secretary of State must lay a copy of it before Parliament.

21　Expiry and repeal of TPIM powers

(1)　Except so far as otherwise provided under this section, the Secretary of State's TPIM powers expire at the end of 5 years beginning with the day on which this Act is passed.

Enforcement

23　Offence

(1)　An individual is guilty of an offence if—

(a)　a TPIM notice is in force in relation to the individual, and

(b)　the individual contravenes, without reasonable excuse, any measure specified in the TPIM notice.

(1A)　Where an individual—

(a)　is subject to a measure specified under paragraph 2 of Schedule 1 (a "travel measure"), and

(b)　leaves the United Kingdom or travels outside the United Kingdom,

subsection (l)(b) has effect, in relation to that act, with the omission of the words "without reasonable excuse".

(2)　If the individual has the permission of the Secretary of State by virtue of Schedule 1 for an act which would, without that permission, contravene such a measure, the individual contravenes that measure by virtue of that act if the act is not in accordance with the terms of the permission.

(3)　An individual guilty of an offence under subsection (1) is liable—

(a)　on conviction on indictment, to imprisonment for a term not exceeding 5 years or to a fine, or to both;

(b)　on summary conviction in England and Wales, to imprisonment for a term not exceeding 12 months or to a fine not exceeding the statutory maximum, or to both;

(c)　on summary conviction in Northern Ireland, to imprisonment for a term not exceeding 6 months or to a fine not exceeding the statutory maximum, or to both;

(d)　on summary conviction in Scotland, to imprisonment for a term not exceeding 12 months or to a fine not exceeding the statutory maximum, or to both.

(3A)　Where an individual commits an offence under subsection (1) by contravening a travel measure, subsection (3)(a) has effect as if "10 years" were substituted for "5 years".

SCHEDULES

SCHEDULE 1
TERRORISM PREVENTION AND INVESTIGATION MEASURES

PART 1
MEASURES

Overnight residence measure

1.   (1)   The Secretary of State may impose restrictions on the individual in relation to the residence in which the individual resides.

(2)   The Secretary of State may, in particular, impose any of the following —
   (a)   a requirement to reside at a specified residence;
   (b)   a requirement to give notice to the Secretary of State of the identity of any other individuals who reside (or will reside) at the specified residence;
   (c)   a requirement, applicable overnight between such hours as are specified, to remain at, or within, the specified residence.

(3)   The specified residence must be —
   (a)   premises that are the individual's own residence, or
   (b)   other premises situated in an agreed locality or in some other locality in the United Kingdom that the Secretary of State considers to be appropriate.

(3A) If there are premises that are the individual's own residence at the time when the notice imposing restrictions under this paragraph is served on the individual, premises more than 200 miles from those premises may be specified under sub-paragraph (3)(b) only if they are in an agreed locality.

(5)   An "agreed locality" is a locality in the United Kingdom which is agreed by the Secretary of State and the individual.

(5A) The specified residence (if it is not the individual's own residence) may be a residence provided by or on behalf of the Secretary of State.

(6)   If the specified residence is provided to the individual by or on behalf of the Secretary of State, the Secretary of State may require the individual to comply with any specified terms of occupancy of that residence (which may be specified by reference to a lease or other document).

(7)   A requirement of the kind mentioned in sub-paragraph (2)(c) must include provision to enable the individual to apply for the permission of the Secretary of State to be away from the specified residence, for the whole or part of any applicable period, on one or more occasions.

(8)   The Secretary of State may grant such permission subject to either or both of the following conditions —
   (a)   the condition that the individual remains overnight at other agreed premises between such hours as the Secretary of State may require;
   (b)   the condition that the individual complies with such other restrictions in relation to the individual's movements whilst away from the specified residence as are so required.

(9)   "Agreed premises" are premises in the United Kingdom which are agreed by the Secretary of State and the individual.

(10) Sub-paragraph (8) is not to be read as limiting —
   (a)   the generality of sub-paragraph (7) of paragraph 13 (power to impose conditions when granting permission), or
   (b)   the power to impose further conditions under that sub-paragraph in connection with permission granted by virtue of sub-paragraph (7) of this paragraph.

(11) In sub-paragraph (7) "applicable period" means a period for which the individual is required to remain at the specified residence by virtue of a requirement of the kind mentioned in sub-paragraph (2)(c).

Travel measure

2.   (1)   The Secretary of State may impose restrictions on the individual leaving a specified area or travelling outside that area.

(2)   The specified area must be—
(a)   the United Kingdom, or
(b)   any area within the United Kingdom that includes the place where the individual will be living.

(3)   The Secretary of State may, in particular, impose any of the following requirements—
(a)   a requirement not to leave the specified area without the permission of the Secretary of State;
(b)   a requirement to give notice to the Secretary of State before leaving that area;
(c)   a requirement not to possess or otherwise control, or seek to obtain, any travel document without the permission of the Secretary of State;
(d)   a requirement to surrender any travel document that is in the possession or control of the individual.

(4)   "Travel document" means—
(a)   the individual's passport, or
(b)   any ticket or other document that permits the individual to make a journey by any means—
(i)   from the specified area to a place outside that area, or
(ii)   between places outside the specified area.

(5)   "Passport" means any of the following—
(a)   a United Kingdom passport (within the meaning of the Immigration Act 1971);
(b)   a passport issued by or on behalf of the authorities of a country or territory outside the United Kingdom, or by or on behalf of an international organisation;
(c)   a document that can be used (in some or all circumstances) instead of a passport.

Exclusion measure

3.   (1)   The Secretary of State may impose restrictions on the individual entering—
(a)   a specified area or place, or
(b)   a place or area of a specified description.

(2)   The Secretary of State may, in particular, impose any of the following requirements in respect of a specified area or place or a specified description of an area or place—
(a)   a requirement not to enter without the permission of the Secretary of State;
(b)   a requirement to give notice to the Secretary of State before entering;
(c)   a requirement not to enter unless other specified conditions are met.

Movement directions measure

4.   (1)   The Secretary of State may impose a requirement for the individual to comply with directions given by a constable in respect of the individual's movements (which may, in particular, include a restriction on movements).

(2)   A constable may give such directions only for the purpose of securing compliance—
(a)   with other specified measures, or
(b)   with a condition imposed under this Act requiring the individual to be escorted by a constable.

(3)   Directions may not remain in effect for a period that is any longer than the constable giving the directions considers necessary for the purpose mentioned in sub-paragraph (2); but that period may not in any event be a period of more than 24 hours.

Financial services measure

5.   (1)   The Secretary of State may impose restrictions on the individual's use of, or access to, such descriptions of financial services as are specified.

(2)   The Secretary of State may, in particular, impose any of the following requirements—
(a)   a requirement not to hold any accounts, without the permission of the Secretary of State, other than the nominated account (see sub-paragraph (3));
(b)   a requirement to close, or to cease to have an interest in, accounts;

(c)   a requirement to comply with specified conditions in relation to the holding of any account (including the nominated account) or any other use of financial services;

(d)   a requirement not to possess, or otherwise control, cash over a total specified value without the permission of the Secretary of State.

(3)   The Secretary of State must allow the individual to hold (at least) one account (the "nominated account") if—

(a)   the individual gives notice to the Secretary of State of the holding of the nominated account, and

(b)   the account is held with a bank.

(4)   In sub-paragraph (3) "bank" means an institution which is incorporated in, or formed under the law of, any part of the United Kingdom and which has permission under Part 4A of the Financial Services and Markets Act 2000 to carry on the regulated activity of accepting deposits (within the meaning of section 22 of that Act, taken with Schedule 2 to that Act and any order under section 22 of that Act).

(5)   The reference in sub-paragraph (2)(d) to possessing or otherwise controlling cash does not include any cash that is held in an account with a person providing financial services (in accordance with any requirements imposed under this paragraph).

(6)   In sub-paragraph (2)(d) "cash" means—

(a)   coins and notes in any currency,

(b)   postal orders,

(c)   cheques of any kind, including travellers' cheques,

(d)   bankers' drafts,

(e)   bearer bonds and bearer shares, and

(f)   such other kinds of monetary instrument as may be specified.

(7)   A reference in this paragraph to the individual holding an account is a reference to an account held with a person providing financial services—

(a)   that is in the individual's name or is held for the individual's benefit (whether held solely in the individual's name or jointly with one or more other persons); or

(b)   in respect of which the individual has power of attorney or can otherwise exercise control.

(8)   In this paragraph "financial services" means any service of a financial nature, including (but not limited to) banking and other financial services consisting of—

(a)   accepting deposits and other repayable funds;

(b)   lending (including consumer credit and mortgage credit);

(c)   payment and money transmission services (including credit, charge and debit cards).

Property measure

6.   (1)   The Secretary of State may impose either or both of the following—

(a)   restrictions on the individual in relation to the transfer of property to, or by, the individual, or

(b)   requirements on the individual in relation to the disclosure of property.

(2)   The Secretary of State may, in particular, impose any of the following requirements—

(a)   a requirement not to transfer money or other property to a person or place outside the United Kingdom without the permission of the Secretary of State;

(b)   a requirement to give notice to the Secretary of State before transferring money or other property to a person or place outside the United Kingdom;

(c)   a requirement to comply with any other specified conditions in relation to the transfer of property to, or by, the individual;

(d)   a requirement to disclose to the Secretary of State such details as may be specified of any property that falls within sub-paragraph (3).

(3)   Property falls within this sub-paragraph if it is property of a specified description—

(a)   in which the individual has an interest of any kind, or

(b)   over which, or in relation to which, the individual may exercise any right (including a right of use or a right to grant access).

(4)   A reference in this paragraph to the transfer of property includes a reference to the arrangement of such a transfer.

(5)   In this paragraph "property" includes rights over, or in relation to, property (including rights of use and rights to grant access); and a reference to the transfer of property includes a reference to the acquisition or disposal of such rights.

Weapons and explosives measure

6A.   (1)   The Secretary of State may impose on the individual—
(a)   a prohibition on possessing offensive weapons, imitation firearms or explosives;
(b)   a prohibition on making an application for a firearm certificate or a shot gun certificate.

(2)   In sub-paragraph (1)(a)—
"offensive weapon" means an article made or adapted for use for causing injury to the person, or intended by the person in possession of it for such use (by that person or another);
"imitation firearm" has the same meaning as in the Firearms Act 1968 or (in relation to Northern Ireland) the Firearms (Northern Ireland) Order 2004 (S1 2004/702 (N.I. 3));
"explosive" means anything that is—
(a)   an explosive within the meaning of the Explosives Act 1875, or
(b)   an explosive substance within the meaning of the Explosive Substances Act 1883.

(3)   For the purposes of sub-paragraph (1)(b)—
(a)   an application for a firearm certificate is an application under section 26A of the Firearms Act 1968 or article 4 of the Firearms (Northern Ireland) Order 2004;
(b)   an application for a shot gun certificate is an application under section 26B of the Firearms Act 1968.

Electronic communication device measure

7.   (1)   The Secretary of State may impose either or both of the following—
(a)   restrictions on the individual's possession or use of electronic communication devices;
(b)   requirements on the individual in relation to the possession or use of electronic communication devices by other persons in the individual's residence.

(2)   The Secretary of State may, in particular, impose—
(a)   a requirement not to possess or use any devices without the permission of the Secretary of State (subject to sub-paragraph (3));
(b)   a requirement that a device may only be possessed or used subject to specified conditions.

(3)   The Secretary of State must allow the individual to possess and use (at least) one of each of the following descriptions of device (subject to any conditions on such use as may be specified under sub-paragraph (2)(b))—
(a)   a telephone operated by connection to a fixed line;
(b)   a computer that provides access to the internet by connection to a fixed line (including any apparatus necessary for that purpose);
(c)   a mobile telephone that does not provide access to the internet.

(4)   The conditions specified under sub-paragraph (2)(b) may, in particular, include conditions in relation to—
(a)   the type or make of a device (which may require the individual to use a device that is supplied or modified by the Secretary of State);
(b)   the manner in which, or the times at which, a device is used;
(c)   the monitoring of such use;
(d)   the granting to a specified description of person of access to the individual's premises for the purpose of the inspection or modification of a device;
(e)   the surrendering to a specified description of person of a device on a temporary basis for the purpose of its inspection or modification at another place.

(5)   An "electronic communication device" means any of the following—
(a)   a device that is capable of storing, transmitting or receiving images, sounds or information by electronic means;
(b)   a component part of such a device;
(c)   an article designed or adapted for use with such a device (including any disc, memory stick, film or other separate article on which images, sound or information may be recorded).

(6) The devices within sub-paragraph (5)(a) include (but are not limited to)—
    (a) computers,
    (b) telephones (whether mobile telephones or telephones operated by connection to a fixed line),
    (c) equipment (not within paragraph (a) or (b)) designed or adapted for the purpose of connecting to the internet, and
    (d) equipment designed or adapted for the purposes of sending or receiving facsimile transmissions.

Association measure

8. (1) The Secretary of State may impose restrictions on the individual's association or communication with other persons.
    (2) The Secretary of State may, in particular, impose any of the following requirements—
        (a) a requirement not to associate or communicate with specified persons, or specified descriptions of persons, without the permission of the Secretary of State;
        (b) a requirement to give notice to the Secretary of State before associating or communicating with other persons (whether at all or in specified circumstances);
        (c) a requirement to comply with any other specified conditions in connection with associating or communicating with other persons.
    (3) An individual associates or communicates with another person if the individual associates or communicates with that person by any means (and for this purpose it is immaterial whether the association or communication is carried out by the individual in person or by or through another individual or means).

Work or studies measure

9. (1) The Secretary of State may impose restrictions on the individual in relation to the individual's work or studies.
    (2) The Secretary of State may, in particular, impose any of the following requirements—
        (a) a requirement not to carry out without the permission of the Secretary of State—
            (i) specified work or work of a specified description, or
            (ii) specified studies or studies of a specified description;
        (b) a requirement to give notice to the Secretary of State before carrying out any work or studies;
        (c) a requirement to comply with any other specified conditions in connection with any work or studies.
    (3) In this paragraph—
    "work" includes any business or occupation (whether paid or unpaid);
    "studies" includes any course of education or training.

Reporting measure

10. (1) The Secretary of State may impose a requirement for the individual—
    (a) to report to such a police station, at such times and in such manner, as the Secretary of State may by notice require, and
    (b) to comply with any directions given by a constable in relation to such reporting.
    (2) Such a notice may, in particular, provide that a requirement to report to a police station is not to apply if conditions specified in the notice are met.

Appointments measure

10A. (1) The Secretary of State may impose a requirement for the individual—
    (a) to attend appointments with specified persons or persons of specified descriptions, and
    (b) to comply with any reasonable directions given by the Secretary of State that relate to matters about which the individual is required to attend an appointment.
    (2) A requirement under sub-paragraph (1)(a) is a requirement to attend appointments—
        (a) at specified times and places, or
        (b) at times and places notified to the individual by persons referred to in that sub-paragraph.

Photography measure

11.   The Secretary of State may impose a requirement for the individual to allow photographs to be taken of the individual at such locations and at such times as the Secretary of State may by notice require.

Monitoring measure

12.   (1)   The Secretary of State may impose requirements for the individual to co-operate with specified arrangements for enabling the individual's movements, communications or other activities to be monitored by electronic or other means.

        (2)   The Secretary of State may, in particular, impose any of the following requirements for co-operation with the specified arrangements—

                (a)   a requirement to submit to procedures required by the arrangements;

                (b)   a requirement to wear or otherwise use apparatus approved by or in accordance with the arrangements;

                (c)   a requirement to maintain such apparatus in a specified manner;

                (d)   a requirement to comply with directions given by persons carrying out functions for the purposes of the arrangements.

        (3)   Directions under sub-paragraph (2)(d) may include directions requiring the individual to grant access to the individual's residence for the purpose of the inspection or modification of any apparatus used or maintained under the arrangements.

SCHEDULE 3
APPEALS AGAINST CONVICTIONS

1.   An individual who has been convicted of an offence under section 23(1) may appeal against the conviction if—

        (a)   a TPIM notice, the extension of a TPIM notice, or the revival of a TPIM notice is quashed, or measures specified in a TPIM notice are quashed; and

        (b)   the individual could not have been convicted had the quashing occurred before the proceedings for the offence were brought.

2.   An appeal under this Schedule is to be made—

        (a)   in the case of a conviction on indictment in England and Wales or Northern Ireland, to the Court of Appeal;

        (b)   in the case of a conviction on indictment in Scotland, to the High Court of Justiciary;

        (c)   in the case of a summary conviction in England and Wales, to the Crown Court;

        (ca)   in the case of a summary conviction in Scotland, to the Sheriff Appeal Court; or

        (d)   in the case of a summary conviction in Northern Ireland, to the county court.

3.   (1)   The right of appeal under this Schedule does not arise until there is no further possibility of an appeal against—

                (a)   the decision to quash the notice, extension, revival or measures, or

                (b)   any decision on an appeal made against that decision.

        (2)   In determining whether there is no further possibility of an appeal against a decision of the kind mentioned in sub-paragraph (1), any power to extend the time for giving notice of application for leave to appeal, or for applying for leave to appeal, must be ignored.

4.   (1)   On an appeal under this Schedule to any court, that court must allow the appeal and quash the conviction.

SCHEDULE 4
PROCEEDINGS RELATING TO TERRORISM PREVENTION AND INVESTIGATION MEASURES

Introductory

1.   In this Schedule—

        "appeal proceedings" means proceedings in the Court of Appeal or the Inner House of the Court of Session on an appeal relating to TPIM proceedings;

        "the relevant court" means—

        (a)   in relation to TPIM proceedings, the court;

(b)   in relation to appeal proceedings, the Court of Appeal or the Inner House of the Court of Session;

"rules of court" means rules for regulating the practice and procedure to be followed in the court, the Court of Appeal or the Inner House of the Court of Session.

Rules of court: general provision

2.   (1)   A person making rules of court relating to TPIM proceedings or appeal proceedings must have regard to the need to secure the following—
       (a)   that the decisions that are the subject of the proceedings are properly reviewed, and
       (b)   that disclosures of information are not made where they would be contrary to the public interest.
      (2)   Rules of court relating to TPIM proceedings or appeal proceedings may make provision—
       (a)   about the mode of proof and about evidence in the proceedings;
       (b)   enabling or requiring the proceedings to be determined without a hearing;
       (c)   about legal representation in the proceedings;
       (d)   enabling the proceedings to take place without full particulars of the reasons for the decisions to which the proceedings relate being given to a party to the proceedings (or to any legal representative of that party);
       (e)   enabling the relevant court to conduct proceedings in the absence of any person, including a party to the proceedings (or any legal representative of that party);
       (f)   about the functions of a person appointed as a special advocate (see paragraph 10);
       (g)   enabling the court to give a party to the proceedings a summary of evidence taken in the party's absence.
      (3)   In this paragraph—
       (a)   references to a party to the proceedings do not include the Secretary of State;
       (b)   references to a party's legal representative do not include a person appointed as a special advocate.
      (4)   Nothing in this paragraph is to be read as restricting the power to make rules of court or the matters to be taken into account when doing so.

Rules of court: disclosure

3.   (1)   Rules of court relating to TPIM proceedings or appeal proceedings must secure that the Secretary of State is required to disclose—
       (a)   material on which the Secretary of State relies,
       (b)   material which adversely affects the Secretary of State's case, and
       (c)   material which supports the case of another party to the proceedings.
      (2)   This paragraph is subject to paragraph 4.
4.   (1)   Rules of court relating to TPIM proceedings or appeal proceedings must secure—
       (a)   that the Secretary of State has the opportunity to make an application to the relevant court for permission not to disclose material otherwise than to the relevant court and any person appointed as a special advocate;
       (b)   that such an application is always considered in the absence of every party to the proceedings (and every party's legal representative);
       (c)   that the relevant court is required to give permission for material not to be disclosed if it considers that the disclosure of the material would be contrary to the public interest;
       (d)   that, if permission is given by the relevant court not to disclose material, it must consider requiring the Secretary of State to provide a summary of the material to every party to the proceedings (and every party's legal representative);
       (e)   that the relevant court is required to ensure that such a summary does not contain material the disclosure of which would be contrary to the public interest.
      (2)   Rules of court relating to TPIM proceedings or appeal proceedings must secure that provision to the effect mentioned in sub-paragraph (3) applies in cases where the Secretary of State—

(a) does not receive the permission of the relevant court to withhold material, but elects not to disclose it, or

(b) is required to provide a party to the proceedings with a summary of material that is withheld, but elects not to provide the summary.

(3) The relevant court must be authorised—

(a) if it considers that the material or anything that is required to be summarised might adversely affect the Secretary of State's case or support the case of a party to the proceedings, to direct that the Secretary of State—

(i) is not to rely on such points in the Secretary of State's case, or

(ii) is to make such concessions or take such other steps as the court may specify, or

(b) in any other case, to ensure that the Secretary of State does not rely on the material or (as the case may be) on that which is required to be summarised.

(4) In this paragraph—

(a) references to a party to the proceedings do not include the Secretary of State;

(b) references to a party's legal representative do not include a person appointed as a special advocate.

Article 6 rights

5. (1) Nothing in paragraphs 2 to 4, or in rules of court made under any of those paragraphs, is to be read as requiring the relevant court to act in a manner inconsistent with Article 6 of the Human Rights Convention.

(2) The "Human Rights Convention" means the Convention within the meaning of the Human Rights Act 1998 (see section 21(1) of that Act).

Rules of court: anonymity

6. (1) Rules of court relating to TPIM proceedings or appeal proceedings may make provision for—

(a) the making by the Secretary of State or the relevant individual of an application to the court for an order requiring anonymity for that individual, and

(b) the making by the court, on such an application, of an order requiring such anonymity;

and the provision made by the rules may allow the application and the order to be made irrespective of whether any other TPIM proceedings have been begun in the court.

(2) Rules of court may provide for the Court of Appeal or the Inner House of the Court of Session to make an order in connection with any appeal proceedings requiring anonymity for the relevant individual.

(3) In sub-paragraphs (1) and (2) the references, in relation to a court, to an order requiring anonymity for the relevant individual are references to an order by that court which imposes such prohibition or restriction as it thinks fit on the disclosure—

(a) by such persons as the court specifies or describes, or

(b) by persons generally,

of the identity of the relevant individual or of any information that would tend to identify the relevant individual.

(4) In this paragraph "relevant individual" means an individual on whom the Secretary of State is proposing to impose, or has imposed, measures.

Initial exercise of rule-making powers by Lord Chancellor

7. (1) The first time after the passing of this Act that rules of court are made in exercise of the powers conferred by this Schedule in relation to proceedings in England and Wales or in Northern Ireland, the rules may be made by the Lord Chancellor instead of by the person who would otherwise make them.

(2) Before making rules of court under sub-paragraph (1), the Lord Chancellor must consult—

(a) in relation to rules applicable to proceedings in England and Wales, the Lord Chief Justice of England and Wales;

(b) in relation to rules applicable to proceedings in Northern Ireland, the Lord Chief Justice of Northern Ireland.

(3)   But the Lord Chancellor is not required to undertake any other consultation before making the rules.

(4)   A requirement to consult under sub-paragraph (2) may be satisfied by consultation that took place wholly or partly before the passing of this Act.

(5)   Rules of court made by the Lord Chancellor under sub-paragraph (1)—
    (a)   must be laid before Parliament, and
    (b)   if not approved by a resolution of each House before the end of 40 days beginning with the day on which they were made, cease to have effect at the end of that period.

(6)   In determining that period of 40 days no account is to be taken of any time during which Parliament is dissolved or prorogued or during which both Houses are adjourned for more than 4 days.

(7)   If rules cease to have effect in accordance with sub-paragraph (5)—
    (a)   that does not affect anything done in previous reliance on the rules, and
    (b)   sub-paragraph (1) applies again as if the rules had not been made.

(8)   The following provisions do not apply to rules of court made by the Lord Chancellor under this paragraph—
    (a)   section 3(6) of the Civil Procedure Act 1997 (Parliamentary procedure for civil procedure rules);
    (b)   section 56(1), (2) and (4) of the Judicature (Northern Ireland) Act 1978 (statutory rules procedure).

(9)   Until the coming into force of section 85 of the Courts Act 2003, the reference in sub-paragraph (8)(a) to section 3(6) of the Civil Procedure Act 1997 is to be read as a reference to section 3(2) of that Act.

Use of advisers

8.   (1)   In any TPIM proceedings or appeal proceedings the relevant court may if it thinks fit—
    (a)   call in aid one or more advisers appointed for the purposes of this paragraph by the Lord Chancellor, and
    (b)   hear and dispose of the proceedings with the assistance of the adviser or advisers.

    (2)   The Lord Chancellor may appoint advisers for the purposes of this paragraph only with the approval of—
    (a)   the Lord President of the Court of Session, in relation to an adviser who may be called in aid wholly or mainly in Scotland;
    (b)   the Lord Chief Justice of Northern Ireland, in relation to an adviser who may be called in aid wholly or mainly in Northern Ireland;
    (c)   the Lord Chief Justice of England and Wales, in any other case.

    (3)   Rules of court may regulate the use of advisers in proceedings who are called in aid under sub-paragraph (1).

    (4)   The Lord Chancellor may pay such remuneration, expenses and allowances to advisers appointed for the purposes of this paragraph as the Lord Chancellor may determine.

9.   (1)   The Lord President of the Court of Session may nominate a judge of the Court of Session who is a member of the First or Second Division of the Inner House of that Court to exercise the function under paragraph 8(2)(a).

    (2)   The Lord Chief Justice of Northern Ireland may nominate any of the following to exercise the function under paragraph 8(2)(b)—
    (a)   the holder of one of the offices listed in Schedule 1 to the Justice (Northern Ireland) Act 2002;
    (b)   a Lord Justice of Appeal (as defined in section 88 of that Act).

    (3)   The Lord Chief Justice of England and Wales may nominate a judicial office holder (as defined in section 109(4) of the Constitutional Reform Act 2005) to exercise the function under paragraph 8(2)(c).

Appointment of special advocate

10.   (1)   The appropriate law officer may appoint a person to represent the interests of a party in any TPIM proceedings or appeal proceedings from which the party (and any legal representative of the party) is excluded.

(2)   A person appointed under sub-paragraph (1) is referred to in this Schedule as appointed as a "special advocate".

(3)   The "appropriate law officer" is—
   (a)   in relation to proceedings in England and Wales, the Attorney General;
   (b)   in relation to proceedings in Scotland, the Advocate General for Scotland;
   (c)   in relation to proceedings in Northern Ireland, the Advocate General for Northern Ireland.

(4)   A person appointed as a special advocate is not responsible to the party to the proceedings whose interests the person is appointed to represent.

(5)   A person may be appointed as a special advocate only if—
   (a)   in the case of an appointment by the Attorney General, the person has a general qualification for the purposes of section 71 of the Courts and Legal Services Act 1990;
   (b)   in the case of an appointment by the Advocate General for Scotland, the person is an advocate or a solicitor who has rights of audience in the Court of Session or the High Court of Justiciary by virtue of section 25A of the Solicitors (Scotland) Act 1980;
   (c)   in the case of an appointment by the Advocate General for Northern Ireland, the person is a member of the Bar of Northern Ireland.

PROTECTION OF FREEDOMS ACT 2012
(2012, c. 9)

An Act to provide for a code of practice about surveillance camera systems and for the appointment and role of the Surveillance Camera Commissioner; to amend the maximum detention period for terrorist suspects; to replace certain stop and search powers and to provide for a related code of practice; to make provision about the trafficking of people for exploitation and about stalking.

[1st May 2012]

PART 2
REGULATION OF SURVEILLANCE

CHAPTER 1
REGULATION OF CCTV AND OTHER SURVEILLANCE CAMERA TECHNOLOGY

Code of practice

29   Code of practice for surveillance camera systems

(1)   The Secretary of State must prepare a code of practice containing guidance about surveillance camera systems.

(2)   Such a code must contain guidance about one or more of the following—
   (a)   the development or use of surveillance camera systems,
   (b)   the use or processing of images or other information obtained by virtue of such systems.

(3)   Such a code may, in particular, include provision about—
   (a)   considerations as to whether to use surveillance camera systems,
   (b)   types of systems or apparatus,
   (c)   technical standards for systems or apparatus,
   (d)   locations for systems or apparatus,
   (e)   the publication of information about systems or apparatus,
   (f)   standards applicable to persons using or maintaining systems or apparatus,
   (g)   standards applicable to persons using or processing information obtained by virtue of systems,
   (h)   access to, or disclosure of, information so obtained,
   (i)   procedures for complaints or consultation.

(4) Such a code—
(a) need not contain provision about every type of surveillance camera system,
(b) may make different provision for different purposes.
(6) In this Chapter "surveillance camera systems" means—
(a) closed circuit television or automatic number plate recognition systems,
(b) any other systems for recording or viewing visual images for surveillance purposes,
(c) any systems for storing, receiving, transmitting, processing or checking images or information obtained by systems falling within paragraph (a) or (b), or
(d) any other systems associated with, or otherwise connected with, systems falling within paragraph (a), (b) or (c).

Procedural requirements

30 Issuing of code

(1) The Secretary of State must lay before Parliament—
(a) a code of practice prepared under section 29, and
(b) a draft of an order providing for the code to come into force.
(2) The Secretary of State must make the order and issue the code if the draft of the order is approved by a resolution of each House of Parliament.
(3) The Secretary of State must not make the order or issue the code unless the draft of the order is so approved.
(4) The Secretary of State must prepare another code of practice under section 29 if—
(a) the draft of the order is not so approved, and
(b) the Secretary of State considers that there is no realistic prospect that it will be so approved.
(5) A code comes into force in accordance with an order under this section.
(6) Such an order—
(a) is to be a statutory instrument, and
(b) may contain transitional, transitory or saving provision.
(7) If a draft of an instrument containing an order under this section would, apart from this subsection, be treated as a hybrid instrument for the purposes of the standing orders of either House of Parliament, it is to proceed in that House as if it were not a hybrid instrument.

32 Publication of code

(1) The Secretary of State must publish the code issued under section 30(2).

Enforcement and Commissioner

33 Effect of code

(1) A relevant authority must have regard to the surveillance camera code when exercising any functions to which the code relates.
(2) A failure on the part of any person to act in accordance with any provision of the surveillance camera code does not of itself make that person liable to criminal or civil proceedings.
(3) The surveillance camera code is admissible in evidence in any such proceedings.
(4) A court or tribunal may, in particular, take into account a failure by a relevant authority to have regard to the surveillance camera code in determining a question in any such proceedings.

34 Commissioner in relation to code

(1) The Secretary of State must appoint a person as the Surveillance Camera Commissioner (in this Chapter "the Commissioner").
(2) The Commissioner is to have the following functions—
(a) encouraging compliance with the surveillance camera code,
(b) reviewing the operation of the code, and
(c) providing advice about the code (including changes to it or breaches of it).

Codes of practice in relation to powers of entry

47   Code of practice in relation to non-devolved powers of entry

(1)   The Secretary of State must prepare a code of practice containing guidance about the exercise of powers of entry and associated powers.

(2)   Such a code may, in particular, include provision about—
    (a)   considerations before exercising, or when exercising, the powers,
    (b)   considerations after exercising the powers (such as the retention of records, or the publication of information, about the exercise of the powers).

(3)   Such a code—
    (a)   must not contain provision about devolved powers of entry and devolved associated powers,
    (b)   need not contain provision about every other type of power of entry or associated power,
    (c)   may make different provision for different purposes.

48   Issuing of code

(1)   The Secretary of State must lay before Parliament—
    (a)   a code of practice prepared under section 47, and
    (b)   a draft of an order providing for the code to come into force.

(2)   The Secretary of State must make the order and issue the code if the draft of the order is approved by a resolution of each House of Parliament.

(3)   The Secretary of State must not make the order or issue the code unless the draft of the order is so approved.

(4)   The Secretary of State must prepare another code of practice under section 47 if—
    (a)   the draft of the order is not so approved, and
    (b)   the Secretary of State considers that there is no realistic prospect that it will be so approved.

(5)   A code comes into force in accordance with an order under this section.

(6)   Such an order—
    (a)   is to be a statutory instrument, and
    (b)   may contain transitional, transitory or saving provision.

(7)   If a draft of an instrument containing an order under this section would, apart from this subsection, be treated as a hybrid instrument for the purposes of the standing orders of either House of Parliament, it is to proceed in that House as if it were not a hybrid instrument.

49   Alteration or replacement of code

(1)   The Secretary of State—
    (a)   must keep the powers of entry code under review ...

50   Publication of code

(1)   The Secretary of State must publish the code issued under section 48(2).

51   Effect of code

(1)   A relevant person must have regard to the powers of entry code when exercising any functions to which the code relates.

(2)   A failure on the part of any person to act in accordance with any provision of the powers of entry code does not of itself make that person liable to criminal or civil proceedings.

(3)   The powers of entry code is admissible in evidence in any such proceedings.

(4)   A court or tribunal may, in particular, take into account a failure by a relevant person to have regard to the powers of entry code in determining a question in any such proceedings.

ANTI-SOCIAL BEHAVIOUR, CRIME AND POLICING ACT 2014
(2014, c. 12)

An Act to make provision about anti-social behaviour, crime and disorder, including provision about recovery of possession of dwelling-houses; to make provision amending the Dangerous Dogs Act 1991, the Police Act 1997, Schedules 7 and 8 to the Terrorism Act 2000, the Extradition Act 2003 and Part 3 of the Police Reform and Social Responsibility Act 2011; to make provision about firearms, about sexual harm and violence and about forced marriage; to make provision about the police, the Independent Police Complaints Commission and the Serious Fraud Office; to make provision about invalid travel documents; to make provision about criminal justice and court fees; and for connected purposes.   [13th March 2014]

PART 1
INJUNCTIONS

1   Power to grant injunctions

(1)   A court may grant an injunction under this section against a person aged 10 or over ("the respondent") if two conditions are met.

(2)   The first condition is that the court is satisfied, on the balance of probabilities, that the respondent has engaged or threatens to engage in anti-social behaviour.

(3)   The second condition is that the court considers it just and convenient to grant the injunction for the purpose of preventing the respondent from engaging in anti-social behaviour.

(4)   An injunction under this section may for the purpose of preventing the respondent from engaging in anti-social behaviour—
   (a)   prohibit the respondent from doing anything described in the injunction;
   (b)   require the respondent to do anything described in the injunction.

(5)   Prohibitions and requirements in an injunction under this section must, so far as practicable, be such as to avoid—
   (a)   any interference with the times, if any, at which the respondent normally works or attends school or any other educational establishment;
   (b)   any conflict with the requirements of any other court order or injunction to which the respondent may be subject.

(6)   An injunction under this section must—
   (a)   specify the period for which it has effect, or
   (b)   state that it has effect until further order.
   In the case of an injunction granted before the respondent has reached the age of 18, a period must be specified and it must be no more than 12 months.

(7)   An injunction under this section may specify periods for which particular prohibitions or requirements have effect.

(8)   An application for an injunction under this section must be made to—
   (a)   a youth court, in the case of a respondent aged under 18;
   (b)   the High Court or the county court, in any other case.
   Paragraph (b) is subject to any rules of court made under section 18(2).

2   Meaning of "anti-social behaviour"

(1)   In this Part "anti-social behaviour" means—
   (a)   conduct that has caused, or is likely to cause, harassment, alarm or distress to any person,
   (b)   conduct capable of causing nuisance or annoyance to a person in relation to that person's occupation of residential premises, or
   (c)   conduct capable of causing housing-related nuisance or annoyance to any person.

(2)   Subsection (1)(b) applies only where the injunction under section 1 is applied for by—
   (a)   a housing provider,
   (b)   a local authority, or
   (c)   a chief officer of police.

(3) In subsection (1)(c) "housing-related" means directly or indirectly relating to the housing management functions of—
    (a) a housing provider, or
    (b) a local authority.

(4) For the purposes of subsection (3) the housing management functions of a housing provider or a local authority include—
    (a) functions conferred by or under an enactment;
    (b) the powers and duties of the housing provider or local authority as the holder of an estate or interest in housing accommodation.

4 Power of arrest

(1) A court granting an injunction under section 1 may attach a power of arrest to a prohibition or requirement of the injunction if the court thinks that—
    (a) the anti-social behaviour in which the respondent has engaged or threatens to engage consists of or includes the use or threatened use of violence against other persons, or
    (b) there is a significant risk of harm to other persons from the respondent.
    "Requirement" here does not include one that has the effect of requiring the respondent to participate in particular activities.

(2) If the court attaches a power of arrest, the injunction may specify a period for which the power is to have effect which is shorter than that of the prohibition or requirement to which it relates.

5 Applications for injunctions

(1) An injunction under section 1 may be granted only on the application of—
    (a) a local authority,
    (b) a housing provider,
    (c) the chief officer of police for a police area,
    (d) the chief constable of the British Transport Police Force,
    (e) Transport for London,
    (f) the Environment Agency,
    (g) the Natural Resources Body for Wales,
    (h) the Secretary of State exercising security management functions, or a Special Health Authority exercising security management functions on the direction of the Secretary of State, or
    (i) the Welsh Ministers exercising security management functions, or a person or body exercising security management functions on the direction of the Welsh Ministers or under arrangements made between the Welsh Ministers and that person or body.

(2) In subsection (1) "security management functions" means—
    (a) the Secretary of State's security management functions within the meaning given by section 195(3) of the National Health Service Act 2006;
    (b) the functions of the Welsh Ministers corresponding to those functions.

(3) A housing provider may make an application only if the application concerns anti-social behaviour that directly or indirectly relates to or affects its housing management functions.

(4) For the purposes of subsection (3) the housing management functions of a housing provider include—
    (a) functions conferred by or under an enactment;
    (b) the powers and duties of the housing provider as the holder of an estate or interest in housing accommodation.

(5) The Secretary of State may by order—
    (a) amend this section;
    (b) amend section 20 in relation to expressions used in this section.

9 Arrest without warrant

(1) Where a power of arrest is attached to a provision of an injunction under section 1, a constable may arrest the respondent without warrant if he or she has reasonable cause to suspect that the respondent is in breach of the provision.

(2) A constable who arrests a person under subsection (1) must inform the person who applied for the injunction.

(3) A person arrested under subsection (1) must, within the period of 24 hours beginning with the time of the arrest, be brought before—

    (a) a judge of the High Court or a judge of the county court, if the injunction was granted by the High Court;

    (b) a judge of the county court, if—

        (i) the injunction was granted by the county court, or

        (ii) the injunction was granted by a youth court but the respondent is aged 18 or over;

    (c) a justice of the peace, if neither paragraph (a) nor paragraph (b) applies.

(4) In calculating when the period of 24 hours ends, Christmas Day, Good Friday and any Sunday are to be disregarded.

(5) The judge before whom a person is brought under subsection (3)(a) or (b) may remand the person if the matter is not disposed of straight away.

(6) The justice of the peace before whom a person is brought under subsection (3)(c) must remand the person to appear before the youth court that granted the injunction.

PART 2
CRIMINAL BEHAVIOUR ORDERS

22   Power to make orders

(1) This section applies where a person ("the offender") is convicted of an offence.

(2) The court may make a criminal behaviour order against the offender if two conditions are met.

(3) The first condition is that the court is satisfied, beyond reasonable doubt, that the offender has engaged in behaviour that caused or was likely to cause harassment, alarm or distress to any person.

(4) The second condition is that the court considers that making the order will help in preventing the offender from engaging in such behaviour.

(5) A criminal behaviour order is an order which, for the purpose of preventing the offender from engaging in such behaviour—

    (a) prohibits the offender from doing anything described in the order;

    (b) requires the offender to do anything described in the order.

(6) The court may make a criminal behaviour order against the offender only if it is made in addition to—

    (a) a sentence imposed in respect of the offence, or

    (b) an order discharging the offender conditionally.

(7) The court may make a criminal behaviour order against the offender only on the application of the prosecution.

(8) The prosecution must find out the views of the local youth offending team before applying for a criminal behaviour order to be made if the offender will be under the age of 18 when the application is made.

(9) Prohibitions and requirements in a criminal behaviour order must, so far as practicable, be such as to avoid—

    (a) any interference with the times, if any, at which the offender normally works or attends school or any other educational establishment;

    (b) any conflict with the requirements of any other court order or injunction to which the offender may be subject.

(10) In this section "local youth offending team" means—

    (a) the youth offending team in whose area it appears to the prosecution that the offender lives, or

    (b) if it appears to the prosecution that the offender lives in more than one such area, whichever one or more of the relevant youth offending teams the prosecution thinks appropriate.

30   Breach of order

(1)   A person who without reasonable excuse—
    (a)   does anything he or she is prohibited from doing by a criminal behaviour order, or
    (b)   fails to do anything he or she is required to do by a criminal behaviour order,
    commits an offence.

(2)   A person guilty of an offence under this section is liable—
    (a)   on summary conviction, to imprisonment for a period not exceeding 6 months or to a fine, or to both;
    (b)   on conviction on indictment, to imprisonment for a period not exceeding 5 years or to a fine, or to both.

(3)   If a person is convicted of an offence under this section, it is not open to the court by or before which the person is convicted to make an order under subsection (1)(b) of section 12 of the Powers of Criminal Courts (Sentencing) Act 2000 (conditional discharge).

(4)   In proceedings for an offence under this section, a copy of the original criminal behaviour order, certified by the proper officer of the court which made it, is admissible as evidence of its having been made and of its contents to the same extent that oral evidence of those things is admissible in those proceedings.

(5)   In relation to any proceedings for an offence under this section that are brought against a person under the age of 18—
    (a)   section 49 of the Children and Young Persons Act 1933 (restrictions on reports of proceedings in which children and young persons are concerned) does not apply in respect of the person;
    (b)   section 45 of the Youth Justice and Criminal Evidence Act 1999 (power to restrict reporting of criminal proceedings involving persons under 18) does so apply.

(6)   If, in relation to any proceedings mentioned in subsection (5), the court does exercise its power to give a direction under section 45 of the Youth Justice and Criminal Evidence Act 1999, it must give its reasons for doing so.

PART 3
DISPERSAL POWERS

34   Authorisations to use powers under section 35

(1)   A police officer of at least the rank of inspector may authorise the use in a specified locality, during a specified period of not more than 48 hours, of the powers given by section 35.
    "Specified" means specified in the authorisation.

(2)   An officer may give such an authorisation only if satisfied on reasonable grounds that the use of those powers in the locality during that period may be necessary for the purpose of removing or reducing the likelihood of—
    (a)   members of the public in the locality being harassed, alarmed or distressed, or
    (b)   the occurrence in the locality of crime or disorder.

(3)   In deciding whether to give such an authorisation an officer must have particular regard to the rights of freedom of expression and freedom of assembly set out in articles 10 and 11 of the Convention.
    "Convention" has the meaning given by section 21(1) of the Human Rights Act 1998.

(4)   An authorisation under this section—
    (a)   must be in writing,
    (b)   must be signed by the officer giving it, and
    (c)   must specify the grounds on which it is given.

35   Directions excluding a person from an area

(1)   If the conditions in subsections (2) and (3) are met and an authorisation is in force under section 34, a constable in uniform may direct a person who is in a public place in the locality specified in the authorisation—
    (a)   to leave the locality (or part of the locality), and
    (b)   not to return to the locality (or part of the locality) for the period specified in the direction ("the exclusion period").

(2) The first condition is that the constable has reasonable grounds to suspect that the behaviour of the person in the locality has contributed or is likely to contribute to—
  (a) members of the public in the locality being harassed, alarmed or distressed, or
  (b) the occurrence in the locality of crime or disorder.

(3) The second condition is that the constable considers that giving a direction to the person is necessary for the purpose of removing or reducing the likelihood of the events mentioned in subsection (2)(a) or (b).

(4) The exclusion period may not exceed 48 hours.
  The period may expire after (as long as it begins during) the period specified in the authorisation under section 34.

(5) A direction under this section—
  (a) must be given in writing, unless that is not reasonably practicable;
  (b) must specify the area to which it relates;
  (c) may impose requirements as to the time by which the person must leave the area and the manner in which the person must do so (including the route).

(6) The constable must (unless it is not reasonably practicable) tell the person to whom the direction is given that failing without reasonable excuse to comply with the direction is an offence.

(7) If the constable reasonably believes that the person to whom the direction is given is under the age of 16, the constable may remove the person to a place where the person lives or a place of safety.

(8) Any constable may withdraw or vary a direction under this section; but a variation must not extend the duration of a direction beyond 48 hours from when it was first given.

(9) Notice of a withdrawal or variation of a direction—
  (a) must be given to the person to whom the direction was given, unless that is not reasonably practicable, and
  (b) if given, must be given in writing unless that is not reasonably practicable.

(10) In this section "public place" means a place to which at the material time the public or a section of the public has access, on payment or otherwise, as of right or by virtue of express or implied permission.

(11) In this Part "exclusion period" has the meaning given by subsection (1)(b).

36   Restrictions

(1) A constable may not give a direction under section 35 to a person who appears to the constable to be under the age of 10.

(2) A constable may not give a direction under section 35 that prevents the person to whom it is given having access to a place where the person lives.

(3) A constable may not give a direction under section 35 that prevents the person to whom it is given attending at a place which the person is—
  (a) required to attend for the purposes of the person's employment, or a contract of services to which the person is a party,
  (b) required to attend by an obligation imposed by or under an enactment or by the order of a court or tribunal, or
  (c) expected to attend for the purposes of education or training or for the purposes of receiving medical treatment,
  at a time when the person is required or expected (as the case may be) to attend there.

(4) A constable may not give a direction to a person under section 35 if the person is one of a group of persons who are—
  (a) engaged in conduct that is lawful under section 220 of the Trade Union and Labour Relations (Consolidation) Act 1992 (peaceful picketing), or
  (b) taking part in a public procession of the kind mentioned in subsection (1) of section 11 of the Public Order Act 1986 in respect of which—
    (i) written notice has been given in accordance with that section, or
    (ii) written notice is not required to be given as provided by subsections (1) and (2) of that section.

(5) In deciding whether to give a direction under section 35 a constable must have particular regard to the rights of freedom of expression and freedom of assembly set out in articles 10 and 11 of the Convention.
  "Convention" has the meaning given by section 21(1) of the Human Rights Act 1998.

38 Record-keeping

(1) A constable who gives a direction under section 35 must make a record of—
    (a) the individual to whom the direction is given,
    (b) the time at which the direction is given, and
    (c) the terms of the direction (including in particular the area to which it relates and the exclusion period).

(2) A constable who withdraws or varies a direction under section 35 must make a record of—
    (a) the time at which the direction is withdrawn or varied,
    (b) whether notice of the withdrawal or variation is given to the person to whom the direction was given and if it is, at what time, and
    (c) if the direction is varied, the terms of the variation.

(3) A constable who gives a direction under section 37 must make a record of—
    (a) the individual to whom the direction is given,
    (b) the time at which the direction is given, and
    (c) the item to which the direction relates.

39 Offences

(1) A person given a direction under section 35 who fails without reasonable excuse to comply with it commits an offence.

(2) A person guilty of an offence under subsection (1) is liable on summary conviction—
    (a) to imprisonment for a period not exceeding 3 months, or
    (b) to a fine not exceeding level 4 on the standard scale.

(3) A person given a direction under section 37 who fails without reasonable excuse to comply with it commits an offence.

(4) A person guilty of an offence under subsection (3) is liable on summary conviction to a fine not exceeding level 2 on the standard scale.

PART 4
COMMUNITY PROTECTION

CHAPTER 1
COMMUNITY PROTECTION NOTICES

43 Power to issue notices

(1) An authorised person may issue a community protection notice to an individual aged 16 or over, or a body, if satisfied on reasonable grounds that—
    (a) the conduct of the individual or body is having a detrimental effect, of a persistent or continuing nature, on the quality of life of those in the locality, and
    (b) the conduct is unreasonable.

(2) In subsection (1) "authorised person" means a person on whom section 53 (or an enactment amended by that section) confers power to issue community protection notices.

(3) A community protection notice is a notice that imposes any of the following requirements on the individual or body issued with it—
    (a) a requirement to stop doing specified things;
    (b) a requirement to do specified things;
    (c) a requirement to take reasonable steps to achieve specified results.

(4) The only requirements that may be imposed are ones that are reasonable to impose in order—
    (a) to prevent the detrimental effect referred to in subsection (1) from continuing or recurring, or
    (b) to reduce that detrimental effect or to reduce the risk of its continuance or recurrence.

(5)   A person (A) may issue a community protection notice to an individual or body (B) only if—

    (a)   B has been given a written warning that the notice will be issued unless B's conduct ceases to have the detrimental effect referred to in subsection (1), and

    (b)   A is satisfied that, despite B having had enough time to deal with the matter, B's conduct is still having that effect.

(6)   A person issuing a community protection notice must before doing so inform any body or individual the person thinks appropriate.

(7)   A community protection notice must—

    (a)   identify the conduct referred to in subsection (1);

    (b)   explain the effect of sections 46 to 51.

(8)   A community protection notice may specify periods within which, or times by which, requirements within subsection (3)(b) or (c) are to be complied with.

52   Fixed penalty notices

(1)   An authorised person may issue a fixed penalty notice to anyone who that person has reason to believe has committed an offence under section 48.

(2)   In subsection (1) "authorised person" means a person on whom section 53 (or an enactment amended by that section) confers power to issue fixed penalty notices under this section.

(3)   A fixed penalty notice is a notice offering the person to whom it is issued the opportunity of discharging any liability to conviction for the offence by payment of a fixed penalty to a local authority specified in the notice.

(4)   The local authority specified under subsection (3) must be—

    (a)   the local authority that issued the community protection notice to which the fixed penalty notice relates;

    (b)   if the community protection notice was not issued by a local authority, the local authority (or, as the case may be, one of the local authorities) that could have issued it.

(5)   Where a person is issued with a notice under this section in respect of an offence—

    (a)   no proceedings may be taken for the offence before the end of the period of 14 days following the date of the notice;

    (b)   the person may not be convicted of the offence if the person pays the fixed penalty before the end of that period.

(6)   A fixed penalty notice must—

    (a)   give reasonably detailed particulars of the circumstances alleged to constitute the offence;

    (b)   state the period during which (because of subsection (5)(a)) proceedings will not be taken for the offence;

    (c)   specify the amount of the fixed penalty;

    (d)   state the name and address of the person to whom the fixed penalty may be paid;

    (e)   specify permissible methods of payment.

(7)   An amount specified under subsection (6)(c) must not be more than £100.

(8)   A fixed penalty notice may specify two amounts under subsection (6)(c) and specify that, if the lower of those amounts is paid within a specified period (of less than 14 days), that is the amount of the fixed penalty.

(9)   Whatever other method may be specified under subsection (6)(e), payment of a fixed penalty may be made by pre-paying and posting to the person whose name is stated under subsection (6)(d), at the stated address, a letter containing the amount of the penalty (in cash or otherwise).

(10)   Where a letter is sent as mentioned in subsection (9), payment is regarded as having been made at the time at which that letter would be delivered in the ordinary course of post.

(11)   In any proceedings, a certificate that—

    (a)   purports to be signed by or on behalf of the chief finance officer of the local authority concerned, and

    (b)   states that payment of a fixed penalty was, or was not, received by the dated specified in the certificate,

is evidence of the facts stated.

(12) In this section "chief finance officer", in relation to a local authority, means the person with responsibility for the authority's financial affairs.

53 Authorised persons

(1) A community protection notice or a fixed penalty notice may be issued by—
  (a) a constable;
  (b) the relevant local authority (see subsections (2) and (3));
  (c) a person designated by the relevant local authority for the purposes of this section.

(2) For a community protection notice, "the relevant local authority" means the local authority (or, as the case may be, any of the local authorities) within whose area the conduct specified in the notice has, according to the notice, been taking place.

(3) For a fixed penalty notice, "the relevant local authority" means the local authority (or, as the case may be, any of the local authorities) within whose area the offence in question is alleged to have taken place.

(4) Only a person of a description specified in an order made by the Secretary of State for the purposes of subsection (1)(c) may be designated under that subsection.

PART 4
COMMUNITY PROTECTION

CHAPTER 2
PUBLIC SPACES PROTECTION ORDERS

59 Power to make orders

(1) A local authority may make a public spaces protection order if satisfied on reasonable grounds that two conditions are met.

(2) The first condition is that—
  (a) activities carried on in a public place within the authority's area have had a detrimental effect on the quality of life of those in the locality, or
  (b) it is likely that activities will be carried on in a public place within that area and that they will have such an effect.

(3) The second condition is that the effect, or likely effect, of the activities—
  (a) is, or is likely to be, of a persistent or continuing nature,
  (b) is, or is likely to be, such as to make the activities unreasonable, and
  (c) justifies the restrictions imposed by the notice.

(4) A public spaces protection order is an order that identifies the public place referred to in subsection (2) ("the restricted area") and—
  (a) prohibits specified things being done in the restricted area,
  (b) requires specified things to be done by persons carrying on specified activities in that area, or
  (c) does both of those things.

(5) The only prohibitions or requirements that may be imposed are ones that are reasonable to impose in order—
  (a) to prevent the detrimental effect referred to in subsection (2) from continuing, occurring or recurring, or
  (b) to reduce that detrimental effect or to reduce the risk of its continuance, occurrence or recurrence.

(6) A prohibition or requirement may be framed—
  (a) so as to apply to all persons, or only to persons in specified categories, or to all persons except those in specified categories;
  (b) so as to apply at all times, or only at specified times, or at all times except those specified;
  (c) so as to apply in all circumstances, or only in specified circumstances, or in all circumstances except those specified.

(7) A public spaces protection order must—
  (a) identify the activities referred to in subsection (2);
  (b) explain the effect of section 63 (where it applies) and section 67;
  (c) specify the period for which the order has effect.

(8)   A public spaces protection order must be published in accordance with regulations made by the Secretary of State.

60   Duration of orders

(1)   A public spaces protection order may not have effect for a period of more than 3 years, unless extended under this section.

(2)   Before the time when a public spaces protection order is due to expire, the local authority that made the order may extend the period for which it has effect if satisfied on reasonable grounds that doing so is necessary to prevent—

     (a)   occurrence or recurrence after that time of the activities identified in the order, or

     (b)   an increase in the frequency or seriousness of those activities after that time.

(3)   An extension under this section—

     (a)   may not be for a period of more than 3 years;

     (b)   must be published in accordance with regulations made by the Secretary of State.

(4)   A public spaces protection order may be extended under this section more than once.

64   Orders restricting public right of way over highway

(1)   A local authority may not make a public spaces protection order that restricts the public right of way over a highway without considering—

     (a)   the likely effect of making the order on the occupiers of premises adjoining or adjacent to the highway;

     (b)   the likely effect of making the order on other persons in the locality;

     (c)   in a case where the highway constitutes a through route, the availability of a reasonably convenient alternative route.

(2)   Before making such an order a local authority must—

     (a)   notify potentially affected persons of the proposed order,

     (b)   inform those persons how they can see a copy of the proposed order,

     (c)   notify those persons of the period within which they may make representations about the proposed order, and

     (d)   consider any representations made.

In this subsection "potentially affected persons" means occupiers of premises adjacent to or adjoining the highway, and any other persons in the locality who are likely to be affected by the proposed order.

(3)   Before a local authority makes a public spaces protection order restricting the public right of way over a highway that is also within the area of another local authority, it must consult that other authority if it thinks it appropriate to do so.

(4)   A public spaces protection order may not restrict the public right of way over a highway for the occupiers of premises adjoining or adjacent to the highway.

(5)   A public spaces protection order may not restrict the public right of way over a highway that is the only or principal means of access to a dwelling.

(6)   In relation to a highway that is the only or principal means of access to premises used for business or recreational purposes, a public spaces protection order may not restrict the public right of way over the highway during periods when the premises are normally used for those purposes.

(7)   A public spaces protection order that restricts the public right of way over a highway may authorise the installation, operation and maintenance of a barrier or barriers for enforcing the restriction.

(8)   A local authority may install, operate and maintain barriers authorised under subsection (7).

(9)   A highway over which the public right of way is restricted by a public spaces protection order does not cease to be regarded as a highway by reason of the restriction (or by reason of any barrier authorised under subsection (7)).

(10)   In this section—

"dwelling" means a building or part of a building occupied, or intended to be occupied, as a separate dwelling;

"highway" has the meaning given by section 328 of the Highways Act 1980.

67 Offence of failing to comply with order

(1) It is an offence for a person without reasonable excuse—

    (a) to do anything that the person is prohibited from doing by a public spaces protection order, or

    (b) to fail to comply with a requirement to which the person is subject under a public spaces protection order.

(2) A person guilty of an offence under this section is liable on summary conviction to a fine not exceeding level 3 on the standard scale.

(3) A person does not commit an offence under this section by failing to comply with a prohibition or requirement that the local authority did not have power to include in the public spaces protection order.

68 Fixed penalty notices

(1) A constable or an authorised person may issue a fixed penalty notice to anyone he or she has reason to believe has committed an offence under section 63 or 67 in relation to a public spaces protection order.

(2) A fixed penalty notice is a notice offering the person to whom it is issued the opportunity of discharging any liability to conviction for the offence by payment of a fixed penalty to a local authority specified in the notice.

(3) The local authority specified under subsection (2) must be the one that made the public spaces protection order.

(4) Where a person is issued with a notice under this section in respect of an offence—

    (a) no proceedings may be taken for the offence before the end of the period of 14 days following the date of the notice;

    (b) the person may not be convicted of the offence if the person pays the fixed penalty before the end of that period.

(5) A fixed penalty notice must—

    (a) give reasonably detailed particulars of the circumstances alleged to constitute the offence;

    (b) state the period during which (because of subsection (4)(a)) proceedings will not be taken for the offence;

    (c) specify the amount of the fixed penalty;

    (d) state the name and address of the person to whom the fixed penalty may be paid;

    (e) specify permissible methods of payment.

(6) An amount specified under subsection (5)(c) must not be more than £100.

(7) A fixed penalty notice may specify two amounts under subsection (5)(c) and specify that, if the lower of those amounts is paid within a specified period (of less than 14 days), that is the amount of the fixed penalty.

(8) Whatever other method may be specified under subsection (5)(e), payment of a fixed penalty may be made by pre-paying and posting to the person whose name is stated under subsection (5)(d), at the stated address, a letter containing the amount of the penalty (in cash or otherwise).

(9) Where a letter is sent as mentioned in subsection (8), payment is regarded as having been made at the time at which that letter would be delivered in the ordinary course of post.

(10) In any proceedings, a certificate that—

    (a) purports to be signed by or on behalf of the chief finance officer of the local authority concerned, and

    (b) states that payment of a fixed penalty was, or was not, received by the dated specified in the certificate,

    is evidence of the facts stated.

(11) In this section—

"authorised person" means a person authorised for the purposes of this section by the local authority that made the order (or authorised by virtue of section 69(2));

"chief finance officer", in relation to a local authority, means the person with responsibility for the authority's financial affairs.

HOUSE OF LORDS REFORM ACT 2014
(2014, c. 24)

An Act to make provision for resignation from the House of Lords; and to make provision for the expulsion of Members of the House of Lords in specified circumstances.   [14th May 2014]

1   Resignation

(1)   A member of the House of Lords who is a peer may retire or otherwise resign as a member of the House of Lords by giving notice in writing to the Clerk of the Parliaments.

(2)   The notice must—

(a)   specify a date from which the resignation is to take effect, and

(b)   be signed by the peer and by a witness.

(3)   At the beginning of that date the peer ceases to be a member of the House of Lords.

(4)   Resignation may not be rescinded.

2   Non-attendance

(1)   A member of the House of Lords who is a peer and does not attend the House of Lords during a Session ceases to be a member of the House at the beginning of the following Session.

(2)   A peer "does not attend the House of Lords during a Session" if, and only if, the Lord Speaker certifies that the peer—

(a)   at no time during the Session attended the House, having regard to attendance records kept by officials of the House, and

(b)   did not have leave of absence in respect of the Session, in accordance with Standing Orders of the House.

(3)   Subsection (1) does not apply to a peer in respect of attendance during a Session if—

(a)   the peer was disqualified from sitting or voting in the House, or suspended from its service, for the whole of the Session, or

(b)   the House resolves that subsection (1) should not apply to the peer by reason of special circumstances.

(4)   Subsection (1) does not apply in respect of attendance during a Session that is less than six months long.

(5)   In this section a reference to attendance is a reference to attending the proceedings of the House (including the proceedings of a Committee of the House).

(6)   This section applies in respect of attendance during the first Session to begin after its coming into force and subsequent Sessions.

3   Conviction of serious offence

(1)   A member of the House of Lords who is convicted of a serious offence ceases to be a member of the House of Lords.

(2)   A person "is convicted of a serious offence" if, and only if, the Lord Speaker certifies that the person, while a member of the House of Lords, has been—

(a)   convicted of a criminal offence, and

(b)   sentenced or ordered to be imprisoned or detained indefinitely or for more than one year.

(3)   It is irrelevant for the purposes of subsection (2)—

(a)   whether the offence is committed at a time when the person is a member of the House of Lords;

(b)   whether any of the offence, conviction, sentence, order, imprisonment or detention occurs in the United Kingdom or elsewhere; (but see subsection (9)).

(4)   The reference in subsection (2) to an offence is only to an offence committed on or after the day on which this section comes into force.

(5)   The reference in subsection (2) to a person being sentenced or ordered to be imprisoned or detained indefinitely or for more than one year does not include such a sentence or order where the sentence or order is suspended.

(6)   A certificate under subsection (2) takes effect when it is issued.

(7)   If a person who has ceased to be a member of the House of Lords in accordance with this section is successful on appeal—
    (a)   the Lord Speaker must issue a further certificate to that effect, and
    (b)   on the issue of that certificate, the original certificate under subsection (2) shall be treated for the purposes of this Act as never having had effect.

(8)   A person who has ceased to be a member of the House of Lords in accordance with this section "is successful on appeal" if, and only if, the Lord Speaker certifies that—
    (a)   the conviction certified under subsection (2)(a) has been quashed, or
    (b)   the sentence or order certified under subsection (2)(b) has been—
        (i)   varied so that it is no longer a sentence or order that the person be imprisoned or detained indefinitely or for more than one year within the meaning of subsection (2)(b), or
        (ii)   replaced with another sentence or order that is not a sentence or order that the person be so imprisoned or detained.

(9)   A certificate under subsection (2) in respect of a conviction outside the United Kingdom may be issued only if the House of Lords resolves that subsection (1) should apply; and where the House does so resolve the Lord Speaker must issue the certificate.

4   Effect of ceasing to be a member

(1)   This section applies where a person ceases to be a member of the House of Lords in accordance with this Act.

(2)   The person becomes disqualified from attending the proceedings of the House of Lords (including the proceedings of a Committee of the House).

(3)   Accordingly, the person shall not be entitled to receive a writ to attend the House (whether under section 1 of the Life Peerages Act 1958, by virtue of the dignity conferred by virtue of appointment as a Lord of Appeal in Ordinary, by virtue of a hereditary peerage or as a Lord Spiritual) and may not attend the House in pursuance of a writ already received.

(4)   If the person is a hereditary peer who is excepted from section 1 of the House of Lords Act 1999 by virtue of section 2 of that Act, the person ceases to be excepted from section 1 of that Act (and accordingly section 3 of that Act applies (removal of disqualification on voting in parliamentary elections or being an MP)).

(5)   If the person is a peer other than a hereditary peer, the person is not, by virtue of that peerage, disqualified for—
    (a)   voting at elections to the House of Commons, or
    (b)   being, or being elected as, a member of that House.

(6)   In relation to a peer who ceases to be a member of the House of Lords in accordance with this Act, any reference in section 1(3) or (4)(b) of the Representation of the People Act 1985 to a register of parliamentary electors is to be read as including—
    (a)   any register of local government electors in Great Britain, and
    (b)   any register of local electors in Northern Ireland,
which was required to be published on any date before the date on which the peer ceased to be a member.

(7)   The Standing Orders of the House required by section 2(4) of the House of Lords Act 1999 (filling of vacancies) must make provision requiring the holding of a by-election to fill any vacancy which arises under this Act among the people excepted from section 1 of that Act in consequence of an election.

(8)   Subject to section 3(7), a person who ceases to be a member of the House of Lords in accordance with this Act may not subsequently become a member of that House.

5   Certificate of Lord Speaker

(1)   A certificate of the Lord Speaker under this Act shall be conclusive for all purposes.

(2)   A certificate may be issued on the Lord Speaker's own initiative.

COUNTER-TERRORISM AND SECURITY ACT 2015
(2015, c. 6)

An Act to make provision in relation to terrorism; to make provision about retention of communications data, about information, authority to carry and security in relation to air, sea and rail transport and about reviews by the Special Immigration Appeals Commission against refusals to issue certificates of naturalisation; and for connected purposes.

[12th February 2015]

CHAPTER 2
TEMPORARY EXCLUSION FROM THE UNITED KINGDOM

Imposition of temporary exclusion orders

2   Temporary exclusion orders

(1)   A "temporary exclusion order" is an order which requires an individual not to return to the United Kingdom unless—

     (a)   the return is in accordance with a permit to return issued by the Secretary of State before the individual began the return, or

     (b)   the return is the result of the individual's deportation to the United Kingdom.

(2)   The Secretary of State may impose a temporary exclusion order on an individual if conditions A to E are met.

(3)   Condition A is that the Secretary of State reasonably suspects that the individual is, or has been, involved in terrorism-related activity outside the United Kingdom.

(4)   Condition B is that the Secretary of State reasonably considers that it is necessary, for purposes connected with protecting members of the public in the United Kingdom from a risk of terrorism, for a temporary exclusion order to be imposed on the individual.

(5)   Condition C is that the Secretary of State reasonably considers that the individual is outside the United Kingdom.

(6)   Condition D is that the individual has the right of abode in the United Kingdom.

(7)   Condition E is that—

     (a)   the court gives the Secretary of State permission under section 3, or

     (b)   the Secretary of State reasonably considers that the urgency of the case requires a temporary exclusion order to be imposed without obtaining such permission.

(8)   During the period that a temporary exclusion order is in force, the Secretary of State must keep under review whether condition B is met.

3   Temporary exclusion orders: prior permission of the court

(1)   This section applies if the Secretary of State—

     (a)   makes the relevant decisions in relation to an individual, and

     (b)   makes an application to the court for permission to impose a temporary exclusion order on the individual.

(2)   The function of the court on the application is to determine whether the relevant decisions of the Secretary of State are obviously flawed.

(3)   The court may consider the application—

     (a)   in the absence of the individual,

     (b)   without the individual having been notified of the application, and

     (c)   without the individual having been given an opportunity (if the individual was aware of the application) of making any representations to the court.

(4)   But that does not limit the matters about which rules of court may be made.

(5)   In determining the application, the court must apply the principles applicable on an application for judicial review.

(6)   In a case where the court determines that any of the relevant decisions of the Secretary of State is obviously flawed, the court may not give permission under this section.

(7)   In any other case, the court must give permission under this section.

(8)   Schedule 2 makes provision for references to the court etc where temporary exclusion orders are imposed in cases of urgency.

(9) Only the Secretary of State may appeal against a determination of the court under—
    (a) this section, or
    (b) Schedule 2;
and such an appeal may only be made on a question of law.

(10) In this section "the relevant decisions" means the decisions that the following conditions are met—
    (a) condition A;
    (b) condition B;
    (c) condition C;
    (d) condition D.

4 Temporary exclusion orders: supplementary provision

(1) The Secretary of State must give notice of the imposition of a temporary exclusion order to the individual on whom it is imposed (the "excluded individual").

(2) Notice of the imposition of a temporary exclusion order must include an explanation of the procedure for making an application under section 6 for a permit to return.

(3) A temporary exclusion order—
    (a) comes into force when notice of its imposition is given; and
    (b) is in force for the period of two years (unless revoked or otherwise brought to an end earlier).

(4) The Secretary of State may revoke a temporary exclusion order at any time.

(5) The Secretary of State must give notice of the revocation of a temporary exclusion order to the excluded individual.

(6) If a temporary exclusion order is revoked, it ceases to be in force when notice of its revocation is given.

(7) The validity of a temporary exclusion order is not affected by the excluded individual—
    (a) returning to the United Kingdom, or
    (b) departing from the United Kingdom.

(8) The imposition of a temporary exclusion order does not prevent a further temporary exclusion order from being imposed on the excluded individual (including in a case where an order ceases to be in force at the expiry of its two year duration).

(9) At the time when a temporary exclusion order comes into force, any British passport held by the excluded individual is invalidated.

(10) During the period when a temporary exclusion order is in force, the issue of a British passport to the excluded individual while he or she is outside the United Kingdom is not valid.

(11) In this section "British passport" means a passport, or other document which enables or facilitates travel from one state to another (except a permit to return), that has been—
    (a) issued by or for Her Majesty's Government in the United Kingdom, and
    (b) issued in respect of a person's status as a British citizen.

Permit to return

5 Permit to return

(1) A "permit to return" is a document giving an individual (who is subject to a temporary exclusion order) permission to return to the United Kingdom.

(2) The permission may be made subject to a requirement that the individual comply with conditions specified in the permit to return.

(3) The individual's failure to comply with a specified condition has the effect of invalidating the permit to return.

(4) A permit to return must state—
    (a) the time at which, or period of time during which, the individual is permitted to arrive on return to the United Kingdom;
    (b) the manner in which the individual is permitted to return to the United Kingdom; and
    (c) the place where the individual is permitted to arrive on return to the United Kingdom.

(5) Provision made under subsection (4)(a) or (c) may, in particular, be framed by reference to the arrival in the United Kingdom of a specific flight, sailing or other transport service.

(6) Provision made under subsection (4)(b) may, in particular, state—

    (a) a route,

    (b) a method of transport,

    (c) an airline, shipping line or other passenger carrier, or

    (d) a flight, sailing or other transport service,

which the individual is permitted to use to return to the United Kingdom.

(7) The Secretary of State may not issue a permit to return except in accordance with section 6 or 7.

(8) It is for the Secretary of State to decide the terms of a permit to return (but this is subject to section 6(3)).

6   Issue of permit to return: application by individual

(1) If an individual applies to the Secretary of State for a permit to return, the Secretary of State must issue a permit within a reasonable period after the application is made.

(2) But the Secretary of State may refuse to issue the permit if—

    (a) the Secretary of State requires the individual to attend an interview with a constable or immigration officer at a time and a place specified by the Secretary of State, and

    (b) the individual fails to attend the interview.

(3) Where a permit to return is issued under this section, the relevant return time must fall within a reasonable period after the application is made.

(4) An application is not valid unless it is made in accordance with the procedure for applications specified by the Secretary of State.

(5) In this section—

"application" means an application made by an individual to the Secretary of State for a permit to return to be issued;

"relevant return time" means—

    (a) the time at which the individual is permitted to arrive on return to the United Kingdom (in a case where the permit to return states such a time), or

    (b) the start of the period of time during which the individual is permitted to arrive on return to the United Kingdom (in a case where the permit to return states such a period).

7   Issue of permit to return: deportation or urgent situation

(1) The Secretary of State must issue a permit to return to an individual if the Secretary of State considers that the individual is to be deported to the United Kingdom.

(2) The Secretary of State may issue a permit to return to an individual if—

    (a) the Secretary of State considers that, because of the urgency of the situation, it is expedient to issue a permit to return even though no application has been made under section 6, and

    (b) there is no duty to issue a permit to return under subsection (1).

(3) Subsection (1) or (2) applies whether or not any request has been made to issue the permit to return under that provision.

8   Permit to return: supplementary provision

(1) The Secretary of State may vary a permit to return.

(2) The Secretary of State may revoke a permit to return issued to an individual only if—

    (a) the permit to return has been issued under section 6 and the individual asks the Secretary of State to revoke it;

    (b) the permit to return has been issued under section 7(1) and the Secretary of State no longer considers that the individual is to be deported to the United Kingdom;

    (c) the permit to return has been issued under section 7(2) and the Secretary of State no longer considers that, because of the urgency of the situation, the issue of the permit to return is expedient;

    (d) the Secretary of State issues a subsequent permit to return to the individual; or

    (e) the Secretary of State considers that the permit to return has been obtained by misrepresentation.

(3) The making of an application for a permit to return to be issued under section 6 (whether or not resulting in a permit to return being issued) does not prevent a subsequent application from being made.

(4) The issuing of a permit to return (whether or not resulting in the individual's return to the United Kingdom) does not prevent a subsequent permit to return from being issued (whether or not the earlier permit is still in force).

Obligations after return to the United Kingdom

9   Obligations after return to the United Kingdom

(1) The Secretary of State may, by notice, impose any or all of the permitted obligations on an individual who—
    (a)   is subject to a temporary exclusion order, and
    (b)   has returned to the United Kingdom.

(2) The "permitted obligations" are—
    (a)   any obligation of a kind that may be imposed (on an individual subject to a TPIM notice) under these provisions of Schedule 1 to the Terrorism Prevention and Investigation Measures Act 2011—
       (i)   paragraph 10 (reporting to police station);
       (ii)   paragraph 10A (attendance at appointments etc);
    (b)   an obligation to notify the police, in such manner as a notice under this section may require, of—
       (i)   the individual's place (or places) of residence, and
       (ii)   any change in the individual's place (or places) of residence.

(3) A notice under this section—
    (a)   comes into force when given to the individual; and
    (b)   is in force until the temporary exclusion order ends (unless the notice is revoked or otherwise brought to an end earlier).

(4) The Secretary of State may, by notice, vary or revoke any notice given under this section.

(5) The variation or revocation of a notice under this section takes effect when the notice of variation or revocation is given to the individual.

(6) The validity of a notice under this section is not affected by the individual—
    (a)   departing from the United Kingdom, or
    (b)   returning to the United Kingdom.

(7) The giving of any notice to an individual under this section does not prevent any further notice under this section from being given to that individual.

Offences and proceedings etc.

10   Offences

(1) An individual subject to a temporary exclusion order is guilty of an offence if, without reasonable excuse, the individual returns to the United Kingdom in contravention of the restriction on return specified in the order.

(2) It is irrelevant for the purposes of subsection (1) whether or not the individual has a passport or other similar identity document.

(3) An individual subject to an obligation imposed under section 9 is guilty of an offence if, without reasonable excuse, the individual does not comply with the obligation.

(4) In a case where a relevant notice has not actually been given to an individual, the fact that the relevant notice is deemed to have been given to the individual under regulations under section 13 does not (of itself) prevent the individual from showing that lack of knowledge of the temporary exclusion order, or of the obligation imposed under section 9, was a reasonable excuse for the purposes of this section.

(5) An individual guilty of an offence under this section is liable—
    (a)   on conviction on indictment, to imprisonment for a term not exceeding 5 years or to a fine, or to both;
    (b)   on summary conviction in England and Wales, to imprisonment for a term not exceeding 12 months or to a fine, or to both;
    (c)   on summary conviction in Northern Ireland, to imprisonment for a term not exceeding 6 months or to a fine not exceeding the statutory maximum, or to both;

(d)   on summary conviction in Scotland, to imprisonment for a term not exceeding 12 months or to a fine not exceeding the statutory maximum, or to both.

(6)   Where an individual is convicted by or before a court of an offence under this section, it is not open to that court to make in respect of the offence—

(a)   an order under section 12(1)(b) of the Powers of Criminal Courts (Sentencing) Act 2000 (conditional discharge);

(b)   an order under section 227A of the Criminal Procedure (Scotland) Act 1995 (community pay-back orders); or

(c)   an order under Article 4(1)(b) of the Criminal Justice (Northern Ireland) Order 1996 (S.I. 1996/3160 (N.I. 24)) (conditional discharge in Northern Ireland).

(7)   In this section—

"relevant notice" means—

(a)   notice of the imposition of a temporary exclusion order, or

(b)   notice under section 9 imposing an obligation;

"restriction on return" means the requirement specified in a temporary exclusion order in accordance with section 2(1).

(8)   In section 2 of the UK Borders Act 2007 (detention at ports), in subsection (1A), for "the individual is subject to a warrant for arrest" substitute "the individual—

(a)   may be liable to be detained by a constable under section 14 of the Criminal Procedure (Scotland) Act 1995 in respect of an offence under section 10(1) of the Counter-Terrorism and Security Act 2015, or

(b)   is subject to a warrant for arrest."

11   Review of decisions relating to temporary exclusion orders

(1)   This section applies where an individual who is subject to a temporary exclusion order is in the United Kingdom.

(2)   The individual may apply to the court to review any of the following decisions of the Secretary of State—

(a)   a decision that any of the following conditions was met in relation to the imposition of the temporary exclusion order—

(i)   condition A;

(ii)   condition B;

(iii)   condition C;

(iv)   condition D;

(b)   a decision to impose the temporary exclusion order;

(c)   a decision that condition B continues to be met;

(d)   a decision to impose any of the permitted obligations on the individual by a notice under section 9.

(3)   On a review under this section, the court must apply the principles applicable on an application for judicial review.

(4)   On a review of a decision within subsection (2)(a) to (c), the court has the following powers (and only those powers)—

(a)   power to quash the temporary exclusion order;

(b)   power to give directions to the Secretary of State for, or in relation to, the revocation of the temporary exclusion order.

(5)   If the court does not exercise either of its powers under subsection (4), the court must decide that the temporary exclusion order is to continue in force.

(6)   On a review of a decision within subsection (2)(d), the court has the following powers (and only those powers)—

(a)   power to quash the permitted obligation in question;

(b)   if that is the only permitted obligation imposed by the notice under section 9, power to quash the notice;

(c)   power to give directions to the Secretary of State for, or in relation to—

(i)   the variation of the notice so far as it relates to that permitted obligation, or

(ii)   if that is the only permitted obligation imposed by the notice, the revocation of the notice.

(7)   If the court does not exercise any of its powers under subsection (6), the court must decide that the notice under section 9 is to continue in force.

(8) If the court exercises a power under subsection (6)(a) or (c)(i), the court must decide that the notice under section 9 is to continue in force subject to that exercise of that power.

(9) The power under this section to quash a temporary exclusion order, permitted obligation or notice under section 9 includes—

(a) in England and Wales or Northern Ireland, power to stay the quashing for a specified time, or pending an appeal or further appeal against the decision to quash; or

(b) in Scotland, power to determine that the quashing is of no effect for a specified time or pending such an appeal or further appeal.

(10) An appeal against a determination of the court on a review under this section may only be made on a question of law.

(11) For the purposes of this section, a failure by the Secretary of State to make a decision whether condition B continues to be met is to be treated as a decision that it continues to be met.

PART 4
AVIATION, SHIPPING AND RAIL

22 Authority-to-carry schemes

(1) The Secretary of State may make one or more schemes requiring a person (a "carrier") to seek authority from the Secretary of State to carry persons on aircraft, ships or trains which are—

(a) arriving, or expected to arrive, in the United Kingdom, or

(b) leaving, or expected to leave, the United Kingdom.

A scheme made under this section is called an "authority-to-carry scheme".

(2) An authority-to-carry scheme must specify or describe—

(a) the classes of carrier to which it applies (which may be all carriers or may be defined by reference to the method of transport or otherwise),

(b) the classes of passengers or crew in respect of whom authority to carry must be sought (which may be all of them or may be defined by reference to nationality, the possession of specified documents or otherwise), and

(c) the classes of passengers or crew in respect of whom authority to carry may be refused.

(3) An authority-to-carry scheme may specify or describe a class of person under subsection (2)(c) only if it is necessary in the public interest.

(4) The Secretary of State may make different authority-to-carry schemes for different purposes and in particular may make different schemes for different types of carrier, journey or person.

(5) An authority-to-carry scheme must set out the process for carriers to request, and for the Secretary of State to grant or refuse, authority to carry, which may include—

(a) a requirement for carriers to provide specified information on passengers or crew by a specified time before travel;

(b) a requirement for carriers to provide the information in a specified manner and form;

(c) a requirement for carriers to be able to receive, in a specified manner and form, communications from the Secretary of State relating to the information provided or granting or refusing authority to carry.

(7) The grant or refusal of authority under an authority-to-carry scheme does not determine whether a person is entitled or permitted to enter the United Kingdom.

PART 5
RISK OF BEING DRAWN INTO TERRORISM

CHAPTER 1
PREVENTING PEOPLE BEING DRAWN INTO TERRORISM

26 General duty on specified authorities

(1) A specified authority must, in the exercise of its functions, have due regard to the need to prevent people from being drawn into terrorism.

(2)   A specified authority is a person or body that is listed in Schedule 6.

(3)   In the case of a specified authority listed in Schedule 6 in terms that refer to the exercise of particular functions or to a particular capacity that it has, the reference in subsection (1) to the authority's functions is to those functions or its functions when acting in that capacity.

(4)   Subsection (1) does not apply to the exercise of—

     (a)   a judicial function;

     (b)   a function exercised on behalf of, or on the instructions of, a person exercising a judicial function;

     (c)   a function in connection with proceedings in the House of Commons or the House of Lords;

     (d)   a function in connection with proceedings in the Scottish Parliament;

     (e)   a function in connection with proceedings in the National Assembly for Wales.

(5)   References to a judicial function include a reference to a judicial function conferred on a person other than a court or tribunal.

27   Power to specify authorities

(1)   The Secretary of State may by regulations made by statutory instrument amend Schedule 6.

(2)   The power under subsection (1) may not be exercised so as to extend the application of section 26(1) to—

     (a)   the exercise of a function referred to in section 26(4);

     (b)   the House of Commons;

     (c)   the House of Lords;

     (d)   the Scottish Parliament;

     (e)   the National Assembly for Wales or the Assembly Commission within the meaning of the Government of Wales Act 2006;

     (f)   the General Synod of the Church of England;

     (g)   the Security Service;

     (h)   the Secret Intelligence Service;

     (i)   the Government Communications Headquarters;

     (j)   any part of Her Majesty's forces, or of the Ministry of Defence, which engages in intelligence activities.

(3)   Regulations under this section may amend this Chapter so as to make consequential or supplemental provision.

(4)   A statutory instrument containing regulations under this section may not be made unless a draft of the instrument has been laid before each House of Parliament and approved by a resolution of each House.

(5)   Subsection (4) does not apply to a statutory instrument containing regulations that only make provision for—

     (a)   the omission of an entry where the authority concerned has ceased to exist, or

     (b)   the variation of an entry in consequence of a change of name or transfer of functions.

(6)   A statutory instrument that falls within subsection (5) is subject to annulment in pursuance of a resolution of either House of Parliament.

28   Power to specify authorities: Welsh and Scottish authorities

(1)   The Secretary of State must consult the Welsh Ministers before making regulations under section 27(1) that—

     (a)   add a Welsh authority to Schedule 6, or

     (b)   amend or remove an entry that relates to a Welsh authority.

(2)   The Secretary of State must consult the Scottish Ministers before making regulations under section 27(1) that—

     (a)   add a Scottish authority to Schedule 6, or

     (b)   amend or remove an entry that relates to a Scottish authority.

31   Freedom of expression in universities etc

(1)   This section applies to a specified authority if it is the proprietor or governing body of—

     (a)   an institution that provides further education (within the meaning given by section 2(3) of the Education Act 1996),

     (b)   an institution that provides courses of a description mentioned in Schedule 6 to the Education Reform Act 1988 (higher education courses), or

     (c)   a post-16 education body within the meaning of the Further and Higher Education (Scotland) Act 2005.

(2)   When carrying out the duty imposed by section 26(1), a specified authority to which this section applies—

     (a)   must have particular regard to the duty to ensure freedom of speech, if it is subject to that duty;

     (aa)   must have particular regard to the need to ensure freedom of speech, if it is the proprietor or governing body of an institution mentioned in subsection (1)(c);

     (b)   must have particular regard to the importance of academic freedom, if it is the proprietor or governing body of a qualifying institution.

(3)   When issuing guidance under section 29 to specified authorities to which this section applies, the Secretary of State—

     (a)   must have particular regard to the duty to ensure freedom of speech, in the case of authorities that are subject to that duty;

     (aa)   must have particular regard to the need to ensure freedom of speech, in the case of authorities that are proprietors or governing bodies of institutions mentioned in subsection (1)(c);

     (b)   must have particular regard to the importance of academic freedom, in the case of authorities that are proprietors or governing bodies of qualifying institutions.

(4)   When considering whether to give directions under section 30 to a specified authority to which this section applies, the Secretary of State—

     (a)   must have particular regard to the duty to ensure freedom of speech, in the case of an authority that is subject to that duty;

     (aa)   must have particular regard to the need to ensure freedom of speech, in the case of authorities that are proprietors or governing bodies of institutions mentioned in subsection (1)(c);

     (b)   must have particular regard to the importance of academic freedom, in the case of an authority that is the proprietor or governing body of a qualifying institution.

(5)   In this section—

"the duty to ensure freedom of speech" means the duty imposed by section 43(1) of the Education (No. 2) Act 1986;

"the need to ensure freedom of speech" means the need to take such steps as are reasonably practicable to ensure that freedom of speech within the law is secured for members, students and employees of the institution in question and for visiting speakers.

"academic freedom" means the freedom referred to in section 202(2)(a) of the Education Reform Act 1988;

"qualifying institution" has the meaning given by section 202(3) of that Act.

CHAPTER 2

SUPPORT ETC FOR PEOPLE VULNERABLE TO BEING DRAWN INTO TERRORISM

36   Assessment and support: local panels

(1)   Each local authority must ensure that a panel of persons is in place for its area—

     (a)   with the function of assessing the extent to which identified individuals are vulnerable to being drawn into terrorism, and

     (b)   with the other functions mentioned in subsection (4).

(2)   "Identified individual", in relation to a panel, means an individual who is referred to the panel by a chief officer of police for an assessment of the kind mentioned in subsection (1)(a).

(3)   A chief officer of police may refer an individual to a panel only if there are reasonable grounds to believe that the individual is vulnerable to being drawn into terrorism.

(4)   The functions of a panel referred to in subsection (1)(b) are—

     (a)   to prepare a plan in respect of identified individuals who the panel considers should be offered support for the purpose of reducing their vulnerability to being drawn into terrorism;

    (b)   if the necessary consent is given, to make arrangements for support to be provided to those individuals in accordance with their support plan;

    (c)   to keep under review the giving of support to an identified individual under a support plan;

    (d)   to revise a support plan, or withdraw support under a plan, if at any time the panel considers it appropriate;

    (e)   to carry out further assessments, after such periods as the panel considers appropriate, of an individual's vulnerability to being drawn into terrorism in cases where—

        (i)   the necessary consent is refused or withdrawn to the giving of support under a support plan, or

        (ii)   the panel has determined that support under a plan should be withdrawn;

    (f)   to prepare a further support plan in such cases if the panel considers it appropriate.

(5)   A support plan must include the following information—

    (a)   how, when and by whom a request for the necessary consent is to be made;

    (b)   the nature of the support to be provided to the identified individual;

    (c)   the persons who are to be responsible for providing it;

    (d)   how and when such support is to be provided.

(6)   Where in the carrying out of its functions under this section a panel determines that support should not be given to an individual under a support plan, the panel—

    (a)   must consider whether the individual ought to be referred to a provider of any health or social care services, and

    (b)   if so, must make such arrangements as the panel considers appropriate for the purpose of referring the individual.

(7)   In exercising its functions under this section a panel must have regard to any guidance given by the Secretary of State about the exercise of those functions.

(8)   Before issuing guidance under subsection (7) the Secretary of State must (whether before or after this Act is passed) consult—

    (a)   the Welsh Ministers so far as the guidance relates to panels in Wales;

    (b)   the Scottish Ministers so far as the guidance relates to panels in Scotland;

    (c)   any person whom the Secretary of State considers appropriate.

37   Membership and proceedings of panels

(1)   The members of a panel must include—

    (a)   the responsible local authority;

    (b)   the chief officer of police for a police area the whole or any part of which is in the area of that authority.

(2)   Each of those members must appoint a person to represent them on the panel; and the representative must be a person whom the member concerned considers to have the required skills and experience.

(3)   Where more than one chief officer of police comes within subsection (1)(b), a person may represent more than one of the chief officers; but at any meeting of the panel at which an identified individual is to be discussed there must be a person present from the police force for the area in which the individual resides to act as the representative.

(4)   A panel may also include such other persons as the responsible local authority considers appropriate (whether generally or in the case of a particular identified individual).

(5)   The chair of a panel is the responsible local authority; but where more than one local authority is the responsible local authority, the authorities may determine that one (or more) of them is to be the chair.

(6)   If a panel cannot reach a unanimous decision on a question arising before it, the question must be decided—

    (a)   according to the opinion of the majority of the panel, or

    (b)   if there is no majority opinion, by the chair.

(7)   Subject to subsection (6), a panel may determine its own procedure.

SCHEDULE 1
SEIZURE OF PASSPORTS ETC FROM PERSONS SUSPECTED
OF INVOLVEMENT IN TERRORISM

Interpretation

1.   (1)   The following definitions have effect for the purposes of this Schedule.
       (2)   "Immigration officer" means a person who is appointed as an immigration officer under paragraph 1 of Schedule 2 to the Immigration Act 1971.
       (3)   "Customs official" means a person who is designated as a general customs official under section 3(1) of the Borders, Citizenship and Immigration Act 2009 or as a customs revenue official under section 11(1) of that Act.
       (4)   "Qualified officer" means an immigration officer or customs official who is designated by the Secretary of State for the purposes of this Schedule.
       (5)   "Senior police officer" means a police officer of at least the rank of superintendent.
       (6)   "Travel document" means anything that is or appears to be—
             (a)   a passport, or
             (b)   a ticket or other document that permits a person to make a journey by any means from a place within Great Britain to a place outside Great Britain, or from a place within Northern Ireland to a place outside the United Kingdom.
       (7)   "Passport" means—
             (a)   a United Kingdom passport (within the meaning of the Immigration Act 1971),
             (b)   a passport issued by or on behalf of the authorities of a country or territory outside the United Kingdom, or by or on behalf of an international organisation, or
             (c)   a document that can be used (in some or all circumstances) instead of a passport.
       (8)   "Port" means—
             (a)   an airport,
             (b)   a sea port,
             (c)   a hoverport,
             (d)   a heliport,
             (e)   a railway station where passenger trains depart for, or arrive from, places outside the United Kingdom, or
             (f)   any other place at which a person is able, or attempting, to get on or off any craft, vessel or vehicle in connection with entering or leaving Great Britain or Northern Ireland.
       (9)   A place is "in the border area" if it is in Northern Ireland and is no more than one mile from the border between Northern Ireland and the Republic of Ireland.
       (10) "Involvement in terrorism-related activity" is any one or more of the following—
             (a)   the commission, preparation or instigation of acts of terrorism;
             (b)   conduct that facilitates the commission, preparation or instigation of such acts, or is intended to do so;
             (c)   conduct that gives encouragement to the commission, preparation or instigation of such acts, or is intended to do so;
             (d)   conduct that gives support or assistance to individuals who are known or believed by the person concerned to be involved in conduct falling within paragraph (a). It is immaterial whether the acts of terrorism in question are specific acts of terrorism or acts of terrorism in general.
       (11) "Terrorism" and "terrorist" have the same meaning as in the Terrorism Act 2000 (see sections 1(1) to (4) and 40 of that Act).
       (12) "Judicial authority" means—
             (a)   in England and Wales, a District Judge (Magistrates' Courts) who is—
                   (i)   designated under paragraph 29(4)(a) of Schedule 8 to the Terrorism Act 2000, or
                   (ii)   designated for the purposes of this Schedule by the Lord Chief Justice of England and Wales;
             (b)   in Scotland, the sheriff;

(c)   in Northern Ireland, a county court judge, or a district judge (magistrates' courts) who is—

    (i)   designated under paragraph 29(4)(c) of Schedule 8 to the Terrorism Act 2000, or

    (ii)   designated for the purposes of this Schedule by the Lord Chief Justice of Northern Ireland.

(13) The Lord Chief Justice may nominate a judicial office holder (as defined in section 109(4) of the Constitutional Reform Act 2005) to exercise his or her functions under sub-paragraph (12)(a)(ii).

(14) The Lord Chief Justice of Northern Ireland may nominate any of the following to exercise his or her functions under sub-paragraph (12)(c)(ii)—

(a)   the holder of one of the offices listed in Schedule 1 to the Justice (Northern Ireland) Act 2002;

(b)   a Lord Justice of Appeal (as defined in section 88 of that Act).

(15) "The 14-day period" and "the 30-day period" have the meanings given by paragraphs 5(2) and 8(7) respectively.

Powers of search and seizure etc

2.   (1)   This paragraph applies in the case of a person at a port in Great Britain if a constable has reasonable grounds to suspect that the person—

(a)   is there with the intention of leaving Great Britain for the purpose of involvement in terrorism-related activity outside the United Kingdom, or

(b)   has arrived in Great Britain with the intention of leaving it soon for that purpose.

(2)   This paragraph applies in the case of a person at a port in Northern Ireland, or in the border area, if a constable has reasonable grounds to suspect that the person—

(a)   is there with the intention of leaving the United Kingdom for the purpose of involvement in terrorism-related activity outside the United Kingdom, or

(b)   has arrived in Northern Ireland with the intention of leaving the United Kingdom soon for that purpose.

(3)   The constable may—

(a)   exercise any of the powers in sub-paragraph (5) in the case of the person, or

(b)   direct a qualified officer to do so.

(4)   A qualified officer must (if able to do so) comply with any direction given by a constable under sub-paragraph (3)(b).

(5)   The powers are—

(a)   to require the person to hand over all travel documents in his or her possession to the constable or (as the case may be) the qualified officer;

(b)   to search for travel documents relating to the person and to take possession of any that the constable or officer finds;

(c)   to inspect any travel document relating to the person;

(d)   to retain any travel document relating to the person that is lawfully in the possession of the constable or officer.

(6)   The power in sub-paragraph (5)(b) is a power to search—

(a)   the person;

(b)   anything that the person has with him or her;

(c)   any vehicle in which the officer believes the person to have been travelling or to be about to travel.

(7)   A constable or qualified officer—

(a)   may stop a person or vehicle for the purpose of exercising a power in sub-paragraph (5)(a) or (b);

(b)   may if necessary use reasonable force for the purpose of exercising a power in sub-paragraph (5)(a) or (b);

(c)   may authorise a person to carry out on the constable's or officer's behalf a search under sub-paragraph (5)(b).

(8)   A constable or qualified officer exercising a power in sub-paragraph (5) (a) or (b) must tell the person that—

(a)   the person is suspected of intending to leave Great Britain or (as the case may be) the United Kingdom for the purpose of involvement in terrorism-related activity outside the United Kingdom, and

   (b) the constable or officer is therefore entitled under this Schedule to exercise the power.

  (9) Where a travel document relating to the person is in the possession of an immigration officer or customs official (whether a qualified officer or not), the constable may direct the officer or official—

   (a) to pass the document to a constable as soon as practicable, and

   (b) in the meantime to retain it.

  The officer or official must comply with any such direction.

Travel documents in possession of immigration officers or customs officials

3. (1) Where—

   (a) a travel document lawfully comes into the possession of an immigration officer or customs official (whether a qualified officer or not) without a power under paragraph 2 being exercised, and

   (b) as soon as possible after taking possession of the document, the officer or official asks a constable whether the constable wishes to give a direction under paragraph 2(9) in relation to the document,

  the officer or official may retain the document until the constable tells him or her whether or not the constable wishes to give such a direction.

  (2) A request under sub-paragraph (1) must be considered as soon as possible.

Authorisation by senior police officer for retention of travel document

4. (1) Where a travel document is in the possession of a constable or qualified officer as a result of the exercise of a power under paragraph 2, the relevant constable must as soon as possible either—

   (a) seek authorisation from a senior police officer for the document to be retained, or

   (b) ensure that the document is returned to the person to whom it relates.

  "The relevant constable" means the constable by whom, or on whose direction, the power was exercised.

  (2) The document may be retained while an application for authorisation is considered.

Persons unable to leave the United Kingdom

14. (1) This paragraph applies where a person's travel documents are retained under this Schedule with the result that, for the period during which they are so retained ("the relevant period"), the person is unable to leave the United Kingdom.

  (2) The Secretary of State may make whatever arrangements he or she thinks appropriate in relation to the person—

   (a) during the relevant period;

   (b) on the relevant period coming to an end.

  (3) If at any time during the relevant period the person does not have leave to enter or remain in the United Kingdom, the person's presence in the United Kingdom at that time is nevertheless not unlawful for the purposes of the Immigration Act 1971.

SCHEDULE 2
URGENT TEMPORARY EXCLUSION ORDERS: REFERENCE TO THE COURT ETC

Application

1. This Schedule applies if the Secretary of State—

  (a) makes the urgent case decisions in relation to an individual, and

  (b) imposes a temporary exclusion order on the individual.

Statement of urgency

2. The temporary exclusion order must include a statement that the Secretary of State reasonably considers that the urgency of the case requires the order to be imposed without obtaining the permission of the court under section 3.

Reference to court

3.　　(1)　Immediately after giving notice of the imposition of the temporary exclusion order, the Secretary of State must refer to the court the imposition of the order on the individual.

　　　(2)　The function of the court on the reference is to consider whether the urgent case decisions were obviously flawed.

　　　(3)　The court's consideration of the reference must begin within the period of 7 days beginning with the day on which notice of the imposition of the temporary exclusion order is given to the individual.

　　　(4)　The court may consider the reference—
　　　　　(a)　in the absence of the individual,
　　　　　(b)　without the individual having been notified of the reference, and
　　　　　(c)　without the individual having been given an opportunity (if the individual was aware of the reference) of making any representations to the court.

　　　(5)　But that does not limit the matters about which rules of court may be made.

Decision by court

4.　　(1)　In a case where the court determines that any of the relevant decisions of the Secretary of State is obviously flawed, the court must quash the temporary exclusion order.

　　　(2)　If sub-paragraph (1) does not apply, the court must confirm the temporary exclusion order.

　　　(3)　If the court determines that the decision of the Secretary of State that the urgency condition is met is obviously flawed, the court must make a declaration of that determination (whether it quashes or confirms the temporary exclusion order under the preceding provisions of this paragraph).

Procedures on reference

5.　　(1)　In determining a reference under paragraph 3, the court must apply the principles applicable on an application for judicial review.

　　　(2)　The court must ensure that the individual is notified of the court's decision on a reference under paragraph 3.

HOUSE OF LORDS (EXPULSION AND SUSPENSION) ACT 2015
(2015, c. 14)

An Act to make provision empowering the House of Lords to expel or suspend members.

[26th March 2015]

1　　Expulsion and suspension of members of the House of Lords

　　(1)　Standing Orders of the House of Lords may make provision under which the House of Lords may by resolution—
　　　(a)　expel a member of the House of Lords, or
　　　(b)　suspend a member of the House of Lords for the period specified in the resolution.

　　(2)　A person expelled by virtue of this section ceases to be a member.

　　(3)　A person suspended by virtue of this section remains a member during the period of suspension, but during that period the person—
　　　(a)　is not entitled to receive writs of summons to attend the House of Lords, and
　　　(b)　despite any writ of summons previously issued to the person, is disqualified from sitting or voting in the House of Lords or a committee of the House of Lords.

　　(4)　A resolution passed by virtue of subsection (1) must state that, in the opinion of the House of Lords, the conduct giving rise to the resolution—
　　　(a)　occurred after the coming into force of this Act, or
　　　(b)　occurred before the coming into force of this Act and was not public knowledge before that time.

EUROPEAN UNION (NOTIFICATION OF WITHDRAWAL) ACT 2017
(2017, c. 9)

An Act to confer power on the Prime Minister to notify, under Article 50(2) of the Treaty on European Union, the United Kingdom's intention to withdraw from the EU.   [16th March 2017]

1   Power to notify withdrawal from the EU

(1)   The Prime Minister may notify, under Article 50(2) of the Treaty on European Union, the United Kingdom's intention to withdraw from the EU.

(2)   This section has effect despite any provision made by or under the European Communities Act 1972 or any other enactment.

PACE CODES
POLICE AND CRIMINAL EVIDENCE ACT 1984 (PACE)
CODE A 2015

CODE OF PRACTICE FOR THE EXERCISE BY:
POLICE OFFICERS OF STATUTORY POWERS OF STOP AND SEARCH
POLICE OFFICERS AND POLICE STAFF OF REQUIREMENTS TO RECORD PUBLIC
ENCOUNTERS

Commencement – Transitional Arrangements

This code applies to any search by a police officer and the recording of
public encounters taking place after 00.00 on 19 March 2015.

1.0   General

1.01   This code of practice must be readily available at all police stations for consultation by
police officers, police staff, detained persons and members of the public.

1.02   The notes for guidance included are not provisions of this code, but are guidance
to police officers and others about its application and interpretation. Provisions in the
annexes to the code are provisions of this code.

1.03   This code governs the exercise by police officers of statutory powers to search a person
or a vehicle without first making an arrest. The main stop and search powers to which this
code applies are set out in Annex A, but that list should not be regarded as definitive (see
Note 1). In addition, it covers requirements on police officers and police staff to record
encounters not governed by statutory powers (see *paragraphs 2.11 and 4.12*). This code
does not apply to:

(a)   the powers of stop and search under:
    (i)   the Aviation Security Act 1982, section 27(2), and
    (ii)   the Police and Criminal Evidence Act 1984 (PACE), section 6(1) (which relates
        specifically to powers of constables employed by statutory undertakers on the
        premises of the statutory undertakers);

(b)   searches carried out for the purposes of examination under Schedule 7 to the Terrorism
Act 2000 and to which the Code of Practice issued under paragraph 6 of Schedule 14
to the Terrorism Act 2000 applies.

(c)   the powers to search persons and vehicles and to stop and search in specified
locations to which the Code of Practice issued under section 47AB of the Terrorism
Act 2000 applies.

1   Principles governing stop and search

1.1   Powers to stop and search must be used fairly, responsibly, with respect for people being
searched and without unlawful discrimination. Under the Equality Act 2010, section 149,
when police officers are carrying out their functions, they also have a duty to have due regard
to the need to eliminate unlawful discrimination, harassment and victimisation, to advance
equality of opportunity between people who share a 'relevant protected characteristic' and
people who do not share it, and to take steps to foster good relations between those
persons (see *Notes 1 and 1A*). The Children Act 2004, section 11, also requires chief police
officers and other specified persons and bodies to ensure that in the discharge of their
functions they have regard to the need to safeguard and promote the welfare of all persons
under the age of 18.

1.2   The intrusion on the liberty of the person stopped or searched must be brief and detention
for the purposes of a search must take place at or near the location of the stop.

1.3   If these fundamental principles are not observed the use of powers to stop and search
may be drawn into question. Failure to use the powers in the proper manner reduces their
effectiveness. Stop and search can play an important role in the detection and prevention
of crime, and using the powers fairly makes them more effective.

1.4   The primary purpose of stop and search powers is to enable officers to allay or confirm
suspicions about individuals without exercising their power of arrest. Officers may be
required to justify the use or authorisation of such powers, in relation both to individual
searches and the overall pattern of their activity in this regard, to their supervisory officers
or in court. Any misuse of the powers is likely to be harmful to policing and lead to mistrust
of the police. Officers must also be able to explain their actions to the member of the public

searched. The misuse of these powers can lead to disciplinary action (see *paragraphs 5.5 and 5.6*).

1.5   An officer must not search a person, even with his or her consent, where no power to search is applicable. Even where a person is prepared to submit to a search voluntarily, the person must not be searched unless the necessary legal power exists, and the search must be in accordance with the relevant power and the provisions of this Code. The only exception, where an officer does not require a specific power, applies to searches of persons entering sports grounds or other premises carried out with their consent given as a condition of entry.

1.6   Evidence obtained from a search to which this Code applies may be open to challenge if the provisions of this Code are not observed.

2   Types of stop and search powers

2.1   This code applies, subject to paragraph 1.03, to powers of stop and search as follows:

(a)   powers which require reasonable grounds for suspicion, before they may be exercised; that articles unlawfully obtained or possessed are being carried such as section 1 of PACE for stolen and prohibited articles and section 23 of the Misuse of Drugs Act 1971 for controlled drugs;

(b)   authorised under section 60 of the Criminal Justice and Public Order Act 1994, based upon a reasonable belief that incidents involving serious violence may take place or that people are carrying dangerous instruments or offensive weapons within any locality in the police area, or that it is expedient to use the powers to find such instruments or weapons that have been used in incidents of serious violence;

(c)   *Not used;*

(d)   the powers in Schedule 5 to the Terrorism Prevention and Investigation Measures (TPIM) Act 2011 to search an individual who has not been arrested, conferred by:

(i)   paragraph 6(2)(a) at the time of serving a TPIM notice;

(ii)   paragraph 8(2)(a) under a search warrant for compliance purposes; and

(iii)   paragraph 10 for public safety purposes.

See *paragraph 2.18A*.

(e)   powers to search a person who has not been arrested in the exercise of a power to search premises (see Code B *paragraph 2.4*).

(a)   Stop and search powers requiring reasonable grounds for suspicion – explanation

General

2.2   Reasonable grounds for suspicion is the legal test which a police officer must satisfy before they can stop and detain individuals or vehicles to search them under powers such as section 1 of PACE (to find stolen or prohibited articles) and section 23 of the Misuse of Drugs Act 1971 (to find controlled drugs). This test must be applied to the particular circumstances in each case and is in two parts:

(i)   *Firstly,* the officer must have formed a *genuine* suspicion in their own mind that they will find the object for which the search power being exercised allows them to search (see Annex A, second column, for examples); and

(ii)   *Secondly,* the suspicion that the object will be found must be reasonable. This means that there must be an *objective* basis for that suspicion based on facts, information and/or intelligence which are relevant to the likelihood that the object in question will be found, so that a reasonable person would be entitled to reach the same conclusion based on the same facts and information and/or intelligence.

Officers must therefore be able to explain the basis for their suspicion by reference to intelligence or information about, or some specific behaviour by, the person concerned (see *paragraphs 3.8(d), 4.6* and *5.5*).

2.2A   The exercise of these stop and search powers depends on the likelihood that the person searched is in possession of an item for which they may be searched; it does not depend on the person concerned being suspected of committing an offence in relation to the object of the search. A police officer who has reasonable grounds to suspect that a person is in *innocent possession* of a stolen or prohibited article, controlled drug or other item for which the officer is empowered to search, may stop and search the person even though there would be no power of arrest. This would apply when a child under the age of criminal responsibility (10 years) is suspected of carrying any such item, even if they knew they had it. (See *Notes 1B* and *1BA*.)

Personal factors can never support reasonable grounds for suspicion

2.2B   Reasonable suspicion can never be supported on the basis of personal factors. This means that unless the police have information or intelligence which *provides a description* of a person suspected of carrying an article for which there is a power to stop and search, the following *cannot be used*, alone or in combination with each other, or in combination with any other factor, as the reason for stopping and searching any individual, including any vehicle which they are driving or are being carried in:

(a)   A person's physical appearance with regard, for example, to any of the 'relevant protected characteristics' set out in the Equality Act 2010, section 149, which are age, disability, gender reassignment, pregnancy and maternity, race, religion or belief, sex and sexual orientation (see *paragraph 1.1* and *Note 1A*), or the fact that the person is known to have a previous conviction; and

(b)   Generalisations or stereotypical images that certain groups or categories of people are more likely to be involved in criminal activity.

2.3   *Not used.*

Reasonable grounds for suspicion based on information and/or intelligence

2.4   Reasonable grounds for suspicion should normally be linked to accurate and current intelligence or information, relating to articles for which there is a power to stop and search, being carried by individuals or being in vehicles in any locality. This would include reports from members of the public or other officers describing:

•   a person who has been seen carrying such an article or a vehicle in which such an article has been seen.

•   crimes committed in relation to which such an article would constitute relevant evidence, for example, property stolen in a theft or burglary, an offensive weapon or bladed or sharply pointed article used to assault or threaten someone or an article used to cause criminal damage to property.

2.4A   Searches based on accurate and current intelligence or information are more likely to be effective. Targeting searches in a particular area at specified crime problems not only increases their effectiveness but also minimises inconvenience to law-abiding members of the public. It also helps in justifying the use of searches both to those who are searched and to the public. This does not, however, prevent stop and search powers being exercised in other locations where such powers may be exercised and reasonable suspicion exists.

2.5   *Not used.*

Reasonable grounds for suspicion and searching groups

2.6   Where there is reliable information or intelligence that members of a group or gang habitually carry knives unlawfully or weapons or controlled drugs, and wear a distinctive item of clothing or other means of identification in order to identify themselves as members of that group or gang, that distinctive item of clothing or other means of identification may provide reasonable grounds to stop and search any person believed to be a member of that group or gang. (See *Note 9*.)

2.6A   A similar approach would apply to particular organised protest groups where there is reliable information or intelligence:

(a)   that the group in question arranges meetings and marches to which one or more members bring articles intended to be used to cause criminal damage and/or injury to others in support of the group's aims;

(b)   that at one or more previous meetings or marches arranged by that group, such articles have been used and resulted in damage and/or injury; and

(c)   that on the subsequent occasion in question, one or more members of the group have brought with them such articles with similar intentions

These circumstances may provide reasonable grounds to stop and search any members of the group to find such articles (see *Note 9A*). See also *paragraphs 2.12* to *2.18*, *"Searches authorised under section 60 of the Criminal Justice and Public Order Act 1994"*, when serious violence is anticipated at meetings and marches.

Reasonable grounds for suspicion based on behaviour, time and location

2.6B   Reasonable suspicion may also exist without specific information or intelligence and on the basis of the behaviour of a person. For example, if an officer encounters someone on the street at night who is obviously trying to hide something, the officer may (depending on the other surrounding circumstances) base such suspicion on the fact that this kind of behaviour is often linked to stolen or prohibited articles being carried. An officer who forms the opinion that a person is acting suspiciously or that they appear to be nervous must be able to explain, with reference to specific aspects of the person's behaviour or conduct which they have observed, why they formed that opinion (see *paragraphs 3.8(d)* and *5.5*). A hunch or instinct which cannot be explained or justified to an objective observer can never amount to reasonable grounds.

2.7 *Not used.*

2.8 *Not used.*

Securing public confidence and promoting community relations

2.8A All police officers must recognise that searches are more likely to be effective, legitimate and secure public confidence when their reasonable grounds for suspicion are based on a range of objective factors. The overall use of these powers is more likely to be effective when up-to-date and accurate intelligence or information is communicated to officers and they are well-informed about local crime patterns. Local senior officers have a duty to ensure that those under their command who exercise stop and search powers have access to such information, and the officers exercising the powers have a duty to acquaint themselves with that information (see *paragraphs 5.1 to 5.6*).

Questioning to decide whether to carry out a search

2.9 An officer who has reasonable grounds for suspicion may detain the person concerned in order to carry out a search. Before carrying out the search the officer may ask questions about the person's behaviour or presence in circumstances which gave rise to the suspicion. As a result of questioning the detained person, the reasonable grounds for suspicion necessary to detain that person may be confirmed or, because of a satisfactory explanation, be dispelled. (See *Notes 2* and *3*.) Questioning may also reveal reasonable grounds to suspect the possession of a different kind of unlawful article from that originally suspected. Reasonable grounds for suspicion however cannot be provided retrospectively by such questioning during a person's detention or by refusal to answer any questions asked.

2.10 If, as a result of questioning before a search, or other circumstances which come to the attention of the officer, there cease to be reasonable grounds for suspecting that an article of a kind for which there is a power to stop and search is being carried, no search may take place. (See *Note 3*.) In the absence of any other lawful power to detain, the person is free to leave at will and must be so informed.

2.11 There is no power to stop or detain a person in order to find grounds for a search. Police officers have many encounters with members of the public which do not involve detaining people against their will and do not require any statutory power for an officer to speak to a person (see *paragraph 4.12* and *Note 1*). However, if reasonable grounds for suspicion emerge during such an encounter, the officer may detain the person to search them, even though no grounds existed when the encounter began. As soon as detention begins, and before searching, the officer must inform the person that they are being detained for the purpose of a search and take action in accordance with *paragraphs 3.8 to 3.11* under "Steps to be taken prior to a search".

(b) **Searches authorised under section 60 of the Criminal Justice and Public Order Act 1994**

2.12 Authority for a constable in uniform to stop and search under section 60 of the Criminal Justice and Public Order Act 1994 may be given if the authorising officer reasonably believes:

(a) that incidents involving serious violence may take place in any locality in the officer's police area, and it is expedient to use these powers to prevent their occurrence;

(b) that persons are carrying dangerous instruments or offensive weapons without good reason in any locality in the officer's police area; or

(c) that an incident involving serious violence has taken place in the officer's police area, a dangerous instrument or offensive weapon used in the incident is being carried by a person in any locality in that police area, and it is expedient to use these powers to find that instrument or weapon.

2.13   An authorisation under section 60 may only be given by an officer of the rank of inspector or above and in writing, or orally if paragraph 2.12(c) applies and it is not practicable to give the authorisation in writing. The authorisation (whether written or oral) must specify the grounds on which it was given, the locality in which the powers may be exercised and the period of time for which they are in force. The period authorised shall be no longer than appears reasonably necessary to prevent, or seek to prevent incidents of serious violence, or to deal with the problem of carrying dangerous instruments or offensive weapons or to find a dangerous instrument or offensive weapon that has been used. It may not exceed 24 hours. An oral authorisation given where paragraph 2.12(c) applies must be recorded in writing as soon as practicable. (See *Notes 10 to 13*.)

2.14   An inspector who gives an authorisation must, as soon as practicable, inform an officer of or above the rank of superintendent. This officer may direct that the authorisation shall be extended for a further 24 hours, if violence or the carrying of dangerous instruments or offensive weapons has occurred, or is suspected to have occurred, and the continued use of the powers is considered necessary to prevent or deal with further such activity or to find a dangerous instrument or offensive weapon used that has been used. That direction must be given in writing unless it is not practicable to do so, in which case it must be recorded in writing as soon as practicable afterwards. (See *Note 12*.)

2.14A   The selection of persons and vehicles under section 60 to be stopped and, if appropriate, searched should reflect an objective assessment of the nature of the incident or weapon in question and the individuals and vehicles thought likely to be associated with that incident or those weapons (see *Notes 10 and 11*). The powers must not be used to stop and search persons and vehicles for reasons unconnected with the purpose of the authorisation. When selecting persons and vehicles to be stopped in response to a specific threat or incident, officers must take care not to discriminate unlawfully against anyone on the grounds of any of the protected characteristics set out in the Equality Act 2010. (See *paragraph 1.1*.)

2.14B   The driver of a vehicle which is stopped under section 60 and any person who is searched under section 60 are entitled to a written statement to that effect if they apply within twelve months from the day the vehicle was stopped or the person was searched. This statement is a record which states that the vehicle was stopped or (as the case may be) that the person was searched under section 60 and it may form part of the search record or be supplied as a separate record.

Powers to require removal of face coverings

2.15   Section 60AA of the Criminal Justice and Public Order Act 1994 also provides a power to demand the removal of disguises. The officer exercising the power must reasonably believe that someone is wearing an item wholly or mainly for the purpose of concealing identity. There is also a power to seize such items where the officer believes that a person intends to wear them for this purpose. There is no power to stop and search for disguises. An officer may seize any such item which is discovered when exercising a power of search for something else, or which is being carried, and which the officer reasonably believes is intended to be used for concealing anyone's identity. This power can only be used if an authorisation given under section 60 or under section 60AA, is in force. (See *Note 4*.)

2.16   Authority under section 60AA for a constable in uniform to require the removal of disguises and to seize them may be given if the authorising officer reasonably believes that activities may take place in any locality in the officer's police area that are likely to involve the commission of offences and it is expedient to use these powers to prevent or control these activities.

2.17   An authorisation under section 60AA may only be given by an officer of the rank of inspector or above, in writing, specifying the grounds on which it was given, the locality in which the powers may be exercised and the period of time for which they are in force. The period authorised shall be no longer than appears reasonably necessary to prevent, or seek to prevent the commission of offences. It may not exceed 24 hours. (See *Notes 10 to 13*.)

2.18   An inspector who gives an authorisation must, as soon as practicable, inform an officer of or above the rank of superintendent. This officer may direct that the authorisation shall be extended for a further 24 hours, if crimes have been committed, or are suspected to have been committed, and the continued use of the powers is considered necessary to prevent or deal with further such activity. This direction must also be given in writing at the time or as soon as practicable afterwards. (See *Note 12*.)

(c)   **Not used**

(d)   **Searches under Schedule 5 to the Terrorism Prevention and Investigation Measures Act 2011**

2.18A   Paragraph 3 of Schedule 5 to the TPIM Act 2011 allows a constable to detain an individual to be searched under the following powers:

(i)   paragraph 6(2)(a) when a TPIM notice is being, or has just been, served on the individual for the purpose of ascertaining whether there is anything on the individual that contravenes measures specified in the notice;

(ii)   paragraph 8(2)(a) in accordance with a warrant to search the individual issued by a justice of the peace in England and Wales, a sheriff in Scotland or a lay magistrate in Northern Ireland who is satisfied that a search is necessary for the purpose of determining whether an individual in respect of whom a TPIM notice is in force is complying with measures specified in the notice (see *paragraph 2.20*); and

(iii)   paragraph 10 to ascertain whether an individual in respect of whom a TPIM notice is in force is in possession of anything that could be used to threaten or harm any person. *See paragraph 2.1(e).*

2.19   The exercise of the powers mentioned in *paragraph 2.18A* does not require the constable to have reasonable grounds to suspect that the individual:

(a)   has been, or is, contravening any of the measures specified in the TPIM notice; or

(b)   has on them anything which:

•   in the case of the power in sub-paragraph (i), contravenes measures specified in the TPIM notice;

•   in the case of the power in sub-paragraph (ii) is not complying with measures specified in the TPIM notice; or

•   in the case of the power in sub-paragraph (iii), could be used to threaten or harm any person.

2.20   A search of an individual on warrant under the power mentioned in paragraph 2.18A(ii) must carried out within 28 days of the issue of the warrant and:

•   the individual may be searched on one occasion only within that period;

•   the search must take place at a reasonable hour unless it appears that this would frustrate the purposes of the search.

2.21   *Not used.*

2.22   *Not used.*

2.23   *Not used.*

2.24   *Not used.*

2.24A   *Not used.*

2.25   *Not used.*

2.26   The powers under Schedule 5 allow a constable to conduct a search of an individual only for specified purposes relating to a TPIM notice as set out above. However, anything found may be seized and retained if there are reasonable grounds for believing that it is or it contains evidence of any offence for use at a trial for that offence or to prevent it being concealed, lost, damaged, altered, or destroyed. However, this would not prevent a search being carried out under other search powers if, in the course of exercising these powers, the officer formed reasonable grounds for suspicion.

(e)   **Powers to search persons in the exercise of a power to search premises**

2.27   The following powers to search premises also authorise the search of a person, not under arrest, who is found on the premises during the course of the search:

(a)   section 139B of the Criminal Justice Act 1988 under which a constable may enter school premises and search the premises and any person on those premises for any bladed or pointed article or offensive weapon;

(b)   under a warrant issued under section 23(3) of the Misuse of Drugs Act 1971 to search premises for drugs or documents but only if the warrant specifically authorises the search of persons found on the premises; and

(c)   under a search warrant or order issued under paragraph 1, 3 or 11 of Schedule 5 to the Terrorism Act 2000 to search premises and any person found there for material likely to be of substantial value to a terrorist investigation.

2.28   Before the power under section 139B of the Criminal Justice Act 1988 may be exercised, the constable must have reasonable grounds to suspect that an offence under section 139A or 139AA of the Criminal Justice Act 1988 (having a bladed or pointed article or offensive weapon on school premises) has been or is being committed. A warrant to search premises and persons found therein may be issued under section 23(3) of the Misuse of Drugs Act 1971 if there are reasonable grounds to suspect that controlled drugs or certain documents are in the possession of a person on the premises.

2.29   The powers in *paragraph 2.27* do not require prior specific grounds to suspect that the person to be searched is in possession of an item for which there is an existing power to search. However, it is still necessary to ensure that the selection and treatment of those searched under these powers is based upon objective factors connected with the search of the premises, and not upon personal prejudice.

3   Conduct of searches

3.1   All stops and searches must be carried out with courtesy, consideration and respect for the person concerned. This has a significant impact on public confidence in the police. Every reasonable effort must be made to minimise the embarrassment that a person being searched may experience. (See *Note 4*.)

3.2   The co-operation of the person to be searched must be sought in every case, even if the person initially objects to the search. A forcible search may be made only if it has been established that the person is unwilling to co-operate or resists. Reasonable force may be used as a last resort if necessary to conduct a search or to detain a person or vehicle for the purposes of a search.

3.3   The length of time for which a person or vehicle may be detained must be reasonable and kept to a minimum. Where the exercise of the power requires reasonable suspicion, the thoroughness and extent of a search must depend on what is suspected of being carried, and by whom. If the suspicion relates to a particular article which is seen to be slipped into a person's pocket, then, in the absence of other grounds for suspicion or an opportunity for the article to be moved elsewhere, the search must be confined to that pocket. In the case of a small article which can readily be concealed, such as a drug, and which might be concealed anywhere on the person, a more extensive search may be necessary. In the case of searches mentioned in *paragraph 2.1(b)* and *(d)*, which do not require reasonable grounds for suspicion, officers may make any reasonable search to look for items for which they are empowered to search. (See *Note 5*.)

3.4   The search must be carried out at or near the place where the person or vehicle was first detained. (See *Note 6*.)

3.5   There is no power to require a person to remove any clothing in public other than an outer coat, jacket or gloves, except under section 60AA of the Criminal Justice and Public Order Act 1994 (which empowers a constable to require a person to remove any item worn to conceal identity). (See *Notes 4* and *6*.) A search in public of a person's clothing which has not been removed must be restricted to superficial examination of outer garments. This does not, however, prevent an officer from placing his or her hand inside the pockets of the outer clothing, or feeling round the inside of collars, socks and shoes if this is reasonably necessary in the circumstances to look for the object of the search or to remove and examine any item reasonably suspected to be the object of the search. For the same reasons, subject to the restrictions on the removal of headgear, a person's hair may also be searched in public. (See *paragraphs 3.1* and *3.3*.)

3.6   Where on reasonable grounds it is considered necessary to conduct a more thorough search (e.g. by requiring a person to take off a T-shirt), this must be done out of public view, for example, in a police van unless *paragraph 3.7* applies, or police station if there is one nearby (see *Note 6*.) Any search involving the removal of more than an outer coat, jacket, gloves, headgear or footwear, or any other item concealing identity, may only be made by an officer of the same sex as the person searched and may not be made in the presence of anyone of the opposite sex unless the person being searched specifically requests it. (See *Code C Annex L* and *Notes 4* and *7*.)

3.7   Searches involving exposure of intimate parts of the body must not be conducted as a routine extension of a less thorough search, simply because nothing is found in the course of the initial search. Searches involving exposure of intimate parts of the body may be carried out only at a nearby police station or other nearby location which is out of public view (but not a police vehicle). These searches must be conducted in accordance with paragraph 11 of Annex A to Code C except that an intimate search mentioned in *paragraph 11(f) of Annex A* to Code C may not be authorised or carried out under any stop and search powers. The other provisions of Code C do not apply to the conduct and recording of searches of persons detained at police stations in the exercise of stop and search powers. (See *Note 7*.)

Steps to be taken prior to a search

3.8   Before any search of a detained person or attended vehicle takes place the officer must take reasonable steps, if not in uniform (see *paragraph 3.9*), to show their warrant card to the person to be searched or in charge of the vehicle to be searched and whether or not in uniform, to give that person the following information:

(a)   that they are being detained for the purposes of a search;

(b)   the officer's name (except in the case of enquiries linked to the investigation of terrorism, or otherwise where the officer reasonably believes that giving their name might put them in danger, in which case a warrant or other identification number shall be given) and the name of the police station to which the officer is attached;

(c)   the legal search power which is being exercised, and

(d)   a clear explanation of:

   (i)   the object of the search in terms of the article or articles for which there is a power to search; and

   (ii)   in the case of:

   •   the power under section 60 of the Criminal Justice and Public Order Act 1994 (see *paragraph 2.1(b)*), the nature of the power, the authorisation and the fact that it has been given;

   •   the powers under Schedule 5 to the Terrorism Prevention and Investigation Measures Act 2011 (see *paragraph 2.1(e)* and *2.18A*):

   —   the fact that a TPIM notice is in force or, (in the case of paragraph 6(2)(a)) that a TPIM notice is being served;

   —   the nature of the power being exercised.

   For a search under paragraph 8 of Schedule 5, the warrant must be produced and the person provided with a copy of it.

   •   all other powers requiring reasonable suspicion (see *paragraph 2.1(a)*), the grounds for that suspicion. This means explaining the basis for the suspicion by reference to information and/or intelligence about, or some specific behaviour by, the person concerned (see *paragraph 2.2*).

(e)   that they are entitled to a copy of the record of the search if one is made (see section 4 below) if they ask within 3 months from the date of the search and:

   (i)   if they are not arrested and taken to a police station as a result of the search and it is practicable to make the record on the spot, that immediately after the search is completed they will be given, if they request, either:

   •   a copy of the record; or

   •   a receipt which explains how they can obtain a copy of the full record or access to an electronic copy of the record; or

   (ii)   if they are arrested and taken to a police station as a result of the search, that the record will be made at the station as part of their custody record and they will be given, if they request, a copy of their custody record which includes a record of the search as soon as practicable whilst they are at the station. (See *Note 16*.)

3.9   Stops and searches under the power mentioned in *paragraph 2.1(b)* may be undertaken only by a constable in uniform.

3.10   The person should also be given information about police powers to stop and search and the individual's rights in these circumstances.

3.11   If the person to be searched, or in charge of a vehicle to be searched, does not appear to understand what is being said, or there is any doubt about the person's ability to understand English, the officer must take reasonable steps to bring information regarding the person's rights and any relevant provisions of this Code to his or her attention. If the person is deaf or cannot understand English and is accompanied by someone, then the officer must try to establish whether that person can interpret or otherwise help the officer to give the required information.

4   Recording requirements

(a)   Searches which do not result in an arrest

4.1   When an officer carries out a search in the exercise of any power to which this Code applies and the search does not result in the person searched or person in charge of the vehicle searched being arrested and taken to a police station, a record must be made of it, electronically or on paper, unless there are exceptional circumstances which make this wholly impracticable (e.g. in situations involving public disorder or when the recording officer's presence is urgently required elsewhere). If a record is to be made, the officer carrying out the search must make the record on the spot unless this is not practicable, in which case, the officer must make the record as soon as practicable after the search is completed. (See *Note 16*.)

4.2   If the record is made at the time, the person who has been searched or who is in charge of the vehicle that has been searched must be asked if they want a copy and if they do, they must be given immediately, either:

- a copy of the record; or
- a receipt which explains how they can obtain a copy of the full record or access to an electronic copy of the record.

4.2A   An officer is not required to provide a copy of the full record or a receipt at the time if they are called to an incident of higher priority. (See *Note 21*.)

(b)   Searches which result in an arrest

4.2B   If a search in the exercise of any power to which this Code applies results in a person being arrested and taken to a police station, the officer carrying out the search is responsible for ensuring that a record of the search is made as part of their custody record. The custody officer must then ensure that the person is asked if they want a copy of the record and, if they do, that they are given a copy as soon as practicable. (See *Note 16*.)

(c)   Record of search

4.3   The record of a search must always include the following information:

(a) A note of the self defined ethnicity, and if different, the ethnicity as perceived by the officer making the search, of the person searched or of the person in charge of the vehicle searched (as the case may be) (see *Note 18*);

(b) The date, time and place the person or vehicle was searched (see *Note 6*);

(c) The object of the search in terms of the article or articles for which there is a power to search;

(d) In the case of:

- the power under section 60 of the Criminal Justice and Public Order Act 1994 (see *paragraph 2.1(b)*), the nature of the power, the authorisation and the fact that it has been given (see Note 17);
- the powers under Schedule 5 to the Terrorism Prevention and Investigation Measures Act 2011 (see *paragraphs 2.1(e)* and *2.18A*):
  - the fact that a TPIM notice is in force or, (in the case of paragraph 6(2) (a)), that a TPIM notice is being served;
  - the nature of the power, and
  - for a search under paragraph 8, the date the search warrant was issued, the fact that the warrant was produced and a copy of it provided and the warrant must also be endorsed by the constable executing it to state whether anything was found and whether anything was seized, and
- all other powers requiring reasonable suspicion (see *paragraph 2.1(a)*), the grounds for that suspicion.

(e) subject to paragraph 3.8(b), the identity of the officer carrying out the search. (See *Note 15*.)

4.3A   For the purposes of completing the search record, there is no requirement to record the name, address and date of birth of the person searched or the person in charge of a vehicle which is searched. The person is under no obligation to provide this information and they should not be asked to provide it for the purpose of completing the record.

4.4   Nothing in *paragraph 4.3* requires the names of police officers to be shown on the search record or any other record required to be made under this Code in the case of enquiries linked to the investigation of terrorism or otherwise where an officer reasonably believes that recording names might endanger the officers. In such cases the record must show the officers' warrant or other identification number and duty station.

4.5   A record is required for each person and each vehicle searched. However, if a person is in a vehicle and both are searched, and the object and grounds of the search are the same, only one record need be completed. If more than one person in a vehicle is searched, separate records for each search of a person must be made. If only a vehicle is searched, the self-defined ethnic background of the person in charge of the vehicle must be recorded, unless the vehicle is unattended.

4.6 The record of the grounds for making a search must, briefly but informatively, explain the reason for suspecting the person concerned, by reference to information and/ or intelligence about, or some specific behaviour by, the person concerned (see *paragraph 2.2*).

4.7 Where officers detain an individual with a view to performing a search, but the need to search is eliminated as a result of questioning the person detained, a search should not be carried out and a record is not required. (See *paragraph 2.10* and *Notes 3 and 22A*.)

4.8 After searching an unattended vehicle, or anything in or on it, an officer must leave a notice in it (or on it, if things on it have been searched without opening it) recording the fact that it has been searched.

4.9 The notice must include the name of the police station to which the officer concerned is attached and state where a copy of the record of the search may be obtained and how (if applicable) an electronic copy may be accessed and where any application for compensation should be directed.

4.10 The vehicle must if practicable be left secure.

4.10A *Not used.*

4.10B *Not used.*

Recording of encounters not governed by statutory powers

4.11 *Not used*

4.12 There is no national requirement for an officer who requests a person in a public place to account for themselves, i.e. their actions, behaviour, presence in an area or possession of anything, to make any record of the encounter or to give the person a receipt. (See *paragraph 2.11* and *Notes 22A and 22B*.)

4.12A *Not used.*

4.13 *Not used.*

4.14 *Not used.*

4.15 *Not used.*

4.16 *Not used.*

4.17 *Not used.*

4.18 *Not used.*

4.19 *Not used.*

4.20 *Not used.*

5 Monitoring and supervising the use of stop and search powers

General

5.1 Any misuse of stop and search powers is likely to be harmful to policing and lead to mistrust of the police by the local community and by the public in general. Supervising officers must monitor the use of stop and search powers and should consider in particular whether there is any evidence that they are being exercised on the basis of stereotyped images or inappropriate generalisations. Supervising officers must satisfy themselves that the practice of officers under their supervision in stopping, searching and recording is fully in accordance with this Code. Supervisors must also examine whether the records reveal any trends or patterns which give cause for concern and, if so, take appropriate action to address this. (See *paragraph 2.8A*.)

5.2 Senior officers with area or force-wide responsibilities must also monitor the broader use of stop and search powers and, where necessary, take action at the relevant level.

5.3 Supervision and monitoring must be supported by the compilation of comprehensive statistical records of stops and searches at force, area and local level. Any apparently disproportionate use of the powers by particular officers or groups of officers or in relation to specific sections of the community should be identified and investigated.

5.4 In order to promote public confidence in the use of the powers, forces, in consultation with police and crime commissioners, must make arrangements for the records to be scrutinised by representatives of the community, and to explain the use of the powers at a local level. (See *Note 19*.)

Suspected misuse of powers by individual officers

5.5 Police supervisors must monitor the use of stop and search powers by individual officers to ensure that they are being applied appropriately and lawfully. Monitoring takes many forms, such as direct supervision of the exercise of the powers, examining stop and search records (particularly examining the officer's documented reasonable grounds for suspicion) and asking the officer to account for the way in which they conducted and recorded particular searches or through complaints about a stop and search that an officer has carried out.

5.6   Where a supervisor identifies issues with the way that an officer has used a stop and search power, the facts of the case will determine whether the standards of professional behaviour as set out in the Code of Ethics (see http://www.college.police.uk/en/20972.htm) have been breached and which formal action is pursued. Improper use might be a result of poor performance or a conduct matter, which will require the supervisor to take appropriate action such as performance or misconduct procedures. It is imperative that supervisors take both timely and appropriate action to deal with all such cases that come to their notice.

Notes for guidance

Officers exercising stop and search powers

1   *This Code does not affect the ability of an officer to speak to or question a person in the ordinary course of the officer's duties without detaining the person or exercising any element of compulsion. It is not the purpose of the code to prohibit such encounters between the police and the community with the co-operation of the person concerned and neither does it affect the principle that all citizens have a duty to help police officers to prevent crime and discover offenders. This is a civic rather than a legal duty; but when a police officer is trying to discover whether, or by whom, an offence has been committed he or she may question any person from whom useful information might be obtained, subject to the restrictions imposed by Code C. A person's unwillingness to reply does not alter this entitlement, but in the absence of a power to arrest, or to detain in order to search, the person is free to leave at will and cannot be compelled to remain with the officer.*

1A   *In paragraphs 1.1 and 2.2B(a), the 'relevant protected characteristics' are: age, disability, gender reassignment, pregnancy and maternity, race, religion or belief, sex and sexual orientation.*

1B   *Innocent possession means that the person does [not] have the guilty knowledge that they are carrying an unlawful item which is required before an arrest on suspicion that the person has committed an offence in respect of the item sought (if arrest is necessary - see PACE Code G) and/or a criminal prosecution) can be considered. It is not uncommon for children under the age of criminal responsibility to be used by older children and adults to carry stolen property, drugs and weapons and, in some cases, firearms, for the criminal benefit of others, either:*

•   *in the hope that police may not suspect they are being used for carrying the items; or*

•   *knowing that if they are suspected of being couriers and are stopped and searched, they cannot be arrested or prosecuted for any criminal offence.*

Stop and search powers therefore allow the police to intervene effectively to break up criminal gangs and groups that use young children to further their criminal activities.

1BA   *Whenever a child under 10 is suspected of carrying unlawful items for someone else, or is found in circumstances which suggest that their welfare and safety may be at risk, the facts should be reported and actioned in accordance with established force safeguarding procedures. This will be in addition to treating them as a potentially vulnerable or intimidated witness in respect of their status as a witness to the serious criminal offence(s) committed by those using them as couriers. Safeguarding considerations will also apply to other persons aged under 18 who are stopped and searched under any of the powers to which this Code applies. See paragraph 1.1 with regard to the requirement under the Children Act 2004, section 11, for chief police officers and other specified persons and bodies, to ensure that in the discharge of their functions, they have regard to the need to safeguard and promote the welfare of all persons under the age of 18.*

2   *In some circumstances preparatory questioning may be unnecessary, but in general a brief conversation or exchange will be desirable not only as a means of avoiding unsuccessful searches, but to explain the grounds for the stop/search, to gain co-operation and reduce any tension there might be surrounding the stop/search.*

3   *Where a person is lawfully detained for the purpose of a search, but no search in the event takes place, the detention will not thereby have been rendered unlawful.*

4   *Many people customarily cover their heads or faces for religious reasons — for example, Muslim women, Sikh men, Sikh or Hindu women, or Rastafarian men or women. A police officer cannot order the removal of a head or face covering except where there is reason to believe that the item is being worn by the individual wholly or mainly for the purpose of disguising identity, not simply because it disguises identity. Where there may be religious sensitivities about ordering the removal of such an item, the officer should permit the item*

to be removed out of public view. Where practicable, the item should be removed in the presence of an officer of the same sex as the person and out of sight of anyone of the opposite sex (see Code C Annex L).

5   A search of a person in public should be completed as soon as possible.

6   A person may be detained under a stop and search power at a place other than where the person was first detained, only if that place, be it a police station or elsewhere, is nearby. Such a place should be located within a reasonable travelling distance using whatever mode of travel (on foot or by car) is appropriate. This applies to all searches under stop and search powers, whether or not they involve the removal of clothing or exposure of intimate parts of the body (see paragraphs 3.6 and 3.7) or take place in or out of public view. It means, for example, that a search under the stop and search power in section 23 of the Misuse of Drugs Act 1971 which involves the compulsory removal of more than a person's outer coat, jacket or gloves cannot be carried out unless a place which is both nearby the place they were first detained and out of public view, is available. If a search involves exposure of intimate parts of the body and a police station is not nearby, particular care must be taken to ensure that the location is suitable in that it enables the search to be conducted in accordance with the requirements of paragraph 11 of Annex A to Code C.

7   A search in the street itself should be regarded as being in public for the purposes of paragraphs 3.6 and 3.7 above, even though it may be empty at the time a search begins. Although there is no power to require a person to do so, there is nothing to prevent an officer from asking a person voluntarily to remove more than an outer coat, jacket or gloves in public.

8   Not used.

9   Other means of identification might include jewellery, insignias, tattoos or other features which are known to identify members of the particular gang or group.

9A   A decision to search individuals believed to be members of a particular group or gang must be judged on a case by case basis according to the circumstances applicable at the time of the proposed searches and in particular, having regard to:
     (a) the number of items suspected of being carried;
     (b) the nature of those items and the risk they pose; and
     (c) the number of individuals to be searched.
     A group search will only be justified if it is a necessary and proportionate approach based on the facts and having regard to the nature of the suspicion in these cases. The extent and thoroughness of the searches must not be excessive.
     The size of the group and the number of individuals it is proposed to search will be a key factor and steps should be taken to identify those who are to be searched to avoid unnecessary inconvenience to unconnected members of the public who are also present.
     The onus is on the police to be satisfied and to demonstrate that their approach to the decision to search is in pursuit of a legitimate aim, necessary and proportionate.

Authorising officers

10   The powers under section 60 are separate from and additional to the normal stop and search powers which require reasonable grounds to suspect an individual of carrying an offensive weapon (or other article). Their overall purpose is to prevent serious violence and the widespread carrying of weapons which might lead to persons being seriously injured by disarming potential offenders or finding weapons that have been used in circumstances where other powers would not be sufficient. They should not therefore be used to replace or circumvent the normal powers for dealing with routine crime problems. A particular example might be an authorisation to prevent serious violence or the carrying of offensive weapons at a sports event by rival team supporters when the expected general appearance and age range of those likely to be responsible, alone, would not be sufficiently distinctive to support reasonable suspicion (see paragraph 2.6). The purpose of the powers under section 60AA is to prevent those involved in intimidatory or violent protests using face coverings to disguise identity.

11   Authorisations under section 60 require a reasonable belief on the part of the authorising officer. This must have an objective basis, for example: intelligence or relevant information such as a history of antagonism and violence between particular groups; previous incidents of violence at, or connected with, particular events or locations; a significant increase in knife-point robberies in a limited area; reports that individuals are regularly carrying weapons in a particular locality; information following an incident in which weapons were used about where the weapons might be found or in the case of section 60AA previous incidents of crimes being committed while wearing face coverings to conceal identity.

12   *It is for the authorising officer to determine the period of time during which the powers mentioned in paragraph 2.1(b) may be exercised. The officer should set the minimum period he or she considers necessary to deal with the risk of violence, the carrying of knives or offensive weapons, or to find dangerous instruments or weapons that have been used. A direction to extend the period authorised under the powers mentioned in paragraph 2.1(b) may be given only once. Thereafter further use of the powers requires a new authorisation.*

13   *It is for the authorising officer to determine the geographical area in which the use of the powers is to be authorised. In doing so the officer may wish to take into account factors such as the nature and venue of the anticipated incident or the incident which has taken place, the number of people who may be in the immediate area of that incident, their access to surrounding areas and the anticipated or actual level of violence. The officer should not set a geographical area which is wider than that he or she believes necessary for the purpose of preventing anticipated violence, the carrying of knives or offensive weapons, or for finding a dangerous instrument or weapon that has been used or, in the case of section 60AA, the prevention of commission of offences. It is particularly important to ensure that constables exercising such powers are fully aware of the locality within which they may be used. The officer giving the authorisation should therefore specify either the streets which form the boundary of the locality or a divisional boundary if appropriate, within the force area. If the power is to be used in response to a threat or incident that straddles police force areas, an officer from each of the forces concerned will need to give an authorisation.*

14   *Not used.*

Recording

15   *Where a stop and search is conducted by more than one officer the identity of all the officers engaged in the search must be recorded on the record. Nothing prevents an officer who is present but not directly involved in searching from completing the record during the course of the encounter.*

16   *When the search results in the person searched or in charge of a vehicle which is searched being arrested, the requirement to make the record of the search as part of the person's custody record does not apply if the person is granted "street bail" after arrest (see section 30A of PACE) to attend a police station and is not taken in custody to the police station An arrested person's entitlement to a copy of the search record which is made as part of their custody record does not affect their entitlement to a copy of their custody record or any other provisions of PACE Code C section 2 (Custody records).*

17   *It is important for monitoring purposes to specify when authority is given for exercising the stop and search power under section 60 of the Criminal Justice and Public Order Act 1994.*

18   *Officers should record the self-defined ethnicity of every person stopped according to the categories used in the 2001 census question listed in Annex B. The person should be asked to select one of the five main categories representing broad ethnic groups and then a more specific cultural background from within this group. The ethnic classification should be coded for recording purposes using the coding system in Annex B. An additional "Not stated" box is available but should not be offered to respondents explicitly. Officers should be aware and explain to members of the public, especially where concerns are raised, that this information is required to obtain a true picture of stop and search activity and to help improve ethnic monitoring, tackle discriminatory practice, and promote effective use of the powers. If the person gives what appears to the officer to be an "incorrect" answer (e.g. a person who appears to be white states that they are black), the officer should record the response that has been given and then record their own perception of the person's ethnic background by using the PNC classification system. If the "Not stated" category is used the reason for this must be recorded on the form.*

19   *Arrangements for public scrutiny of records should take account of the right to confidentiality of those stopped and searched. Anonymised forms and/or statistics generated from records should be the focus of the examinations by members of the public. The groups that are consulted should always include children and young persons.*

20   *Not used.*

21   *In situations where it is not practicable to provide a written copy of the record or immediate access to an electronic copy of the record or a receipt of the search at the time (see paragraph 4.2A above), the officer should consider giving the person details of the station which they may attend for a copy of the record. A receipt may take the form of a simple business card which includes sufficient information to locate the record should the person ask for copy, for example, the date and place of the search, and a reference number or the name of the officer who carried out the search (unless paragraph 4.4 applies).*

22   Not used.

22A   Where there are concerns which make it necessary to monitor any local disproportionality, forces have discretion to direct officers to record the self-defined ethnicity of persons they request to account for themselves in a public place or who they detain with a view to searching but do not search. Guidance should be provided locally and efforts made to minimise the bureaucracy involved. Records should be closely monitored and supervised in line with paragraphs 5.1 to 5.6, and forces can suspend or re-instate recording of these encounters as appropriate.

22B   A person who is asked to account for themselves should, if they request, be given information about how they can report their dissatisfaction about how they have been treated.

Definition of offensive weapon

23   'Offensive weapon' is defined as "any article made or adapted for use for causing injury to the person, or intended by the person having it with him for such use by him or by someone else". There are three categories of offensive weapons: those made for causing injury to the person; those adapted for such a purpose; and those not so made or adapted, but carried with the intention of causing injury to the person. A firearm, as defined by section 57 of the Firearms Act 1968, would fall within the definition of offensive weapon if any of the criteria above apply.

24   Not used.

25   Not used.

POLICE AND CRIMINAL EVIDENCE ACT 1984 (PACE)
CODE B 2013

REVISED CODE OF PRACTICE FOR SEARCHES OF PREMISES BY POLICE OFFICERS
AND THE SEIZURE OF PROPERTY FOUND BY POLICE OFFICERS
ON PERSONS OR PREMISES

Commencement – Transitional Arrangements

This Code applies to applications for warrants made after 00.00 on 27 October 2013 and to searches and seizures taking place after 00.00 on 27 October 2013.

1   Introduction

1.1   This Code of Practice deals with police powers to:
        • search premises
        • seize and retain property found on premises and persons

1.1A   These powers may be used to find:
        • property and material relating to a crime
        • wanted persons
        • children who abscond from local authority accommodation where they have been remanded or committed by a court

1.2   A justice of the peace may issue a search warrant granting powers of entry, search and seizure, e.g. warrants to search for stolen property, drugs, firearms and evidence of serious offences. Police also have powers without a search warrant. The main ones provided by the Police and Criminal Evidence Act 1984 (PACE) include powers to search premises:
        • to make an arrest
        • after an arrest

1.3   The right to privacy and respect for personal property are key principles of the Human Rights Act 1998. Powers of entry, search and seizure should be fully and clearly justified before use because they may significantly interfere with the occupier's privacy. Officers should consider if the necessary objectives can be met by less intrusive means.

1.3A   Powers to search and seize must be used fairly, responsibly, with respect for people who occupy premises being searched or are in charge of property being seized and without unlawful discrimination. Under the Equality Act 2010, section 149, when police officers are carrying out their functions, they also have a duty to have due regard to the need to eliminate unlawful discrimination, harassment and victimisation, to advance equality of opportunity between people who share a relevant protected characteristic and people who do not share it, and to take steps to foster good relations between those persons. See Note 1A.

1.4   In all cases, police should therefore:
- exercise their powers courteously and with respect for persons and property
- only use reasonable force when this is considered necessary and proportionate to the circumstances

1.5   If the provisions of PACE and this Code are not observed, evidence obtained from a search may be open to question.

Note for Guidance

1A   In paragraph 1.3A, 'relevant protected characteristic' includes: age, disability, gender reassignment, pregnancy and maternity, race, religion/belief, sex and sexual orientation.

2   General

2.1   This Code must be readily available at all police stations for consultation by:
- police officers
- police staff
- detained persons
- members of the public

2.2   The Notes for Guidance included are not provisions of this Code.

2.3   This Code applies to searches of premises:

(a)   by police for the purposes of an investigation into an alleged offence, with the occupier's consent, other than:
- routine scene of crime searches;
- calls to a fire or burglary made by or on behalf of an occupier or searches following the activation of fire or burglar alarms or discovery of insecure premises;
- searches when paragraph 5.4 applies;
- bomb threat calls;

(b)   under powers conferred on police officers by PACE, sections 17, 18 and 32;

(c)   undertaken in pursuance of search warrants issued to and executed by constables in accordance with PACE, sections 15 and 16 (see Note 2A);

(d)   subject to paragraph 2.6, under any other power given to police to enter premises with or without a search warrant for any purpose connected with the investigation into an alleged or suspected offence. (See Note 2B.)

For the purposes of this Code, 'premises' as defined in PACE, section 23, includes any place, vehicle, vessel, aircraft, hovercraft, tent or movable structure and any offshore installation as defined in the Mineral Workings (Offshore Installations) Act 1971, section 1. (See Note 2D.)

2.4   A person who has not been arrested but is searched during a search of premises should be searched in accordance with Code A. (See Note 2C.)

2.5   This Code does not apply to the exercise of a statutory power to enter premises or to inspect goods, equipment or procedures if the exercise of that power is not dependent on the existence of grounds for suspecting that an offence may have been committed and the person exercising the power has no reasonable grounds for such suspicion.

2.6   This Code does not affect any directions or requirements of a search warrant, order or other power to search and seize lawfully exercised in England or Wales that any item or evidence seized under that warrant, order or power be handed over to a police force, court, tribunal, or other authority outside England or Wales. For example, warrants and orders issued in Scotland or Northern Ireland (see Note 2B(f)) and search warrants and powers provided for in sections 14 to 17 of the Crime (International Co-operation) Act 2003.

2.7   When this Code requires the prior authority or agreement of an officer of at least inspector or superintendent rank, that authority may be given by a sergeant or chief inspector authorised to perform the functions of the higher rank under PACE, section 107.

2.8   Written records required under this Code not made in the search record shall, unless otherwise specified, be made:
- in the recording officer's pocket book ('pocket book' includes any official report book issued to police officers) or
- on forms provided for the purpose

2.9   Nothing in this Code requires the identity of officers, or anyone accompanying them during a search of premises, to be recorded or disclosed:

(a)   in the case of enquiries linked to the investigation of terrorism; or

(b)   if officers reasonably believe recording or disclosing their names might put them in danger.

In these cases officers should use warrant or other identification numbers and the name of their police station. Police staff should use any identification number provided to them by the police force. (See *Note 2E.*)

2.10 The 'officer in charge of the search' means the officer assigned specific duties and responsibilities under this Code. Whenever there is a search of premises to which this Code applies one officer must act as the officer in charge of the search. (See *Note 2F.*)

2.11 In this Code:

    (a) 'designated person' means a person other than a police officer, designated under the Police Reform Act 2002, Part 4 who has specified powers and duties of police officers conferred or imposed on them. (See *Note 2G.*)

    (b) any reference to a police officer includes a designated person acting in the exercise or performance of the powers and duties conferred or imposed on them by their designation.

    (c) a person authorised to accompany police officers or designated persons in the execution of a warrant has the same powers as a constable in the execution of the warrant and the search and seizure of anything related to the warrant. These powers must be exercised in the company and under the supervision of a police officer. (See *Note 3C.*)

2.12 If a power conferred on a designated person:

    (a) allows reasonable force to be used when exercised by a police officer, a designated person exercising that power has the same entitlement to use force;

    (b) includes power to use force to enter any premises, that power is not exercisable by that designated person except:

        (i) in the company and under the supervision of a police officer; or

        (ii) for the purpose of:
- saving life or limb; or
- preventing serious damage to property.

2.13 Designated persons must have regard to any relevant provisions of the Codes of Practice.

Notes for guidance

2A *PACE sections 15 and 16 apply to all search warrants issued to and executed by constables under any enactment, e.g. search warrants issued by a:*

    (a) justice of the peace under the:
- *Theft Act 1968, section 26 – stolen property;*
- *Misuse of Drugs Act 1971, section 23 – controlled drugs;*
- *PACE, section 8 – evidence of an indictable offence;*
- *Terrorism Act 2000, Schedule 5, paragraph 1;*
- *Terrorism Prevention and Investigation Measures Act 2011, Schedule 5, paragraph 8(2)(b) search of premises for compliance purposes (see paragraph 10.1).*

    (b) Circuit judge under:
- *PACE, Schedule 1;*
- *Terrorism Act 2000, Schedule 5, paragraph 11.*

2B *Examples of the other powers in paragraph 2.3(d) include:*

    (a) Road Traffic Act 1988, section 6E(1) giving police power to enter premises under section 6E(1) to:
- *require a person to provide a specimen of breath; or*
- *arrest a person following:*
  - *a positive breath test;*
  - *failure to provide a specimen of breath;*

    (b) Transport and Works Act 1992, section 30(4) giving police powers to enter premises mirroring the powers in (a) in relation to specified persons working on transport systems to which the Act applies;

    (c) Criminal Justice Act 1988, section 139B giving police power to enter and search school premises for offensive weapons, bladed or pointed articles;

    (d) Terrorism Act 2000, Schedule 5, paragraphs 3 and 15 empowering a superintendent in urgent cases to give written authority for police to enter and search premises for the purposes of a terrorist investigation;

    (e) Explosives Act 1875, section 73(b) empowering a superintendent to give written authority for police to enter premises, examine and search them for explosives;

(f)   *search warrants and production orders or the equivalent issued in Scotland or Northern Ireland endorsed under the Summary Jurisdiction (Process) Act 1881 or the Petty Sessions (Ireland) Act 1851 respectively for execution in England and Wales.*

(g)   *Terrorism Prevention and Investigation Measures Act 2011, Schedule 5, paragraphs 5(1), 6(2)(b) and 7(2), searches relating to TPIM notices (see paragraph 10.1).*

2C   *The Criminal Justice Act 1988, section 139B provides that a constable who has reasonable grounds to suspect an offence under the Criminal Justice Act 1988, section 139A or 139AAhas or is being committed may enter school premises and search the premises and any persons on the premises for any bladed or pointed article or offensive weapon. Persons may be searched under a warrant issued under the Misuse of Drugs Act 1971, section 23(3) to search premises for drugs or documents only if the warrant specifically authorises the search of persons on the premises. Powers to search premises under certain terrorism provisions also authorise the search of persons on the premises, for example, under paragraphs 1, 2, 11 and 15 of Schedule 5 to the Terrorism Act 2000 and section 52 of the Anti-terrorism, Crime and Security Act 2001.*

2D   *The Immigration Act 1971, Part III and Schedule 2 gives immigration officers powers to enter and search premises, seize and retain property, with and without a search warrant. These are similar to the powers available to police under search warrants issued by a justice of the peace and without a warrant under PACE, sections 17, 18, 19 and 32 except they only apply to specified offences under the Immigration Act 1971 and immigration control powers. For certain types of investigations and enquiries these powers avoid the need for the Immigration Service to rely on police officers becoming directly involved. When exercising these powers, immigration officers are required by the Immigration and Asylum Act 1999, section 145 to have regard to this Code's corresponding provisions. When immigration officers are dealing with persons or property at police stations, police officers should give appropriate assistance to help them discharge their specific duties and responsibilities.*

2E   *The purpose of paragraph 2.9(b) is to protect those involved in serious organised crime investigations or arrests of particularly violent suspects when there is reliable information that those arrested or their associates may threaten or cause harm to the officers or anyone accompanying them during a search of premises. In cases of doubt, an officer of inspector rank or above should be consulted.*

2F   *For the purposes of paragraph 2.10, the officer in charge of the search should normally be the most senior officer present. Some exceptions are:*

(a)   *a supervising officer who attends or assists at the scene of a premises search may appoint an officer of lower rank as officer in charge of the search if that officer is:*
- *more conversant with the facts;*
- *a more appropriate officer to be in charge of the search;*

(b)   *when all officers in a premises search are the same rank. The supervising officer if available, must make sure one of them is appointed officer in charge of the search, otherwise the officers themselves must nominate one of their number as the officer in charge;*

(c)   *a senior officer assisting in a specialist role. This officer need not be regarded as having a general supervisory role over the conduct of the search or be appointed or expected to act as the officer in charge of the search.*

Except in (c), nothing in this Note diminishes the role and responsibilities of a supervisory officer who is present at the search or knows of a search taking place.

2G   *An officer of the rank of inspector or above may direct a designated investigating officer not to wear a uniform for the purposes of a specific operation.*

3   Search warrants and production orders

(a)   Before making an application

3.1   When information appears to justify an application, the officer must take reasonable steps to check the information is accurate, recent and not provided maliciously or irresponsibly. An application may not be made on the basis of information from an anonymous source if corroboration has not been sought. (See *Note 3A*.)

3.2   The officer shall ascertain as specifically as possible the nature of the articles concerned and their location.

3.3   The officer shall make reasonable enquiries to:
- (i)   establish if:
  - anything is known about the likely occupier of the premises and the nature of the premises themselves;
  - the premises have been searched previously and how recently;
- (ii) obtain any other relevant information.

3.4   An application:
- (a) to a justice of the peace for a search warrant or to a Circuit judge for a search warrant or production order under PACE, Schedule 1 must be supported by a signed written authority from an officer of inspector rank or above:

  Note: If the case is an urgent application to a justice of the peace and an inspector or above is not readily available, the next most senior officer on duty can give the written authority.
- (b) to a circuit judge under the Terrorism Act 2000, Schedule 5 for:
  - a production order;
  - search warrant; or
  - an order requiring an explanation of material seized or produced under such a warrant or production order, must be supported by a signed written authority from an officer of superintendent rank or above.

3.5   Except in a case of urgency, if there is reason to believe a search might have an adverse effect on relations between the police and the community, the officer in charge shall consult the local police/community liaison officer:
- before the search; or
- in urgent cases, as soon as practicable after the search

(b)   Making an application

3.6   A search warrant application must be supported in writing, specifying:
- (a) the enactment under which the application is made (see *Note 2A*);
- (b) (i)   whether the warrant is to authorise entry and search of:
  - one set of premises; or
  - if the application is under PACE section 8, or Schedule 1, paragraph 12, more than one set of specified premises or all premises occupied or controlled by a specified person, and
  - (ii) the premises to be searched;
- (c) the object of the search (see *Note 3B*);
- (d) the grounds for the application, including, when the purpose of the proposed search is to find evidence of an alleged offence, an indication of how the evidence relates to the investigation;
- (da) Where the application is under PACE section 8, or Schedule 1, paragraph 12 for a single warrant to enter and search:
  - (i)   more than one set of specified premises; the officer must specify each set of premises which it is desired to enter and search;
  - (ii) all premises occupied or controlled by a specified person; the officer must specify;
    - as many sets of premises which it is desired to enter and search as it is reasonably practicable to specify;
    - the person who is in occupation or control of those premises and any others which it is desired to search;
    - why it is necessary to search more premises than those which can be specified, and
    - why it is not reasonably practicable to specify all the premises which it is desired to enter and search;
- (db) Whether an application under PACE section 8 is for a warrant authorising entry and search on more than one occasion, and if so, the officer must state the grounds for this and whether the desired number of entries authorised is unlimited or a specified maximum;
- (e) That there are no reasonable grounds to believe the material to be sought, when making application to a:
  - (i)   justice of the peace or a Circuit judge consists of or includes items subject to legal privilege;

(ii)   justice of the peace, consists of or includes excluded material or special procedure material;

Note: this does not affect the additional powers of seizure in the Criminal Justice and Police Act 2001, Part 2 covered in *paragraph 7.7* (see *Note 3B*).

(f)   if applicable, a request for the warrant to authorise a person or persons to accompany the officer who executes the warrant. (See *Note 3C*.)

3.7   A search warrant application under PACE, Schedule 1, paragraph 12(a), shall if appropriate indicate why it is believed service of notice of an application for a production order may seriously prejudice the investigation. Applications for search warrants under the Terrorism Act 2000, Schedule 5, paragraph 11 must indicate why a production order would not be appropriate.

3.8   If a search warrant application is refused, a further application may not be made for those premises unless supported by additional grounds.

Notes for guidance

3A   *The identity of an informant need not be disclosed when making an application, but the officer should be prepared to answer any questions the magistrate or judge may have about:*
- *the accuracy of previous information from that source, and*
- *any other related matters*

3B   *The information supporting a search warrant application should be as specific as possible, particularly in relation to the articles or persons being sought and where in the premises it is suspected they may be found. The meaning of 'items subject to legal privilege', 'excluded material' and 'special procedure material' are defined by PACE, sections 10, 11 and 14 respectively.*

3C   *Under PACE, section 16(2), a search warrant may authorise persons other than police officers to accompany the constable who executes the warrant. This includes, e.g. any suitably qualified or skilled person or an expert in a particular field whose presence is needed to help accurately identify the material sought or to advise where certain evidence is most likely to be found and how it should be dealt with. It does not give them any right to force entry, but it gives them the right to be on the premises during the search and to search for or seize property without the occupier's permission.*

4   Entry without warrant – particular powers

(a)   Making an arrest etc

4.1   The conditions under which an officer may enter and search premises without a warrant are set out in PACE, section 17. It should be noted that this section does not create or confer any powers of arrest. See other powers in *Note 2B(a)*.

(b)   Search of premises where arrest takes place or the arrested person was immediately before arrest

4.2   When a person has been arrested for an indictable offence, a police officer has power under PACE, section 32 to search the premises where the person was arrested or where the person was immediately before being arrested.

(c)   Search of premises occupied or controlled by the arrested person

4.3   The specific powers to search premises which are occupied or controlled by a person arrested for an indictable offence are set out in PACE, section 18. They may not be exercised, except if section 18(5) applies, unless an officer of inspector rank or above has given written authority. That authority should only be given when the authorising officer is satisfied that the premises are occupied or controlled by the arrested person and that the necessary grounds exist. If possible the authorising officer should record the authority on the Notice of Powers and Rights and, subject to *paragraph 2.9*, sign the Notice. The record of the grounds for the search and the nature of the evidence sought as required by section 18(7) of the Act should be made in:
- the custody record if there is one, otherwise
- the officer's pocket book, or
- the search record

5   Search with consent

5.1   Subject to *paragraph 5.4*, if it is proposed to search premises with the consent of a person entitled to grant entry the consent must, if practicable, be given in writing on the Notice of Powers and Rights before the search. The officer must make any necessary enquiries to be satisfied the person is in a position to give such consent. (See *Notes 5A* and *5B*.)

5.2   Before seeking consent the officer in charge of the search shall state the purpose of the proposed search and its extent. This information must be as specific as possible, particularly regarding the articles or persons being sought and the parts of the premises to be searched. The person concerned must be clearly informed they are not obliged to consent, that any consent given can be withdrawn at any time, including before the search starts or while it is underway and anything seized may be produced in evidence. If at the time the person is not suspected of an offence, the officer shall say this when stating the purpose of the search.

5.3   An officer cannot enter and search or continue to search premises under *paragraph 5.1* if consent is given under duress or withdrawn before the search is completed.

5.4   It is unnecessary to seek consent under *paragraphs 5.1* and *5.2* if this would cause disproportionate inconvenience to the person concerned. (See *Note 5C*.)

Notes for guidance

5A   *In a lodging house, hostel or similar accommodation, every reasonable effort should be made to obtain the consent of the tenant, lodger or occupier. A search should not be made solely on the basis of the landlord's consent.*

5B   *If the intention is to search premises under the authority of a warrant or a power of entry and search without warrant, and the occupier of the premises co-operates in accordance with paragraph 6.4, there is no need to obtain written consent.*

5C   *Paragraph 5.4 is intended to apply when it is reasonable to assume innocent occupiers would agree to, and expect, police to take the proposed action, e.g. if:*

- *a suspect has fled the scene of a crime or to evade arrest and it is necessary quickly to check surrounding gardens and readily accessible places to see if the suspect is hiding, or*
- *police have arrested someone in the night after a pursuit and it is necessary to make a brief check of gardens along the pursuit route to see if stolen or incriminating articles have been discarded.*

6   Searching premises – general considerations

(a)   Time of searches

6.1   Searches made under warrant must be made within three calendar months of the date the warrant is issued or within the period specified in the enactment under which the warrant is issued if this is shorter.

6.2   Searches must be made at a reasonable hour unless this might frustrate the purpose of the search.

6.3   When the extent or complexity of a search mean it is likely to take a long time, the officer in charge of the search may consider using the seize and sift powers referred to in *section 7*.

6.3A   A warrant under PACE, section 8 may authorise entry to and search of premises on more than one occasion if, on the application, the justice of the peace is satisfied that it is necessary to authorise multiple entries in order to achieve the purpose for which the warrant is issued. No premises may be entered or searched on any subsequent occasions without the prior written authority of an officer of the rank of inspector who is not involved in the investigation. All other warrants authorise entry on one occasion only.

6.3B   Where a warrant under PACE section 8, or Schedule 1, paragraph 12 authorises entry to and search of all premises occupied or controlled by a specified person, no premises which are not specified in the warrant may be entered and searched without the prior written authority of an officer of the rank of inspector who is not involved in the investigation.

(b)   Entry other than with consent

6.4   The officer in charge of the search shall first try to communicate with the occupier, or any other person entitled to grant access to the premises, explain the authority under which entry is sought and ask the occupier to allow entry, unless:

(i)   the search premises are unoccupied;

      (ii)   the occupier and any other person entitled to grant access are absent;

      (iii)   there are reasonable grounds for believing that alerting the occupier or any other person entitled to grant access would frustrate the object of the search or endanger officers or other people.

6.5   Unless *sub-paragraph 6.4(iii)* applies, if the premises are occupied the officer, subject to *paragraph 2.9*, shall, before the search begins:

      (i)   identify him or herself, show their warrant card (if not in uniform) and state the purpose of, and grounds for, the search, and

      (ii)   identify and introduce any person accompanying the officer on the search (such persons should carry identification for production on request) and briefly describe that person's role in the process.

6.6   Reasonable and proportionate force may be used if necessary to enter premises if the officer in charge of the search is satisfied the premises are those specified in any warrant, or in exercise of the powers described in paragraphs 4.1 to 4.3, and if:

      (i)   the occupier or any other person entitled to grant access has refused entry;

      (ii)   it is impossible to communicate with the occupier or any other person entitled to grant access; or

      (iii)   any of the provisions of *paragraph 6.4* apply.

(c)   **Notice of Powers and Rights**

6.7   If an officer conducts a search to which this Code applies the officer shall, unless it is impracticable to do so, provide the occupier with a copy of a Notice in a standard format:

      (i)   specifying if the search is made under warrant, with consent, or in the exercise of the powers described in *paragraphs 4.1* to *4.3*. Note: the notice format shall provide for authority or consent to be indicated (see *paragraphs 4.3* and *5.1*);

      (ii)   summarising the extent of the powers of search and seizure conferred by PACE and other relevant legislation as appropriate;

      (iii)   explaining the rights of the occupier and the owner of the property seized;

      (iv)   explaining compensation may be payable in appropriate cases for damages caused entering and searching premises, and giving the address to send a compensation application (see *Note 6A*), and

      (v)   stating this Code is available at any police station.

6.8   If the occupier is:

- present; copies of the Notice and warrant shall, if practicable, be given to them before the search begins, unless the officer in charge of the search reasonably believes this would frustrate the object of the search or endanger officers or other people;

- not present; copies of the Notice and warrant shall be left in a prominent place on the premises or appropriate part of the premises and endorsed, subject to *paragraph 2.9* with the name of the officer in charge of the search, the date and time of the search

      The warrant shall be endorsed to show this has been done.

(d)   **Conduct of searches**

6.9   Premises may be searched only to the extent necessary to achieve the purpose of the search, having regard to the size and nature of whatever is sought.

6.9A   A search may not continue under:

- a warrant's authority once all the things specified in that warrant have been found;

- any other power once the object of that search has been achieved.

6.9B   No search may continue once the officer in charge of the search is satisfied whatever is being sought is not on the premises (see *Note 6B*). This does not prevent a further search of the same premises if additional grounds come to light supporting a further application for a search warrant or exercise or further exercise of another power. For example, when, as a result of new information, it is believed articles previously not found or additional articles are on the premises.

6.10   Searches must be conducted with due consideration for the property and privacy of the occupier and with no more disturbance than necessary. Reasonable force may be used only when necessary and proportionate because the co-operation of the occupier cannot be obtained or is insufficient for the purpose. (See *Note 6C*.)

6.11   A friend, neighbour or other person must be allowed to witness the search if the occupier wishes unless the officer in charge of the search has reasonable grounds for believing the presence of the person asked for would seriously hinder the investigation or endanger officers or other people. A search need not be unreasonably delayed for this purpose. A record of the action taken should be made on the premises search record including the grounds for refusing the occupier's request.

6.12   A person is not required to be cautioned prior to being asked questions that are solely necessary for the purpose of furthering the proper and effective conduct of a search, see Code C, *paragraph 10.1(c)*. For example, questions to discover the occupier of specified premises, to find a key to open a locked drawer or cupboard or to otherwise seek co-operation during the search or to determine if a particular item is liable to be seized.

6.12A   If questioning goes beyond what is necessary for the purpose of the exemption in Code C, the exchange is likely to constitute an interview as defined by Code C, *paragraph 11.1A* and would require the associated safeguards included in Code C, *section 10*.

(e)   Leaving premises

6.13   If premises have been entered by force, before leaving the officer in charge of the search must make sure they are secure by:
- arranging for the occupier or their agent to be present;
- any other appropriate means.

(f)   Searches under PACE Schedule 1 or the Terrorism Act 2000, Schedule 5

6.14   An officer shall be appointed as the officer in charge of the search (see *paragraph 2.10*), in respect of any search made under a warrant issued under PACE Act 1984, Schedule 1 or the Terrorism Act 2000, Schedule 5. They are responsible for making sure the search is conducted with discretion and in a manner that causes the least possible disruption to any business or other activities carried out on the premises.

6.15   Once the officer in charge of the search is satisfied material may not be taken from the premises without their knowledge, they shall ask for the documents or other records concerned. The officer in charge of the search may also ask to see the index to files held on the premises, and the officers conducting the search may inspect any files which, according to the index, appear to contain the material sought. A more extensive search of the premises may be made only if:
- the person responsible for them refuses to:
  - produce the material sought, or
  - allow access to the index.
- it appears the index is:
  - inaccurate, or
  - incomplete.
- for any other reason the officer in charge of the search has reasonable grounds for believing such a search is necessary in order to find the material sought.

Notes for guidance

6A   *Whether compensation is appropriate depends on the circumstances in each case. Compensation for damage caused when effecting entry is unlikely to be appropriate if the search was lawful, and the force used can be shown to be reasonable, proportionate and necessary to effect entry. If the wrong premises are searched by mistake everything possible should be done at the earliest opportunity to allay any sense of grievance and there should normally be a strong presumption in favour of paying compensation.*

6B   *It is important that, when possible, all those involved in a search are fully briefed about any powers to be exercised and the extent and limits within which it should be conducted.*

6C   *In all cases the number of officers and other persons involved in executing the warrant should be determined by what is reasonable and necessary according to the particular circumstances.*

7   Seizure and retention of property

(a)   Seizure

7.1   Subject to *paragraph 7.2*, an officer who is searching any person or premises under any statutory power or with the consent of the occupier may seize anything:
(a)   covered by a warrant;

(b)   the officer has reasonable grounds for believing is evidence of an offence or has been obtained in consequence of the commission of an offence but only if seizure is necessary to prevent the items being concealed, lost, disposed of, altered, damaged, destroyed or tampered with;

(c)   covered by the powers in the Criminal Justice and Police Act 2001, Part 2 allowing an officer to seize property from persons or premises and retain it for sifting or examination elsewhere.

See *Note 7B*.

7.2   No item may be seized which an officer has reasonable grounds for believing to be subject to legal privilege, as defined in PACE, section 10, other than under the Criminal Justice and Police Act 2001, Part 2.

7.3   Officers must be aware of the provisions in the Criminal Justice and Police Act 2001, section 59, allowing for applications to a judicial authority for the return of property seized and the subsequent duty to secure in section 60. (See *paragraph 7.12(iii)*.)

7.4   An officer may decide it is not appropriate to seize property because of an explanation from the person holding it but may nevertheless have reasonable grounds for believing it was obtained in consequence of an offence by some person. In these circumstances, the officer should identify the property to the holder, inform the holder of their suspicions and explain the holder may be liable to civil or criminal proceedings if they dispose of, alter or destroy the property.

7.5   An officer may arrange to photograph, image or copy, any document or other article they have the power to seize in accordance with *paragraph 7.1*. This is subject to specific restrictions on the examination, imaging or copying of certain property seized under the Criminal Justice and Police Act 2001, Part 2. An officer must have regard to their statutory obligation to retain an original document or other article only when a photograph or copy is not sufficient.

7.6   If an officer considers information stored in any electronic form and accessible from the premises could be used in evidence, they may require the information to be produced in a form:

•   which can be taken away and in which it is visible and legible, or

•   from which it can readily be produced in a visible and legible form.

(b)   Criminal Justice and Police Act 2001: Specific procedures for seize and sift powers

7.7   The Criminal Justice and Police Act 2001, Part 2 gives officers limited powers to seize property from premises or persons so they can sift or examine it elsewhere. Officers must be careful they only exercise these powers when it is essential and they do not remove any more material than necessary. The removal of large volumes of material, much of which may not ultimately be retainable, may have serious implications for the owners, particularly when they are involved in business or activities such as journalism or the provision of medical services. Officers must carefully consider if removing copies or images of relevant material or data would be a satisfactory alternative to removing originals. When originals are taken, officers must be prepared to facilitate the provision of copies or images for the owners when reasonably practicable. (See *Note 7C*.)

7.8   Property seized under the Criminal Justice and Police Act 2001, sections 50 or 51 must be kept securely and separately from any material seized under other powers. An examination under section 53 to determine which elements may be retained must be carried out at the earliest practicable time, having due regard to the desirability of allowing the person from whom the property was seized, or a person with an interest in the property, an opportunity of being present or represented at the examination.

7.8A   All reasonable steps should be taken to accommodate an interested person's request to be present, provided the request is reasonable and subject to the need to prevent harm to, interference with, or unreasonable delay to the investigatory process. If an examination proceeds in the absence of an interested person who asked to attend or their representative, the officer who exercised the relevant seizure power must give that person a written notice of why the examination was carried out in those circumstances. If it is necessary for security reasons or to maintain confidentiality officers may exclude interested persons from decryption or other processes which facilitate the examination but do not form part of it. (See *Note 7D*.)

7.9   It is the responsibility of the officer in charge of the investigation to make sure property is returned in accordance with sections 53 to 55. Material which there is no power to retain must be:
- separated from the rest of the seized property, and
- returned as soon as reasonably practicable after examination of all the seized property.

7.9A Delay is only warranted if very clear and compelling reasons exist, for example:
- the unavailability of the person to whom the material is to be returned, or
- the need to agree a convenient time to return a large volume of material

7.9B Legally privileged, excluded or special procedure material which cannot be retained must be returned:
- as soon as reasonably practicable, and
- without waiting for the whole examination.

7.9C As set out in section 58, material must be returned to the person from whom it was seized, except when it is clear some other person has a better right to it. (See *Note 7E*.)

7.10 When an officer involved in the investigation has reasonable grounds to believe a person with a relevant interest in property seized under section 50 or 51 intends to make an application under section 59 for the return of any legally privileged, special procedure or excluded material, the officer in charge of the investigation should be informed as soon as practicable and the material seized should be kept secure in accordance with section 61. (See *Note 7C*.)

7.11 The officer in charge of the investigation is responsible for making sure property is properly secured. Securing involves making sure the property is not examined, copied, imaged or put to any other use except at the request, or with the consent, of the applicant or in accordance with the directions of the appropriate judicial authority. Any request, consent or directions must be recorded in writing and signed by both the initiator and the officer in charge of the investigation. (See *Notes 7F* and *7G*.)

7.12 When an officer exercises a power of seizure conferred by sections 50 or 51 they shall provide the occupier of the premises or the person from whom the property is being seized with a written notice:
- (i)   specifying what has been seized under the powers conferred by that section;
- (ii)   specifying the grounds for those powers;
- (iii) setting out the effect of sections 59 to 61 covering the grounds for a person with a relevant interest in seized property to apply to a judicial authority for its return and the duty of officers to secure property in certain circumstances when an application is made, and
- (iv)   specifying the name and address of the person to whom:
  - notice of an application to the appropriate judicial authority in respect of any of the seized property must be given;
  - an application may be made to allow attendance at the initial examination of the property.

7.13 If the occupier is not present but there is someone in charge of the premises, the notice shall be given to them. If no suitable person is available, so the notice will easily be found it should either be:
- left in a prominent place on the premises, or
- attached to the exterior of the premises.

(c)   Retention

7.14 Subject to *paragraph 7.15*, anything seized in accordance with the above provisions may be retained only for as long as is necessary. It may be retained, among other purposes:
- (i)   for use as evidence at a trial for an offence;
- (ii)   to facilitate the use in any investigation or proceedings of anything to which it is inextricably linked (see *Note 7H*);
- (iii) for forensic examination or other investigation in connection with an offence;
- (iv)   in order to establish its lawful owner when there are reasonable grounds for believing it has been stolen or obtained by the commission of an offence.

7.15 Property shall not be retained under *paragraph 7.14(i)*, *(ii)* or *(iii)* if a copy or image would be sufficient.

(d)   Rights of owners etc

7.16   If property is retained, the person who had custody or control of it immediately before seizure must, on request, be provided with a list or description of the property within a reasonable time.

7.17   That person or their representative must be allowed supervised access to the property to examine it or have it photographed or copied, or must be provided with a photograph or copy, in either case within a reasonable time of any request and at their own expense, unless the officer in charge of an investigation has reasonable grounds for believing this would:

(i)   prejudice the investigation of any offence or criminal proceedings; or

(ii)   lead to the commission of an offence by providing access to unlawful material such as pornography;

A record of the grounds shall be made when access is denied.

Notes for guidance

7A   *Any person claiming property seized by the police may apply to a magistrates' court under the Police (Property) Act 1897 for its possession and should, if appropriate, be advised of this procedure.*

7B   *The powers of seizure conferred by PACE, sections 18(2) and 19(3) extend to the seizure of the whole premises when it is physically possible to seize and retain the premises in their totality and practical considerations make seizure desirable. For example, police may remove premises such as tents, vehicles or caravans to a police station for the purpose of preserving evidence.*

7C   *Officers should consider reaching agreement with owners and/or other interested parties on the procedures for examining a specific set of property, rather than awaiting the judicial authority's determination. Agreement can sometimes give a quicker and more satisfactory route for all concerned and minimise costs and legal complexities.*

7D   *What constitutes a relevant interest in specific material may depend on the nature of that material and the circumstances in which it is seized. Anyone with a reasonable claim to ownership of the material and anyone entrusted with its safe keeping by the owner should be considered.*

7E   *Requirements to secure and return property apply equally to all copies, images or other material created because of seizure of the original property.*

7F   *The mechanics of securing property vary according to the circumstances; "bagging up", i.e. placing material in sealed bags or containers and strict subsequent control of access is the appropriate procedure in many cases.*

7G   *When material is seized under the powers of seizure conferred by PACE, the duty to retain it under the Code of Practice issued under the Criminal Procedure and Investigations Act 1996 is subject to the provisions on retention of seized material in PACE, section 22.*

7H   *Paragraph 7.14 (ii) applies if inextricably linked material is seized under the Criminal Justice and Police Act 2001, sections 50 or 51. Inextricably linked material is material it is not reasonably practicable to separate from other linked material without prejudicing the use of that other material in any investigation or proceedings. For example, it may not be possible to separate items of data held on computer disk without damaging their evidential integrity. Inextricably linked material must not be examined, imaged, copied or used for any purpose other than for proving the source and/or integrity of the linked material.*

8   Action after searches

8.1   If premises are searched in circumstances where this Code applies, unless the exceptions in *paragraph 2.3(a)* apply, on arrival at a police station the officer in charge of the search shall make or have made a record of the search, to include:

(i)   the address of the searched premises;

(ii)   the date, time and duration of the search;

(iii)   the authority used for the search:

•   if the search was made in exercise of a statutory power to search premises without warrant, the power which was used for the search:

•   if the search was made under a warrant or with written consent;

—   a copy of the warrant and the written authority to apply for it, see *paragraph 3.4*; or

—   the written consent;

      shall be appended to the record or the record shall show the location of the copy warrant or consent;

(iv)   subject to *paragraph 2.9*, the names of:
- the officer(s) in charge of the search;
- all other officers and authorised persons who conducted the search;

(v)   the names of any people on the premises if they are known;

(vi)   any grounds for refusing the occupier's request to have someone present during the search, see *paragraph 6.11*;

(vii)   a list of any articles seized or the location of a list and, if not covered by a warrant, the grounds for their seizure;

(viii)   whether force was used, and the reason;

(ix)   details of any damage caused during the search, and the circumstances;

(x)   if applicable, the reason it was not practicable:
    (a)   to give the occupier a copy of the Notice of Powers and Rights, see paragraph 6.7;
    (b)   before the search to give the occupier a copy of the Notice, see *paragraph 6.8*;

(xi)   when the occupier was not present, the place where copies of the Notice of Powers and Rights and search warrant were left on the premises, see *paragraph 6.8*.

8.2   On each occasion when premises are searched under warrant, the warrant authorising the search on that occasion shall be endorsed to show:

(i)   if any articles specified in the warrant were found and the address where found;

(ii)   if any other articles were seized;

(iii)   the date and time it was executed and if present, the name of the occupier or if the occupier is not present the name of the person in charge of the premises;

(iv)   subject to *paragraph 2.9*, the names of the officers who executed it and any authorised persons who accompanied them, and

(v)   if a copy, together with a copy of the Notice of Powers and Rights was:
- handed to the occupier, or
- endorsed as required by *paragraph 6.8*; and left on the premises and where.

8.3   Any warrant shall be returned within three calendar months of its issue or sooner on completion of the search(es) authorised by that warrant, if it was issued by a:
- justice of the peace, to the designated officer for the local justice area in which the justice was acting when issuing the warrant; or
- judge, to the appropriate officer of the court concerned,

9   Search registers

9.1   A search register will be maintained at each sub-divisional or equivalent police station. All search records required under *paragraph 8.1* shall be made, copied, or referred to in the register. (See *Note 9A*.)

Note for guidance

9A   *Paragraph 9.1 also applies to search records made by immigration officers. In these cases, a search register must also be maintained at an immigration office. (See also Note 2D.)*

10   Searches under Schedule 5 to the Terrorism Prevention and Investigation Measures Act 2011

10.1   This Code applies to the powers of constables under Schedule 5 to the Terrorism Prevention and Investigation Measures Act 2011 relating to TPIM notices to enter and search premises subject to the modifications in the following paragraphs.

10.2   In paragraph 2.3(d), the reference to the investigation into an alleged or suspected offence include the enforcement of terrorism prevention and investigation measures which may be imposed on an individual by a TPIM notice in accordance with the Terrorism Prevention and Investigation Measures Act 2011.

10.3   References to the purpose and object of the entry and search of premises, the nature of articles sought and what may be seized and retained include (as appropriate):

(a)   in relation to the power to search *without a search warrant in paragraph 5* (for purposes of serving TPIM notice), finding the individual on whom the notice is to be served.

(b)   in relation to the power to search *without a search warrant in paragraph 6* (at time of serving TPIM notice), ascertaining whether there is anything in the premises, that contravenes measures specified in the notice. (See *Note 10A*.)

(c) in relation to the power to search *without a search warrant* under *paragraph 7* (suspected absconding), ascertaining whether a person has absconded or if there is anything on the premises which will assist in the pursuit or arrest of an individual in respect of whom a TPIM notice is force who is reasonably suspected of having absconded.

(d) in relation to the power to search *under a search warrant* issued under *paragraph 8* (for compliance purposes), determining whether an individual in respect of whom a TPIM notice is in force is complying with measures specified in the notice. (See *Note 10A*.)

Note for guidance

10A *Searches of individuals under Schedule 5, paragraphs 6(2)(a) (at time of serving TPIM notice) and 8(2)(a) (for compliance purposes) must be conducted and recorded in accordance with Code A. See Code A paragraph 2.18A for details.*

POLICE AND CRIMINAL EVIDENCE ACT 1984 (PACE) CODE C 2017

REVISED CODE OF PRACTICE FOR THE DETENTION, TREATMENT AND QUESTIONING OF PERSONS BY POLICE OFFICERS

Commencement - Transitional Arrangements

This Code applies to people in police detention after 00.00 on 23 February 2017, notwithstanding that their period of detention may have commenced before that time.

1 General

1.0 The powers and procedures in this Code must be used fairly, responsibly, with respect for the people to whom they apply and without unlawful discrimination. Under the Equality Act 2010, section 149 (Public sector Equality Duty), police forces must, in carrying out their functions, have due regard to the need to eliminate unlawful discrimination, harassment, victimisation and any other conduct which is prohibited by that Act, to advance equality of opportunity between people who share a relevant protected characteristic and people who do not share it, and to foster good relations between those persons. The Equality Act also makes it unlawful for police officers to discriminate against, harass or victimise any person on the grounds of the 'protected characteristics' of age, disability, gender reassignment, race, religion or belief, sex and sexual orientation, marriage and civil partnership, pregnancy and maternity, when using their powers. See *Notes 1A* and *1AA*.

1.1 All persons in custody must be dealt with expeditiously, and released as soon as the need for detention no longer applies.

1.1A A custody officer must perform the functions in this Code as soon as practicable. A custody officer will not be in breach of this Code if delay is justifiable and reasonable steps are taken to prevent unnecessary delay. The custody record shall show when a delay has occurred and the reason. See *Note 1H*.

1.2 This Code of Practice must be readily available at all police stations for consultation by: police officers;
- police staff;
- detained persons;
- members of the public.

1.3 The provisions of this Code:
- include the *Annexes*
- do not include the *Notes for Guidance*.

1.4 If an officer has any suspicion, or is told in good faith, that a person of any age may be mentally disordered or otherwise mentally vulnerable, in the absence of clear evidence to dispel that suspicion, the person shall be treated as such for the purposes of this Code. See *Note 1G*.

1.5 Anyone who appears to be under 18, shall, in the absence of clear evidence that they are older and subject to *paragraph 1.5A*, be treated as a juvenile for the purposes of this Code and any other Code. See *Note 1L*

1.5A *Paragraph 1.5* does not change the statutory provisions in section 65(1) of PACE (appropriate consent) which require the consent of a juvenile's parent or guardian.

In this Code, section 65(1) is relevant to Annex A *paragraphs 2(b) and 2B* (Intimate searches) and *Annex K paragraphs 1(b) and 3* (X-Ray and ultrasound scan). In Code D (Identification), section 65(1) is relevant to para*graph 2.12* and *Note 2A*, which apply to identification procedures, to taking fingerprints, samples, footwear impressions, photographs and to evidential searches and examinations.

1.6 If a person appears to be blind, seriously visually impaired, deaf, unable to read or speak or has difficulty orally because of a speech impediment, they shall be treated as such for the purposes of this Code in the absence of clear evidence to the contrary.

1.7 'The appropriate adult' means, in the case of a:

  (a) juvenile:

    (i) the parent, guardian or, if the juvenile is in the care of a local authority or voluntary organisation, a person representing that authority or organisation (see *Note 1B*);

    (ii) a social worker of a local authority (see *Note 1C*);

    (iii) failing these, some other responsible adult aged 18 or over who is *not*:

      — a police officer;

      — employed by the police;

      — under the direction or control of the chief officer of a police force; or

      — a person who provides services under contractual arrangements (but without being employed by the chief officer of a police force), to assist that force in relation to the discharge of its chief officer's functions,

    whether or not they are on duty at the time.

    See *Note 1F*.

  (b) person who is mentally disordered or mentally vulnerable: See *Note 1D*.

    (i) a relative, guardian or other person responsible for their care or custody;

    (ii) someone experienced in dealing with mentally disordered or mentally vulnerable people but who is not:

      — a police officer;

      — employed by the police;

      — under the direction or control of the chief officer of a police force; or

      — a person who provides services under contractual arrangements (but without being employed by the chief officer of a police force), to assist that force in relation to the discharge of its chief officer's functions,

    whether or not they are on duty at the time;

    (iii) failing these, some other responsible adult aged 18 or over other than a person described in the bullet points in *sub-paragraph (b)(ii)* above.

    See *Note 1F*.

1.8 If this Code requires a person be given certain information, they do not have to be given it if at the time they are incapable of understanding what is said, are violent or may become violent or in urgent need of medical attention, but they must be given it as soon as practicable.

1.9 References to a custody officer include any police officer who, for the time being, is performing the functions of a custody officer.

1.9A When this Code requires the prior authority or agreement of an officer of at least inspector or superintendent rank, that authority may be given by a sergeant or chief inspector authorised to perform the functions of the higher rank under the Police and Criminal Evidence Act 1984 (PACE), section 107.

1.10 Subject to *paragraph 1.12*, this Code applies to people in custody at police stations in England and Wales, whether or not they have been arrested, and to those removed to a police station as a place of safety under the Mental Health Act 1983, sections 135 and 136, as a last resort (see paragraph 3.16). *Section 15* applies solely to people in police detention, e.g. those brought to a police station under arrest or arrested at a police station for an offence after going there voluntarily.

1.11   No part of this Code applies to a detained person:
        (a) to whom PACE Code H applies because:
              • they are detained following arrest under section 41 of the Terrorism Act 2000 (TACT) and not charged; or
              • an authorisation has been given under section 22 of the Counter-Terrorism Act 2008 (CTACT) (post-charge questioning of terrorist suspects) to interview them.
        (b) to whom the Code of Practice issued under paragraph 6 of Schedule 14 to TACT applies because they are detained for examination under Schedule 7 to TACT.

1.12   This Code does not apply to people in custody:
        (i)   arrested by officers under the Criminal Justice and Public Order Act 1994, section 136(2) on warrants issued in Scotland, or arrested or detained without warrant under section 137(2) by officers from a police force in Scotland. In these cases, police powers and duties and the person's rights and entitlements whilst at a police station in England or Wales are the same as those in Scotland;
        (ii)   arrested under the Immigration and Asylum Act 1999, section 142(3) in order to have their fingerprints taken;
        (iii) whose detention has been authorised under Schedules 2 or 3 to the Immigration Act 1971 or section 62 of the Nationality, Immigration and Asylum Act 2002;
        (iv)   who are convicted or remanded prisoners held in police cells on behalf of the Prison Service under the Imprisonment (Temporary Provisions) Act 1980;
        (v)   Not used.
        (vi)   detained for searches under stop and search powers except as required by Code A.
        The provisions on conditions of detention and treatment in *sections 8* and *9* must be considered as the minimum standards of treatment for such detainees.

1.13   In this Code:
        (a) 'designated person' means a person other than a police officer, who has specified powers and duties conferred or imposed on them by designation under section 38 or 39 of the Police Reform Act 2002;
        (b) reference to a police officer includes a designated person acting in the exercise or performance of the powers and duties conferred or imposed on them by their designation;
        (c) where a search or other procedure to which this Code applies may only be carried out or observed by a person of the same sex as the detainee, the gender of the detainee and other parties present should be established and recorded in line with Annex L of this Code.

1.14   Designated persons are entitled to use reasonable force as follows:
        (a) when exercising a power conferred on them which allows a police officer exercising that power to use reasonable force, a designated person has the same entitlement to use force; and
        (b) at other times when carrying out duties conferred or imposed on them that also entitle them to use reasonable force, for example:
              • when at a police station carrying out the duty to keep detainees for whom they are responsible under control and to assist any police officer or designated person to keep any detainee under control and to prevent their escape;
              • when securing, or assisting any police officer or designated person in securing, the detention of a person at a police station;
              • when escorting, or assisting any police officer or designated person in escorting, a detainee within a police station;
              • for the purpose of saving life or limb; or
              • preventing serious damage to property.

1.15   Nothing in this Code prevents the custody officer, or other police officer or designated person (see *paragraph 1.13*) given custody of the detainee by the custody officer, from allowing another person (see *(a)* and *(b)* below) to carry out individual procedures or tasks at the police station if the law allows. However, the officer or designated person given custody remains responsible for making sure the procedures and tasks are carried out correctly in accordance with the Codes of Practice (see *paragraph 3.5* and *Note 3F*). The other person who is allowed to carry out the procedures or tasks must be someone who *at that time*, is:

(a) under the direction and control of the chief officer of the force responsible for the police station in question; or

(b) providing services under contractual arrangements (but without being employed by the chief officer the police force), to assist a police force in relation to the discharge of its chief officer's functions.

1.16 Designated persons and others mentioned in *sub-paragraphs (a)* and *(b)* of *paragraph 1.15,* must have regard to any relevant provisions of the Codes of Practice.

1.17 In any provision of this or any other Code which allows or requires police officers or police staff to make a record in their report book, the reference to report book shall include any official report book or electronic recording device issued to them that enables the record in question to be made and dealt with in accordance with that provision. References in this and any other Code to written records, forms and signatures include electronic records and forms and electronic confirmation that identifies the person making the record or completing the form.

Chief officers must be satisfied as to the integrity and security of the devices, records and forms to which this *paragraph* applies and that use of those devices, records and forms satisfies relevant data protection legislation.

Notes for Guidance

1A *Although certain sections of this Code apply specifically to people in custody at police stations, those there voluntarily to assist with an investigation should be treated with no less consideration, e.g. offered refreshments at appropriate times, and enjoy an absolute right to obtain legal advice or communicate with anyone outside the police station.*

1AA *In paragraph 1.0, under the Equality Act 2010, section 149, the 'relevant protected characteristics' are age, disability, gender reassignment, pregnancy and maternity, race, religion/belief and sex and sexual orientation. For further detailed guidance and advice on the Equality Act, see: https://www.gov.uk/guidance/equality-act-2010-guidance.*

1B *A person, including a parent or guardian, should not be an appropriate adult if they:*
- *are:*
  - — *suspected of involvement in the offence; the victim;*
  - — *a witness;*
  - — *involved in the investigation.*
- *received admissions prior to attending to act as the appropriate adult.*

Note: If a juvenile's parent is estranged from the juvenile, they should not be asked to act as the appropriate adult if the juvenile expressly and specifically objects to their presence.

1C *If a juvenile admits an offence to, or in the presence of, a social worker or member of a youth offending team other than during the time that person is acting as the juvenile's appropriate adult, another appropriate adult should be appointed in the interest of fairness.*

1D *In the case of people who are mentally disordered or otherwise mentally vulnerable, it may be more satisfactory if the appropriate adult is someone experienced or trained in their care rather than a relative lacking such qualifications. But if the detainee prefers a relative to a better qualified stranger or objects to a particular person their wishes should, if practicable, be respected.*

1E *A detainee should always be given an opportunity, when an appropriate adult is called to the police station, to consult privately with a solicitor in the appropriate adult's absence if they want. An appropriate adult is not subject to legal privilege.*

1F *A solicitor or independent custody visitor who is present at the police station and acting in that capacity, may not be the appropriate adult.*

1G *'Mentally vulnerable' applies to any detainee who, because of their mental state or capacity, may not understand the significance of what is said, of questions or of their replies. 'Mental disorder' is defined in the Mental Health Act 1983, section 1(2) as 'any disorder or disability of mind'. When the custody officer has any doubt about the mental state or capacity of a detainee, that detainee should be treated as mentally vulnerable and an appropriate adult called.*

1H *Paragraph 1.1A is intended to cover delays which may occur in processing detainees e.g. if:*
- *a large number of suspects are brought into the station simultaneously to be placed in custody;*
- *interview rooms are all being used;*
- *there are difficulties contacting an appropriate adult, solicitor or interpreter.*

1I   *The custody officer must remind the appropriate adult and detainee about the right to legal advice and record any reasons for waiving it in accordance with section 6.*

1J   *Not used.*

1K   *This Code does not affect the principle that all citizens have a duty to help police officers to prevent crime and discover offenders. This is a civic rather than a legal duty; but when police officers are trying to discover whether, or by whom, offences have been committed they are entitled to question any person from whom they think useful information can be obtained, subject to the restrictions imposed by this Code. A person's declaration that they are unwilling to reply does not alter this entitlement.*

1L   *Paragraph 1.5 reflects the statutory definition of 'arrested juvenile' in section 37(15) of PACE. This section was amended by section 42 of the Criminal Justice and Courts Act 2015 with effect from 26 October 2015, and includes anyone who appears to be under the age of 18. This definition applies for the purposes of the detention and bail provisions in sections 34 to 51 of PACE.*

1M   *Not used.*

2   Custody records

2.1A   When a person:
- is brought to a police station under arrest
- is arrested at the police station having attended there voluntarily or
- attends a police station to answer bail

they must be brought before the custody officer as soon as practicable after their arrival at the station or if applicable, following their arrest after attending the police station voluntarily. This applies to both designated and non-designated police stations. A person is deemed to be "at a police station" for these purposes if they are within the boundary of any building or enclosed yard which forms part of that police station.

2.1   A separate custody record must be opened as soon as practicable for each person brought to a police station under arrest or arrested at the station having gone there voluntarily or attending a police station in answer to street bail. All information recorded under this Code must be recorded as soon as practicable in the custody record unless otherwise specified. Any audio or video recording made in the custody area is not part of the custody record.

2.2   If any action requires the authority of an officer of a specified rank, subject to *paragraph 2.6A*, their name and rank must be noted in the custody record.

2.3   The custody officer is responsible for the custody record's accuracy and completeness and for making sure the record or copy of the record accompanies a detainee if they are transferred to another police station. The record shall show the:
- time and reason for transfer;
- time a person is released from detention.

2.3A   If a person is arrested and taken to a police station as a result of a search in the exercise of any stop and search power to which PACE Code A (Stop and search) or the 'search powers code' issued under TACT applies, the officer carrying out the search is responsible for ensuring that the record of that stop and search is made as part of the person's custody record. The custody officer must then ensure that the person is asked if they want a copy of the search record and if they do, that they are given a copy as soon as practicable. The person's entitlement to a copy of the search record which is made as part of their custody record is in addition to, and does not affect, their entitlement to a copy of their custody record or any other provisions of section 2 (Custody records) of this Code. (See Code A *paragraph 4.2B* and the TACT search powers code *paragraph 5.3.5*).

2.4   The detainee's solicitor and appropriate adult must be permitted to inspect the whole of the detainee's custody record as soon as practicable after their arrival at the station and at any other time on request, whilst the person is detained. This includes the following *specific* records relating to the reasons for the detainee's arrest and detention and the offence concerned to which *paragraph 3.1(b)* refers:
     (a)   The information about the circumstances and reasons for the detainee's arrest as recorded in the custody record in accordance with *paragraph 4.3 of Code G*. This applies to any further offences for which the detainee is arrested whilst in custody;
     (b)   The record of the grounds for each authorisation to keep the person in custody. The authorisations to which this applies are the same as those described at items *(i)(a)* to *(d)* in the table in *paragraph 2 of Annex M* of this Code.

Access to the records in *sub-paragraphs (a)* and *(b)* is *in addition* to the requirements in *paragraphs 3.4(b), 11.1A, 15.0, 15,7A(c) and 16.7A* to make certain documents and materials available and to provide information about the offence and the reasons for arrest and detention.

Access to the custody record for the purposes of this paragraph must be arranged and agreed with the custody officer and may not unreasonably interfere with the custody officer's duties. A record shall be made when access is allowed and whether it includes the records described in *sub-paragraphs (a)* and *(b)* above.

2.4A When a detainee leaves police detention or is taken before a court they, their legal representative or appropriate adult shall be given, on request, a copy of the custody record as soon as practicable. This entitlement lasts for 12 months after release.

2.5 The detainee, appropriate adult or legal representative shall be permitted to inspect the original custody record after the detainee has left police detention provided they give reasonable notice of their request. Any such inspection shall be noted in the custody record.

2.6 Subject to *paragraph 2.6A*, all entries in custody records must be timed and signed by the maker. Records entered on computer shall be timed and contain the operator's identification.

2.6A Nothing in this Code requires the identity of officers or other police staff to be recorded or disclosed:

(a) *Not used.*

(b) if the officer or police staff reasonably believe recording or disclosing their name might put them in danger.

In these cases, they shall use their warrant or other identification numbers and the name of their police station. See *Note 2A*.

2.7 The fact and time of any detainee's refusal to sign a custody record, when asked in accordance with this Code, must be recorded.

Note for Guidance

2A *The purpose of paragraph 2.6A(b) is to protect those involved in serious organised crime investigations or arrests of particularly violent suspects when there is reliable information that those arrested or their associates may threaten or cause harm to those involved. In cases of doubt, an officer of inspector rank or above should be consulted.*

3 Initial action

(a) Detained persons – normal procedure

3.1 When a person is brought to a police station under arrest or arrested at the station having gone there voluntarily, the custody officer must make sure the person is told clearly about:

(a) the following continuing rights, which may be exercised at any stage during the period in custody:

(i) their right to consult privately with a solicitor and that free independent legal advice is available as in *section 6*;

(ii) their right to have someone informed of their arrest as in *section 5*;

(iii) their right to consult the Codes of Practice (see *Note 3D*); and

(iv) if applicable, their right to interpretation and translation (see *paragraph 3.12*) and their right to communicate with their High Commission, Embassy or Consulate (see *paragraph 3.12A*).

(b) their right to be informed about the offence and (as the case may be) any further offences for which they are arrested whilst in custody and why they have been arrested and detained in accordance with *paragraphs 2.4, 3.4(a)* and *11.1A* of this Code and *paragraph 3.3* of *Code G*.

3.2 The detainee must also be given a written notice, which contains information:

(a) to allow them to exercise their rights by setting out:

(i) their rights under *paragraph 3.1, paragraph 3.12* and *3.12A*;

(ii) the arrangements for obtaining legal advice, see *section 6*;

(iii) their right to a copy of the custody record as in *paragraph 2.4A*;

(iv) their right to remain silent as set out in the caution in the terms prescribed in *section 10*;

>   (v)   their right to have access to materials and documents which are essential to effectively challenging the lawfulness of their arrest and detention for any offence and (as the case may be) any further offences for which they are arrested whilst in custody, in accordance with *paragraphs 3.4(b), 15.0, 15.7A(c)* and *16.7A* of this Code;
>
>   (vi)   the maximum period for which they may be kept in police detention without being charged, when detention must be reviewed and when release is required;
>
>   (vii)   their right to medical assistance in accordance with *section 9* of this Code;
>
>   (viii)   their right, if they are prosecuted, to have access to the evidence in the case before their trial in accordance with the Criminal Procedure and Investigations Act 1996, the Attorney General's Guidelines on Disclosure, the common law and the Criminal Procedure Rules; and

    (b)   briefly setting out their other entitlements while in custody, by:

>   (i)   mentioning:
> - the provisions relating to the conduct of interviews;
> - the circumstances in which an appropriate adult should be available to assist the detainee and their statutory rights to make representations whenever the need for their detention is reviewed;
>
>   (ii)   listing the entitlements in this Code, concerning;
> - reasonable standards of physical comfort;
> - adequate food and drink;
> - access to toilets and washing facilities, clothing, medical attention, and exercise when practicable.

    See *Note 3A*.

3.2A   The detainee must be given an opportunity to read the notice and shall be asked to sign the custody record to acknowledge receipt of the notice. Any refusal to sign must be recorded on the custody record.

3.3   *Not used.*

3.3A   An 'easy read' illustrated version should also be provided if available (see *Note 3A*).

3.4   (a)   The custody officer shall:

- record the offence(s) that the detainee has been arrested for and the reason(s) for the arrest on the custody record. See *paragraph 10.3 and Code G paragraphs 2.2 and 4.3*;
- note on the custody record any comment the detainee makes in relation to the arresting officer's account but shall not invite comment. If the arresting officer is not physically present when the detainee is brought to a police station, the arresting officer's account must be made available to the custody officer remotely or by a third party on the arresting officer's behalf. If the custody officer authorises a person's detention, subject to *paragraph 1.8*, that officer must record the grounds for detention in the detainee's presence and at the same time, inform them of the grounds. The detainee must be informed of the grounds for their detention before they are questioned about any offence;
- note any comment the detainee makes in respect of the decision to detain them but shall not invite comment;
- not put specific questions to the detainee regarding their involvement in any offence, nor in respect of any comments they may make in response to the arresting officer's account or the decision to place them in detention. Such an exchange is likely to constitute an interview as in *paragraph 11.1A* and require the associated safeguards in *section 11*.

    Note: This *sub-paragraph* also applies to any further offences and grounds for detention which come to light whilst the person is detained.

    See *paragraph 11.13* in respect of unsolicited comments.

    (b)   Documents and materials which are essential to effectively challenging the lawfulness of the detainee's arrest and detention must be made available to the detainee or their solicitor. Documents and materials will be "essential" for this purpose if they are capable of undermining the reasons and grounds which make the detainee's arrest and detention *necessary*. The decision about whether particular documents or materials must be made available for the purpose of this requirement therefore rests with the custody officer who determines whether detention is necessary, in consultation with the investigating officer who has the knowledge of the documents and materials in a particular case necessary to inform that decision. A note should be made in the detainee's custody record of the *fact* that documents or materials have been made available under this sub-paragraph and when. The investigating officer should make a separate note of what is made available and how it is made available in a particular case. This sub-paragraph also applies (with modifications) for the purposes of *sections 15 (Reviews and extensions of detention)* and *16 (Charging detained persons)*. See *Note 3ZA* and *paragraphs 15.0* and *16.7A*.

3.5   The custody officer or other custody staff as directed by the custody officer shall:
   (a)   ask the detainee whether at this time, they:
      (i)   would like legal advice, see *paragraph 6.5*;
      (ii)   want someone informed of their detention, see *section 5*;
   (b)   ask the detainee to sign the custody record to confirm their decisions in respect of (a);
   (c)   determine whether the detainee:
      (i)   is, or might be, in need of medical treatment or attention, see *section 9*;
      (ii)   requires:
      •   an appropriate adult (see *paragraphs 1.4, 1.5, 1.5A* and *3.15*);
      •   help to check documentation (see *paragraph 3.20*);
      •   an interpreter (see *paragraph 3.12 and Note 13B*).
   (d)   record the decision in respect of (c).
      Where any duties under this paragraph have been carried out by custody staff at the direction of the custody officer, the outcomes shall, as soon as practicable, be reported to the custody officer who retains overall responsibility for the detainee's care and treatment and ensuring that it complies with this Code. See *Note 3F*.

3.6   When the needs mentioned in *paragraph 3.5(c)* are being determined, the custody officer is responsible for initiating an assessment to consider whether the detainee is likely to present specific risks to custody staff, any individual who may have contact with detainee (e.g. legal advisers, medical staff) or themselves. This risk assessment must include the taking of reasonable steps to establish the detainee's identity and to obtain information about the detainee that is relevant to their safe custody, security and welfare and risks to others. Such assessments should therefore always include a check on the Police National Computer (PNC), to be carried out as soon as practicable, to identify any risks that have been highlighted in relation to the detainee. Although such assessments are primarily the custody officer's responsibility, it may be necessary for them to consult and involve others, e.g. the arresting officer or an appropriate healthcare professional, see *paragraph 9.13*. Other records held by or on behalf of the police and other UK law enforcement authorities that might provide information relevant to the detainee's safe custody, security and welfare and risk to others and to confirming their identity should also be checked. Reasons for delaying the initiation or completion of the assessment must be recorded.

3.7   Chief officers should ensure that arrangements for proper and effective risk assessments required by *paragraph 3.6* are implemented in respect of all detainees at police stations in their area.

3.8   Risk assessments must follow a structured process which clearly defines the categories of risk to be considered and the results must be incorporated in the detainee's custody record. The custody officer is responsible for making sure those responsible for the detainee's custody are appropriately briefed about the risks. If no specific risks are identified by the assessment, that should be noted in the custody record. See *Note 3E* and *paragraph 9.14*.

3.8A   The content of any risk assessment and any analysis of the level of risk relating to the person's detention is not required to be shown or provided to the detainee or any person acting on behalf of the detainee. But information should not be withheld from any person acting on the detainee's behalf, for example, an appropriate adult, solicitor or interpreter, if to do so might put that person at risk.

3.9   The custody officer is responsible for implementing the response to any specific risk assessment, e.g.:
   •   reducing opportunities for self harm;
   •   calling an appropriate healthcare professional;
   •   increasing levels of monitoring or observation;
   •   reducing the risk to those who come into contact with the detainee.
   See *Note 3E*.

3.10   Risk assessment is an ongoing process and assessments must always be subject to review if circumstances change.

3.11   If video cameras are installed in the custody area, notices shall be prominently displayed showing cameras are in use. Any request to have video cameras switched off shall be refused.

(b)   *Detained persons – special groups*

3.12   If the detainee appears to be someone who does not speak or understand English or who has a hearing or speech impediment, the custody officer must ensure:

(a)   that without delay, arrangements *(see paragraph 13.1ZA)* are made for the detainee to have the assistance of an interpreter in the action under *paragraphs 3.1 to 3.5*. If the person appears to have a hearing or speech impediment, the reference to 'interpreter' includes appropriate assistance necessary to comply with *paragraphs 3.1 to 3.5*. See *paragraph 13.1C* if the detainee is in Wales. See *section 13* and *Note 13B;*

(b)   that in addition to the continuing rights set out in *paragraph 3.1(a)(i)* to *(iv)*, the detainee is told clearly about their right to interpretation and translation;

(c)   that the written notice given to the detainee in accordance with *paragraph 3.2* is in a language the detainee understands and includes the right to interpretation and translation together with information about the provisions in *section 13* and *Annex M*, which explain how the right applies (see *Note 3A*); and

(d)   that if the translation of the notice is not available, the information in the notice is given through an interpreter and a written translation provided without undue delay.

3.12A   If the detainee is a citizen of an independent Commonwealth country or a national of a foreign country, including the Republic of Ireland, the custody officer must ensure that in addition to the continuing rights set out in *paragraph 3.1(a)(i)* to *(iv)*, they are informed as soon as practicable about their rights of communication with their High Commission, Embassy or Consulate set out in *section 7*. This right must be included in the written notice given to the detainee in accordance with *paragraph 3.2*.

3.13   If the detainee is a juvenile, the custody officer must, if it is practicable, ascertain the identity of a person responsible for their welfare. That person:

- may be:
  - the parent or guardian;
  - if the juvenile is in local authority or voluntary organisation care, or is otherwise being looked after under the Children Act 1989, a person appointed by that authority or organisation to have responsibility for the juvenile's welfare;
  - any other person who has, for the time being, assumed responsibility for the juvenile's welfare.
- must be informed as soon as practicable that the juvenile has been arrested, why they have been arrested and where they are detained. This right is in addition to the juvenile's right in *section 5* not to be held incommunicado. See *Note 3C*.

3.14   If a juvenile is known to be subject to a court order under which a person or organisation is given any degree of statutory responsibility to supervise or otherwise monitor them, reasonable steps must also be taken to notify that person or organisation (the 'responsible officer'). The responsible officer will normally be a member of a Youth Offending Team, except for a curfew order which involves electronic monitoring when the contractor providing the monitoring will normally be the responsible officer.

3.15   If the detainee is a juvenile, mentally disordered or otherwise mentally vulnerable, the custody officer must, as soon as practicable:

- inform the appropriate adult, who in the case of a juvenile may or may not be a person responsible for their welfare, as in *paragraph 3.13*, of:
  - the grounds for their detention;
  - their whereabouts.
- ask the adult to come to the police station to see the detainee.

3.16   It is imperative that a mentally disordered or otherwise mentally vulnerable person, detained under the Mental Health Act 1983, section 136, be assessed as soon as possible. A police station should only be used as a place of safety as a last resort but if that assessment is to take place at the police station, an approved mental health professional and a registered medical practitioner shall be called to the station as soon as possible to carry it out. See

Note 9D. The appropriate adult has no role in the assessment process and their presence is not required. Once the detainee has been assessed and suitable arrangements made for their treatment or care, they can no longer be detained under section 136. A detainee must be immediately discharged from detention under section 136 if a registered medical practitioner, having examined them, concludes they are not mentally disordered within the meaning of the Act.

3.17 If the appropriate adult is:
- already at the police station, the provisions of *paragraphs 3.1* to *3.5* must be complied with in the appropriate adult's presence;
- not at the station when these provisions are complied with, they must be complied with again in the presence of the appropriate adult when they arrive,

and a copy of the notice given to the detainee in accordance with *paragraph 3.2*, shall also be given to the appropriate adult.

3.18 The detainee shall be advised that:
- the duties of the appropriate adult include giving advice and assistance;
- they can consult privately with the appropriate adult at any time.

3.19 If the detainee, or appropriate adult on the detainee's behalf, asks for a solicitor to be called to give legal advice, the provisions of *section 6* apply.

3.20 If the detainee is blind, seriously visually impaired or unable to read, the custody officer shall make sure their solicitor, relative, appropriate adult or some other person likely to take an interest in them and not involved in the investigation is available to help check any documentation. When this Code requires written consent or signing the person assisting may be asked to sign instead, if the detainee prefers. This paragraph does not require an appropriate adult to be called solely to assist in checking and signing documentation for a person who is not a juvenile, or mentally disordered or otherwise mentally vulnerable (see *paragraph 3.15* and *Note 13C*).

3.20A The Children and Young Persons Act 1933, section 31, requires that arrangements must be made for ensuring that a girl under the age of 18, while detained in a police station, is under the care of a woman. See *Note 3G.* It also requires that arrangements must be made for preventing any person under 18, while being detained in a police station, from associating with an adult charged with any offence, unless that adult is a relative or the adult is jointly charged with the same offence as the person under 18.

(c) *Persons attending a police station or elsewhere voluntarily*

3.21 Anybody attending a police station or other location (see *paragraph 3.22*) voluntarily to assist police with the investigation of an offence may leave at will unless arrested. See *Note 1K.* The person may only be prevented from leaving at will if their arrest on suspicion of committing the offence is necessary in accordance with Code G. See *Code G Note 2G.*
(a) If during an interview it is decided that their arrest is necessary, they must:
- be informed at once that they are under arrest and of the grounds and reasons as required by *Code G,* and
- be brought before the custody officer at the police station where they are arrested or, as the case may be, at the police station to which they are taken after being arrested elsewhere. The custody officer is then responsible for making sure that a custody record is opened and that they are notified of their rights in the same way as other detainees as required by this Code.
(b) If they are not arrested but are cautioned as in *section 10*, the person who gives the caution must, at the same time, inform them they are not under arrest and they are not obliged to remain at the station or other location, but if they agree to remain, they may obtain free and independent legal advice if they want. They shall also be given a copy of the notice explaining the arrangements for obtaining legal advice and told that the right to legal advice includes the right to speak with a solicitor on the telephone and be asked if they want advice. If advice is requested, the interviewer is responsible for securing its provision without delay by contacting the Defence Solicitor Call Centre. The interviewer is responsible for confirming that the suspect has given their agreement to be interviewed voluntarily. In the case of a juvenile or mentally vulnerable suspect, this must be given in the presence of the appropriate adult and for a juvenile, the agreement of a parent or guardian of the juvenile is also required. The interviewer must ensure that other provisions of this Code and Codes E

and F concerning the conduct and recording of interviews of suspects and the rights and entitlements and safeguards for suspects who have been arrested and detained are followed insofar as they can be applied to suspects who are not under arrest. This includes:

- informing them of the offence and, as the case may be, any further offences, they are suspected of and the grounds and reasons for that suspicion and their right to be so informed (see *paragraph 3.1(b)*);
- the caution as required in *section 10*;
- determining whether they require an appropriate adult and help to check documentation (see *paragraph 3.5(c)(ii)*); and
- determining whether they require an interpreter and the provision of interpretation and translation services and informing them of that right. See *paragraphs 3.1(a)(iv), 3.5(c) (ii)* and *3.12, Note 6B* and *section 13*.

but does not include any requirement to provide a written notice in addition to that above which concerns the arrangements for obtaining legal advice.

3.22 If the other location mentioned in *paragraph 3.21* is any place or premises for which the interviewer requires the person's informed consent to remain, for example, the person's home, then the references that the person is 'not obliged to remain' and that they 'may leave at will' mean that the person may also withdraw their consent and require the interviewer to leave.

(d) Documentation

3.23 The grounds for a person's detention shall be recorded, in the person's presence if practicable. See *paragraph 1.8*.

3.24 Action taken under *paragraphs 3.12* to *3.20* shall be recorded.

(e) Persons answering street bail

3.25 When a person is answering street bail, the custody officer should link any documentation held in relation to arrest with the custody record. Any further action shall be recorded on the custody record in accordance with paragraphs 3.23 and 3.24 above.

(f) Requirements for suspects to be informed of certain rights

3.26 The provisions of this section identify the information which must be given to suspects who have been cautioned in accordance with *section 10 of this Code* according to whether or not they have been arrested and detained. It includes information required by *EU Directive 2012/13* on the right to information in criminal proceedings. If a complaint is made by or on behalf of such a suspect that the information and (as the case may be) access to records and documents has not been provided as required, the matter shall be reported to an inspector to deal with as a complaint for the purposes of *paragraph 9.2*, or *paragraph 12.9* if the challenge is made during an interview. This would include, for example:

  (a) in the case of a detained suspect:
  - not informing them of their rights (see *paragraph 3.1*);
  - not giving them a copy of the Notice (see *paragraph 3.2(a)*);
  - not providing an opportunity to read the notice (see *paragraph 3.2A*);
  - not providing the required information (see *paragraphs 3.2(a), 3.12(b)* and, *3.12A*;
  - not allowing access to the custody record (see *paragraph 2.4*);
  - not providing a translation of the Notice (see *paragraph 3.12(c)* and *(d)*); and
  (b) in the case of a suspect who is not detained:
  - not informing them of their rights or providing the required information (see *paragraph 3.21(b)*).

Notes for Guidance

3ZA *For the purposes of paragraphs 3.4(b) and 15.0:*

  (a) *Investigating officers are responsible for bringing to the attention of the officer who is responsible for authorising the suspect's detention or (as the case may be) continued detention (before or after charge), any documents and materials in their possession or control which appear to undermine the need to keep the suspect in custody. In accordance with Part IV of PACE, this officer will be either the custody officer, the officer reviewing the need for detention before or after charge (PACE, section 40), or the officer considering the need to extend detention without charge from 24 to 36 hours (PACE, section 42) who is then responsible for determining, which, if any, of those documents and materials are capable of undermining the need to detain the suspect and must therefore be made available to the suspect or their solicitor.*

(b)   *the way in which documents and materials are 'made available', is a matter for the investigating officer to determine on a case by case basis and having regard to the nature and volume of the documents and materials involved. For example, they may be made available by supplying a copy or allowing supervised access to view. However, for view only access, it will be necessary to demonstrate that sufficient time is allowed for the suspect and solicitor to view and consider the documents and materials in question.*

3A   *For access to currently available notices, including 'easy-read' versions, see https://www.gov.uk/guidance/notice-of-rights-and-entitlements-a-persons-rights-in-police-detention.*

3B   *Not used.*

3C   *If the juvenile is in local authority or voluntary organisation care but living with their parents or other adults responsible for their welfare, although there is no legal obligation to inform them, they should normally be contacted, as well as the authority or organisation unless they are suspected of involvement in the offence concerned. Even if the juvenile is not living with their parents, consideration should be given to informing them.*

3D   *The right to consult the Codes of Practice does not entitle the person concerned to delay unreasonably any necessary investigative or administrative action whilst they do so. Examples of action which need not be delayed unreasonably include:*
- *procedures requiring the provision of breath, blood or urine specimens under the Road Traffic Act 1988 or the Transport and Works Act 1992;*
- *searching detainees at the police station;*
- *taking fingerprints, footwear impressions or non-intimate samples without consent for evidential purposes.*

3E   *The Detention and Custody Authorised Professional Practice (APP) produced by the College of Policing (see http://www.app.college.police.uk) provides more detailed guidance on risk assessments and identifies key risk areas which should always be considered. See Home Office Circular 34/2007 (Safety of solicitors and probationary representatives at police stations).*

3F   *A custody officer or other officer who, in accordance with this Code, allows or directs the carrying out of any task or action relating to a detainee's care, treatment, rights and entitlements to another officer or any other person, must be satisfied that the officer or person concerned is suitable, trained and competent to carry out the task or action in question.*

3G   *Guidance for police officers and police staff on the operational application of section 31 of the Children and Young Persons Act 1933 has been published by the College of Policing and is available at: https://www.app.college.police.uk/app-content/detention-and-custody-2/detainee-care/children-and- young-persons/#girls.*

4   Detainee's property

(a)   Action

4.1   The custody officer is responsible for:
- (a)   ascertaining what property a detainee:
    - (i)   has with them when they come to the police station, whether on:
        - arrest or re-detention on answering to bail;
        - commitment to prison custody on the order or sentence of a court;
        - lodgement at the police station with a view to their production in court from prison custody;
        - transfer from detention at another station or hospital;
        - detention under the Mental Health Act 1983, section 135 or 136;
        - remand into police custody on the authority of a court.
    - (ii)   might have acquired for an unlawful or harmful purpose while in custody;
- (b)   the safekeeping of any property taken from a detainee which remains at the police station.

The custody officer may search the detainee or authorise their being searched to the extent they consider necessary, provided a search of intimate parts of the body or involving the removal of more than outer clothing is only made as in *Annex A*. A search may only be carried out by an officer of the same sex as the detainee. See *Note 4A* and *Annex L*.

4.2   Detainees may retain clothing and personal effects at their own risk unless the custody officer considers they may use them to cause harm to themselves or others, interfere with evidence, damage property, effect an escape or they are needed as evidence. In this event the custody officer may withhold such articles as they consider necessary and must tell the detainee why.

4.3   Personal effects are those items a detainee may lawfully need, use or refer to while in detention but do not include cash and other items of value.

(b)   Documentation

4.4   It is a matter for the custody officer to determine whether a record should be made of the property a detained person has with him or had taken from him on arrest. Any record made is not required to be kept as part of the custody record but the custody record should be noted as to where such a record exists and that record shall be treated as being part of the custody record for the purpose of this and any other Code of Practice (see *paragraphs 2.4, 2.4A* and *2.5*). Whenever a record is made the detainee shall be allowed to check and sign the record of property as correct. Any refusal to sign shall be recorded.

4.5   If a detainee is not allowed to keep any article of clothing or personal effects, the reason must be recorded.

Notes for Guidance

4A   *PACE, Section 54(1) and paragraph 4.1 require a detainee to be searched when it is clear the custody officer will have continuing duties in relation to that detainee or when that detainee's behaviour or offence makes an inventory appropriate. They do not require every detainee to be searched, e.g. if it is clear a person will only be detained for a short period and is not to be placed in a cell, the custody officer may decide not to search them. In such a case the custody record will be endorsed 'not searched', paragraph 4.4 will not apply, and the detainee will be invited to sign the entry. If the detainee refuses, the custody officer will be obliged to ascertain what property they have in accordance with paragraph 4.1.*

4B   *Paragraph 4.4 does not require the custody officer to record on the custody record property in the detainee's possession on arrest if, by virtue of its nature, quantity or size, it is not practicable to remove it to the police station.*

4C   *Paragraph 4.4 does not require items of clothing worn by the person to be recorded unless withheld by the custody officer as in paragraph 4.2.*

5   Right not to be held incommunicado

(a)   Action

5.1   Subject to *paragraph 5.7B*, any person arrested and held in custody at a police station or other premises may, on request, have one person known to them or likely to take an interest in their welfare informed at public expense of their whereabouts as soon as practicable. If the person cannot be contacted the detainee may choose up to two alternatives. If they cannot be contacted, the person in charge of detention or the investigation has discretion to allow further attempts until the information has been conveyed. See *Notes 5C* and *5D*.

5.2   The exercise of the above right in respect of each person nominated may be delayed only in accordance with *Annex B*.

5.3   The above right may be exercised each time a detainee is taken to another police station.

5.4   If the detainee agrees, they may at the custody officer's discretion, receive visits from friends, family or others likely to take an interest in their welfare, or in whose welfare the detainee has an interest. See *Note 5B*.

5.5   If a friend, relative or person with an interest in the detainee's welfare enquires about their whereabouts, this information shall be given if the suspect agrees and *Annex B* does not apply. See *Note 5D*.

5.6   The detainee shall be given writing materials, on request, and allowed to telephone one person for a reasonable time, see *Notes 5A* and *5E*. Either or both of these privileges may be denied or delayed if an officer of inspector rank or above considers sending a letter or making a telephone call may result in any of the consequences in:

(a) *Annex B paragraphs 1* and *2* and the person is detained in connection with an indictable offence;

(b) *Not used.*

Nothing in this paragraph permits the restriction or denial of the rights in *paragraphs 5.1 and 6.1.*

5.7 Before any letter or message is sent, or telephone call made, the detainee shall be informed that what they say in any letter, call or message (other than in a communication to a solicitor) may be read or listened to and may be given in evidence. A telephone call may be terminated if it is being abused. The costs can be at public expense at the custody officer's discretion.

5.7A Any delay or denial of the rights in this section should be proportionate and should last no longer than necessary.

5.7B In the case of a person in police custody for specific purposes and periods in accordance with a direction under the Crime (Sentences) Act 1997, Schedule 1 (productions from prison etc.), the exercise of the rights in this section shall be subject to any additional conditions specified in the direction for the purpose of regulating the detainee's contact and communication with others whilst in police custody. See *Note 5F.*

(b)   Documentation

5.8 A record must be kept of any:

(a) request made under this section and the action taken;

(b) letters, messages or telephone calls made or received or visit received;

(c) refusal by the detainee to have information about them given to an outside enquirer. The detainee must be asked to countersign the record accordingly and any refusal recorded.

Notes for Guidance

5A   *A person may request an interpreter to interpret a telephone call or translate a letter.*

5B   *At the custody officer's discretion and subject to the detainee's consent, visits should be allowed when possible, subject to having sufficient personnel to supervise a visit and any possible hindrance to the investigation.*

5C   *If the detainee does not know anyone to contact for advice or support or cannot contact a friend or relative, the custody officer should bear in mind any local voluntary bodies or other organisations who might be able to help. Paragraph 6.1 applies if legal advice is required.*

5D   *In some circumstances it may not be appropriate to use the telephone to disclose information under paragraphs 5.1 and 5.5.*

5E   *The telephone call at paragraph 5.6 is in addition to any communication under paragraphs 5.1 and 6.1.*

5F   *Prison Service Instruction 26/2012 (Production of Prisoners at the Request of Warranted Law Enforcement Agencies) provides detailed guidance and instructions for police officers and Governors and Directors of Prisons regarding applications for prisoners to be transferred to police custody and their safe custody and treatment while in police custody.*

6   Right to legal advice

(a)   Action

6.1 Unless *Annex B* applies, all detainees must be informed that they may at any time consult and communicate privately with a solicitor, whether in person, in writing or by telephone, and that free independent legal advice is available. See *paragraph 3.1, Notes 1I, 6B and 6J*

6.2 *Not used.*

6.3 A poster advertising the right to legal advice must be prominently displayed in the charging area of every police station. See *Note 6H.*

6.4 No police officer should, at any time, do or say anything with the intention of dissuading any person who is entitled to legal advice in accordance with this Code, whether or not they have been arrested and are detained, from obtaining legal advice. See *Note 6ZA.*

6.5 The exercise of the right of access to legal advice may be delayed only as in *Annex B.* Whenever legal advice is requested, and unless *Annex B* applies, the custody officer must act without delay to secure the provision of such advice. If the detainee has the right to speak to a solicitor in person but declines to exercise the right the officer should point out that the right includes the right to speak with a solicitor on the telephone. If the detainee continues to waive this right, or a detainee whose right to free legal advice is limited to telephone advice from the Criminal Defence Service (CDS) Direct (*see Note 6B*) declines to exercise that right, the officer should ask them why and any reasons should be recorded on the custody record or the interview record as appropriate. Reminders of the right to legal advice must be given as in *paragraphs 3.5, 11.2, 15.4, 16.4, 16.5, 2B of Annex A, 3 of Annex K* and *5 of Annex M* of this Code and Code D, *paragraphs 3.17(ii)* and *6.3*. Once it is clear a detainee does not want to speak to a solicitor in person or by telephone they should cease to be asked their reasons. See *Note 6K*.

6.5A   In the case of a person who is a juvenile or is mentally disordered or otherwise mentally vulnerable, an appropriate adult should consider whether legal advice from a solicitor is required. If such a detained person wants to exercise the right to legal advice, the appropriate action should be taken and should not be delayed until the appropriate adult arrives. If the person indicates that they do not want legal advice, the appropriate adult has the right to ask for a solicitor to attend if this would be in the best interests of the person. However, the person cannot be forced to see the solicitor if they are adamant that they do not wish to do so.

6.6   A detainee who wants legal advice may not be interviewed or continue to be interviewed until they have received such advice unless:

(a)   *Annex B* applies, when the restriction on drawing adverse inferences from silence in *Annex C* will apply because the detainee is not allowed an opportunity to consult a solicitor; or

(b)   an officer of superintendent rank or above has reasonable grounds for believing that:

(i)   the consequent delay might:

- lead to interference with, or harm to, evidence connected with an offence;
- lead to interference with, or physical harm to, other people;
- lead to serious loss of, or damage to, property;
- lead to alerting other people suspected of having committed an offence but not yet arrested for it;
- hinder the recovery of property obtained in consequence of the commission of an offence.

See *Note 6A*

(ii)   when a solicitor, including a duty solicitor, has been contacted and has agreed to attend, awaiting their arrival would cause unreasonable delay to the process of investigation.

Note: In these cases the restriction on drawing adverse inferences from silence in *Annex C* will apply because the detainee is not allowed an opportunity to consult a solicitor.

(c)   the solicitor the detainee has nominated or selected from a list:

(i)   cannot be contacted;

(ii)   has previously indicated they do not wish to be contacted; or

(iii)   having been contacted, has declined to attend; and

- the detainee has been advised of the Duty Solicitor Scheme but has declined to ask for the duty solicitor;
- in these circumstances the interview may be started or continued without further delay provided an officer of inspector rank or above has agreed to the interview proceeding.

Note: The restriction on drawing adverse inferences from silence in *Annex C* will not apply because the detainee is allowed an opportunity to consult the duty solicitor;

(d)   the detainee changes their mind about wanting legal advice or (as the case may be) about wanting a solicitor present at the interview and states that they no longer wish to speak to a solicitor. In these circumstances, the interview may be started or continued without delay provided that:

(i)   an officer of inspector rank or above:

- speaks to the detainee to enquire about the reasons for their change of mind (see *Note 6K*), and
- makes, or directs the making of, reasonable efforts to ascertain the solicitor's expected time of arrival and to inform the solicitor that the suspect has stated that they wish to change their mind and the reason (if given);

(ii) the detainee's reason for their change of mind (if given) and the outcome of the action in (i) are recorded in the custody record;

(iii) the detainee, after being informed of the outcome of the action in (i) above, confirms in writing that they want the interview to proceed without speaking or further speaking to a solicitor or (as the case may be) without a solicitor being present and do not wish to wait for a solicitor by signing an entry to this effect in the custody record;

(iv) an officer of inspector rank or above is satisfied that it is proper for the interview to proceed in these circumstances and:

- gives authority in writing for the interview to proceed and, if the authority is not recorded in the custody record, the officer must ensure that the custody record shows the date and time of the authority and where it is recorded, and

- takes, or directs the taking of, reasonable steps to inform the solicitor that the authority has been given and the time when the interview is expected to commence and records or causes to be recorded, the outcome of this action in the custody record.

(v) When the interview starts and the interviewer reminds the suspect of their right to legal advice (see *paragraph 11.2*, Code E *paragraph 4.5* and Code F *paragraph 4.5*), the interviewer shall then ensure that the following is recorded in the written interview record or the interview record made in accordance with Code E or F:

- confirmation that the detainee has changed their mind about wanting legal advice or (as the case may be) about wanting a solicitor present and the reasons for it if given;

- the fact that authority for the interview to proceed has been given and, subject to *paragraph 2.6A,* the name of the authorising officer;

- that if the solicitor arrives at the station before the interview is completed, the detainee will be so informed without delay and *a break will be taken* to allow them to speak to the solicitor if they wish, unless *paragraph 6.6(a)* applies, and

- that at any time during the interview, the detainee may again ask for legal advice and that if they do, a break will be taken to allow them to speak to the solicitor, unless *paragraph 6.6(a), (b), or (c)* applies.

Note: In these circumstances, the restriction on drawing adverse inferences from silence in *Annex C* will not apply because the detainee is allowed an opportunity to consult a solicitor if they wish.

6.7　If *paragraph 6.6(a)* applies, where the reason for authorising the delay ceases to apply, there may be no further delay in permitting the exercise of the right in the absence of a further authorisation unless *paragraph 6.6(b), (c)* or *(d)* applies. If *paragraph 6.6(b)(i)* applies, once sufficient information has been obtained to avert the risk, questioning must cease until the detainee has received legal advice unless *paragraph 6.6(a), (b)(ii), (c)* or *(d)* applies.

6.8　A detainee who has been permitted to consult a solicitor shall be entitled on request to have the solicitor present when they are interviewed unless one of the exceptions in *paragraph 6.6* applies.

6.9　The solicitor may only be required to leave the interview if their conduct is such that the interviewer is unable properly to put questions to the suspect. See *Notes 6D* and *6E*.

6.10　If the interviewer considers a solicitor is acting in such a way, they will stop the interview and consult an officer not below superintendent rank, if one is readily available, and otherwise an officer not below inspector rank not connected with the investigation. After speaking to the solicitor, the officer consulted will decide if the interview should continue in the presence of that solicitor. If they decide it should not, the suspect will be given the opportunity to consult another solicitor before the interview continues and that solicitor given an opportunity to be present at the interview. *See Note 6E*.

6.11　The removal of a solicitor from an interview is a serious step and, if it occurs, the officer of superintendent rank or above who took the decision will consider if the incident should be reported to the Solicitors Regulatory Authority. If the decision to remove the solicitor has been taken by an officer below superintendent rank, the facts must be reported to an officer of superintendent rank or above, who will similarly consider whether a report to the

Solicitors Regulatory Authority would be appropriate. When the solicitor concerned is a duty solicitor, the report should be both to the Solicitors Regulatory Authority and to the Legal Aid Agency.

6.12 'Solicitor' in this Code means:
- a solicitor who holds a current practising certificate;
- an accredited or probationary representative included on the register of representatives maintained by the Legal Aid Agency.

6.12A An accredited or probationary representative sent to provide advice by, and on behalf of, a solicitor shall be admitted to the police station for this purpose unless an officer of inspector rank or above considers such a visit will hinder the investigation and directs otherwise. Hindering the investigation does not include giving proper legal advice to a detainee as in *Note 6D*. Once admitted to the police station, *paragraphs 6.6* to *6.10* apply.

6.13 In exercising their discretion under *paragraph 6.12A*, the officer should take into account in particular:
- whether:
  - the identity and status of an accredited or probationary representative have been satisfactorily established;
  - they are of suitable character to provide legal advice, e.g. a person with a criminal record is unlikely to be suitable unless the conviction was for a minor offence and not recent.
- any other matters in any written letter of authorisation provided by the solicitor on whose behalf the person is attending the police station. See *Note 6F*.

6.14 If the inspector refuses access to an accredited or probationary representative or a decision is taken that such a person should not be permitted to remain at an interview, the inspector must notify the solicitor on whose behalf the representative was acting and give them an opportunity to make alternative arrangements. The detainee must be informed and the custody record noted.

6.15 If a solicitor arrives at the station to see a particular person, that person must, unless *Annex B* applies, be so informed whether or not they are being interviewed and asked if they would like to see the solicitor. This applies even if the detainee has declined legal advice or, having requested it, subsequently agreed to be interviewed without receiving advice. The solicitor's attendance and the detainee's decision must be noted in the custody record.

(b) Documentation

6.16 Any request for legal advice and the action taken shall be recorded.

6.17 A record shall be made in the interview record if a detainee asks for legal advice and an interview is begun either in the absence of a solicitor or their representative, or they have been required to leave an interview.

Notes for Guidance

6ZA No police officer or police staff shall indicate to any suspect, except to answer a direct question, that the period for which they are liable to be detained, or if not detained, the time taken to complete the interview, might be reduced:
- *if they do not ask for legal advice or do not want a solicitor present when they are interviewed; or*
- *if they have asked for legal advice or (as the case may be) asked for a solicitor to be present when they are interviewed but change their mind and agree to be interviewed without waiting for a solicitor.*

6A In considering if paragraph 6.6(b) applies, the officer should, if practicable, ask the solicitor for an estimate of how long it will take to come to the station and relate this to the time detention is permitted, the time of day (i.e. whether the rest period under paragraph 12.2 is imminent) and the requirements of other investigations. If the solicitor is on their way or is to set off immediately, it will not normally be appropriate to begin an interview before they arrive. If it appears necessary to begin an interview before the solicitor's arrival, they should be given an indication of how long the police would be able to wait before 6.6(b) applies so there is an opportunity to make arrangements for someone else to provide legal advice.

6B A detainee has a right to free legal advice and to be represented by a solicitor. This Note for Guidance explains the arrangements which enable detainees to obtain legal advice. An outline of these arrangements is also included in the Notice of Rights and Entitlements given to detainees in accordance with paragraph 3.2. The arrangements also apply, with appropriate modifications, to persons attending a police station or other location voluntarily who are cautioned prior to being interviewed. See paragraph 3.21.

When a detainee asks for free legal advice, the Defence Solicitor Call Centre (DSCC) must be informed of the request.

Free legal advice will be limited to telephone advice provided by CDS Direct if a detainee is:
- detained for a non-imprisonable offence;
- arrested on a bench warrant for failing to appear and being held for production at court (except where the solicitor has clear documentary evidence available that would result in the client being released from custody);
- arrested for drink driving (driving/in charge with excess alcohol, failing to provide a specimen, driving/in charge whilst unfit through drink), or
- detained in relation to breach of police or court bail conditions

unless one or more exceptions apply, in which case the DSCC should arrange for advice to be given by a solicitor at the police station, for example:
- the police want to interview the detainee or carry out an eye-witness identification procedure;
- the detainee needs an appropriate adult;
- the detainee is unable to communicate over the telephone;
- the detainee alleges serious misconduct by the police;
- the investigation includes another offence not included in the list,
- the solicitor to be assigned is already at the police station.

When free advice is not limited to telephone advice, a detainee can ask for free advice from a solicitor they know or if they do not know a solicitor or the solicitor they know cannot be contacted, from the duty solicitor.

To arrange free legal advice, the police should telephone the DSCC. The call centre will decide whether legal advice should be limited to telephone advice from CDS Direct, or whether a solicitor known to the detainee or the duty solicitor should speak to the detainee. When a detainee wants to pay for legal advice themselves:
- the DSCC will contact a solicitor of their choice on their behalf;
- they may, when free advice is only available by telephone from CDS Direct, still speak to a solicitor of their choice on the telephone for advice, but the solicitor would not be paid by legal aid and may ask the person to pay for the advice;
- they should be given an opportunity to consult a specific solicitor or another solicitor from that solicitor's firm. If this solicitor is not available, they may choose up to two alternatives. If these alternatives are not available, the custody officer has discretion to allow further attempts until a solicitor has been contacted and agreed to provide advice;
- they are entitled to a private consultation with their chosen solicitor on the telephone or the solicitor may decide to come to the police station;
- If their chosen solicitor cannot be contacted, the DSCC may still be called to arrange free legal advice.

Apart from carrying out duties necessary to implement these arrangements, an officer must not advise the suspect about any particular firm of solicitors.

6B1 Not used.
6B2 Not used.
6C Not used.
6D The solicitor's only role in the police station is to protect and advance the legal rights of their client. On occasions this may require the solicitor to give advice which has the effect of the client avoiding giving evidence which strengthens a prosecution case. The solicitor may intervene in order to seek clarification, challenge an improper question to their client or the manner in which it is put, advise their client not to reply to particular questions, or if they wish to give their client further legal advice. Paragraph 6.9 only applies if the solicitor's approach or conduct prevents or unreasonably obstructs proper questions being put to the suspect or the suspect's response being recorded. Examples of unacceptable conduct include answering questions on a suspect's behalf or providing written replies for the suspect to quote.

6E   *An officer who takes the decision to exclude a solicitor must be in a position to satisfy the court the decision was properly made. In order to do this they may need to witness what is happening.*

6F   *If an officer of at least inspector rank considers a particular solicitor or firm of solicitors is persistently sending probationary representatives who are unsuited to provide legal advice, they should inform an officer of at least superintendent rank, who may wish to take the matter up with the Solicitors Regulation Authority.*

6G   *Subject to the constraints of Annex B, a solicitor may advise more than one client in an investigation if they wish. Any question of a conflict of interest is for the solicitor under their professional code of conduct. If, however, waiting for a solicitor to give advice to one client may lead to unreasonable delay to the interview with another, the provisions of paragraph 6.6(b) may apply.*

6H   *In addition to a poster in English, a poster or posters containing translations into Welsh, the main minority ethnic languages and the principal European languages should be displayed wherever they are likely to be helpful and it is practicable to do so.*

6I   *Not used.*

6J   *Whenever a detainee exercises their right to legal advice by consulting or communicating with a solicitor, they must be allowed to do so in private. This right to consult or communicate in private is fundamental. If the requirement for privacy is compromised because what is said or written by the detainee or solicitor for the purpose of giving and receiving legal advice is overheard, listened to, or read by others without the informed consent of the detainee, the right will effectively have been denied. When a detainee speaks to a solicitor on the telephone, they should be allowed to do so in private unless this is impractical because of the design and layout of the custody area or the location of telephones. However, the normal expectation should be that facilities will be available, unless they are being used, at all police stations to enable detainees to speak in private to a solicitor either face to face or over the telephone.*

6K   *A detainee is not obliged to give reasons for declining legal advice and should not be pressed to do so.*

7   Citizens of independent Commonwealth countries or foreign nationals

(a)   Action

7.1   A detainee who is a citizen of an independent Commonwealth country or a national of a foreign country, including the Republic of Ireland, has the right, upon request, to communicate at any time with the appropriate High Commission, Embassy or Consulate. That detainee must be informed as soon as practicable of this right and asked if they want to have their High Commission, Embassy or Consulate told of their whereabouts and the grounds for their detention. Such a request should be acted upon as soon as practicable. See *Note 7A*.

7.2   A detainee who is a citizen of a country with which a bilateral consular convention or agreement is in force requiring notification of arrest must also be informed that subject to *paragraph 7.4*, notification of their arrest will be sent to the appropriate High Commission, Embassy or Consulate as soon as practicable, whether or not they request it. A list of the countries to which this requirement currently applies and contact details for the relevant High Commissions, Embassies and Consulates can be obtained from the Consular Directorate of the Foreign and Commonwealth Office (FCO) as follows:
- from the FCO web pages:
  - https://gov.uk/government/publications/table-of-consular-conventions-and-mandatory-notification- obligations, and
  - https://www.gov.uk/government/publications/foreign-embassies-in-the-uk
- by telephone to 020 7008 3100,
- by email to fcocorrespondence@fco.gov.uk.
- by letter to the Foreign and Commonwealth Office, King Charles Street, London, SW1A 2AH.

7.3   Consular officers may, if the detainee agrees, visit one of their nationals in police detention to talk to them and, if required, to arrange for legal advice. Such visits shall take place out of the hearing of a police officer.

7.4 Notwithstanding the provisions of consular conventions, if the detainee claims that they are a refugee or have applied or intend to apply for asylum, the custody officer must ensure that UK Visas and Immigration (UKVI) (formerly the UK Border Agency) is informed as soon as practicable of the claim. UKVI will then determine whether compliance with relevant international obligations requires notification of the arrest to be sent and will inform the custody officer as to what action police need to take.

(b) Documentation

7.5 A record shall be made:
- when a detainee is informed of their rights under this section and of any requirement in paragraph 7.2;
- of any communications with a High Commission, Embassy or Consulate, and
- of any communications with UKVI about a detainee's claim to be a refugee or to be seeking asylum and the resulting action taken by police.

Note for Guidance

7A *The exercise of the rights in this section may not be interfered with even though Annex B applies.*

8 Conditions of detention

(a) Action

8.1 So far as it is practicable, not more than one detainee should be detained in each cell. See *Note 8C*.

8.2 Cells in use must be adequately heated, cleaned and ventilated. They must be adequately lit, subject to such dimming as is compatible with safety and security to allow people detained overnight to sleep. No additional restraints shall be used within a locked cell unless absolutely necessary and then only restraint equipment, approved for use in that force by the chief officer, which is reasonable and necessary in the circumstances having regard to the detainee's demeanour and with a view to ensuring their safety and the safety of others. If a detainee is deaf, mentally disordered or otherwise mentally vulnerable, particular care must be taken when deciding whether to use any form of approved restraints.

8.3 Blankets, mattresses, pillows and other bedding supplied shall be of a reasonable standard and in a clean and sanitary condition. See *Note 8A*.

8.4 Access to toilet and washing facilities must be provided.

8.5 If it is necessary to remove a detainee's clothes for the purposes of investigation, for hygiene, health reasons or cleaning, replacement clothing of a reasonable standard of comfort and cleanliness shall be provided. A detainee may not be interviewed unless adequate clothing has been offered.

8.6 At least two light meals and one main meal should be offered in any 24-hour period. See *Note 8B*. Drinks should be provided at meal times and upon reasonable request between meals. Whenever necessary, advice shall be sought from the appropriate healthcare professional, see *Note 9A*, on medical and dietary matters. As far as practicable, meals provided shall offer a varied diet and meet any specific dietary needs or religious beliefs the detainee may have. The detainee may, at the custody officer's discretion, have meals supplied by their family or friends at their expense. See *Note 8A*.

8.7 Brief outdoor exercise shall be offered daily if practicable.

8.8 A juvenile shall not be placed in a police cell unless no other secure accommodation is available and the custody officer considers it is not practicable to supervise them if they are not placed in a cell or that a cell provides more comfortable accommodation than other secure accommodation in the station. A juvenile may not be placed in a cell with a detained adult.

(b) Documentation

8.9 A record must be kept of replacement clothing and meals offered.

8.10 If a juvenile is placed in a cell, the reason must be recorded.

8.11 The use of any restraints on a detainee whilst in a cell, the reasons for it and, if appropriate, the arrangements for enhanced supervision of the detainee whilst so restrained, shall be recorded. See *paragraph 3.9*.

Notes for Guidance

8A   The provisions in paragraph 8.3 and 8.6 respectively are of particular importance in the case of a person likely to be detained for an extended period. In deciding whether to allow meals to be supplied by family or friends, the custody officer is entitled to take account of the risk of items being concealed in any food or package and the officer's duties and responsibilities under food handling legislation.

8B   Meals should, so far as practicable, be offered at recognised meal times, or at other times that take account of when the detainee last had a meal.

8C   The Detention and Custody Authorised Professional Practice (APP) produced by the College of Policing (see http://www.app.college.police.uk) provides more detailed guidance on matters concerning detainee healthcare and treatment and associated forensic issues which should be read in conjunction with sections 8 and 9 of this Code.

9   Care and treatment of detained persons

(a)   General

9.1   Nothing in this section prevents the police from calling an appropriate healthcare professional to examine a detainee for the purposes of obtaining evidence relating to any offence in which the detainee is suspected of being involved. See *Notes 9A and 8C.*

9.2   If a complaint is made by, or on behalf of, a detainee about their treatment since their arrest, or it comes to notice that a detainee may have been treated improperly, a report must be made as soon as practicable to an officer of inspector rank or above not connected with the investigation. If the matter concerns a possible assault or the possibility of the unnecessary or unreasonable use of force, an appropriate healthcare professional must also be called as soon as practicable.

9.3   Detainees should be visited at least every hour. If no reasonably foreseeable risk was identified in a risk assessment, see *paragraphs 3.6 to 3.10*, there is no need to wake a sleeping detainee. Those suspected of being under the influence of drink or drugs or both or of having swallowed drugs, see *Note 9CA*, or whose level of consciousness causes concern must, subject to any clinical directions given by the appropriate healthcare professional, see *paragraph 9.13*:
- be visited and roused at least every half hour;
- have their condition assessed as in *Annex H;*
- and clinical treatment arranged if appropriate.

See *Notes 9B, 9C* and *9H*

9.4   When arrangements are made to secure clinical attention for a detainee, the custody officer must make sure all relevant information which might assist in the treatment of the detainee's condition is made available to the responsible healthcare professional. This applies whether or not the healthcare professional asks for such information. Any officer or police staff with relevant information must inform the custody officer as soon as practicable.

(b)   Clinical treatment and attention

9.5   The custody officer must make sure a detainee receives appropriate clinical attention as soon as reasonably practicable if the person:
(a)   appears to be suffering from physical illness; or
(b)   is injured; or
(c)   appears to be suffering from a mental disorder; or
(d)   appears to need clinical attention.

9.5A   This applies even if the detainee makes no request for clinical attention and whether or not they have already received clinical attention elsewhere. If the need for attention appears urgent, e.g. when indicated as in *Annex H*, the nearest available healthcare professional or an ambulance must be called immediately.

9.5B   The custody officer must also consider the need for clinical attention as set out in *Note 9C* in relation to those suffering the effects of alcohol or drugs.

9.5   *Paragraph 9.5 is not meant to prevent or delay the transfer to a hospital if necessary of a person detained under the Mental Health Act 1983, section 136. See Note 9D. When an assessment under that Act is to take place at a police station (see paragraph 3.16) the custody officer must consider whether an appropriate healthcare professional should be called to conduct an initial clinical check on the detainee. This applies particularly* when there is likely to be any significant delay in the arrival of a suitably qualified medical practitioner.

9.7 If it appears to the custody officer, or they are told, that a person brought to a station under arrest may be suffering from an infectious disease or condition, the custody officer must take reasonable steps to safeguard the health of the detainee and others at the station. In deciding what action to take, advice must be sought from an appropriate healthcare professional. See *Note 9E*. The custody officer has discretion to isolate the person and their property until clinical directions have been obtained.

9.8 If a detainee requests a clinical examination, an appropriate healthcare professional must be called as soon as practicable to assess the detainee's clinical needs. If a safe and appropriate care plan cannot be provided, the appropriate healthcare professional's advice must be sought. The detainee may also be examined by a medical practitioner of their choice at their expense.

9.9 If a detainee is required to take or apply any medication in compliance with clinical directions prescribed before their detention, the custody officer must consult the appropriate healthcare professional before the use of the medication. Subject to the restrictions in *paragraph 9.10,* the custody officer is responsible for the safekeeping of any medication and for making sure the detainee is given the opportunity to take or apply prescribed or approved medication. Any such consultation and its outcome shall be noted in the custody record.

9.10 No police officer may administer or supervise the self-administration of medically prescribed controlled drugs of the types and forms listed in the Misuse of Drugs Regulations 2001, Schedule 2 or 3. A detainee may only self-administer such drugs under the personal supervision of the registered medical practitioner authorising their use or other appropriate healthcare professional. The custody officer may supervise the self-administration of, or authorise other custody staff to supervise the self-administration of, drugs listed in Schedule 4 or 5 if the officer has consulted the appropriate healthcare professional authorising their use and both are satisfied self-administration will not expose the detainee, police officers or anyone else to the risk of harm or injury.

9.11 When appropriate healthcare professionals administer drugs or authorise the use of other medications, supervise their self-administration or consult with the custody officer about allowing self-administration of drugs listed in Schedule 4 or 5, it must be within current medicines legislation and the scope of practice as determined by their relevant statutory regulatory body.

9.12 If a detainee has in their possession, or claims to need, medication relating to a heart condition, diabetes, epilepsy or a condition of comparable potential seriousness then, even though *paragraph 9.5* may not apply, the advice of the appropriate healthcare professional must be obtained.

9.13 Whenever the appropriate healthcare professional is called in accordance with this section to examine or treat a detainee, the custody officer shall ask for their opinion about:
- any risks or problems which police need to take into account when making decisions about the detainee's continued detention;
- when to carry out an interview if applicable; and
- the need for safeguards.

9.14 When clinical directions are given by the appropriate healthcare professional, whether orally or in writing, and the custody officer has any doubts or is in any way uncertain about any aspect of the directions, the custody officer shall ask for clarification. It is particularly important that directions concerning the frequency of visits are clear, precise and capable of being implemented. See *Note 9F.*

(c) Documentation

9.15 A record must be made in the custody record of:
(a) the arrangements made for an examination by an appropriate healthcare professional under *paragraph 9.2* and of any complaint reported under that paragraph together with any relevant remarks by the custody officer;
(b) any arrangements made in accordance with *paragraph 9.5*;
(c) any request for a clinical examination under *paragraph 9.8* and any arrangements made in response;

    (d)   the injury, ailment, condition or other reason which made it necessary to make the arrangements in (a) to (c); See *Note 9G*.

    (e)   any clinical directions and advice, including any further clarifications, given to police by a healthcare professional concerning the care and treatment of the detainee in connection with any of the arrangements made in (a) to (c); See *Notes 9E* and *9F*.

    (f)   if applicable, the responses received when attempting to rouse a person using the procedure in *Annex H*. See *Note 9H*.

9.16   If a healthcare professional does not record their clinical findings in the custody record, the record must show where they are recorded. See *Note 9G*. However, information which is necessary to custody staff to ensure the effective ongoing care and well being of the detainee must be recorded openly in the custody record, see *paragraph 3.8* and *Annex G, paragraph 7*.

9.17   Subject to the requirements of *Section 4*, the custody record shall include:

- a record of all medication a detainee has in their possession on arrival at the police station;
- a note of any such medication they claim to need but do not have with them.

Notes for Guidance

9A   *A 'healthcare professional' means a clinically qualified person working within the scope of practice as determined by their relevant statutory regulatory body. Whether a healthcare professional is 'appropriate' depends on the circumstances of the duties they carry out at the time.*

9B   *Whenever possible juveniles and mentally vulnerable detainees should be visited more frequently.*

9C   *A detainee who appears drunk or behaves abnormally may be suffering from illness, the effects of drugs or may have sustained injury, particularly a head injury which is not apparent. A detainee needing or dependent on certain drugs, including alcohol, may experience harmful effects within a short time of being deprived of their supply. In these circumstances, when there is any doubt, police should always act urgently to call an appropriate healthcare professional or an ambulance. Paragraph 9.5 does not apply to minor ailments or injuries which do not need attention. However, all such ailments or injuries must be recorded in the custody record and any doubt must be resolved in favour of calling the appropriate healthcare professional.*

9CA   *Paragraph 9.3 would apply to a person in police custody by order of a magistrates' court under the Criminal Justice Act 1988, section 152 (as amended by the Drugs Act 2005, section 8) to facilitate the recovery of evidence after being charged with drug possession or drug trafficking and suspected of having swallowed drugs. In the case of the healthcare needs of a person who has swallowed drugs, the custody officer, subject to any clinical directions, should consider the necessity for rousing every half hour. This does not negate the need for regular visiting of the suspect in the cell.*

9D   *Whenever practicable, arrangements should be made for persons detained for assessment under the Mental Health Act 1983, section 136 to be taken to a hospital. Chapter 10 of the Mental Health Act 1983 Code of Practice (as revised) provides more detailed guidance about arranging assessments under section 136 and transferring detainees from police stations to other places of safety.*

9E   *It is important to respect a person's right to privacy and information about their health must be kept confidential and only disclosed with their consent or in accordance with clinical advice when it is necessary to protect the detainee's health or that of others who come into contact with them.*

9F   *The custody officer should always seek to clarify directions that the detainee requires constant observation or supervision and should ask the appropriate healthcare professional to explain precisely what action needs to be taken to implement such directions.*

9G   *Paragraphs 9.15 and 9.16 do not require any information about the cause of any injury, ailment or condition to be recorded on the custody record if it appears capable of providing evidence of an offence.*

9H   *The purpose of recording a person's responses when attempting to rouse them using the procedure in Annex H is to enable any change in the individual's consciousness level to be noted and clinical treatment arranged if appropriate.*

10 Cautions

(a) When a caution must be given

10.1 A person whom there are grounds to suspect of an offence, see *Note 10A*, must be cautioned before any questions about an offence, or further questions if the answers provide the grounds for suspicion, are put to them if either the suspect's answers or silence, (i.e. failure or refusal to answer or answer satisfactorily) may be given in evidence to a court in a prosecution. A person need not be cautioned if questions are for other necessary purposes, e.g.:

(a) solely to establish their identity or ownership of any vehicle;

(b) to obtain information in accordance with any relevant statutory requirement, see *paragraph 10.9*;

(c) in furtherance of the proper and effective conduct of a search, e.g. to determine the need to search in the exercise of powers of stop and search or to seek co-operation while carrying out a search; or

(d) to seek verification of a written record as in *paragraph 11.13*.

(e) *Not used.*

10.2 Whenever a person not under arrest is initially cautioned, or reminded that they are under caution, that person must at the same time be told they are not under arrest and must be informed of the provisions of *paragraph 3.21* which explain that they need to agree to be interviewed, how they may obtain legal advice according to whether they are at a police station or elsewhere and the other rights and entitlements that apply to a voluntary interview. See *Note 10C*.

10.3 A person who is arrested, or further arrested, must be informed at the time if practicable or, if not, as soon as it becomes practicable thereafter, that they are under arrest and of the grounds and reasons for their arrest, see paragraph 3.4, *Note 10B* and *Code G, paragraphs 2.2 and 4.3*.

10.4 As required by *Code G, section 3*, a person who is arrested, or further arrested, must also be cautioned unless:

(a) it is impracticable to do so by reason of their condition or behaviour at the time;

(b) they have already been cautioned immediately prior to arrest as in *paragraph 10.1*.

(b) Terms of the cautions

10.5 The caution which must be given on:

(a) arrest; or

(b) all other occasions before a person is charged or informed they may be prosecuted; see *section 16*,

should, unless the restriction on drawing adverse inferences from silence applies, see *Annex C*, be in the following terms:

"You do not have to say anything. But it may harm your defence if you do not mention when questioned something which you later rely on in Court. Anything you do say may be given in evidence."

Where the use of the Welsh Language is appropriate, a constable may provide the caution directly in Welsh in the following terms:

"Does dim rhaid i chi ddweud dim byd. Ond gall niweidio eich amddiffyniad os na fyddwch chi'n sôn, wrth gael eich holi, am rywbeth y byddwch chi'n dibynnu arno nes ymlaen yn y Llys. Gall unrhyw beth yr ydych yn ei ddweud gael ei roi fel tystiolaeth."

See *Note 10G*

10.6 *Annex C, paragraph 2* sets out the alternative terms of the caution to be used when the restriction on drawing adverse inferences from silence applies.

10.7 Minor deviations from the words of any caution given in accordance with this Code do not constitute a breach of this Code, provided the sense of the relevant caution is preserved. See *Note 10D*.

10.8 After any break in questioning under caution, the person being questioned must be made aware they remain under caution. If there is any doubt the relevant caution should be given again in full when the interview resumes. See *Note 10E*.

10.9 When, despite being cautioned, a person fails to co-operate or to answer particular questions which may affect their immediate treatment, the person should be informed of any relevant consequences and that those consequences are not affected by the caution. Examples are when a person's refusal to provide:

- their name and address when charged may make them liable to detention;
- particulars and information in accordance with a statutory requirement, e.g. under the Road Traffic Act 1988, may amount to an offence or may make the person liable to a further arrest.

(c)   ***Special warnings under the Criminal Justice and Public Order Act 1994, sections 36 and 37***

10.10   When a suspect interviewed at a police station or authorised place of detention after arrest fails or refuses to answer certain questions, or to answer satisfactorily, after due warning, see *Note 10F*, a court or jury may draw such inferences as appear proper under the Criminal Justice and Public Order Act 1994, sections 36 and 37. Such inferences may only be drawn when:

    (a)   the restriction on drawing adverse inferences from silence, see *Annex C,* does not apply; and

    (b)   the suspect is arrested by a constable and fails or refuses to account for any objects, marks or substances, or marks on such objects found:

       - on their person;
       - in or on their clothing or footwear;
       - otherwise in their possession; or
       - in the place they were arrested;

    (c)   the arrested suspect was found by a constable at a place at or about the time the offence for which that officer has arrested them is alleged to have been committed, and the suspect fails or refuses to account for their presence there.

       When the restriction on drawing adverse inferences from silence applies, the suspect may still be asked to account for any of the matters in (*b*) or (c) but the special warning described in *paragraph 10.11* will not apply and must not be given.

10.11   For an inference to be drawn when a suspect fails or refuses to answer a question about one of these matters or to answer it satisfactorily, the suspect must first be told in ordinary language:

    (a)   what offence is being investigated;
    (b)   what fact they are being asked to account for;
    (c)   this fact may be due to them taking part in the commission of the offence;
    (d)   a court may draw a proper inference if they fail or refuse to account for this fact; and
    (e)   a record is being made of the interview and it may be given in evidence if they are brought to trial.

(d)   ***Juveniles and persons who are mentally disordered or otherwise mentally vulnerable***

10.11A The information required in paragraph 10.11 must not be given to a suspect who is a juvenile or who is mentally disordered or otherwise mentally vulnerable unless the appropriate adult is present.

10.12   If a juvenile or a person who is mentally disordered or otherwise mentally vulnerable is cautioned in the absence of the appropriate adult, the caution must be repeated in the adult's presence.

10.12A *Not used.*

(e)   ***Documentation***

10.13   A record shall be made when a caution is given under this section, either in the interviewer's report book or in the interview record.

Notes for Guidance

10A   *There must be some reasonable, objective grounds for the suspicion, based on known facts or information which are relevant to the likelihood the offence has been committed and the person to be questioned committed it.*

10B   *An arrested person must be given sufficient information to enable them to understand that they have been deprived of their liberty and the reason they have been arrested, e.g. when a person is arrested on suspicion of committing an offence they must be informed of the suspected offence's nature, when and where it was committed. The suspect must also be informed of the reason or reasons why the arrest is considered necessary. Vague or technical language should be avoided.*

10C *The restriction on drawing inferences from silence, see Annex C, paragraph 1, does not apply to a person who has not been detained and who therefore cannot be prevented from seeking legal advice if they want, see paragraph 3.21.*

10D *If it appears a person does not understand the caution, the person giving it should explain it in their own words.*

10E *It may be necessary to show to the court that nothing occurred during an interview break or between interviews which influenced the suspect's recorded evidence. After a break in an interview or at the beginning of a subsequent interview, the interviewer should summarise the reason for the break and confirm this with the suspect.*

10F *The Criminal Justice and Public Order Act 1994, sections 36 and 37 apply only to suspects who have been arrested by a constable or an officer of Revenue and Customs and are given the relevant warning by the police or Revenue and Customs officer who made the arrest or who is investigating the offence. They do not apply to any interviews with suspects who have not been arrested.*

10G *Nothing in this Code requires a caution to be given or repeated when informing a person not under arrest they may be prosecuted for an offence. However, a court will not be able to draw any inferences under the Criminal Justice and Public Order Act 1994, section 34, if the person was not cautioned.*

11 Interviews – general

(a) Action

11.1A An interview is the questioning of a person regarding their involvement or suspected involvement in a criminal offence or offences which, under paragraph 10.1, must be carried out under caution. Before a person is interviewed, they and, if they are represented, their solicitor must be given sufficient information to enable them to understand the nature of any such offence, and why they are suspected of committing it (see *paragraphs 3.4(a)* and *10.3*), in order to allow for the effective exercise of the rights of the defence. However, whilst the information must always be sufficient for the person to understand the nature of any offence (see *Note 11ZA*), this does not require the disclosure of details at a time which might prejudice the criminal investigation. The decision about what needs to be disclosed for the purpose of this requirement therefore rests with the investigating officer who has sufficient knowledge of the case to make that decision. The officer who discloses the information shall make a record of the information disclosed and when it was disclosed. This record may be made in the interview record, in the officer's report book or other form provided for this purpose. Procedures under the Road Traffic Act 1988, section 7 or the Transport and Works Act 1992, section 31 do not constitute interviewing for the purpose of this Code.

11.1 Following a decision to arrest a suspect, they must not be interviewed about the relevant offence except at a police station or other authorised place of detention, unless the consequent delay would be likely to:

(a) lead to:
- interference with, or harm to, evidence connected with an offence;
- interference with, or physical harm to, other people; or
- serious loss of, or damage to, property;

(b) lead to alerting other people suspected of committing an offence but not yet arrested for it; or

(c) hinder the recovery of property obtained in consequence of the commission of an offence.

Interviewing in any of these circumstances shall cease once the relevant risk has been averted or the necessary questions have been put in order to attempt to avert that risk.

11.2 Immediately prior to the commencement or re-commencement of any interview at a police station or other authorised place of detention, the interviewer should remind the suspect of their entitlement to free legal advice and that the interview can be delayed for legal advice to be obtained, unless one of the exceptions in *paragraph 6.6* applies. It is the interviewer's responsibility to make sure all reminders are recorded in the interview record.

11.3   *Not used.*

11.4   At the beginning of an interview the interviewer, after cautioning the suspect, see *section 10*, shall put to them any significant statement or silence which occurred in the presence and hearing of a police officer or other police staff before the start of the interview and which have not been put to the suspect in the course of a previous interview. See *Note 11A*. The interviewer shall ask the suspect whether they confirm or deny that earlier statement or silence and if they want to add anything.

11.4A   A significant statement is one which appears capable of being used in evidence against the suspect, in particular a direct admission of guilt. A significant silence is a failure or refusal to answer a question or answer satisfactorily when under caution, which might, allowing for the restriction on drawing adverse inferences from silence, see *Annex C*, give rise to an inference under the Criminal Justice and Public Order Act 1994, Part III.

11.5   No interviewer may try to obtain answers or elicit a statement by the use of oppression. Except as in *paragraph 10.9*, no interviewer shall indicate, except to answer a direct question, what action will be taken by the police if the person being questioned answers questions, makes a statement or refuses to do either. If the person asks directly what action will be taken if they answer questions, make a statement or refuse to do either, the interviewer may inform them what action the police propose to take provided that action is itself proper and warranted.

11.6   The interview or further interview of a person about an offence with which that person has not been charged or for which they have not been informed they may be prosecuted, must cease when:

(a)   the officer in charge of the investigation is satisfied all the questions they consider relevant to obtaining accurate and reliable information about the offence have been put to the suspect, this includes allowing the suspect an opportunity to give an innocent explanation and asking questions to test if the explanation is accurate and reliable, e.g. to clear up ambiguities or clarify what the suspect said;

(b)   the officer in charge of the investigation has taken account of any other available evidence; and

(c)   the officer in charge of the investigation, or in the case of a detained suspect, the custody officer, see *paragraph 16.1*, reasonably believes there is sufficient evidence to provide a realistic prospect of conviction for that offence. See *Note 11B*.

This paragraph does not prevent officers in revenue cases or acting under the confiscation provisions of the Criminal Justice Act 1988 or the Drug Trafficking Act 1994 from inviting suspects to complete a formal question and answer record after the interview is concluded.

(b)   Interview records

11.7   (a)   An accurate record must be made of each interview, whether or not the interview takes place at a police station.

(b)   The record must state the place of interview, the time it begins and ends, any interview breaks and, subject to *paragraph 2.6A*, the names of all those present; and must be made on the forms provided for this purpose or in the interviewer's report book or in accordance with Codes of Practice E or F.

(c)   Any written record must be made and completed during the interview, unless this would not be practicable or would interfere with the conduct of the interview, and must constitute either a verbatim record of what has been said or, failing this, an account of the interview which adequately and accurately summarises it.

11.8   If a written record is not made during the interview it must be made as soon as practicable after its completion.

11.9   Written interview records must be timed and signed by the maker.

11.10   If a written record is not completed during the interview the reason must be recorded in the interview record.

11.11   Unless it is impracticable, the person interviewed shall be given the opportunity to read the interview record and to sign it as correct or to indicate how they consider it inaccurate. If the person interviewed cannot read or refuses to read the record or sign it, the senior interviewer present shall read it to them and ask whether they would like to sign it as correct or make their mark or to indicate how they consider it inaccurate. The interviewer shall certify on the interview record itself what has occurred. See *Note 11E*.

11.12 If the appropriate adult or the person's solicitor is present during the interview, they should also be given an opportunity to read and sign the interview record or any written statement taken down during the interview.

11.13 A record shall be made of any comments made by a suspect, including unsolicited comments, which are outside the context of an interview but which might be relevant to the offence. Any such record must be timed and signed by the maker. When practicable the suspect shall be given the opportunity to read that record and to sign it as correct or to indicate how they consider it inaccurate. See *Note 11E*.

11.14 Any refusal by a person to sign an interview record when asked in accordance with this Code must itself be recorded.

(c) *Juveniles and mentally disordered or otherwise mentally vulnerable people*

11.15 A juvenile or person who is mentally disordered or otherwise mentally vulnerable must not be interviewed regarding their involvement or suspected involvement in a criminal offence or offences, or asked to provide or sign a written statement under caution or record of interview, in the absence of the appropriate adult unless *paragraphs 11.1 or 11.18 to 11.20* apply. See *Note 11C*.

11.16 Juveniles may only be interviewed at their place of education in exceptional circumstances and only when the principal or their nominee agrees. Every effort should be made to notify the parent(s) or other person responsible for the juvenile's welfare and the appropriate adult, if this is a different person, that the police want to interview the juvenile and reasonable time should be allowed to enable the appropriate adult to be present at the interview. If awaiting the appropriate adult would cause unreasonable delay, and unless the juvenile is suspected of an offence against the educational establishment, the principal or their nominee can act as the appropriate adult for the purposes of the interview.

11.17 If an appropriate adult is present at an interview, they shall be informed:
- that they are not expected to act simply as an observer; and
- that the purpose of their presence is to:
  - advise the person being interviewed;
  - observe whether the interview is being conducted properly and fairly; and
  - facilitate communication with the person being interviewed.

11.17A The appropriate adult may be required to leave the interview if their conduct is such that the interviewer is unable properly to put questions to the suspect. This will include situations where the appropriate adult's approach or conduct prevents or unreasonably obstructs proper questions being put to the suspect or the suspect's responses being recorded (see *Note 11F*). If the interviewer considers an appropriate adult is acting in such a way, they will stop the interview and consult an officer not below superintendent rank, if one is readily available, and otherwise an officer not below inspector rank not connected with the investigation. After speaking to the appropriate adult, the officer consulted must remind the adult that their role under *paragraph 11.17* does not allow them to obstruct proper questioning and give the adult an opportunity to respond. The officer consulted will then decide if the interview should continue without the attendance of that appropriate adult. If they decide it should, another appropriate adult must be obtained before the interview continues, unless the provisions of *paragraph 11.18* below apply.

(d) *Vulnerable suspects – urgent interviews at police stations*

11.18 The following interviews may take place only if an officer of superintendent rank or above considers delaying the interview will lead to the consequences in *paragraph 11.1(a) to (c)*, and is satisfied the interview would not significantly harm the person's physical or mental state (see *Annex G*):
(a) an interview of a detained juvenile or person who is mentally disordered or otherwise mentally vulnerable without the appropriate adult being present;
(b) an interview of anyone detained other than in *(a)* who appears unable to:
  - appreciate the significance of questions and their answers; or
  - understand what is happening because of the effects of drink, drugs or any illness, ailment or condition;
(c) an interview, without an interpreter having been arranged, of a detained person whom the custody officer has determined requires an interpreter (see *paragraphs 3.5(c)(ii)* and *3.12*) which is carried out by an interviewer speaking the suspect's own language

or (as the case may be) otherwise establishing effective communication which is sufficient to enable the necessary questions to be asked and answered in order to avert the consequences. See *paragraphs 13.2* and *13.5*.

11.19 These interviews may not continue once sufficient information has been obtained to avert the consequences in *paragraph 11.1(a)* to *(c)*.

11.20 A record shall be made of the grounds for any decision to interview a person under *paragraph 11.18*.

Notes for Guidance

11ZA   The requirement in paragraph 11.1A for a suspect to be given sufficient information about the offence applies prior to the interview and whether or not they are legally represented. What is sufficient will depend on the circumstances of the case, but it should normally include, as a minimum, a description of the facts relating to the suspected offence that are known to the officer, including the time and place in question. This aims to avoid suspects being confused or unclear about what they are supposed to have done and to help an innocent suspect to clear the matter up more quickly.

11A   Paragraph 11.4 does not prevent the interviewer from putting significant statements and silences to a suspect again at a later stage or a further interview.

11B   The Criminal Procedure and Investigations Act 1996 Code of Practice, paragraph 3.5 states 'In conducting an investigation, the investigator should pursue all reasonable lines of enquiry, whether these point towards or away from the suspect. What is reasonable will depend on the particular circumstances.' Interviewers should keep this in mind when deciding what questions to ask in an interview.

11C   Although juveniles or people who are mentally disordered or otherwise mentally vulnerable are often capable of providing reliable evidence, they may, without knowing or wishing to do so, be particularly prone in certain circumstances to provide information that may be unreliable, misleading or self-incriminating. Special care should always be taken when questioning such a person, and the appropriate adult should be involved if there is any doubt about a person's age, mental state or capacity. Because of the risk of unreliable evidence it is also important to obtain corroboration of any facts admitted whenever possible.

11D   Juveniles should not be arrested at their place of education unless this is unavoidable. When a juvenile is arrested at their place of education, the principal or their nominee must be informed.

11E   Significant statements described in paragraph 11.4 will always be relevant to the offence and must be recorded. When a suspect agrees to read records of interviews and other comments and sign them as correct, they should be asked to endorse the record with, e.g. 'I agree that this is a correct record of what was said' and add their signature. If the suspect does not agree with the record, the interviewer should record the details of any disagreement and ask the suspect to read these details and sign them to the effect that they accurately reflect their disagreement. Any refusal to sign should be recorded.

11F   The appropriate adult may intervene if they consider it is necessary to help the suspect understand any question asked and to help the suspect to answer any question. Paragraph 11.17A only applies if the appropriate adult's approach or conduct prevents or unreasonably obstructs proper questions being put to the suspect or the suspect's response being recorded. Examples of unacceptable conduct include answering questions on a suspect's behalf or providing written replies for the suspect to quote. An officer who takes the decision to exclude an appropriate adult must be in a position to satisfy the court the decision was properly made. In order to do this they may need to witness what is happening and give the suspect's solicitor (if they have one) who witnessed what happened, an opportunity to comment.

12   Interviews in police stations

(a)   Action

12.1   If a police officer wants to interview or conduct enquiries which require the presence of a detainee, the custody officer is responsible for deciding whether to deliver the detainee into the officer's custody. An investigating officer who is given custody of a detainee takes over responsibility for the detainee's care and safe custody for the purposes of this Code until they return the detainee to the custody officer when they must report the manner in which they complied with the Code whilst having custody of the detainee.

12.2   Except as below, in any period of 24 hours a detainee must be allowed a continuous period of at least 8 hours for rest, free from questioning, travel or any interruption in connection with the investigation concerned. This period should normally be at night or other appropriate time which takes account of when the detainee last slept or rested. If a detainee is arrested at a police station after going there voluntarily, the period of 24 hours runs from the time of their arrest and not the time of arrival at the police station. The period may not be interrupted or delayed, except:

(a)   when there are reasonable grounds for believing not delaying or interrupting the period would:
  (i)   involve a risk of harm to people or serious loss of, or damage to, property;
  (ii)   delay unnecessarily the person's release from custody; or
  (iii) otherwise prejudice the outcome of the investigation;

(b)   at the request of the detainee, their appropriate adult or legal representative;

(c)   when a delay or interruption is necessary in order to:
  (i)   comply with the legal obligations and duties arising under section 15; or
  (ii)   to take action required under *section 9* or in accordance with medical advice.

If the period is interrupted in accordance with *(a)*, a fresh period must be allowed. Interruptions under *(b)* and *(c)* do not require a fresh period to be allowed.

12.3   Before a detainee is interviewed, the custody officer, in consultation with the officer in charge of the investigation and appropriate healthcare professionals as necessary, shall assess whether the detainee is fit enough to be interviewed. This means determining and considering the risks to the detainee's physical and mental state if the interview took place and determining what safeguards are needed to allow the interview to take place. See *Annex G*. The custody officer shall not allow a detainee to be interviewed if the custody officer considers it would cause significant harm to the detainee's physical or mental state. Vulnerable suspects listed at *paragraph 11.18* shall be treated as always being at some risk during an interview and these persons may not be interviewed except in accordance with *paragraphs 11.18* to *11.20*.

12.4   As far as practicable interviews shall take place in interview rooms which are adequately heated, lit and ventilated.

12.5   A suspect whose detention without charge has been authorised under PACE because the detention is necessary for an interview to obtain evidence of the offence for which they have been arrested may choose not to answer questions but police do not require the suspect's consent or agreement to interview them for this purpose. If a suspect takes steps to prevent themselves being questioned or further questioned, e.g. by refusing to leave their cell to go to a suitable interview room or by trying to leave the interview room, they shall be advised their consent or agreement to interview is not required. The suspect shall be cautioned as in *section 10*, and informed if they fail or refuse to co-operate, the interview may take place in the cell and that their failure or refusal to co-operate may be given in evidence. The suspect shall then be invited to co-operate and go into the interview room.

12.6   People being questioned or making statements shall not be required to stand.

12.7   Before the interview commences each interviewer shall, subject to *paragraph 2.6A*, identify themselves and any other persons present to the interviewee.

12.8   Breaks from interviewing should be made at recognised meal times or at other times that take account of when an interviewee last had a meal. Short refreshment breaks shall be provided at approximately two hour intervals, subject to the interviewer's discretion to delay a break if there are reasonable grounds for believing it would:

(i)   involve a:
  •   risk of harm to people;
  •   serious loss of, or damage to, property;
(ii)   unnecessarily delay the detainee's release; or
(iii) otherwise prejudice the outcome of the investigation.

See *Note 12B*

12.9   If during the interview a complaint is made by or on behalf of the interviewee concerning the provisions of any of the Codes, or it comes to the interviewer's notice that the interviewee may have been treated improperly, the interviewer should:

(i)   record the matter in the interview record; and
(ii)   inform the custody officer, who is then responsible for dealing with it as in *section 9*.

(b)   Documentation

12.10   A record must be made of the:
- time a detainee is not in the custody of the custody officer, and why
- reason for any refusal to deliver the detainee out of that custody.

12.11   A record shall be made of:
(a)   the reasons it was not practicable to use an interview room; and
(b)   any action taken as in *paragraph 12.5.*
The record shall be made on the custody record or in the interview record for action taken whilst an interview record is being kept, with a brief reference to this effect in the custody record.

12.12   Any decision to delay a break in an interview must be recorded, with reasons, in the interview record.

12.13   All written statements made at police stations under caution shall be written on forms provided for the purpose.

12.14   All written statements made under caution shall be taken in accordance with *Annex D.* Before a person makes a written statement under caution at a police station, they shall be reminded about the right to legal advice. See *Note 12A.*

Notes for Guidance

12A   *It is not normally necessary to ask for a written statement if the interview was recorded in writing and the record signed in accordance with paragraph 11.11 or audibly or visually recorded in accordance with Code E or F. Statements under caution should normally be taken in these circumstances only at the person's express wish. A person may however be asked if they want to make such a statement.*

12B   *Meal breaks should normally last at least 45 minutes and shorter breaks after two hours should last at least 15 minutes. If the interviewer delays a break in accordance with paragraph 12.8 and prolongs the interview, a longer break should be provided. If there is a short interview and another short interview is contemplated, the length of the break may be reduced if there are reasonable grounds to believe this is necessary to avoid any of the consequences in paragraph 12.8(i) to (iii).*

13   Interpreters

(a)   General

13.1   Chief officers are responsible for making arrangements (see *paragraph 13.1ZA*) to provide appropriately qualified independent persons to act as interpreters and to provide translations of essential documents for:
(a)   detained suspects who, in accordance with *paragraph 3.5(c)(ii)*, the custody officer has determined require an interpreter, and
(b)   suspects who are not under arrest but are cautioned as in *section 10* who, in accordance with *paragraph 3.21(b)*, the interviewer has determined require an interpreter. In these cases, the responsibilities of the custody officer are, if appropriate, assigned to the interviewer. An interviewer who has any doubts about whether and what arrangements for an interpreter must be made or about how the provisions of this section should be applied to a suspect who is not under arrest should seek advice from an officer of the rank of sergeant or above.
If the suspect has a hearing or speech impediment, references to 'interpreter' and 'interpretation' in this Code include arrangements for appropriate assistance necessary to establish effective communication with that person. See *paragraph 13.1C* below if the person is in Wales.

13.1ZA References in *paragraph 13.1* above and elsewhere in this Code (see *paragraphs 3.12(a), 13.2, 13.2A, 13.5, 13.6, 13.9, 13.10, 13.10A, 13.10D* and *13.11 below* and in any other Code, to making arrangements for an interpreter to assist a suspect, mean making arrangements for the interpreter to be *physically* present in the same location as the suspect *unless* the provisions in *paragraph 13.12* below, and Part 1 of *Annex N*, allow live-link interpretation to be used.

13.1A   The arrangements *must* comply with the minimum requirements set out in *Directive 2010/64/EU* of the European Parliament and of the Council of 20 October 2010 on the right to interpretation and translation in criminal proceedings (see *Note 13A*). The provisions *of this* Code implement the requirements for those to whom this Code applies. These requirements include the following:

- That the arrangements made and the quality of interpretation and translation provided shall be sufficient to '*safeguard the fairness of the proceedings, in particular by ensuring that suspected or accused persons have knowledge of the cases against them and are able to exercise their right of defence*'. This term which is used by the Directive means that the suspect must be able to understand their position and be able to communicate effectively with police officers, interviewers, solicitors and appropriate adults as provided for by this and any other Code in the same way as a suspect who can speak and understand English and who does not have a hearing or speech impediment and who would therefore not require an interpreter. See *paragraphs 13.12 to 13.14* and *Annex N* for application to live-link interpretation.
- The provision of a written translation of all documents considered essential for the person to exercise their right of defence and to '*safeguard the fairness of the proceedings*' as described above. For the purposes of this Code, this includes any decision to authorise a person to be detained and details of any offence(s) with which the person has been charged or for which they have been told they may be prosecuted, see *Annex M*.
- Procedures to help determine:
  - whether a suspect can speak and understand English and needs the assistance of an interpreter, see *paragraph 13.1* and *Notes 13B* and *13C*; and
  - whether another interpreter should be arranged or another translation should be provided when a suspect complains about the quality of either or both, see *paragraphs 13.10A* and *13.10C*.

13.1B All reasonable attempts should be made to make the suspect understand that interpretation and translation will be provided at public expense.

13.1C With regard to persons in Wales, nothing in this or any other Code affects the application of the Welsh Language Schemes produced by police and crime commissioners in Wales in accordance with the Welsh Language Act 1993. See paragraphs 3.12 and 13.1.

(b)   *Interviewing suspects – foreign languages*

13.2 Unless *paragraphs 11.1 or 11.18(c)* apply, a suspect who for the purposes of this Code requires an interpreter because they do not appear to speak or understand English (see *paragraphs 3.5(c)(ii)* and *3.12*) must not be interviewed unless arrangements are made for a person capable of interpreting to assist the suspect to understand and communicate.

13.2A If a person who is a juvenile or is mentally disordered or mentally vulnerable is interviewed and the person acting as the appropriate adult does not appear to speak or understand English, arrangements must be made for an interpreter to assist communication between the person, the appropriate adult and the interviewer, unless the interview is urgent and *paragraphs 11.1 or 11.18(c)* apply.

13.3 When a written record of the interview is made (see *paragraph 11.7*), the interviewer shall make sure the interpreter makes a note of the interview at the time in the person's language for use in the event of the interpreter being called to give evidence, and certifies its accuracy. The interviewer should allow sufficient time for the interpreter to note each question and answer after each is put, given and interpreted. The person should be allowed to read the record or have it read to them and sign it as correct or indicate the respects in which they consider it inaccurate. If an audio or visual record of the interview is made, the arrangements in Code E or F shall apply. See *paragraphs 13.12* to *13.14* and *Annex N* for application to live-link interpretation.

13.4 In the case of a person making a statement under caution (see *Annex D*) to a police officer or other police staff in a language other than English:
   (a)   the interpreter shall record the statement in the language it is made;
   (b)   the person shall be invited to sign it;
   (c)   an official English translation shall be made in due course. See *paragraphs 13.12* to *13.14* and *Annex N* for application to live-link interpretation.

(c)   *Interviewing suspects who have a hearing or speech impediment*

13.5 Unless *paragraphs 11.1 or 11.18(c)* (urgent interviews) apply, a suspect who for the purposes of this Code requires an interpreter or other appropriate assistance to enable effective communication with them because they appear to have a hearing or speech impediment (see *paragraphs 3.5(c)(ii)* and *3.12*) must not be interviewed without arrangements having been made to provide an independent person capable of interpreting or of providing other appropriate assistance.

13.6   An interpreter should also be arranged if a person who is a juvenile or who is mentally disordered or mentally vulnerable is interviewed and the person who is present as the appropriate adult, appears to have a hearing or speech impediment, unless the interview is urgent and *paragraphs 11.1 or 11.18(c)* apply.

13.7   If a written record of the interview is made, the interviewer shall make sure the interpreter is allowed to read the record and certify its accuracy in the event of the interpreter being called to give evidence. If an audio or visual recording is made, the arrangements in Code E or F apply.

See *paragraphs 13.12* to *13.14* and *Annex N* for application to live-link interpretation.

(d)   Additional rules for detained persons

13.8   *Not used.*

13.9   If *paragraph 6.1* applies and the detainee cannot communicate with the solicitor because of language, hearing or speech difficulties, arrangements must be made for an interpreter to enable communication. A police officer or any other police staff may not be used for this purpose.

13.10   After the custody officer has determined that a detainee requires an interpreter (see *paragraph 3.5(c)(ii)*) and following the initial action in *paragraphs 3.1 to 3.5*, arrangements must also be made for an interpreter to:
- explain the grounds and reasons for any authorisation for their *continued* detention, before or after charge and any information about the authorisation given to them by the authorising officer and which is recorded in the custody record. See *paragraphs 15.3, 15.4* and *15.16(a)* and *(b)*;
- to provide interpretation at the magistrates' court for the hearing of an application for a warrant of further detention or any extension or further extension of such warrant to explain any grounds and reasons for the application and any information about the authorisation of their further detention given to them by the court (see PACE, sections 43 and 44 and *paragraphs 15.2* and *15.16(c)*); and
- explain any offence with which the detainee is charged or for which they are informed they may be prosecuted and any other information about the offence given to them by or on behalf of the custody officer, see *paragraphs 16.1* and *16.3*.

13.10A If a detainee complains that they are not satisfied with the quality of interpretation, the custody officer or (as the case may be) the interviewer, is responsible for deciding whether to make arrangements for a different interpreter in accordance with the procedures set out in the arrangements made by the chief officer, see *paragraph 13.1A*.

(e)   Translations of essential documents

13.10B Written translations, oral translations and oral summaries of essential documents in a language the detainee understands shall be provided in accordance with Annex M (Translations of documents and records).

13.10C If a detainee complains that they are not satisfied with the quality of the translation, the custody officer or (as the case may be) the interviewer, is responsible for deciding whether a further translation should be provided in accordance with the procedures set out in the arrangements made by the chief officer, see *paragraph 13.1A*.

(f)   Decisions not to provide interpretation and translation.

13.10D If a suspect challenges a decision:
- made by the custody officer or (as the case may be) by the interviewer, in accordance with this Code (see *paragraphs 3.5(c)(ii)* and *3.21(b)*) that they do not require an interpreter, or
- made in accordance with *paragraphs 13.10A, 13.10B* or *13.10C* not to make arrangements to provide a different interpreter or another translation or not to translate a requested document,

the matter shall be reported to an inspector to deal with as a complaint for the purposes of *paragraph 9.2* or *paragraph 12.9* if the challenge is made during an interview.

(g) Documentation

13.11 The following must be recorded in the custody record or, as applicable, the interview record:

(a) Action taken to arrange for an interpreter, including the live-link requirements in Annex N as applicable;

(b) Action taken when a detainee is not satisfied about the standard of interpretation or translation provided, see *paragraphs 13.10A* and *13.10C*;

(c) When an urgent interview is carried out in accordance with *paragraph 13.2* or *13.5* in the absence of an interpreter;

(d) When a detainee has been assisted by an interpreter for the purpose of providing or being given information or being interviewed;

(e) Action taken in accordance with Annex M when:
- a written translation of an essential document is provided;
- an oral translation or oral summary of an essential document is provided instead of a written translation and the authorising officer's reason(s) why this would not prejudice the fairness of the proceedings (see *Annex M, paragraph 3*);
- a suspect waives their right to a translation of an essential document (see *Annex M, paragraph 4*);
- when representations that a document which is not included in the table is essential and that a translation should be provided are refused and the reason for the refusal (see *Annex M, paragraph 8*).

(h) Live-link interpretation

13.12 In this section and in Annex N, 'live-link interpretation' means an arrangement to enable communication between the suspect and an interpreter who is not *physically* present with the suspect. The arrangement must ensure that anything said by any person in the suspect's presence and hearing can be interpreted in the same way as if the interpreter was physically present at that time. The communication must be by audio *and* visual means for the purpose of an interview, and for all other purposes it may be *either*; by audio and visual means, or by audio means *only*, as follows:

(a) Audio and visual communication

This applies for the purposes of an interview conducted and recorded in accordance with Code E (Audio recording) or Code F (Visual recording) and during that interview, live link interpretation must *enable*:

(i) the suspect, the interviewer, solicitor, appropriate adult and any other person *physically* present with the suspect at any time during the interview and an interpreter who is not *physically* present, to *see* and *hear* each other; and

(ii) the interview to be conducted and recorded in accordance with the provisions of Codes C, E and F, subject to the modifications in Part 2 of Annex N.

(b) Audio and visual or audio without visual communication.

This applies to communication for the purposes of any provision of this or any other Code except as described in (a), which requires or permits information to be given to, sought from, or provided by a suspect, whether orally or in writing, which would include communication between the suspect and their solicitor and/or appropriate adult, and for these cases, live link interpretation must:

(i) *enable* the suspect, the person giving or seeking that information, any other person *physically* present with the suspect at that time and an interpreter who is not so present, to either *see* and *hear* each other, or to *hear without seeing* each other (for example by using a telephone); and

(ii) enable that information to be given to, sought from, or provided by, the suspect in accordance with the provisions of this or any other Code that apply to that information, as modified for the purposes of the live-link, by Part 2 of Annex N.

13.12A The requirement in *sub-paragraphs 13.12(a)(ii)* and *(b)(ii)*, that live-link interpretation must enable compliance with the relevant provisions of the Codes C, E and F, means that the arrangements must provide for any written or electronic record of what the suspect says in their own language which is made by the interpreter, to be securely transmitted without delay so that the suspect can be invited to read, check and if appropriate, sign or otherwise confirm that the record is correct or make corrections to the record.

13.13   Chief officers must be satisfied that live-link interpretation used in their force area for the purposes of *paragraphs 3.12(a)* and *(b)*, provides for accurate and secure communication with the suspect. This includes ensuring that at any time during which live link interpretation is being used: a person cannot see, hear or otherwise obtain access to any communications between the suspect and interpreter or communicate with the suspect or interpreter unless so authorised or allowed by the custody officer or, in the case of an interview, the interviewer and that as applicable, the confidentiality of any private consultation between a suspect and their solicitor and appropriate adult (see *paragraphs 13.2A, 13.6* and *13.9*) is maintained. See *Annex N paragraph 4*.

Notes for Guidance

13A   *Chief officers have discretion when determining the individuals or organisations they use to provide interpretation and translation services for their forces provided that these are compatible with the requirements of the Directive. One example which chief officers may wish to consider is the Ministry of Justice commercial agreements for interpretation and translation services.*

13B   *A procedure for determining whether a person needs an interpreter might involve a telephone interpreter service or using cue cards or similar visual aids which enable the detainee to indicate their ability to speak and understand English and their preferred language. This could be confirmed through an interpreter who could also assess the extent to which the person can speak and understand English.*

13C   *There should also be a procedure for determining whether a suspect who requires an interpreter requires assistance in accordance with paragraph 3.20 to help them check and if applicable, sign any documentation.*

14   Questioning – special restrictions

14.1   If a person is arrested by one police force on behalf of another and the lawful period of detention in respect of that offence has not yet commenced in accordance with PACE, section 41, no questions may be put to them about the offence while they are in transit between the forces except to clarify any voluntary statement they make.

14.2   If a person is in police detention at a hospital, they may not be questioned without the agreement of a responsible doctor. See *Note 14A*.

Note for Guidance

14A   *If questioning takes place at a hospital under paragraph 14.2, or on the way to or from a hospital, the period of questioning concerned counts towards the total period of detention permitted.*

15   Reviews and extensions of detention

(a)   Persons detained under PACE

15.0   The requirement in *paragraph 3.4(b)* that documents and materials essential to challenging the lawfulness of the detainee's arrest and detention must be made available to the detainee or their solicitor, applies for the purposes of this section as follows:

(a)   The officer reviewing the need for detention without charge (*PACE, section 40*), or (as the case may be) the officer considering the need to extend detention without charge from 24 to 36 hours (*PACE, section 42*), is responsible, in consultation with the investigating officer, for deciding which documents and materials are essential and must be made available.

(b)   When *paragraph 15.7A* applies (application for a warrant of further detention or extension of such a warrant), the officer making the application is responsible for deciding which documents and materials are essential and must be made available *before* the hearing. See *Note 3ZA*.

15.1   The review officer is responsible under PACE, section 40 for periodically determining if a person's detention, before or after charge, continues to be necessary. This requirement continues throughout the detention period and, except as in *paragraph 15.10*, the review officer must be present at the police station holding the detainee. See *Notes 15A* and *15B*.

15.2   Under PACE, section 42, an officer of superintendent rank or above who is responsible for the station holding the detainee may give authority any time after the second review to extend the maximum period the person may be detained without charge by up to 12 hours. Further detention without charge may be authorised only by a magistrates' court in accordance with PACE, sections 43 and 44. See *Notes 15C, 15D* and *15E*.

15.2A An authorisation under section 42(1) of PACE extends the maximum period of detention permitted before charge for indictable offences from 24 hours to 36 hours. Detaining a juvenile or mentally vulnerable person for longer than 24 hours will be dependent on the circumstances of the case and with regard to the person's:

    (a)   special vulnerability;

    (b)   the legal obligation to provide an opportunity for representations to be made prior to a decision about extending detention;

    (c)   the need to consult and consider the views of any appropriate adult; and

    (d)   any alternatives to police custody.

15.3 Before deciding whether to authorise continued detention the officer responsible under *paragraph 15.1* or *15.2* shall give an opportunity to make representations about the detention to:

    (a)   the detainee, unless in the case of a review as in *paragraph 15.1*, the detainee is asleep;

    (b)   the detainee's solicitor if available at the time; and

    (c)   the appropriate adult if available at the time.

See *Note 15CA*

15.3A Other people having an interest in the detainee's welfare may also make representations at the authorising officer's discretion.

15.3B Subject to *paragraph 15.10*, the representations may be made orally in person or by telephone or in writing. The authorising officer may, however, refuse to hear oral representations from the detainee if the officer considers them unfit to make representations because of their condition or behaviour. See *Note 15C*.

15.3C The decision on whether the review takes place in person or by telephone or by video conferencing (see *Note 15G*) is a matter for the review officer. In determining the form the review may take, the review officer must always take full account of the needs of the person in custody. The benefits of carrying out a review in person should always be considered, based on the individual circumstances of each case with specific additional consideration if the person is:

    (a)   a juvenile (and the age of the juvenile); or

    (b)   suspected of being mentally vulnerable; or

    (c)   in need of medical attention for other than routine minor ailments; or

    (d)   subject to presentational or community issues around their detention.

15.4 Before conducting a review or determining whether to extend the maximum period of detention without charge, the officer responsible must make sure the detainee is reminded of their entitlement to free legal advice, see *paragraph 6.5*, unless in the case of a review the person is asleep.

15.5 If, after considering any representations, the review officer under *paragraph 15.1* decides to keep the detainee in detention or the superintendent under *paragraph 15.2* extends the maximum period for which they may be detained without charge, then any comment made by the detainee shall be recorded. If applicable, the officer shall be informed of the comment as soon as practicable. See also *paragraphs 11.4* and *11.13*.

15.6 No officer shall put specific questions to the detainee:

    •   regarding their involvement in any offence; or

    •   in respect of any comments they may make:

        —   when given the opportunity to make representations; or

        —   in response to a decision to keep them in detention or extend the maximum period of detention.

Such an exchange could constitute an interview as in *paragraph 11.1A* and would be subject to the associated safeguards in *section 11* and, in respect of a person who has been charged, *paragraph 16.5*. See also *paragraph 11.13*.

15.7 A detainee who is asleep at a review, see *paragraph 15.1*, and whose continued detention is authorised must be informed about the decision and reason as soon as practicable after waking.

15.7A When an application is made to a magistrates' court under PACE, section 43 for a warrant of further detention to extend detention without charge of a person arrested for an *indictable offence*, or under section 44, to extend or further extend that warrant, the detainee:

    (a)   must be brought to court for the hearing of the application;

    (b)   is entitled to be legally represented if they wish, in which case, *Annex B* cannot apply; and

    (c)   must be given a copy of the information which supports the application and states:

        (i)   the nature of the offence for which the person to whom the application relates has been arrested;

        (ii)   the general nature of the evidence on which the person was arrested;

        (iii)   what inquiries about the offence have been made and what further inquiries are proposed;

        (iv)   the reasons for believing continued detention is necessary for the purposes of the further inquiries;

Note: A warrant of further detention can only be issued or extended if the court has reasonable grounds for believing that the person's further detention is necessary for the purpose of obtaining evidence of an indictable offence for which the person has been arrested and that the investigation is being conducted diligently and expeditiously. See *paragraph 15.0(b)*.

15.8   *Not used.*

(b)   *Review of detention by telephone and video conferencing facilities*

15.9   PACE, section 40A provides that the officer responsible under section 40 for reviewing the detention of a person who has not been charged, need not attend the police station holding the detainee and may carry out the review by telephone.

15.9A PACE, section 45A(2) provides that the officer responsible under section 40 for reviewing the detention of a person who has not been charged, need not attend the police station holding the detainee and may carry out the review by video conferencing facilities. See *Note 15G.*

15.9B A telephone review is not permitted where facilities for review by video conferencing exist and it is practicable to use them.

15.9C The review officer can decide at any stage that a telephone review or review by video conferencing should be terminated and that the review will be conducted in person. The reasons for doing so should be noted in the custody record. See *Note 15F.*

15.10 When a review is carried out by telephone or by video conferencing facilities, an officer at the station holding the detainee shall be required by the review officer to fulfil that officer's obligations under PACE section 40 and this Code by:

    (a)   making any record connected with the review in the detainee's custody record;

    (b)   if applicable, making the record in (*a*) in the presence of the detainee; and

    (c)   for a review by telephone, giving the detainee information about the review.

15.11 When a review is carried out by telephone or by video conferencing facilities, the requirement in *paragraph 15.3* will be satisfied:

    (a)   if facilities exist for the immediate transmission of written representations to the review officer, e.g. fax or email message, by allowing those who are given the opportunity to make representations, to make their representations:

        (i)   orally by telephone or (as the case may be) by means of the video conferencing facilities; or

        (ii)   in writing using the facilities for the immediate transmission of written representations; and

    (b)   in all other cases, by allowing those who are given the opportunity to make representations, to make their representations orally by telephone or by means of the video conferencing facilities.

(c)   *Documentation*

15.12 It is the officer's responsibility to make sure all reminders given under *paragraph 15.4* are noted in the custody record.

15.13 The grounds for, and extent of, any delay in conducting a review shall be recorded.

15.14 When a review is carried out by telephone or video conferencing facilities, a record shall be made of:

    (a)   the reason the review officer did not attend the station holding the detainee;

    (b)   the place the review officer was;

    (c)   the method representations, oral or written, were made to the review officer, see *paragraph 15.11.*

15.15 Any written representations shall be retained.
15.16 A record shall be made as soon as practicable of:
   (a) the outcome of each review of detention before or after charge, and if *paragraph 15.7* applies, of when the person was informed and by whom;
   (b) the outcome of any determination under PACE, section 42 by a superintendent whether to extend the maximum period of detention without charge beyond 24 hours from the relevant time. If an authorisation is given, the record shall state the number of hours and minutes by which the detention period is extended or further extended.
   (c) the outcome of each application under PACE, section 43, for a warrant of further detention or under section 44, for an extension or further extension of that warrant. If a warrant for further detention is granted under section 43 or extended or further extended under 44, the record shall state the detention period authorised by the warrant and the date and time it was granted or (as the case may be) the period by which the warrant is extended or further extended.

   Note: Any period during which a person is released on bail does not count towards the maximum period of detention without charge allowed under PACE, sections 41 to 44.

Notes for Guidance

15A *Review officer for the purposes of:*
   • *PACE, sections 40, 40A and 45A means, in the case of a person arrested but not charged, an officer of at least inspector rank not directly involved in the investigation and, if a person has been arrested and charged, the custody officer.*
15B *The detention of persons in police custody not subject to the statutory review requirement in paragraph 15.1 should still be reviewed periodically as a matter of good practice. Such reviews can be carried out by an officer of the rank of sergeant or above. The purpose of such reviews is to check the particular power under which a detainee is held continues to apply, any associated conditions are complied with and to make sure appropriate action is taken to deal with any changes. This includes the detainee's prompt release when the power no longer applies, or their transfer if the power requires the detainee be taken elsewhere as soon as the necessary arrangements are made. Examples include persons:*
   (a) *arrested on warrant because they failed to answer bail to appear at court;*
   (b) *arrested under the Bail Act 1976, section 7(3) for breaching a condition of bail granted after charge;*
   (c) *in police custody for specific purposes and periods under the Crime (Sentences) Act 1997, Schedule 1;*
   (d) *convicted, or remand prisoners, held in police stations on behalf of the Prison Service under the Imprisonment (Temporary Provisions) Act 1980, section 6;*
   (e) *being detained to prevent them causing a breach of the peace;*
   (f) *detained at police stations on behalf of Immigration Enforcement (formerly the UK Immigration Service);*
   (g) *detained by order of a magistrates' court under the Criminal Justice Act 1988, section 152 (as amended by the Drugs Act 2005, section 8) to facilitate the recovery of evidence after being charged with drug possession or drug trafficking and suspected of having swallowed drugs.*
   The detention of persons remanded into police detention by order of a court under the Magistrates' Courts Act 1980, section 128 is subject to a statutory requirement to review that detention. This is to make sure the detainee is taken back to court no later than the end of the period authorised by the court or when the need for their detention by police ceases, whichever is the sooner.
15C *In the case of a review of detention, but not an extension, the detainee need not be woken for the review. However, if the detainee is likely to be asleep, e.g. during a period of rest allowed as in paragraph 12.2, at the latest time a review or authorisation to extend detention may take place, the officer should, if the legal obligations and time constraints permit, bring forward the procedure to allow the detainee to make representations. A detainee not asleep during the review must be present when the grounds for their continued detention are recorded and must at the same time be informed of those grounds unless the review officer considers the person is incapable of understanding what is said, violent or likely to become violent or in urgent need of medical attention.*

15CA   *In paragraph 15.3(b) and (c), 'available' includes being contactable in time to enable them to make representations remotely by telephone or other electronic means or in person by attending the station. Reasonable efforts should therefore be made to give the solicitor and appropriate adult sufficient notice of the time the decision is expected to be made so that they can make themselves available.*

15D   *An application to a Magistrates' Court under PACE, sections 43 or 44 for a warrant of further detention or its extension should be made between 10am and 9pm, and if possible during normal court hours. It will not usually be practicable to arrange for a court to sit specially outside the hours of 10am to 9pm. If it appears a special sitting may be needed outside normal court hours but between 10am and 9pm, the clerk to the justices should be given notice and informed of this possibility, while the court is sitting if possible.*

15E   *In paragraph 15.2, the officer responsible for the station holding the detainee includes a superintendent or above who, in accordance with their force operational policy or police regulations, is given that responsibility on a temporary basis whilst the appointed long-term holder is off duty or otherwise unavailable.*

15F   *The provisions of PACE, section 40A allowing telephone reviews do not apply to reviews of detention after charge by the custody officer. When video conferencing is not required, they allow the use of a telephone to carry out a review of detention before charge. The procedure under PACE, section 42 must be done in person.*

15G   *Video conferencing facilities means any facilities (whether a live television link or other facilities) by means of which the review can be carried out with the review officer, the detainee concerned and the detainee's solicitor all being able to both see and to hear each other. The use of video conferencing facilities for decisions about detention under section 45A of PACE is subject to regulations made by the Secretary of State being in force.*

16   Charging detained persons

(a)   Action

16.1   When the officer in charge of the investigation reasonably believes there is sufficient evidence to provide a realistic prospect of conviction for the offence (see *paragraph 11.6*), they shall without delay, and subject to the following qualification, inform the custody officer who will be responsible for considering whether the detainee should be charged. See *Notes 11B* and *16A*. When a person is detained in respect of more than one offence it is permissible to delay informing the custody officer until the above conditions are satisfied in respect of all the offences, but see *paragraph 11.6*. If the detainee is a juvenile, mentally disordered or otherwise mentally vulnerable, any resulting action shall be taken in the presence of the appropriate adult if they are present at the time. See *Notes 16B* and *16C*.

16.1A   Where guidance issued by the Director of Public Prosecutions under PACE, section 37A is in force the custody officer must comply with that Guidance in deciding how to act in dealing with the detainee. See *Notes 16AA* and *16AB*.

16.1B   Where in compliance with the DPP's Guidance the custody officer decides that the case should be immediately referred to the CPS to make the charging decision, consultation should take place with a Crown Prosecutor as soon as is reasonably practicable. Where the Crown Prosecutor is unable to make the charging decision on the information available at that time, the detainee may be released without charge and on bail (with conditions if necessary) under section 37(7)(a). In such circumstances, the detainee should be informed that they are being released to enable the Director of Public Prosecutions to make a decision under section 37B.

16.2   When a detainee is charged with or informed they may be prosecuted for an offence, see *Note 16B*, they shall, unless the restriction on drawing adverse inferences from silence applies, see *Annex C*, be cautioned as follows:

> *'You do not have to say anything. But it may harm your defence if you do not mention now something which you later rely on in court. Anything you do say may be given in evidence.'*

Where the use of the Welsh Language is appropriate, a constable may provide the caution directly in Welsh in the following terms:

> *'Does dim rhaid i chi ddweud dim byd. Ond gall niweidio eich amddiffyniad os na fyddwch chi'n sôn, yn awr, am rywbeth y byddwch chi'n dibynnu arno nes ymlaen yn y llys. Gall unrhyw beth yr ydych yn ei ddweud gael ei roi fel tystiolaeth.'*

Annex C, paragraph 2 sets out the alternative terms of the caution to be used when the restriction on drawing adverse inferences from silence applies.

16.3   When a detainee is charged they shall be given a written notice showing particulars of the offence and, subject to *paragraph 2.6A*, the officer's name and the case reference number. As far as possible the particulars of the charge shall be stated in simple terms, but they shall also show the precise offence in law with which the detainee is charged. The notice shall begin:

    'You are charged with the offence(s) shown below.' Followed by the caution.

    If the detainee is a juvenile, mentally disordered or otherwise mentally vulnerable, a copy of the notice should also be given to the appropriate adult.

16.4   If, after a detainee has been charged with or informed they may be prosecuted for an offence, an officer wants to tell them about any written statement or interview with another person relating to such an offence, the detainee shall either be handed a true copy of the written statement or the content of the interview record brought to their attention. Nothing shall be done to invite any reply or comment except to:

(a)   caution the detainee, *'You do not have to say anything, but anything you do say may be given in evidence.'*;

    Where the use of the Welsh Language is appropriate, caution the detainee in the following terms:

    'Does dim rhaid i chi ddweud dim byd, ond gall unrhyw beth yr ydych yn ei ddweud gael ei roi fel tystiolaeth.'

    and

(b)   remind the detainee about their right to legal advice.

16.4A If the detainee:

- cannot read, the document may be read to them;
- is a juvenile, mentally disordered or otherwise mentally vulnerable, the appropriate adult shall also be given a copy, or the interview record shall be brought to their attention.

16.5   A detainee may not be interviewed about an offence after they have been charged with, or informed they may be prosecuted for it, unless the interview is necessary:

- to prevent or minimise harm or loss to some other person, or the public
- to clear up an ambiguity in a previous answer or statement
- in the interests of justice for the detainee to have put to them, and have an opportunity to comment on, information concerning the offence which has come to light since they were charged or informed they might be prosecuted

Before any such interview, the interviewer shall:

(a)   caution the detainee, *'You do not have to say anything, but anything you do say may be given in evidence.'*

    Where the use of the Welsh Language is appropriate, the interviewer shall caution the detainee: *'Does dim rhaid i chi ddweud dim byd, ond gall unrhyw beth yr ydych yn ei ddweud gael ei roi fel tystiolaeth.'*

(b)   remind the detainee about their right to legal advice. See *Note 16B*

16.6   The provisions of *paragraphs 16.2 to 16.5* must be complied with in the appropriate adult's presence if they are already at the police station. If they are not at the police station then these provisions must be complied with again in their presence when they arrive unless the detainee has been released. See *Note 16C*.

16.7   When a juvenile is charged with an offence and the custody officer authorises their continued detention after charge, the custody officer must make arrangements for the juvenile to be taken into the care of a local authority to be detained pending appearance in court *unless* the custody officer certifies in accordance with PACE, section 38(6), that:

(a)   for any juvenile; it is impracticable to do so and the reasons why it is impracticable must be set out in the certificate that must be produced to the court; or,

(b)   in the case of a juvenile of at least 12 years old, no secure accommodation is available and other accommodation would not be adequate to protect the public from serious harm from that juvenile. See *Note 16D*.

Note: Chief officers should ensure that the operation of these provisions at police stations in their areas is subject to supervision and monitoring by an officer of the rank of inspector or above.

16.7A The requirement in *paragraph 3.4(b)* that documents and materials essential to effectively challenging the lawfulness of the detainee's arrest and detention must be made available to the detainee and, if they are represented, their solicitor, applies for the purposes of this section and a person's detention after charge. This means that the custody officer making the bail decision (PACE, section 38) or reviewing the need for detention after charge (*PACE, section 40*), is responsible for determining what, if any, documents or materials are essential and must be made available to the detainee or their solicitor. See *Note 3ZA*.

(b) Documentation

16.8   A record shall be made of anything a detainee says when charged.

16.9   Any questions put in an interview after charge and answers given relating to the offence shall be recorded in full during the interview on forms for that purpose and the record signed by the detainee or, if they refuse, by the interviewer and any third parties present. If the questions are audibly recorded or visually recorded the arrangements in Code E or F apply.

16.10   If arrangements for a juvenile's transfer into local authority care as in *paragraph 16.7* are not made, the custody officer must record the reasons in a certificate which must be produced before the court with the juvenile. See *Note 16D*.

Notes for Guidance

16A   *The custody officer must take into account alternatives to prosecution under the Crime and Disorder Act 1998 applicable to persons under 18, and in national guidance on the cautioning of offenders applicable to persons aged 18 and over.*

16AA   *When a person is arrested under the provisions of the Criminal Justice Act 2003 which allow a person to be re-tried after being acquitted of a serious offence which is a qualifying offence specified in Schedule 5 to that Act and not precluded from further prosecution by virtue of section 75(3) of that Act the detention provisions of PACE are modified and make an officer of the rank of superintendent or above who has not been directly involved in the investigation responsible for determining whether the evidence is sufficient to charge.*

16AB   *Where Guidance issued by the Director of Public Prosecutions under section 37B is in force, a custody officer who determines in accordance with that Guidance that there is sufficient evidence to charge the detainee, may detain that person for no longer than is reasonably necessary to decide how that person is to be dealt with under PACE, section 37(7)(a) to (d), including, where appropriate, consultation with the Duty Prosecutor. The period is subject to the maximum period of detention before charge determined by PACE, sections 41 to 44. Where in accordance with the Guidance the case is referred to the CPS for decision, the custody officer should ensure that an officer involved in the investigation sends to the CPS such information as is specified in the Guidance.*

16B   *The giving of a warning or the service of the Notice of Intended Prosecution required by the Road Traffic Offenders Act 1988, section 1 does not amount to informing a detainee they may be prosecuted for an offence and so does not preclude further questioning in relation to that offence.*

16C   *There is no power under PACE to detain a person and delay action under paragraphs 16.2 to 16.5 solely to await the arrival of the appropriate adult. Reasonable efforts should therefore be made to give the appropriate adult sufficient notice of the time the decision (charge etc.) is to be implemented so that they can be present. If the appropriate adult is not, or cannot be, present at that time, the detainee should be released on bail to return for the decision to be implemented when the adult is present, unless the custody officer determines that the absence of the appropriate adult makes the detainee unsuitable for bail for this purpose. After charge, bail cannot be refused, or release on bail delayed, simply because an appropriate adult is not available, unless the absence of that adult provides the custody officer with the necessary grounds to authorise detention after charge under PACE, section 38.*

16D   *Except as in paragraph 16.7, neither a juvenile's behaviour nor the nature of the offence provides grounds for the custody officer to decide it is impracticable to arrange the juvenile's transfer to local authority care. Impracticability concerns the transport and travel requirements and the lack of secure accommodation which is provided for the purposes of restricting liberty does not make it impracticable to transfer the juvenile. The availability of secure accommodation is only a factor in relation to a juvenile aged 12 or over when other local authority accommodation would not be adequate to protect the public from serious harm from them. The obligation to transfer a juvenile to local authority accommodation applies as much to a juvenile charged during the daytime as to a juvenile to be held overnight, subject to a requirement to bring the juvenile before a court under PACE, section 46.*

17 Testing persons for the presence of specified Class A drugs

(a) Action

17.1 This section of Code C applies only in selected police stations in police areas where the provisions for drug testing under section 63B of PACE (as amended by section 5 of the Criminal Justice Act 2003 and section 7 of the Drugs Act 2005) are in force and in respect of which the Secretary of State has given a notification to the relevant chief officer of police that arrangements for the taking of samples have been made. Such a notification will cover either a police area as a whole or particular stations within a police area. The notification indicates whether the testing applies to those arrested or charged or under the age of 18 as the case may be and testing can only take place in respect of the persons so indicated in the notification. Testing cannot be carried out unless the relevant notification has been given and has not been withdrawn. See *Note 17F*.

17.2 A sample of urine or a non-intimate sample may be taken from a person in police detention for the purpose of ascertaining whether they have any specified Class A drug in their body only where they have been brought before the custody officer and:

(a) either the arrest condition, see *paragraph 17.3*, or the charge condition, see *paragraph 17.4* is met;

(b) the age condition see *paragraph 17.5*, is met;

(c) the notification condition is met in relation to the arrest condition, the charge condition, or the age condition, as the case may be. (Testing on charge and/or arrest must be specifically provided for in the notification for the power to apply. In addition, the fact that testing of under 18s is authorised must be expressly provided for in the notification before the power to test such persons applies.). See *paragraph 17.1*; and

(d) a police officer has requested the person concerned to give the sample (the request condition).

17.3 The arrest condition is met where the detainee:

(a) has been arrested for a trigger offence, see Note 17E, but not charged with that offence; or

(b) has been arrested for any other offence but not charged with that offence and a police officer of inspector rank or above, who has reasonable grounds for suspecting that their misuse of any specified Class A drug caused or contributed to the offence, has authorised the sample to be taken.

17.4 The charge condition is met where the detainee:

(a) has been charged with a trigger offence, or

(b) has been charged with any other offence and a police officer of inspector rank or above, who has reasonable grounds for suspecting that the detainee's misuse of any specified Class A drug caused or contributed to the offence, has authorised the sample to be taken.

17.5 The age condition is met where:

(a) in the case of a detainee who has been arrested but not charged as in *paragraph 17.3*, they are aged 18 or over;

(b) in the case of a detainee who has been charged as in *paragraph 17.4*, they are aged 14 or over.

17.6 Before requesting a sample from the person concerned, an officer must:

(a) inform them that the purpose of taking the sample is for drug testing under PACE. This is to ascertain whether they have a specified Class A drug present in their body;

(b) warn them that if, when so requested, they fail without good cause to provide a sample they may be liable to prosecution;

(c) where the taking of the sample has been authorised by an inspector or above in accordance with *paragraph 17.3(b)* or *17.4(b)* above, inform them that the authorisation has been given and the grounds for giving it;

(d) remind them of the following rights, which may be exercised at any stage during the period in custody:

(i) the right to have someone informed of their arrest [see section 5];

(ii) the right to consult privately with a solicitor and that free independent legal advice is available [see section 6]; and

(iii) the right to consult these Codes of Practice [see section 3].

17.7   In the case of a person who has not attained the age specified in section 63B(5A) of PACE—
        (a)   the making of the request for a sample under *paragraph 17.2(d)* above;
        (b)   the giving of the warning and the information under *paragraph 17.6* above; and
        (c)   the taking of the sample,
        may not take place except in the presence of an appropriate adult. See *Note 17G*.

17.8   Authorisation by an officer of the rank of inspector or above within *paragraph 17.3(b)* or
        17.4(b) may be given orally or in writing but, if it is given orally, it must be confirmed in
        writing as soon as practicable.

17.9   If a sample is taken from a detainee who has been arrested for an offence but not charged
        with that offence as in *paragraph 17.3*, no further sample may be taken during the same
        continuous period of detention. If during that same period the charge condition is also met
        in respect of that detainee, the sample which has been taken shall be treated as being
        taken by virtue of the charge condition, see *paragraph 17.4*, being met.

17.10   A detainee from whom a sample may be taken may be detained for up to six hours from
        the time of charge if the custody officer reasonably believes the detention is necessary
        to enable a sample to be taken. Where the arrest condition is met, a detainee whom the
        custody officer has decided to release on bail without charge may continue to be detained,
        but not beyond 24 hours from the relevant time (as defined in section 41(2) of PACE), to
        enable a sample to be taken.

17.11   A detainee in respect of whom the arrest condition is met, but not the charge condition,
        see *paragraphs 17.3* and *17.4*, and whose release would be required before a sample can
        be taken had they not continued to be detained as a result of being arrested for a further
        offence which does not satisfy the arrest condition, may have a sample taken at any time
        within 24 hours after the arrest for the offence that satisfies the arrest condition.

(b)   Documentation

17.12   The following must be recorded in the custody record:
        (a)   if a sample is taken following authorisation by an officer of the rank of inspector or
              above, the authorisation and the grounds for suspicion;
        (b)   the giving of a warning of the consequences of failure to provide a sample;
        (c)   the time at which the sample was given; and
        (d)   the time of charge or, where the arrest condition is being relied upon, the time of arrest
              and, where applicable, the fact that a sample taken after arrest but before charge is
              to be treated as being taken by virtue of the charge condition, where that is met in the
              same period of continuous detention. See *paragraph 17.9*.

(c)   General

17.13   A sample may only be taken by a prescribed person. See *Note 17C*.

17.14   Force may not be used to take any sample for the purpose of drug testing.

17.15   The terms "Class A drug" and "misuse" have the same meanings as in the Misuse of Drugs
        Act 1971. "Specified" (in relation to a Class A drug) and "trigger offence" have the same
        meanings as in Part III of the Criminal Justice and Court Services Act 2000.

17.16   Any sample taken:
        (a)   may not be used for any purpose other than to ascertain whether the person concerned
              has a specified Class A drug present in his body; and
        (b)   can be disposed of as clinical waste unless it is to be sent for further analysis in cases
              where the test result is disputed at the point when the result is known, including on the
              basis that medication has been taken, or for quality assurance purposes.

(d)   Assessment of misuse of drugs

17.17   Under the provisions of Part 3 of the Drugs Act 2005, where a detainee has tested positive
        for a specified Class A drug under section 63B of PACE a police officer may, at any time
        before the person's release from the police station, impose a requirement on the detainee
        to attend an initial assessment of their drug misuse by a suitably qualified person and to
        remain for its duration. Where such a requirement is imposed, the officer must, at the same
        time, impose a second requirement on the detainee to attend and remain for a follow-up
        assessment. The officer must inform the detainee that the second requirement will cease
        to have effect if, at the initial assessment they are informed that a follow-up assessment is
        not necessary These requirements may only be imposed on a person if:
        (a)   they have reached the age of 18

(b) notification has been given by the Secretary of State to the relevant chief officer of police that arrangements for conducting initial and follow-up assessments have been made for those from whom samples for testing have been taken at the police station where the detainee is in custody.

17.18 When imposing a requirement to attend an initial assessment and a follow-up assessment the police officer must:
(a) inform the person of the time and place at which the initial assessment is to take place;
(b) explain that this information will be confirmed in writing; and
(c) warn the person that they may be liable to prosecution if they fail without good cause to attend the initial assessment and remain for its duration and if they fail to attend the follow-up assessment and remain for its duration (if so required).

17.19 Where a police officer has imposed a requirement to attend an initial assessment and a follow-up assessment in accordance with *paragraph 17.17*, he must, before the person is released from detention, give the person notice in writing which:
(a) confirms their requirement to attend and remain for the duration of the assessments; and
(b) confirms the information and repeats the warning referred to in *paragraph 17.18*.

17.20 The following must be recorded in the custody record:
(a) that the requirement to attend an initial assessment and a follow-up assessment has been imposed; and
(b) the information, explanation, warning and notice given in accordance with *paragraphs 17.17* and *17.19*.

17.21 Where a notice is given in accordance with paragraph 17.19, a police officer can give the person a further notice in writing which informs the person of any change to the time or place at which the initial assessment is to take place and which repeats the warning referred to in *paragraph 17.18(c)*.

17.22 Part 3 of the Drugs Act 2005 also requires police officers to have regard to any guidance issued by the Secretary of State in respect of the assessment provisions.

Notes for Guidance

17A When warning a person who is asked to provide a urine or non-intimate sample in accordance with paragraph 17.6(b), the following form of words may be used:
"You do not have to provide a sample, but I must warn you that if you fail or refuse without good cause to do so, you will commit an offence for which you may be imprisoned, or fined, or both".
Where the Welsh language is appropriate, the following form of words may be used:
"Does dim rhaid i chi roi sampl, ond mae'n rhaid i mi eich rhybuddio y byddwch chi'n cyflawni trosedd os byddwch chi'n methu neu yn gwrthod gwneud hynny heb reswm da, ac y gellir, oherwydd hynny, eich carcharu, eich dirwyo, neu'r ddau."

17B *A sample has to be sufficient and suitable. A sufficient sample is sufficient in quantity and quality to enable drug-testing analysis to take place. A suitable sample is one which by its nature, is suitable for a particular form of drug analysis.*

17C *A prescribed person in paragraph 17.13 is one who is prescribed in regulations made by the Secretary of State under section 63B(6) of the Police and Criminal Evidence Act 1984. [The regulations are currently contained in regulation SI 2001 No. 2645, the Police and Criminal Evidence Act 1984 (Drug Testing Persons in Police Detention) (Prescribed Persons) Regulations 2001.]*

17D *Samples, and the information derived from them, may not be subsequently used in the investigation of any offence or in evidence against the persons from whom they were taken.*

17E *Trigger offences are:*
1. *Offences under the following provisions of the Theft Act 1968:*
   section 1   (theft)
   section 8   (robbery)
   section 9   (burglary)
   section 10   (aggravated burglary)
   section 12   (taking a motor vehicle or other conveyance without authority)
   section 12A (aggravated vehicle-taking)
   section 22   (handling stolen goods)
   section 25   (going equipped for stealing etc.)

2.   Offences under the following provisions of the Misuse of Drugs Act 1971, if committed in respect of a specified Class A drug:–

section 4   (restriction on production and supply of controlled drugs)
section 5(2)   (possession of a controlled drug)
section 5(3)   (possession of a controlled drug with intent to supply)

3.   Offences under the following provisions of the Fraud Act 2006:

section 1   (fraud)
section 6   (possession etc. of articles for use in frauds)
section 7   (making or supplying articles for use in frauds)

3A.   An offence under section 1(1) of the Criminal Attempts Act 1981 if committed in respect of an offence under

(a)   any of the following provisions of the Theft Act 1968:

section 1   (theft)
section 8   (robbery)
section 9   (burglary)
section 22   (handling stolen goods)

(b)   section 1 of the Fraud Act 2006 (fraud)

4.   Offences under the following provisions of the Vagrancy Act 1824:

section 3   (begging)
section 4   (persistent begging)

17F   The power to take samples is subject to notification by the Secretary of State that appropriate arrangements for the taking of samples have been made for the police area as a whole or for the particular police station concerned for whichever of the following is specified in the notification:

(a)   persons in respect of whom the arrest condition is met;
(b)   persons in respect of whom the charge condition is met;
(c)   persons who have not attained the age of 18.

Note: Notification is treated as having been given for the purposes of the charge condition in relation to a police area, if testing (on charge) under section 63B(2) of PACE was in force immediately before section 7 of the Drugs Act 2005 was brought into force; and for the purposes of the age condition, in relation to a police area or police station, if immediately before that day, notification that arrangements had been made for the taking of samples from persons under the age of 18 (those aged 14-17) had been given and had not been withdrawn.

17G   Appropriate adult in paragraph 17.7 means the person's–

(a)   parent or guardian or, if they are in the care of a local authority or voluntary organisation, a person representing that authority or organisation; or
(b)   a social worker of a local authority; or
(c)   if no person falling within (a) or (b) above is available, any responsible person aged 18 or over who is not:
    –   a police officer; employed by the police;
    –   under the direction or control of the chief officer of police force; or
    –   a person who provides services under contractual arrangements (but without being employed by the chief officer of a police force), to assist that force in relation to the discharge of its chief officer's functions
    whether or not they are on duty at the time.

Note: Paragraph 1.5 extends this Note to the person called to fulfil the role of the appropriate adult for a 17-year old detainee for the purposes of paragraph 17.7.

ANNEX B
DELAY IN NOTIFYING ARREST OR ALLOWING ACCESS TO LEGAL ADVICE

A   Persons detained under PACE

1.   The exercise of the rights in *Section 5* or *Section 6*, or both, may be delayed if the person is in police detention, as in PACE, section 118(2), in connection with an indictable offence, has not yet been charged with an offence and an officer of superintendent rank or above,

or inspector rank or above only for the rights in *Section 5*, has reasonable grounds for believing their exercise will:

(i) lead to:
- interference with, or harm to, evidence connected with an indictable offence; or
- interference with, or physical harm to, other people; or

(ii) lead to alerting other people suspected of having committed an indictable offence but not yet arrested for it; or

(iii) hinder the recovery of property obtained in consequence of the commission of such an offence.

2. These rights may also be delayed if the officer has reasonable grounds to believe that:

(i) the person detained for an indictable offence has benefited from their criminal conduct (decided in accordance with Part 2 of the Proceeds of Crime Act 2002); and

(ii) the recovery of the value of the property constituting that benefit will be hindered by the exercise of either right.

3. Authority to delay a detainee's right to consult privately with a solicitor may be given only if the authorising officer has reasonable grounds to believe the solicitor the detainee wants to consult will, inadvertently or otherwise, pass on a message from the detainee or act in some other way which will have any of the consequences specified under *paragraphs 1 or 2*. In these circumstances, the detainee must be allowed to choose another solicitor. See *Note B3*.

4. If the detainee wishes to see a solicitor, access to that solicitor may not be delayed on the grounds they might advise the detainee not to answer questions or the solicitor was initially asked to attend the police station by someone else. In the latter case, the detainee must be told the solicitor has come to the police station at another person's request, and must be asked to sign the custody record to signify whether they want to see the solicitor.

5. The fact the grounds for delaying notification of arrest may be satisfied does not automatically mean the grounds for delaying access to legal advice will also be satisfied.

6. These rights may be delayed only for as long as grounds exist and in no case beyond 36 hours after the relevant time as in PACE, section 41. If the grounds cease to apply within this time, the detainee must, as soon as practicable, be asked if they want to exercise either right, the custody record must be noted accordingly, and action taken in accordance with the relevant section of the Code.

7. A detained person must be permitted to consult a solicitor for a reasonable time before any court hearing.

B *Not* **used**

C **Documentation**

13. The grounds for action under this Annex shall be recorded and the detainee informed of them as soon as practicable.

14. Any reply given by a detainee under *paragraphs 6 or 11* must be recorded and the detainee asked to endorse the record in relation to whether they want to receive legal advice at this point.

D **Cautions and special warnings**

15. When a suspect detained at a police station is interviewed during any period for which access to legal advice has been delayed under this Annex, the court or jury may not draw adverse inferences from their silence.

Notes for Guidance

B1 Even if Annex B applies in the case of a juvenile, or a person who is mentally disordered or otherwise mentally vulnerable, action to inform the appropriate adult and the person responsible for a juvenile's welfare, if that is a different person, must nevertheless be taken as in paragraph 3.13 and 3.15.

B2 In the case of Commonwealth citizens and foreign nationals, see Note 7A.

B3 A decision to delay access to a specific solicitor is likely to be a rare occurrence and only when it can be shown the suspect is capable of misleading that particular solicitor and there is more than a substantial risk that the suspect will succeed in causing information to be conveyed which will lead to one or more of the specified consequences.

ANNEX L
ESTABLISHING GENDER OF PERSONS FOR THE PURPOSE OF SEARCHING

1.   Certain provisions of this and other PACE Codes explicitly state that searches and other procedures may only be carried out by, or in the presence of, persons of the same sex as the person subject to the search or other procedure. See *Note L1.*

2.   All searches and procedures must be carried out with courtesy, consideration and respect for the person concerned. Police officers should show particular sensitivity when dealing with transgender individuals (including transsexual persons) and transvestite persons (see *Notes L2, L3 and L4).*

(a)   Consideration

3.   In law, the gender (and accordingly the sex) of an individual is their gender as registered at birth unless they have been issued with a Gender Recognition Certificate (GRC) under the Gender Recognition Act 2004 (GRA), in which case the person's gender is their acquired gender. This means that if the acquired gender is the male gender, the person's sex becomes that of a man and, if it is the female gender, the person's sex becomes that of a woman and they must be treated as their acquired gender.

4.   When establishing whether the person concerned should be treated as being male or female for the purposes of these searches and procedures, the following approach which is designed to minimise embarrassment and secure the person's co-operation should be followed:

(a)   The person must not be asked whether they have a GRC (see paragraph 8);

(b)   If there is no doubt as to as to whether the person concerned should be treated as being male or female, they should be dealt with as being of that sex.

(c)   If at any time (including during the search or carrying out the procedure) there is doubt as to whether the person should be treated, or continue to be treated, as being male or female:

(i)   the person should be asked what gender they consider themselves to be. If they express a preference to be dealt with as a particular gender, they should be asked to indicate and confirm their preference by signing the custody record or, if a custody record has not been opened, the search record or the officer's notebook. Subject to (ii) below, the person should be treated according to their preference;

(ii)   if there are grounds to doubt that the preference in (i) accurately reflects the person's predominant lifestyle, for example, if they ask to be treated as a woman but documents and other information make it clear that they live predominantly as a man, or vice versa, they should be treated according to what appears to be their predominant lifestyle and not their stated preference;

(iii)   If the person is unwilling to express a preference as in (i) above, efforts should be made to determine their predominant lifestyle and they should be treated as such. For example, if they appear to live predominantly as a woman, they should be treated as being female; or

(iv)   if none of the above apply, the person should be dealt with according to what reasonably appears to have been their sex as registered at birth.

5.   Once a decision has been made about which gender an individual is to be treated as, each officer responsible for the search or procedure should where possible be advised before the search or procedure starts of any doubts as to the person's gender and the person informed that the doubts have been disclosed. This is important so as to maintain the dignity of the person and any officers concerned.

(b)   Documentation

6.   The person's gender as established under *paragraph 4(c)(i)* to *(iv)* above must be recorded in the person's custody record or, if a custody record has not been opened, on the search record or in the officer's notebook.

7.   Where the person elects which gender they consider themselves to be under *paragraph 4(b)(i)* but, following *4(b)(ii)* is not treated in accordance with their preference, the reason must be recorded in the search record, in the officer's notebook or, if applicable, in the person's custody record.

(c)   Disclosure of information

8.   Section 22 of the GRA defines any information relating to a person's application for a GRC or to a successful applicant's gender before it became their acquired gender as 'protected information'. Nothing in this Annex is to be read as authorising or permitting any police officer or any police staff who has acquired such information when acting in their official capacity to disclose that information to any other person in contravention of the GRA. Disclosure includes making a record of 'protected information' which is read by others.

Notes for Guidance

L1   Provisions to which paragraph 1 applies include:
- *In Code C; paragraph 4.1 and Annex A paragraphs 5, 6, and 11 (searches, strip and intimate searches of detainees under sections 54 and 55 of PACE);*
- *In Code A; paragraphs 2.8 and 3.6 and Note 4;*
- *In Code D; paragraph 5.5 and Note 5F (searches, examinations and photographing of detainees under section 54A of PACE) and paragraph 6.9 (taking samples);*
- *In Code H; paragraph 4.1 and Annex A paragraphs 6, 7 and 12 (searches, strip and intimate searches under sections 54 and 55 of PACE of persons arrested under section 41 of the Terrorism Act 2000).*

L2   While there is no agreed definition of transgender (or trans), it is generally used as an umbrella term to describe people whose gender identity (self-identification as being a woman, man, neither or both) differs from the sex they were registered as at birth. The term includes, but is not limited to, transsexual people.

L3   Transsexual means a person who is proposing to undergo, is undergoing or has undergone a process (or part of a process) for the purpose of gender reassignment, which is a protected characteristic under the Equality Act 2010 (see paragraph 1.0), by changing physiological or other attributes of their sex. This includes aspects of gender such as dress and title. It would apply to a woman making the transition to being a man and a man making the transition to being a woman, as well as to a person who has only just started out on the process of gender reassignment and to a person who has completed the process. Both would share the characteristic of gender reassignment with each having the characteristics of one sex, but with certain characteristics of the other sex.

L4   Transvestite means a person of one gender who dresses in the clothes of a person of the opposite gender. However, a transvestite does not live permanently in the gender opposite to their birth sex.

L5   Chief officers are responsible for providing corresponding operational guidance and instructions for the deployment of transgender officers and staff under their direction and control to duties which involve carrying out, or being present at, any of the searches and procedures described in paragraph 1. The guidance and instructions must comply with the Equality Act 2010 and should therefore complement the approach in this Annex.

POLICE AND CRIMINAL EVIDENCE ACT (PACE) 1984
CODE G 2012

REVISED CODE OF PRACTICE FOR THE STATUTORY POWER OF ARREST
BY POLICE OFFICERS

Commencement – Transitional Arrangements

This Code applies to any arrest made by a police officer after 00:00 on 12 November 2012

1   Introduction

1.1   This Code of Practice deals with the statutory power of police to arrest a person who is involved, or suspected of being involved, in a criminal offence. The power of arrest must be used fairly, responsibly, with respect for people suspected of committing offences and without unlawful discrimination. The Equality Act 2010 makes it unlawful for police officers to discriminate against, harass or victimise any person on the grounds of the 'protected characteristics' of age, disability, gender reassignment, race, religion or belief, sex and sexual orientation, marriage and civil partnership, pregnancy and maternity when using their powers. When police forces are carrying out their functions they also have a duty to have regard to the need to eliminate unlawful discrimination, harassment and victimisation and to take steps to foster good relations.

1.2   The exercise of the power of arrest represents an obvious and significant interference with the Right to Liberty and Security under Article 5 of the European Convention on Human Rights set out in Part I of Schedule 1 to the Human Rights Act 1998.

1.3   The use of the power must be fully justified and officers exercising the power should consider if the necessary objectives can be met by other, less intrusive means. Absence of justification for exercising the power of arrest may lead to challenges should the case proceed to court. It could also lead to civil claims against police for unlawful arrest and false imprisonment. When the power of arrest is exercised it is essential that it is exercised in a non-discriminatory and proportionate manner which is compatible with the Right to Liberty under Article 5. *See Note 1B.*

1.4   Section 24 of the Police and Criminal Evidence Act 1984 (as substituted by section 110 of the Serious Organised Crime and Police Act 2005) provides the statutory power for a constable to arrest without warrant for all offences. If the provisions of the Act and this Code are not observed, both the arrest and the conduct of any subsequent investigation may be open to question.

1.5   This Code of Practice must be readily available at all police stations for consultation by police officers and police staff, detained persons and members of the public.

1.6   The *Notes for Guidance* are not provisions of this code.

2   Elements of Arrest under section 24 PACE

2.1   A lawful arrest requires two elements:

A person's involvement or suspected involvement or attempted involvement in the commission of a criminal offence;

AND

  Reasonable grounds for *believing* that the person's arrest is necessary.
  - both elements must be satisfied, and
  - it can never be necessary to arrest a person unless there are reasonable grounds to suspect them of committing an offence.

2.2   The arrested person must be informed that they have been arrested, even if this fact is obvious, and of the relevant circumstances of the arrest in relation to both the above elements. The custody officer must be informed of these matters on arrival at the police station. See *paragraphs 2.9, 3.3* and *Note 3* and *Code C paragraph 3.4.*

(a)   **'Involvement in the commission of an offence'**

2.3   A constable may arrest without warrant in relation to any offence (see *Notes 1* and *1A*) anyone:
  - who is about to commit an offence <u>or</u> is in the act of committing an offence;
  - whom the officer has reasonable grounds for suspecting is about to commit an offence <u>or</u> to be committing an offence;
  - whom the officer has reasonable grounds to suspect of being guilty of an offence which he or she has reasonable grounds for suspecting has been committed;
  - anyone who is guilty of an offence which has been committed or anyone whom the officer has reasonable grounds for suspecting to be guilty of that offence.

2.3A   There must be some reasonable, objective grounds for the suspicion, based on known facts and information which are relevant to the likelihood the offence has been committed and the person liable to arrest committed it. See *Notes 2* and *2A.*

(b)   **Necessity criteria**

2.4   The power of arrest is <u>only</u> exercisable if the constable has reasonable grounds for *believing* that it is necessary to arrest the person. The statutory criteria for what may constitute necessity are set out in paragraph 2.9 and it remains an operational decision at the discretion of the constable to decide:
  - which one or more of the necessity criteria (if any) applies to the individual; and
  - if any of the criteria do apply, whether to arrest, grant street bail after arrest, report for summons or for charging by post, issue a penalty notice or take any other action that is open to the officer.

2.5   In applying the criteria, the arresting officer has to be satisfied that at least one of the reasons supporting the need for arrest is satisfied.

2.6   Extending the power of arrest to all offences provides a constable with the ability to use that power to deal with any situation. However applying the necessity criteria requires the constable to examine and justify the reason or reasons why a person needs to be arrested or (as the case may be) further arrested, for an offence for the custody officer to decide whether to authorise their detention for that offence. See *Note 2C*

2.7   The criteria in paragraph 2.9 below which are set out in section 24 of PACE as substituted by section 110 of the Serious Organised Crime and Police Act 2005 <u>are</u> exhaustive. However, the circumstances that may satisfy those criteria remain a matter for the operational discretion of individual officers. Some examples are given to illustrate what those circumstances might be and what officers might consider when deciding whether arrest is necessary.

2.8   In considering the individual circumstances, the constable must take into account the situation of the victim, the nature of the offence, the circumstances of the suspect and the needs of the investigative process.

2.9   When it is practicable to tell a person why their arrest is necessary (as required by paragraphs 2.2, 3.3 and *Note 3*), the constable should outline the facts, information and other circumstances which provide the grounds for believing that their arrest is necessary and which the officer considers satisfy one or more of the statutory criteria in sub-paragraphs (a) to (f), namely:

(a)   to enable the name of the person in question to be ascertained (in the case where the constable does not know, and cannot readily ascertain, the person's name, or has reasonable grounds for doubting whether a name given by the person as his name is his real name):

An officer might decide that a person's name cannot be readily ascertained if they fail or refuse to give it when asked, particularly after being warned that failure or refusal is likely to make their arrest necessary (see *Note 2D*). Grounds to doubt a name given may arise if the person appears reluctant or hesitant when asked to give their name or to verify the name they have given.

Where mobile fingerprinting is available and the suspect's name cannot be ascertained or is doubted, the officer should consider using the power under section 61(6A) of PACE (see *Code D paragraph 4.3(e)*) to take and check the fingerprints of a suspect as this may avoid the need to arrest solely to enable their name to be ascertained.

(b)   correspondingly as regards the person's address:

An officer might decide that a person's address cannot be readily ascertained if they fail or refuse to give it when asked, particularly after being warned that such a failure or refusal is likely to make their arrest necessary. See *Note 2D*. Grounds to doubt an address given may arise if the person appears reluctant or hesitant when asked to give their address or is unable to provide verifiable details of the locality they claim to live in.

When considering reporting to consider summons or charging by post as alternatives to arrest, an address would be satisfactory if the person will be at it for a sufficiently long period for it to be possible to serve them with the summons or requisition and charge; or, that some other person at that address specified by the person will accept service on their behalf. When considering issuing a penalty notice, the address should be one where the person will be in the event of enforcement action if the person does not pay the penalty or is convicted and fined after a court hearing.

(c)   to prevent the person in question:

(i)   causing physical injury to himself or any other person;
       This might apply where the suspect has already used or threatened violence against others and it is thought likely that they may assault others if they are not arrested. See *Note 2D*

(ii)   suffering physical injury;
       This might apply where the suspect's behaviour and actions are believed likely to provoke, or have provoked, others to want to assault the suspect unless the suspect is arrested for their own protection. See *Note 2D*

(iii) causing loss or damage to property;

This might apply where the suspect is a known persistent offender with a history of serial offending against property (theft and criminal damage) and it is thought likely that they may continue offending if they are not arrested.

(iv)   committing an offence against public decency (only applies where members of the public going about their normal business cannot reasonably be expected to avoid the person in question);

This might apply when an offence against public decency is being committed in a place to which the public have access and is likely to be repeated in that or some other public place at a time when the public are likely to encounter the suspect. See *Note 2D*

(v)   causing an unlawful obstruction of the highway;

This might apply to any offence where its commission causes an unlawful obstruction which it is believed may continue or be repeated if the person is not arrested, particularly if the person has been warned that they are causing an obstruction. See *Note 2D*

(d)   to protect a child or other vulnerable person from the person in question.

This might apply when the health (physical or mental) or welfare of a child or vulnerable person is likely to be harmed or is at risk of being harmed, if the person is not arrested in cases where it is not practicable and appropriate to make alternative arrangements to prevent the suspect from having any harmful or potentially harmful contact with the child or vulnerable person.

(e)   to allow the prompt and effective investigation of the offence or of the conduct of the person in question. See *Note 2E*

This may arise when it is thought likely that unless the person is arrested and then either taken in custody to the police station or granted 'street bail' to attend the station later, see *Note 2J*, further action considered necessary to properly investigate their involvement in the offence would be frustrated, unreasonably delayed or otherwise hindered and therefore be impracticable. Examples of such actions include:

(i)   *interviewing the suspect* on occasions when the person's voluntary attendance is not considered to be a practicable alternative to arrest, because for example:
   - it is thought unlikely that the person would attend the police station voluntarily to be interviewed.
   - it is necessary to interview the suspect about the outcome of other investigative action for which their arrest is necessary, see (ii) to (v) below.
   - arrest would enable the special warning to be given in accordance with Code C paragraphs 10.10 and 10.11 when the suspect is found:
     - in possession of incriminating objects, or at a place where such objects are found;
     - at or near the scene of the crime at or about the time it was committed.
   - the person has made false statements and/or presented false evidence;
   - it is thought likely that the person:
     - may steal or destroy evidence;
     - may collude or make contact with, co-suspects or conspirators;
     - may intimidate or threaten or make contact with, witnesses. See *Notes 2F and 2G*

(ii)   when considering arrest in connection with the investigation of an *indictable offence* (see *Note 6*), there is a need:
   - to enter and search without a search warrant any premises occupied or controlled by the arrested person or where the person was when arrested or immediately before arrest;
   - to prevent the arrested person from having contact with others;
   - to detain the arrested person for more than 24 hours before charge.

(iii) when considering arrest in connection with any *recordable offence* and it is necessary to secure or preserve evidence of that offence by taking fingerprints, footwear impressions or samples from the suspect for evidential comparison or matching with other material relating to that offence, for example, from the crime scene. See *Note 2H*

(iv) when considering arrest in connection with any offence and it is necessary to search, examine or photograph the person to obtain evidence. See *Note 2H*

(v) when considering arrest in connection with an offence to which the statutory Class A drug testing requirements in Code C section 17 apply, to enable testing when it is thought that drug misuse might have caused or contributed to the offence. See *Note 2I*.

(f) to prevent any prosecution for the offence from being hindered by the disappearance of the person in question.

This may arise when it is thought that:

- if the person is not arrested they are unlikely to attend court if they are prosecuted;
- the address given is not a satisfactory address for service of a summons or a written charge and requisition to appear at court because the person will not be at it for a sufficiently long period for the summons or charge and requisition to be served and no other person at that specified address will accept service on their behalf.

3   Information to be given on Arrest

(a)   *Cautions — when a caution must be given*

3.1   Code C paragraphs 10.1 and 10.2 set out the requirement for a person whom there are grounds to suspect of an offence (see *Note 2*) to be cautioned before being questioned or further questioned about an offence.

3.2   *Not used.*

3.3   A person who is arrested, or further arrested, must be informed at the time if practicable, or if not, as soon as it becomes practicable thereafter, that they are under arrest and of the grounds and reasons for their arrest, see paragraphs 2.2 and *Note 3.*

3.4   A person who is arrested, or further arrested, must be cautioned unless:

(a) it is impracticable to do so by reason of their condition or behaviour at the time;

(b) they have already been cautioned immediately prior to arrest as in *paragraph 3.1.*

(b)   *Terms of the caution (Taken from Code C section 10)*

3.5   The caution, which must be given on arrest, should be in the following terms:

"You do not have to say anything. But it may harm your defence if you do not mention when questioned something which you later rely on in Court. Anything you do say may be given in evidence."

Where the use of the Welsh Language is appropriate, a constable may provide the caution directly in Welsh in the following terms:

"Does dim rhaid i chi ddweud dim byd. Ond gall niweidio eich amddiffyniad os na fyddwch chi'n sôn, wrth gael eich holi, am rywbeth y byddwch chi'n dibynnu arno nes ymlaen yn y Llys. Gall unrhyw beth yr ydych yn ei ddweud gael ei roi fel tystiolaeth."

See *Note 4*

3.6   Minor deviations from the words of any caution given in accordance with this Code do not constitute a breach of this Code, provided the sense of the relevant caution is preserved. See *Note 5*

3.7   *Not used.*

4   Records of Arrest

(a) General

4.1   The arresting officer is required to record in his pocket book or by other methods used for recording information:

- the nature and circumstances of the offence leading to the arrest;
- the reason or reasons why arrest was necessary;
- the giving of the caution; and
- anything said by the person at the time of arrest.

4.2   Such a record should be made at the time of the arrest unless impracticable to do. If not made at that time, the record should then be completed as soon as possible thereafter.

4.3   On arrival at the police station or after being first arrested at the police station, the arrested person must be brought before the custody officer as soon as practicable and a custody record must be opened in accordance with section 2 of Code C. The information given by the arresting officer on the circumstances and reason or reasons for arrest shall be recorded as part of the custody record. Alternatively, a copy of the record made by the officer in accordance with paragraph 4.1 above shall be attached as part of the custody record. See *paragraph 2.2* and *Code C paragraphs 3.4* and *10.3*.

4.4   The custody record will serve as a record of the arrest. Copies of the custody record will be provided in accordance with paragraphs 2.4 and 2.4A of Code C and access for inspection of the original record in accordance with paragraph 2.5 of Code C.

(b)   **Interviews and arrests**

4.5   Records of interview, significant statements or silences will be treated in the same way as set out in sections 10 and 11 of Code C and in Codes E and F (audio and visual recording of interviews).

Notes for Guidance

1   *For the purposes of this Code, 'offence' means any statutory or common law offence for which a person may be tried by a magistrates' court or the Crown court and punished if convicted. Statutory offences include assault, rape, criminal damage, theft, robbery, burglary, fraud, possession of controlled drugs and offences under road traffic, liquor licensing, gambling and immigration legislation and local government byelaws. Common law offences include murder, manslaughter, kidnapping, false imprisonment, perverting the course of justice and escape from lawful custody.*

1A   *This code does not apply to powers of arrest conferred on constables under any arrest warrant, for example, a warrant issued under the Magistrates' Courts Act 1980, sections 1 or 13, or the Bail Act 1976, section 7(1), or to the powers of constables to arrest without warrant other than under section 24 of PACE for an offence. These other powers to arrest without warrant do not depend on the arrested person committing any specific offence and include:*

- *PACE, section 46A, arrest of person who fails to answer police bail to attend police station or is suspected of breaching any condition of that bail for the custody officer to decide whether they should be kept in police detention which applies whether or not the person commits an offence under section 6 of the Bail Act 1976 (e.g. failing without reasonable cause to surrender to custody);*
- *Bail Act 1976, section 7(3), arrest of person bailed to attend court who is suspected of breaching, or is believed likely to breach, any condition of bail to take them to court for bail to be re-considered;*
- *Children & Young Persons Act 1969, section 32(1A) (absconding) – arrest to return the person to the place where they are required to reside;*
- *Immigration Act 1971, Schedule 2 to arrest a person liable to examination to determine their right to remain in the UK;*
- *Mental Health Act 1983, section 136 to remove person suffering from mental disorder to place of safety for assessment;*
- *Prison Act 1952, section 49, arrest to return person unlawfully at large to the prison etc. where they are liable to be detained;*
- *Road Traffic Act 1988, section 6D arrest of driver following the outcome of a preliminary roadside test requirement to enable the driver to be required to provide an evidential sample;*
- *Common law power to stop or prevent a Breach of the Peace - after arrest a person aged 18 or over may be brought before a justice of the peace court to show cause why they should not be bound over to keep the peace - not criminal proceedings.*

1B   *Juveniles should not be arrested at their place of education unless this is unavoidable. When a juvenile is arrested at their place of education, the principal or their nominee must be informed. (From Code C Note 11D)*

2   *Facts and information relevant to a person's suspected involvement in an offence should not be confined to those which tend to indicate the person has committed or attempted to commit the offence. Before making a decision to arrest, a constable should take account of any facts and information that are available, including claims of innocence made by the person, that might dispel the suspicion.*

2A   *Particular examples of facts and information which might point to a person's innocence and may tend to dispel suspicion include those which relate to the statutory defence provided* by the Criminal Law Act 1967, section 3(1) which allows the use of reasonable force in the prevention of crime or making an arrest and the common law of self-defence. This may be relevant when a person appears, or claims, to have been acting reasonably in defence of themselves or others or to prevent their property or the property of others from being stolen, destroyed or damaged, particularly if the offence alleged is based on the use of unlawful force, e.g. a criminal assault. When investigating allegations involving the use of force by school staff, the power given to all school staff under the Education and Inspections Act 2006, section 93, to use reasonable force to prevent their pupils from committing any offence, injuring persons, damaging property or prejudicing the maintenance of good order and discipline may be similarly relevant. The Association of Chief Police Officers and the Crown Prosecution Service have published joint guidance to help the public understand the meaning of reasonable force and what to expect from the police and CPS in cases which involve claims of self defence. Separate advice for school staff on their powers to use reasonable force is available from the Department for Education

2B If a constable who is dealing with an allegation of crime and considering the need to arrest becomes an investigator for the purposes of the Code of Practice under the Criminal Procedure and Investigations Act 1996, the officer should, in accordance with paragraph 3.5 of that Code, "pursue all reasonable lines of inquiry, whether these point towards or away from the suspect. What is reasonable in each case will depend on the particular circumstances."

2C For a constable to have reasonable grounds for believing it necessary to arrest, he or she is not required to be satisfied that there is no viable alternative to arrest. However, it does mean that in all cases, the officer should consider that arrest is the practical, sensible and proportionate option in all the circumstances at the time the decision is made. This applies equally to a person in police detention after being arrested for an offence who is suspected of involvement in a further offence and the necessity to arrest them for that further offence is being considered.

2D Although a warning is not expressly required, officers should if practicable, consider whether a warning which points out their offending behaviour, and explains why, if they do not stop, the resulting consequences may make their arrest necessary. Such a warning might:
- if heeded, avoid the need to arrest, or
- if it is ignored, support the need to arrest and also help prove the mental element of certain offences, for example, the person's intent or awareness, or help to rebut a defence that they were acting reasonably.

A person who is warned that they may be liable to arrest if their real name and address cannot be ascertained, should be given a reasonable opportunity to establish their real name and address before deciding that either or both are unknown and cannot be readily ascertained or that there are reasonable grounds to doubt that a name and address they have given is their real name and address. They should be told why their name is not known and cannot be readily ascertained and (as the case may be) of the grounds for doubting that a name and address they have given is their real name and address, including, for example, the reason why a particular document the person has produced to verify their real name and/or address, is not sufficient.

2E The meaning of "prompt" should be considered on a case by case basis taking account of all the circumstances. It indicates that the progress of the investigation should not be delayed to the extent that it would adversely affect the effectiveness of the investigation. The arresting officer also has discretion to release the arrested person on 'street bail' as an alternative to taking the person directly to the station. See Note 2J.

2F An officer who believes that it is necessary to interview the person suspected of committing the offence must then consider whether their arrest is necessary in order to carry out the interview. The officer is not required to interrogate the suspect to determine whether they will attend a police station voluntarily to be interviewed but they must consider whether the suspect's voluntary attendance is a practicable alternative for carrying out the interview. If it is, then arrest would not be necessary. Conversely, an officer who considers this option but is not satisfied that it is a practicable alternative, may have reasonable grounds for deciding that the arrest is necessary at the outset 'on the street'. Without such considerations, the officer would not be able to establish that arrest was necessary in order to interview.

Circumstances which suggest that a person's arrest 'on the street' would not be necessary to interview them might be where the officer:

- *is satisfied as to their identity and address and that they will attend the police station voluntarily to be interviewed, either immediately or by arrangement at a future date and time; and*
- *is not aware of any other circumstances which indicate that voluntary attendance would not be a practicable alternative. See paragraph 2.9(e)(i) to (v).*

When making arrangements for the person's voluntary attendance, the officer should tell the person:

- *that to properly investigate their suspected involvement in the offence they must be interviewed under caution at the police station, but in the circumstances their arrest for this purpose will not be necessary if they attend the police station voluntarily to be interviewed;*
- *that if they attend voluntarily, they will be entitled to free legal advice before, and to have a solicitor present at, the interview;*
- *that the date and time of the interview will take account of their circumstances and the needs of the investigation; and*
- *that if they do not agree to attend voluntarily at a time which meets the needs of the investigation, or having so agreed, fail to attend, or having attended, fail to remain for the interview to be completed, their arrest will be necessary to enable them to be interviewed.*

2G   *When the person attends the police station voluntarily for interview by arrangement as in Note 2F above, their arrest on arrival at the station prior to interview would only be justified if:*

- *new information coming to light after the arrangements were made indicates that from that time, voluntary attendance ceased to be a practicable alternative and the person's arrest became necessary; and*
- *it was not reasonably practicable for the person to be arrested before they attended the station.*

If a person who attends the police station voluntarily to be interviewed decides to leave before the interview is complete, the police would at that point be entitled to consider whether their arrest was necessary to carry out the interview. The possibility that the person might decide to leave during the interview is therefore not a valid reason for arresting them before the interview has commenced. See Code C paragraph 3.21.

2H   *The necessity criteria do not permit arrest solely to enable the routine taking, checking (speculative searching) and retention of fingerprints, samples, footwear impressions and photographs when there are no prior grounds to believe that checking and comparing the fingerprints etc. or taking a photograph would provide relevant evidence of the person's involvement in the offence concerned or would help to ascertain or verify their real identity.*

2I   *The necessity criteria do not permit arrest for an offence solely because it happens to be one of the statutory drug testing "trigger offences" (see Code C Note 17E) when there is no suspicion that Class A drug misuse might have caused or contributed to the offence.*

2J   *Having determined that the necessity criteria have been met and having made the arrest, the officer can then consider the use of street bail on the basis of the effective and efficient progress of the investigation of the offence in question. It gives the officer discretion to compel the person to attend a police station at a date/time that best suits the overall needs of the particular investigation. Its use is not confined to dealing with child care issues or allowing officers to attend to more urgent operational duties and granting street bail does not retrospectively negate the need to arrest.*

3   *An arrested person must be given sufficient information to enable them to understand they have been deprived of their liberty and the reason they have been arrested, as soon as practicable after the arrest, e.g. when a person is arrested on suspicion of committing an offence they must be informed of the nature of the suspected offence and when and where it was committed. The suspect must also be informed of the reason or reasons why arrest is considered necessary. Vague or technical language should be avoided. When explaining why one or more of the arrest criteria apply, it is not necessary to disclose any specific details that might undermine or otherwise adversely affect any investigative processes. An example might be the conduct of a formal interview when prior disclosure of such details*

might give the suspect an opportunity to fabricate an innocent explanation or to otherwise conceal lies from the interviewer.

4   *Nothing in this Code requires a caution to be given or repeated when informing a person not under arrest they may be prosecuted for an offence. However, a court will not be able to draw any inferences under the Criminal Justice and Public Order Act 1994, section 34, if the person was not cautioned.*

5   *If it appears a person does not understand the caution, the person giving it should explain it in their own words.*

6   *Certain powers available as the result of an arrest – for example, entry and search of premises, detention without charge beyond 24 hours, holding a person incommunicado and delaying access to legal advice – only apply in respect of indictable offences and are subject to the specific requirements on authorisation as set out in PACE and the relevant Code of Practice.*

COURT RULES
CIVIL PROCEDURE RULES 1998, PART 54

I JUDICIAL REVIEW

54.1 Scope and interpretation

(1) This Section of this Part contains rules about judicial review.

(2) In this Section—

    (a) a 'claim for judicial review' means a claim to review the lawfulness of—

        (i) an enactment; or

        (ii) a decision, action or failure to act in relation to the exercise of a public function.

    (e) 'the judicial review procedure' means the Part 8 procedure as modified by this Section;

    (f) 'interested party' means any person (other than the claimant and defendant) who is directly affected by the claim; and

    (g) 'court' means the High Court, unless otherwise stated.

(Rule 8.1(6)(b) provides that a rule or practice direction may, in relation to a specified type of proceedings, disapply or modify any of the rules set out in Part 8 as they apply to those proceedings)

54.1A Who may exercise the powers of the High Court

(1) A court officer assigned to the Administrative Court office who is—

    (a) a barrister; or

    (b) a solicitor,

may exercise the jurisdiction of the High Court with regard to the matters set out in paragraph (2) with the consent of the President of the Queen's Bench Division.

(2) The matters referred to in paragraph (1) are—

    (a) any matter incidental to any proceedings in the High Court;

    (b) any other matter where there is no substantial dispute between the parties; and

    (c) the dismissal of an appeal or application where a party has failed to comply with any order, rule or practice direction.

(3) A court officer may not decide an application for—

    (a) permission to bring judicial review proceedings;

    (b) an injunction;

    (c) a stay of any proceedings, other than a temporary stay of any order or decision of the lower court over a period when the High Court is not sitting or cannot conveniently be convened, unless the parties seek a stay by consent.

(4) Decisions of a court officer may be made without a hearing.

(5) A party may request any decision of a court officer to be reviewed by a judge of the High Court.

(6) At the request of a party, a hearing will be held to reconsider a decision of a court officer, made without a hearing.

(7) A request under paragraph (5) or (6) must be filed within 7 days after the party is served with notice of the decision.

54.2 When this Section must be used

The judicial review procedure must be used in a claim for judicial review where the claimant is seeking—

(a) a mandatory order;

(b) a prohibiting order;

(c) a quashing order; or

(d) an injunction under section 30 of the Senior Courts Act 1981 (restraining a person from acting in any office in which he is not entitled to act).

54.3 When this Section may be used

(1) The judicial review procedure may be used in a claim for judicial review where the claimant is seeking—

(a) a declaration; or

(b) an injunction.

(Section 31(2) of the Senior Courts Act 1981 sets out the circumstances in which the court may grant a declaration or injunction in a claim for judicial review)

(Where the claimant is seeking a declaration or injunction in addition to one of the remedies listed in rule 54.2, the judicial review procedure must be used)

(2)   A claim for judicial review may include a claim for damages, restitution or the recovery of a sum due but may not seek such a remedy alone.

(Section 31(4) of the Senior Courts Act sets out the circumstances in which the court may award damages, restitution or the recovery of a sum due on a claim for judicial review)

54.4   Permission required

The court's permission to proceed is required in a claim for judicial review whether started under this Section or transferred to the Administrative Court.

54.5   Time limit for filing claim form

(A1) In this rule—

'the planning acts' has the same meaning as in section 336 of the Town and Country Planning Act 1990;

'decision governed by the Public Contracts Regulations 2015' means any decision the legality of which is or may be affected by a duty owed to an economic operator by virtue of regulations 89 or 90 of those Regulations (and for this purpose it does not matter that the claimant is not an economic operator); and

'economic operator' has the same meaning as in regulation 2(1) of the Public Contracts Regulations 2015.

(1)   The claim form must be filed—

    (a)   promptly; and

    (b)   in any event not later than 3 months after the grounds to make the claim first arose.

(2)   The time limits in this rule may not be extended by agreement between the parties.

(3)   This rule does not apply when any other enactment specifies a shorter time limit for making the claim for judicial review.

(4)   Paragraph (1) does not apply in the cases specified in paragraphs (5) and (6).

(5)   Where the application for judicial review relates to a decision made by the Secretary of State or local planning authority under the planning acts, the claim form must be filed not later than six weeks after the grounds to make the claim first arose.

(6)   Where the application for judicial review relates to a decision governed by the Public Contracts Regulations 2015, the claim form must be filed within the time within which an economic operator would have been required by regulation 92 of those Regulations (and disregarding the rest of that regulation) to start any proceedings under those Regulations in respect of that decision.

54.6   Claim form

(1)   In addition to the matters set out in rule 8.2 (contents of the claim form) the claimant must also state—

    (a)   the name and address of any person he considers to be an interested party;

    (b)   that he is requesting permission to proceed with a claim for judicial review;

    (c)   any remedy (including any interim remedy) he is claiming; and

    (d)   where appropriate, the grounds on which it is contended that the claim is an Aarhus Convention claim.

(Rules 45.41 to 45.44 make provision about costs in Aarhus Convention claims.)

(Part 25 sets out how to apply for an interim remedy)

(2)   The claim form must be accompanied by the documents required by Practice Direction 54A.

54.7   Service of claim form

The claim form must be served on—

(a)   the defendant; and

(b)   unless the court otherwise directs, any person the claimant considers to be an interested party,

within 7 days after the date of issue.

54.7A Judicial review of decisions of the Upper Tribunal

(1) This rule applies where an application is made, following refusal by the Upper Tribunal of permission to appeal against a decision of the First Tier Tribunal, for judicial review—

    (a) of the decision of the Upper Tribunal refusing permission to appeal; or

    (b) which relates to the decision of the First Tier Tribunal which was the subject of the application for permission to appeal.

(2) Where this rule applies—

    (a) the application may not include any other claim, whether against the Upper Tribunal or not; and

    (b) any such other claim must be the subject of a separate application.

(3) The claim form and the supporting documents required by paragraph (4) must be filed no later than 16 days after the date on which notice of the Upper Tribunal's decision was sent to the applicant.

(4) The supporting documents are—

    (a) the decision of the Upper Tribunal to which the application relates, and any document giving reasons for the decision;

    (b) the grounds of appeal to the Upper Tribunal and any documents which were sent with them;

    (c) the decision of the First Tier Tribunal, the application to that Tribunal for permission to appeal and its reasons for refusing permission; and

    (d) any other documents essential to the claim.

(5) The claim form and supporting documents must be served on the Upper Tribunal and any other interested party no later than 7 days after the date of issue.

(6) The Upper Tribunal and any person served with the claim form who wishes to take part in the proceedings for judicial review must, no later than 21 days after service of the claim form, file and serve on the applicant and any other party an acknowledgment of service in the relevant practice form.

(7) The court will give permission to proceed only if it considers—

    (a) that there is an arguable case, which has a reasonable prospect of success, that both the decision of the Upper Tribunal refusing permission to appeal and the decision of the First Tier Tribunal against which permission to appeal was sought are wrong in law; and

    (b) that either—

        (i) the claim raises an important point of principle or practice; or

        (ii) there is some other compelling reason to hear it.

(8) If the application for permission is refused on paper without an oral hearing, rule 54.12(3) (request for reconsideration at a hearing) does not apply.

(9) If permission to apply for judicial review is granted—

    (a) if the Upper Tribunal or any interested party wishes there to be a hearing of the substantive application, it must make its request for such a hearing no later than 14 days after service of the order granting permission; and

    (b) if no request for a hearing is made within that period, the court will make a final order quashing the refusal of permission without a further hearing.

(10) The power to make a final order under paragraph (9)(b) may be exercised by the Master of the Crown Office or a Master of the Administrative Court.

54.8 Acknowledgment of service

(1) Any person served with the claim form who wishes to take part in the judicial review must file an acknowledgment of service in the relevant practice form in accordance with the following provisions of this rule.

(2) Any acknowledgment of service must be—

    (a) filed not more than 21 days after service of the claim form; and

    (b) served on—

        (i) the claimant; and

        (ii) subject to any direction under rule 54.7(b), any other person named in the claim form,

    as soon as practicable and, in any event, not later than 7 days after it is filed.

(3) The time limits under this rule may not be extended by agreement between the parties.

(4)   The acknowledgment of service—
    (a)   must—
        (i)   where the person filing it intends to contest the claim, set out a summary of his grounds for doing so; and
        (ii)   state the name and address of any person the person filing it considers to be an interested party; and
    (b)   may include or be accompanied by an application for directions.
(5)   Rule 10.3(2) does not apply.
(Section 31(3C) of the Senior Courts Act 1981(1) requires the court, where it is asked to do so by the defendant, to consider whether the outcome for the claimant would have been substantially different if the conduct complained of had not occurred.)

54.9 Failure to file acknowledgment of service

(1)   Where a person served with the claim form has failed to file an acknowledgment of service in accordance with rule 54.8, he—
    (a)   may not take part in a hearing to decide whether permission should be given unless the court allows him to do so; but
    (b)   provided he complies with rule 54.14 or any other direction of the court regarding the filing and service of—
        (i)   detailed grounds for contesting the claim or supporting it on additional grounds; and
        (ii)   any written evidence,
    may take part in the hearing of the judicial review.
(2)   Where that person takes part in the hearing of the judicial review, the court may take his failure to file an acknowledgment of service into account when deciding what order to make about costs.
(3)   Rule 8.4 does not apply.

54.10 Permission given

(1)   Where permission to proceed is given the court may also give directions.
(2)   Directions under paragraph (1) may include—
    (a)   a stay of proceedings to which the claim relates;
    (b)   directions requiring the proceedings to be heard by a Divisional Court.

54.11 Service of order giving or refusing permission

The court will serve—
(a)   the order giving or refusing permission; and
(b)   any directions,
on—
    (i)   the claimant;
    (ii)   the defendant; and
    (iii)   any other person who filed an acknowledgment of service.

54.11A Permission decision where court requires a hearing

(1)   This rule applies where the court wishes to hear submissions on—
    (a)   whether it is highly likely that the outcome for the claimant would not have been substantially different if the conduct complained of had not occurred; and if so
    (b)   whether there are reasons of exceptional public interest which make it nevertheless appropriate to give permission.
(2)   The court may direct a hearing to determine whether to give permission.
(3)   The claimant, defendant and any other person who has filed an acknowledgment of service must be given at least 2 days' notice of the hearing date.
(4)   The court may give directions requiring the proceedings to be heard by a Divisional Court.
(5)   The court must give its reasons for giving or refusing permission.

54.12 Permission decision without a hearing

(1)   This rule applies where the court, without a hearing—
    (a)   refuses permission to proceed; or

      (b)   gives permission to proceed—
           (i)   subject to conditions; or
           (ii)   on certain grounds only.

(2)   The court will serve its reasons for making the decision when it serves the order giving or refusing permission in accordance with rule 54.11.

(3)   Subject to paragraph (7), the claimant may not appeal but may request the decision to be reconsidered at a hearing.

(4)   A request under paragraph (3) must be filed within 7 days after service of the reasons under paragraph (2).

(5)   The claimant, defendant and any other person who has filed an acknowledgment of service will be given at least 2 days' notice of the hearing date.

(6)   The court may give directions requiring the proceedings to be heard by a Divisional Court.

(7)   Where the court refuses permission to proceed and records the fact that the application is totally without merit in accordance with rule 23.12, the claimant may not request that decision to be reconsidered at a hearing.

54.13 Defendant etc. may not apply to set aside

Neither the defendant nor any other person served with the claim form may apply to set aside an order giving permission to proceed.

54.14 Response

(1)   A defendant and any other person served with the claim form who wishes to contest the claim or support it on additional grounds must file and serve—
      (a)   detailed grounds for contesting the claim or supporting it on additional grounds; and
      (b)   any written evidence,
    within 35 days after service of the order giving permission.

(2)   The following rules do not apply—
      (a)   rule 8.5 (3) and 8.5 (4) (defendant to file and serve written evidence at the same time as acknowledgment of service); and
      (b)   rule 8.5 (5) and 8.5(6) (claimant to file and serve any reply within 14 days).

54.15 Where claimant seeks to rely on additional grounds

The court's permission is required if a claimant seeks to rely on grounds other than those for which he has been given permission to proceed.

54.16 Evidence

(1)   Rule 8.6 (1) does not apply.

(2)   No written evidence may be relied on unless—
      (a)   it has been served in accordance with any—
           (i)   rule under this Section; or
           (ii)   direction of the court; or
      (b)   the court gives permission.

54.17 Court's powers to hear any person

(1)   Any person may apply for permission—
      (a)   to file evidence; or
      (b)   make representations at the hearing of the judicial review.

(2)   An application under paragraph (1) should be made promptly.

54.18 Judicial review may be decided without a hearing

The court may decide the claim for judicial review without a hearing where all the parties agree.

54.19 Court's powers in respect of quashing orders

(1)   This rule applies where the court makes a quashing order in respect of the decision to which the claim relates.

(2)   The court may—
      (a)   (i)   remit the matter to the decision-maker; and

      (ii)   direct it to reconsider the matter and reach a decision in accordance with the judgment of the court; or
   (b)   in so far as any enactment permits, substitute its own decision for the decision to which the claim relates.
(Section 31 of the Senior Courts Act 1981 enables the High Court, subject to certain conditions, to substitute its own decision for the decision in question.)

54.20 Transfer

The court may
   (a)   order a claim to continue as if it had not been started under this Section; and
   (b)   where it does so, give directions about the future management of the claim.
(Part 30 (transfer) applies to transfers to and from the Administrative Court)

CIVIL PROCEDURE RULES 1998, PD 54A — JUDICIAL REVIEW

SECTION I
GENERAL PROVISIONS RELATING TO JUDICIAL REVIEW

The Court

2.1   Part 54 claims for judicial review are dealt with in the Administrative Court.

Rule 54.5 – Time limit for filing claim form

4.1   Where the claim is for a quashing order in respect of a judgment, order or conviction, the date when the grounds to make the claim first arose, for the purposes of rule 54.5(1)(b), is the date of that judgment, order or conviction.

Rule 54.6 – claim form

Interested parties

5.1   Where the claim for judicial review relates to proceedings in a court or tribunal, any other parties to those proceedings must be named in the claim form as interested parties under rule 54.6(1)(a) (and therefore served with the claim form under rule 54.7(b)).

5.2   For example, in a claim by a defendant in a criminal case in the Magistrates or Crown Court for judicial review of a decision in that case, the prosecution must always be named as an interested party.

Human rights

5.3   Where the claimant is seeking to raise any issue under the Human Rights Act 1998, or seeks a remedy available under that Act, the claim form must include the information required by paragraph 15 of Practice Direction 16.

Devolution issues

5.4   Where the claimant intends to raise a devolution issue, the claim form must:
   (1)   specify that the applicant wishes to raise a devolution issue and identify the relevant provisions of the Government of Wales Act 2006, the Northern Ireland Act 1998 or the Scotland Act 1998; and
   (2)   contain a summary of the facts, circumstances and points of law on the basis of which it is alleged that a devolution issue arises.

5.5   In this practice direction 'devolution issue' has the same meaning as in paragraph 1, schedule 9 to the Government of Wales Act 2006; paragraph 1, schedule 10 to the Northern Ireland Act 1998; and paragraph 1, schedule 6 of the Scotland Act 1998.

Claim form

5.6   The claim form must include or be accompanied by—
   (1)   a detailed statement of the claimant's grounds for bringing the claim for judicial review;
   (2)   a statement of the facts relied on;

(3)   any application to extend the time limit for filing the claim form;

(4)   any application for directions.

5.7   In addition, the claim form must be accompanied by

(1)   any written evidence in support of the claim or application to extend time;

(2)   a copy of any order that the claimant seeks to have quashed;

(3)   where the claim for judicial review relates to a decision of a court or tribunal, an approved copy of the reasons for reaching that decision;

(4)   copies of any documents on which the claimant proposes to rely;

(5)   copies of any relevant statutory material; and

(6)   a list of essential documents for advance reading by the court (with page references to the passages relied on).

5.8   Where it is not possible to file all the above documents, the claimant must indicate which documents have not been filed and the reasons why they are not currently available.

Bundle of documents

5.9   The claimant must file two copies of a paginated and indexed bundle containing all the documents referred to in paragraphs 5.6 and 5.7.

5.10   Attention is drawn to rules 8.5(1) and 8.5(7).

Rule 54.7 – service of claim form

6.1   Except as required by rules 54.11 or 54.12(2), the Administrative Court will not serve documents and service must be effected by the parties.

Rule 54.8 – acknowledgment of service

7.1   Attention is drawn to rule 8.3(2) and the relevant practice direction and to rule 10.5.

Rule 54.10 – permission given

Directions

8.1   Case management directions under rule 54.10(1) may include directions about serving the claim form and any evidence on other persons.

8.2   Where a claim is made under the Human Rights Act 1998, a direction may be made for giving notice to the Crown or joining the Crown as a party. Attention is drawn to rule 19.4A and paragraph 6 of Practice Direction 19A.

Permission without a hearing

8.4   The court will generally, in the first instance, consider the question of permission without a hearing.

Permission hearing

8.5   Neither the defendant nor any other interested party need attend a hearing on the question of permission unless the court directs otherwise.

8.6   Where the defendant or any party does attend a hearing, the court will not generally make an order for costs against the claimant.

Rule 54.11 – service of order giving or refusing permission

9.1   An order refusing permission or giving it subject to conditions or on certain grounds only must set out or be accompanied by the court's reasons for coming to that decision.

Rule 54.14 – response

10.1   Where the party filing the detailed grounds intends to rely on documents not already filed, he must file a paginated bundle of those documents when he files the detailed grounds.

Rule 54.15 – where claimant seeks to rely on additional grounds

11.1   Where the claimant intends to apply to rely on additional grounds at the hearing of the claim for judicial review, he must give notice to the court and to any other person served with the claim form no later than 7 clear days before the hearing (or the warned date where appropriate).

Rule 54.16 – evidence

12.1   Disclosure is not required unless the court orders otherwise.

Rule 54.17 – court's powers to hear any person

13.1   Where all the parties consent, the court may deal with an application under rule 54.17 without a hearing.

13.2   Where the court gives permission for a person to file evidence or make representations at the hearing of the claim for judicial review, it may do so on conditions and may give case management directions.

13.3   An application for permission should be made by letter to the Administrative Court office, identifying the claim, explaining who the applicant is and indicating why and in what form the applicant wants to participate in the hearing.

13.4   If the applicant is seeking a prospective order as to costs, the letter should say what kind of order and on what grounds.

13.5   Applications to intervene must be made at the earliest reasonable opportunity, since it will usually be essential not to delay the hearing.

Rule 54.20 – transfer

14.1   Attention is drawn to rule 30.5.

14.2   In deciding whether a claim is suitable for transfer to the Administrative Court, the court will consider whether it raises issues of public law to which Part 54 should apply.

Skeleton arguments

15.1   The claimant must file and serve a skeleton argument not less than 21 working days before the date of the hearing of the judicial review (or the warned date).

15.2   The defendant and any other party wishing to make representations at the hearing of the judicial review must file and serve a skeleton argument not less than 14 working days before the date of the hearing of the judicial review (or the warned date).

15.3   Skeleton arguments must contain:

    (1)   a time estimate for the complete hearing, including delivery of judgment;

    (2)   a list of issues;

    (3)   a list of the legal points to be taken (together with any relevant authorities with page references to the passages relied on);

    (4)   a chronology of events (with page references to the bundle of documents (see paragraph 16.1);

    (5)   a list of essential documents for the advance reading of the court (with page references to the passages relied on) (if different from that filed with the claim form) and a time estimate for that reading; and

    (6)   a list of persons referred to.

Bundle of documents to be filed

16.1   The claimant must file a paginated and indexed bundle of all relevant documents required for the hearing of the judicial review when he files his skeleton argument.

16.2   The bundle must also include those documents required by the defendant and any other party who is to make representations at the hearing.

Agreed final order

17.1   If the parties agree about the final order to be made in a claim for judicial review, the claimant must file at the court a document (with 2 copies) signed by all the parties setting out the terms of the proposed agreed order together with a short statement of the matters relied on as justifying the proposed agreed order and copies of any authorities or statutory provisions relied on.

17.2   The court will consider the documents referred to in paragraph 17.1 and will make the order if satisfied that the order should be made.

17.3   If the court is not satisfied that the order should be made, a hearing date will be set.

17.4   Where the agreement relates to an order for costs only, the parties need only file a document signed by all the parties setting out the terms of the proposed order.

SECTION III

APPLICATIONS FOR PERMISSION TO APPLY FOR JUDICIAL REVIEW OF DECISIONS OF THE UPPER TRIBUNAL

19.1   A person who makes an application for permission to apply for judicial review of the decision of the Upper Tribunal refusing permission to appeal must file a claim form which must—

(a)   state on its face that the application is made under Rule 54.7A;

(b)   set out succinctly the grounds on which it is argued that the criteria in Rule 54.7A(7) are met; and

(c)   be accompanied by the supporting documents required under Rule 54.7A(4).

19.2   If the Upper Tribunal or any interested party wishes there to be a hearing of the substantive application under Rule 54.7A(9), it must make its request in writing (by letter copied to the claimant) for such a hearing no later than 14 days after service of the order granting permission.

INTERNATIONAL CONVENTIONS
CONVENTION FOR THE PROTECTION OF HUMAN RIGHTS AND FUNDAMENTAL FREEDOMS AS AMENDED BY PROTOCOLS NO. 11 AND NO. 14

Rome, 4.XI.1950

The governments signatory hereto, being members of the Council of Europe,

Considering the Universal Declaration of Human Rights proclaimed by the General Assembly of the United Nations on 10th December 1948;

Considering that this Declaration aims at securing the universal and effective recognition and observance of the Rights therein declared;

Considering that the aim of the Council of Europe is the achievement of greater unity between its members and that one of the methods by which that aim is to be pursued is the maintenance and further realisation of human rights and fundamental freedoms;

Reaffirming their profound belief in those fundamental freedoms which are the foundation of justice and peace in the world and are best maintained on the one hand by an effective political democracy and on the other by a common understanding and observance of the human rights upon which they depend;

Being resolved, as the governments of European countries which are like-minded and have a common heritage of political traditions, ideals, freedom and the rule of law, to take the first steps for the collective enforcement of certain of the rights stated in the Universal Declaration,

Have agreed as follows:

Article 1 – Obligation to respect human rights

The High Contracting Parties shall secure to everyone within their jurisdiction the rights and freedoms defined in Section I of this Convention.

SECTION I – RIGHTS AND FREEDOMS

Article 2 – Right to life

1   Everyone's right to life shall be protected by law. No one shall be deprived of his life intentionally save in the execution of a sentence of a court following his conviction of a crime for which this penalty is provided by law.

2   Deprivation of life shall not be regarded as inflicted in contravention of this article when it results from the use of force which is no more than absolutely necessary:

    a   in defence of any person from unlawful violence;

    b   in order to effect a lawful arrest or to prevent the escape of a person lawfully detained;

    c   in action lawfully taken for the purpose of quelling a riot or insurrection.

Article 3 – Prohibition of torture

No one shall be subjected to torture or to inhuman or degrading treatment or punishment.

Article 4 – Prohibition of slavery and forced labour

1   No one shall be held in slavery or servitude.

2   No one shall be required to perform forced or compulsory labour.

3   For the purpose of this article the term "forced or compulsory labour" shall not include:

    a   any work required to be done in the ordinary course of detention imposed according to the provisions of Article 5 of this Convention or during conditional release from such detention;

    b   any service of a military character or, in case of conscientious objectors in countries where they are recognised, service exacted instead of compulsory military service;

    c   any service exacted in case of an emergency or calamity threatening the life or well-being of the community;

    d   any work or service which forms part of normal civic obligations.

Article 5 – Right to liberty and security

1   Everyone has the right to liberty and security of person. No one shall be deprived of his liberty save in the following cases and in accordance with a procedure prescribed by law:

    a   the lawful detention of a person after conviction by a competent court;

b   the lawful arrest or detention of a person for non-compliance with the lawful order of a court or in order to secure the fulfilment of any obligation prescribed by law;

c   the lawful arrest or detention of a person effected for the purpose of bringing him before the competent legal authority on reasonable suspicion of having committed an offence or when it is reasonably considered necessary to prevent his committing an offence or fleeing after having done so;

d   the detention of a minor by lawful order for the purpose of educational supervision or his lawful detention for the purpose of bringing him before the competent legal authority;

e   the lawful detention of persons for the prevention of the spreading of infectious diseases, of persons of unsound mind, alcoholics or drug addicts or vagrants;

f   the lawful arrest or detention of a person to prevent his effecting an unauthorised entry into the country or of a person against whom action is being taken with a view to deportation or extradition.

2   Everyone who is arrested shall be informed promptly, in a language which he understands, of the reasons for his arrest and of any charge against him.

3   Everyone arrested or detained in accordance with the provisions of paragraph 1.c of this article shall be brought promptly before a judge or other officer authorised by law to exercise judicial power and shall be entitled to trial within a reasonable time or to release pending trial. Release may be conditioned by guarantees to appear for trial.

4   Everyone who is deprived of his liberty by arrest or detention shall be entitled to take proceedings by which the lawfulness of his detention shall be decided speedily by a court and his release ordered if the detention is not lawful.

5   Everyone who has been the victim of arrest or detention in contravention of the provisions of this article shall have an enforceable right to compensation.

Article 6 – Right to a fair trial

1   In the determination of his civil rights and obligations or of any criminal charge against him, everyone is entitled to a fair and public hearing within a reasonable time by an independent and impartial tribunal established by law. Judgment shall be pronounced publicly but the press and public may be excluded from all or part of the trial in the interests of morals, public order or national security in a democratic society, where the interests of juveniles or the protection of the private life of the parties so require, or to the extent strictly necessary in the opinion of the court in special circumstances where publicity would prejudice the interests of justice.

2   Everyone charged with a criminal offence shall be presumed innocent until proved guilty according to law.

3   Everyone charged with a criminal offence has the following minimum rights:

a   to be informed promptly, in a language which he understands and in detail, of the nature and cause of the accusation against him;

b   to have adequate time and facilities for the preparation of his defence;

c   to defend himself in person or through legal assistance of his own choosing or, if he has not sufficient means to pay for legal assistance, to be given it free when the interests of justice so require;

d   to examine or have examined witnesses against him and to obtain the attendance and examination of witnesses on his behalf under the same conditions as witnesses against him;

e   to have the free assistance of an interpreter if he cannot understand or speak the language used in court.

Article 7 – No punishment without law

1   No one shall be held guilty of any criminal offence on account of any act or omission which did not constitute a criminal offence under national or international law at the time when it was committed. Nor shall a heavier penalty be imposed than the one that was applicable at the time the criminal offence was committed.

2   This article shall not prejudice the trial and punishment of any person for any act or omission which, at the time when it was committed, was criminal according to the general principles of law recognised by civilised nations.

Article 8 – Right to respect for private and family life

1   Everyone has the right to respect for his private and family life, his home and his correspondence.

2   There shall be no interference by a public authority with the exercise of this right except such as is in accordance with the law and is necessary in a democratic society in the interests of national security, public safety or the economic well-being of the country, for the prevention of disorder or crime, for the protection of health or morals, or for the protection of the rights and freedoms of others.

Article 9 – Freedom of thought, conscience and religion

1   Everyone has the right to freedom of thought, conscience and religion; this right includes freedom to change his religion or belief and freedom, either alone or in community with others and in public or private, to manifest his religion or belief, in worship, teaching, practice and observance.

2   Freedom to manifest one's religion or beliefs shall be subject only to such limitations as are prescribed by law and are necessary in a democratic society in the interests of public safety, for the protection of public order, health or morals, or for the protection of the rights and freedoms of others.

Article 10 – Freedom of expression

1   Everyone has the right to freedom of expression. This right shall include freedom to hold opinions and to receive and impart information and ideas without interference by public authority and regardless of frontiers. This article shall not prevent States from requiring the licensing of broadcasting, television or cinema enterprises.

2   The exercise of these freedoms, since it carries with it duties and responsibilities, may be subject to such formalities, conditions, restrictions or penalties as are prescribed by law and are necessary in a democratic society, in the interests of national security, territorial integrity or public safety, for the prevention of disorder or crime, for the protection of health or morals, for the protection of the reputation or rights of others, for preventing the disclosure of information received in confidence, or for maintaining the authority and impartiality of the judiciary.

Article 11 – Freedom of assembly and association

1   Everyone has the right to freedom of peaceful assembly and to freedom of association with others, including the right to form and to join trade unions for the protection of his interests.

2   No restrictions shall be placed on the exercise of these rights other than such as are prescribed by law and are necessary in a democratic society in the interests of national security or public safety, for the prevention of disorder or crime, for the protection of health or morals or for the protection of the rights and freedoms of others. This article shall not prevent the imposition of lawful restrictions on the exercise of these rights by members of the armed forces, of the police or of the administration of the State.

Article 12 – Right to marry

Men and women of marriageable age have the right to marry and to found a family, according to the national laws governing the exercise of this right.

Article 13 – Right to an effective remedy

Everyone whose rights and freedoms as set forth in this Convention are violated shall have an effective remedy before a national authority notwithstanding that the violation has been committed by persons acting in an official capacity.

Article 14 – Prohibition of discrimination

The enjoyment of the rights and freedoms set forth in this Convention shall be secured without discrimination on any ground such as sex, race, colour, language, religion, political or other opinion, national or social origin, association with a national minority, property, birth or other status.

Article 15 – Derogation in time of emergency

1   In time of war or other public emergency threatening the life of the nation any High Contracting Party may take measures derogating from its obligations under this Convention to the extent strictly required by the exigencies of the situation, provided that such measures are not inconsistent with its other obligations under international law.

2   No derogation from Article 2, except in respect of deaths resulting from lawful acts of war, or from Articles 3, 4 (paragraph 1) and 7 shall be made under this provision.

3   Any High Contracting Party availing itself of this right of derogation shall keep the Secretary General of the Council of Europe fully informed of the measures which it has taken and the reasons therefor. It shall also inform the Secretary General of the Council of Europe when such measures have ceased to operate and the provisions of the Convention are again being fully executed.

SECTION II – EUROPEAN COURT OF HUMAN RIGHTS

Article 19 – Establishment of the Court

To ensure the observance of the engagements undertaken by the High Contracting Parties in the Convention and the Protocols thereto, there shall be set up a European Court of Human Rights, hereinafter referred to as "the Court". It shall function on a permanent basis.

Article 20 – Number of judges

The Court shall consist of a number of judges equal to that of the High Contracting Parties.

Article 21 – Criteria for office

1   The judges shall be of high moral character and must either possess the qualifications required for appointment to high judicial office or be jurisconsults of recognised competence.

2   The judges shall sit on the Court in their individual capacity.

3   During their term of office the judges shall not engage in any activity which is incompatible with their independence, impartiality or with the demands of a full-time office; all questions arising from the application of this paragraph shall be decided by the Court.

Article 22 – Election of judges

1   The judges shall be elected by the Parliamentary Assembly with respect to each High Contracting Party by a majority of votes cast from a list of three candidates nominated by the High Contracting Party.

Article 23 – Terms of office and dismissal

1   The judges shall be elected for a period of nine years. They may not be re-elected.

2   The terms of office of judges shall expire when they reach the age of 70.

3   The judges shall hold office until replaced. They shall, however, continue to deal with such cases as they already have under consideration.

4   No judge may be dismissed from office unless the other judges decide by a majority of two-thirds that that judge has ceased to fulfil the required conditions.

Article 24 – Registry and rapporteurs

1   The Court shall have a registry, the functions and organisation of which shall be laid down in the rules of the Court.

2   When sitting in a single-judge formation, the Court shall be assisted by rapporteurs who shall function under the authority of the President of the Court. They shall form part of the Court's registry.

Article 25 – Plenary Court

The plenary Court shall

a   elect its President and one or two Vice-Presidents for a period of three years; they may be re-elected;

b   set up Chambers, constituted for a fixed period of time;

c   elect the Presidents of the Chambers of the Court; they may be re-elected;

d   adopt the rules of the Court;

e   elect the Registrar and one or more Deputy Registrars;

f   make any request under Article 26, paragraph 2.

Article 26 – Single-judge formation, committees, Chambers and Grand Chamber

1   To consider cases brought before it, the Court shall sit in a single-judge formation, in committees of three judges, in Chambers of seven judges and in a Grand Chamber of seventeen judges. The Court's Chambers shall set up committees for a fixed period of time.

2   At the request of the plenary Court, the Committee of Ministers may, by a unanimous decision and for a fixed period, reduce to five the number of judges of the Chambers.

3   When sitting as a single judge, a judge shall not examine any application against the High Contracting Party in respect of which that judge has been elected.

4   There shall sit as an *ex officio* member of the Chamber and the Grand Chamber the judge elected in respect of the High Contracting Party concerned. If there is none or if that judge is unable to sit, a person chosen by the President of the Court from a list submitted in advance by that Party shall sit in the capacity of judge.

5   The Grand Chamber shall also include the President of the Court, the Vice-Presidents, the Presidents of the Chambers and other judges chosen in accordance with the rules of the Court. When a case is referred to the Grand Chamber under Article 43, no judge from the Chamber which rendered the judgment shall sit in the Grand Chamber, with the exception of the President of the Chamber and the judge who sat in respect of the High Contracting Party concerned.

Article 27 – Competence of single judges

1   A single judge may declare inadmissible or strike out of the Court's list of cases an application submitted under Article 34, where such a decision can be taken without further examination.

2   The decision shall be final.

3   If the single judge does not declare an application inadmissible or strike it out, that judge shall forward it to a committee or to a Chamber for further examination.

Article 28 – Competence of committees

1   In respect of an application submitted under Article 34, a committee may, by a unanimous vote,

a   declare it inadmissible or strike it out of its list of cases, where such decision can be taken without further examination; or

b   declare it admissible and render at the same time a judgment on the merits, if the underlying question in the case, concerning the interpretation or the application of the Convention or the Protocols thereto, is already the subject of well-established case-law of the Court.

2   Decisions and judgments under paragraph 1 shall be final.

3   If the judge elected in respect of the High Contracting Party concerned is not a member of the committee, the committee may at any stage of the proceedings invite that judge to take the place of one of the members of the committee, having regard to all relevant factors, including whether that Party has contested the application of the procedure under paragraph 1.b.

Article 29 – Decisions by Chambers on admissibility and merits

1   If no decision is taken under Article 27 or 28, or no judgment rendered under Article 28, a Chamber shall decide on the admissibility and merits of individual applications submitted under Article 34. The decision on admissibility may be taken separately.

2   A Chamber shall decide on the admissibility and merits of inter-State applications submitted under Article 33. The decision on admissibility shall be taken separately unless the Court, in exceptional cases, decides otherwise.

Article 30 – Relinquishment of jurisdiction to the Grand Chamber

Where a case pending before a Chamber raises a serious question affecting the interpretation of the Convention or the protocols thereto, or where the resolution of a question before the Chamber might have a result inconsistent with a judgment previously delivered by the Court, the Chamber may, at any time before it has rendered its judgment, relinquish jurisdiction in favour of the Grand Chamber, unless one of the parties to the case objects.

Article 31 – Powers of the Grand Chamber

The Grand Chamber shall

a   determine applications submitted either under Article 33 or Article 34 when a Chamber has relinquished jurisdiction under Article 30 or when the case has been referred to it under Article 43;

b   decide on issues referred to the Court by the Committee of Ministers in accordance with Article 46, paragraph 4; and

c   consider requests for advisory opinions submitted under Article 47.

Article 32 – Jurisdiction of the Court

1   The jurisdiction of the Court shall extend to all matters concerning the interpretation and application of the Convention and the protocols thereto which are referred to it as provided in Articles 33, 34, 46 and 47.

2   In the event of dispute as to whether the Court has jurisdiction, the Court shall decide.

Article 33 – Inter-State cases

Any High Contracting Party may refer to the Court any alleged breach of the provisions of the Convention and the protocols thereto by another High Contracting Party.

Article 34 – Individual applications

The Court may receive applications from any person, non-governmental organisation or group of individuals claiming to be the victim of a violation by one of the High Contracting Parties of the rights set forth in the Convention or the protocols thereto. The High Contracting Parties undertake not to hinder in any way the effective exercise of this right.

Article 35 – Admissibility criteria

1   The Court may only deal with the matter after all domestic remedies have been exhausted, according to the generally recognised rules of international law, and within a period of six months from the date on which the final decision was taken.

2   The Court shall not deal with any application submitted under Article 34 that

a   is anonymous; or

b   is substantially the same as a matter that has already been examined by the Court or has already been submitted to another procedure of international investigation or settlement and contains no relevant new information.

3   The Court shall declare inadmissible any individual application submitted under Article 34 if it considers that:

a   the application is incompatible with the provisions of the Convention or the Protocols thereto, manifestly ill-founded, or an abuse of the right of individual application; or

b   the applicant has not suffered a significant disadvantage, unless respect for human rights as defined in the Convention and the Protocols thereto requires an examination of the application on the merits and provided that no case may be rejected on this ground which has not been duly considered by a domestic tribunal.

4   The Court shall reject any application which it considers inadmissible under this Article. It may do so at any stage of the proceedings.

Article 36 – Third party intervention

1   In all cases before a Chamber or the Grand Chamber, a High Contracting Party one of whose nationals is an applicant shall have the right to submit written comments and to take part in hearings.

2   The President of the Court may, in the interest of the proper administration of justice, invite any High Contracting Party which is not a party to the proceedings or any person concerned who is not the applicant to submit written comments or take part in hearings.

3   In all cases before a Chamber or the Grand Chamber, the Council of Europe Commissioner for Human Rights may submit written comments and take part in hearings.

Article 37 – Striking out applications

1   The Court may at any stage of the proceedings decide to strike an application out of its list of cases where the circumstances lead to the conclusion that

a   the applicant does not intend to pursue his application; or

b   the matter has been resolved; or

c   for any other reason established by the Court, it is no longer justified to continue the examination of the application.

However, the Court shall continue the examination of the application if respect for human rights as defined in the Convention and the protocols thereto so requires.

2   The Court may decide to restore an application to its list of cases if it considers that the circumstances justify such a course.

Article 38 – Examination of the case

The Court shall examine the case together with the representatives of the parties and, if need be, undertake an investigation, for the effective conduct of which the High Contracting Parties concerned shall furnish all necessary facilities.

Article 39 – Friendly settlements

1   At any stage of the proceedings, the Court may place itself at the disposal of the parties concerned with a view to securing a friendly settlement of the matter on the basis of respect for human rights as defined in the Convention and the Protocols thereto.
2   Proceedings conducted under paragraph 1 shall be confidential.
3   If a friendly settlement is effected, the Court shall strike the case out of its list by means of a decision which shall be confined to a brief statement of the facts and of the solution reached.
4   This decision shall be transmitted to the Committee of Ministers, which shall supervise the execution of the terms of the friendly settlement as set out in the decision.

Article 40 – Public hearings and access to documents

1   Hearings shall be in public unless the Court in exceptional circumstances decides otherwise.
2   Documents deposited with the Registrar shall be accessible to the public unless the President of the Court decides otherwise.

Article 41 – Just satisfaction

If the Court finds that there has been a violation of the Convention or the protocols thereto, and if the internal law of the High Contracting Party concerned allows only partial reparation to be made, the Court shall, if necessary, afford just satisfaction to the injured party.

Article 42 – Judgments of Chambers

Judgments of Chambers shall become final in accordance with the provisions of Article 44, paragraph 2.

Article 43 – Referral to the Grand Chamber

1   Within a period of three months from the date of the judgment of the Chamber, any party to the case may, in exceptional cases, request that the case be referred to the Grand Chamber.
2   A panel of five judges of the Grand Chamber shall accept the request if the case raises a serious question affecting the interpretation or application of the Convention or the protocols thereto, or a serious issue of general importance.
3   If the panel accepts the request, the Grand Chamber shall decide the case by means of a judgment.

Article 44 – Final judgments

1   The judgment of the Grand Chamber shall be final.
2   The judgment of a Chamber shall become final
         a   when the parties declare that they will not request that the case be referred to the Grand Chamber; or
         b   three months after the date of the judgment, if reference of the case to the Grand Chamber has not been requested; or
         c   when the panel of the Grand Chamber rejects the request to refer under Article 43.
3   The final judgment shall be published.

Article 45 – Reasons for judgments and decisions

1   Reasons shall be given for judgments as well as for decisions declaring applications admissible or inadmissible.
2   If a judgment does not represent, in whole or in part, the unanimous opinion of the judges, any judge shall be entitled to deliver a separate opinion.

Article 46 – Binding force and execution of judgments

1   The High Contracting Parties undertake to abide by the final judgment of the Court in any case to which they are parties.

2   The final judgment of the Court shall be transmitted to the Committee of Ministers, which shall supervise its execution.

3   If the Committee of Ministers considers that the supervision of the execution of a final judgment is hindered by a problem of interpretation of the judgment, it may refer the matter to the Court for a ruling on the question of interpretation. A referral decision shall require a majority vote of two thirds of the representatives entitled to sit on the Committee.

4   If the Committee of Ministers considers that a High Contracting Party refuses to abide by a final judgment in a case to which it is a party, it may, after serving formal notice on that Party and by decision adopted by a majority vote of two thirds of the representatives entitled to sit on the Committee, refer to the Court the question whether that Party has failed to fulfil its obligation under paragraph 1.

5   If the Court finds a violation of paragraph 1, it shall refer the case to the Committee of Ministers for consideration of the measures to be taken. If the Court finds no violation of paragraph 1, it shall refer the case to the Committee of Ministers, which shall close its examination of the case.

Article 47 – Advisory opinions

1   The Court may, at the request of the Committee of Ministers, give advisory opinions on legal questions concerning the interpretation of the Convention and the Protocols thereto.

2   Such opinions shall not deal with any question relating to the content or scope of the rights or freedoms defined in Section I of the Convention and the Protocols thereto, or with any other question which the Court or the Committee of Ministers might have to consider in consequence of any such proceedings as could be instituted in accordance with the Convention.

3   Decisions of the Committee of Ministers to request an advisory opinion of the Court shall require a majority vote of the representatives entitled to sit on the committee.

Article 48 – Advisory jurisdiction of the Court

The Court shall decide whether a request for an advisory opinion submitted by the Committee of Ministers is within its competence as defined in Article 47.

Article 49 – Reasons for advisory opinions

1   Reasons shall be given for advisory opinions of the Court.

2   If the advisory opinion does not represent, in whole or in part, the unanimous opinion of the judges, any judge shall be entitled to deliver a separate opinion.

SECTION III – MISCELLANEOUS PROVISIONS

Article 53 – Safeguard for existing human rights

Nothing in this Convention shall be construed as limiting or derogating from any of the human rights and fundamental freedoms which may be ensured under the laws of any High Contracting Party or under any other agreement to which it is a Party.

Article 58 – Denunciation

1   A High Contracting Party may denounce the present Convention only after the expiry of five years from the date on which it became a party to it and after six months' notice contained in a notification addressed to the Secretary General of the Council of Europe, who shall inform the other High Contracting Parties.

2   Such a denunciation shall not have the effect of releasing the High Contracting Party concerned from its obligations under this Convention in respect of any act which, being capable of constituting a violation of such obligations, may have been performed by it before the date at which the denunciation became effective.

3   Any High Contracting Party which shall cease to be a member of the Council of Europe shall cease to be a Party to this Convention under the same conditions.

4   The Convention may be denounced in accordance with the provisions of the preceding paragraphs in respect of any territory to which it has been declared to extend under the terms of Article 56.

Protocol to the Convention for the Protection of Human Rights and Fundamental Freedoms

PARIS, 20.III.1952

Article 1 – Protection of property

Every natural or legal person is entitled to the peaceful enjoyment of his possessions. No one shall be deprived of his possessions except in the public interest and subject to the conditions provided for by law and by the general principles of international law.

The preceding provisions shall not, however, in any way impair the right of a State to enforce such laws as it deems necessary to control the use of property in accordance with the general interest or to secure the payment of taxes or other contributions or penalties.

Article 2 – Right to education

No person shall be denied the right to education. In the exercise of any functions which it assumes in relation to education and to teaching, the State shall respect the right of parents to ensure such education and teaching in conformity with their own religious and philosophical convictions.

Article 3 – Right to free elections

The High Contracting Parties undertake to hold free elections at reasonable intervals by secret ballot, under conditions which will ensure the free expression of the opinion of the people in the choice of the legislature.

Protocol No. 6 to the Convention for the Protection of Human Rights and Fundamental Freedoms concerning the abolition of the death penalty

STRASBOURG, 28.IV.1983

Article 1 – Abolition of the death penalty

The death penalty shall be abolished. No-one shall be condemned to such penalty or executed.

Article 2 – Death penalty in time of war

A State may make provision in its law for the death penalty in respect of acts committed in time of war or of imminent threat of war; such penalty shall be applied only in the instances laid down in the law and in accordance with its provisions. The State shall communicate to the Secretary General of the Council of Europe the relevant provisions of that law.

Protocol No. 13 to the Convention for the Protection of Human Rights and Fundamental Freedoms, concerning the abolition of the death penalty in all circumstances

VILNIUS, 3.V.2002

Article 1 – Abolition of the death penalty

The death penalty shall be abolished. No one shall be condemned to such penalty or executed.

Article 2 – Prohibition of derogations

No derogation from the provisions of this Protocol shall be made under Article 15 of the Convention.

Article 3 – Prohibition of reservations

No reservation may be made under Article 57 of the Convention in respect of the provisions of this Protocol.

TREATY ON EUROPEAN UNION
(CONSOLIDATED – LISBON TREATY)

Article 50

1.   Any Member State may decide to withdraw from the Union in accordance with its own constitutional requirements.

2.   A Member State which decides to withdraw shall notify the European Council of its intention. In the light of the guidelines provided by the European Council, the Union shall negotiate and conclude an agreement with that State, setting out the arrangements for its withdrawal, taking account of the framework for its future relationship with the Union. That agreement shall be negotiated in accordance with Article 218(3) of the Treaty on the Functioning of the European Union. It shall be concluded on behalf of the Union by the Council, acting by a qualified majority, after obtaining the consent of the European Parliament.

3.   The Treaties shall cease to apply to the State in question from the date of entry into force of the withdrawal agreement or, failing that, two years after the notification referred to in paragraph 2, unless the European Council, in agreement with the Member State concerned, unanimously decides to extend this period.

4.   For the purposes of paragraphs 2 and 3, the member of the European Council or of the Council representing the withdrawing Member State shall not participate in the discussions of the European Council or Council or in decisions concerning it.
   A qualified majority shall be defined in accordance with Article 238(3)(b) of the Treaty on the Functioning of the European Union.

5.   If a State which has withdrawn from the Union asks to rejoin, its request shall be subject to the procedure referred to in Article 49.

INDEX

CPI Antony Rowe

Chippenham, UK

2018-01-02 21:53